BURPEE®

The Complete
Flower Gardener

BURPEE®

The Complete
FlowerGardener

The Comprehensive Guide
to Growing Flowers Organically

Karan Davis Cutler
and
Barbara W. Ellis

Photography by Jerry Pavia

Wiley Publishing, Inc.

Published by John Wiley & Sons, Inc., Hoboken, New Jersey
Published simultaneously in Canada

For general information on our other products and services or for technical support,
please contact our Customer Care Department within the United States at (800)
762-2974, outside the United States at (317) 572-3993 or fax (317) 572-4002.

Wiley also publishes its books in a variety of electronic formats. Some content that
appears in print may not be available in electronic books. For more information
about Wiley products, visit our web site at www.wiley.com.

Library of Congress Cataloging-in-Publication Data
Cutler, Karan Davis.
    Burpee-the complete flower gardener : the comprehensive guide to growing
flowers organically / Karan Davis Cutler and Barbara W. Ellis.
        p. cm.
    Includes index.
    ISBN   978-0-7645-4324-1 (cloth)
    1. Flower gardening. 2. Organic gardening. I. Ellis, Barbara W. II. Title.
    SB405.C88 2006
    635.9—dc22

                                                2006016016

Printed in the United States of America
10 9 8 7 6 5 4 3 2 1

For Ellen Esslinger Davis,

who grew flowers nearly every one

of her 100 years

PHOTOGRAPHY CREDITS

Unless otherwise noted below, all photographs are by Jerry Pavia.

Scott Bauer, ARS/USDA: 153

Bonide Products: 159

Brent and Becky's Bulbs: 324

The Color Wheel Co.: 110, 111

Karan Davis Cutler: iv–v, vi all, 9, 10, 11, 16, 18, 20, 21, 24, 33, 35, 38, 43, 49, 57, 60, 66, 68, 74, 82, 95, 104 top, 104 bottom, 108, 109 top, 109 middle, 113, 114 left, 114 right, 115, 116–117, 118 bottom, 119, 120, 121, 139, 146–147, 149, 157, 168, 170, 174 top, 174 bottom, 185, 191, 210, 220, 224, 230 top, 249 top, 249 bottom, 251, 257, 261, 265, 267 bottom, 274, 275 top, 291, 292–293, 298, 299 top, 309, 318 left, 319, 322, 326, 333, 337, 338, 352 top, 352 middle, 353, 354, 364, 365 top, 371 top, 376, 385, 388, 393 top, 393 bottom, 396 bottom, 404 top, 404 bottom, 412 bottom, 413 top, 413 bottom, 416 top, 420, 424 bottom, 428 bottom, 440, 454 bottom, 458, 467, 470, 471, 472, 473, 474

Netherlands Flower Bulb Information Center: 7

Neil Soderstrom: ii, 23, 51, 52, 56, 62–3, 65, 72, 75, 79, 80, 81, 83, 89, 100–1, 107, 118 top, 122, 123, 124, 125, 126, 128, 129, 130, 132, 134, 136, 140, 142, 143, 152, 155, 158, 160, 162, 165, 166, 173, 179, 187, 190, 193, 194–5, 197, 199, 200, 202, 204, 206, 207, 209

U. S. National Arboretum, USDA-ARS: 465

W. Atlee Burpee & Co.: 1, 5, 29, 47, 63, 85, 117, 147, 177, 195, 458

ACKNOWLEDGMENTS

We've gratefully taken advantage of the knowledge and help of others when writing this book. Special thanks goes to Stephen J. Cutler and Peter Evans, who always show Herculean forbearance. We appreciate the help we received from Kathleen Fisher; Sydney Eddison; Jerry Pavia; Neil Soderstrom; Don Zeidler and Thomas Nally, W. Atlee Burpee & Co.; Sally Ferguson, Netherlands Flower Bulb Information Center; Susan Romanoff, Gardener's Supply Company; Ken Haines, The Color Wheel Company; Lorry Hulbert, Bonide Products, Inc.; Scott Kunst, Old House Gardens; Nona Wolfram-Koivula and Macie Zorn, All-America Selections; Robert Longsworth, Oberlin College; Brent and Becky Heath, Brent & Becky's Bulbs; Nancy Vanatta, ARS Photo Unit, USDA; Ramon Jordon, Floral & Nursery Plants Research Unit, U.S. National Arboretum; Kevin P. Walek, American Hosta Society, Janice Dowdeswell, Dowdeswell's Delphiniums; William C. Welch and Nancy Volkman, Texas A&M University; Jim Alston, Park Seed Co.; Gary L. Wade, USDA Forest Service; Eric Post, Pennsylvania State University; Richard A. Criley, University of Hawaii; R. Anson Eaglin, USDA; Arthur Cameron, Michigan State University.

At John Wiley & Sons, we'd especially like to thank Anne Ficklen, a savvy editor with more patience than authors deserve but not more than they appreciate, and the book's designer, Holly Wittenberg, editorial assistants Jessica DeSanta and Charleen Barila, and production editor Ava Wilder.

CONTENTS

Introduction
1

PART I
Flower Gardening from the Ground Up
3

CHAPTER ONE
The World of Flowers: Understanding Plant Basics
5

CHAPTER TWO
Where Does Your Garden Grow: Taking Stock of Local Conditions
29

CHAPTER THREE
Home Ground: Assessing Your Garden Site
47

CHAPTER FOUR
Terra Wonderful: Making Great Soil for Growing Flowers
63

CHAPTER FIVE
Balancing Act: Creating Borders and Beds
85

CHAPTER SIX
Garden Work: Planting and Tending Flowers
117

CHAPTER SEVEN
Bugs and Other Bothers: Handling Problems in the Flower Garden
147

CHAPTER EIGHT
Being Single-Minded: Creating Gardens of Special Delight
177

CHAPTER NINE
Tool Talk: Equipping the Flower Gardener
195

PART II
Plant Portraits
213

Achillea 214
Aconitum 215
Ageratum houstonianum 217
Alcea rosea 218
Alchemilla mollis 221
Allium 222
Amsonia tabernaemontana 225
Anemone 226
Anthemis tinctoria 228
Antirrhinum majus 230

Aquilegia 232
Aruncus 234
Asclepias tuberosa 235
Aster 237
Astilbe 240
Baptisia australis 242
Begonia 244
Bergenia 247
Brachyscome iberidifolia 248
Bracteantha bracteata 249
Calendula officinalis 250
Campanula 252
Canna × generalis 256
Catharanthus roseus 258
Celosia argentea 260
Centaurea 261
Centranthus ruber 264
Chrysanthemum × morifolium 265
Cimicifuga 268
Cleome hassleriana 269
Convallaria majalis 270
Coreopsis 272
Corydalis 275
Cosmos 276
Crocus 279
Dahlia 284
Delphinium 287
Dianthus 290
Dicentra 293
Dictamnus albus 295
Digitalis 296
Echinacea purpurea 298
Echinops ritro 300
Epimedium 302
Eryngium 303
Eschscholzia californica 304
Eupatorium 306
Euphorbia 308
Filipendula 310
Fritillaria 311
Fuchsia 314

Gaillardia 315
Galium odoratum 316
Gazania ringens 317
Geranium 319
Geum 323
Gladiolus × hortulanus 324
Gomphrena 326
Gypsophila 327
Helenium autumnale 329
Helianthus 331
Helleborus 334
Hemerocallis 335
Heuchera 338
Hibiscus moscheutos 341
Hosta 343
Hyacinthus orientalis 346
Iberis 348
Impatiens 350
Ipomoea 351
Iris 354
Kniphofia uvaria 360
Leucanthemum × superbum 361
Liatris 363
Ligularia 364
Lilium 366
Limonium 370
Linum 372
Liriope 373
Lobelia 374
Lobularia maritima 376
Lunaria annua 378
Lupinus 379
Lychnis 381
Lysimachia 382
Malva 384
Matthiola incana 385
Monarda 387
Myosotis sylvatica 388
Narcissus 390
Nepeta 394
Nicotiana 395
Nigella damascena 397

Oenothera 398
Paeonia 399
Papaver 402
Pelargonium 405
Penstemon 407
Perovskia atriplicifolia 409
Petunia 411
Phlox 414
Physostegia virginiana 417
Platycodon grandiflora 418
Portulaca grandiflora 419
Potentilla 421
Primula 422
Pulmonaria 425
Rodgersia 426
Rudbeckia 427
Salvia 429
Scabiosa caucasica 431
Sedum 433
Stachys byzantina 434
Tagetes 435
Thalictrum 438
Tradescantia 439
Tropaeolum majus 441
Tulipa 442
Verbascum 448
Verbena 449
Veronica 450
Viola 452
Zinnia 454

PART III
Appendix
457

Appendix
458

Index
474

Introduction

*W*ould that we all lived in a time when we could walk deep into a baronial garden and enjoy galleries of natural masterpieces and hear symphonies created on the wing. But, in truth, flowers need not the canvas of an old English garden to portray their beauty, nor birds to sing their songs. Today's home gardener can look at a single rose on a well-tended plant and experience all the magnificence of nature.

The age of the regal garden is past, except for the botanical museums, and in its stead grow a plethora of plants and flowers at many a home in designs inspired by imagination to display, arrange, and enjoy to the fullest throughout the year.

From late winter's first bloom on a witch hazel to the surprise of an early spring crocus to the splendor of daffodils, tulips, forsythias, and azaleas, the garden cherishes each warming day as it heralds the dawn of a new season.

Soon the garden explodes with the first summer flowers and showers us with colors, textures, and delights. Now is the time of bounty and great joy.

To achieve such wonders, it is important to respect the garden and tend to its needs.

Like people, plants have different likes and dislikes, so before madly circling every photo in the new seed catalog, it's best to understand what the plant enjoys and what your garden has to offer. Don't waste effort and face disappointment trying to coax an acid-loving plant into blooming in your alkaline soil. Have the soil tested and then amend it organically to create an optimum home for as many flowers as possible.

We tend to link compost to growing vegetables, but flowering plants need nutrients as well. Discover simple but effective techniques herein, and notice the tremendous difference a rich, loamy soil can make in the flower garden.

Then select those specimens that will perform best in your soil and growing conditions. A shade-loving plant will not tolerate daylong blazing sun,

and a sun worshipper won't bloom in deep shade. See Part II of this volume for an alphabetical listing of flowering-plant portraits.

At the Burpee Trial Gardens at Fordhook Farm in Doylestown, Pennsylvania, new plants are grown under a variety of conditions to determine the optimum planting medium and site. We've taken the guesswork out of flower selection by including precise growing information with every flower-seed packet or plant and posted expanded explanations on the company web site: www. burpee.com.

Armed with an array of compatible plant choices, patrol your property with an eye for suitable growing sites. Places for beds and borders, themed gardens, and nooks and crannies where a splash of color will surprise or startle should all be noted and included on a property sketch.

Themed gardens are a special delight. Moonlight or soft lighting creates magic in a white garden. Plant moonflowers to add a powerful fragrance to an exotic summer's eve.

A patriot's garden decked in red, white, and blue flowers is perfect for a themed Fourth of July party.

And a child's birthday party held in a secret chamber within a dramatic stand of majestic sunflowers will resound with giggles and glee.

Adventures in flower gardening can be enjoyed at every level. Beds and borders can be sized to fit a variety of schedules and for those lucky enough to have the luxury of time, the flower garden knows no boundaries for the creative soul.

But for those with multiple demands on their time, flowering oases can provide peace and satisfaction. Within these pages are all the tools needed to create a living Monet, Van Gogh, or Renoir. So take up your gloves and spades and begin a wonderful journey into the world of flower gardening.

GEORGE BALL JR.
President, W. Atlee Burpee & Co.

1

PART I

Flower Gardening from the Ground Up

History is unambiguous about the first English immigrants to America: They were a practical lot. They stuffed their pockets and pouches and trunks with the seeds of food and medicinal plants, not the seeds of ornamental plants. The hefty garden order shipped from England to John Winthrop Jr., in 1631, included only a handful of flowers. Such a hardheaded approach didn't last, of course. Within three decades of the Pilgrims' 1620 landing, the colonists were growing scores of ornamentals, including a bevy of eye-catching but largely impractical blossoms, such as bellflowers, candytuft, Canterbury bells, daffodils, gladioli, hollyhocks, snapdragons, and tulips.

Flower gardeners today—whether we tend a single window box or maintain a dozen beds and borders—are spiritual descendents of those pioneers. We are members of "Adam's profession," bewitched by the ever-changing claims and bliss of growing flowers. Once you are seized by *furor hortensis*, as the Earl of Chesterfield described the delights of horticulture in 1751, your garden will give you, as his did him, "More pleasure than kingdoms do kings." The true object of gardening, he wrote, is to enrich, not extend.

Flower gardens do enrich the lives of their makers. They are eternally interesting and rewarding, as well as challenging, demanding, and frustrating. And while the goal should be to enjoy and enrich, it doesn't take long before you will want to extend. The temptations are countless: a few more pots for the patio; a cold frame to get a head start in spring; a new bed of shade plants under the beech tree; and more.

November and December may slow *furor hortensis* in most parts of North America, but January brings seed and plant catalogs and the excitement of new cultivars, better weather, and bigger blooms. There's no resisting, and there's no end of fun. Welcome to the *familia hortensis*.

Spring Beauty. *'Apricot Beauty' and other Early Single Division tulips provide lush color to the home garden; especially when you use all plants of the same color. Poet Amy Lowell liked their erect bearing: "Marshalled like soldiers . . . the tulips stand arrayed."*

CHAPTER ONE

The World of Flowers: Understanding Plant Basics

*I am not a greedy person
except about flowers and plants,
and then I become fanatically greedy.*

May Sarton, *Plant Dreaming Deep*, 1968

THERE IS A GARDENFUL OF PRACTICAL REASONS TO grow flowers: daffodils and irises to fill vases, chrysanthemums and pinks to fashion corsages, statice and strawflowers to make wreaths, nasturtiums and violets to garnish foods, bee balm and goldenrod to brew teas, marigolds and cosmos to produce dyes, lavender

Flowers as Models. *Calla lilies (*Zantedeschia *spp.) are tender natives of southern Africa. Their striking blossoms have been as irresistible to artists as they are to gardeners.*

and lilies to generate fragrance. There are flowers for drying and pressing, flowers for curing ills, flowers for attracting bees, birds, and other wildlife, flowers for turning children into gardeners, vining flowers for screening out the neighbors, and more.

With so many hardheaded incentives, don't forget that flowers are inherently lovely, worth growing solely for themselves. Artists and poets, the keenest of seers, have always known that "beauty is its own excuse for being," as Ralph Waldo Emerson phrased it more than 150 years ago. It's not an accident that most great painters, both Western and Eastern, have used flowers as subjects. Just a fragmentary list of those who have recreated blooms on paper or canvas includes Renoir, Manet, van Gogh, Cézanne, Matisse, Chagall, Dali, Warhol, Yun Bing, and Hokusai.

In addition to roses, which are the preeminent floral posers, artists have been seduced often by irises, lilies, sunflowers, daisies, tulips, chrysanthemums, and dahlias. American artist Georgia O'Keeffe is reputed to have said that she hated flowers and painted them only because "they're cheaper than models and they don't move." Her comment surely was facetious, for her reputation stands in part on her provocative calla lily portraits. Perhaps Marc Chagall was closer to the truth when he wrote, "Art is the unceasing effort to compete with the beauty of flowers and never succeeding."

Flowers have interested and inspired writers as well. Medieval literature is littered with flowers, as are Chaucer's *Canterbury Tales* and Shakespeare's plays; the Romantic poets' focus on flowers was second only to their obsession with matters of the heart. Flowers appear as crucial symbols in the works of Hawthorne, Poe, Faulkner, and other major American

OFFICIAL FLORICULTURE

Flowers have served as national symbols for centuries: the rose in England, the *fleur-de-lis* in France, the chrysanthemum in Japan. The tulip is the official flower of the Netherlands, despite being a native of the Middle East and Central Asia, and orchids are symbolic of a half dozen South and Central American nations. Mexico's flower is the dahlia, Finland's is the lily-of-the-valley (*Convallaria majalis*), and the Flanders, or corn, poppy (*Papaver rhoeas*) represents both Belgium and Poland. The lotus (*Nelumbo* spp.) is the official flower of India, and if you've seen *The Sound of Music*, it comes as no surprise that Austria's national flower is edelweiss (*Leontopodium alpinum*). Although the historian-critic Lewis Mumford quipped that the American national flower was "the concrete clover leaf," in fact, it is the rose, designated officially in 1986.

writers, and they even figure in popular mysteries, most famously in the books by Rex Stout, whose detective Nero Wolfe is a dedicated orchid grower.

Mythology, too, teems with flowers. In a Persian narrative, the first tulip springs from the spot where a distraught lover jumped to his demise. English folklore is more benign vis-à-vis tulips, which were reputedly used by pillywiggins (fairies that tend spring flowers) as cradles for their babies. According to Hindustani legend, the tulip immersed itself in blood while in a jealous passion, which explains the

FLOR, FLORA, FLOWER

The flora half of flora and fauna comes from *flor*, "flower" in Latin. Flora was the Roman goddess of spring flowers and "all that flourishes." She was celebrated in spring at *Floralia*, a licentious festival featuring X-rated art and naked women. Flora's partner, fauna, refers to Faunus, the Roman god of animals, the fields, and shepherds. In Greece, Faunus was known as Pan, a pipe-playing, fun-loving god depicted as half man and half goat.

red markings, or wound, that many tulips carry in their centers.

Peonies and chrysanthemums recur in Chinese and Japanese myths, and European mythology brims with flowers. Dozens of accounts attribute the common name of various *Myosotis* species—forget-me-nots—to foolhardy lovers drowning in rivers while trying to pick flowers for their ladyloves. "*Vergiss mich nicht*," calls out a German knight about to go under for the third time, "Do not forget me." And scores of classical myths revolve around irises, narcissi, crocuses, daphnes, asters, peonies, and hyacinths, to list only a few species.

The link between words and flowers reached an apex in the Victorian era with the "language of flowers," a *lingua botanica* that assigned character traits and emotions to specific blossoms. Sending a *tussie-mussie*—a circular bouquet jampacked with flowers—also sent a message of love, sympathy, or another sentiment. Scores of "flower dictionaries" were published; cosmos, for example, stood for modesty; hosta for devotion; narcissi, egotism; violets, modesty and faithfulness. No flower was without an attribute, and most had many attributes, making it necessary for recipients of tussie-mussies to read between the petals.

To the amazement of many, books about the language of flowers continue to be published. Such books may seem hopelessly outdated, but *Tussie-Mussies: The Victorian Art of Expressing Yourself in the Language of Flowers* (1993) is one of many titles that preserves the genre, even updates it with suggested flower combinations for communicating "support during a difficult divorce" and "congratulations on a successful diet."

Flowers on Paper. *Botanical illustrations of tulips, like this drawing by Crispijn van de Passe the Younger labeled "Tulipa bononiensis," helped create the wildly speculative bulb market in 17th-century Holland known as "Tulipomania."*

Blessed Be the Names

The common names of flowers—the North Carolina garden writer Elizabeth Lawrence called them "sweet country names" in *Gardening for Love* (1987)—always carry a story. In Scandinavia, for instance, legend has it that foxbells once rang out warnings to foxes that they were in danger. The mysterious peals so frightened hunters that they stopped killing foxes, and thus the gods removed the clappers from the bells, rendering the flowers silent.

It would be fun to fill a flower bed on the basis of common names alone, perhaps a small plot bursting not only with foxbells, but with witch's thimbles, goblin gloves, lushmore, fairies' petticoats, Virgin's fingers, lion's mouth, popdocks, fairy caps, rabbit flower, throatwort, and Pan's sweethearts. Plant them all, though, and the bed would contain only one flower, the common foxglove (*Digitalis purpurea*).

Foxglove's many aliases highlight a problem with common names: Most flowers have more than one.

Plant Names. *The foxglove's genus name,* Digitalis, *refers to a chemical in its leaves that stimulates the heart. Though safe when prescribed by a physician, digitalis never should be self-prescribed.*

Worse still, the same common names are used for different flowers. When British gardeners talk about daisies, they are referring to the English daisy, a low-growing perennial that blooms in late spring. Americans using the same term are likely to be thinking of a 3-foot Shasta daisy (*Leucanthemum × superbum*), one of Luther Burbank's most enduring breeding successes. Or they may have ox-eye daisy in mind, those intrepid roadside flowers, or golden Marguerites, or Michaelmas daisies, or Swan River daisies, or Transvaal daisies, or any of a dozen other daisylike flowers.

To identify who's really who, it's important to know something about scientific names, the tongue-tangling appellations that tend to intimidate new gardeners (and more than a few experienced ones). Scientific names—also referred to as botanical names, Latin names, and Latin binomials—are the gold standard, the internationally accepted names for plants. One plant, one name, any time, any place.

For centuries scientists tried to agree on how to classify and name plants but didn't achieve a consensus until the Swedish naturalist Carolus Linnaeus came along with his binomial system. Linnaeus based naming on his understanding of plants' reproductive parts, an approach that scandalized conservatives, but his system nevertheless was accepted in 1753. In the Linnaean scheme, all plants are members of the kingdom Plantae, one of the five basic groups of living things, then distributed in increasingly smaller categories: division, class, order, family, genus, and species.

In the garden, every plant goes by at least two Latin or Latinlike names: a *genus name* and a *species name*, or specific epithet. (A genus is a group of similar plants within a family; a species is a distinct plant within the genus.) For example, the genus name for all poppies—and there are dozens—is *Papaver*, a word that comes from Latin. The opium poppy is one type, or species, of poppy. Its species name is *somniferum*, which means "sleep-producing." So the opium poppy's full scientific name is *Papaver somniferum*. (The second time it's written in a text, it becomes *P. somniferum*.) In print, scientific names are set in italics or underlined, with the genus name capitalized. *Papaver* spp. is shorthand for referring to all the species in the poppy genus. Species names often refer to a characteristic of the plant: its origin, its discoverer, its color, or some other quality. *Viola biflora*, twin-flowered violet, has biflora, or paired, yellow flowers, while *V. tricolor*, Johnny-jump-up, has flowers of three colors: yellow, blue, and purple.

Just as different flowers have the same genus name—there are hundreds of different lilies, or *Lilium* species—flowers from different genera can have the same species name (or variation of the name). There's not only *Viola odorata* (sweet violet) but *Oenothera odorata* (sweet sundrops) and *Reseda odorata* (mignonette). *Odorata* and its variants mean "fragrant," so any flower with a form of *odorata* in its name, like *Lathyrus odoratus*, or sweet pea, should smell good.

Most garden flowers have a third, or *cultivar*, name, which is placed in single quotation marks, such as *Papaver somniferum* 'White Cloud'. A cultivar—gardeners often call them varieties, although botanists make distinctions between cultivars and varieties—is usually a plant that has been developed by people rather than by Mother Nature. (The term *cultivar* is short for cultivated variety; the abbreviation "cvs." stands for cultivars.) Cultivars must differ in some way from the species. 'White Cloud', for example, is an opium poppy with double white flowers, while ordinary opium poppies, plain old *Papaver somniferum*, have single flowers not only in white but also in shades of pink, purple, and red.

The point of all these taxonomic tags—*taxonomy* is the science of classifying plants, and the people who do the work are called *taxonomists*—is to ensure that gardeners are planting the flower they think they're planting. It's worth trying to learn flowers' scientific names. Plants like petunia and zinnia, whose genus name is the same as their common name, are easy. Other scientific names can be a real chore to remember.

One last note: Scientific names aren't eternal. As botanists make new discoveries about known plants, taxonomists sometimes change their scientific names according to the rules set down in the *International Code of Botanical Nomenclature*. Common morning glory, for example, was *Convolvulus purpureus* and *Pharbitis purpurea* before it became *Ipomoea purpurea*. Fortunately, name changes don't occur every day. Chrysanthemum is another genus with more than one alias.

Bigger and Better. *The opium poppy,* Papaver somniferum *'Peony Flowered', gets its cultivar name from its large, frilly blooms, which resemble those of double peonies.*

Life Style

While not all plants blossom—ferns are a notable example—most plants do produce flowers, including trees, woody shrubs and vines, and *herbs*, the omnibus word for plants with soft rather than woody stems. Flower gardeners spend most of their time with herbs, or *herbaceous plants*, which they often group on the basis of how long they live. (Trees and woody plants are outside the scope of this book.)

ANNUALS

Annuals are herbaceous plants that have, as American writer Richardson Wright put it, "a short life and a merry one." Bachelor's buttons (*Centaurea cyanus*), cosmos, marigolds, zinnias, and other annuals do everything in one garden season: They germinate or sprout, bloom, produce seeds, and die. All their energy is directed toward bringing forth seeds to produce the next generation before they are killed by the cold.

Easy Annuals. *Zinnias are one of many undemanding, sun-loving annual flowers. Gardeners can choose from hundreds of brilliantly colorful cultivars if they start with seeds rather than purchase nursery-grown plants.*

Traditionally, garden writers have been dismissive of annuals—too easy to grow, too bright, too common—but annuals are useful and handsome flowers. They have a long bloom time, are less expensive than perennials, and provide instant gratification. There are annuals for every inclination: subtle and gaudy hues, ground creepers and climbers, big and small blooms, intricate and simple forms. There are annuals for dry and wet spots, for large and small spaces, for sun and shade. Most annuals are simple to cultivate, but there is a smattering of demanding species for gardeners seeking a challenge.

BIENNIALS

There aren't many herbaceous *biennials*, plants with lives that extend over two growing seasons. Canterbury bells (*Campanula medium*), common foxglove (*Digitalis purpurea*), money plant (*Lunaria annua*), and other biennials germinate and produce foliage and strong roots the first year, then go dormant. The second year they resprout, flower, set seeds, and die.

That two-season life cycle isn't written in stone. If seeded very early, some biennials will bloom in their first year. Many biennials reliably *self-seed*—drop seeds in the garden that will sprout the next

---

A PLACE TO BEGIN

Annuals aren't foolproof plants, but most are easy to grow and reward their growers with colorful blooms that keep coming throughout the garden season. If you're new to gardening, begin with some of these nearly foolproof flowers.

Ageratum (*Ageratum houstonianum*)

Annual phlox (*Phlox drummondii*)

Calliopsis/plains coreopsis
    (*Coreopsis tinctoria*)

Cockscomb (*Celosia argentea*)

Cosmos (*Cosmos bipinnatus, C. sulphureus*)

Impatiens (*Impatiens walleriana*)

Marigolds (*Tagetes* spp.)

Moss rose (*Portulaca grandiflora*)

Nasturtium (*Tropaeolum majus*)

Petunia (*Petunia* × *hybrida*)

Spider flower (*Cleome hassleriana*)

Sweet alyssum (*Lobularia maritima*)

Zinnias (*Zinnia* spp.)

SPEED DEMONS

*S*ome annuals grow so quickly that there's no need to start them indoors or to buy plants at the garden center. These are a few of the annuals that can be sown in most gardens right where they'll flower. Rough up the soil a bit to provide a seedbed, but don't forget that most annuals need only average soil: Pour on the fertilizer, and you'll get elephantine plants and no flowers.

Calliopsis/plains coreopsis (*Coreopsis tinctoria*)

Cosmos (*Cosmos bipinnatus, C. sulphureus*)

Marigolds (*Tagetes* spp.)

Morning glory (*Ipomoea tricolor*)

Nasturtium (*Tropaeolum majus*)

Night-scented stock (*Matthiola longipetala*)

Pot marigold (*Calendula officinalis*)

Snow-on-the-mountain (*Euphorbia marginata*)

Sunflower (*Helianthus annuus*)

Sweet alyssum (*Lobularia maritima*)

Zinnia (*Zinnia elegans*)

spring—so that you may never have to replant even though your original plants die.

PERENNIALS

The word *perennial* comes from the Latin for "perpetual" or "enduring." Herbaceous perennials aren't always perpetual, but they are plants that live three years or more in the right climate. (The adage about perennials is: "The first year they sleep, the second they creep, the third they leap.") Perennials are the meat-and-potatoes of most flower borders, dying to the ground in winter in cold regions but faithfully resprouting in spring. These flowers, as the poet and son of a Michigan nurseryman Theodore Roethke wrote, "deep in their roots . . . keep the light."

As a rule, perennials bloom for a shorter time and produce fewer seeds than annuals and biennials do.

Garden Stalwarts. *Hybrid peonies with single blooms need less support than double-flowered cultivars. Few perennials can match the peony's elegant beauty, its usefulness in beds and borders, its handsome foliage, or its longevity in the garden.*

They're more difficult to grow from seed, but their flowers also have more complicated shapes and forms and subtler colors. Their leaves also have more varied shapes and textures. It is this visual diversity—and the fact that there are perennials that will flourish in all settings and conditions—that makes vigorous plants like fern-leaf yarrow (*Achillea filipendulina*), purple coneflower (*Echinacea purpurea*), and daylilies so popular with gardeners.

Being perennial and being *hardy* are not the same thing. (For more information about plant hardiness, see Chapter 2, page 29.) Perenniality is a matter of genetics, while hardiness refers to a plant's ability to survive in a particular climate. Still, most perennials are flowers you can depend on and are easy to cultivate and willing to grow and increase without pampering. While a few species called *short-lived perennials* conk out in two or three seasons, most perennials live for many years. A few have octogenarian genes and are likely to outlast those who plant them. The hardest part of growing perennials is curbing your enthusiasm: You'll want one of everything.

BULBOUS FLOWERS

The word *bulb* is used by gardeners to refer to any of the flowers that grow from specialized underground structures. (The formal term for any bulbous plant is geophyte.) All bulbous plants have a *dormant period*, a time when they aren't actively growing. It can be during cold or hot weather, depending on the plant and the location. Most bulbous plants return year after year if they have the right conditions and receive good care.

True bulbs, such as tulips and lilies, are made up of food-storing fleshy scales, tightly joined in some plants, more loosely packed together in others. Roots grow from the wider end. Each bulb contains an undeveloped plant, or embryo, as well as stored food to support its growth. Many bulbs multiply underground and can be dug, separated, and replanted elsewhere. Most hardy bulbs must be planted in the fall; they flower in the spring.

Corms look much like bulbs and store food, but they are actually swollen underground stems, solid inside rather than layered or scaled. At the end of the garden season, the corm dries up and a new corm forms just above the old one at the base of the stem. Corms also produce offsets called *cormels*, which will produce flowering plants in 2 or 3 years. Like true bulbs, corm roots grow from the wider end. Some species of gayfeathers (*Liatris* spp.) grow from corms, as do crocuses and gladioli.

Rhizomes are specialized food-storing stems that grow horizontally, either underground or along the surface of the soil, and produce both roots and shoots. Bearded iris are the most familiar rhizomatous garden flower; they have thick, fleshy rhizomes that grow slowly and create dense plant clumps. Lily-of-the-valley (*Convallaria majalis*) is also rhizomatous, but its long, thin rhizomes—which are dug and sold as *pips*—race through the soil, producing new plants as they go. Plants with rhizomes that can be dug and stored without soil are often sold with bulbs and corms. Gardeners propagate, or create, new plants by cutting the rhizome into pieces.

Tuberous plants include both species that grow from stem tubers, such as tuberous begonias and cyclamens, and flowers like dahlias that grow from tuberous roots. The botanical differences aren't terribly important to home gardeners, except to know that stem tubers have eyes, or buds, like a potato's; a piece of tuber that has at least one eye will produce a new plant. Plants with tuberous roots have buds located at the top of the tuber, so any tuber segment must be attached to a piece of the *crown*—the place where the roots and stem join—for it to produce new plants.

Point of Origin

No one disputes that *angiosperms*, or flowering plants, are both the youngest and largest plant group on earth, but the experts do disagree on how many angiosperms there are. Prominent botanists recently have estimated that the total is at least 425,000 flowering trees, shrubs, and herbs, nearly twice the traditionally cited number of 235,000. Add subspecies, varieties, cultivars, and the new species discovered each year (2,000 or more), and the sum is even greater.

About two-thirds of these flowering species are tropicals, plants that originate between the Tropic of Cancer and the Tropic of Capricorn, the belt that circles the middle of the globe. The rest occur in temperate areas, either north or south of tropical latitudes. Where people were born

Opening Day. *'February Gold' and other hardy daffodils signal the beginning of the garden season. The United States now imports nearly 110 million narcissus bulbs from Holland each year, and thousands more are grown domestically.*

isn't all that important (unless they want to be president); once they invest in a winter wardrobe, those who got their start in life in southern Florida can live just fine in northern Minnesota. In contrast, tropical

ONE LEAF OR TWO?

Botanists recognize two subclasses of angiosperms based on the number of *seed leaves*, or *cotyledons*, the plant has: *Monocotyledons* have one, *dicotyledons* two. (Cotyledons are the embryonic leaves contained in a seed and normally are the first leaves to appear when a seed sprouts.) There are other differences. Monocotyledons, or monocots, such as lilies and daffodils, tend to have fleshy or fibrous roots or grow from bulbs or bulblike organs; to have long, narrow leaves with parallel veins and little or no leaf stalk; and to have flower parts in multiples of three. Dicotyledons, or dicots, including geraniums (*Geranium* spp. and *Pelargonium* spp.), peonies, and phlox, are likely to have taproots or fibrous roots; to have broad or compound leaves with net-veining; and to have leaf stalks. Dicotyledonous flowers typically have flower parts in fours or fives.

plants that call Miami, Florida, home are unlikely to adapt to the conditions in Duluth, Minnesota, where January's mean temperature is 8.5°F, shockingly cold compared with Miami's mean of 67.3°F. Geography is critical to plants: Where they originate—where they are *native*—largely determines where else they can grow or, at the least, how gardeners must treat them. There are no reliable fur coats for plants.

A majority of our favorite garden plants are travelers, not native-born Americans but "green immigrants," to borrow the title of a book by Claire Shaver Haughton. Brought here both intentionally and unintentionally, many of these *exotic*, or *non-native*, species have made themselves at home in North America and live happily in our beds and borders. Foxglove (*Digitalis purpurea*), tulips, daffodils, daylilies, petunias, cosmos—they're all immigrants. "My flowers are near and foreign," the American poet Emily Dickinson wrote to a friend in 1866, "and I have but to cross the floor to stand in the Spice Islands."

Some species here on green cards have adapted too well. Freed from natural competition and controls, they jumped the garden fence and naturalized in the wild so enthusiastically that they now threaten native plants and ecosystems. Purple loosestrife (*Lythrum salicaria*) is one; its spikes of colorful blooms are undeniably pretty, but it has become a floral menace from the East Coast to the West. Noninvasive garden substitutes for purple loosestrife include spike gayfeather (*Liatris spicata*), Chinese astilbe (*Astilbe chinensis*), spike speedwells (*Veronica spicata* 'Red Fox' and other cultivars), hybrid sage (*Salvia × sylvestris* 'Rose Queen'), and tree mallow (*Malva sylvestris* 'Zebrina').

If some flowers make themselves too much at home, others balk in new environments and must be grown differently from the way they grow in their natural settings. *Impatiens walleriana*, the primogenitor of most of our garden impatiens, is a perennial

PLANT HUNTERS

Plant hunters, who deserve credit for many of our favorite garden flowers, are among the most interesting figures in history. Humans have been moving plants from one location to another since the dawn of time, but written records go back only to 1495 B.C., when an Egyptian queen imported frankincense trees from what is now Somalia. The settlement of North America was accompanied by a rush in botanical travelers, both to the New World from the Old and from the New World to the Old. The greatest contribution that can be made to any nation, Thomas Jefferson wrote, "is to add a useful plant to its culture."

Perhaps the most determined plant collector on record was the Englishman E. H. Wilson, who later became the director of the Arnold Arboretum in Boston, Massachusetts. So devoted was Wilson that he nearly died in China after finding the fragrant regal lily (*Lilium regale*). Wilson survived infection and other complications when a boulder smashed his leg in 1910, but he was left crippled with what he referred to as his "lily limp." Despite his handicap, he collected and introduced more plants—about 3,000 species—than anyone else in history.

BOTANICAL BULLIES

*W*hile no garden need contain only indigenous plants, some exotic species have proved so aggressive that responsible gardeners don't grow them. Many of the worst invasive species are woody plants. Perhaps the worst of the worst is kudzu (*Pueraria lobata*), which was brought to the United States from Japan by Thomas Hogg in the late 19th century. It quickly escaped from cultivation and is now known as "the vine that ate the South."

While there is every reason to be cautious, species that are invasive in one region may not be invasive everywhere. Baby's breath (*Gypsophila paniculata*), for example, is a pest on the West Coast but is well behaved in New England. Consult local conservation organizations to determine which exotic flowers (and other plants) are treacherous in your region. Most states maintain lists of species that should not be grown. Among North America's potential floral villains are:

Baby's breath (*Gypsophila paniculata*)

Bachelor's button (*Centaurea cyanus*)

Canada thistle (*Cirsium arvense*)

Common mullein (*Verbascum thapsus*)

Common toadflax (*Linaria vulgaris*)

Crown vetch (*Coronilla varia*)

Dame's rocket (*Hesperis matronalis*)

Globe centaurea/giant knapweed (*Centaurea macrocephala*)

Madagascar periwinkle (*Catharanthus roseus*)

Mugwort (*Artemisia vulgaris*)

Nodding thistle (*Carduus nutans*)

Ox-eye daisy (*Leucanthemum vulgare*)

Periwinkle/myrtle (*Vinca major, V. minor*)

Purple loosestrife (*Lythrum salicaria*)

Scotch broom (*Cytisus scoparius*)

Sulfur cinquefoil (*Potentilla recta*)

Tawny daylily (*Hemerocallis fulva*)

Roadside Blooms. *Ox-eye daisies* (Leucanthemum vulgare) *may seem like quintessential American flowers, but in fact they are floral expatriates from Europe and Asia that have naturalized with great success throughout North America.*

in its native East Africa. It's also perennial in balmy San Clemente, California, but in Kansas and other places where winters are cold, gardeners must handle impatiens as if they were annuals. Similarly, dahlias, natives of Central America, can stay in the ground year after year in places where the mercury doesn't go below 32°F; but in Montana, gardeners must dig dahlia tubers and store them indoors over the winter.

While winter temperature is the most important factor in how we grow plants that aren't native to a region, it's not the only consideration. Mobile, Alabama, and Tucson, Arizona, have similar mean temperatures in January—about 51°F—but Mobile receives an average of nearly 5 inches of rain during that month, while Tucson gets less than 1 inch. Desert species from Asia may thrive in Tucson, but they won't thrive in Mobile. Other factors that influence how a plant adapts—or doesn't adapt—include how humid or hot it gets in summer, what are the nighttime temperatures, and how long the sun shines during the growing season.

How do you know if a flower labeled "perennial" will be perennial in your garden or whether you can leave a bulbous plant in the ground over winter? First, check the information in Plant Portraits, which begin on page 213. Ask other gardeners in your neighborhood, and don't be shy about quizzing the people at local nurseries and garden centers. Your USDA Hardiness Zone rating and microclimate are additional guides to whether or not a flower will thrive in your garden. (See Chapter 2, page 29, for information about hardiness zones and microclimates.) Watch, too, for the climate-related terms used in garden books and on plant labels. (One warning: The words *tender* and *hardy* don't have anything to do with whether or not a plant is easy to grow, long-lived, or pest- or disease-resistant. They have to do with how sensitive a plant is to cold.)

Terms to Grow By

What does all this mean when you're pushing a cart through a garden center or perusing the pages of a mail-order catalog? Understanding a few commonly used terms will help you sort through all the tempting offerings.

Hardy perennials are flowers that are able to grow outside all year round in most North American gardens. Goat's beard (*Aruncus dioicus*), daylilies, and garden phlox (*Phlox paniculata*) are good examples.

Tender perennials, in contrast, can grow outside all year in mild climates but not in cold regions where the ground freezes. Wax begonias (*Begonia semperflorens*), black-eyed Susan vine (*Thunbergia alta*), and petunias persist in warm regions, but don't expect them to reappear in spring in frosty realms. Tender perennials often are tagged with the phrase "perennial grown as an annual."

Cool-weather annuals, also called hardy annuals, are annual species—such as bachelor's button (*Centaurea cyanus*), sweet alyssum (*Lobularia maritima*), snapdragon (*Antirrhinum majus*), and sweet peas (*Lathyrus odoratus*)—that prefer cool conditions;

Tender Treasure. *This 'Karma Amanda' dahlia has long-lasting blooms. Bred especially for cutting, its tubers, like those of other dahlias, must be overwintered indoors in cold regions, then replanted outdoors in spring.*

some are able to survive light frosts. They may die out when the mercury climbs in warm climates but will continue to flower all summer in gardens where temperatures are more moderate.

Warm-weather annuals, or tender annuals, such as cockscomb (*Celosia argentea*), scarlet sage (*Salvia splendens*), and flowering tobacco (*Nicotiana alta*), thrive in heat and are sensitive to even a whisper of frost. Some annuals fall in the middle, between these two extremes, and they're sometimes referred to as half-hardy annuals. These, including strawflower (*Bracteantha bracteata*), spider flower (*Cleome hassleriana*), and baby's breath (*Gypsophila elegans*), do best in warm but not torrid conditions.

Hardy bulbs—flowers such as daffodils, crocuses, and many lilies—tolerate very cold winters. They are grown as perennials in temperate climates, left in the ground to resprout in spring.

Tender bulbs, in contrast, can't endure gelid winters. In all but the warmest parts of North America, these natives of tropical and subtropical regions must be treated as if they were annuals and replaced each year or grown as tender perennials and dug and overwintered indoors. Dahlias, cannas, tuberous begonias (*Begonia tuberhybrida* hybrids), and gladioli are examples of tender bulbs.

One last point: Labels like "tender" or "cool weather" don't just tell what kind of protection from cold a plant might need. They also signal that you may need to give a plant shade during the hottest part of the day, or extra water, or that you must start it indoors, long before it is warm enough to plant it outside. What a plant needs depends on where *it* was from and where *you* are located. Like politics, all gardening is local.

Botany Basics

Experienced gardeners know more than the names of the flowers they grow. They know about plants themselves. Botanists can tell you that African marigolds (*Tagetes erecta*) have leaves that are "pinnate, narrowly lanceolate to lanceolate, acute, sharply toothed," but that sort of detail isn't a prerequisite to or a guarantee for growing healthy African marigolds. Knowing all the terms for foliage and flower shapes and margin and vein patterns is a worthy accomplishment, but it's not the place to begin. A little basic anatomy is more useful: roots, stems, and leaves. If you have all three, you have a living plant.

ROOTS

It's easy to forget about roots. They're usually below ground and out of sight, yet they are as crucial as a plant's visible parts. They not only fasten the plant in the soil and support the stem but also take up minerals and water, largely through their tips and hairs, which are then moved up through the plant. They store food for the plant to use in the future. "Young buds sleep in the root's white core," John Keats wrote in 1818, which is a line from "Faery Song I" that proves the poet was also a botanist.

Garden flowers typically have one of two root systems: tap or fibrous. *Taproots* are fleshy and generally long and unbranched. Typically, they're shaped something like a carrot, which is an edible root, but they also may be branched. Taproots plunge deep into the earth, giving the aboveground plant resistance to drought and wind. Mature flowering plants with taproots, such as globe thistle (*Echinops ritro*), Oriental poppy (*Papaver orientale*), and sea holly (*Eryngium maritimum*), are difficult to transplant and nearly impossible to *divide*, or separate, into several plants.

Most garden flowers have *fibrous roots*, which makes them relatively easy to transplant or to propagate by dividing. Fibrous roots grow more out than down and are well branched. The roots can be thin, even stringy, or thick and fleshy, as is the case with daylilies. And there can be lots of them: The world record is held by a single winter rye plant with roots that totaled 387 miles in length.

Roots cannot produce leaves, but they can sprout more roots and stems. As long as a plant is alive, its roots keep growing, always on the lookout for moisture and food. Like things living aboveground, roots need oxygen and will survive only where it's available. If the soil is too wet or too compacted, most roots suffocate and die. The better its root system, the better a plant grows. "Good roots, good plant" is country wisdom based in science.

STEMS

Stems are the plant's plumbing, carrying water and nutrients to the leaves and sugars back to the roots. And they bear the plant's *buds*, which are

Up and Away. *The dark blue flowers of 'Blue Dawn' morning glory (Ipomoea acuminata) fade from blue to mauve, creating a bicolor effect; this fast-growing tender perennial can climb 12 feet or more in one season.*

undeveloped shoots, as well as leaves and flowers. Stems vary widely and can be round or square, smooth or hairy. Some stems stand erect like plebes at attention; others sprout at an angle; and the stems of vines are limber and require support. A few flowers have underground or ground-hugging stems, but most flower stems are aboveground, upright, fairly rigid, and easy to see.

Also visible are the stem *nodes*, the irregular joints along the stems where shoots, leaves, and flowers are attached. Each stem has an *apical bud*, a bud located at its tip, that not only controls how long a stem grows but influences the development of the *lateral buds* that form along the stem. Gardeners often pinch off the apical bud on plants to encourage lateral buds to sprout and produce a bushier plant.

Internodes are the stem segments between the nodes. Every species has its own genetic instructions as to the length of the internodes, and thus the length of the stem. Vining species like morning glories (*Ipomoea* spp.) have long stems, while other flowers, such as some *Sedum* species, have short ones. Stem length is affected by growing conditions as well as DNA. Plants that get too little light, for instance, produce long, spindly stems. (Rhizomes, which may be aboveground or below, technically are stems, not roots, since they have nodes, internodes, and buds.)

LEAVES

Leaves, as elementary school teachers like to say, are food factories. Through magic called *photosynthesis*, leaves make the sugars and other compounds that plants need to grow. Photosynthesis requires light, chlorophyll, carbon dioxide, and water, and leaves are engineered either to have or to obtain all four. Designed to catch light, most leaves are flat and positioned to avoid being shaded by other leaves on the plant. They have pores, primarily on their undersides, which allow them to take in carbon dioxide, to emit oxygen, and to regulate water loss.

What's important to the gardener is that photosynthesis is vital to a plant's ability to develop, to produce flowers, and even to survive. Cut off a lily's stalk or a daffodil's leaves before they wither and their bulbs will not be able to replenish their food supply and to create the embryos that are next year's flowers. Mow down crocus foliage while it's still green and the plants will not produce new corms to take the place of the old ones. Most leaves are unable to repair themselves if they are damaged. Removing a large share of the leaves of any flowering plant—annual, biennial, perennial, or bulbous—forces it to use its energy to produce new leaves at the expense of producing blooms. Keep pruning a plant's leaves and eventually the plant will die.

When a seed sprouts, the first leaves to appear are the *cotyledons*, or *seed leaves*. They are followed by

FIRST-STRING FOLIAGE

*F*lowers don't need a public relations department, but leaves do, at least among new gardeners. Flowers, remember, bloom for only a few days or weeks, while leaves are present throughout the garden season. Most plants have unassuming foliage, but some have leaves that are highly ornamental. Variegated foliage typically combines green with white, silver, or gold.

Artemisias (*Artemisia* spp.); silver, white

Beardtongue (*Penstemon digitalis*) 'Husker Red'; red

Caladiums (*Caladium* cvs.); white, red, pink, variegated

Canna (*Canna* × *generalis*); maroon, yellow, variegated

Coleus (*Solenostemon scutellarioides*); yellow, red, purple, variegated

Coral bells/heucheras (*Heuchera* cvs.); purple, red, variegated

Hostas (*Hosta* cvs.); gold, blue-green, variegated

Lamb's ear (*Stachys byzantina*); white

Lilyturfs (*Liriope* cvs.); variegated

Lungworts (*Pulmonaria* spp.); variegated

Sedums/stonecrops (*Sedum* spp.); 'Vera Jameson', red; 'Matrona', pink/russet; 'Purple Emperor', purple

Snow-on-the-mountain (*Euphorbia marginata*); variegated

Spotted deadnettles (*Lamium maculatum* cvs.); variegated

Variegated obedient plant (*Physostegia virginiana* 'Variegata'); variegated

Variegated Solomon's seal (*Polygonatum odoratum* var. *thunbergii* 'Variegatum'); variegated

Variegated sweet iris (*Iris pallida* 'Variegata'); variegated

Foliage as Flowers. *Some plants, such as this caladium, are grown primarily for their ornamental leaves rather than their blooms. Caladiums are warm-climate plants but can be grown in containers in northern gardens.*

Botanists use scores of terms to describe leaf shapes, leaf divisions, leaf bases, leaf tips, and more. An ovate leaf is egg-shaped; deltoid is the formal word for a triangular leaf. A leaf with an entire margin has edges that are smooth—no teeth, lobes, or other interruptions; a leaf with toothed edges has dentate margins. *The American Horticultural Society A–Z Encyclopedia of Garden Plants* (1996) and other general garden encyclopedias (see Appendix, page 457, for more titles) provide extensive lists of plant terminology, all the words used to describe plant, leaf, and flower shapes and arrangements.

Knowing the language of horticulture—the difference between a single and double flower, for example—helps gardeners read catalogs and books more intelligently, but not knowing every technical term won't keep anyone from growing healthy plants. Once bitten by the garden bug, however, learning more about the details is inescapable.

As for leaves, what gardeners do need to know from the start is that they come in an amazing pomp of colors, textures, shapes, and sizes. In some flowering plants, such as caladiums (*Caladium* cvs.), coleus (*Solenostemon scutellarioides*), and hosta, the leaves are the main attraction, far more ornamental than the flowers. Tropical plants especially are blessed with eye-catching leaves, but even run-of-the-mill foliage is a garden asset.

Parsing Flowers

As vital as roots, stems, and leaves are, blooms get center stage in the garden. Botany texts describe flowers as "modified or specialized shoots," but they are far more to gardeners: They are the plant's glory. The German poet Goethe called them "the beautiful hieroglyphics of nature by which she indicates how much she loves us." Flowers may do all this, but they are also utilitarian, a plant's *raison d'être*, the main stop on its route to immortality. Reproduction occurs in flowers. The fact that they enchant us with a raft of colors and forms and textures and fragrances is icing on the cake.

Botanists have generated a mountain of technical flower lingo, beginning with *inflorescence*, which is the formal term for the flowering part of a plant. There are big and little flowers, and dozens of bloom forms: trumpets, funnels, tubes, bells, wheels, pompons, cups, and many more. In some species, a flower

the plant's *true leaves*, which may look different from the seed leaves. Mature foliage consists of the leaf itself, or *leaf blade*, and the *petiole*, the stalk by which the leaf is attached to the plant. (In some plants, the leaf has no petiole and is attached directly to the stem.) If there is just a single leaf blade growing from the petiole, as with coral bells (*Heuchera* spp.) or hostas, it is a *simple leaf*. A *compound leaf* consists of several leaflets growing from one petiole; astilbes and marigolds have compound leaves.

is a flower is a flower, a single bloom on a stalk, like a tulip's. Other species, like sweet woodruff (*Galium odoratum*), are more complicated and bear flowers in combinations and different arrangements.

Baby's breath (*Gypsophila paniculata*) has a *panicle* arrangement: many flowers on a many-branched stem. *Umbel* flowers, such as the ornamental onion star of Persia (*Allium christophii*) resemble umbrellas, with each flower stalk originating from a single axis. The blooms of common foxglove (*Digitalis purpurea*), gladioli, and other species with a *spike* arrangement are attached directly to upright stems. Plants with a *raceme* arrangement, such as hollyhock (*Alcea rosea*), have a single upright stem with flowers attached by individual stalks, or *pedicels*.

Whatever their color, size, shape, or arrangement, most flowers have four parts: sepals, petals, stamen, and pistil. (Flowers with all four parts are *complete*; those missing one or more parts are *incomplete*.) At the base of a bloom are the *sepals* (pronounced "SEA-pulls"), the green leaflike wrappers that protect the flower bud. Collectively the sepals are known as the *calyx*, Greek for "covering." When the bud is ready to open, the sepals fold back to allow the petals to unfurl.

White or brilliantly hued, plain or marked, aromatic or scentless, the *petals* are the most conspicuous part of nearly all flowers. Collectively known as the *corolla*, petals are a flower's cleavage, its come-hither means of attracting bees and other pollinators—and gardeners. In addition to a gallery of colors and stripes, spots, and streaks, petals can be *single*, as they are in most cosmos, or *doubled*, as they are in the old-fashioned *Paeonia officinalis*

'Rubra Plena'. They can be *reflexed*, meaning pointing backward, as they are in cyclamens (*Cyclamen* spp.), or recurved, fused, semidoubled, and more. In *The Mikado*, Nanki-Poo and Ko-Ko are celebrating petals when they sing of the "flowers that bloom in the spring, tra la."

The forms, colors, markings, and fragrances of flower petals in the wild are not random but intentional, botanical examples of good marketing. Like contemporary ads targeted at a specific audience, petals have evolved to entice exactly the right pollinators. Hummingbirds, for example, are bewitched by the color red, so plants like bee balms (*Monarda* spp.) and torch lilies (*Kniphofia* spp.) with shapes that require long beaks to reach the nectar—the hummingbird's payoff for carrying the pollen from one bloom to another—tend to be red.

In the Public Broadcasting System's television series *The Private Life of Plants*, host David Attenborough showed viewers what an insect sees. Under ultraviolet light—which replicates an insect's perception—a yellow evening primrose (*Oenothera macrocarpa*) has markings that point pollinators to its nectar and pollen. Foxgloves (*Digitalis* spp.) and

Spider Flower. *Most Cleome hassleriana cultivars are large, erect plants with scented blossoms in hues of white, pink, and pale purple. Cleomes, old-time favorites, often self-seed, reappearing year after year, despite being annuals.*

EXCEPTIONS TO THE RULE

In some flowers, including begonias, lilies, irises, and tulips, the sepals and petals are indistinguishable and are referred to as *tepals*. Anemones, or windflowers (*Anemone* spp.), are among the flowers that don't have sepals. The green leaflike parts at the base of the flowers in some species aren't sepals but modified leaves called *bracts*. A few flowers—poinsettia (*Euphorbia pulcherrima*) and calla lilies (*Zantedeschia* cvs.) are examples—have what appear to be petals but are actually bracts that surround a tight cluster of true flowers.

pansies have similar roadmaps, but theirs are visible to human eyes. Similarly, the colorful "eyes" of many daylily cultivars serve as targets at which pollinators can aim (while also being a joy to gardeners).

Sepals and petals are sterile—essential in attracting pollinators but not directly involved in producing seeds. That process belongs to what biologists call a flower's *essential organs*, its stamen and pistil. The *stamen* is the male part of the flower and contains the pollen-making anthers. (The prim and proper Mrs. William Starr Dana, writing a children's botany book in 1896, called the anthers "dust boxes." When you see flowers, she wrote, "I hope that you children . . . will try to carry away in your minds a clear idea of the size and shape of their dust boxes.") The *pistil*, which contains a *stigma* and a *style*, is the female part of the flower.

Flowers are either *perfect*—containing both male and female parts—or *imperfect*, containing either male or female parts but not both. Most garden flowers, such as petunias, snapdragon (*Antirrhinum majus*), and lilies, are perfect. Imperfect flowers are either *monoecious* (separate male and female flowers are produced on the same plant) or *dioecious* (a plant produces either male or female flowers). Begonias and castor bean (*Ricinus communis*) are examples of monoecious flowers. Goat's beard (*Aruncus dioicus*) bears dioecious flowers, so if you want flowers *and* seeds from goat's beard, you need to have both female and male plants in your garden.

Sex and Reproduction in the Garden

Flowering plants reproduce by asexual and sexual methods. Many species do both. *Asexual*, or *vegetative*, *reproduction*—the creation of progeny from a single parent—is rare in the animal kingdom but is common among plants. Species with a G rating include those that reproduce from above- and underground stems, as iris and lily-of-the-valley (*Convallaria majalis*) do and flowers like lilies and crocuses, which form new bulbs or corms. Other plants propagate by sending up new stems from their roots, and some plants multiply through *fragmentation*, wherein a piece of a plant breaks off, falls to the ground, roots, and grows. Asexual reproduction guarantees another generation because the plant doesn't require outside help.

Gardeners and commercial growers propagate herbaceous plants vegetatively by rooting cuttings, dividing clumps, and tissue culturing, or micropropagating. (For more information on propagating plants, see "Spreading the Joy," page 139.) Asexual reproduction assures conformity. New plants will be identical to their parent: They will have exactly the same traits, good or bad, everything from flower color to the ability to resist or not resist diseases. Vegetative propagation is far faster than growing plants from

Plant to Pollinator. *The reproductive parts of this 'Sigudilla' daylily are displayed prominently, their placement and the bloom's yellow eye carefully designed to facilitate pollination by bees, insects, and other beneficial wildlife.*

Garden Helpers. *Many flowers, including these asters, depend on butterflies and other wildlife to produce seeds, which is one of many reasons why using toxic chemicals in the garden is not in the home gardener's best interest.*

seeds, but what it lacks is genetic variation. With asexual reproduction, there are no new colors or forms or adaptations to insects and weather.

In contrast, *sexual reproduction*, the union of female and male reproductive cells, ensures genetic variation. Many offspring will be similar to their parents and to one another but not necessarily identical, and some may be altogether different. Sexual reproduction is not only how most plants multiply, but it is the way that they improve their chances of survival, adapting over generations to their environment—to cold or heat, for example—or becoming more alluring to pollinators. Plant breeders depend on sexual reproduction to create different and better—and some not-so-different and not-so-better—flowers for our gardens.

Pollination—the transfer of pollen from the anthers to the stigma—comes about in two ways: *self-pollination* within a single flower or from one flower to another flower on the same plant or *cross-pollination* between the flower of one plant to the flower of another plant. Self-pollinating flowers tend to have fewer and smaller blooms and be monocolored and unscented; their descendents have less genetic variability than those of cross-pollinating flowers. Cross-pollinating species usually have many and larger flowers that are brightly colored, marked, and scented. Because of the genetic variety of cross-pollination, these plants tend to be stronger and more successful. Not surprisingly, evolution has produced more cross- than self-pollinating plants.

Cross-pollinating species have an Achilles' heel, however. Flowers can't move about and find mates as animals do. They need help getting the pollen from the anthers to the stigma. Or, as Mrs. William Starr Dana modestly explained in *Plants and Their Children* (1896), they need help getting "the wonderful golden dust that turns flowers into apples as easily as Cinderella's fairy godmother turned rats into ponies" into the "seedbox."

Wind is one of two prime helpers, as hay fever victims know; the other is wildlife. Since wind-pollinated flowers don't require cooperation from the animal kingdom, they tend to be less showy but produce huge amounts of nonsticky pollen to compensate for their inefficient technique. Species that need aid from wildlife—the majority of all flowering plants—typically have flowers that are nectar-bearing as well as brightly colored, patterned, or fragrant. Insects and other animals in their search for food move pollen from one flower to another. (Research suggests that a single bee may visit as many as 50,000 flowers during its lifetime.)

Some flowers, such as goldenrods (*Solidago* spp.), attract a mix of pollinators, but most species are selective. The *coevolution* of plants and animals—plants have adapted to attract particular animals, and animals have learned that particular plants are a good source of food—has created partnerships that guarantee that pollination takes place. Different colors attract different pollinators; other pollinators depend on scent. Most animals like the same fragrances that gardeners like, but even flowers with off odors have their devotees. Our native skunk cabbage (*Symplocarpus foetidus*) is Chanel No. 5 to flies. Flowers that need perching rather than hovering wildlife have evolved with landing platforms. The "mouth" of the common snapdragon (*Antirrhinum majus*), for example, is designed to open when a pollinator of the correct weight—a bumblebee—lands on its lower lip.

Whether accomplished alone or with assistance, pollination's objective is a fruit containing viable seeds that will disperse, germinate, and thrive. New Englander Celia Thaxter, writing in 1894, called seeds more amazing than genies in bottles: "In this tiny casket lie folded roots, stalks, leaves, buds, flowers, seed-vessels . . . all that goes to make up a plant which is as gigantic in proportion to the bounds that confine it as the oak is to the acorn." How seeds are distributed is a subject unto itself, with wind, water, and animals the primary carriers. Gardeners are also major seed emissaries.

Fooling with Mother Nature

Gardeners are not only seed emissaries; they, along with botanists and commercial breeders, are botanical tricksters, changing wild plants for their own needs. As a result, a majority of the herbaceous flowers grown in North American gardens are cultivated varieties, plants altered by humans through selection or more sophisticated breeding methods. *Artificial selection*—people saving and replanting the seeds of the strongest or tallest plant, or the seeds from the plant with the largest or the bluest

Prize Winner. *The daisy Rudbeckia hirta 'Indian Summer' is a 1995 All-America Selections winner. Plants must be widely adaptable to win an award, capable of thriving in home gardens throughout most of North America and performing as well as or better than cultivars already in commerce.*

flowers—has been going on for at least 10,000 years. It is the oldest and simplest way to modify plants.

But it is not the only way. The Assyrians and Babylonians were hand-pollinating date palms in the 8th century B.C. In the 1500s, Dutch growers transformed the tiny wild *Hyacinthus orientalis* into the sturdy, fragrant Dutch hyacinth we cultivate today. The London nurseryman Thomas Fairchild produced the first documented artificial hybrid in 1691. Called "Fairchild's mule," the flower's father was a sweet William, its mother a carnation. In 1866 Gregor Mendel laid out the mathematics of genetics in *Experiments in Plant Hybridization*. Things got seriously complicated in the 20th century: pure-line theory, dominant alleles, chromosome inversion, trisomics, monoploids, diploids, polyploids, backcrosses, F_1 hybrids, interspecific crosses, and much more.

Artificial selection and breeding technology have refashioned some flowers so drastically that our Victorian ancestors wouldn't know them. No 19th-century gardener would recognize 'Teddy Bear' as *Helianthus annuus*. It is a 2-foot plant topped by a shaggy, doubled, petalless flower that has none of a classic sunflower's appeal. We can buy pansies without faces, snapdragons (*Antirrhinum majus*) with no snap, and sweet peas (*Lathyrus odoratus*) that aren't sweet. New and different are not always better.

Flower breeders have been intent on creating new colors and shapes, decreasing or increasing plant size, changing plant form, lengthening bloom time, and improving resistance to diseases and insects and tolerance to heat and cold. The benefits are undeniable: daylilies like 'Stella de Oro', with flowers that stay open for more than a day; 'Profusion Cherry', an award-winning zinnia that is mildew-tolerant and heat- and drought-resistant; and 'Feather Daisy', a compact, semidouble Shasta daisy (*Leucanthemum × superbum*) that doesn't require staking.

Increasingly, our gardens are filled with *hybrids* rather than open-pollinates. *Open-pollinated cultivars*, or OPs, are plants that pollinate on their own and bear seeds that produce offspring pretty much like themselves. Hybrids are artificial crosses—occasionally accidental crosses—between different plants of the same species, between different species, or between plants from different genera.

Hybrids should be identified by a multiplication sign in their name—such as *Leucanthemum × superbum*, the Shasta daisy's formal moniker—but nurseries, seed companies, and garden writers often omit it. In truth, the details of the crossing and recrossing and reverse crossing are so convoluted that the names of grandparents and parents often are lost, or concealed, by breeders. As a result, many hybrid cultivars are listed only by their genus and cultivar name. *Lilium* 'Genteel Lady', for example, is a fragrant Oriental hybrid lily with white, bowl-shaped flowers marked by lavender-pink spots. Despite being both genteel and a lady, neither we nor she has any idea who was her father.

Creating a hybrid demands a knowledge of genetics, tedious hand-pollinating, and careful record keeping, and it can take a decade or more to fashion a cultivar with the desired combination of traits. The *crème de la crème* of hybrids is the F_1 hybrid, the result of crossing two inbred, or stable, plant lines in meticulously controlled conditions, using one as the male parent and the other as the female parent. F_1 hybrids are highly uniform and have what is called "hybrid vigor," the potential to grow faster or bigger or better, or have superior adaptability to different conditions, such as heat or cold.

The down side? In addition to a much higher price tag for a packet of seeds or a nursery-grown plant, gardeners can't save seeds from hybrids for next year's garden. Actually they can, but they will be

Old-Timer. *The origins of the ubiquitous* Hemerocallis fulva *are lost in time. Known as the common daylily, the tawny daylily, and the ditch lily, it was an early European immigrant to North America. Although it spreads vigorously, it rarely produces seeds.*

disappointed by the results. Seeds from hybrid plants do not *come true*: They do not yield uniform seedlings with all the characteristics of their two parents. Some hybrids, such as the popular marigold triploid hybrids, which are crosses between tall African marigolds and compact French marigolds, rarely produce *any* seeds. Those they do bear often don't germinate, and those that germinate don't come true.

While many gardeners believe that the advantages of hybrids outweigh any of their disadvantages, the unstinting emphasis by commercial breeders on hybrid cultivars has hatched an interest in old and OP cultivars. The champion of this movement—and a recipient of the MacArthur Foundation Genius Award—is Kent Whealy and his colleagues at Seed Savers Exchange. Whealy has focused on vegetables and fruits, while his wife, Diane, has established the Flower and Herb Exchange, an effort to preserve older, or *heirloom*, garden flowers, wildflowers, and herbs. Scott Kunst at Old House Gardens in Michigan has done similar work in behalf of bulbous flowers. (See Appendix, page 457, for more information.)

HEIRLOOM BEAUTIES

*I*f you want to grow flowers that your grandmother grew (or even her great-great grandmother grew), there are plenty of older cultivars still available thanks to horticultural preservationists. These heirloom plants, named varieties that are at least 50 years old, deserve a place in today's gardens. New is not always better, as this sample of old-timers proves.

Astilbes (*Astilbe arendsii*) 'Bridal Veil', 1929; *A. japonica* 'Gladstone', before 1934

Bearded irises (*Iris* Bearded Hybrids) 'Honorabile', 1840; 'Wabash', 1937; 'Great Lakes', 1942; 'Amigo', 1943; 'Ola Kala', 1948

Bachelor's button (*Centaurea cyanus*) 'Jubilee Gem', before 1937

Bee balm (*Monarda didyma*) 'Cambridge Scarlet', before 1908

Cosmos (*Cosmos bipinnatus*) *C. sulphureus* 'Sunset', circa 1895; 'Sensation', 1936

Crocuses (*Crocus chrysanthus*) *C.* × *luteus* 'Dutch Yellow'/'Yellow Mammoth', 1665; 'Snowbunting', 1914

Crown imperial (*Fritillaria imperialis*) 'Lutea', 1665

Daffodils (*Narcissus* cvs.) 'King Alfred', 1899; 'Mrs. R. O. Blackhouse', 1921

Dahlias (*Dahlia* cvs.) 'Kaiser Wilhelm', 1892; 'Jersey Beauty', 1923; 'Bishop of Llandaff', 1927

Daylilies (*Hemerocallis* cvs.) 'Hyperion', 1924, 'Thelma Perry', 1925

Everlasting pea (*Lathyrus latifolius*) 'Pink Beauty', before 1924

Fairies' toadflax (*Linaria maroccana*) 'Fairy Bouquet', 1872

Fall-blooming, or Japanese, anemone (*Anemone* × *hybrida*) 'Honorine Jobert', 1851

Feverfew (*Tanacetum parthenium*) 'Flore Pleno', before 1700

Flowering tobacco (*Nicotiana alata*) 'Lime Green', before 1950

Garden phlox (*Phlox paniculata*) 'Trapis Blanc', 1901; 'Bridesmaid', 1910; 'Rijnstroom', 1910; 'Bright Eyes', 1934

Gladioli (*Gladiolus* cvs.) 'Carolina Primrose', 1908; 'Atom', 1946; 'Spick & Span', 1946

Hollyhock (*Alcea rosea*) 'Indian Spring', before 1930

Hyacinth (*Hyacinth orientalis*) 'Marie', 1860; 'Lady Derby', 1875; 'Distinction', 1880

Japanese iris (*Iris ensata*) 'Goldbound', 1885

Lilies (*Lilium* cvs.) *L. lancifolium* 'Splendens' 1804; *L. speciosum* 'Rubrum', 1830; 'Mrs. R. O. Blackhouse', 1921; 'Fire King', 1933

Lupines (*Lupinus* cvs.) 'Russell Hybrids', 1937

Marigold (*Tagetes patula*) 'Naughty Marietta', 1947

Mexican sunflower (*Tithonia rotundifolia*) 'Red Torch', 1951

Morning glory (*Ipomoea nil*) 'Scarlet O'Hara', circa 1939

Nasturtium (*Tropaeolum majus*) 'Empress of India', 1884

New England aster (*Aster novae-angliae*) 'Mrs. S. T. Wright', before 1907

Oriental poppy (*Papaver orientale*) 'Princess Victoria Louise', by 1930

Peonies (*Paeonia* cvs.) 'Francis Ortegat', 1850; 'Festiva Maxima', 1851; 'Duchesse de Nemours', 1856; 'Sarah Bernhardt', 1906

Pot marigold (*Calendula officinalis*) 'Orange King', before 1850

Sedum/stonecrop (*Sedum*) 'Autumn Joy', before 1920

Snapdragon (*Antirrhinum majus*) 'Sawyer's Mixed', before 1600

Sneezewort (*Achillea ptarmica*) 'The Pearl', circa 1850

Sweet pea (*Lathyrus odoratus*) 'Cupani', 1699; 'Painted Lady', 1737; 'Mrs. Willmont', 1901; 'Lord Nelson', 1907

Tawny daylily (*Hemerocallis fulva*) 'Europa', 1700s

Tulips (*Tulipa* cvs.) 'Prince of Austria', 1860; 'Rosamunde Huykman', 1895; 'Generaal de Wet', 1904; 'Lac Van Rijn', 1620; 'Fantasy', 1910; 'Zomerschoon', 1620

American Gold. *Native rough-and-tumble flowers like gloriosa daisies (Rudbeckia hirta 'Gloriosa') are widely adapted to many regions. Understanding the conditions in your garden and choosing appropriate plants is critical to growing flowers successfully.*

CHAPTER TWO

Where Does Your Garden Grow: Taking Stock of Local Conditions

I try to accept what nature hands me and work with it.

Dorothy Sucher, *The Invisible Garden*, 1999

GOOD ADVICE FOR ANY GARDENER IS THE horticultural version of look before you leap: Plan before you plant. That doesn't mean creating exhaustively detailed, exact-scale blueprints and unequivocal plant lists before you step outside with a spade; it means taking time to consider a few basic questions. Already you know you want to grow flowers, but why do you want to? There are dozens of good reasons: flowers for vases, flowers for drying, flowers to brighten the landscape, flowers to hide the neighbor's garbage can, flowers for pressing, flowers for fragrance, flowers for dyes or potpourri, and plenty more.

Chances are that you have not one but multiple reasons, so thinking ahead will help you know what kind of flower garden or gardens to create and what plants it (or they) should contain.

If filling vases is the goal, you're going to need flowers with sturdy stems and staying power, garden peonies like the fragrant pink 'Mrs. Franklin D. Roosevelt' or 'Burpee's Climax' marigold, not daylilies, whose blooms stay open only one day, or the ground-hugging moss rose (*Portulaca grandiflora*). And since you'll be cutting most of the flowers, you won't want the garden bordering the front walk or the patio. (See Chapter 8, page 177, for information about creating special gardens.)

In addition to resolving why you're growing flowers and what kind of plot they will need, judge how much time you have, how much energy you have, and what size pocketbook you have. As the English writer Rudyard Kipling put it, "Gardens are not made by singing 'Oh, how beautiful,' and sitting in the shade."

Labor-free gardens are imaginary things, like unicorns and fairies, but limiting the size of your gardens and choosing species that demand less rather than more care will reduce the time and energy required. Don't let your imagination get too far ahead of your judgement. And while plants, seeds, soil amendments, and tools don't grow on trees, there are ways to do things on the cheap or, at least, on the cheaper. Starting plants from seeds and making compost are two obvious money-saving enterprises.

As for the proverbial green thumb, Henry Beard and Roy McKie (*Gardening: A Gardener's Dictionary*, 1982) explain that it is simply a "common condition suffered by gardeners in which the skin of the thumb develops a greenish hue as a result of handling large amounts of currency at nurseries." All kidding aside, a green thumb—the ability to make plants grow—is learned, not inherited.

The Big Picture

In addition to outlining what you want to do in the garden, think about what is possible in terms of your climate and weather. They determine what flowers are most likely to succeed in your location. *Climate* refers to the prevailing conditions of a particular spot, a composite averaged over time. *Weather* is what's happening today. As television forecasters like to say, "Climate is what you are supposed to get, weather is what you do get." With an annual average of less than 8 inches of rain per year, Phoenix, Arizona, has a dry climate, but its weather today may have been rainy.

Scientists divide the globe into climate regions, or zones: tropical, subtropical, desert, savannah, temperate, and polar. North America (and Hawaii) includes all those zones, from tropical in southern Mexico and southern Florida, to polar in northern

BLOOM TIME

*L*atitude influences when flowers blossom, so just because your cousin's Siberian iris (*Iris sibirica*) is flowering in St. Louis, Missouri, doesn't mean yours in Denver, Colorado, will be. The rule of thumb is that for every degree of latitude, up or down, there is a difference of three or four days. A wonderful guide to bloom times is Joseph Hudak's *Gardening with Perennials Month by Month* (2nd ed., 1993), a book worth buying or borrowing from your local library. Hudak used his 40 years of gardening experience to document the flowering times of more than 700 species in his Boston, Massachusetts, location. To establish when the same plant will bloom in your garden, determine your latitude, find the difference between it and that of Boston, which is about 43°, and do the math. For example, bee balm (*Monarda didyma*) begins flowering in mid-June in Boston, but it would flower about two weeks earlier in Cincinnati, Ohio, latitude 39°. (The formula is straightforward: 43° − 39° = plus 4° × 4 days = plus 16 days.) If you don't know your latitude, go to the web site of the U.S. Geological Survey (geonames.usgs.gov/pls/gnis/web_query.gnis_web_query_form) and look it up.

DEAR DIARY

Our weather memories are notoriously bad and often are disproved by the official numbers. Climate and weather records are available for many North American cities, but if there are no National Weather Service data for your location, check with the Cooperative Extension Service or local airport, or log on to the National Weather Service (www.nws.noaa.gov).

Better still, keep your own records. A weather diary is an essential garden tool, and daily entries make it the most helpful. Note high and low temperatures and rainfall amounts, and record when plants start or stop flowering and other garden events. Several years of entries are necessary before you can draw conclusions—for example, that your frost-free date usually coincides with the maple trees leafing or the start of the Little League season. Even the best of records aren't foolproof, but they will make your garden more weatherproof.

Canada and Alaska. Your climate not only determines what flowers will flourish in your beds and borders, it determines how you grow them. Gardeners in both San Diego, California, and Bismarck, North Dakota, can grow impatiens, but San Diegans can grow them outdoors 365 days a year, while Bismarckians, with only 135 frost-free days a year, must treat impatiens as if they were annuals.

Climate is affected by latitude, by elevation, by the lay of the land, and by the direction the wind blows. The farther you are from the equator—which changes the angle of the sun's rays and the length and intensity of light—the colder and longer your winter, and the cooler and shorter your growing season. The latitude of Austin, Texas, is about 14 degrees south of Green Bay, Wisconsin's. On average, Austin gardeners have 125 more days each year to grow flowers than do Packers' fans. And 125 days is a lifetime in the garden, long enough to sow sunflower seeds *and* pick the flowers they produce.

While latitude is important, it's not all-important. Elevation counts too. The higher you're perched, the fewer the days above freezing there will be and the colder it will be in both

Local Conditions. *The strong stems of 'Attila' tulips make them a good choice for garden beds that are exposed to moderate winds.*

MOUNTAIN CLIMBERS

People in high places may have *carte blanche* in five-star hotels, but they have special challenges in the garden. Elevation, nutrient-poor soils, and compressed growing seasons are conditions few envy. Despite the limitations, high-altitude gardeners can grow many flowers, and experts insist that at high-elevations, blooms have richer colors. Provided they have good snow cover, these are some of the perennials most likely to succeed at 8,000 feet; plants marked with an asterisk are hardy to 10,000 feet.

Alpine poppy (*Papaver alpinum*)★

Autumn Joy sedum (*Sedum* 'Autumn Joy')

Bleeding heart (*Dicentra spectabilis*)★

Candytuft (*Iberis sempervirens*)★

Clustered bellflower (*Campanula glomerata*)

Columbines (*Aquilegia* spp.)★

Delphinium (*Delphinium elatum*)★

Eastern pasque flower (*Pulsatilla patens*)★

Garden phlox (*Phlox paniculata*)

Iceland poppy (*Papaver croceum*)★

Lupine (*Lupinus polyphyllus*)

Meadow anemone (*Anemone canadensis*)

Mountain bluet (*Centaurea montana*)

Orange coneflower (*Rudbeckia fulgida*)

Painted daisy (*Tanacetum coccineum*)★

Peonies (*Paeonia* cvs.)

Shasta daisy (*Leucanthemum × superbum*)

Siberian iris (*Iris sibirica*)

Spike speedwell (*Veronica spicata*)

Sweet William (*Dianthus barbatus*)★

Yarrows (*Achillea* spp.)

Zinnia (*Zinnia elegans*)

Tough Character. *Spike speedwell* (Veronica spicata 'Goodness Grows') *not only flowers from late spring into autumn, it thrives at high altitudes, attracts butterflies, is deer-resistant, and makes a fine cut flower. (In earlier times the plant was sometimes known as thunderbolts because picking it was reputed to bring on thunder and lightning.)*

summer and winter. Temperatures drop from 3°F to 5°F for every 1,000 feet of elevation above mean sea level. When gardeners at the base of a mountain get rain in spring or fall, those in the clouds are likely to get snow. Colder temperatures mean plants on top of Old Smokey grow more slowly than they would at sea level, so high-flying gardeners need to look for short-season cultivars. One bright note is that high-altitude gardens usually get a winter-long snow cover. Snow is a superb mulch, insulating and

protecting perennial and bulbous plants from cryogenic temperatures that they couldn't survive if the ground were bare.

Mountains affect not only those gardening on them but those living near them. In North America, the prevailing winds blow from west to east. Gardeners located west of mountain ranges tend to have more cloudy, wet days than they want, whereas those downwind must invest in sprinkler systems, hoses, and watering cans. Combine mountains with a nearby ocean—such as the northwest combo of the Cascade range and the Pacific—and the contrast is astonishing. Olympia, Washington, west of the Cascades, gets about 50 inches of rain a year, while Spokane, Washington, east of the mountains, receives less than 17 inches.

Facing Facts

Perhaps not just original sin but jealousy originated in the garden. It is the *green*-eyed monster, after all, and the grass is always *greener* in someone else's yard. In truth, gardeners are an envious lot: Those in Bakersfield, California, would trade their souls for more rain, and residents of Barrow, Alaska, where there is less than a week of frost-free days each year, would kill for a couple of months with temperatures in the 60s. Hell may not have limits—Doctor Faustus claimed it didn't—but gardens do.

According to no less an expert than British garden maven Gertrude Jekyll, "There is no spot of ground, however arid, bare or ugly, that cannot be tamed into such a state as may give the impression of beauty and delight." That reassuring pronouncement is heightened by the fact that much of North America falls in the temperate zone, one with four distinct seasons that receives at least 30 inches of precipitation each year and has average summer temperatures above 60°F. That means most of us can grow an immense variety of flowers in our yards and on our decks, patios, and rooftops. Within the temperate zone, however, there are different climates, and within climates different microclimates. The trick is to discover what flowers will prosper where you hang your hat.

Native Sons and Daughters. *Colorful 'Calypso Mix' is a hybrid monkey flower, a tender perennial and descendent of the native North American Mimulus species. Most gardeners grow monkey flowers as if they were annuals, replanting them each year.*

JUST LIKE HOME

One tip-off to which species will like your garden's conditions comes from their geographic origins. (The study of what naturally grows where is called *plant geography*.) Many of our favorite garden flowers didn't come from down the street: Plants travel more than jet-setters, constantly crisscrossing oceans and continents. The welcome mat is always out for a beautiful flower, whatever language it speaks.

Place of origin discloses what garden conditions best suit a plant's needs—what it takes to succeed in cultivation. Flowers from hot, arid regions, such as the California poppy (*Eschscholzia californica*), are used to sun, sandy soil, and drought. Plant them in shade and clay soil, water them every day, fertilize them every week, and they'll be dead before you learn to pronounce *Eschscholzia*.

Knowing who hails from where also is fun in its own right. *Primula vulgaris*, the ancestor of many of our garden primroses, comes from England, whereas summer's familiar red-zonal geranium (*Pelargonium × hortorum*) got its start in South Africa. White Easter lily (*Lilium longiflorum*) is a native of the Ryukyu Islands off southern Japan, where it is known as *teppo-yuri*, or blunderbuss lily, a reference to the wide mouth of its blossom. Most asters are North Americans; *Aster novae-angliae*, New England aster, suggests as much in its name. Sun-loving cosmos (*Cosmos* spp.) come from the southern United States and Central America. Yellow monkey flower (*Mimulus guttatus*) is one of the many native plants first described by Meriwether Lewis during his western journey with William Clark; with the help of Sacajawea, who, he wrote, "has been of great Service to me as a pilot through this Country," Lewis collected the flower on July 4, 1806, near what is now Missoula, Montana.

Don't fret if the flowers you want to grow come from the Mediterranean and you live on the prairie, or if they come from the tropics and you garden in Maine. Flowers don't have to be natives—they just have to be able to cope with your garden's conditions. Most flowers are astonishingly flexible and with a gardener's help can survive in conditions quite unlike those where they were born. You may have to make adjustments: Upstate New Yorkers can grow zonal geraniums (*Pelargonium × hortorum*) but as annuals, not perennials; gardeners in South Carolina can grow pansies but only during the few months when temperatures are cool. You *can* take the flower out of the country, and, to some degree, you also can take the country out of the flower.

ZONING IN

Another guide as to whether a plant species will do well at your address is how *hardy* it is, how much cold can it endure in winter. To help gardeners determine plant hardiness, the United States Department of Agriculture created the *Hardiness Zone Map*. It divides North America into 11 zones based on the average annual minimum temperature. You'll see these hardiness zone numbers listed when you read about perennial and bulbous flowers (and shrubs and trees) or look at plant labels and plant catalogs. (Annual flowers, since they only live for one growing season, don't have hardiness-zone numbers.)

Hardiness zone ratings of plants are hugely useful guides, but they aren't written in stone. Hands-on gardeners know that many species and cultivars are far hardier than the experts say. Yellow corydalis (*Corydalis lutea*), a perennial with fernlike foliage and bright yellow blooms, is regularly labeled Zone 6; but Vermonters who have good snow cover in winter grow corydalis in Zone 4a. Being a little skeptical about the hardiness designation of a flower species or cultivar isn't a bad idea. At the same time, you can only push the envelope so far. Trying to grow a plant that clearly is not hardy in your region is like skating on thin ice.

WHERE AM I?

The USDA Hardiness Zone Map is reproduced in garden books and posted at many garden centers and nurseries; it's also available through County Extension Service offices (see Appendix, page 457, for a reprint of this map). Computer-savvy gardeners can use an online map that allows zooming in on different regions by going to www.usna.usda.gov/Hardzone/ushzmap. html. If you can't determine your hardiness zone, ask another gardener or a professional at your local nursery or garden center.

Hardy Soul. *'Summer Wine' is one of hundreds of daylilies that can survive winter in USDA Zone 2, where the average minimum temperature ranges from −40°F to −50°F. Daylilies are one of the least problematic perennials.*

Most North American gardens fall into USDA Hardiness Zones 4, 5, 6, 7, and 8, and their owners can grow a huge range of flowers. Plant hardiness, however, isn't just a matter of winter's average low temperature. There are other factors that affect a plant's capacity to survive goose bump–producing winters.

Plant vigor. Flowering plants that are stressed during the growing season—that don't have the conditions they need, including adequate light, water, or fertilizer—are less able to withstand cold temperatures.

Plant genetics. Hardiness is in the genes, which explains why two cultivars of the same species can have different hardiness ratings. However, plants can acclimatize to some degree over time. Buying locally grown perennial plants is hardiness insurance, because good growers propagate from their most vigorous, winter-tough plants.

Soil. Plants that should be hardy but are growing in a wet site often die from root rot in winter. Conversely, gardeners with fertile, well-drained soil may be able to grow flowers designated one hardiness zone warmer than their own.

Wind. Like people, plants are susceptible to *wind chill*, when the air feels colder than the thermometer reads. Gardeners without protection from polar gusts should be cautious and purchase plants rated one zone colder than their own.

Snow. Snow keeps soil temperatures stable and protects plants during winter. Gardeners with a deep, constant snow cover often can grow flowers rated one or two zones warmer than their own.

MORE LIMITS TO CONSIDER

How cold it gets in winter is only one climate hurdle. Other factors that bear on how well a plant performs are the length of the growing season, hottest summer temperatures, and the amount of sun and rain. Talk to neighbors, other gardeners, and local experts for help with choosing flowers that will succeed in your garden. Visit nearby gardens and nurseries and consult the professionals at the closest Cooperative Extension Service office. People who are gardening near your location are going to be the most helpful.

The growing season. The length of the growing season—the number of days between the last frost in spring and the first frost in autumn—is crucial horticultural information. Annual flowers that need 200 days to get from seed to blossoms must be sown indoors in many parts of North America to get a head start on the season. Perennial asters (*Aster* spp.), which loiter before they bloom in late summer, may be cut down by frost before their buds

open in short-season gardens. The difference in the length of growing seasons across North America is substantial: a meager 67 days in Laramie, Wyoming; 157 in Denver, Colorado; 185 in Springfield, Illinois; 199 in New York City (thanks in part to all that concrete); 217 in Portland, Oregon; 244 in Mobile, Alabama; and 365 in Miami, Florida. (For garden-season lengths and dates of first and last frosts of selected cities, see Appendix, page 457.)

Local gardeners and garden professionals will know the most about when it's safe—or at least *should* be safe—to set out tender plants and when it's likely that Jack Frost will put an end to the flower garden. Garden books, nursery and seed catalogs, and seed packets often give general information about the time it takes *in ideal conditions* from *germination*—the seeds sprouting—to the first flowers. Additional information about specific flowers is included in Plant Portraits, beginning on page 213.

Heat. High temperatures can be a problem for plants, making it difficult for them to *respire*, the botanical version of breathing. Cultivating flowers in hot, dry regions requires extra water, shade during the hottest part of the day, and mulch to help keep the soil cool and moist. In the South, where it often is hot and humid in summer, flowers may need more sun and better air circulation in order to avoid diseases such as mildew. Gardeners in New Orleans, Louisiana, not only must deal with the

(continues on page 39)

WHEN THE DOGWOODS BLOOM

Well before the National Oceanic and Atmospheric Administration (NOAA) became everyone's weather handicapper, gardeners relied on phenological, or recurring natural, signs to help them know when to do what in the garden. The word *phenology* comes from the Greek word *phaino*, "to show or appear." What was once local lore ("sow corn when oak leaves are the size of a squirrel's ear") long ago turned into a worldwide network of gardeners and scientists. The Norwegians began keeping formal records in the 1850s, the Finns in the 1890s, and now there are established phenological networks throughout North America, such as Plantwatch, a Canadian network that recruits school children to "track the green wave of spring."

Because phenology data reflect local differences in temperature, rainfall, and day length, they are highly reliable predictors of local conditions, far better than a single indicator like standard frost-free dates, which have only a 50 percent probability. It takes a few years of observation and notes to establish horticultural guideposts. Any event can be recorded: the day the bluebirds return; the first appearance of fireflies or mosquitoes; or the first leaves on the weeping willow. In time the correlations will become clear. When phoebes nest in the yard and crocuses flower, temperatures are unlikely to fall below freezing; or wait until the lilacs bloom before you set out tender flowers, such as impatiens. And for the record, "When the dogwood flowers appear / Frost will not again be here."

LEGENDS OF THE FALL

*E*veryone knows about garden chrysanthemums—nurseries and garden centers are crammed with almost nothing else beginning in August—but there are other fine perennial and bulbous plants for the autumn garden. Reliable *Rudbeckia* 'Goldsturm' starts blooming in late summer and hangs on through September, enough to qualify it for a place on the autumn honor role, and dahlias wait until September to do their best. Other end-of-the-season candidates include:

American bugbane (*Cimicifuga americana*)

Asters (*Aster* spp.)

Autumn crocuses (*Colchicum autumnale,*
    C. speciosum, C. hybrids)

Autumn daffodil (*Sternbergia lutea*)

Black snakeroot (*Cimicifuga racemosa*)

Boltonia (*Boltonia asteroides*) 'Snowbank'

Catmint (*Nepeta subsessilis*)

Closed bottle gentian (*Gentiana andrewsii*)

Crocuses (*Crocus speciosus, C. sativus*)

Fall-blooming, or Japanese, anemones (*Anemone
    hupehensis, A.* × *hybrida, A. tomentosa*)

Goldenrods (*Solidago* spp.)

Ironweed (*Vernonia noveboracensis*)

Japanese onion (*Allium thunbergii*) 'Ozawa'

Joe-Pye weeds (*Eupatorium* spp.)

Nippon daisy (*Nipponanthemum nipponicum*)

Obedient plant (*Physostegia virginiana*)

Perennial sunflowers (*Helianthus* spp.)

Russian sage (*Perovskia atriplicifolia*)

Sedums/stonecrops (*Sedum* cvs.) 'Autumn Joy',
    'Frosty Morn', 'Vera Jameson', *S. sieboldii*

Sneezeweed (*Helenium autumnale*)

Tall gayfeather (*Liatris scariosa*) 'September Glory'

Toad lilies (*Tricyrtis* spp.)

Turtleheads (*Chelone* spp.)

American Gold. *Vigorous and hardy native flowers like black-eyed Susans* (Rudbeckia fulgida) *and early goldenrod* (Solidago juncea) *help end the garden season on a colorful note. Both are easy to grow and maintain in the home garden.*

Everyday Beauty. *Like many common annual flowers, hybrid petunias need warm temperatures and sunshine to thrive. The colorful petunias sold today are descendents of seeds collected in South America by French explorers 200 years ago.*

SOME LIKE IT HOT

Gardeners may hate high temperatures, but there is a gold mine of annual flowers that are willing to put up with heat. Some are technically perennials or biennials, but most North American gardeners treat these species as annuals and replant them each year. Not only do these plants endure high temperatures, but they are happy in sandy soil. Adding compost to the soil helps retain moisture and provides needed nutrients. But don't overfeed annuals: Too much fertilizer produces lush leaves at the expense of blooms.

Annual baby's breath (*Gypsophila elegans*)

Annual phlox (*Phlox drummondii*)

Black-eyed Susan (*Rudbeckia hirta*)

California poppy (*Eschscholzia californica*)

Calliopsis/plains coreopsis (*Coreopsis tinctoria*)

Cockscomb (*Celosia argentea*)

Cosmos (*Cosmos bipinnatus, C. sulphureus*)

Creeping zinnia (*Sanvitalia procumbens*)

Four-o'clock (*Mirabilis jalapa*)

Golden Marguerite (*Anthemis tinctoria*)

Madagascar periwinkle (*Catharanthus roseus*)

Moss rose (*Portulaca grandiflora*)

Petunia (*Petunia* × *hybrida*)

Scarlet sage (*Salvia splendens*)

Sea pink/common thrift (*Armeria maritima*)

Spider flower (*Cleome hassleriana*)

Statice (*Limonium sinuatum*)

Sunflower (*Helianthus annuus*)

Verbenas (*Verbena* spp.)

Zinnias (*Zinnia* spp.)

DRY BONES

*S*pring-flowering bulbs, such as tulips, crocuses, hyacinths, and daffodils, are successful in moderately dry sites, as are these sun-loving perennials and annuals. Always begin with organically rich soil—which will help hold what moisture there is—and remember that dry doesn't mean waterless: All garden flowers need some moisture. Most of these flowers also crave sun.

African daisy/Cape marigold (*Dimorphotheca sinuata*)

Bachelor's button (*Centaurea cyanus*)

Black-eyed Susan (*Rudbeckia hirta*)

Blanket flowers (*Gaillardia* spp.)

Butterfly weed (*Asclepias tuberosa*)

Calliopsis/plains coreopsis (*Coreopsis tinctoria*)

Cockscomb (*Celosia argentea*)

Cosmos (*Cosmos bipinnatus, C. sulphureus*)

Creeping zinnia (*Sanvitalia procumbens*)

Gas plant (*Dianthus* var. *purpureus*)

Gazanias (*Gazania* hybrids)

Globe thistle (*Echinops ritro*)

Goldenrods (*Solidago* spp.)

Marigolds (*Tagetes* spp.)

Moss rose (*Portulaca grandiflora*)

Nasturtium (*Tropaeolum majus*)

Petunia (*Petunia* × *hybrida*)

Phlox (*Phlox* spp.)

Pot marigold (*Calendula officinalis*)

Purple coneflower (*Echinacea purpurea*)

Scarlet sage (*Salvia splendens*)

Sea holly (*Eryngium amethystinum*)

Sea pink/common thrift (*Armeria maritima*)

Sedums/stonecrops (*Sedum* spp.)

Statice (*Limonium sinuatum*)

Sunflower (*Helianthus annuus*)

Sweet alyssum (*Lobularia maritima*)

Tall gayfeather (*Liatris scariosa*)

Verbenas (*Verbena* spp.)

Yarrows (*Achillea* spp.)

Zinnias (*Zinnia* spp.)

---

effects of hurricanes, they must deal with a location where the mean temperature is 82.7°F in July, and there is only 58 percent possible sun but 6.2 inches of rain and an average morning relative humidity of 91 percent. Flower growers in the Big Easy know adversity.

Some plants, such as bellflowers (*Campanula* spp.) and delphiniums, are nearly impossible to grow if you live where sunstroke is as common as dandelions in lawns. Peonies, daffodils, and tulips are among the flowers that love cold in winter and won't live on unless they have enough *chilling days,* days when the mercury falls below 32°F.

Average temperature. The average temperature during a garden season also affects what flowers will grow well. Green Bay, Wisconsin, has only 119 days between its last and first frosts, but its mean temperature in July and August is nearly 70°F. Compare that with San Francisco, California, which has about 310 frost-free days but a mean temperature in July and August of only 60°F. Many plants won't grow when the mercury is below 50°F and only poke along when it's 60°F. There may be enough time to get sunflowers to bloom in the city by the bay, but there may not be enough heat.

Sun and Rain. Plants can't do without sun and rain or, at least, without light and water. North American locations differ substantially in the amount of sun and rain they receive. Boise, Idaho, for instance, gets 87 percent of possible sunshine in July, whereas Pittsburgh, Pennsylvania, gets only 57 percent. Rain, too, is unevenly rationed: Bakersfield, California, averages zero precipitation in the month of July, while Fort Myers, Florida, gets 8.98 inches.

Gardeners must chose plants carefully if their climate is lean in the sun or rain department. Water can be provided—although environmentally responsible gardeners will want to plant drought-proof species if they live in regions where rain is as rare as hen's teeth—but sun is pretty much an absolute. If your location is a cloudy one or your garden is shaded by trees or structures that can't be changed, choose flowers that are willing to thrive in the shadows.

COOL CHARACTERS

Gardeners with cool weather in summer, such as those living in the Pacific Northwest or the far north, must forego heat-loving, sun-worshiping species, but there is still plenty to fill their pots, window boxes, beds, and borders. Among the most reliable choices are these perennials.

Astilbes (*Astilbe* cvs.)

Bellflowers (*Campanula* spp.)

Bergenias (*Bergenia* spp.)

Columbines (*Aquilegia* spp.)

Coral bells/heucheras (*Heuchera* spp.)

Cyclamens (*Cyclamen* spp.)

Delphiniums (*Delphinium* cvs.)

English daisy (*Bellis perennis*)

Geums/avens (*Geum* spp.)

Hellebores (*Helleborus* spp.)

Hostas (*Hosta* cvs.)

Lady's mantle (*Alchemilla mollis*)

Lungworts (*Pulmonaria* spp.)

Lupine (*Lupinus* 'Russell Hybrids')

Oriental poppy (*Papaver orientalis*)

Pasqueflower (*Pulsatilla vulgaris*)

Primroses (*Primula* spp.)

Siberian bugloss (*Brunnera macrophylla*)

Speedwells (*Veronica* spp.)

Thread-leaved coreopsis (*Coreopsis verticillata*)

Violas (*Viola* spp.)

Yarrow (*Achillea millefolium*)

Eye Candy. *Oriental poppies* (Papaver orientalis) *flower in late spring, die back once the mercury rises, and resprout in fall. Their blooms, which are the largest of all poppy species, are notable for their brightly colored petals resembling crepe paper.*

Working with Your Landscape

The Enlightenment poet Alexander Pope wisely advised gardeners, "Consult the genius of the place in all." Whether you're beginning from scratch or have inherited a garden, *know where you are*. Take a careful look before you begin digging and planting. Your garden space is a *microclimate*, a place that may have prevailing conditions slightly—or greatly—different from the surrounding landscape, and there are a zillion microclimates within every climate zone. For example, if your flower garden is alongside a house, it will be warmer because of heat loss from the building and the solar energy absorbed by it. If you're gardening on a north slope, conditions will be colder than normal, but if you're planting on a southern slope, conditions may be one or two zones warmer than what the USDA Hardiness Zone map indicates for the region.

Large bodies of water moderate temperatures, as grape growers along the shores of Lake Erie know. Anyone blessed with a waterfront address—salt or fresh water—is likely to have an additional week or three to grow plants than someone living 100 miles from the shore and cooler conditions in summer and warmer conditions in winter.

City gardeners can expect summer temperatures as much as 10°F hotter than the surrounding countryside's. Caused by the replacement of vegetation with concrete and asphalt and called the urban heat–island effect, the higher temperatures may lengthen the growing season by several weeks. They also mean that flowers must be watered more frequently.

Climates can't be changed, but microclimates can be modulated:

- **To Warm Things Up.** Windbreaks—walls, fences, and hedges—that block wind will make a site warmer. So will the amount of sun a site receives, especially afternoon sun. Eliminating objects that shade a site will make it warmer. Organically rich soil heats up more quickly than does heavy clay soil, and well-drained soil stays warmer than wet soil. Raised and mulch-free beds tend to warm up more quickly in spring.

- **To Cool Things Off.** A northern or eastern exposure is cooler than a southern or western one. Shade—from trees, shrubs, fences, hedges, and more—lowers temperatures, especially afternoon shade. Mulching keeps the soil moist and roots cool, and watering can give flowers just the help they need to survive excessive heat.

Landscape design is outside the scope of this book, but it is important to decide what you want flowers to do for you and your landscape. Are you gone in July and August and want flowers in spring, or do you want flowers from June until the first frost? Does your flower garden have a particular purpose? Are your flowers intended for the vase? Do you need flowering vines to obscure an ugly fence or to climb a post? Want fragrant flowers to scent the patio at dusk? Will the flower beds you imagine complement the style of your house? (For resources on garden design, see Appendix, page 457.)

OLD SALTS

Flower beds located near the ocean or close to streets that are treated with deicing salt in winter need to be filled with species that are salt-tolerant. A number of ornamental grasses, such as feather reed grass (*Calamagrostis* × *acutiflora* 'Karl Foerster') are salt-tolerant, as are these perennial flowers, all judged most likely to succeed despite salt spray from the Seven Seas or from the local highway department.

Bee balm (*Monarda didyma*)
Coral bells/heucheras (*Heuchera* cvs.)
Daylilies (*Hemerocallis* cvs.)
Hostas (*Hosta* cvs.)
Lilyturf (*Liriope muscari*)
Obedient plant (*Physostegia virginiana*)
Pinks (*Dianthus* spp.)
Rose campion (*Lychnis coronaria*)
Sea hollies (*Eryngium* spp.)
Sea lavender (*Limonium latifolium*)
Sea pink/common thrift (*Armeria maritima* 'Splendens')
Sedums/stonecrops (*Sedum* spp.)

Now look at your garden canvas, the space you have to work with. What *can* you do? Do you have an acre of treeless land or room for only a half-dozen containers and a window box? Are you starting from scratch or are there established beds and borders? Winter is the ideal time to see a garden's basic structure and gauge its exposure. Herbaceous flowers disappear in winter in most parts of North America, leaving the permanent elements, the *hardscape*. Unless your wallet is exceptionally large, the hardscape is there to stay.

Hardscape levies limits: For most gardeners, houses and driveways can't be moved, nor can the roots of big trees or underground wires, pipes, and tanks. More than one country gardener has discovered that the ground over the septic tank is not the best place to dig. Veteran city gardeners know that planting flowers where neighborhood children cut through to reach the next street is certain disaster, unless the flowers are accompanied by a chain-link fence topped with barbed wire.

To avoid common mistakes, diagram what is already in place in your landscape. Use graph paper and try to keep to scale. To simplify measurements, make each grid on the paper equal to 1 foot, but don't agonize over measurements. (If you prefer pixels to paper, you may want to purchase an inexpensive software program.) Outline all the immovable objects on the graph paper: property lines, house, patio, deck, porch, garage, shed, driveway, fence, walls, large trees and shrubs, sandbox, compost pile, soccer field, walkways, whatever. And indicate direction on your drawing: north, south, east, and west.

Next, take notes about what's going on and what you like and don't like. What beds already exist and what grows in them? (You may want to recruit a neighborhood gardener to help you identify what you already have.) If you want to see flowers from your patio, where could they go? Where does the sun shine? Where is it shady? Does the wind roar through one corner of your property? Where does the ground stay wet or dry out at a minute's notice? Where do your children play soccer? Do you like straight lines or curves? Do you like formal gardens

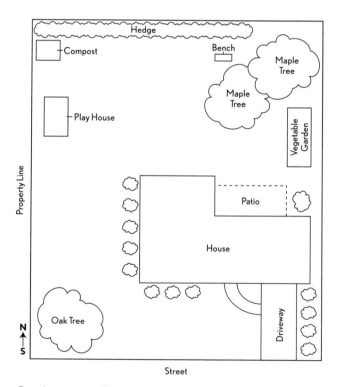

Gardening on Paper. *Before heading to the garden center for peonies and petunias, make a simple drawing of your yard to establish where best to grow flowers. As you add plants to your landscape, add them to your diagram as well.*

or more casual designs? What style best fits the architecture of your house?

Now the task is to combine what you want—a formal border 100 feet long and filled with sun-loving perennials, for instance, or an informal bed of woodland plants—with what is possible. No direct sun? Forget the perennial border. No shade? Forget the woodland garden. Flower gardens don't exist in isolation, so you must accept the limitations of your space. No space is hopeless, however; soil and drainage can be improved, rainfall can be supplemented, and there are flowers for both sun and shade. Last, ask yourself once again: How much time and energy can I give to digging, planting, pulling weeds, trimming, and deadheading and the other chores that all gardens require? If you answer "one," based on a

1 to 10 scale, forget beds and borders and consider growing a few flowers in containers.

Be of Good Courage

You only have to peruse one or two coffee-table garden books to be convinced that everyone has a yard containing a mammoth, spic-and-span herbaceous border filled with color-coordinated flowers forever in full bloom, backed by a moss-covered stone wall, and graced with garden furniture imported from France. Even visiting modest gardens may be intimidating. Yet looking at what others have done can and should be both inspirational and helpful. Don't be overwhelmed. Established gardens once were new.

Easy Lilies. *'Yellow Pixie', an Asiatic hybrid lily, is one of many "pot," or "patio," lilies now available to home gardeners. Very hardy, quick to multiply, and easy to grow, up-facing pot lilies are less than 2 feet tall, which makes them ideal for planting in containers.*

Everyday gardeners have plenty of wisdom to pass on, so make an effort to meet them. They hang out at nurseries, garden centers, botanical gardens, and at garden lectures and plant-society meetings. Most are generous spirits, eager to talk about their successes and their failures. You may want to join a garden club, even if you haven't planted a single flower, or enroll in a Master Gardener course. (The course covers the basics of plant science and home horticulture; phone your local Cooperative Extension Service and ask if a Master Gardener program is available in your area.)

Soak up all you can from others, but keep in mind that there is no "right" way to design a bed or border or yard. No two flower gardens are exactly the same. It's your space, and you can do whatever you want with it. If you want a round bed filled with fire-engine-red salvia, orange cannas, and one plastic pink flamingo, create it. If you want to plant a dozen different daylilies in a straight line, do it. If you want to follow a plan you found in a magazine, go ahead. Of all the elements in a home landscape—trees, shrubs, walkways, fences, and more—flowers are by far the easiest to change, the least expensive to buy, and the quickest to establish.

If you overworry about floundering, consider some of these guidelines. These are not rules, things gardeners *must* do, but a few basics on which nearly all gardeners agree.

Take notes. See as many gardens as you can—both public and private—and record what you like and don't like. Look for specific flowers or combinations of flowers that please you; notice the way flowers are integrated into the landscape. Are you drawn to fancy-free gardens, or do you prefer straight lines and orderly patterns? You may want to photograph particular flowers or gardens for reference.

Start small. Like Rome, a garden isn't created in a day. Or even a season. Rather than panicking that you must do everything at once, choose one part of your landscape, such as your curb lawn or a bare spot by the back door, and begin there. The standard wisdom is to give any established garden a year before you change it, but if you know you hate rhododendrons or roses or wisteria, don't wait: Rip them out.

Trust in dumb luck. One thing in the garden always leads to something else, often something good. Keep a sharp eye out, and you'll see plants that beg to be neighbors, or beg not to be! Planting diagrams are useful, but they aren't the last word—don't be afraid to stick in plants that aren't on the design. You don't even have to have a design. Let your garden grow. As it grows, so will your confidence and skill.

Insist on instant gratification. Careful planning is sensible, but don't let it stop you from *gardening*. As Sydney Eddison writes in *The Self-Taught Gardener* (1997), too many garden books approach garden-making "as if it were arithmetic—theory and technique first, plants and pleasure last." Instead, she writes, "you should go outside and play as soon as possible." Buy some annuals and stick them in the garden or in a pot, so you can have blooms *now*.

Simple is usually better. You'll eventually arrive at flower gardens that please you, but when you're starting out, keep things simple. Opt for beds with fewer angles or curves or patterns filled with fewer different kinds of flowers. Rather than a bed with one peony, one gloriosa daisy (*Rudbeckia hirta*), one daylily, one lily, one blanket flower (*Gaillardia aristata*), one large-flowered coreopsis (*Coreopsis grandiflora*), one zinnia, and one zonal geranium (*Pelargonium × hortorum*), create an eye-popping blast of yellow, gold, and red with five 'Early Sunrise' coreopsis, five 'Dazzler' blanket flowers, and five 'Autumn Colors' gloriosa daisies. (For more information about creating beds and borders, see Chapter 5, page 85.)

Begin with easy plants. To increase your chances of success, begin with flowers that are easy to grow. Lists differ by garden location and conditions, but among the most nondemanding perennials for a sunny site are Siberian iris (*Iris sibirica*), peonies, daylilies, rudbeckias, and purple coneflower (*Echinacea purpurea*). For partial shade, try hostas, astilbes, goat's beards (*Aruncus* spp.), bleeding hearts (*Dicentra* spp.), and lungworts (*Pulmonaria* spp.). Marigolds (*Tagetes* spp.), spider flower (*Cleome hassleriana*), zinnias, and cosmos are easy to grow annuals in a sunny site; in shade, nothing compares with impatiens. (For a list of easy to grow annuals, see "A Place to Begin," page 10.) Daffodils and crocuses are two hardy bulbs that are close to foolproof. All these are common flowers for a good reason: They are common because they almost never fail.

Flower gardens are not permanent exhibits. No garden is made once and for all, like a museum diorama. Like it or not, gardens change over time on their own. Plants get larger and multiply, and plants die. Trees grow taller and shade beds that once were sunny, or they die and let in sun where once it was shady. And gardeners change gardens. They discover new flowers and tire of old ones. They make beds larger and smaller; they move plants. If your garden doesn't please you, or if some plants are unsuccessful, you can make changes. There's always next year in the garden. Changing the garden, frankly, is more than half the fun.

Plan Ahead. *Handsome combinations like the blue catmint* (Nepeta × faassenii) *and the pale yellow flowers of* Achillea 'Moonshine' *along this walkway are not usually achieved by accident. Repeating the same color creates a sense of unity and order.*

Welcome Home. *Even a handsome weathered brick walkway is enhanced when edged by flowers. Choose low-growing species that have long bloom times and foliage that remains neat and attractive after the plants stop flowering.*

CHAPTER THREE

Home Ground: Assessing Your Garden Site

*B*e it ever so humble,
there's no place like home.

J. Howard Payne, *Clari, the Maid of Milan,* 1823

THERE MAY BE NO PLACE LIKE HOME, BUT MOST gardeners would improve "home" a bit if they could. Less wind, perhaps, and more sun. Better soil, more rain. Or less rain, less humidity. In a perfect world, we'd all have lightly sheltered, sunny gardens with rock-free, perfectly draining, organically rich soil, a southern exposure, a long growing season, and enough gentle rain to keep plants happy. But the world is not perfect, and your garden site also is unlikely to be perfect, to have the ideal attributes for growing flowers. Rather than railing about its limitations, get to know them—and get to know your garden's virtues.

47

There are places in North America where it's impossible to grow flowers outdoors, but there aren't many. Use a wide-angle lens when you first look at your site's *topography*, by definition "the configuration of a surface including its relief and the position of its natural and man-made features." Flat or on a hillside? Wet or dry? Windy or still? Sunny or shady? One- or two-story house? Flower gardens that relate naturally to their topography—harmonize with it and are in scale—are the most successful and satisfying. In *Gardens Are for People* (1955), the American landscape designer Thomas Church wrote that the unity of the garden and its site, including its buildings, was fundamental.

First of all, track the pattern of the sun. Your property's *exposure*, its relationship to the sun, is defined by its topography. To grow sun-loving flowers, such as sunflowers and dahlias, a southern or southwestern exposure is required in most parts of North America. There are precise ways to measure when and for how long the sun shines in every nook and cranny of your property, but they require exact latitude data plus an understanding of altitude, azimuth, and magnetic deviation, as well as skill with graph paper, compass, protractor, and plumb bob. For most gardeners, a little patience and a sharp eye are enough: Record where and for how long the sun shines each week *throughout* the growing season.

If you can, avoid placing a flower garden in a low spot where cold air stagnates and late spring or early fall frosts are routine. (The top of a hill normally is windier and drier than the bottom of a hill; south and southwest exposures are warmer and sunnier but also dry out more quickly.) Stay away from solidly enclosed spots, like a small area boxed in by a building or a tall, solid fence; these places won't get the sun and breezes that most garden flowers need. Good air circulation discourages many plant diseases, especially in the Southeast and other humid regions. If your garden location demands a barrier for privacy or discouraging intruders, make sure it isn't one that it keeps plants from getting all the fresh air and light they need.

After taking a general inventory, focus on what you have in terms of wind, water, sun, and soil. They are flower garden basics.

Wind Worthy. *The multicolored blossoms of* Paeonia lactiflora *'Bowl of Beauty', a popular, fragrant Japanese peony, aren't immune to strong breezes but withstand them better than the heavy double blooms produced by many garden peonies.*

CLIMB HIGH

*W*oody vines, such as clematis, wisteria, and bougainvillea, are well-documented breeze-blockers that are better known than perennial and annual climbers because nearly all provide protection in summer *and* winter. All vines have one thing in common: They need something sturdy to ascend. Most of these climbers are grown as annuals, except in tropical gardens, and all of them produce flowers. Several species have ornamental fruits as well. Even the perennials on this list, remember, won't block the wind in winter except in gardens where winter feels like summer.

Balloon vine (*Cardiospermum halicacabum*)

Balsam pear / bitter gourd (*Momordica charantia*)

Black-eyed Susan vine (*Thunbergia alata*)

Blue trumpet vine (*Thunbergia grandiflora*)

Bottle gourd (*Lagenaria siceraria*)

Canary creeper (*Tropaeolum peregrinum*)

Chicabiddy / creeping gloxinia (*Maurandya scandens*)

Chilean glory vine (*Eccremocarpus scaber*)

Climbing nasturtium (*Tropaeolum majus*)

Cup-and-saucer vine (*Cobaea scandens*)

Hyacinth bean (*Lablab purpureus*)

Moonflower (*Ipomoea alba*)

Morning glories (*Ipomoea* spp.)

Purple bell vine (*Rhodochiton atrosanguineum*)

Scarlet runner bean (*Phaseolus coccineus*)

Spanish flag (*Ipomoea lobata*)

Sweet pea (*Lathyrus odoratus*)

Twining snapdragon (*Maurandella antirrhiniflora*)

Daisies on a Vine. Thunbergia alata, *black-eyed Susan vine, is a fast-growing perennial that flowers from summer through fall. Hardy in warm climates, this tropical climber ascends by twining and is superb for creating privacy with its dense foliage and profusion of blooms.*

Blowin' in the Wind

Fresh air and good air circulation are vital to keeping plants and their growers happy. As Thomas Hill, who wrote the first English-language how-to garden book (*The Gardener's Labyrinth*, 1577) explained: "Evile aire . . . doth not only annoy and currupt the plants . . . but choke and dul the spirits of men." And women.

Zephyr breezes and fresh air are one thing, but face-numbing, bone-chilling wind is something else. At worst, mistral winds kill plants; at best, they retard growth. Moreover, blustery winds make quick work of many tall flowers, toppling delphiniums and tattering the blossoms of bearded iris and Oriental poppies (*Papaver orientale*).

And it's not just cold winds. Hot winds, like the Santa Anas that blow from east to west into southern California gardens, dehydrate plants, especially nonnative flowers that aren't adapted to arid conditions. Finally, wind compounds the effects of both cold and heat, and it works hand in hand with sun. If you block the wind and not the sun, the temperature rises; block the sun and not the wind, and the temperature falls. Wind, after sun and water, has the greatest impact on plant growth.

If wind roars unrelentingly through your property—minicyclones in the 15 mph range—consider installing permanent windbreaks, such as fences, trees, shrubs, and vines. Most gardens call for protection on their north or west side, but it's not unusual for prevailing winds to come from one direction in winter and a different direction in summer. Before you plant or build, make sure of the direction of the breezes you want to block. If you install a barrier on the wrong side of the garden, you'll have cold

LIVING FENCES

*T*hese woody shrubs, some of which bear flowers and ornamental fruits, are good wind-blocking candidates. You don't want to create a solid barrier, but you may want to set plants closer to each other than is normally recommended.

Autumn olive (*Elaeagnus umbellata*); deciduous, Zone 3

Bamboos (*Phyllostachys* spp.); broad-leaved evergreen, Zone 6/7

Barberries (*Berberis* spp.); deciduous, Zone 4

Carolina allspice/sweet shrub (*Calycanthus floridus*); deciduous, Zone 4

Common boxwood (*Buxus sempervirens*); broad-leaved evergreen, Zone 5

Common lilac (*Syringa vulgaris*); deciduous, Zone 3

Firethorns (*Pyracantha* spp.); deciduous/broad-leaved evergreen, Zone 5

Forsythias (*Forsythia* spp.); deciduous, Zone 4

Fragrant honeysuckle (*Lonicera fragrantissima*); deciduous, Zone 4

Heavenly bamboo (*Nandina domestica*); broad-leaved evergreen, Zone 7

Hollies (*Ilex* spp.); broad-leaved evergreen/deciduous, Zone 5

Japanese photinia (*Photinia glabra*); broad-leaved evergreen, Zone 7

Mock orange (*Philadelphus coronarius*); deciduous, Zone 4

Peegee hydrangea (*Hydrangea paniculata*); deciduous, Zone 3

Privets (*Ligustrum* spp.); deciduous/broad-leaved evergreen, Zone 3

Rugosa rose (*Rosa rugosa*); deciduous, Zone 3

Spireas (*Spiraea* spp.); deciduous, Zone 3

Viburnums (*Viburnum* spp.); deciduous, Zone 3

Virginia sweet spire (*Itea virginica*); deciduous, Zone 5

Yews (*Taxus* spp.); evergreen, Zone 3

---

air swirling around and settling on your lilies or hot air drying them out. The windbreak, of course, should be set perpendicular to the direction of the prevailing wind.

A windbreak has to be higher than the plants it protects, but it's not necessary to recreate the Berlin Wall. The horizontal zone of protection is about six times the height of the barrier—more if the ground slopes down, less if the ground rises. Semiopen structures, such as picket fences, do a better job than solid ones, which can create vicious downdrafts and turbulence on the leeward side, and they don't blow over in a gale. Tests show that a curved or S-shaped windbreak is more effective than a straight one.

Live windbreaks are an attractive solution but are like children: They grow up. Vines and shrubs can be set closer to the flower garden than trees can, but don't forget that the wide-ranging roots of even moderately tall woody plants like lilacs will swipe moisture and nutrients from an adjacent flower bed. One way to discourage roots from sneaking into your flower garden is to dig a 2-foot-deep trench between the garden and the windbreak, sever any roots you encounter, line the trench with a weed-suppressing fabric, and refill the trench with soil.

Typically the best plants for blocking winds are native species, which are adapted to your climate. Using plants of varied heights—a mix of deciduous and evergreen and small trees and shrubs—also gives year-round wind protection and reduces the chance that diseases or insects will decimate the windbreak in one fell swoop. Stagger plants, setting them in several rows rather than a single line—tall species farther from your garden, shortest nearer your garden. You get bonus points for creating a living windbreak: They are attractive backdrops to flower gardens, are lures for birds and other wildlife, and shut out street noise, shortcutting walkers, and nosy neighbors.

Cold spring winds that come and then go can be tamed by temporary barriers, such as cloches or floating row covers placed over tender flowers or a small fence made of burlap or a commercial wind fabric.

Not only do small covers and fences reduce the wind speed by as much as 50 percent, they can raise the air temperature several degrees on the leeward side, which may be just enough to keep your zinnia seedlings from freezing.

Gardeners in very windy sites can help themselves by using mulches, which reduce water loss from the soil, and by planting low-growing plants, which are better able to deal with stiff breezes. Flowers with small leaves and deep roots also are better designed to tolerate heavy winds. Avoid tall plants with large leaves, such as ligularias (*Ligularia* spp.), and be prepared to stake delphiniums and other tall species with long stems. Some perennials are able to withstand brisk breezes despite being tall. A short list includes fall-blooming, or Japanese, anemones (*Anemone hupehensis*, A. × *hybrida*, A. *tomentosa*), gayfeathers (*Liatris* spp.), spider flower (*Cleome hassleriana*), purple coneflower (*Echinacea purpurea*), Joe-Pye weeds (*Eupatorium* spp.), goldenrods (*Solidago* spp.), and foxtail lilies (*Eremurus* spp.).

Garden Scenery. *Trees and shrubs create a good-looking backdrop for flower beds and borders while protecting taller plants, such as these bee balms* (Monarda *spp.) and coneflower* (Echinacea purpurea), *from devastation by strong winds.*

Water, Water, Everywhere

Unfortunately, water isn't everywhere. As the English journalist Reginal Arkell expressed it in *Green Fingers* (1934):

> *A Gardener's life*
> *Is full of sweets and sours;*
> *He gets the sunshine*
> *When he needs the showers.*

How true. Even a quick look at a weather map reveals that some parts of North America get all the rain a flower garden needs, some far less. Plants, like gardeners themselves, are largely made of water (70 percent of a person's weight, about 90 percent of a plant's). Without water there would be neither flowers nor the people who grow them.

If it does rain at your house, and rains often and long, don't choose a low spot for growing flowers. Sodden soil is air-poor soil, and plant roots need air as well as moisture. (In fact, roots don't grow in the soil itself, they grow in the spaces between the soil particles.) Anywhere water pools for more than two days after a rain is the wrong place for a flower garden, unless you're prepared to raise the level of the soil or drain the area. Both solutions can be expensive, especially the second, which requires not only drainage tiles and dry wells but mammoth excavation equipment. In wet spots, sticking to plants that love moist soil is a third, cheaper option.

There are two simple ways to determine your soil's *porosity*, its ability to drain. To test a damp site, dig a square hole 1 foot deep and just as wide, and fill it with water. After 24 hours, refill the hole and wait. If the hole isn't empty after 12 hours, the

Water Wise. *Testing the soil's porosity before you plant is always wise. If a foot-square test hole doesn't drain after 36 hours, choose another location for growing flowers.*

soil is not porous enough for plants to live in easily. To test if soil is too porous—it drains too quickly—water the site to a depth of 6 inches. If after 48 hours the top 6 inches of soil are dry, the soil needs to be made less porous. Gardeners in arid regions with too little rain sometimes make sunken beds to conserve moisture, or they install permanent irrigation systems. (For information about improving soil, see Chapter 4, page 63.)

You can't make the sun shine, but you can make it rain. How much you can make it rain depends on where you live. Water covers three-quarters of the earth's surface, but less than 5 percent of it is fresh water, and it's needed for more than growing flowers. (Studies show that an individual who used about 5 gallons of water a day in 1900 now uses more than 100 gallons a day.) Everyone should be water-wise, but gardeners in areas where water is as scarce as bee balm without hummingbirds must be particularly conservation-minded.

One approach in arid regions is to become a *xeriscaper*, someone who cultivates drought-tolerant plants, many of which have foliage that is silver or gray, hairy or waxy, and long and narrow. *De rigueur* in xeri-gardens are drip irrigation systems, labyrinths of PVC lines equipped with emitters, pressure regulators, and computerized timers that can cut water use in half. (For a list of flowers that don't fuss when conditions are dry, see "Dry Bones," page 39; for more information on xeriscaping, see Appendix, page 457.)

Xeriplants. *Plants like lamb's ear* (Stachys byzantina), *licorice plant* (Helichrysum petiolatum), *Victoria rosemary* (Westringia rosariniformis), *and lavender* (Lavandula angustifolia) *are good choices for gardens that receive little rain.*

RISING TO THE OCCASION

Raised beds—gardens elevated above ground level—are more than a solution to sites that are too wet to grow most flowers. They're also a way of dealing with problematic soil conditions, such as high acidity or poor texture, and a way out of forcing gardeners with sore backs and other infirmities to hang up their trowels. Raised beds also warm up more quickly in spring, a boon to cold-climate gardeners. Despite being *à la mode*, raised beds have been around for centuries. The German abbot Walahfrid Strabo, known as Walahfrid the Squinter, described surrounding his 9th-century herb garden "with planks" and raising it "a little above the level ground" to keep it from washing away.

A height between 6 and 12 inches is typical, but a very wet spot or a very bad back may compel something higher. Bed size depends on what you plan to grow, but be sure you can reach the center of the bed from two sides so you don't have to walk in the bed to care for the flowers.

Freestanding raised beds are easy to make—just pull up soil from the surrounding area or purchase a truckload of soil—but they erode easily. Planting the perimeter with a flowering ground cover, such as lesser periwinkle (*Vinca minor*), will help prevent soil from washing away.

Raised beds contained in a wood, brick, or stone frame are more time-consuming and expensive to build, but they are erosion-proof and their edges add a decorative element to the landscape. (Do not use lumber treated with creosote or pentachlorophenol, which can leach into the soil and damage plants.)

Be sure to loosen the existing soil of a raised bed to a depth of at least 2 feet, then add enough additional soil and organic matter to reach the desired height. Commercial topsoil normally contains few nutrients and little organic matter. Before you plant, amend it with generous amounts—a 50:50 ratio—of compost and other organic matter, let it settle for a week or two, then add more organic matter if necessary.

The obvious signs of not enough moisture are sagging leaves and stems, and even modest wilting can be permanently damaging to plants, especially young plants. Other red flags? Look for leaves that curl, lose their luster, or turn gray-green or yellow, or for blooms that slow or stop. Check the soil before you water, because too much moisture also causes wilting. If it's dry to a depth of 3 or 4 inches, you need to add water. Another easy test is to dig down 3 inches, take a handful of soil, and squeeze it. If it forms a ball, there's enough moisture. Annuals tend to need more water than perennials, which have larger root systems. All flowers growing in containers demand scrutiny; in hot weather, they may require daily watering.

In torrid, dry regions, it may take 2 inches of water per week to keep flowers happy, but the general touchstone is 1 inch a week, plus another ½ inch for every 10 degrees above 60°F. That means that a rainless week with temperatures in the 80s calls for 2 inches of gardener-made rain. To calculate how many gallons it will take to add 1 inch of water to your garden, multiply the area of the garden by 0.083. Then multiply that product number by 7.5. For a 10 × 10–foot garden, the math would be 10 × 10 = 100 × 0.083 = 8.3 × 7.5 = 62.25 gallons of water.

The only advantage of watering with a hose and nozzle is the pleasure it sometimes gives the gardener. Unless you direct the flow only to the plants that need it and are stupendously patient, hand watering with a hose is both wasteful and unlikely to deliver enough water to be genuinely helpful. "When you are wet to the skin you contentedly declare your garden has had enough," Czech playwright Karel Čapek mused in *The Gardener's Year* (1929), and "you go in to get dry. In the meantime the garden said 'Ouf,' lapped up your water without a wink, and is as dry and thirsty as it was before."

Overhead lawn sprinklers also waste water through evaporation—the loss can be 70 percent on a day that is dry, sunny, and windy—and they wet everything in their range, not just the flowers. If you use an overhead sprinkler (and they are wonderfully convenient), don't turn it on and walk away. To calculate how long you need to run it, set two or three coffee cans in the garden. After sprinkling for 30 minutes, measure the water in the cans to get a rough idea of how much water your garden is receiving.

To keep track of rainfall, install a rain gauge. Don't worry about tenths of inches; instead, combine what the gauge tells you and what your plants tell you. Plants are the ultimate authority: If there has been no rain but your flowers look healthy, forget watering and consider yourself lucky.

When you water isn't important if you're using a drip irrigation system or a soaker hose. Gardeners in hot, humid climates who use overhead sprinklers should water in the early morning, so that plant leaves can dry before nightfall. (Wet foliage encourages many plant diseases.) In hot, dry climates use sprinklers in the evening or early morning to lessen evaporation. In cool, northern gardens, water in midmorning so that you're not pouring cold water on plants just waking up from a cold night.

The amount of water flowers need is influenced not only by where they are growing but by the soil in which they are growing. (For more about soil, see Chapter 4, page 63.) Flowers growing in sandy soils, which drain quickly, typically need more than 1 inch of water per week. Loam soils are in the middle; they retain water better than sandy soils but less well than

Damp Spots. *The award-winning, 3-foot Siberian iris 'Caesar's Brother' blooms in spring and tolerates a wide range of conditions, but it does best in fertile soil that is very wet and slightly acid.*

WET FEET

Some flowers are content with soil that stays damp. That's *damp*, not sopping, although some of the plants on this list will also grow in sopping soil and even standing water—plants that grow in constantly wet conditions are marked with an asterisk (*). For the most part, the flowers listed here need moist soil that is rich in organic matter and drains but is still too wet for sages (*Salvia* spp.), California poppy (*Eschscholzia californica*), and spider flower (*Cleome hassleriana*).

Anise hyssop (*Agastache foeniculum*)

Astilbes (*Astilbe* cvs.)

Bee balms (*Monarda* spp.)

Blue vervain (*Verbena hastata*)

Buttercups (*Ranunculus* spp.)

Canada lily (*Lilium canadense*)

Canterbury bells (*Campanula medium*)

Flags/flag irises (*Iris virginica, I. pseudacorus*)*

Forget-me-not (*Myosotis scorpioides*)*

Goatsbeard (*Aruncus dioicus*)

Green and gold/golden star (*Chrysogonum virginicum*)

Hostas (*Hosta* cvs.)

Japanese primrose (*Primula japonica*)*

Joe-Pye weeds (*Eupatorium* spp.)*

Labrador violet (*Viola labradorica*)

Ligularias (*Ligularia* spp.)*

Lobelias (*Lobelia* spp.)*

Meadow rues (*Thalictrum* spp.)

Monkey flowers (*Mimulus* spp.)*

Pot marigold (*Calendula officinalis*)

Rose mallow (*Hibiscus moscheutos*)

Scarlet rose mallow (*Hibiscus coccineusi*)*

Siberian iris (*Iris sibirica*)

Snakeroots (*Cimicifuga* spp.)

Sneezeweed (*Helenium autumnale*)*

Spiderworts (*Tradescantia* Andersoniana Group)

Spike gayfeather (*Liatris spicata*)

Swamp milkweed (*Asclepias incarnata*)*

Sweet flag (*Acorus gramineus*)*

Sweet pea (*Lathyrus odoratus*)

Turtleheads (*Chelone* spp.)*

clayey soils. One inch a week should be adequate if there's no rain. Clay soils take the most time to dry out. Flowers growing in heavy clay soil usually need less than 1 inch of water per week. Whatever its water-holding characteristic, adding organic matter to soil always helps: It makes sandy soil retain moisture better and clay soil drain better.

Established perennial flowers often do fine on less than 1 inch of water, while newly planted annuals and perennials usually need more than 1 inch. But when your plants droop, you need to respond quickly; water-stressed plants are highly susceptible to vascular damage and to pests and diseases. A quick hosing in the heat of the day cools plants off but provides no moisture to their roots, the organ designed to absorb water. To be most effective *and* most efficient:

Water slowly and deeply. Water needs to reach plants' roots; just wetting the soil surface discourages deep root development. (Flowers with shallow roots, such as bee balms [*Monarda* spp.], can be given less water but must be watered more often.) Remember that most of the water from heavy rains runs off and is of little value to garden plants. Plants don't just need an inch of rain—they need an inch that sinks into the soil. Don't water so much that the ground becomes soggy, and don't rewater if the soil is still wet.

Water plants, not the ground. Direct water where it's needed: around your plants. If you live where it's necessary to water often, consider investing in a permanent drip irrigation system. Or, for much less money, purchase a *soaker*, or *drip, hose*, which is a hose punctured with small holes from one end to the other that you lay on the ground, snaking it between your plants. Soaker hoses not only conserve water compared with sprinklers—as much as 60

Low Tech. *Watering cans aren't cutting edge, but they are effective. According to a 16th-century authority, gardeners should take care with plants, "lest cloying them too much with water, they after wax feeble and perish."*

percent—they water without wetting plant leaves. And remember hand watering; even in this digital age, watering cans are as effective as ever. (For information about watering equipment, see Chapter 9, page 195.)

Mulch. Mulch lowers the temperature of the soil and helps it retain moisture. A 2- or 3-inch layer of mulch will reduce how often you must water and will discourage weeds. (For more information about mulches, see Chapter 6, page 117.)

Weed. Weeds use water too, so don't make your flowers compete. In a contest, the weeds always win.

Group like-minded flowers. Watering is more efficient if species with similar moisture requirements are planted together.

Improve the soil. Soil rich in organic matter hangs on to nearly every drop of water it receives. Add compost and other organic matter to the garden every chance you get, and if you're making a new bed, loosen the soil to a depth of at least 1 foot, then amend the soil with organic matter. Don't overfertilize: Plants growing at a normal rate need less water than those that are overfed.

Recycle water. Gray water from the laundry, kitchen sink, and bath or shower is safe to use in a flower garden. Don't recycle water that contains borax or chlorine bleach, and always pour gray water on the soil, not on the plants. Catching rainwater is another environmentally friendly act that can benefit your flower garden.

The American philosopher Loren Eiseley wrote, "If there is magic on this planet it is contained in water." Watching a thirsty plant come back to life after being watered is one example of that magic, although many gardeners might agree with those who insist that while gardening requires lots of water, much of it is in the form of perspiration.

Let There Be Light, Please

Wind can be blocked, water can be pumped, soil can be improved, but light is something gardeners outside of Hollywood can't supply. Shaded beds and borders are slow to warm in spring, and they cool quickly in autumn. Experts consider light the transcendent consideration when locating a garden. You can take down trees and shrubs, even move walls, fences, and buildings, but you can't change your property's fundamental exposure. Midsummer, when trees and shrubs have leafed out, is the best time to measure what's shading what and when.

The east side of your house—or of any tall screen—gets morning sun and shade in the afternoon; the west side receives morning shade and sun in the afternoon. The south side receives sun most of the day, while the north side gets little direct sun. If you can, plant east or south of tall barriers; a shady woodland garden can go on their north side. Not only do big trees and shrubs create shade but their roots can extend beyond 75 feet and compete with other plants for moisture and food. If you grow flowers near large woody plants, be prepared to water and fertilize. (For plants that can succeed under a tree, see Chapter 8, page 177.)

Like teenagers, the lion's share of best-loved garden flowers are enthusiastic sunbathers. At a minimum, these species need six hours of full sun every day, and eight hours is even better. (Full sun is unobstructed sunlight.) When you see flowers labeled "full sun" in catalogs, garden magazines, and books, don't expect an Oscar-winning performance unless you give them exactly that: at least six hours of direct sun, ideally from midmorning to midafternoon.

Flowers, being an adaptable caboodle, will put up with variations in light—and light does vary. There is a giant difference between getting six hours of warm

SUN WORSHIPERS

All plants are *phototropic*—they reach for the light—but only a few are *heliotropic*: Their flowers track the sun, literally. (Tropism is growth toward or away from a stimulus.) Many vines are *thigmotropic*, meaning they twist around objects they encounter, and most plant roots stretch toward water, making them *hydrotropic*.) The annual sunflower (*Helianthus annuus*) is the best-known example of heliotropism. In *Metamorphoses*, Book IV, Ovid told the story of Clytie, a maiden who fell in love with but was rejected by the sun god. Her jealousy got her turned into the sunflower, which is why the sunflower keeps its eye on the sun.

Perforate St. Johnswort (*Hypericum perforatum*), tansy-leaved aster/Tahoka daisy (*Machaeranthera tanacetifolia*), and some *Echinacea*, *Ranunculus*, and *Viola* species also are heliotropic. Sun-tracking flowers are most common in alpine and arctic environments, presumably an evolutionary adaptation prompted by the need to collect heat. Or maybe it's jealousy.

Sunflower Trail. *In* My Ántonia *(1918), Willa Cather repeated the legend that the first Mormans traveling west from Missouri spread sunflower seeds as they went, creating floral road signs for the many settlers who followed them.*

PHOTO WHAT?

Photoperiodism refers to plants' physiological responses, such as vegetative growth and flowering time, to variations in daylight. The phenomenon, discovered about 1920 by two USDA scientists working with tobacco plants, led to dividing plants into three groups. Every species has a unique schedule, but generally *short-day plants*, such as poinsettia (*Euphorbia pulcherrima*), some violets (*Viola* spp.), chrysanthemums, and Japanese morning glory (*Ipomoea nil*), only flower when daylight lasts about eight hours and night lasts 16. Flowering in *long-day plants*, including asters, stonecrops (*Sedum* spp.), baby's breaths (*Gypsophila* spp.), and California poppy (*Eschscholzia californica*), is triggered by nights that are much shorter than the days. Flowering in the third and largest group, *day-neutral plants*, is triggered by things other than light.

Understanding photoperiodism has allowed the flower industry to give us all sorts of out-of-season blossoms, including chrysanthemums at Easter. Plants must be in controlled conditions for growers to take full advantage of their photoperiodic tendencies, but urban dwellers gardening under streetlights often discover that some of their perennials bloom early and that their fall-flowering plants never blossom at all. Too much light, actually, not enough dark—for it is the length of night, not day—is crucial. It's really noctoperiodism, not photoperiodism.

---

morning sun and shade in the afternoon and getting shade in the morning and six hours of sizzling afternoon sun, at least from a flower's perspective. Morning sun may not be enough to ensure lush blooming and erect stems for a Shasta daisy (*Leucanthemum* × *superbum*), but it is adequate for bee balm (*Monarda didyma*); afternoon sun is too strong for bleeding hearts (*Dicentra* spp.) but not too much for an orange coneflower (*Rudbeckia fulgida*).

Light is less intense in northern regions—a function of latitude and the sun's angle—especially in late summer when days grow shorter. Flowers, such as yellow corydalis (*Corydalis lutea*) and creeping phlox (*Phlox stolonifera*), that benefit from afternoon shade in hot, sunny regions are altogether happy in full sun in the North. If you have the freedom to choose between morning and afternoon sun as a garden site, *always* pick the former.

Light affects plants in many ways. Too little sun and their stems elongate and become spindly, what gardeners call "leggy." Meager light can reduce flowering or stop it altogether, and it can change the time a plant flowers (usually delaying it). If your garden site gets full sun, choose flowers that demand full sun; if the site is shady, fill it with flowers that prefer shade. Trying to grow sun worshipers like thread-leaved coreopsis (*Coreopsis verticillata*) in the shade or shade-lovers like Lenten roses (*Helleborus* × *hybridus*) in full sun is as futile as spraying for grasshoppers.

Light also affects bloom color. Some plants that grow best in full sun have better color when they get protection during the brightest part of the day. According to daylily expert Sydney Eddison (*A Passion for Daylilies*, 1992), all dark-colored *Hemerocallis*, despite being sun-lovers, look better when they have some afternoon shade. In fact, most red, purple, lavender, and blue flowers fade somewhat if grown in full sun in parts of the country where tin roofs are too hot for cats to tread.

Gardeners don't have to count only the sunny days, as the ubiquitous sundial adage advises. There is a truckload of flowers content with half-sunny days and quarter-sunny days, as well as flowers that don't want any direct sun at all. (Don't confuse not wanting direct sun with not needing light. All garden flowers need light, and they especially need light to bloom well.) Most shade-loving species don't produce the big, bold, bright blossoms that are the glory of sun-rich gardens. And the majority bloom in the spring. Adding a few long-blooming, shade-tolerant flowers, such as impatiens (*Impatiens walleriana*), will provide color throughout the growing season.

Like morning and afternoon sun, morning shade is different from afternoon shade and from full shade, which is no direct sun and little light. One solution for the dense shade thrown by deciduous trees and shrubs is a garden of spring bulbs, daffodils, crocuses,

PLANTS FOR THE SHADOWS

*N*either full nor midday sun is wanted by these annuals and perennials. All succeed with only three or four hours of sun, preferably morning sun. Some of the flowers listed as annuals are technically biennials or perennials that are treated as annuals in most North American gardens. Flowers growing in hot regions require more shade than those north of the Mason-Dixon line.

ANNUALS

Annual candytuft (*Iberis umbellata*)

Black-eyed Susan vine (*Thunbergia alata*)

Bush violet (*Browallia speciosa*)

Common foxglove (*Digitalis purpurea*)

Edging lobelia (*Lobelia erinus*)

Flowering tobacco (*Nicotiana alta*)

Forget-me-not (*Myosotis sylvatica*)

Four-o'clock (*Mirabilis jalapa*)

Garden balsam (*Impatiens balsamina*)

Impatiens (*Impatiens walleriana*)

Madagascar periwinkle (*Catharanthus roseus*)

Mignonette (*Reseda odorata*)

Monkey flowers (*Mimulus* spp.)

Morning glory (*Ipomoea tricolor*)

Pansy (*Viola* × *wittrockiana*)

Persian violet (*Exacum affine*)

Snow-on-the-mountain (*Euphorbia marginata*)

Tuberous begonias (*Begonia tuberhybrida* hybrids)

Wax begonia (*Begonia semperflorens*)

PERENNIALS

Astilbes (*Astilbe* cvs.)

Bergenias (*Bergenia* spp.)

Bleeding hearts (*Dicentra* spp.)

Bloodroot (*Sanguinaria canadensis*)

Celandine poppy (*Stylophorum diphyllum*)

Coral bells/heucheras (*Heuchera* spp.)

Creeping phlox (*Phlox stolonifera*)

Fall-blooming Japanese anemones (*Anemone hupehensis, A.* × *hybrida, A. tomentosa*)

Foamflower (*Tiarella cordifolia*)

Goat's beard (*Aruncus dioicus*)

Hardy geraniums/cranesbills (*Geranium* spp.)

Hostas (*Hosta* cvs.)

Lady's mantle (*Alchemilla mollis*)

Lenten rose (*Helleborus* × *hybridus*)

Ligularias (*Ligularia* spp.)

Lily-of-the-valley (*Convallaria majalis*)

Lilyturfs (*Liriope* spp.)

Lungworts (*Pulmonaria* spp.)

Primroses (*Primula* spp.)

Rodgersias (*Rodgersia* spp.)

Snakeroots (*Cimicifuga* spp.)

Solomon's seals (*Polygonatum* spp.)

Sweet woodruff (*Galium odoratum*)

Violets (*Viola* spp.)

Wild blue phlox (*Phlox divaricata*)

Yellow corydalis (*Corydalis lutea*)

Woodland Sprite. *Yellow corydalis (C. lutea), with its lark-like blooms, can be grown in full sun in regions with cool summers but needs midday shade in gardens where summer is hot.*

Fade Out. *Some flowers, such as the hybrid Ageratum 'Artist Alto Blue' tend to fade in regions where the sun is relentless. Giving plants some shade during the brightest part of the day will help preserve their color.*

grape hyacinths (*Muscari* spp.), and similar species that bloom before woody plants are in leaf. Another solution is a woodland garden populated primarily by native plants that thrive in the shadows.

As important as light is, don't rush to cut down a 100-year-old maple or a 100-foot white pine. Sometimes raising a tree's canopy—removing its lower branches—will admit enough light to keep plants healthy and blooming. Thinning out the canopies of deciduous trees is another way to let in more light. To keep tall flower species, such as spider flower (*Cleome hassleriana*) and plume poppy (*Macleaya cordata*), from shading smaller neighbors, place them on the north side of beds and borders. If you're planting in rows, as you might in a cutting garden, run the rows from east to west to maximize light and locate tall species on the north side of the plot.

Practical Matters

It's not just wind, water, and light that affect where a garden can grow; pragmatic concerns enter the mix too. Fortunately, if the mix isn't quite right—if your garden turns out not to be in the right place—you can take a mulligan. Do-overs are permitted in flower gardening as well as in golf.

As a rule, place flower gardens:

Near but not too near the beaten path. To show off what you've grown, you want family and friends to walk close to your flowers—but not on them.

Close to the faucet. Having the garden near the water source saves time, walking, and buying the second or third length of hose.

Convenient to tools and supplies. Daily garden jobs don't get done if you must run to the basement every time you need a hoe or trowel.

Where you can see them. You've worked hard. Looking at the results is one of the most satisfying parts of growing flowers.

Above all, don't forget your own schedule. If you spend summers at the seashore or in the mountains, make sure your gardens are planted with flowers that bloom in spring and fall. If you have only an hour or two a week that you can spend gardening, grow flowers in containers. Or keep your beds or borders small and keep them filled with low-care plants.

To keep garden work to a minimum, include spring-flowering hardy bulbs, such as daffodils, and many hardy perennials, including fernleaf yarrow (*Achillea filipendulina*), daylilies, astilbes, rudbeckias, thread-leaved coreopsis (*Coreopsis verticillata*), globe thistle (*Echinops ritro*), meadowsweets (*Filipendula* spp.), Siberian iris (*Iris sibirica*), and Russian sage (*Perovskia atriplicifolia*).

Down Under. *Crape myrtles* (Lagerstroemia indica) *are ideal for shading flowers that want less sun, such as these Hosta cultivars and colorful foxgloves* (Digitalis purpurea). *The trees' handsome bark is a garden bonus.*

Weather Duo. *Dusty miller* (Senecio cineraria) *and the AAS winning* Zinnia elegans *'Profusion Orange' not only combine well visually but they have similar cultural requirements. 'Profusion Orange' is a cross of two zinnia species and is highly resistant to disease.*

CHAPTER FOUR

Terra Wonderful: Making Great Soil for Growing Flowers

*I find that a real gardener is not
a man who cultivates flowers;
he is a man who cultivates the soil.*

Karel Čapek, *The Gardener's Year*, 1931

"TO DIG AND DELVE IN NICE CLEAN DIRT / CAN DO a mortal little hurt." That doggerel comes from the American humorist John Kendrick Bangs. Gardeners tend to call it soil, not dirt, which is what we sweep under the rug or get on our politicians. Whatever the appellation, including "planting medium," it's what plants call home. It keeps them in their place and provides the oxygen, water, and nutrients they need to survive. Soil long has been a preoccupation with vegetable gardeners. Flower gardeners need to catch up.

What your soil is like depends on where you live, but most North American gardeners are sitting atop soil that has two clear-cut layers above bedrock: *subsoil* and *topsoil*. Subsoil—scientists call it the *accumulation horizon*—consists of fine particles that have leached downward. Only the roots of very big plants, mostly trees and shrubs, reach into the subsoil. Topsoil, the uppermost layer, is where flower roots and lots of other living things reside. The deeper the topsoil, the better; the richer the topsoil, the better. There are dozens of adages about soil, all of which echo the familiar "Good soil makes good gardeners." And good soil does make good gardeners, because good soil makes good plants.

And what makes good garden soil? Balanced texture, good structure, moderate pH, ample nutrients, and an excessively generous supply of organic matter. And how do you know your soil is good, able to grow morning glories that stretch to the sky? The simplest test is the presence of earthworms. Earthworms—Aristotle called them "the intestines of the soil"—are a fussy bunch despite their lowly status. (Earthworms also were a keen interest of Charles Darwin, who published his classic findings—*The Formation of Vegetable Mould, through the Action of Worms with Observations on Their Habits*—in 1881.) Lowly or not, earthworms require moist, organically rich soil, exactly what many flowering plants require. If the ground dries out or is too wet, or is contaminated by chemicals or hasn't enough organic matter, worms move up and out. Unable to move out, plants will die out.

Take a *spit* of soil, a shovelful of dirt. If it contains one or two earthworms, you probably are starting with fertile topsoil. Not all topsoil is fit for gardening, however. "Every earth is not . . . recommended, for the yeeld of Garden herbs," the Englishman Thomas Hill wrote in 1577. Or for the "yeeld" of garden flowers. If your spit of soil contains no worms, if it's suitable for filling an hourglass, or if it's the right consistency for making bricks, there's work to be done. And even if your soil is good to begin with, you need to keep improving it. Garden soil, like a garden and many other things in life, is a work in progress.

Soil Texture and Structure

It may come as a surprise that soil isn't solid matter. About half of what we think of as soil is—or *should be*—air and water. The other half consists of bits of rocks and minerals and, if you're lucky, a fecund stew of organic life and material. The proportions of those bits of rocks and minerals make up a soil's *texture*. Measuring their proportions tells you what kind of soil you have and what extra help it may need from you in order to grow flowers well.

TEXTURE

Scientists categorize soils based on the size of their particles, beginning with boulders, the largest particles, then descending through cobbles, pebbles, and gravel. New England's stone walls are a reminder that some soils are cursed with larger particles than others. Most North American gardeners don't have to deal with boulders—which, to soil scientists, is any rock larger than 10 inches across—or even gravel. Most of us have soils that consist of a mix of the three smallest types of particles: *sand*, *silt*, and *clay*.

The size difference between particles of sand, silt, and clay seems insignificant until you consider the equal weight of each. A pound of sand contains 2½ million particles; a pound of silt contains 2½ billion particles; and a pound of clay contains 40 trillion particles.

Sand particles are the largest and most irregular of the three types, which is why sandy soil is easy to cultivate whether dry or wet. Sandy soil is pale and feels gritty; it warms quickly in spring and drains even faster, losing, or leaching, nutrients in the process. Clay particles, the smallest of the three, are too small to be seen without an electron microscope. Clay soils can be red, gray, or brown. They feel sticky when wet and retain moisture and nutrients better than sand or silt, but they are slow to warm in spring and to dry after rain. Silt falls in the middle. Its particles also are too small for the naked eye to see. When they dry out completely, they are difficult to rewet, but once wet, they absorb and retain water and nutrients. Silty soil feels slippery because its particles are sometimes coated with clay. Soil that contains a mix of the three is called *loam*. When gardeners dream, their soil is loam.

You can get a general idea of your soil's texture by scooping up a handful of damp soil. Squeeze it, then

On the Rocks. *Gardeners not blessed with loam still can grow many colorful flowers, such as yellow Kamtschat stonecrop (Sedum kamtschaticum), white American mountain mint (Pycnanthemum tenuifolium), and lavender Russian sage (Perovskia atriplicifolia).*

FLOWERS FOR THE SANDBOX

*W*ell, not for the sandbox but for sandy soil, which tends to be dry and infertile. These flowers can tolerate those conditions, but adding loads of organic matter to the soil will make their lives easier and better. Don't forget that even plants that are adapted to growing in sandy soil may need watering when there is little rain.

Bearded irises (*Iris* Bearded Hybrids)

Blanket flowers (*Gaillardia* spp.)

California poppy (*Eschscholzia californica*)

Cockscomb (*Celosia cristata*)

Common lupine (*Lupinus perennis*)

Cosmos (*Cosmos bipinnatus, C. sulphureus*)

Creeping zinnia (*Sanvitalia procumbens*)

Daylilies (*Hemerocallis* cvs.)

Gayfeathers (*Liatris* spp., except *L. spicata,
    L. pycnostachya*)

Hairy beard-tongue (*Penstemon hirsutus*)

Hoary vervain (*Verbena stricta*)

Lance-leaved coreopsis (*Coreopsis lanceolata*)

Madagascar periwinkle (*Catharanthus roseus*)

Moss rose (*Portulaca grandiflora*)

Nasturtium (*Tropaeolum majus*)

Petunia (*Petunia* × *hybrida*)

Russian sage (*Perovskia atriplicifolia*)

Scarlet sage (*Salvia splendens*)

Sea lavender (*Limonium latifolium*)

Sedums/stonecrops (*Sedum* spp.)

Snow-in-summer (*Cerastium tomentosum*)

Snow-on-the-mountain (*Euphorbia marginata*)

Spider flower (*Cleome hassleriana*)

Statice (*Limonium sinuatum*)

Strawflower (*Bracteantha bracteata*)

Torch lily (*Kniphofia uvaria*)

Verbenas (*Verbena* spp.)

Yarrows (*Achillea* spp.)

Zinnias (*Zinnia* spp.)

Bearded Ladies. *There is a rainbow of bearded irises, and all grow happily in light, moderately rich soil. Heavy soil and too much fertilizer, especially too much high-nitrogen fertilizer, encourages iris rhizomes to rot.*

open your hand. If the soil is loose, it is mainly sand. If it forms a ball, sticky and smooth, the soil is mostly clay. And if forms a ball that crumbles when you open your fist, the soil consists primarily of silt particles.

A more precise method of evaluating the soil texture of your garden requires only a lidded, straight-sided, clear-glass quart jar, a ruler, and the U.S. Department of Agriculture (USDA) Soil Texture Triangle (see at right). Fill the jar one-quarter full of dry pulverized soil that you've dug vertically, like a core sample (remove any stones or large bits of organic matter), add 1 tablespoon of powdered dishwashing detergent or 1 teaspoon of Calgon or another water softener to help keep the soil particles separate, and add water until the jar is three-quarters full. Screw on the lid and shake vigorously for at least three minutes.

Set the jar down, and after one minute, measure the layer of sand, which will fall to the bottom, from the jar's side. After two or three hours, measure the silt layer, which will lie on top of the sand. Wait at least 24 hours to measure the

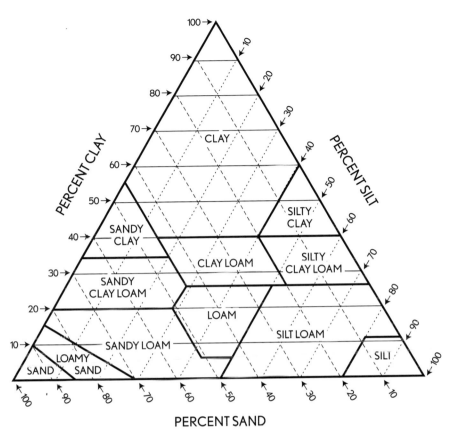

Garden Triangulation. *To determine your soil's texture, locate its percentages of sand, silt, and clay on the corresponding side of the USDA Soil Texture Triangle. From each point draw a straight line inward that is parallel to the dotted lines extending from that side. The area where the three lines intersect is your soil's classification.*

clay layer, which forms atop the silt (it may look more like muddy water than a solid). To determine the percentage of each, add the three measurements, then divide that total into each measurement and multiply by 100. If the jar contained ½ inch of sand, 1 inch of silt, and 2½ inches of clay, for a total of 4 inches, the results would be: 12.5 percent sand ($0.5 \div 4 \times 100$),

25 percent silt ($1 \div 4 \times 100$), and 62.5 percent clay ($2.5 \div 4 \times 100$).

Trying to improve a sandy soil's texture by adding clay or a clayey soil's texture by adding sand is everyone's first impulse, but it is a wrong one. That's because soil texture is literally writ in billions of bits of stone, and attempting to alter it by adding clay or sand is impractical. According to the experts, it would take between 3 and 5 tons of sand to temper a 10×50–foot flower border that has clay soil, and the change would be both modest and temporary.

STRUCTURE

Gardeners can compensate for a soil's texture by improving its structure. *Soil structure* is the degree to which soil particles bind together, or *aggregate*. Sand particles hardly aggregate at all, while clay particles can aggregate so tightly they become

HEAVY AND LIGHT

Gardeners often talk about soil being *heavy* or *light*. When they do, they are describing its texture, the size and mix of its particles. Heavy soils, which have a high clay content, retain moisture and compact easily. Light soils have a high sand content and tend to be dry and lacking a good supply of the nutrients that plants need to grow and flourish.

CLAY BUSTERS

Many North American native grasses and flowers, such as gray-headed coneflower (*Ratibida pinnata*), are adapted to heavy clay soil. So are these garden perennials. Despite their roots' ability to penetrate clay, all will be happier if you amend the soil with generous amounts of compost, leaf mold, or other organic matter. In addition to loosening the soil, organic matter will improve its ability to drain excess moisture.

Asters (*Aster* spp.)

Astilbes (*Astilbe* cvs.)

Black-eyed Susan (*Rudbeckia hirta*)

Compass plant (*Silphium laciniatum*)

Daylilies (*Hemerocallis* cvs.)

Garden phlox (*Phlox paniculata*)

Gayfeathers (*Liatris* spp.)

Goatsbeard (*Aruncus dioicus*)

Goldenrods (*Solidago* spp.)

Lady's mantle (*Alchemilla mollis*)

Ox-eye (*Heliopsis helianthoides*)

Purple coneflower (*Echinacea purpurea*)

Russian sage (*Perovskia atriplicifolia*)

Sedums/stonecrops (*Sedum* cvs.) 'Autumn Joy'

Speedwells (*Veronica* spp.)

Wild bergamot (*Monarda fistulosa*)

rototiller too long, too often, or when the ground is soppy wet or bone dry affects structure *negatively* by pulverizing the soil aggregates and reducing its pore space. (Cultivating wet soil compacts it; cultivating arid soil pulverizes it.) Even hand digging in very wet or dry soil is harmful, as is any action that destroys aggregates or compacts soil, such as walking on it. That familiar sign just as well could read, "Keep Off the Soil."

Every kind of garden soil will benefit from regular infusions of organic matter, whether from compost, mulch, chopped leaves, or other sources. Some other improvement tactics, directed at particular types of problem soil, include:

Wet, heavy soil. Add organic matter; provide drainage; create raised beds; change location.

Dry, light soil. Add organic matter; mulch; water frequently or irrigate; create sunken beds.

Saline soil. Add organic matter; mulch; improve drainage; add gypsum and wash away excessive salts by drenching the soil with fresh water; irrigate often with fresh water.

Disease-infected soil. Adjust soil pH to appropriate levels; keep plants healthy; grow disease-resistant varieties; mulch; rotate crops; solarize soil. (See "Death by Sun," page 81, for directions.)

Old Reliable. *Handsome* Rudbeckia fulgida *var.* sullivantii *'Goldsturm' has been touted for more than 50 years because it is a long-lived, low-maintenance perennial that thrives in all but soppy wet soils. The cultivar name is German for "gold storm."*

almost impenetrable. Soils with good structure—*friable soils*—have particles that cling together loosely so that there is pore space between them. It's in this open pore space, ideally about half the soil's volume, that air, water, roots, and underground life move. Friable soil retains moisture and nutrients yet drains well. It's easy to dig, doesn't turn into mud when it rains, and doesn't blow away when the sun blazes and there is no rain.

Normal physical events, such as cycles of freezing and thawing, tend to aggregate soil particles, and adding organic matter—whatever kind of soil you have—also improves soil structure by encouraging soil particles to aggregate. On the flip side, even well-meaning gardeners use soil management techniques that destroy structure. For example, using a

A Cut Above. *Raised beds are a good and relatively simple solution for gardeners who have problem soils or problem backs. The brick retaining wall in this raised bed is not only handsome, it keeps the bed's soil from washing away.*

Life Below Ground

It's easy to forget that there is a superabundance of living organisms residing in the darkness beneath our feet. Ninety-five percent of healthy soil may be rock, air, and water, but 5 percent of soil is or once was alive. Soil is animal and vegetable as well as mineral. It's the animal and vegetable portion, the organic portion, that makes soil different from disintegrated rock.

That organic 5 percent consists of billons and billions of micro- and not-so-micro flora and fauna. Billions and billions is not double-talk: It's a jungle down there. Scientists estimate that the top foot of a square acre of ground may contain as many as 3 tons of living organisms. Roots, bulbs, and other rootlike plant parts constitute most of the *macroflora* in the soil, along with algae, bacteria, fungi, and viruses. (One bacterium, *actinomyces*, is responsible for soil's "freshly dug" fragrance.) An inventory of subsurface fauna includes both part- and full-time residents, such as woodchucks, voles, moles, snakes, slugs, grubs, millipedes, beetles, ants, wireworms, earthworms, and more animals you can see, as well as nematodes, protozoa, and other life that must be magnified to be visible.

All the life in netherland below our feet is necessary to healthy soil, although gardeners wouldn't call some of these inhabitants friends. Voles adore dining on succulent roots; slugs love chewing through plant leaves as much as cutworms like chewing through young stems; verticillium wilt, a fungus, infects flowers through their roots. Oddly enough, making certain that the soil is teeming with living things is the best weapon against the few subterranean troublemakers. (For information about dealing with pests and diseases, see Chapter 7, page 147.)

HUMUS HOMILY

Humus, completely decayed organic matter, is a horticultural icon. If a gardener had visited the garden of Eden, Karel Čapek wrote in 1931, he would have ignored Eve, sniffed excitedly, and exclaimed, "Good Lord, what humus!" That's because humus, although it isn't overly rich in nutrients, can retain both nutrients and water in the soil for plants to use. Moreover, it makes soil friable—easy to work—by improving its structure. Gardeners often use the word *humus* to refer to any organic matter, but true humus has come to the end of the decomposition process. Organic matter that is still decaying is more accurately called *active humus*.

Below-ground organisms occupy themselves by traveling up, down, and through the soil, stirring and aerating it as they go. Many soil organisms, especially earthworms, improve soil structure and thus tilth, aeration, and drainage by exuding substances that help soil particles clump together. And soil organisms are nonstop gourmands, constantly digesting roots, stems, leaves, and each other. The larger organisms start the process and the microorganisms conclude it by breaking down the residue left by their bigger neighbors. The final result is *humus*, the dark organic matter that remains when decomposition is complete.

The decomposition processes release nitrogen, phosphorus, and other important foods in a form that plants can use, as well as acids that dissolve rock particles, thereby releasing minerals to plants. Keeping the decomposition cycle going is the best recipe for fertile, friable soil. By making sure that the top 8 inches of soil—the layer where most organisms dwell and where most flower roots grow—is well supplied with organic matter, the decomposition cycle should not end.

Pssssssst, Soil pH

Remember using litmus paper in elementary school to determine whether Pepsi Cola was acid or alkaline? (Answer: acid.) Soils give varied results when their pH is measured—pH is an acronym for *potential hydrogen*—and where your soil falls on the pH scale, whether it is acid or alkaline or neutral, has consequences for the organisms it contains, for which nutrients are available to plants, and for plants themselves.

The pH scale goes from 0 to 14; a score of 7.0 is neutral. Anything above 7.0 is *alkaline*, or sweet, and anything below 7.0 is *acid*, or sour. The scale is logarithmic, not arithmetic, which means 6.0 is ten times more acid than 7.0, not two times. Small differences

Floral Litmus Test. *One clue to a soil's pH is revealed in the blooms of the bigleaf hydrangea (H. macrophylla). Blue flowers normally indicate acid soil, whereas pink and purple flowers are fairly reliable signs of sweeter soil.*

PINK AND BLUE

Changing a soil's pH isn't child's play, but testing a soil's pH is simple. You can do it yourself—both simple and complex soil-test kits are available from garden centers and online firms (a pack of litmus strips is less than $5; electronic meters more than $100). Better still, have your soil tested by professionals through your local state university or Cooperative Extension Service; private laboratories also test soil but usually charge far more than public institutions. (See Appendix, page 457, for more information about soil testing.) Once you've tested your soil—or had it tested—there is no reason to retest *unless* your flowers tell you something is wrong.

in pH numbers mean huge differences in soils. Like the majority of garden flowers, most underground organisms do well in a near-neutral pH of 6.5. If soil is extremely acidic or alkaline, the life it needs to grow flowers is going to move elsewhere.

All the nutrients plants need but three (hydrogen, oxygen, and carbon) are acquired from the soil—and they are most available in soil that is rich in organic matter and that has a pH between 6.2 and 7.2. (See "Food for Flowers," below, for more information about plant nutrients.) Gardeners in regions where rainfall is heavy, such as the Pacific Northwest and many areas east of the Mississippi River, or where acid rain is a problem, as it is in New England, are likely to have acid soils. Gardeners in arid regions with low rainfall—the Rocky Mountain states, the Great Plains, the Southwest—typically have soil that is neutral or alkaline. Clayey soils, which derive from granite, are normally acid, while sandy soils, which originate from limestone, are usually alkaline. Building foundations often leach lime into the soil, making the soil alongside houses and other structures— prime garden locations—highly alkaline.

Garden flowers that develop *interveinal chlorosis*— their leaves turn yellow or white but the veins in the leaves stay green—may be an indication that a soil's pH is out of kilter, either too sour or too sweet. Gardening is always local, however. Your neighbor may have acid soil, and you may not have acid soil. The proof of the garden pudding is in the plants: If your flowers are thriving, assume your soil's pH is within healthy limits. But if they aren't thriving, test your soil's pH. Testing is also a good thing to do if you're creating a new garden.

Most gardeners don't have soil that registers anywhere near the extremes of the pH scale, and most garden flowers are relatively undemanding. They grow well in soil that is moderately acid, neutral, or moderately alkaline (6.0 to 7.2). Sweet woodruff (*Galium odoratum*) is about as unparticular as they come: It survives in soils with pH readings anywhere from 4.0 to 8.0. A soil's pH becomes an important consideration when selecting plants *only* when it always stays well above or below neutral.

The traditional remedy is to add lime to acid soils, sulfur to alkaline soils. Even with recommendations from a professional test, changing soil pH is an inexact science, and it isn't accomplished in a day. Small changes in pH are easier than large ones;

clayey soil and soil rich in organic matter change more slowly than does sandy soil; acid soil is more easily modified than is alkaline soil. The general rule is that soil pH can be boosted or lowered 1 point a year *at most*. Fall is the best season for adjusting pH because there are no young, tender plants to be damaged, and the additives will have all winter to dissolve before plants start their new growth.

You can help stabilize pH levels by incorporating organic matter in the soil. In fact, adding only organic matter—composted sawdust will lower pH and wood ashes will raise pH—may be all that's called for. (Most organic matter raises soil pH slightly. Even oak leaves, which are acid when fresh, have a net alkaline effect as decomposition progresses.) If your soil needs a big-time adjustment, be sure to follow the recommended rates provided by your soil test or the recommendations that appear on the bags of sulfur, lime, or whatever additive you're using.

Food for Flowers

Plants take hydrogen, oxygen, and carbon from the air and water (and change them into food, starches and sugars, through photosynthesis), but the rest of what they need, the mineral nutrients, are absorbed through their roots. Agronomists—soil scientists— divide these nutrients into groups based on the amounts plants require.

Making Amends. *A range of organic fertilizers, such as gypsum, rock phosphate, compost, alfalfa meal, limestone, greensand, and cow manure, are available at local garden centers and farm stores and from mail-order companies.*

The *macronutrients*, the elements that plants need in largest amounts, are nitrogen (N), phosphorus (P), and potassium (K). Plants require all three to develop well, but the second and third, phosphorus and potassium, are the most important for growing flowers; perennials, especially, want greater amounts of phosphorus. Plants also need smaller amounts of calcium, magnesium, and sulfur, along with smaller still amounts of iron, zinc, copper, boron, manganese, molybdenum, chlorine, and nickel. Gardeners describe soil that has liberal amounts of all the necessary nutrients as *fertile* or *rich*.

Plant nutrients are consequential to overall metabolic processes, but they also have particular roles.

- Nitrogen promotes growth of dark green stems and leaves.
- Phosphorus encourages rapid growth and promotes seedling growth, strong stems and roots, and flowering.
- Potassium, or potash, increases plant vigor, flowering, and resistance to disease, cold, heat, and drought.

Soil nutrients, which are used up by plants and lost through erosion and leaching, must be replenished. Your flowers will provide the best evidence as to whether the soil contains the nutrients they need.

Spindly stems, smaller than normal or pale, yellowish, purplish, mottled, or curled leaves, stunted growth, and a lack of flowers are all signs that the soil may need a nutritional boost.

Nearly all bags of fertilizer, organic and synthetic, carry three numbers separated by hyphens, such as 10-10-10. The numbers represent the percentage by net weight of nitrogen, phosphorus, and potassium, or N-P-K, that the product contains. A 100-pound bag labeled 10-20-10 contains 10 percent nitrogen, 20 percent phosphorus, and 10 percent potassium. *Complete fertilizers* are products that contain at least some amount of all three major nutrients, N-P-K.

Organic products often have low numbers, but don't let that alarm you. By law the numbers must refer to the percentage of nitrogen, phosphorus, and potassium that is *immediately available* to plants. Organic additives usually release their nutrients slowly, not all at once. Rock phosphate, for example, is about 30 percent phosphorus but only 3 percent is immediately available, so a bag of rock phosphate would be labeled 0-3-0, not 0-30-0.

One of the cardinal rules of good gardening is to give the soil more than you take away. An unnamed English vicar famous for his garden had a unique method for renourishing his soil. When asked how he grew such lush roses, he confessed, "I bury a cat under each bush." While dead cats aren't a fertilizer that most gardeners would care to use, the vicar's successful approach comes down on the organic side of the organic/natural versus synthetic/chemical debate, a debate that continues to rage.

Organic fertilizers, such as bonemeal and fish emulsion, contain meaningful amounts of the basic elements plants need to grow; most also improve soil structure. *Organic soil amendments*, such as grass clippings or composted leaves, are materials that improve soil structure; they also contain nutrients in small amounts. When used in conjunction with fertilizers and amendments, the word *organic* means the material came from an animal, plant, or naturally occurring substance. They can be divided into four loose groups.

Animal manures. Animal wastes contain nitrogen, phosphorus, and potassium, making them complete fertilizers, plus smaller amounts of sulfur, calcium, and micronutrients, and are a good source of organic matter. Fresh manures, which are rich in nitrogen, can burn plants and should be composted before being used.

FLORAL DIETERS

*W*hile few plants turn up their noses at fertile soil, many flowers are satisfied with run-of-the-mill soil. Some species are downright nutritional martyrs, willing to grow and bloom in *thin soil*, soil that is not rich in nutrients. If you're beginning with poor soil, try some of these plants to get your flower garden started.

Baby's-breath (*Gypsophila paniculata*)

Bachelor's button (*Centaurea cyanus*)

Blanket flowers (*Gaillardia* spp.)

Blue daisy (*Felicia amelloides*)

Butter-and-eggs (*Linaria vulgaris*)

California poppy (*Eschscholzia californica*)

Calliopsis/plains coreopsis (*Coreopsis tinctoria*)

Candytufts (*Iberis sempervirens, I. umbellata*)

Cockscomb (*Celosia argentea*)

Crested iris (*Iris cristata*)

Farewell-to-spring (*Clarkia unguiculata*)

Flanders poppy/corn poppy (*Papaver rhoeas*)

Flowering tobaccos (*Nicotiana* spp.)

Forget-me-not (*Myosotis sylvatica*)

Four-o'clock (*Mirabilis jalapa*)

Harebell speedwell (*Veronica prostrata*)

Lily-of-the-valley (*Convallaria majalis*)

Love-lies-bleeding (*Amaranthus caudatus*)

Maiden pink (*Dianthus deltoides*)

Mexican poppy (*Argemone grandiflora*)

Morning glories (*Ipomoea* spp.)

Moss phlox (*Phlox subulata*)

Moss rose (*Portulaca grandiflora*)

Nasturtium (*Tropaeolum majus*)

Petunia (*Petunia × hybrida*)

Snow-in-summer (*Cerastium tomentosum*)

Spider flower (*Cleome hassleriana*)

Sunflower (*Helianthus annuus*)

Sweet alyssum (*Lobularia maritima*)

Wall rock cress (*Arabis caucasica*)

Wild cranesbill (*Geranium maculatum*)

Yarrows (*Achillea* spp.)

Carefree Celosia. *Plumed coxcomb like this* C. argentea *'Pampas Plum' is a tender perennial that most gardeners treat as an annual. Willing to grow in poor soils, easy to grow celosias also tolerate heat and humidity.*

Composted matter. Compost is a first-class soil additive. Its nutrient value depends on what was added to the compost pile, but well-made compost is a complete fertilizer and also contains a wide array of micronutrients. Good compost contains everything flowers need to flourish.

Dried animal parts. Materials such as blood meal and bonemeal provide a variety of nutrients depending on the material used. Bonemeal is rich in phosphorus and calcium, whereas blood meal is high in immediately available nitrogen; fish meal is more balanced, scoring about 5-3-3.

Rock powders. These, including limestone and granite meal, are normally not complete fertilizers but are rich in specific nutrients.

In contrast with organic fertilizers and additives, *synthetic fertilizers*—some gardeners call them chemical fertilizers—are products that don't occur naturally. Urea, a source of nitrogen made by reacting ammonia with carbon dioxide, is a synthetic fertilizer, as are popular products such as Miracle-Gro and Gold'n Gro, and generic bags of 10-10-10, 5-10-5, and other denominations.

Plants can't distinguish between the nutrients that come from Mother Nature and those made in chemical plants, but soils and the organisms they contain know the difference. That's because organic fertilizers and amendments don't just feed plants, they feed and improve the soil. Unlike synthetic products, which are immediately available to plants, most organic materials are slow acting: They must be converted by soil organisms before they can be used by plants. That makes them safe to apply in large amounts at one time. Overdosing soil with chemical fertilizers not only can damage plants but can reduce and destroy macro- and microbiotic activity in the soil. Once the life underground is gone, the soil is dead and can do nothing except anchor plants. Except for air, water, and sun, plants will be entirely dependent on their grower.

Many organic products do not contain a balanced supply of nitrogen, phosphorus, and potassium; they are more likely to be high in one nutrient and low in or missing the other two. Most, however, contain many micronutrients, not just the N-P-K threesome that comes in a bag of 10-10-10. Gardeners who consistently add a variety of organic materials to their garden— animal manures, composted matter, dried animal products, and rock powders—will have fertile soil. Be a little cautious with high-nitrogen substances, such as blood meal, fish emulsion, and especially fresh animal manures: Too much nitrogen yields giant-sized plants but very few flowers. As a general rule, a little-too-little fertilizer is better than much-too-much, even if the fertilizer is organic.

Making Soil Better

What are gardeners to do to improve soil that has poor texture or structure? With soil that is infertile? One answer fits all: Feed the soil. Add organic matter. *Adding organic matter is the single most important and effective thing gardeners can do to improve garden soil.*

Organic matter nourishes the underground menagerie; it helps the soil retain moisture and nutrients; it makes soil drain better; it moderates and stabilizes soil pH; it increases soil fertility. Heavy clay soil? Add organic matter. Sandy soil? Add organic matter. Infertile soil? Add organic matter. Organic matter won't turn clay or sand into loam, that golden mean of soils, and it won't supply a complete stockpile of nutrients overnight, but it will produce soil that behaves like loam and is increasingly fertile.

It's difficult to imagine a garden containing too much organic matter, but if you can see pieces of leaves, stems, and other organic materials when you dig, your soil likely needs only maintenance, not a total overhaul. If there are no signs of organic matter in the shovelful, begin building compost bins and seek out a local manure source. Dark, fertile soil isn't created overnight—or even in one year—but it can be done in far less than a decade. If your soil is poor, add organic matter every time you have a tool in the ground, be it for digging or planting or cultivating. Any organic matter will improve *any* garden soil—potato peelings to fish meal, buckwheat hulls to cow dung—but some materials are especially helpful to particular kinds of soil.

Gardeners with warm, sandy soil need to add large quantities of organic matter and add them often. Sandy soil is improved fastest by adding

Brown Gold. *Adding compost to gardens is the best thing gardeners can do to improve the soil. If you can't make your own, you can buy compost at local garden centers. With compost, more is better. Try to add some every year.*

composted and other partially decayed matter, but it also needs materials that will decay more slowly, such as bark or pine needles. Silty soil is most helped by shredded leaves, cocoa hulls, hay, straw, dry leaves, and other bulky materials, which will improve drainage and aeration, and reduce crusting. Clayey soil is bettered quickest by adding bulky materials, such as half-decayed plant refuse, animal manures, shredded pine bark, straw, and *green manures*. (Green manures are crops of grasses, legumes, and other plants that are grown just to be plowed back into the soil. Used widely by vegetable gardeners, they are inappropriate for most flower gardens, but may be useful in cutting gardens.)

Adding organic materials to your soil is never out of season, although what effect it has depends on what you add, when you add it, and how you add it. Fresh matter breaks down faster than straw and other dry matter do; organic materials that have been chopped or shredded decay more quickly than those that are whole; and organic matter that is incorporated into the soil decomposes sooner than organic matter that is spread on the soil's surface. Last, organic matter decomposes more rapidly in soil that is moist and warm than in soil that is dry or cold.

Gardeners should add at least 1 inch of chopped or fine organic matter (or 4 inches of bulky matter) to soil each year *at a minimum*. Two or three times that amount is even better, especially if your soil has poor structure or lacks nutrients. Most commercial products, including manures, cocoa hulls, and compost, are measured in cubic yards whether they're sold bagged or in bulk. To estimate how much you'll need in cubic yards, multiply the length (in feet) of the garden by its width (in feet) by the thickness of the layer of the organic material (in inches). Then divide the product by 324. The math for adding 2 inches of composted manure to a 20 × 5–foot flower border would be: 20 feet × 5 feet × 2 = 200; 200 ÷ 324 = .617 cubic yards.

Vegetable growers begin with a blank slate each year, which makes it easy to incorporate organic matter in the soil. Not so flower gardeners, who have beds and borders filled with perennials and bulbs and other permanent plants. Even if you must work around established plants, it's possible to add plenty of compost or other organic matter to your soil. Start in early spring and dig as much compost, leaf mold, or other composted organic matter—at least 1 inch—into the soil as you can. Once the ground has warmed, mulch between plants; keep the soil mulched throughout the summer. In late fall, incorporate the old mulch into the soil and lay down a mulch for winter. When spring comes, begin the cycle again.

Each organic material has its own merits, and all organic materials improve the soil. But the best of the best is compost. Its nutrient value is relatively low—good homemade compost scores from 0.5-0.5-0.5 to 4-4-4; dry commercial compost about 1-1-1—but its ability to improve the soil's structure and feed microorganisms is unsurpassed, and fertility will follow. Compost is the *crème de la crème*, the *pièce de résistance*, the best in show, the big rock candy mountain of organic matter.

THE GREAT NITROGEN HEIST

Thick organic mulches—matter used to cover bare ground—and Herculean quantities of organic matter added to the soil can steal nitrogen away from plants. (Prime offenders are dry leaves, wood chips, ground corncobs, sawdust, pine needles, and other dry, bulky, low-nitrogen matter.) Plant foliage that turns yellow and growth that slows are two indications that the soil's nitrogen is depleted. Adding blood meal, coffee grounds, cottonseed meal, fish emulsion and meal, soybean meal, and animal manures will resupply nitrogen to the soil. (For more information about mulches, see "Much Ado About Mulch," page 131.)

Compost Does Happen

Trust the bumper sticker, COMPOST HAPPENS. *Compost* is decayed organic matter. Toss grass clippings, leaves, and weeds in a pile and eventually they decompose, the *happening* part of the compost slogan. Composting is a way to use yard, garden, and kitchen refuse rather than adding them to the local landfill. Its chemistry doesn't pollute, its raw materials are free, and it takes no special talents. And compost returns to the soil what plants take from it.

Turning weeds and leaves into "brown gold" is horticultural alchemy, but this alchemy is not a guarded secret: Combine organic materials in a pile,

Refuse Refuge. *This simple wood and wire bin is both a destination for yard and kitchen debris and the starting place for making compost. Some gardeners don't bother with bins and simply pile their waste in an out-of-the-way spot.*

keep the pile aerated and moist, and stand back while the microorganisms do the rest. Even piles that aren't aerated and kept moist will decompose after several years. Called *cold*, or *anaerobic*, *composting*, the laissez-faire approach calls only for piling on. No measuring or layering or moistening or turning or covering or uncovering. Cold composting is slow, though, and the temperature inside the pile is unlikely to reach 100°F, which means that disease organisms and weed seeds may survive.

Most gardeners take a composting path somewhere between cold composting and schemes so complicated that they could be a full-time job. Flower growers interested in dotting every "i" in the compost process should consult books devoted entirely to the subject, such as the Brooklyn Botanic Garden's *Easy Compost* (1997). Those who don't see composting as a religious experience and don't want to purchase multiscreen digital thermometers with 10-foot probes have only to repeat the mantra "compost happens."

Gardeners with an out-of-the-way spot may be content with freestanding compost piles, but limited space or a penchant for tidiness calls for containers of some sort. If both space and organic waste are in small supply, consider converting a plastic or metal trash can by cutting out its bottom and drilling two dozen nickel-sized holes for aeration around the sides and in the lid. Set it on wood chips or bricks for good drainage. Or purchase a plastic stationary or tumble bin; both are widely available at local garden centers or from mail-order firms. (See "Composting," page 206, for more information about commercial compost containers.) A tumbling composter looks like a plastic barrel on a frame; it turns, or tumbles, with a

GREEN AND BROWN, WET AND DRY

Compost will "happen" faster if you maintain a 3:1 carbon to nitrogen balance. High-carbon matter is usually brown and dry, high-nitrogen matter green and succulent.

High carbon: dry cornstalks, dry garden debris, dry leaves, newsprint, pine needles, sawdust, straw and hay, wood chips

High nitrogen: animal manures, coffee grounds, fresh garden debris, fresh leaves, grass clippings, kitchen waste, seaweed, sod

flick of the wrist, mixing its contents and accelerating their decomposition.

Gardeners with elbow room can make compost bins out of concrete blocks, bricks, wood, or wire. They should be three-sided, 3- to 5-feet square, and no more than 5 feet high. Block or brick bins should be made without mortar and with space between the blocks or bricks for aeration. Prefab picket fencing or wood pallets are excellent for bin making. Nail or wire the corners together, and use a ½-inch fence wire for the fourth side to keep the compost in and easily accessible and to keep animals out. Or make a round compost bin entirely from ½-inch fence wire. Or create an organic bin from bales of hay or straw; eventually both the bin and its contents will become compost. To make turning piles easier—or to accommodate all your yard and kitchen refuse—construct two or three side-by-side containers, then move the compost matter from one bin to the next.

If you want to speed up the compost process, follow a few simple rules:

Limit size. Tests indicate that compost binds that contain between 3 and 5 cubic feet of organic matter are the most efficient. To cover 100 square feet of garden 1 inch deep takes about 9 cubic feet of finished compost.

Balance carbon and nitrogen. Make sure the compost pile has the correct balance of materials, both high-nitrogen and high-carbon. The ideal ratio will not only quicken the decomposition pace but ensure that the materials heat up enough to kill pathogens and weed seeds. The gold standard is three

parts dry materials that are high in carbon, such as straw, newsprint, pine needles, leaves, and sawdust, to one part green or wet matter, high-nitrogen refuse, such as kitchen waste, pulled weeds, grass clippings, and fresh animal manures. If the proportions aren't approximately 3:1—carbon to nitrogen—there may be problems. Too much dry material (carbon) and decomposition moves at glacial speed; too much green matter (nitrogen) and the odor will have the neighbors calling City Hall.

Add microorganisms. Adding a little soil, turf, or animal manure to a compost pile or bin will ensure that it contains the microorganisms that do the decomposing.

Chop or shred. Cutting organic matter into small pieces expedites decomposition, especially with woody matter like shrub stems and twigs. Every time you shred or chop a grapefruit or watermelon rind before you add it to the compost pile, you speed the decay process.

Layer the pile. Layering the organic matter you compost hastens decomposition. Layering means alternately adding high-carbon materials, *the dry, brown stuff*; then a thickness of *succulent, green stuff*, the high-nitrogen matter; and lastly a layer of dirt—then starting all over again. You don't have to weigh or measure; just try to add three parts of brown (C) for every one part green (N).

Keep the pile aerated. The microorganisms at work in a compost pile need air. The usual recommendation for providing it is to turn the pile, which is more difficult than it sounds. A better alternative is to fork the decomposing materials into a new pile or into a second bin located next to the first. Creating a base of wood chips or other coarse matter also helps aerate the pile, as does limiting its size.

Keep the pile moist, not soggy. Composting matter needs to be damp but not soppy wet. Find a well-drained location for your pile or container or elevate it so that it doesn't become waterlogged. Shape piles so water runs off rather than pools. Gardeners in rainy climates may need a loose cover to prevent their compost from getting too wet, whereas gardeners in arid regions may need to wet their compost and to cover it to retain moisture.

Making useable compost very quickly—*hot composting*—is demanding. Gardeners must stockpile organic matter to create an entire pile at one time, be exact about the C:N proportions and layer them properly, monitor the pile's temperature and moisture and make appropriate adjustments, and turn the pile every three or four days. Microorganisms in hot composting are so active that the internal temperature of the pile can reach 160°F, high enough to kill pathogens, weed seeds, and bits of sprouting root but also high enough to kill friendly microorganisms. If all the conditions are met, hot composting should produce a finished product in less than three months.

Fast, slow, or somewhere in between, many gardeners maintain more than one compost pile or bin so there is always a place to toss last night's watermelon rinds or the purple clover they just pulled out of the cutting garden. Don't add large woody matter, such as tree limbs, unless they are chipped, shredded, or chopped first. Leave out any matter that may carry pathogens, such as pet feces and diseased plants, or grass clippings or other matter that's been sprayed with a pesticide or herbicide. Don't include meat waste or bones, which will attract skunks, rats, raccoons, and other wildlife. Anything allelopathic, such as eucalyptus and black walnut leaves, or poisonous, such as

Helping Mother Nature. *If a compost pile doesn't decompose, it may be too dry and need watering. Covering the pile with a tarp will help retain moisture.*

oleander or castor bean, should be destroyed rather than composted.

However it's made, compost will do wonders for any garden soil and the flowers it grows. Dig it into the soil. Add it to planting holes. Use it as a mulch. Like kindness, you can't have enough.

If compost is the Cadillac of organic matter, *leaf mold*—a fungus-rich compost made from decayed leaves—is the Rolls Royce. It's considered so valuable in England (where it's spelled as one word) that an illegal trade has developed in leaf mold pilfered from forest and woodland floors. Just as not all leaf mold is legal, not all leaves are equal: Leathery leaves, including oak, rhododendron, and photinia, and the needles of fir species rot very slowly. All leaves decompose more quickly if they are shredded or chopped first.

Making leaf mold is a cold-composting process that relies on fungi and takes time. Think Crock-Pot, not pressure cooker. Gardeners with a small supply of leaves can compost them in black polyethylene garbage bags. Fill the bags with *wet* leaves, punch a few holes in the sides, tie the top, and hide the bags away for a year or 18 months.

FIXING COMPOSTING PROBLEMS

Compost piles don't always perform as quickly and simply as experts claim. These are some of the common problems and their probable solutions.

Pile never heats up. No heat means that the carbon to nitrogen balance is off or that the pile is either waterlogged or too dry. Add animal manures, grass clippings, and other high-nitrogen matter. If pile is sodden, turn it and add more high-carbon materials. If the pile is dry, spray it with water and add manure or other high-nitrogen materials.

Pile barely heats. Pile is too small. If it is less than 2 or 3 feet high, make it bigger. And it may be too dry or have too little high-nitrogen matter. Add more organic matter, and turn the pile.

Matter doesn't decompose. Remove the materials and add them to a new pile; don't add woody materials, or shred them before adding.

Pile smells. Pile is too wet or contains too much high-nitrogen matter. Turn the pile; add more dry matter.

Pile is dry and doesn't decompose. Turn the pile and wet it thoroughly; cover the pile with a loose tarp to retain moisture.

If raking leaves is a predominate autumn activity at your house, build a large wire or wood bin, fill it with leaves, wet them, and wait. In two or three years—faster in warm parts of North America, slower in cold ones—you'll have crumbly, sweet-smelling leaf mold that's well worth stealing.

Breaking Ground

Don't be demoralized if the site of your future flower garden is as weedy and neglected as the secret garden before Mary, Dickon, and Colin rolled up their sleeves. Clearing and opening the soil may take elbow grease, but the process is straightforward: Remove all existing vegetation and prepare the soil for planting. *The important thing is to do it right the first time.* Everyone who sticks a few plants in haphazardly prepared ground comes to regret it, for it means far more work in the long run.

Once you've chosen a site for growing flowers, do all you can to ready it completely before you plant. Most of us are not sagacious enough—or are too impatient—to begin a year ahead, but if you wait until the day you want to plant, preparing the soil is twice as hard and will be half as successful as getting a head start on the job.

Farsighted or last minute, begin by marking the boundaries of the garden. (For information about making beds and borders, see Chapter 5, page 85.) Straight-sided beds can be outlined with stakes and string; to delineate less formal designs, use rope or garden hose. If there has never been a garden in this site, you may want to test the soil's pH and fertility.

CLEARING THE SOIL

Whether you're starting from scratch—on a site that's never been a garden—or reclaiming a bed that contains more weeds than flowers, the first job is to clear the soil, to remove every last plant. Once the garden's boundaries are defined, remove any debris, cut down any woody plants and grub out their roots, and mow the site. (If you're restoring an old bed, dig any plants you want to save and set them aside before you mow.) What's left is the sod, all the grasses, and other low-growing plants. These, too, *and* all their roots must be removed or they will resprout. In a contest between crabgrass and

Bed Making. *Removing turf by hand is an essential step in creating a new, weed-free flower garden. You can use the turf to repair lawns and fill in low spots, or add it to the compost pile.*

bleeding heart (*Dicentra spectabilis*), crabgrass always wins. Or, as Shakespeare expressed it in *Richard III*, "sweet flowers are slow and weeds make haste."

If you just turn the soil—dig a spadeful of dirt and flip it upside down—most of the weeds and grasses will resurface. "Weeds are always growing,"

William Lawson wrote in 1618 (*A New Orchard and Garden*), and "the earth, is full of seed in her bowels, and any stirring gives them heat of sun, and being laid near day, they grow." Using a rototiller gives the same result, and trying to pull all the weeds by hand isn't much better. Even tiny pieces of root that are left behind will send up new plants. The temptation is to reach for a *herbicide*, a chemical solution for killing plants.

There is a smattering of organic herbicides on the market, including Burnout II, which is made from lemon and vinegar juices; Weed-A-Tak, made from clove, wintergreen, peppermint, and other oils; and Concern Fast-Acting Weed Killer, which is made from ammoniated soap. Most organic products are slower and less effective than chemical herbicides, especially on perennial and woody plants, and must be applied several times. Chemical herbicides are deadly effective, but they also tend to persist in the soil and poison groundwater. As the current idiom puts it, "Don't go there."

Instead, choose an organic product or one of these three methods to clear the ground.

Death by shade. A back-saving technique is to turn off the sun by laying down black plastic. Plants can't live without light, so keeping them in the dark is guaranteed to kill nearly anything that grows there. Begin at least ten months before you want to plant, and be sure to use boards, bricks, or some other device to keep the plastic in place.

Heavy cardboard or thick layers—at least 1 inch—of newsprint are alternatives to black plas-

TILLER BEWARE

Gasoline-driven *tillers*, or *rototillers*, are fabulous for saving time and preventing aching muscles, but if not used properly they are *too good* at their job. Overtilling—running a tiller back and forth and back and forth over a garden bed—pulverizes the soil. The surface may look smooth and inviting but gone are the underground pore spaces that are crucial to getting air, water, and nutrients to plant roots. The goal is soil that resembles crumbled corn bread, not cornmeal. If you think you've overtilled, add compost or other organic matter to the soil, but turn it in by hand. If you are creating a large flower garden, don't hesitate to use a rototiller, but follow the rules:

Never till when the soil is wet. If a squeezed handful of soil doesn't crumble when you open your hand, it's too wet.

Never till when the soil is completely dry. If a squeezed handful of soil won't form a ball, it's too dry. Water the area, wait one day, and till.

Stop after one pass. That should be enough to loosen and aerate the soil and to prepare it for planting.

The Hand Test. *Digging or tilling wet soil can damage its structure. Use a simple squeeze test to determine if your soil is dry enough to be worked—if a compressed handful doesn't crumble, it's too wet.*

tic. Hose them after laying them down, then cover with a thick layer of organic matter. After a year they decompose and can be turned into the soil. Or spread wedges of hay or straw—at least 6 inches— over the area. It may begin to sprout a few weeds as it decomposes. If it does, spread another 6-inch layer, even a third or fourth layer. In a couple of seasons the turf will be gone, and the hay will have turned into compost, which can be dug into the soil.

Death by sun. Instead of blocking the sun, consider harnessing it: *Solarizing* uses the heat the sun generates to kill surface vegetation. While effective, solarization is not as good at killing turf and weeds as darkness is; moreover, gardeners in cool regions may not have enough hot days for solarization to be successful. The best time to solarize soil is midsummer, when days are long, hot, and sunny. First mow and water the site, then cover it with 0.5- to 4-mil clear plastic. Pull the plastic as tight as possible and seal the edges with soil. The cover must stay in place for at least eight weeks. And it must be kept sealed: If heat escapes, the vegetation under the plastic will grow better than ever, not die.

Under sealed plastic, the top few inches of soil will register as much as 20°F warmer than soil not covered with plastic, reaching temperatures well over 100°F on blazingly hot days. Heat can destroy beneficial as well as pathogenic underground life, but research suggests that helpful bacteria, fungi, and other organisms are quick to recolonize solarized soil. Still, it's wise to add plenty of compost and other organic matter to soil after it has been solarized.

Death by spade. There are gasoline-powered machines designed to strip sod, but for a small- or medium-sized flower garden a spade works fine. A shovel also works, although the flat blade of a spade

Deceptively Tough. Nectaroscordum siculum *spp.* bulgaricum, *an attention-grabbing member of the lily family, is sturdier than it looks and thrives in most soils. A superb cut flower, its garlic odor indoors is off-putting to some who would question its common name Sicilian honey garlic.*

removes less soil. That's the goal: to remove all the vegetation but as little soil as possible. (For more information about garden tools, see Chapter 9, page 195.)

After watering the area, start on one edge of the garden. Insert the spade vertically into the sod, about 1 or 2 inches deep; lower the handle of the spade so its blade is nearly parallel to the soil's surface; push forward until the spade's blade is completely underground; and then lift the spadeful of sod and set it aside. Don't throw out the sod. It can be used to patch or fill low spots in the lawn or added, upside down, to the compost pile.

TURNING THE SOIL

Turning the soil is what farmers do when they plow and what home gardeners do when they use a roto-tiller or dig a plot by hand. Turning loosens and aerates the soil, and it should be combined with adding organic matter and other needed additives. Fall is the ideal time to turn the soil because frost will break up large clods over the winter, but turning can be done any time the ground isn't frozen. If it's soppy wet, let it dry first. Or if it's bone dry, wet it first.

After the garden plot has been cleared—but before you begin digging or tilling—apply any additives that a soil test shows are needed and cover the area with a thick layer of organic matter, 3 inches or more. This not only enriches the soil but also replaces the couple of inches that were lost if you removed the sod.

Most gardeners can turn a small or medium garden by hand. "The operation of digging . . . [is] a fine healthy occupation, not only from its calling the muscles into vigorous action, but from the smell of the new earth." That observation comes from Jane Loudon (*The Lady's Country Companion*, 1845), a lady who likely had no firsthand knowledge of digging, but its message is no less valuable: Digging is both exhausting and pleasurable.

The best tool for the job is a spading fork, but a shovel or spade works nearly as well. (For more information about garden tools, see Chapter 9, page 195.) As long as the soil's texture isn't extreme—either very sandy or very clayey—digging to the depth of the spading fork, about 1 foot, is deep enough. Eighteen inches is better if the soil is extremely light or heavy. Eighteen inches is also better if you're planting mostly perennials; or you can turn the garden to a depth of 1 foot but dig a deeper hole for each perennial when you plant it. And every time you dig a planting hole, add organic matter.

Digging to the depth of the spading fork—one spit—and turning the soil over is known as *single digging*. Begin on one side of the garden and work facing out, so you don't walk on the soil you've just prepared. Insert the fork fully, and then lift the forkful of soil and flip it over, back into the space it came from. Use the fork to break up big clods of dirt and to mix the organic matter into the soil. Then finish the job by raking the soil surface smooth with a garden rake.

Gardeners with very light or very heavy soil— soil that stays waterlogged or that has become compacted by many seasons of teenagers playing basketball or other causes—will have to do more than single digging. A rototiller is one option; *double-digging* is the other. Double-digging, be warned, is like dirty dancing: Most of us would rather watch someone else do it than do it ourselves. That's because it is hard work and takes more than a little time, since it requires both digging and moving dirt. It is what you do, newspaper columnist Jack Aulis wrote, "to loosen the soil's basement."

Double-digging was once the standard practice of all estate and most home gardeners, and it's still recommended in garden books. Also known as *bastard trenching*, double-digging is *comme il faut* in France and a long-standing tradition in England. And it is an opportunity to tone up your muscles while creating soil that is gloriously ready to grow everything from asters to zinnias. Here's how to double-dig:

1. Establish the boundaries of the bed, remove the sod (see "Death by Spade," page 82, for instructions), and set it aside.
2. Begin on one side of the garden and dig a trench 1 foot wide and 1 foot, or 1 spit, deep. Set the soil aside in a wheelbarrow or on a tarp.
3. Use a spading fork to loosen the subsoil another foot deep for a total of 2 feet.
4. Cover the loosened subsoil with a layer of sod, grass side down.
5. Cover the sod with 2 to 4 inches of compost or other decomposed organic matter.
6. Dig a second trench, 1 foot wide and 1 foot deep, adjoining the first trench. Place the soil from the second trench on top of the organic matter in the first trench.
7. Loosen the subsoil in the second trench to a depth of 1 foot and cover the loosened soil with sod, grass side down, and 2 to 4 inches of organic matter.

The Root of the Matter. *Plants need well-drained soil, so don't fail to dig deeply when preparing a new flower garden. Double-diggers use a spading fork to loosen the soil to a depth of 2 feet.*

8. Dig a third trench, 1 foot wide and 1 foot deep, adjoining the second trench. Place the soil from the third trench on top of the organic matter in the second trench.
9. Continue this pattern until the entire garden plot is dug. Fill the last trench with turf and topsoil that was set aside from the first trench.
10. Cover the garden with another 2 or 3 inches of organic matter; work it in with a spading fork, and rake the plot smooth.

Single or double, by hand or machine, your garden soil is now turned, enriched, and smoothed. If you can curb your enthusiasm, let it settle for a week or two before you begin planting. Then the fun really begins.

Garden Pictures. *Combining white arum lilies (*Zantedeschia aethiopica*) and colorful* Cineraria *hybrids in the garden is possible in only very warm parts of North America. Gardeners in cooler climates usually grow these plants in containers or cultivate them indoors.*

CHAPTER FIVE

Balancing Act: Creating Borders and Beds

this is the garden: colors come and go,
frail azures fluttering from the night's outer wing
strong silent greens serenely lingering,
absolute lights like baths of golden snow.

E. E. Cummings, *Tulips and Chimneys*, 1923

CREATING SUCCESSFUL FLOWER GARDENS IS WORK for a virtuoso juggler. It requires keeping many balls in the air: the color ball, the height ball, the width ball, the shape ball, the bloom-time ball, the foliage ball, the texture ball, the cultural-need ball, and more. And keeping them in the air with a flair. Even the most ambitious garden maker can't grow every flower, so choosing plants that will harmonize and produce a pleasing picture is vital.

Strictly speaking, a flower *bed* is an island of plants that can be viewed from all sides, whereas a *border* has a backdrop of some sort—a fence, a wall, a hedge, perhaps—so that it is seen primarily from one side. A flower bed typically is located near a terrace, deck, or other structure and is meant to be viewed from up close. An *island bed*—also called a perennial island—is a flower bed that's located out in the lawn, like an island of color surrounded by a sea of grass. Both island beds and perennial borders are usually viewed first from a distance, across the lawn.

It helps if the backdrop for a perennial border accents the flowers' colors and forms. Dark backdrops, including the greens of deciduous shrubs and evergreens, are ideal for showing off most flowers. A *foundation planting* is a kind of border, with the building foundation serving as the backdrop. Most foundation gardens consist mainly of woody plants, especially evergreen species, so that there is year-round foliage, but nothing prevents you from including flowers in a foundation planting.

Both beds and borders are legacies from other parts of the world, especially England and Europe. There are some differences in planning for each, but the terms often are used interchangeably. Beds, borders, and island beds can be formal or informal, can be filled entirely with herbaceous plants, or can be *mixed* and contain woody as well as herbaceous plants.

The conventional advice for flower gardeners is to:

- Put beds and borders where you can see them.
- Place formal gardens near the house, informal gardens away from the house.
- Set tall plants at the back of a border or the middle of a bed.
- Mass plants for effect; drifts of three or five plants are commonly recommended.

Dynamic Duo. *Vivid color combinations like this spring duet—red azaleas and purple-blue Dalmation bellflower (*Campanula portenschlagiana*)—will have heads turning. These hues would be toned down in a shaded location.*

FILLING THE MIXED GARDEN

A mixed bed or border is one that contains both herbaceous and woody plants, such as shrubs and small trees. Mixed gardens provide year-round interest, especially in regions where herbaceous plants die back in winter. Any woody plant with attractive foliage that doesn't grow too large or dispatch colonizing stolons or suckers can serve, although it's an advantage if the plant has handsome flowers. There are thousands of possibilities, but these species and cultivars are a place to begin.

Beautybush (*Kolkwitzia amabilis*);
6–10 feet (Zones 4–8)

Blue mist shrubs (*Caryopteris × clandonensis*) 'Dark Knight' and other cvs.; 2–4 feet (Zones 6–9)

Butterfly bush (*Buddleja davidii*);
up to 10 feet (Zones 5–9)

Cinquefoils (*Potentilla fruticosa* cvs. and *P. fruticosa* var. *dahurica*); 2–3 feet (Zones 2–7)

Dwarf Alberta spruce (*Picea glauca* var. *albertiana*) 'Conica'; 6–8 feet (Zones 2–6/7)

Dwarf blue spruces (*Picea pungens* f. *glauca*) dwarf cvs.; 2–4 feet (Zones 3–7/8)

Dwarf common spruces (*Picea abies*) 'Humilis', 'Procumbens', 2–3 feet (Zones 3–7/8)

The Mixed Garden. *Many gardeners add roses like 'Sun Flare', a disease-resistant floribunda, to herbaceous flower gardens. Lemon-yellow 'Sun Flare' won an All America Rose Selections (AARS) award in 1983 and is still widely planted.*

Dwarf hemlock (*Tsuga canadensis*) 'Bennett'; 2–5 feet (Zones 4–7/8)

Dwarf Korean lilac (*Syringa meyeri*) 'Paladin'; 4 feet (Zones 3–7)

Dwarf white pine (*Pinus strobus*) 'Nana'; 2 feet (Zones 3–7)

Eastern redbud (*Cercis canadensis*); up to 30 feet (Zones 4–9)

Floribunda roses (*Rosa* cvs.) 'Iceberg', 'Cherish', and others; 2–5 feet (Zones 5–9)

Golden St. John's wort (*Hypericum frondosum*); 3 feet (Zones 5–8)

Japanese barberries (*Berberis thunbergii*) 'Atropurpurea Nana', 'Monler'/'Gold Nugget'; 1–4 feet (Zones 4–8)

Japanese hollies (*Ilex crenata*) 'Golden Gem', 'Bee Hive'; 2–4 feet (Zones 5–7/8)

Japanese kerria (*Kerria japonica*); 3–6 feet (Zones 4–9)

Japanese red pine (*Pinus densiflora*) 'Oculus Draconis'; 8–10 feet (Zones 3/4–7)

Japanese spireas (*Spiraea japonica*) 'Little Princess', 'Monhub', 'Bullata', 'Nana', 'Goldflame'; up to 3 feet (Zones 4–8)

Polyantha roses (*Rosa* cvs.) 'The Fairy', 'Orange Triumph', and others; 2–4 feet (Zones 5–9)

Slender deutzias (*Deutzia crenata* var. *nakaiana*) 'Nikko' and other cvs.; 3–6 feet (Zones 5–8)

Thread-leaved Japanese maples (*Acer palmatum* var. *dissectum*) 'Dissectum Atropurpureum' and others; up to 6 feet (Zones 5/6–9)

Tutsan (*Hypericum androsaemum*) 'Albury Purple'; 2–3 feet (Zones 6–8)

Variegated red twig dogwoods (*Cornus alba*) 'Elegantissima', 'Spaethii'; 10 feet (Zones 3–7)

Variegated wintercreepers (*Euonymus fortunei*) 'Emerald Gaiety' and others; 3–4 feet (Zones 5–8)

You can't go wrong with any of these guidelines, but you don't have to follow them. It's your garden, and you should have fun and do what pleases you. If you want to write your children's names in red salvia edged with orange marigolds, do it. If you want to plant only white flowers, as English gardener and writer Vita Sackville-West did in one garden, do it. If you want to grow only flowers that bloom in spring or only annual flowers, do it. If you want a crazy quilt of blooms by the front door, do it. Your garden should reflect you and your style. It should make you smile.

However, all gardeners discover that what makes them smile changes over time. They encounter new flowers and new colors and forms and combinations. They opt for flowers like Siberian iris (*Iris sibirica*), astilbes, and purple coneflower (*Echinacea purpurea*) that are easy to grow and discard species that require mollycoddling. They learn that gooseneck loosestrife (*Lysimachia clethroides*) is too aggressive for a small city garden and that an 8-foot plume poppy (*Macleaya cordata*) is too large for one. Or that hollyhocks (*Alcea rosea*) attract more Japanese beetles than hummingbirds and that the fragile blooms of bearded irises never escape damage by rain and wind.

Other changes come as well. Beds and borders that once were sunny turn shady as trees and shrubs mature; plants die because they are in the wrong site, and they die for no apparent reason at all. Gardens are transitory. "A garden plan," garden designer Penelope Hobhouse explained in *On Gardening* (1994), "is not like an architectural blueprint, it can and must be revised. . . . It is not only the planning, planting and anticipation that makes gardening enthralling, there is also the pleasure of changing and adjusting as the expected or unexpected happens."

Getting Started

Despite the innumerable books and articles about "natural gardens," every garden is manufactured, "a gesture against the wild, / The ungovernable sea of grass," the Welsh poet R. S. Thomas wrote in *A Book of Gardens* (1963). A design turns a collection of plants into a garden. Flower garden design is just one part of landscape design, a subject that is beyond the scope of this book (see Appendix, page 457, for books on design). Nevertheless, the two topics have

FINDING INSPIRATION

*I*f you're making your first garden, take advantage of what others already know and do. Plagiarism may be an indictable offense in print, but in the garden it is a form of flattery. Visit private and public gardens—take a camera and notebook along—and don't be shy about asking questions. There are scores of coffee-table books filled with pictures of gardens that will give you ideas. Garden-plan books, too, are useful, and many include to-scale designs and plant lists. Look at them and learn, but never feel you must follow them to the letter.

much in common, including concern about scale and proportion, unity, rhythm, balance, texture, and color. These are terms that gardeners share with visual artists. Creating a garden, not incidentally, often is likened to painting, with space the canvas and plants rather than oils the medium.

Ornamental gardens should square with their owners' needs. Creating a beautiful scene, providing privacy, hiding the trash cans, and having flowers to cut and give away—all these are good reasons for making flower beds and borders. Gardens also need to square with the existing layout of the site. A flower border that must be walked around to get to the car, a flower bed cheek-by-jowl with a badminton court—these are gardens you'll find yourself relocating in only a few seasons. (For more information about the garden site basics, see Chapter 2, page 29.) A sensible combination of beauty and utility is a prerequisite for a home garden.

The most pleasing beds and borders are ones that relate to their surroundings. House, open space, and gardens need to harmonize. A highly formal garden is likely to look out of place in front of an A-frame. A tiny round bed filled with brightly colored flowers adrift in a four-acre ocean of lawn will look out of scale. One clue to the kind of garden style called for is your house's architecture. If it is symmetrical (are there identical windows on each side of a centered front door?), a symmetrical garden will fit nicely. Symmetrical, or formal, gardens are characterized by order: straight lines, geometric plantings, and a limited number of colors and textures. Houses

Garden Portals. *A gate can be both decorative and functional. This simple doorway supports a climbing rose; at the same time, it helps close off the garden from unwelcome visitors, such as the neighbor's overly curious golden retriever.*

with off-center doors and windows normally call for asymmetrical, or informal, gardens and with plantings that echo nature's apparent randomness.

Horticulture books often recommend creating *garden rooms*, an idea rooted in the aesthetic advantages of creating a coherent composition. (The term *garden* comes from *gart*, the Old High German word for "enclosure.") The approach is to divide a space into several gardens that are separated by fences, hedges, trees, shrubs, or other permanent or quasi-permanent element. Like a picture in a frame, a garden looks better if it has clear limits, things that anchor it to its space. The anchor might be the property boundary, the side of a building, a wall, or even a large tree with the garden set around its base.

Most home gardeners don't have 200-year-old yew hedges or ancient brick-and-stone walls that make creating garden rooms easy, as many British gardeners do, but the idea of making several small gardens rather than one huge garden is worth considering. One bed could contain species that bloom in spring and fall. Daffodils, tulips, crocuses, bleeding hearts (*Dicentra* spp.), basket-of-gold (*Aurinia saxatilis*), and lungworts (*Pulmonaria* spp.) bloom in spring, while asters, Nippon daisy (*Nipponanthemum nipponicum*), fall-blooming anemones (*Anemone* spp.), Russian sage (*Perovskia atriplicifolia*), goldenrods (*Solidago* spp.), and sneezeweed (*Helenium autumnale*) bloom in the fall. Another bed, filled largely with annual flowers, could take center stage in summer. One bed could be filled with jazzy colors—reds and golds—and another planted with flowers that bloom in soft pinks and blues and produces a more restful mood. Perhaps a bed is planted to attract butterflies or one is filled with edible flowers and vegetables.

Just as horticultural taste has evolved over the decades, it's inevitable that some of the beds and borders you create this year you'll want to refashion two years hence. For most gardeners, design springs from doing. That said, it's still worth considering the counsel of experts. Theirs aren't hard-and-fast design decrees but worthy ideas born of centuries of experience.

SIZE AND SCALE

How big a garden should be rests partly on how much room there is. To be in scale, flower gardens need to fit comfortably in the space available. One common design principle is the larger the site, the larger the beds and borders. Another is to use large plants in large spaces, smaller plants in smaller spaces. Gardens also need to match up with your house and other permanent features, the things professionals call hardscape. Three-inch pansies planted in front of a 15-foot wood fence are woefully undersized.

Moreover, the elements *within* the flower garden—primarily plants—need to be in proportion to one another. A bed filled entirely with globe thistle (*Echinops ritro*), hollyhock (*Alcea rosea*), plume poppy (*Macleaya cordata*), and other species

Lilliputian Layout. *A small patio garden filled with edging lobelia (L. erinus), pincushion flowers (Scabiosa cvs.), common foxglove (Digitalis purpurea), and other easy to grow flowers can make a big visual statement.*

6 to 8 feet across. If you make them smaller, they look skimpy (unless the yard is tiny). Make them much wider, and you have to walk *in* them to work among the plants. If yours is an ample space and you want room to plant more flowers, make sure you create paths so you can walk in the garden without trampling the plants.

Borders, which are set in front of some sort of backdrop, can be any size; but if you have the room, one 10 or 12 feet wide and 25 or 30 feet long is a good place to start. Twelve feet sounds like a lot, but you'll want to leave a walkway in the back of the border for access and air circulation, so all of that 12 feet won't be available for plants. Here, too, a narrow maintenance path—mulched or furnished with small stepping-stones—down the center will put all the plants within easy reach for pruning, feeding, and other care. In a small yard with limited space, 2- to 3-foot-wide borders may make the most sense.

5 feet or taller would be grossly disproportionate if it were edged with ground-hugging plants like sweet alyssum (*Lobularia maritima*).

How big a garden is or should be depends, too, on the time, energy, and money you're willing to spend. "Let us not pretend that money makes no difference," Pamela Harper wrote in *Color Echoes* (1994), but "abundant time spent working in a garden goes a long way toward compensating for a limited budget." If you are short on time, energy, and money, but notably the first two, be conservative. You'll be more pleased with one fair-sized, well-composed, well-maintained bed than with a half-dozen large beds that are choked with quack grass and creeping Charlie. It's easier to make gardens larger—or create new ones—than it is to recover large gardens that are overgrown and weedy.

While it's important not to overextend, a common mistake of beginners is to make gardens so small that plants must be crammed together. If possible, island beds, whatever their shape, should be

SHAPE AND STYLE

Bed and border shapes depend on your site and your druthers. Symmetrical buildings can be surrounded by asymmetrical gardens and vice versa. And there's no reason not to have both symmetrical and asymmetrical gardens in the same expanse as long as they aren't at visual war with each other. However, many experts advise that beds and borders, whatever their shape, have similar lines—either straight or curved—and angles to create an overall unity. Or they suggest that symmetrical and asymmetrical gardens be separated by an expanse of lawn or another dividing element.

If your site is level, both formal (geometric) and informal shapes will work well, especially geometrical shapes that relate to a built element like a driveway or fence. "A formal garden is like a bud

Casual Chic. *Allowing low-growing plants to meander into pathways softens straight lines and creates an informal mood. The combination of violet and yellow is a classic complementary color scheme that is often used in gardens.*

in a vase," the French novelist Marcel Proust wrote, "magnificent, elegant, and somehow naturally artificial." Regular shapes with straight lines are stable and dignified. Linear plans are effective in large properties but may be less so in small yards, where they accentuate the limited space.

The ultimate in formal gardens is Versailles, designed by André Le Nôtre in the 17th century, but formal beds and borders can be traced back to ancient Egypt, through the Classical Age, the Middle Ages, the Renaissance, the Industrial Revolution, and into the present. Formal gardens demand order

and pattern in their plantings as well as their layout. One characteristic is *bilateral symmetry*: borders and beds, perhaps separated by a walkway, that mirror each other. Formal designs lead the eye away from the immediate to the garden as a whole and to the center of their plan, which explains why formal gardens typically have some sort of centerpiece, such as a fountain, sundial, statue, or small tree.

A good place to begin laying out a formal garden is at the front or back door. From there draw a straight line to the end of the proposed garden. This axis—which is usually a walkway or lawn—divides

the garden in half. Additional axes can be created to intersect the main axis and create smaller beds, but they should be in balance: whatever their geometric shape, each bed should be identical to the one on the opposite side of the axis. Formal herb gardens are an example of this simple design. Handsome and reassuring, formal gardens also require much care to keep them symmetrical and tidy.

Informal bed and border shapes are tailor-made for sites on hillsides or with irregular grades; if possible, the garden shape should take its cue from the land. "Plans," the English garden writer William Robinson wrote, "should be made on the ground to fit the place, and not the place made to suit some plan out of a book" (*The English Flower Garden*, 1883).

Informal (asymmetrical) designs call for relaxed planting schemes, irregular clumps or drifts of plants rather than plants growing in meticulous patterns. Informal gardens are idiosyncratic, they wander, they surprise. But they shouldn't be formless or without order. Beneath their offhand look is a design: a limit of one or two bold curves, which work better than a half-dozen random curves; a repetition of plants, forms, and colors; a seemingly unrehearsed balance, perhaps created by a large plant counterpoised by a group of small plants. Like formal designs, many informal gardens have an axis with beds on both sides, but it will be a meandering axis rather than a straight one, and the beds won't mirror each other. "Sweet disorder," Vita Sackville-West explained, "has to be judiciously arranged."

Any flower bed or border is improved by exact measurements. They are mandatory if the design is formal—even small differences in size or angle become obvious. But seemingly haphazard gardens also are bettered if their curves are similar in shape or degree or if they follow curves that already exist, such as a winding path or—if you're so lucky—a stream. Use a hose or rope to delineate curvilinear beds or borders, stakes and strings for geometrical ones.

You can begin a design on graph paper or on the computer—there are several programs for home gardeners—but mark out the garden on the ground too. Then stand back and visualize what it will look like when filled with flowers. It's possible to see changes that need to be made even before you begin to dig. Straight lines can become curves and curves can be straightened. It's easy to change the outlines of a garden.

Unity and Harmony

Whether the design is formal or informal, flower gardens are most pleasing if they create a sense of unity and wholeness, if they look complete. Too many elements—too many different flowers, shapes, angles, or colors—and the overall effect becomes muddled and chaotic.

Alternately, too little variety, too much repetition, too careful the balance, too restrained the colors, and the result can be dull and predictable. Gardeners use many techniques to create unity and harmony.

REPETITION AND PROGRESSION

Repeating specific plants, shapes, and colors is one way to tie a garden together and turn a botanical collection into a horticultural picture. Fifty yards of alternating red and white zonal geraniums (*Pelargonium* × *hortorum*) loses its force, but a color that recurs less rigidly throughout a garden creates a sense of coherence and consonance. Repeating patterns, shapes, and colors also establishes what designers call visual rhythm and moves the eye in a particular direction.

Repetition is easier in a large garden than a small one. *Mass planting*—filling a bed or border with a single plant—is the transcendent form of repetition. The effect of a huge array of nothing but red tulips, such as 'Bing Crosby', is breathtaking, which is why mass plantings are used in public gardens, where space isn't at a premium. In a confined space, however, the technique loses its power;

moreover, planting only one cultivar means that there will be flowers for only a short time unless you're willing to replant the bed throughout the garden season.

If your space is limited—or even if it isn't—remember that repetitive doesn't have to mean identical. Rather than plant three large clumps of a red daylily such as *Hemerocallis* 'Scarlet Orbit', you can echo their red color with bee balm (*Monarda didyma*) 'Cambridge Scarlet' and scarlet sage (*Salvia splendens*) 'Empire Red'. Or you can underplant pink Darwin tulips, such as 'Pink Impression', with a pink forget-me-not (*Myosotis sylvatica*) 'Victoria Rose' or purple tulips with a purple-and-white pansy, such as 'Bingo Purple Blotch'—or reproduce the verticality of Siberian iris (*Iris sibirica*) with

THAT'S GEE-KELL

The most influential garden designer of the last 150 years is the British artist-turned-gardener Gertrude Jekyll (1843–1932). Turning her back on fussy designs filled with annual bedding flowers, Jekyll championed a more informal, natural look—some call it "controlled wilderness"—that emphasized sophisticated harmonies of flower colors, attention to plant shapes and textures, and planting species that were site-appropriate. Two of her best-known books—recently reissued by Timber Press—are *Wood and Garden* (1899), which traces a year in her garden, and *Colour in the Flower Garden* (1908).

Color Echoes. *Repeating colors creates coherence and cadence in a flower garden. This border contains many different flowers but is held together by two recurring colors. Pastel hues like mauve create a sense of calm and have a relaxing effect.*

hollyhock (*Alcea rosea*), gayfeathers (*Liatris* spp.), delphiniums, gladioli, or obedient plant (*Physostegia virginiana*).

Another way to establish unity is *progression*, or *sequence*—moving in graded steps from tall flowers to short, fine-textured to coarse-textured plants, or the shade, tone, and tint of a single color (or colors that are next to each other on a color wheel, such as orange, yellow-orange, and yellow). Gertrude Jekyll was famous for her designs based on sequential colors, beginning at one end of a border with gray, pale blue, yellow, and pink, moving to strong yellows, oranges, and reds in the middle of the border, then continuing in an inverse sequence to the other end.

FOCUS AND BALANCE

Just as the front door is normally the focal point in a front yard, having an element that draws the eye is another way to tie things together in a bed or border. The point of emphasis might be a modest tree, a water feature, a small statue, a sundial, a bench, a particularly spectacular plant, or the summit of a color progression. A garden design should flow from the focal point, which means it—plant, pool, bench, whatever—should be the first thing to go into the bed. One warning: Small beds can be

Keep Off the Grasses. *Ornamental grasses like this hardy Japanese silver grass (*Miscanthus sinensis *'Graziella') add strong verticality to flower gardens. The showy white flowers appear in early fall and hang on into winter.*

SPLENDOR IN THE GRASSES

Ornamental grasses have been invading flower gardens in droves ever since feather reed grass 'Karl Foerster' was named the 2001 Perennial Plant of the Year. Tall and short, erect and arching, green and colored, plain and striped, ornamental grasses are carefree in nature. And they are more than foliage plants, for many produce handsome flowers. Experts divide grasses into two groups: cool-season grasses, which flower in early summer, and warm-season grasses, which flower in fall. Make sure any perennial grasses you plant are cold hardy in your location. These grasses have notable blooms.

Annual fountain grass (*Pennisetum setaceum*); annual

Blue oat grass (*Helictotrichon sempervirens*); cool season; Zones 4–9

Eulalia grasses (*Miscanthus sinensis* cvs.); warm season; Zones 4–9

Feather grasses (*Stipa* spp.); cool season; Zones 7–10

Feather reed grasses (*Calamagrostis* × *acutiflora*) 'Carl Foerster', 'Overdam'; cool season; Zones 5–9

Feathertop (*Pennisetum villosum*); annual

Fountain grass (*Pennisetum alopecuroides*); warm season; Zones 5/6–9

Pampas grass (*Cortaderia selloana*); warm season; Zones 7–10

Quaking grass (*Briza maxima*); annual

Ravenna grass (*Saccharum ravennae*); warm season; Zones 6–9

Variegated giant reed (*Arundo donax* var. *variegata*); warm season; Zones 5/6–10

Variegated hakone grass (*Hakonechloa macra* 'Aureola'); warm season; Zones 5–9

overwhelmed by even a miniscule garden ornament. If your garden is undersized, you may want to stick with a specimen plant, such as a very small Japanese maple (*Acer palmatum* 'Shindeshojo') or an ornamental grass, as its focal point.

Formal gardens have an inherent unity by virtue of their balanced layout, but asymmetrical gardens also use balance to create coherence. Traditional Japanese gardens are ideal examples: Their elements rarely are symmetrical, yet they are meticulously chosen and placed to produce balance. Home gardeners can use the same techniques. For instance, a tree peony (*Paeonia suffruticosa*) with large leaves can be offset by a mass of willow-leaved sunflower (*Helianthus salicifolius*), which has fine-textured foliage.

Or a tall plant can be balanced by an equivalently horizontal one or several horizontal ones: yellow-banded porcupine grass (*Miscanthus sinensis* 'Strictus') next to yellow-flowering thread-leaved coreopsis (*Coreopsis verticillata*), for example. Or one color can be counterpoised by its complementary color: an orange daylily such as 'Home Run' or orange Oriental poppies like 'China Boy' planted next to blue lupines such as *Lupinus perennis* 'Gallery Blue' or *Delphinium* 'Blue Jay'. The balance, while not symmetrical, still pulls the plants together into a united whole.

BOUNDARIES

Maintaining a tidy edge between a border or bed and the lawn—creating a clear boundary—is another technique gardeners use to define a garden's limits and accent its shape. Well-defined edges, in addition to unifying and setting off the garden, have practical merits: They help keep mulches from washing away; they make it easier to mow; they keep turf from growing into the garden and aggressive flowers from spreading into the lawn.

In horticulture, the term *aggressive* is relative. Flowers that take over in North Carolina may be no problem in Montana or Maine. Some plants spread easily—yellow-flowered *Corydalis lutea* is a good example—but also are easy to control. Others are less so. Check with local gardeners, but keep an eye on the flowers listed below, all handsome but often too willing to push out demure neighbors either by self-seeding or invasive roots. You don't have to exclude them, but you may have to curb them by removing seed heads or dividing frequently.

Creeping bellflower (*Campanula rapunculoides*)

Feverfew (*Tanacetum parthenium*)

Garlic chives (*Allium tuberosum*)

Goldenrods (*Solidago* spp.)

Gooseneck loosestrife (*Lysimachia clethroides*)

Heath aster (*Aster ericoides*)

Lily-of-the-valley (*Convallaria majalis*)

Ox-eye daisy (*Leucanthemum vulgare*)

Ozark sundrop (*Oenothera macrocarpa*)

Perennial sunflowers (*Helianthus* spp.)

Plume poppies (*Macleaya* spp.)

Showy evening primrose (*Oenothera speciosa*)

Star-of-Bethlehem (*Ornithogalum umbellatum*)

Violets (*Viola* spp.)

The simplest edge is a shallow trench, but it requires regular maintenance to keep it weed and grass free. Flower gardens also can be rimmed with woody plants, such as boxwoods (*Buxus* spp.), and with bricks, flagstones, or wood; there are commercial metal and plastic products too, although many are obtrusive if not downright ugly. Low-growing perennials or annuals that have good foliage throughout the garden season are another solution for establishing a boundary. Among the best annuals for the task are dwarf marigolds, including 'Jaguar', 'Nugget Supreme Yellow', and 'Scarlet Starlet'; ageratum (*Ageratum houstonianum*), including 'Blue Lagoon', 'Hawaii Hybrid', and 'Blue Danube'; edging lobelia (*Lobelia erinus*), such as 'Blue Moon' and 'Crystal Palace'; and scarlet sage (*Salvia splendens*), including 'Vista Red', 'Hotline Pink', and 'Hotline Blue'.

Perennials commonly used to edge gardens include wooly yarrow (*Achillea tomentosa*), lady's mantle (*Alchemilla mollis*), dwarf basket-of-gold (*Aurinia saxatilis* var. *compacta*), alpine rock cress (*Arabis alpina*), dwarf goat's beard (*Aruncus aesthusifolius*), bergenias (*Bergenia* spp.), pinks (*Dianthus* spp.), cushion spurge (*Euphorbia polychroma*), sweet woodruff (*Galium odoratum*), coral bells or heucheras (*Heuchera* cvs.), lavenders (*Lavandula* spp.), lilyturfs (*Liriope* spp.), sedums or stonecrops (*Sedum* spp.), lamb's ear (*Stachys byzantina*), and thymes (*Thymus* spp.). Low-growing speedwells, such as *Veronica peduncularis* 'Georgia Blue', *V. spicata*, and

Keeping an Edge. *A neat boundary sets off a flower garden. Be sure to use plants that have good foliage throughout the growing season, like these grasslike lilyturf (Liriope muscari 'Variegata') plants. Lamb's ear (Stachys byzantina) is another popular edger.*

V. prostrata, can be used as edgers, as can the many small hostas that maintain a neat habit throughout the garden season, including 'Gold Heart', 'Pacific Blue Edger', 'Lakeside Cup Cake', 'Radiant Edger', and 'Cherub'. Low-growing hardy geraniums, or cranesbills, including *Geranium dalmaticum*, *G. cinereum* 'Ballerina', and *G. × cantabrigiense* 'Karmina', also are attractive perennials for edging.

Choosing Plants

Selecting plants for a flower garden is like scratching a mosquito bite: Once you start, it's hard to stop. Experts agree that variety is important; at the same time, simplicity is fundamental to a well-designed flower garden. One way to achieve simplicity is not to buy every pretty flower you see. Limit the number of colors to two or three; limit the number of genera, species, and cultivars; and plant flowers in groups of three or five rather than setting them individually throughout a garden. Like too many cooks and the proverbial broth, too many different plants can spoil a garden.

Most beginning gardeners want droves of flowers in bloom from day one. If you're creating new gardens, rely on annuals for the first few seasons. They peak the same year they're planted, and most stay in bloom for several months. Perennials, which are more expensive than annuals, take a couple of

In the Shadows. *A spot under the trees is perfect for hostas, the preeminent shade plant for home gardens. There are hundreds of* Hosta *cultivars, all grown for their showy leaves rather than their less impressive flowers.*

years to reach full size. Going slow with planting perennials also gives you time to see many different flowers before you dip into your wallet. Bulbous flowers, such as lilies, typically blossom the first year they're in the ground—but you have to anticipate. Daffodils and tulips, for example, must be planted in fall in order to bloom the next spring.

Knowing when a plant blooms is important, but knowing what conditions it needs to succeed is more important: what kind of soil, how much light, how much moisture, and more. Finally, gardeners have to think ahead. How large will the plant get? Is it aggressive, likely to overpower other plants, or is it well behaved and unlikely to spread? If it's a

CULTURAL REQUIREMENTS

Flower breeders have made our plant choices nearly infinite, but on-the-ground realities make them finite. All gardeners must take into account their climate, exposure, and soil conditions and whether they meet the needs—gardeners call them *"cultural requirements"* or *"demands"*—of each flower. (For more information about climate, see Chapter 2, page 29; for information about exposure, see Chapter 3, page 47; for information about soil, see Chapter 4, page 63.)

Planting perennial flowers that are marginally hardy, as the saying goes, is like spitting into the wind. Dahlias won't survive North Dakota winters. And perennials that need a period of cold each year, such as most peonies, won't prosper in Miami, Florida. Sun-loving annual flowers like baby's breath (*Gypsophila* spp.), cockscomb (*Celosia argentea*), zinnias, gazanias (*Gazania* Hybrids), marigolds, and moss rose (*Portulaca grandiflora*) will never succeed in the shade, whereas lungworts (*Pulmonaria* spp.), common bleeding heart (*Dicentra spectabilis*), impatiens, and forget-me-nots (*Myosotis* spp.) won't do their best in blazing sun.

Likewise, a garden with heavy clay soil is the wrong setting for flowers that prefer light sandy soil. If the ground is wet and dense, don't plant delphiniums, spider flower (*Cleome hassleriana*), or hollyhock (*Alcea rosea*). But you can plant hairy penstemon (*Penstemon hirsutus*), wild lupine (*Lupinus perennis*), hoary vervain (*Verbena stricta*), and butterfly weed (*Asclepias tuberosa*).

There are two messages from Mother Nature, and Mother really does know best. First, accept and work with the conditions you have. Second, give plants what they want. For lists of flowers for different conditions, see the lists throughout Chapters 1 through 4, and consult the Plant Portraits section (beginning on page 213) for information about the cultural preferences of specific flowers.

PLANT SIZE AND SHAPE

There are dozens of different shapes, or forms, of both plants and blossoms, and they have an impact on the overall appearance of any garden. Size—height and width—also has an effect. There are choices as diminutive as purple-pink flowered wooly thyme (*Thymus pseudolanuginosus*), which is only ¾ inch

perennial or bulbous species, is it hardy in your region? Try to answer these questions before you buy, but don't be afraid to add a flower that you see and like even if you don't know everything about it. Garden centers usually sell only plants that are suitable for local conditions, and what's thriving in a neighbor's garden also is a guide to what will do well in yours.

A Hullabaloo of Plants. *This garden not only contains vivid colors but many shapes and heights, from the upright scarlet sage (Salvia splendens) that edges the bed to the self-sowing yellow Rudbeckia hirta 'Indian Summer', a prize-winning black-eyed Susan with softball-size blooms.*

tall, to giant plants like the 10-foot high and equally wide plume poppy (*Macleaya cordata*).

Including plants of different heights and girths makes any garden more interesting than one in which all plants have similar measurements. One informal guide about plant height, to keep a garden in proportion, is that the tallest plants should not be taller than two-thirds the width of the border, or half the width of a bed. The "stair-step" approach is the standard recommendation for borders: short plants in the front, medium in the middle, tall in the back. Flower beds normally place the tallest plants in the middle and surround them with shorter species.

These are good general rules, but don't follow them religiously. Breaking up a stair-step progression will make the garden look more natural. Bring some tall plants forward and set some shorter plants back, but make sure that the tall flowers you bring forward aren't too dense to see through. Fall-blooming anemones (*Anemone* spp.) and annual cosmos (*Cosmos bipinnatus*) are possible choices; all are open and airy in form.

In addition to its height and width, every flowering plant has a general shape—gardeners refer to it as the plant's *habit*. Reduced to their most basic, the forms are:

Vertical, or upright. Plants with a vertical, or upright, habit often are used as an accent in the garden. Good examples of the vertical habit are delphiniums, irises, lilies, garden phlox (*Phlox paniculata*), foxglove (*Digitalis purpurea*), and cannas. Upright plants can be tightly vertical as are cardinal flower (*Lobelia cardinalis*), whorled loosestrife (*Lysimachia punctata*), and mulleins (*Verbascum* spp.), or they can have a looser form, as do meadow rues (*Thalictrum* spp.) and columbines (*Aquilegia* spp.). Tall, single-stemmed plants should be planted in groups of three or more to avoid looking like a lone cactus in the middle of barren desert.

Mounded. Plants that are mounding can form clumps that are round, vase-shaped, pyramidal, or other shapes. They are represented by astilbes, peonies, garden chrysanthemums, dwarf dahlias, French marigold (*Tagetes patula*), coral bells, or heucheras (*Heuchera* spp.), bleeding hearts (*Dicentra* spp.), blanket flowers (*Gaillardia* spp.), most hostas, baby's breaths (*Gypsophila* spp.), and many more. Mounded plants can look like a platoon of turtles unless they're grouped in irregular drifts, so don't set them in a straight row.

Horizontal, or prostrate. These are mat-forming plants that are meant for the front of the flower garden or for underplanting. Among the common, and good, choices are rock cress (*Arabis caucasica*); low-growing hardy geraniums, or cranesbills, such as *Geranium farreri* and *G. cinereum*; moss phlox and creeping phlox (*Phlox subulata* and *P. stolonifera*); many *Sedum* species; lilyturfs (*Liriope* spp.); and a whole group of prostrate speedwells, including *Veronica alpina*, *V. repens*, *V. cinerea*, and *V. prostrata*.

Climbing. Plants with climbing habits are the last major form. Familiar herbaceous climbers include sweet pea (*Lathyrus odoratus*); morning glory and its many cousins (*Ipomoea* spp.); balloon vine, or love-in-a-puff (*Cardiospermum halicacabum*); and black-eyed Susan vine (*Thunbergia alata*).

RISING TO THE OCCASION

Tall plants give gardens a sense of permanence—their height makes them seem enduring, nearly as lasting as trees. Tall plants belong in the back of the border or the center of the bed. Their only failing? Many must be staked to withstand windy weather or to hold up their large blossoms. There are tall annuals—cosmos, sunflowers, and spider flower (*Cleome hassleriana*) are three examples—but these perennials are a good place to begin for filling in the back row.

Big-leaved ligularia (*Ligularia dentata*)

Blue false indigo (*Baptisia australis*)

Bronze fennel (*Foeniculum vulgare* 'Purpureum')

Common rose mallow (*Hibiscus moscheutos*)

Delphiniums (*Delphinium* cvs.)

Foxtail lilies (*Eremurus* spp.)

Giant coneflower (*Rudbeckia maxima*)

Giant globe thistle (*Echinops sphaerocephalus*)

Goat's beard (*Aruncus dioicus*)

Hollyhock (*Alcea rosea*)

Joe-Pye weeds (*Eupatorium* spp.)

Meadowsweets (*Filipendula* spp.)

Olympic mullein (*Verbascum olympicum*)

Ornamental rhubarb (*Rheum palmatum* 'Atrosanguineum')

Perennial sunflowers (*Helianthus* spp.)

Plume poppy (*Macleaya cordata*)

Ragged coneflower (*Rudbeckia laciniata*)

Russian sage (*Perovskia atriplicifolia*)

Sneezeweed (*Helenium autumnale*)

Tartarian aster (*Aster tataricus*)

Mounds of Flowers. *Long-flowering Paris, or Marguerite, daisy (*Argyranthemum frutescens*) is a tender perennial that most gardeners treat as an annual. It requires full sun and forms a large mound that is as wide as it is high.*

AVERAGE JOES

Flowers of medium height are the Rodney Dangerfields of the garden: They get no respect. Or, at least, they do not get as much as they deserve, for they are the core of most beds and borders. These are some of the most reliable perennials in the "average" category, 2 to 4 feet tall.

Astilbes (*Astilbe* cvs.), including 'Avalanche', 'Spinell', 'Red Fanal', 'Deutschland'

Bee balms (*Monarda* spp.)

Black-eyed Susan (*Rudbeckia fulgida*), including 'Goldsturm'

Bleeding heart (*Dicentra spectabilis*)

Butterfly weed (*Asclepias tuberosa*)

Daylilies (*Hemerocallis* cvs.)

Fall-blooming, or Japanese, anemones (*Anemone hupehensis, A. × hybrida, A. tomentosa*)

Garden phlox (*Phlox paniculata*)

Gooseneck loosestrife (*Lysimachia clethroides*)

Hostas (*Hosta* cvs.)

Large-flowered coreopsis (*Coreopsis grandiflora*)

Lavender (*Lavandula angustifolia*)

Lupines (*Lupinus* spp.), including Russell Hybrids

Peonies (*Paeonia* cvs.)

Purple coneflower (*Echinacea purpurea*)

Rose campion (Lychnis coronaria)

Sea hollies (*Eryngium* spp.)

Siberian iris (*Iris sibirica*)

Solomon's seal (*Polygonatum biflorum*)

Flower blossoms also come in many shapes, combinations, and sizes: single, double, and composite, small to giant. (For more information on bloom forms, see Chapter 1, page 5.) A flower garden with only one plant or bloom form would be boring, but don't overdo it. Too many different shapes and sizes make a garden look muddled.

PLANT TEXTURE

Texture refers to an object's surface qualities, anything that can be seen or felt. In the garden, the term is used most to describe plant foliage. Are the leaves soft and furry like lamb's ears (*Stachys byzantina*) or prickly like globe thistles' (*Echinops* spp.) and the leaves of sea hollies (*Eryngium* spp.)? Are they smooth and waxy like the leaves of lilies, bearded irises, and *Sedum* 'Autumn Joy' or glossy like European wild ginger (*Asarum europaeum*)? Or are they like bee balm (*Monarda didyma*) and lungworts (*Pulmonaria* spp.), which, because their leaves are covered with tiny hairs, have a dull appearance? Do the leaves catch droplets of water and transform them into diamonds as the foliage of lady's mantle (*Alchemilla mollis*) and Icelandic poppy (*Papaver croceum*) do?

Light influences how plants appear, and the amount of light that is reflected from any surface is affected by its texture. Plants with glossy leaves, such as bear's breeches (*Acanthus mollis*) and bergenias (*Bergenia* spp.), glow, drawing attention to themselves. In contrast, flowers with dull, or matte, leaves tend to recede from view. The detail of fine-textured leaves is lost when viewed from a distance, but up close finely dissected foliage, like that of astilbes, creates delicate patterns of light and shadow.

Some genera—*Hosta* is a superb example—offer a wealth of leaf features all by themselves. Hosta leaves range from heart shaped to narrow strap shaped; leaf margins, or edges, are always entire, never lobed or toothed, but they vary from flat to rippled and crimped. Leaves can be wavy, twisted, arched, convex, or cupped, and their surfaces can be anything from smooth to puckered, always with clearly visible veining. All hosta leaves are smooth and hairless, but their "finish" can be matte, satiny, shiny, or waxy. Hosta leaf colors range from near-yellow through green to deep blue, and there are all sorts of variegated options: hostas with white or gold leaf edges and green centers, with white or gold centers and green edges, and more. 'Blue Angel' has enormous heavily textured, nubby blue-gray leaves, whereas 'Blue Mouse Ears' has small, round, relatively smooth leaves. 'Abiqua Drinking Gourd' has cupped, intensely puckered leaves; 'Alligator Shoes' has variegated leaves with a crinkly texture, but 'Geisha', another variegated cultivar, has narrow, smooth foliage that is twisted. *Hosta gracillima* has narrow leaves with ruffled

In Praise of Foliage. *The unusual leaves of dusty miller (Artemisia stelleriana) are notable because of their shape and color. Also known as sagewort, beach wormwood, and old woman, the name "dusty miller" comes from the leaves' white color.*

The foliage of most garden flowers—from asters and bellflowers (*Campanula* spp.) to lungworts (*Pulmonaria* spp.) and peonies—falls in the middle of the scale, with medium texture. Flowers with bold foliage include cannas, bergenias (*Bergenia* spp.), large-leaved hostas, ligularias (*Ligularia* spp.), bear's breeches (*Acanthus* spp.), and, of course, caladiums (*Caladium bicolor*).

Caladiums, heat-loving perennials that grow from stem tubers, are the very definition of bold leaves. While they produce flowers, caladiums' *raison d'être* is their flamboyant foliage. In politico-speak, "It's the leaves, stupid." Caladium leaves can be spotted, splotched, veined, and edged in combinations of green, white, and all shades of red. Each leaf is a *tour de force* of pattern and color. Far-south gardeners can set caladiums in their beds and borders, but cold-climate growers don't have to miss out: They can grow them in containers, starting them indoors, then moving them outside once the danger of frost is well past.

Pleasing gardens usually have a mix of leaf textures: glossy and matte, fine and bold. Too many plants with the same texture is boring, but too many textures may produce a feeling of disharmony. A basic rule is to keep the number of

margins or edges; 'Sunshine Glory' has large green-and-gold variegated leaves with the texture of seersucker. The list goes on and on. According to the American Hosta Society (AHS), there are at least 6,000 named cultivars in commerce—about 3,000 of which are registered with the AHS—and while many are similar, no two are exactly alike.

Plant texture is also measured on a fine to coarse scale. Flowers with fine texture include many linear- and strap-leaved plants like ornamental grasses, crocosmias (*Crocosmia* spp.), daylilies, and Siberian iris (*Iris sibirica*). Plants with narrow, airy foliage are fine-textured as well, such as English lavender (*Lavandula angustifolia*), thread-leaved coreopsis (*Coreopsis verticillata*), cosmos, and love-in-a-mist (*Nigella damascena*). Plants with finely dissected leaves also are fine textured, including yarrows (*Achillea* spp.), marigolds, bloody cranesbill (*Geranium sanguineum*), and sweet woodruff (*Galium odoratum*). Plants that produce mounds of small flowers—baby's breaths (*Gypsophila* spp.), for example—also add texture to the garden.

Colorful Caladiums. *Gardeners grow caladiums exclusively for their stunning leaves. These perennials make good container plants in northern gardens, where it is too cold to overwinter them.*

different textures small when the number of colors is great and vice versa.

BLOOM TIME

The dream of most new gardeners is to have a garden that is always full of flowers, always at its peak. Even with a huge space for growing flowers, that's a terribly ambitious goal. All flower gardens ebb and flow. Before you begin planting, think about when you want your garden to shine. Do you go away in August? Do you throw garden parties in June? Choose plants accordingly.

While no flower garden is always at a pinnacle, there's no reason why there can't be something in bloom from early spring until the snow flies. Victorian gardeners solved this problem by *carpet bedding*, planting masses of bright-colored flowers that bloomed and then were removed and replaced by another mass of bright-hued flowers. Their approach was as labor-intensive as it was colorful, and most contemporary gardeners don't have enough time or energy to follow the tradition. But it is possible to have a succession of blossoms by combining annual, perennial, and bulbous flowers. What it takes is knowledge of what blooms when and for how long.

You might want to think of your garden as a time-share condo: When one flower—or one bed—is done, you need another to take its place. Good seed companies and nurseries, such as daylily specialists Bloomingfields Farm in Connecticut, provide precise information in their print and online catalogs about when plants flower. Creating a succession of blossoms typically means using many different plants, although there are some genera—*Hemerocallis*, or daylilies, for one—with cultivars that are early-, mid-, and late-season bloomers, for a little more than four

PLAY IT AGAIN, STELLA

Introduced in 1975, 'Stella de Oro' has become "the most popular and widely-grown daylily of all time," according to the Oakes Daylilies nursery (www.oakesdaylilies.com) in Tennessee. The secret of its success? 'Stella de Oro' blooms on and off throughout the summer. *Reblooming* daylilies like Stella, which offer another way to produce a succession of flowers, are commonplace now, and specialist nurseries offer dozens of cultivars. This list of All-America Selections winners, each a rebloomer, is one place to begin.

'Bitsy', yellow

'Black-Eyed Stella', melon, darker eye

'Bryan Paul', deep red, yellow throat

'Chorus Line', medium pink and rose, small chartreuse throat

'Frankly Scarlet', scarlet, small gold throat

'Judith', glowing pink, vivid pink eye

'Lady Lucille', deep orange

'Leebea Orange Crush', rich orange, rose red eye

'Lullaby Baby', near white

'Plum Perfect', plum, yellow throat

'Star Struck', gold melon, double

Success Story. *The compact daylily 'Stella de Oro' is one of the most widely planted perennials of any genus. Named for a cookie, she was only the second miniature* Hemerocallis *to win a Stout Medal, the highest prize for daylilies.*

months of bloom in all. Most daylily cultivars flower for a month, and there are more than 55,000 registered daylily cultivars available to home gardeners. For information about the most popular cultivars, what cultivars will thrive in your region, or where to buy daylilies—visit the web site of the American Hemerocallis Society at www.daylilies.org.

The Plant Portraits section, which begins on page 213, provides general information about when flowers bloom. Consult local gardeners about more specific bloom times in your location; for perennial flowers, see "Bloom Time," page 30. Garden centers sell annuals that have been pushed to flower earlier than is natural; many will continue to bloom until the first frost. Perennials bloom for shorter periods of time and are less easy to manipulate.

Every season has its stars, flowers with showy blooms and luminous colors. Depend on these popular flowers at these times, remembering that flowers that begin blooming in one season often continue into the next and that times differ from one region to another.

Spring. Bulbous flowers are the essence of spring—crocuses, daffodils, tulips, giant ornamental onion (*Allium giganteum*), crown imperial (*Fritillaria imperialis*), foxtail lilies (*Eremurus* spp.), and more. These are bright, colorful flowers and look wonderful massed in plantings of one color or flower or in combinations. Familiar spring perennials include Grecian windflower (*Anemone blanda*), columbines (*Aquilegia* spp.), rock cress (*Arabis caucasica*), basket-of-gold (*Aurinia saxatilis*), bergenias (*Bergenia* spp.), lily-of-the-valley (*Convallaria majalis*), bleeding hearts (*Dicentra* spp.), hellebores (*Helleborus* spp.), epimediums or barrenworts (*Epimedium* spp.), primroses (*Primula* spp.), perennial candytuft (*Iberis sempervirens*), fernleaf peony (*Paeonia tenuifolia*), moss phlox (*Phlox subulata*), and lungworts (*Pulmonaria* spp.).

Early summer. The stretch between late spring and high summer is showtime for some of the garden's most eye-popping blossoms, such as delphiniums, irises, peonies, Asiatic lilies (*Lilium* Asiatic Hybrids), and Oriental poppy (*Papaver orientale*). Other familiar early summer blooms include lady's mantle (*Alchemilla mollis*), goat's beard (*Aruncus dioicus*), astilbes, mountain bluet (*Centaurea montana*), coreopsis, pinks (*Dianthus* spp.), foxglove (*Digitalis purpurea*), baby's breath (*Gypsophila paniculata*), coral bells or heucheras (*Heuchera* spp.), red-hot poker (*Kniphofia uvaria*), catmints (*Nepeta* spp.),

blue sage (*Salvia nemorosa*), painted daisy (*Tanacetum coccineum*), spiderworts (*Tradescantia* Andersoniana Group), and speedwells (*Veronica* spp.). It's possible to have annuals in bloom by early summer if they are sown early, including snapdragon (*Antirrhinum majus*), pot marigold (*Calendula officinalis*), California poppy (*Eschscholzia californica*), annual baby's breath (*Gypsophila elegans*), globe candytuft (*Iberis umbellata*), common stock (*Matthiola incana*), forget-me-not (*Myosotis sylvatica*), and nasturtium (*Tropaeolum majus*).

Midsummer. Daylilies are one highlight of midsummer. Other midsummer regulars are yarrows (*Achillea* spp.), golden Marguerite (*Anthemis tinctoria*), butterfly weed (*Asclepias tuberosa*), Shasta daisy (*Leucanthemum* × *superbum*), purple coneflower (*Echinacea purpurea*), gayfeathers (*Liatris* spp.), lilies, sea lavender (*Limonium latifolium*), bee balm (*Monarda didyma*), Russian sage (*Perovskia atriplicifolia*), and balloon flower (*Platycodon grandiflorus*). Midsummer is also the time when many annuals, such as cosmos (*Cosmos bipinnatus* and *C. sulphureus*), strawflower (*Bracteantha bracteata*), flowering tobaccos (*Nicotiana* spp.), petunias, scarlet sage (*Salvia splendens*), marigolds, nasturtium (*Tropaeolum majus*), and zinnias come into full flower.

Late summer and fall. There are wonderful flowers that blossom as the garden season moves toward its close. Garden phlox (*Phlox paniculata*) and rudbeckias, such as *Rudbeckia fulgida* var. *sullivantii* 'Goldsturm', reign in the garden in late summer. From late summer through fall, beds and borders are filled with asters and chrysanthemums. This is the time, too, for monkshoods (*Aconitum* spp.); fall-blooming, or Japanese, anemones (*Anemone hupehensis, A. × hybrida, A. tomentosa*); boltonia (*Boltonia asteroides*); Joe-Pye weeds (*Eupatorium* spp.); gentians (*Gentiana* spp.); sneezeweeds (*Helenium* spp.); late-blooming tall gayfeather (*Liatris scariosa*); big-leaved ligularia (*Ligularia dentata*); Chinese lantern (*Physalis alkekengi*); obedient plant (*Physostegia virginiana*); ragged coneflower (*Rudbeckia laciniata*); sedums and stonecrops (*Sedum* spp., especially *S.* 'Autumn Joy'); and goldenrods (*Solidago* spp.). Tall annual flowers, including spider flower (*Cleome hassleriana*), cosmos, and sunflowers, are another feature of late summer, as are cannas and dahlias, two tender bulbous plants.

Creating a succession of blooms is never easy, but it's easier in a sunny garden than in a shady one. Most shade-loving flowers blossom in spring and early summer; to keep the blossoms coming, include shade-tolerant annuals with long bloom times, such as impatiens and wax begonias (*Begonia semperflorens*).

FLOWERS UNDER AND FLOWERS OVER

Few home borders or beds are large enough to hold all the plants required for an endless parade of whopping, bright-hued blossoms. But no garden need be bloomless if you choose flowers that blossom at different times during the garden season and if you *overplant, underplant,* and *interplant.* These are techniques gardeners use to keep every inch of their beds productive. The terms overlap in practice but technically are different.

Overplanting. This literally means setting one flower on top of another. For example, daffodils, most other spring bulbs, and Oriental poppy (*Papaver orientale*) have leaves that die back after flowering ends, leaving the ground bare. Once their foliage has browned, they can be overplanted with shallow-rooted annuals, such as strawflower (*Bracteantha bracteata*) or scarlet sage (*Salvia splendens*). (Overplanting also is used to describe crowding many

plants into a small space to create an excess of blooms and colors. Cottage gardens—a style that emphasizes a slapdash of many colors and forms—are overplanted in this sense.)

Underplanting. Setting shorter plants in the shadow of taller ones, or underplanting, is another way to keep a garden in bloom. Gardeners most often underplant woody shrubs—roses and lilacs, for example—but tall, vertical flowers, such as lilies, can be underplanted with flowers of medium height, such as dwarf dahlias, astilbes, hybrid sage (*Salvia × sylvestris*), and fall-blooming anemones (*Anemone* spp.). Or underplant medium-sized perennials with species that are even shorter, such as sweet woodruff (*Galium odoratum*), wood sorrel (*Oxalis acetosella*), forget-me-nots (*Myosotis* spp.), fringed bleeding heart (*Dicentra eximia*), and pansies. Flowers that develop slowly, such as asters, can be underplanted with spring-flowering perennials like violets, candytuft (*Iberis sempervirens*), and creeping phlox (*Phlox stolonifera*). The so-called "minor bulbs"—crocuses, snowdrops (*Galanthus* spp.), winter aconite (*Eranthis hyemalis*), grape hyacinths (*Muscari* spp.), Siberian squill (*Scilla siberica*), and more—are also good choices for underplanting.

Interplanting. The third variation, interplanting, involves setting fast-maturing plants next to species that develop more slowly, or placing short-lived plants between slow-growing, long-lived ones. Siberian iris (*Iris sibirica*) and bleeding heart (*Dicentra spectabilis*) bloom early in the season and can be interplanted with purple coneflower (*Echinacea purpurea*) or garden phlox (*Phlox paniculata*), which flower weeks later. Most peonies have an ultimate spread of about 3 feet but take as many as five years to reach that width. While you're waiting, interplant with Shasta daisy (*Leucanthemum × superbum*), a fast-growing, short-lived plant that will provide a full look and plenty of flowers until the peonies establish themselves.

Lilium 'Enchantment', an Asiatic Hybrid lily, and *Hosta fortunei* 'Aureomarginata' is another

Onward and Upward. *Underplanting is a good way to make the most of your garden space. Here the violet ornamental onion* Allium *'Globemaster' grows up through the fragrant yellow blooms of* Paeonia lactiflora *'Cheddar Cheese'.*

fine combination, with the lily stems rising between the hosta's leaves. Hardy bulbs and annual flowers also are ideal for interplanting in perennial beds and borders. You can buy annuals that are already in flower and will continue to bloom until fall, or until they are pushed out by their perennial neighbors. Good choices for a sunny garden include Madagascar periwinkle (*Catharanthus roseus*), California poppy (*Eschscholzia californica*), gazanias (*Gazania* cvs.), petunias, and marigolds.

Color

Color, even color in the garden, is a complicated, book-length subject. There are good volumes on hues and horticulture, beginning with the seminal *Colour in the Flower Garden* by Gertrude Jekyll, first published in 1908, through *Colour in Your Garden* by Penelope Hobhouse (1985) to Sydney Eddison's *The Gardener's Palette* (2002), a wonderfully clear and helpful book. Here, though, are a few of the basics of using color in the garden.

The three *primary colors*, or *hues*, as every child who ever had a box of paints knows, are red, yellow, and blue. Other colors are created by mixing these three together. Red and yellow make orange; yellow and blue make green; and blue and red make violet or purple. These three—orange, green, and violet—

are the *secondary colors*; they, and the three primary colors, are the stuff of rainbows. The six *tertiary colors* are a combination of one primary and one secondary color: For example, yellow and orange form yellow-orange, blue and violet make blue-violet.

If you add black to one of these colors and darken it, you get *shades* of that color; add white to lighten a color and you get *tints* of that color (which are sometimes referred to as pastels); add gray to dull a color and you get *tones* of that color.

Colors differ in *value*, whether they are light or dark. The lightest, or most *luminous*, colors are orange, yellow-orange, and yellow-green; blue, blue-violet, violet, and red-violet are the darkest. One color-harmony rule: Mix tints of light colors with shades of dark colors, not vice versa. Put another way, a pale orange looks fine with dark blue, but bright orange and pale blue don't combine well.

Isaac Newton was the first to understand that light, not pigment, was the source of color. But the first color circle, or wheel, printed in color was created by the English engraver and naturalist Moses Harris a century after Newton. Today there are more colors than Newton or Harris ever imagined, but only 12 appear on a modern *artist's color wheel*—a circular display arranged by the colors' relationships to one another.

Thanks to Connecticut author Sydney Eddison, there now is a color wheel designed just for gardeners

Color Coalitions. *Multicolored flowers can offer good ideas for possible color unions in the garden. These eye-popping hybrid fuchsia blossoms bring together hues that you might not expect to combine successfully.*

HINTS FROM MOTHER NATURE

*P*lants themselves supply clues as to what colors look good together. Those that combine more than one color in their foliage—like cultivars of hostas, cannas, caladiums, and coleus (*Solenostemon scutellarioides*) do—or in their flowers—as tulips, marigolds, pansies, and daylilies do—are a fairly reliable guide to combining colors in the garden. Put an accent on *fairly*. Flower breeders have created multicolored blossoms that are abominations: see new daylilies that combine murky purple and dark red with gold and yellow. So, pick species rather than cultivars, plants like New England asters (*Aster novae-angliae*), that haven't strayed too far from Mother Nature for your color template. You can't go wrong with violet and yellow.

THE BIG THREE

King yellow. In his book on chromatics, the German poet Goethe (1749–1832) classified colors as positive and negative. Yellow was "the king of positive tones," embodying cheerfulness and liveliness. Goethe's analyses were decidedly unscientific, but few would disagree with his conclusion: Yellow is the brightest in the color spectrum and is happy, highly visible, and uplifting. There are scores of yellow flowers, including the dandelion, but better choices include dahlias, marigolds, strawflower (*Bracteantha bracteata*), zinnias, irises, daylilies, lilies, daffodils, tulips, and sundrops (*Oenothera* spp.).

True blue. Bluenose. Blue laws. Blue language. Feeling blue. Not all of blue's connotations are positive, but it's still the color most sought by flower gardeners and breeders, who continue to struggle to create a blue rose. Pure blues are hard to find, but begin with delphiniums, campanulas, bearded irises (*Iris* Bearded Hybrids), Himalayan blue poppy (*Meconopsis betonicifolia*), Virginia bluebell (*Mertensia virginica*), and Siberian squill (*Scilla siberica*). If you want to exhaust the horticultural possibilities of the hue, consult *A Book of Blue Flowers* by Robert Geneve (Timber Press, 2000).

Red-letter flowers. It is supposed that red was the first color perceived by humans and that it held magical qualities. Red still represents love, passion, and danger. It attracts attention, catches the eye. Our emotional reaction to red has an explanation in science: Red light is scattered, or weakened, less than other colors. Put another way, a little red can go a long way—out of or in the garden. Tulips, zonal geranium (*Pelargonium* × *hortorum*), begonias, zinnias, geum (*Geum chiloense*), lilies, dahlias, Flanders or corn poppy (*Papaver rhoeas*), and peonies are among the garden's best redheads.

(www.thegardenercolorwheel.com). It is Cliffs Notes for flower growers. The wheel provides a quick and easy way to see "where all the colors belong and how they will relate to one another." And, according to Eddison and other color experts, what looks best together is either a combination of colors that are closely related or widely different.

Books about color in the garden often catalog hues as either "warm" and "aggressive" or "cool" and "receding." If you divide the color

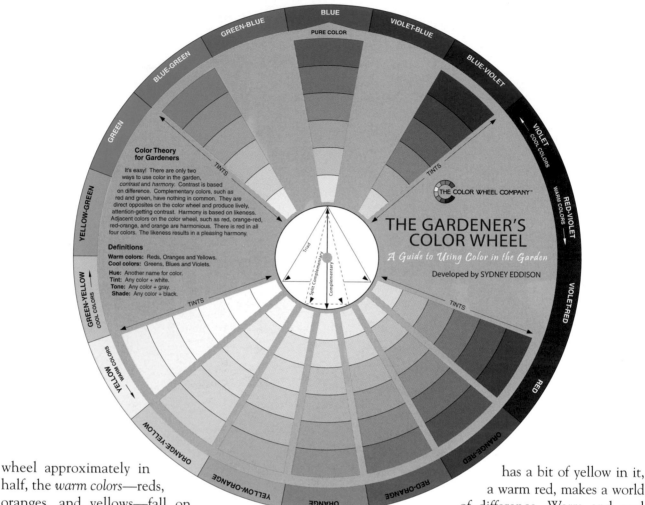

Color Theory for Gardeners

It's easy! There are only two ways to use color in the garden, *contrast* and *harmony*. Contrast is based on difference. Complementary colors, such as red and green, have nothing in common. They are direct opposites on the color wheel and produce lively, attention-getting contrast. Harmony is based on likeness. Adjacent colors on the color wheel, such as red, orange-red, red-orange, and orange are harmonious. There is red in all four colors. The likeness results in a pleasing harmony.

Definitions

Warm colors: Reds, Oranges and Yellows.
Cool colors: Greens, Blues and Violets.

Hue: Another name for color.
Tint: Any color + white.
Tone: Any color + gray.
Shade: Any color + black.

THE COLOR WHEEL COMPANY™

THE GARDENER'S COLOR WHEEL
A Guide to Using Color in the Garden

Developed by SYDNEY EDDISON

wheel approximately in half, the *warm colors*—reds, oranges, and yellows—fall on one side, and *cool colors*—blues, violets, and greens—on the other. Warm colors are eye-catching and lively, cool colors calm and peaceful. Warm colors advance, or look closer than they are, whereas cool colors fade or appear farther away than they actually are. You can trick the eye and make a garden look larger by using flowers with cool colors. Similarly, a border appears larger if flowers with warm colors are placed in the front and those with cool colors in the rear. Nothing but reds, yellows, and oranges in a cramped space may be claustrophobic.

Of course it doesn't stop there. Every primary color is split; it has warmer or cooler versions. Red-orange, for instance, is warmer than red-violet: The red-orange dahlia 'Mars' is downright hot compared with the red-violet bearded iris 'Raspberry Jam'. It's not necessary to approach flowers with a thermometer but look discerningly, because nearly all blooms are combinations of colors, not pure colors. Whether it's a red that contains some blue, a cool red, or a red that

has a bit of yellow in it, a warm red, makes a world of difference. Warm and cool variations of the same hue often clash.

Pinks that have blue in them are incompatible with pink flowers that have red in them. Learning to see the small differences of in-between colors makes a giant difference in the garden.

Hot hues are softened by delicate, open foliage such as bleeding hearts (*Dicentra* spp.), thread-leaved coreopsis (*Coreopsis verticillata*), Swan River daisy (*Brachyscome iberidifolia*), yellow corydalis (*Corydalis lutea*), California poppy (*Eschscholzia california*), cosmos, meadow rues (*Thalictrum* spp.), love-in-a-mist (*Nigella damascena*), annual baby's breath (*Gypsophila elegans*), and columbines (*Aquilegia* spp.). Tuck a blazing orange daylily such as 'Home Run' next to the ferny foliage of a low-growing cosmos cultivar and it won't look nearly so orange.

Light, which affects a color's value, also influences how we see colors in the garden. Colors look warmer in morning light, cooler at dusk. Shady locations appear brighter when they contain light-colored flowers—white, light yellow, lavender, pale blue—but shade dampens the brilliance of hot colors, and dark flowers. The violet blooms of Siberian iris (*Iris sibirica*) 'Caesar's Brother' may disappear altogether in a dark corner. Bright sun fades pastels, but pink, peach, pale yellow, and sky blue shine on overcast days.

If you have trouble choosing a tie or matching skirt and sweater, remember that color theory offers two ways to combine colors: harmonies or contrasts. *Color harmonies*, closely related hues, communicate serenity and unity; designs based on *color contrasts*, hues that are very different, are lively, horticultural exclamation points screaming "look at me." All gardeners learn as they go, but rather than planting a garden willy-nilly with a dozen colors, start with one of the *four basic color schemes*.

Complementary color schemes. These combine two colors that are opposite on the color wheel, such as blue and orange, red and green, yellow and violet, or yellow-orange and

blue-violet. Complementary colors, such as violet verbena 'Tapien Blue Violet' and dwarf yellow snapdragons (*Antirrhinum majus* 'Sonnet Yellow'), orange pot marigolds (*Calendula officinalis*) and cobalt blue edging lobelia (*Lobelia erinus*), or red zonal geraniums (*Pelargonium* × *hortorum*) with dahlia 'Sunny Yellow', intensify each other when used together. They are contrasts to the max, contrasts that may be too garish for some gardeners' taste.

A complementary scheme in the garden might be the violet bearded iris 'Viola' and the early blooming yellow daylily 'Cabbage Flower'; an orange daylily such as 'Kwanso' combined with delphinium 'Blue Jay'; or a yellow trumpet daffodil such as 'Lemon Glow' underplanted with a violet crocus such as 'Twilight'.

One variation of complementary designs is to choose a color and combine it with the colors adjacent to its complement. The combination, known as a *split complement*, could team yellow with red-violet and blue-violet or violet

Dialing for Colors. *Take advantage of the new gardener's color wheel when choosing flowers for beds and borders. The wheel clarifies relationships between hues and may help you avoid combining flowers that won't mix well and find those that will.*

Cool Colors. *A sense of calm is created by the blues and violets in this spring garden. Cool colors tend to recede, making a garden look larger than it is. Warm colors have the opposite effect.*

color wheel, as are blue, green, and yellow. Most triadic combinations, like the autumn foliage triad of red, orange, and yellow, are vibrant, filled with energy.

Analogous color schemes. These feature three hues that lie side by side on a 12-color wheel, such as orange, yellow-orange, and yellow or violet, blue-violet, and blue. They are neighbors, closely related, and thus combine easily, exuding harmony and order. Translated in the early spring garden, an analogous harmony could consist of the red-orange crown imperial (*Fritillaria imperialis*) 'Rubra Maxima', yellow-orange 'Orange Emperor' tulips, and the yellow trumpet daffodil 'Dutch Master'.

Analogous designs are the meat-and-potatoes of garden design books. Because they are predictable combinations—and safe bets in the garden—they look "right" and blend together in expected and pleasing ways. They can be warm combinations or cool. The center color of the three—red-orange, for instance, in a red, red-orange, and orange trio—bridges the gulf between red and orange, and experts recommend using it as the predominate hue. Gardeners can enlarge any analogous color palette by using tints, tones, and shades of any of the base colors, such as teal, magenta, and mango (versions of blue-green, red-violet, and yellow-orange).

Monochromatic color schemes. These use different shades, tints, and tones of a single color. For example, red-flowered 'Jacob Cline' bee balm (*Monarda didyma*), 'Magnus', which is a pink-flowered purple coneflower (*Echinacea purpurea*), and purplish pink-flowered *Astilbe chinensis* var. *pumila* represent

with yellow-green and yellow-orange. Split-complementary alliances can be every bit as flashy as complementary designs. A bed featuring yellow daffodils such as 'Sweetness' and red-violet 'Maytime' tulips interplanted with blue-violet twin-leaf squill (*Scilla bifolia*) or English bluebell (*Hyacinthoides non-scripta*) will have everyone's head turning.

Another variation is a *triadic design*: using three colors, a triad, equidistant from one another on the color wheel. The three primary colors—red, yellow, and blue—are a triad. So are orange, violet, and green or blue-green, yellow-orange, and red-violet. Triads also can be combinations separated by one color on the

A Bit of Everything. *Combining many bright colors creates a lively entry to the front door. The exuberance of polychromatic beds is likely to bring a smile to the face of any visitor.*

TWO DOZEN COMBINATIONS TO TRY

There are tens of thousands of possible plant combinations for home gardens. If you need help getting started, try one or more of these 24 plant duets—some warm, some cool, and all interesting. These pairs are only a beginning. Don't be shy about adding other species and cultivars and other colors.

Blue and gray: spike speedwell (*Veronica spicata*) 'Goodness Grows' and lamb's ears (*Stachys byzantina*)

Blue and orange: globe thistle (*Echinops ritro*) 'Blue Glow' and daylily 'Staghorn Sumac'

Blue and yellow: grape hyacinth (*Muscari botryoides*) and cushion spurge (*Euphorbia polychroma*)

Green and white: hosta 'Undulata Albomarginata' and white bleeding heart (*Dicentra spectabilis*) 'Alba'

Lavender and white-yellow: chives (*Allium schoenoprasum*) and Roman chamomile (*Chamaemelum nobile*)

Lavender-blue and gray: ageratum (*Ageratum houstonianum*) 'Blue Danube' and dusty miller (*Centaurea cineraria*) 'Silver Dust'

Lilac-pink and blue: bellflower (*Campanula latiloba*) 'Hidcote Amethyst' and foothill penstemon (*Penstemon heterophyllus*) 'Züriblau'

Orange and white: red-hot poker (*Kniphofia* cv.) 'Prince Igor' and globe thistle (*Echinops sphaerocephalus*) 'Arctic Glow'

Pink and pink: peony 'Sarah Bernhardt' and masterwort (*Astrantia major*) 'Magnum Blush'

Red and white: cinquefoil (*Potentilla* cvs.) 'Gibson's Scarlet' and peony 'Festiva Maxima'

Red and white: tulip 'Apeldoorn' and daffodil 'Empress of Ireland'

Red and yellow: bee balm (*Monarda didyma*) 'Cambridge Scarlet' and ligularia (*Ligularia stenocephala*) 'The Rocket'

Red-violet and blue-violet: hardy geranium or cranesbill (*Geranium* cv.) 'Ann Folkard' and hybrid sage (*Salvia* × *sylvestris*) 'May Night'

Rose and rose: columbine meadow rue (*Thalictrum aquilegifolium*) and peony 'Monsieur Jules Elite'

Violet and mauve: Siberian iris (*Iris sibirica*) 'Purple Sensation' and tree mallow (*Malva sylvestris*)

Violet and yellow-gold: New England aster (*Aster novae-angliae*) 'Purple Dome' and goldenrod (*Solidago* hybrids) 'Goldenmosa'

White and blue: astilbe 'Bridal Veil' and Serbian bellflower (*Campanula poscharskyana*)

White and lavender-blue: tulip 'Candy Club' and wild blue phlox (*Phlox divaricata*)

White and silver: wild sweet William (*Phlox maculata*) 'Miss Lingard' and 'Miss Willmott's ghost' (*Eryngium giganteum*)

White and white: garden phlox (*Phlox paniculata*) 'David' and Shasta daisy (*Leucanthemum* × *superbum*)

Yellow and orange: daylilies 'Big Bird' and 'Jerome'

Yellow and orange: thread-leaved coreopsis (*Coreopsis verticillata*) 'Zagreb' and butterfly weed (*Asclepias tuberosa*)

Yellow and yellow: solidaster (× *Solidaster luteus*) 'Lemore' and blanket flower (*Gaillardia aristata*)

Yellow-green and blue-violet: lady's mantle (*Alchemilla mollis*) and showy geranium (*Geranium* × *magnificum*)

The Power of White. *White flowers always draw attention to themselves; rather than moderate hues that don't mix well, they emphasize the clash.*

Kissin' Cousins. *These closely related colors—the lavender's violet blooms and the pink flowers of the showy evening primrose (*Oenothera speciosa*)—are a dazzling combination. Equally stunning together are these two garden chrysanthemums (*Chrysanthemum × morifolium*), perfect for analogous schemes. Nurseries and garden centers are well stocked in fall with mums in scores of colors.*

different forms of red. Delphiniums alone could provide a dozen gradations of blue, and a late-summer yellow garden could combine a goldenrod such as *Solidago rugosa* 'Fireworks', ox-eye (*Heliopsis helianthoides*) 'Summer Sun', and a sneezeweed (*Helenium* spp.) such as 'Pumilum Magnificum'.

Although the possibilities are vast if you choose a color like red, which has many variants, monochromatic gardens are not as easy as they might seem. A limited palette can make choosing colors easier, but monochromatic schemes depend heavily on plant textures and forms to create interest.

Polychromatic color schemes. These are horticultural crazy quilts, multicolored garden jumbles that often make heavy use of annual and tender flower species. At their best, they are lively, spontaneous, and visually pleasing. If your bent is free-and-easy, bordering on hodgepodge, a polychromatic garden is just the ticket.

Successful polychromatic gardens—the standard is the English cottage garden or Monet's gardens at Giverny—are wonderfully colorful and exuberant, but sometimes so much can be too much. A random approach to color in the garden produces blunders as well as happy accidents, so don't hesitate to make changes. If the scheme is too brilliantly red, for example, add tints, tones, and shades of red rather than more pure red to calm things down. Don't put a 'Mixed' cultivar of one flower, such as 'Sonnet Mixed' snapdragon (*Antirrhinum majus*) next to a mass of a 'Mixed' cultivar of different species, such as zinnia 'Parasol Mixed' or 'Inca Mixed' marigold

(*Tagetes erecta*). Many cultivars come in separate colors as well as mixes, and mail-order seed suppliers sell colors separately when they can. Garden centers also often offer market packs of plants in mixes as well as solid colors.

These four schemes (and their variations) aren't the be-all and end-all of color combinations. Common in gardens are designs based on *dyads*, two colors on the wheel that are separated by only one color, such as yellow and orange. The two colors in a dyad are close enough to be related but can be different enough to create visual tension. Red-violet hardy geranium (*Geranium* spp.) 'Diva' and blue-violet hybrid sage (*Salvia × sylvestris*) 'May Night' are separated by one color, violet, but the contrast between the two is striking nevertheless.

Some dyads are problematic. Blue and violet *ought* to combine well but rarely do, neither do warm pinks and cool pinks nor warm reds and cool reds. Moreover not all duets are dyads; popular garden duos include blue and pink, blue and white, green and white, lime green and orange, orange and violet, red and yellow, violet and gray, yellow and blue, and yellow and violet.

Remember that the more alike colors are—the closer they are to each other on a color wheel—the more compatible they are; the farther apart they are, the greater their potential impact but also the greater their chance of not mixing successfully. Color combinations didn't come from Olympus or from Mount Sinai. Combinations are neither right nor wrong; they are a matter of taste. Moreover, light, distance, cultural conditions, color combinations, texture, and even genetic differences affect flower colors. Put another way, your 'Taplow Blue' globe thistle (*Echinops bannaticus*) may not look nearly as blue as the one blooming in someone else's garden. Learn to see the subtle differences in color and then experiment. It only takes a spade and a little muscle to change a garden's color scheme.

THE "OTHER" COLORS

In Robert Frost's "Mending Wall' (1914), the narrator's neighbor insists, "good fences make good neighbors." The narrator in the poem isn't sure this is true, but good fences—in the form of plants that are predominately green, gray, and other neutral tones—do make good neighbors in the garden. When paced between hues that rankle side by side, they tone down their differences and achieve visual peace. These hues also bring out the best in other colors and create unity.

Since gardens always contain more leaves than flowers, they also contain more green (and all its variations) than any other color. Green serves as cool scenery for more vivid hues, willing to remain in the background and stabilize and unify beds and borders. Although green is ubiquitous, it isn't dull: Apple green, chartreuse, emerald, jade, kelly green, olive, pea green, shamrock, turquoise, and verdant green are but a handful of the color's possibilities.

Taking advantage of different greens also is a way to add color to a garden. Among the choices are the blue-green leaves of hosta 'Blue Umbrellas', the chartreuse leaves of hosta 'Hooser Harmony', the gold-green leaves of hosta 'Sum and Substance', the purple-green leaves of bugbane (*Cimicifuga simplex*) 'Green Spice', the lime-green leaves of *Heuchera* 'Lime Rickey', and the black-green leaves of 'Preston Park' dahlia. (For more plants with colorful leaves, see "First-String Foliage," page 19.)

Gray and silver, two neutral hues, bring out the best in other colors. They combine with practically anything, which is one reason why gray fences and stone

Supporting Cast. *The gray and silver leaves of the* Senecio *species are superb at both combining with and accenting other colors. Like supporting actors, they make the stars of the garden look better.*

walls are such wonderful border backdrops. Leaves are the primary source of gray and silver in plants. Garden favorites include lamb's ear (*Stachys byzantina*), cultivars of *Artemisia* such as 'Silver Mound' and 'Powis Castle', and other species and cultivars including globe thistles (*Echinops* spp.), sea hollies (*Eryngium* spp.), Olympic mullein (*Verbascum olympicum*), lavenders (*Lavandula* spp.), catmints (*Nepeta* spp.), lungworts (*Pulmonaria* spp.), spotted deadnettle (*Lamium maculatum*), and more. Southwestern gardeners have an enormous group of desert plants to choose from—scores of succulents and cacti that are not hardy in most parts of North America.

White is the lightest color, ideal for dark corners, cloudy days, or an evening garden. No one can ignore white flowers. "In the garden," Sydney Eddison wrote in *The Gardener's Palette*, "white has star quality, the capacity to turn all heads." As a result, white is not the color to choose to reconcile clashing hues. The combination of a coral-red peony and a red-violet peony will not be improved by a white peony placed between them. Henry Mitchell (*The Essential Earthman*, 1981) went so far as to say that white, rather than "a great pacifier of warring colors . . . eggs the warriors on." At the same time, white has many virtues. It clashes with nothing, makes warm colors even more vivid—think of Santa's red-and-white clothes—and combines wonderfully with cool colors. Pastels and white are garden clichés.

There are as many rules for designing beds and borders as there are beds and borders, and most rules come with exceptions, such as the advice to limit the plants with warm colors, vivid reds, and brilliant golds to 15 percent. Yet a garden filled with nothing but gold and red—marigolds, daylilies, bee balms (*Monarda* spp.), dahlias, zinnias, scarlet sage (*Salvia splendens*), and California poppy (*Eschscholzia californica*) can be as exciting and satisfying as a fireworks display. Over time, most gardeners move things around and find the plant and color combinations that please them. The experts have much to say, but in the end each garden should please the garden's maker. If it does that, it is a success.

The Virtues of Annuals. *Colorful annual flowers like scarlet sage (Salvia splendens 'Dwarf Red') are widely available at garden centers and nurseries in spring. Planting a dozen or more adds instant color to the garden that will last until autumn.*

CHAPTER SIX

Garden Work: Planting and Tending Flowers

I will go root away
The noisome weeds which without profit suck
The soil's fertility from wholesome flowers.

William Shakespeare, *Richard III*

EVERY HANDS-ON GARDENER KNOWS THAT THE word *garden* is a verb as well as a noun. It's not only *the garden*, it's *I garden, he and she garden, you garden, we garden, they garden*. Elizabeth Lawrence, who wrote a column for the *Charlotte Observer* in North Carolina for two decades and was a hands-on gardener for more than twice that time, observed that every garden "demands as much of its maker as he has to give." Or as she has to give. But nothing else, she went on, "will give as great a return for the amount of effort put into it."

117

The amount of effort your garden requires depends on the size, the flowers you choose to grow and how you grow them, and your penchant for tidiness. Big gardens, finicky flowers, and an unswerving commitment to order and neatness require more time and work than small plots, self-sufficient flowers, and the ability to tolerate a few spent blooms and weeds. No matter if your effort is great or modest, gardening, John Evelyn wrote in 1666 (*Kalendarium Hortense*), is "a labour full of tranquility and satisfaction . . . and such as contributes to the most serious contemplation, experience, health and longevity."

Once the design is made, the soil is prepared, and the flowers are chosen—subjects covered in previous chapters—it's time to plant. And to tend. And to experience some of that tranquility, satisfaction, and good health that Evelyn ascribed to garden labor.

sunflowers, and cosmos, are easily propagated from seed. (For more flowers that are easy to grow from seed, see "Speed Demons," page 11.)

Sizing Up Seeds. *The seeds of many flowers, such as these* Cleome hassleriana *seeds, are large enough to handle easily; in comparison, the seeds of Iceland poppy (*Papaver nudicaule*) are tiny and number more than 3½ million per pound.*

Flowers for the Garden

Where do flowers come from? If you jump past the biological basics, the flowers in your garden will come either from seeds or bulbs that you plant, cuttings that you root, divisions that you make, or plants that you buy. Home gardeners who are short on time and patience fill their gardens with flowers that someone else has grown, and practically all gardeners buy at least some of their plants.

That's because many flower species are either extremely difficult to grow or grow too slowly to start from seeds; furthermore, seeds for many perennial cultivars—nearly all named daylilies and peonies, for instance—are not available because they won't *come true*, meaning their seeds won't yield plants that resemble their parents. If you want to add 'Cheddar Charm', a spectacular white peony with a gold center, or the popular 'Stella de Oro' daylily, you'll have to buy a plant. In contrast, many annuals, flowers such as marigolds,

Easy Cosmos. *Annual cosmos (*Cosmos bipinnatus*), like 'Sonata Mix', grow so quickly from seeds that buying plants is unnecessary for most home gardeners.*

Starting from Seed

Seeds, which surely belong on Mother Nature's Top Ten Miracles list, are plants in limbo, tiny bundles of roots, stems, leaves, and flowers with a genetic imperative to germinate and grow. Seeds aren't unfailing, but as philosopher Henry David Thoreau put it, you "can have great faith in a seed. . . . Convince me that you have a seed there, and I am prepared to expect wonders." The New England writer Celia Thaxter, a contemporary of Thoreau, expressed the same awe: "Of all the wonderful things in the wonderful universe of God, nothing seems to me more surprising than the planting of a seed in the blank earth and the result thereof."

There is great variety in the shape, color, and size of seeds. While some flower seeds are large enough for easy handling—sunflowers and nasturtium (*Tropaeolum majus*) are examples—none approaches the 40-pound leviathans produced by the double coconut (*Lodoicea seychellarum*). In fact,

Pretty Primroses. *Hardy* Primula × polyanthus *cultivars are among the perennials that are easy to grow from seed. Their blooms rise from a rosette of puckered leaves.*

FAST AND SLOW

Although you can grow many perennial and biennial flowers from seed, it isn't the same as growing annual species. There are rarely blossoms the first year, and sometimes not even the second; moreover, many garden perennials are hybrids and must be propagated vegetatively. If you are patient, try some of these familiar flowers, all of which are *relatively* easy to begin from seed. Since the plants typically cost $8 each, growing them from seed is a real money saver.

Blanket flowers (*Gaillardia* spp.)

Columbines (*Aquilegia* spp.)

Delphiniums (*Delphinium* spp.)

English daisy (*Bellis perennis*)

Forget-me-nots (*Myosotis* spp.)

Foxglove (*Digitalis purpurea*)

Geums/avens (*Geum* spp.)

Goldenrods (*Solidago* spp.)

Hollyhock (*Alcea rosea*)

Joe-Pye weeds (*Eupatorium* spp.)

Lady's mantle (*Alchemilla mollis*)

Lamb's ear (*Stachys byzantina*)

Lobelias (*Lobelia* spp.)

Lupines (*Lupinus* spp.)

Milky bellflower (*Campanula lactiflora*)

Orange coneflowers (*Rudbeckia* spp.)

Ox-eye (*Heliopsis helianthoides*)

Pinks (*Dianthus* spp.)

Poppies (*Papaver* spp.)

Primroses (*Primula* spp.)

Purple coneflower (*Echinacea purpurea*)

Rose campion (*Lychnis coronarius*)

Rose mallow (*Hibiscus moscheutos*)

Shasta daisy (*Leucanthemum* × *superbum*)

Sneezeweed (*Helenium autumnale*)

Torch lily (*Kniphofia uvaria*)

Valerian (*Centranthus ruber*)

Wild blue phlox (*Phlox divaricata*)

COLD BEGINNINGS

Sowing hardy perennials and some cool-weather annuals in pots and setting the pots outdoors is the best of all worlds: It gives plants a head start on spring; it stratifies the seeds; it produces sturdy seedlings; it frees space indoors for seeds that need warmth; and it requires less of the gardener's attention and time. In late winter, fill flowerpots with a soilless medium, moisten it, and sow the seeds *slightly* more thickly than the seed packet recommends. Label each pot. You may want to mulch the pot surface with *very* small pea gravel to prevent the soil from washing out and to discourage weeds and moss. (The gravel is sold in pet shops for aquarium use; garden centers also may carry it.) Set the pots outside in a protected place, such as under a conifer or next to the north wall of a building. If the location receives no moisture, be sure to keep the pots' soil moist, but be careful not to overwater. Once the seedlings have two sets of true leaves, you can transplant them to larger or individual pots and feed them.

most garden flowers have tiny seeds: a whopping 200,000 seeds per ounce for snapdragon (*Antirrhinum majus*); 50,000 per ounce for heliotrope, or cherry pie (*Heliotropium arborescens*); 45,000 seeds per ounce for strawflower (*Bracteantha bracteata*); and 10,000 per ounce for *Verbena* species. For some gardeners, sowing seeds requires reading glasses.

In addition to being fun and satisfying, starting with seeds has other advantages. It's inexpensive compared to buying plants. A packet of 100 seeds of *Cosmos bipinnatus* 'Sensation' is about $2, whereas a pack of six small starter plants runs two or three times that figure. Moreover, beginning with seeds is the only way to have access to less common flowers and cultivars. Even the best garden centers sell only a limited number of cultivars—two Shasta daisies (*Leucanthemum* × *superbum*), perhaps, and one sweet pea (*Lathyrus odoratus*). Begin with seeds and you can choose from a dozen Shastas, including 'Becky', the 2003 Perennial Plant of the Year, and from hundreds of sweet peas, more than a dozen colors as well as striped, spotted, and bicolored cultivars.

It's easy to grab packets of seed off the racks at the supermarket or hardware store, but a better approach is to buy directly from mail-order seed companies and nurseries. Getting on mailing lists is simple—most firms don't charge for their catalogs—or you can do some searching in online catalogs. One of the great joys of winter-bound gardeners is poring over catalogs' glorious flower photographs and fantasizing about next year's beds and borders. Seed companies may have a broad selection of flowers, as Burpee, Swallowtail Garden Seeds, and Thompson & Morgan do, or they may specialize. The Connecticut firm Select Seeds (www.selectseeds.com) focuses on heirloom flowers; Fragrant Garden Nursery in Brookings, Oregon, only sells sweet pea seeds (*Lathyrus odoratus*); the specialty of Van Dyke Zinnias (www.redbudfarms.com), in Stockbridge, Michigan, is obvious.

Local garden clubs, botanical gardens, plant societies, and other nonprofit organizations, which often sponsor seed exchanges, are another good source of flower seeds, as are online seed exchanges like the one sponsored by www.gardenweb.com. If you're interested in old-fashioned and nonhybrid flowers, join the Flower and Herb Exchange (FHE), which gives you access to the seeds of hundreds of flowers that are available nowhere else. (For more information about FHE and a list of seed and plant companies, see Appendix, page 457.)

Giving Seeds the Cold Shoulder. *The seeds of* Primula veris *and many other perennials can be stratified by sowing them in pots in fall and setting them outdoors to overwinter.*

Most commercial flower seeds have a *germination rate*—the percentage of seeds that will sprout—of 70 percent or higher. (And of the seeds that sprout, about 70 percent will become healthy plants.) Seeds that do germinate are *viable*. Some flower seeds remain viable for a long time (the record is held by sacred lotus seeds, which sprouted after 1,200 years in storage), but others, such as lavenders (*Lavandula* spp.), degrade after only a year or two. Seed packets from commercial sources should be stamped with a packing date. If your seeds aren't fresh—leftover from last year or a gift with their age unknown—do a germination test to make sure they are viable before you plant. Here's how:

1. Sprinkle a dozen seeds between two damp paper towels.
2. Roll up the towels and place them in an unsealed plastic bag.
3. Place the bag in a warm (75°F) location.
4. Keep the toweling damp and check the seeds daily.

Even with ideal conditions most seeds take a week or two to germinate, although some, such as annual sunflowers, sprout in a couple of days. If the germinate rate is less than 50 percent (divide the number of seeds that sprout by the number of seeds tested) or if germination takes far longer than the specifications on the seed packet, buy new seeds. "Bad seed," George Washington observed more than 200 years ago, "is a robbery of the worst kind: for your pocket-book not only suffers by it, but your preparations are lost and a season passes away unimproved." If the germination rate is between 55 and 65 percent, use the seeds but sow more thickly than recommended.

Good Reading. *Seed packets contain an astonishing amount of useful information, all designed to help home gardeners know when, where, and how to plant and grow flowers.*

Age isn't the only thing that affects germination. Sowing too deep or not firming the soil, soil temperature that is too high or too low, over- or underwatering, and contaminated soil and diseases can keep seeds from sprouting. If you don't see any signs of life a month after sowing viable seeds, start again.

SPECIAL HANDLING

Some flower seeds require special treatment to germinate well or to germinate at all. Hard-shelled seeds, such as those of morning glories (*Ipomoea* spp.), should be *scarified* before they're sown. Scarifying, which is nothing more than scratching or nicking the seed's coating, speeds germination. The easiest way to scarify seeds is to rub them *gently* on a piece of fine sandpaper. Germination is also accelerated in

some species—cannas for one—if seeds are soaked in water for a few hours before they are sown.

The seeds of other flowers need a period of moist cold or freezing—called "*stratification*"—to germinate. Among the seeds that need to be stratified are those of bleeding heart (*Dicentra spectabilis*), spider flower (*Cleome hassleriana*), and primroses (*Primula* spp.). If you purchase seeds from a commercial seed firm, stratification either will have been done for you or there will be specific directions on the packet. To stratify *most* seeds, place them on a piece of moist paper toweling in a sealed glass jar and store in the refrigerator—not the freezer—for five to eight weeks. Keep an eye out that no mold forms in the container. Or sow them in pots and set them outdoors, five to eight weeks before the last frost. (See "Cold Beginnings," page 120.)

Covering seeds with soil is the traditional planting practice—the rule of thumb is to bury a seed twice as deep as its diameter—but a good number of seeds, including those of columbines (*Aquilegia* spp,) feverfew (*Tanacetum parthenium*), flowering tobaccos (*Nicotiana* spp.), foxglove (*Digitalis purpurea*), poppies (*Papaver* spp.), spider flower (*Cleome hassleriana*), and coreopsis, need light to germinate readily. (For information about the germination needs of specific flowers, see Plant Portraits, beginning on page 213.)

Seed catalogs and packets—especially seed packets—contain a wealth of information about sowing seeds, including planting depths, germination temperatures and rates, the number of days from germination to blooms, and much more. A good online source of detailed germination information for specific flowers is Tom Clothier's Garden Walk and Talk at tomclothier.hort.net.

IN GOOD TIME

"When should I sow seeds?" is a common question for which there is no easy answer. Fortunately for gardeners, most seed packets carry a recommended planting time or "days to bloom" figure, the number of days *on average* between either sowing or germination and the first flowers. To know when you should start seeds, use that number in conjunction with the length of your *growing season*, the time between the last spring frost and first fall frost. If the flower you want to grow takes 140 days to bloom and the time between your soil warming up and the first frost in autumn is 110 days, you either must start seeds indoors or grow some other flower. (For more information about frost-free dates and determining the length of your growing season, see Chapter 2, page 29, and Appendix, page 457.)

Everyone wants a garden filled with blooms as early in spring as possible, but don't be in a rush. If seedlings are kept too long indoors, they won't flourish once they are transplanted to the garden. And seeds sown too early outdoors are likely to rot in the cold, wet soil. In sowing seeds, it's better late than nothing.

Sowing Outdoors

Many annual flowers, such as marigolds and sunflowers, sprout and grow so quickly that they can be sown right in the garden; others, such as larkspur (*Consolida ajacis*) and California poppy (*Eschscholzia californica*) dislike being disturbed and do better if they're sown where they are to grow. Direct seeding outdoors is also recommended for annuals that need cool temperatures to germinate well, such as spider flower (*Cleome hassleriana*) and pot marigold (*Calendula officinalis*).

Beginning outdoors isn't the safest approach, however. The temperature can rise and fall; the ground can become too wet or dry; the sun can fail to shine or shine too brightly; weeds can take over; diseases and pests can attack. Direct seeding carries risks. Above all, seeds rot quickly in cold, sodden soil. It's not possible to turn March into July, but you can help the soil warm by roughing it up and removing any mulch or plant debris. Spreading clear plastic over the planting area—seal the edges of the plastic with soil—also will raise soil temperature, as much as 20°F. Cold can literally be murder on tender *seedlings*, or infant plants, too. Be sure to work with your average frost-free date so that emerging seedlings won't be killed or set back by low temperatures.

Make sure as well that the planting bed is prepared carefully, free of stones, clods, and weeds, and raked smooth. (For information on preparing garden soil, see Chapter 4, page 63.) Sow seeds once the soil is warm, a minimum of 55°F for most annual

flowers. Then follow the seed packet instructions for planting depth. Water gently if the soil is dry, and keep the soil damp—but not soppy wet—until the seeds sprout. Mark where you've sown, as most seedling leaves look alike; you don't want to be pulling up baby zinnia plants, thinking they are weeds.

Sowing Indoors

Many gardeners get an edge on spring by beginning seeds indoors, especially seeds of tender perennials and slow-growing annuals, such as scarlet sage (*Salvia splendens*). Beginning inside rather than in the garden also gives you absolute control of the factors that affect germination and seedling growth: light, temperature, moisture, and soil. Visions of flats of healthy young plants resting on the windowsill are seductive, especially when you're suffering from cabin fever, but don't jump the gun. If the frost-free date is May 15, sowing zinnia seeds indoors in March will produce plants that must twiddle their thumbs for two months before they can go into the garden. By then they will be tall and spindly, anemic plants that won't do well even after they're relocated outdoors.

A greenhouse is a first-rate setting for raising healthy *transplants*, young plants that will be moved to the garden, but you don't need one to start flower seeds indoors. What you do need are viable seeds, a sterile seed-starting medium, containers with good drainage, heat, and moisture. Seeds don't need fertilizer to germinate; they already contain all the nutrients necessary for them to sprout.

Germination Housekeeping. *Containers used for starting seeds should be rinsed with a bleach solution to kill any pathogens.*

Containers. Garden centers and mail-order retailers offer an array of seed-starting systems, but specialized equipment isn't required. You can begin seeds in nearly anything that is at least 1½ inches deep and has drainage holes: clay and plastic pots, plastic and wood flats, peat pots, cottage cheese and yogurt containers, paper cups, and more. If you use an undivided container, a clay *azalea pot*, which is shallower than an ordinary flowerpot, is preferable. Or make a traditional wood flat, something about 2 inches deep. The bottom should be made of slats set ¼ inch apart for drainage; line the flat with newspaper so the seed-starting mix won't wash away. (For detailed information about containers, see "Seed Starting," page 203.)

You can sow dozens of seeds in one 6- or 8-inch container, then transplant the seedlings to individual quarters, either small pots or celled flats, to keep their roots from tangling and give them room to grow. It's even easier to begin seeds in individual containers—sowing two to four seeds in each cell—which eliminates the need to transplant as soon as the new plants emerge. Whatever containers you choose, make sure they have drainage holes. Second, make sure they are clean. If you've used them before, wash them thoroughly, dip them in a 10 percent bleach solution (1 cup bleach to 9 cups water), and rinse in clear water.

Seed-starting media. Dirt—a.k.a. soil—is fine in the garden, but a medium for sprouting seeds indoors should be loose, light, uniform, and sterile, to avoid damping-off and other soil-borne diseases. Garden centers sell mixes just for germinating seeds that are soilless, sterile, lightweight, and water-retentive. Most contain no nutrients—check the package label for contents—so you must fertilize once your seeds sprout, or move the seedlings to containers filled with an enriched medium. (Commercial *seed-starting mixes* typically lack nutrients and are different from *potting mixes*, which usually contain nutrients.)

Heat. Seeds sprout more quickly in warm soil. Or, as Englishman Thomas Hill expressed it in 1577 (*The Gardener's Labyrinth*), "Seeds bestowed in hot places, doe sooner yeeld their stems and leaves." Bestow your containers where the soil temperature will be between 70°F and 75°F day and night. Air temperature should be between 70°F and 75°F during the day and at least 60°F at night.

The top of a refrigerator, radiator, furnace, or floor register may be a good spot for germination,

P SOWING STEP BY STEP

*P*lants in the wild take care of themselves, reseeding each year to ensure survival. Garden cultivars are a more dependent crowd. Their seeds may sprout *in spite of* what you do, but to increase your chance of success, follow these steps:

1. Before you sow, premoisten the seed-starting medium by placing it in a bucket and adding small amounts of warm water. Stir and add more water until the mixture is thoroughly damp.
2. Fill each container to the top, then tap it lightly on a hard surface to settle the sowing mix. The mix should be about ½ inch below the lip of the container to allow for watering. Place the containers on a tray or flat.
3. Follow the packet directions for sowing the seeds, or set them twice as deep as their diameter. Don't sow so thickly that the emerging plants will be crowded, which invites diseases.
4. Unless the packet directions say otherwise, cover the seeds lightly with vermiculite or milled sphagnum peat, then firm gently with your hand.
5. Label the container with the name of the flower and the date.
6. Mist the soil surface until it is damp. Then cover the container loosely with plastic wrap or some other cover to retain humidity, or place it in an *unsealed* plastic bag.
7. Ensure that containers are well ventilated by removing the covers for several hours each day. If you see signs of mold, remove the covers altogether.

Keeping the Medium Moist. *Covering the seed-starting medium keeps it from drying out; once the seeds germinate, remove the covers and move the containers into bright light.*

but make sure it isn't too warm and doesn't dry out the seed-starting mix. A windowsill is not a good spot for sprouting seeds. Seeds don't need bright light to sprout, and while daytime temperatures may be warm, the temperature on windowsills falls during the night. If you plan to start more than a container or two of seeds, invest in a *propagation*, or *heat*, *mat*. It's a reliable way to ensure your seeds get the warmth they need. (For more information about heat mats, see "More Seed-Starting Helpers," page 205.)

Moisture. Seeds require constant moisture to germinate, but even a little too much water may cause them to rot. If the soil surface looks or feels even slightly dry, water may be needed. Be especially alert if you're providing bottom heat: Most of the seed-starting mix below the surface may dry out before the surface does. Water gently or mist, then pour off any water that drains through the bottom of the containers. Or set the containers in a tray of water and let the moisture wick up into the seed-starting mix, then drain. If there is any sign of mold on the soil surface, remove the cover and stop watering. Clay containers dry out more quickly than plastic pots and flats, so expect to water them more often. Indoors or out, if your seeds don't germinate it's probably for one or more of five reasons:

- Seeds were planted too deeply.
- Seeds didn't get enough moisture.
- Seeds got too much moisture.
- Seeds were old and not viable.
- Soil was either too warm or too cold.

Despite these potential dangers, most seeds *do* sprout, even in less-than-ideal conditions. To be on the safe side, however, remember the adage about sowing seeds: "One for blackbird, one for the crow / One for the cutworm, and one to grow."

Up and at 'Em

Turn your back for a day or three and seeds will have done their job. Karol Čapek described the process in *The Gardener's Year* (1931). "Almost any plant grows from under the seed upwards, lifting the seed on its head like a cap. . . . It is simply a wonder of Nature; and this athletic deed is performed until one day it

drops it and throws it away; and now it stands there, naked and fragile, bulky or lean, and has on its top two such ridiculously small leaves."

Those "two such ridiculously small leaves" are cotyledons, or seed leaves, which are temporary and soon replaced by true leaves. (Monocotyledonous flowers, such as iris send up tiny narrow shoots similar to the leaves of the mature plant.) The minute you see shoots emerging, remove the container covers and set your plants into bright light. Newborn plants are fragile for their first few days. Make sure they don't wilt from lack of water, but take care that you don't drown their tender roots by overwatering.

The Marvel of Seeds. *Still wearing the remainder of its seed like a cap on its head, this tiny sunflower (Helianthus annuus) seedling will develop into a 6-foot plant in only a couple of months.*

THE FACTS OF LIGHT

Seedlings need bright light for good growth, lots and lots of bright light, more than most windowsills can provide. Without it, seedlings will elongate, a condition gardeners call "leggy." There are plenty of pricey lighted plant stands for sale, but a single tabletop fluorescent fixture may be all you need; for more coverage, buy an inexpensive, 4-foot industrial light fixture that holds two bulbs. Most are suspended by chains and can be raised as your seedlings grow. Special "grow lights" aren't necessary. Set the bulbs about 3 inches above the plants and leave them on between 14 and 16 hours a day. A timer will make the job easier.

Fluorescent bulbs have the disadvantage of low intensity. Once plants are taller than 8 or 9 inches, the light from fluorescent bulbs won't reach the bottom leaves; however, most seedlings should be ready to go outdoors before they are taller than 9 inches. Don't use incandescent bulbs: They give off heat as well as light and can burn plant leaves.

MOBILE HOMES

Any container that drains well and has room for roots to grow is a good temporary home for a seedling. Seedlings can be transplanted as soon as their true leaves appear (or in the case of lily species and other monocotyledons, when they are about 1 inch tall). Use a small knife to lift each seedling—if several are entangled, gently shake them to separate their roots—then reset it in its own *small* pot or celled flat. If you hold the seedling, hold it by its leaves, not its stem, which is fragile and easily damaged.

Roots emerging from a container's drainage holes indicate that plants are *potbound*—their roots have filled the container—a sign that it's time to move the plant to *slightly* larger pots or cells. Again, don't *overpot*, which is growing small plants in huge containers. Overpotting is lethal, because the large amount of potting mix contains more moisture than the roots can use. You may have to move your seedlings to larger containers—a job known as *potting on* or *potting up*—several times. How may times will depend on how long your plants stay indoors and how vigorously they grow.

Replant seedlings at the same depth or *very slightly* deeper than they were growing previously, and gently firm the soil around the stems. Water

Changing Addresses. *Plants sown indoors will need to be moved to new quarters as they grow; biodegradable containers like this peat pot can be set in the garden, pot and all.*

thoroughly. Ease the transition to new quarters by setting the containers in a shaded location for 24 hours, then move them back into a sunny or lighted place. (If you sowed seeds in cell packs or individual containers, you may not need to repot. Instead, thin to one or two plants by cutting off the weaker seedlings with scissors. *Cut* them, don't *pull*, as this can disturb the roots of the seedlings you want to keep.)

Garden soil, which often contains disease organisms and weed seeds, is great in the garden but it's not great for growing plants indoors. If fed, infant seedlings can continue to grow in a sterile seed-starting mix, but tests show that they do better in a medium that contains basic plant nutrients.

(For more information about plant nutrients, see "Food for Flowers," page 72.) Garden centers sell a wide array of enriched *potting soils*, or mixes, or you can make your own. If you purchase potting soil, buy only as much as you can use immediately. Research done in 2002 indicted that both the chemical and physical properties of commercial soils change over time with "possibly significant effects on plant growth."

There are advantages to using a sterile potting soil—no chance of soilborne diseases, for one—but soil sterility isn't as significant in growing seedlings as it is in starting seeds. In fact, studies show that potting soils containing compost, leaf mold, or other materials that contain beneficial soil organisms produce stronger plants, and that the plants' adjustment to being moved outdoors is smoother. Basic potting soil is a little like chicken soup: The ingredients are few but the recipes are many. An easy *nonsterile* recipe that makes 2 gallons of potting mix is 4 quarts compost, 4 quarts vermiculite or perlite, and ¼ cup balanced organic fertilizer. This organic recipe contains all the nutrients young plants need, but they won't be instantly available, so feed your seedlings with a diluted liquid organic fertilizer. (See "Feed Me, Seymour," page 127.)

From the Bottom Up. *Seedlings are exacting about moisture. Watering from below guarantees that all the soil gets wet but keeps the leaves dry, which helps prevent damping-off.*

Moisture Lite

Seedlings are often killed because they get either too much or too little moisture. Remember that they're plants, not tadpoles, and their roots need oxygen as well as water. Overly wet soil invites root and stem rot as well as diseases, especially damping-off, a fungus that can wipe out healthy seedlings overnight—all of them.

Wilting can be a sign of too much moisture, but it's more likely evidence of not enough. Seedlings that receive so little water that they wilt don't have the resources to recover—watering 36 hours after the fact won't restore them to good health. Seedlings growing on a sunny windowsill are likely to dry out more quickly than those under artificial lights, so check those containers often, especially plants growing in small cell trays.

The trick is to keep the soil mix moist. Not dry, not soggy. The best approach is to water from below because it ensures that more than the top inch of soil gets wet: Fill a tray with water and set the seedling containers in it to soak up the moisture. Having all the soil mix damp encourages deep root growth. After several hours—when the medium surface looks and feels wet—either pour off the remaining water or move the containers out of the tray and allow any excess water to drain. Don't let the containers sit in the water longer than necessary. It's good to mist seedlings occasionally, but do it when they are receiving light and not at dusk or just before you turn off the lights.

Cool, Fresh Air

Put away the heating mats and move off the refrigerator: Seedlings don't need bottom heat. Or much heat at all. Heat promotes fast, spindly growth. For all but a few tropical species, turn the thermostat to between 65°F—70°F during the day, 5°F cooler at night. These lower temperatures, which are cooler than many living rooms, promote compact, sturdy plants.

Seedlings also need good ventilation. Stagnant air invites problems with pests and diseases. Seedlings don't thrive in drafty conditions, but a small fan on the low setting aimed near, but not at, seedlings is an easy way to upgrade air circulation. Make sure, too, that plants have enough room to grow. Once they begin to bump into each other, it's time for potting on. Or thinning—it's much better to have six sturdy, vigorous zinnias to transplant to the garden than a dozen leggy, pale plants, the product of crowded conditions.

Feed Me, Seymour

Like Audrey II, the man-eating plant in *The Little Shop of Horrors*, young plants must be fed. If seedlings are growing in a commercial potting mix that contains fertilizer, additional feeding shouldn't be necessary. But if the potting mix's nutrients come from compost or other organic materials (which are not immediately available to plants) or if it's a sterile mix, the gardener has to provide the necessary nutrients. (For more information about plant nutrients and fertilizers, see "Food for Flowers," page 72.) *Foliar feeding*—applying a liquid fertilizer to plant leaves—is the best way to meet the immediate needs of seedlings because foliar fertilizers are absorbed 20 times faster than are fertilizers applied to the soil.

Feed seedlings with a liquid fertilizer mixed at *one-third the strength* recommended on the package. Any all-purpose liquid fertilizer works, and there are organic as well as chemical products for sale. Omega 6/6/6 and Brix Mix are two well-known organic products. Many gardeners swear by fish emulsion, but it's smelly when used indoors. Another popular

organic fertilizer for seedlings is compost tea, which you can purchase or make yourself.

Feed seedlings every 10 to 14 days, but don't overdo things. Too much fertilizer is as bad as too little, maybe worse. It can burn plant roots and encourages thin, weak growth. If the seedlings' leaves start curling under, they're likely getting too much to eat. If their leaves become discolored—tinged with yellow, red, purple, or brown—they're not getting enough to eat. Slow growth is another sign that plants need to be fed.

Tall and thin may be mandatory for fashion models but is unwelcome in seedlings. If your plants are leggy, they need more light, less fertilizer, and probably less heat. To help encourage branching and stocky growth, pinch off the growing tips of plants that have one main stem like zinnias do. Don't pinch back lilies and other monocotyledonous flowers.

Buying Ready-Made

Starting from seed isn't possible for many garden flowers; for others—most perennial species, for example—it's possible but takes several years before the first bloom appears. Starting from seed also isn't an option for many flower gardeners. If you don't have the time, energy, patience, or space to grow seedlings, or you're looking for cultivars that can't be sown from seed, head for the local nursery or garden center. Before you hand your credit card to the checkout clerk, make sure that you're not buying:

- Plants with yellow or wilted leaves, which indicate poor care
- Plants growing in dry soil, which may already be stressed
- Plants that are spindly and tall—leggy plants have received too little light and are permanently damaged
- Plants that have signs of disease or insects (look at the leaves' undersides)
- Plants that are pot bound
- Plants that have obviously outgrown their containers or are growing in oversized containers
- Plants that are already in flower

The last item on the list is hard to avoid, since *forcing*, or pushing, flowers to bloom early is standard practice in the nursery industry. If you have a choice,

---

TEA TIME

*W*atering with compost tea provides a balanced meal for plants. To make this horticultural cocktail, fill a large container with equal parts of compost and water. Let the brew seep for several days, stirring occasionally, and then screen it through cheesecloth or a sieve. (Or place the compost in a cloth bag and immerse it in the water; after it has seeped, remove the bag.) Dilute the liquid until it is the color of weak tea before watering seedlings. And count your blessings: Not only are you feeding your plants but you're giving them protection against a raft of diseases. Gardeners interested in the subtleties of compost tea can consult the bible on the subject, Elaine Ingham's *The Compost Tea Brewing Manual*, now in its third edition (2002).

pick plants that aren't blooming; they are younger and tolerate transplanting better. If all the plants for sale are in bloom, remove the blossoms before you set them in your garden. Hard as it is to do, removing the flowers encourages vegetative growth—roots, stems, leaves—which will result in larger, more vigorous plants. And more flowers in the long run. As the shoe ad says, "Just do it."

Small is almost always better than large when buying perennial plants. Small plants have spent less time in containers and under lights; they're easier to transplant; and they recover and grow more quickly after being transplanted. At the garden center, look for perennials that have dense, deep green foliage, and strong stems. Short and stocky is better with annuals, too. They're typically sold in either six-packs or undivided containers, or flats. Flat-grown plants are sometimes cheaper but will have intermingled roots. Try not to damage them as you separate the plants.

Perennials are normally available in individual containers, usually 4- or 6-inch plastic pots. The larger the plant, the more expensive it will be. It's a good idea to slip the plant out of its container and check the root system (healthy roots are white, not brown or black), but be careful not to damage the plant. To be polite, ask the clerk to do it for you. If he or she refuses, shop somewhere else.

Annual flower plants, species such as marigolds and impatiens, aren't sold by most mail-order companies. But mail-order companies are the premier source of perennial flowers, including bulbous species, offering scores more cultivars than almost any local nursery can. As with seed companies, some nurseries sell a bit of everything and some nurseries specialize. Cricket Hill Garden in Thomaston, Connecticut, is a source of peonies, especially tree peonies; Ashwood Garden in Glouster, Ohio, sells daylilies, more than 1,000 cultivars. If you shop by mail—either from a catalog or on the web—don't be shocked at what comes in the UPS box. The bearded iris that was described as "a display of God's artistic work . . . gently ruffled, medium saffron yellow, shaded with mustard" in the catalog will arrive as a green stub growing out of a shriveled rhizome.

Don't throw up your hands (or throw in the towel). Mail-order nurseries typically ship *dormant* plants, plants that are not actively growing; and they usually ship them *bare root*, not in pots or other containers. (It's possible to buy two-year-old perennials

Plants in the Buff. *Bare-root plants like these bearded irises don't look like much when they arrive, but they recover quickly once set in the garden; most will flower in their first season.*

shipped in containers, but they are pricey.) Some nurseries—both local and mail-order—also sell inexpensive *liners*, which are young perennials (less than one year) growing in cell-packs or small containers. Most will require a season in the garden before they bloom, but dormant plants—which are usually two years old or older—should flower their first year in the garden. They may be unpromising in March, but they'll be impressive in July.

When plants arrive by mail—bare root or in containers—remove them from the package and inspect them carefully. If they don't look healthy or are damaged, phone the seller. Mail-order firms are astonishingly helpful, anxious to please, and full of good will and good advice. If it's too early for the plants to go into the garden, pot up bare root purchases in standard potting soil, set them and any container-grown plants in a cool, protected location that gets morning sun, and keep them watered. Cold frames are ideal for holding plants until they can be set in the garden. (Or, if it's warm enough but their permanent site isn't ready, *heel-in* your new plants: Plant them temporarily in a protected location that has rich, friable soil, then move them when their spot in the flower garden is available.)

BUYING BULBS

Nurseries selling bulbous plants like tulips and gladioli mail the bulbs, corms, tubers, or rhizomes only at the proper time of year: fall for spring-flowering species, spring for summer-bloomers. They should be planted immediately. Dig individual holes or larger areas for a mass planting. Don't forget to loosen and enrich the soil *beneath* where the bulb or corm will sit, as that's where its roots will grow.

Try to make sure you're setting things right side up. There may be small root remnants on the bottom of the bulb or rhizome to guide you, but if you're not sure ask another gardener or the people at your local nursery. Most bulbous plants come with specific instructions, but the standard wisdom is to plant bulbs and corms at a depth three times their diameter. If your soil is heavy, plant less deeply; if your winters are bitterly cold, plant more deeply. Most tubers and rhizomes should be set just below the soil surface.

There are more than 15,000 named daffodils, most of which are only available from mail-order firms; the same is true of tulips, iris, lilies, and other bulbous flowers. If you buy locally, purchase from a nursery or garden center; avoid inexpensive bags of bulbs sold by national discount stores.

Tough Love

Young plants—those you've grown and those you've purchased—are used to mild, stable conditions, not stiff winds, drying sun, cold temperatures, and thunderstorms. As a result, they need time to adjust before they go into the garden, a process known as *hardening off*. A gradual introduction reduces the shock of moving from warm, protected conditions to the real world.

Begin two or three weeks before your region's frost-free date or once the weather has settled and temperatures are consistently above freezing. (For more information about frost-free and transplanting dates, see Chapter 2, page 29, and Appendix, page 457.) Cut back on watering and stop fertilizing. A week before the local transplant date, begin setting plants—in their containers—outside for a few hours each day in a protected location, somewhere that is out of the wind but gets bright, indirect light. Bring the plants indoors each night. Increase their time outside and their exposure to sun and wind; after a week or so, the plants can stay outside overnight. Give them another two or three days in their containers, then transplant them to the garden.

Cold frames, which are small, unheated greenhouses, are ideal for hardening off seedlings and transplants. (For more information on cold frames, see "More Seed-Starting Helpers," page 205.) If you use one, make sure to open its lid during the day—a closed cold frame on a sunny day quickly becomes a hot frame where plants can cook.

THE GREAT OUTDOORS

Some of the hardiest perennials can go outdoors before the frost-free date, when the soil and air are still cold, but most young plants need hospitable conditions to survive in the garden. Transplanting is always a jolt to plants, even to those that have been

Greenhouses on the Cheap. *Like an unheated greenhouse, cold frames create the perfect conditions for hardening off seedlings and transplants. It may be necessary to open the lid on sunny days to prevent plants from overheating.*

hardened off, but the shock is reduced if you wait until the danger of frost has passed and follow these guidelines.

Pick the right weather. Transplant on an overcast day; sun and wind wilt young plants. Misty, cloudy weather is perfect, even if you get damp while you transplant, but avoid transplanting in the rain.

Soak before moving. Thirty minutes before transplanting, immerse plant containers in a weak solution of liquid organic fertilizer. (Soak the roots of bareroot plants.)

Dig a nice home. Make the planting hole wider and slightly deeper than the root ball of the flower you're transplanting, then set it at the same depth or *very slightly* deeper than it was growing in its container. Most root growth will be horizontal, not vertical; planting too deep retards good root growth. The plant's *crown*—the place where the roots meet the plant stems—should be at or only slightly below the soil surface.

Remove the plant from its container. Press on the bottom of the cell or tap the edge of the pot on a hard surface. Try not to disturb the roots, and don't expose them to the air any longer than necessary. If the plant is pot bound, knead the soil ball to loosen the roots before replanting.

Seedlings that are growing in peat or newspaper pots—or any biodegradable container—can be set in the garden *in* their containers. To encourage outward root growth, remove the bottom of the pot and make a few slits in the sides of the pot. If you've used compressed peat pellets, remove the netting that surrounds the peat.

Finally, remove the top edge of any biodegradable pot so that it doesn't extend above the soil surface. If left on, it can wick moisture away from the plant's roots.

Firm the soil around the plant. Then water the soil thoroughly with a half-strength liquid organic fertilizer that is high in phosphorus. (For more information about fertilizers, see "Food for Flowers," page 72.)

Label the plant. All gardeners think they will remember what they planted where. Very few do.

Deadhead and pinch. Remove any blooms, which allows the plant's energy to go toward vegetative growth, and pinch back transplants that are spindly to encourage branching.

Planting Out. *Moving a dwarf bleeding heart (*Dicentra formosa *'Luxuriant') or any young plant from a container to the garden is a shock. Try to disturb the plant's roots as little as possible when you remove it from its pot and set it in the ground.*

Provide protection. Protect new transplants from sun and wind during their first week outdoors with a piece of floating row cover, a cloche of some kind, or a wood shingle or piece of cardboard propped alongside them. In torrid regions, spray transplants with a commercial *antitranspirant*, or *antidessicant*, a substance that reduces water loss. Wilt-Pruf, a natural product derived from the resin of pine trees that has been around for more than 50 years, is a good choice and widely available in aerosol or pump-spray versions.

Install stakes. Plants that are likely to require help staying erect when they mature—lilies, peonies, climbing plants, and others—need attention now. Getting basic props set now reduces the chance of damaging roots or bulbs. Once plants begin to grow, tie them to or guide them through the support you've installed.

ELBOW ROOM

Many gardeners set plants more closely than the standard recommendations when creating new beds and borders. That's fine for the first year, but once perennial plants mature and spread, they must be *divided*—dug up and separated into several plants—or moved or discarded to keep the garden from becoming too crowded. (For more information about dividing plants, see "Spreading the Joy," page 139.) Most perennials will eventually need dividing, but giving them elbow room from the start postpones this chore. Moreover, crowding hinders normal plant growth and increases the chances of diseases developing. Good air circulation is as important outdoors as in.

You want to set plants so they fill in all the available space without crowding one another. A standard recommendation is that plants should be spaced at a distance equal to their mature height, but that makes no sense for tall, narrow plants like lilies, each of which may have one 5-foot stalk. A better guide is the plant's form. Tall, slender, upright plants like lilies can be spaced about one-quarter as far apart as their mature height. Tall, bushy plants like hollyhock (*Alcea rosea*) need more room; space them about one-half as far apart as their mature height. Shorter, bushy plants like hardy geraniums, or cranesbills (*Geraniums* spp.), and thread-leaved corcopsis (*Coreopsis verticillata*) need to be set about as far apart as their mature height. Space moss phlox (*Phlox subulata*) and other ground cover plants about twice as far apart as their mature height; it will take several seasons for them to fill in, but they will fill in.

If the aim is a solid mass of plants, reduce the spacing, or do more under-, over-, and interplanting. (For information about packing plants into beds and borders, see "Flowers Under and Flowers Over," page 107.) But if your flower bed is centered around a Chinese tree peony that cost $150 and will grow 4 or 5 feet tall and 4 feet wide, as 'Purple Butterfly in the Wind' will, give it extra room to strut its stuff. And if your initial calculations are wrong, you can always add more plants—or remove some.

Much Ado about Mulch

Once new plants—small or large, annual, biennial, or perennial—are moved to the garden, *mulch* them by spreading a layer of organic matter over the bare soil. Mulches have a bevy of merits. They keep the soil surface from crusting and prevent erosion; they reduce soil compaction created by heavy rains and walking; they help soil maintain a uniform temperature, keeping it warmer when the mercury falls and cooler when temperatures go up; they conserve moisture; they suppress weeds; they reduce the need to cultivate the soil; they reduce soilborne diseases being spread by rain splatter; they add organic matter and nutrients to the soil and improve its structure; they insulate roots and bulbs in winter and help prevent plants from lifting out of the ground; and they make beds and borders look trim and well kept.

Despite these merits, one thing is certain: More isn't better when mulching. A very deep layer of mulch—4 inches or more—slows the soil from warming in spring. Deep mulch can cake and keep moisture from reaching plant roots, or it can absorb all the rainfall so that no water reaches the soil. In rainy years, a thick mulch may become water-logged and keep the soil too wet, which encourages rot. And a deep layer of mulch can harbor pests, so much so that gardeners in damp climates with slug and snail problems may want to forego mulch altogether, especially if they're growing susceptible flowers like hostas.

MULCH MATH

Garden centers typically sell mulches in 2- or 3-cubic-foot bags. To determine how many 2-cubic-foot bags are needed to cover a garden with 2 inches of mulch, divide the area of the garden by 12 square feet. For 3-cubic-foot bags, divide by 18 square feet. To do the math for a 25 × 6-foot garden using 2-cubic-foot bags: 25 feet × 6 feet = 150 square feet ÷ 12 square feet = 12.5 (2-cubic-foot) bags. Bulk mulch is normally sold by the cubic yard. To calculate how much you'll need in cubic yards, multiply the area of the garden by the thickness of the mulch (2 inches) and divide the product by 324.

Another thing is certain: Adding mulch to a garden year in and year out builds wonderful soil for growing flowers, soil that is fertile and friable. As Sydney Eddison observed in *The Self-Taught Gardener* (1997), "It is almost impossible to overstate the case for an organic mulch." A friend, she wrote, added "bales of hay by the hundred and truckloads of manure," and now "a telephone pole would sprout leaves in [her] soil."

The best time to lay down mulch is after the soil has warmed. That's midspring in most North American gardens but earlier in hot regions. (And mulch immediately after setting any plant in the garden.) Remove as many weeds as possible before mulching and loosen the top inch or two of soil with a hoe or rake. Two inches of mulch is enough. Mulching doesn't have to be a one time only event, after all. Begin with 2 inches in midspring, then add more as the old mulch breaks down. Never mulch *over* plants, which can cause them to rot. Water thoroughly after mulching to keep the mulch from becoming a horticultural blotter that draws all the moisture from the soil.

Other mulching pointers? Gardens located in the shade tend to be damp and normally need less mulch than sunny gardens do. Gardeners in cold climates may want to choose dark-colored mulches that absorb light and warm the soil, whereas gardeners in hot regions, where the soil can get too warm, should apply a light-colored mulch that reflects light. Grass clippings and other fine-particled mulches decay faster than coarse, woody mulches like pine bark. Compost and leaf mold are at the top of most gardeners' All-Star Mulches list. Some mulches are better suited to flower gardens than others, but every mulch has its champion. These are the main contenders, with a scorecard for each.

Animal bedding. Widely available; cost varies; a mix of manure and straw and hay or wood shavings that decomposes quickly but may not be attractive; improves soil structure and adds nutrients.

Cocoa hulls. Not available everywhere; expensive; attractive texture and dark color; highly absorbent but can become waterlogged and moldy if applied too thickly; slow to break down. (Cottonseed and buckwheat hulls are similar and available regionally.) Cocoa mulch is potentially toxic to dogs.

Compost. Widely available; expensive unless you make your own; attractive; good water penetration and retention; adds nutrients to the soil and

The Merits of Mulch. *Mulching perennial flowers like these hostas with compost will improve the soil, feed the plants, retain moisture, and help keep the soil free of weeds.*

improves its structure; breaks down quickly. An outstanding all-purpose mulch (see "Compost *Does* Happen," page 76).

Grass clippings. Widely available; free; often contain weed seeds and mat easily; good source of nitrogen; avoid clippings that have been treated with herbicides; apply only 1 inch deep; breaks down rapidly.

Ground corncobs. Not available everywhere; inexpensive; light color (aged cobs are dark) and attractive; good moisture retention; provide food for underground organisms but can deplete soil nitrogen.

Hay. Widely available; inexpensive; poor appearance unless chopped; good water penetration and absorption; adds nutrients to the soil; may contain weed seeds; breaks down quickly; used mostly by vegetable gardeners. (Salt hay, slender grasses that grow in mashes, also makes a good mulch; it contains no weed seeds but is not widely available.)

Leaf mold. Rarely sold but can be made at by home gardeners (see Chapter 4, page 63); excellent soil additive and source of nutrients; attractive; fair water penetration; good water retention; breaks down rapidly; a superb mulch for flower gardens.

Leaves. Widely available; free; attractive; good soil additive and source of nutrients; shred before using to avoid matting and speed decomposition. (If you don't have a shredder but do have a string trimmer, fill a garbage can with leaves and use the trimmer to shred them, or use a rotary lawn mower to chop them.) A fine, all-around mulch.

Oyster shells. Regionally available; expensive; attractive; good water penetration; raise soil pH; slow to break down.

Pine needles. Regionally available; inexpensive or free; attractive; good water penetration; a potential fire hazard in dry climates; slow to break down.

Sawdust. Widely available; inexpensive; fair appearance; fair water penetration and retention; compacts easily; draws nitrogen from the soil; breaks down slowly.

Sphagnum peat moss. Widely available; moderately expensive; lowers soil pH; contains no nutrients; highly water-absorbent but mats and crusts easily; very slow to break down; use as a soil conditioner, not a mulch.

Straw. Widely available from wheat, timothy, oats, rye, or barley; inexpensive; largely free of weed seeds; easy to apply but unattractive unless chopped; can rob nitrogen from the soil as it decays; a fire hazard in dry regions. Used primarily by vegetable gardeners.

Wood bark. Widely available; moderately expensive to expensive; attractive, good water penetration; slow to break down; a good all-around mulch. Redwood bark, where available, is especially attractive but more expensive and is only fair at retaining water; it discourages earthworms. Cedar bark tends to crust, preventing water from reaching the soil; choose pine or hardwood bark if available. Fresh bark can be toxic to young plants; bagged bark mulch has been aged and is safe to use.

Wood chips. Widely available; moderately expensive; attractive; good water penetration; breaks down very slowly.

Wood shavings. Widely available; inexpensive; attractive; good water penetration, fair water retention; break down rapidly, taking nitrogen from the soil.

Mineral mulches—stones, crushed stone, and gravel—have the advantages of being free of diseases and weed seeds and are moderately permanent. They look most at home in rock gardens, however, and do almost nothing to improve the soil and little to suppress weeds unless they are applied over a *landscape fabric*, or *geotextile*. These are polypropylene or polyester materials that block weeds and reduce surface evaporation at the same time they allow oxygen, water, and fertilizer to reach the soil.

Almost all commercial landscapers and some gardeners cover new beds and borders with landscape fabric, cutting holes for plants, and then conceal the fabric with several inches of organic mulch or soil. And most home gardeners wish they hadn't after they do. Landscape fabric seems bent on making its way to the surface; adding new plants can be difficult; weeds inevitably emerge; and fabric doesn't enrich the soil in any way. Landscape fabric may have a place in shrub borders but far less so in flower gardens.

In addition to mulching in spring and when new plants are set out, gardeners in cold climates often apply a winter mulch, usually just after the soil freezes, to protect perennials from *heaving*, lifting out of the ground. (Mulching before the ground freezes won't do any harm, but it will delay the ground from freezing.) All organic mulches break down over time, so before you apply a new layer, incorporate as much of the old mulch into the soil as you can with a spade, hoe, or rake.

MULCH TO DYE FOR

*D*yed mulch is the latest in the Things-No-One-Ever-Needed Department. Hues include red, orange, gold, green, and black. Its sole merit is that most are made from shipping pallets and other waste wood that normally would end up in landfills. The dyes are nontoxic, but scientists have discovered that the waste woods often contain traces of arsenic and other toxins that can leech into the soil and poison plants and soil organisms. Add ugly and you have two reasons to avoid dyed mulches.

Garden Chores

Flowering plants, although an inherently rugged band, solicit some help from their growers in order to thrive: fertilizer when the soil lacks nutrients; water when it doesn't rain; help in combating weeds, diseases, and pests; and more. Depending on where you live, on the flowers you grow, and on how well you've prepared the soil, those chores can take a great deal of time or, lucky you, very little time.

FOOD AND DRINK

Most flowers are not *heavy feeders*, plants that need jumbo amounts of fertilizer to thrive. Established plants growing in fertile soil normally don't need to be fed at all—the soil is doing it for you. Such plants not only grow and flower vigorously but they are less susceptible to diseases and pests. In contrast, plants growing in thin, or nutrient-poor, soil tend to be small, pale, and spindly and to grow slowly. Too much fertilizer generates rank growth, lots of stems and leaves but small roots and few flowers. As William Longgood observed in *Voices from the Earth* (1991), overfed plants are like "people whose energies are devoted so completely to their appearance that there is no other development."

Plants aren't coy about telling their growers that they are hungry. (For more information about plant nutrition, see "Food for Flowers," page 72.) These are some of signs to watch for.

- Stunted, pale growth; small, yellow or bluish leaves; and thin, weak stems indicate a nitrogen deficiency.
- Stunted growth; poor root development; small leaves with purplish or reddish undersides; purple or red leaf veins and stems; leaf mottling; and weak stems indicate a phosphorus deficiency.
- Yellow leaf tips and margins; leaves that curl under, are mottled, or have brown edges; weak stems; poor root development; and general lack of vigor indicates a potassium deficiency.
- General lack of vigor; dieback of new growth; small, distorted leaves; flower petals wilt; and lack of growth indicates a calcium deficiency.
- Lower leaves yellowed; yellow leaf margins; brown or purplish patches on leaves; and stunted flowers indicate a magnesium deficiency.
- Stunted and slow growth, and pale or yellow leaves indicate a sulfur deficiency.

There are specific remedies for specific deficiencies, but plant language is an inexact dialect. It's not always easy to know precisely what are the nutritional insufficiencies. A lack of copper causes shoot dieback, but so does a lack of calcium; too little iron can lead to pale leaves and weak stems, but so does a nitrogen deficiency. Rather than spend time and money trying to pinpoint the precise cause, focus

Heavy Feeders. *Chrysanthemums, including these colorful hybrid Korean mums, are among the perennial flowers than need extra doses of fertilizer during the growing season.*

on improving the soil. Start by *topdressing* or *side-dressing* the garden: Spread a layer of compost or balanced organic fertilizer around plants, then work it into the top few inches of the soil.

If your flowers are in dire straits, water them with compost tea. Fish and kelp emulsions also are balanced fertilizers, but a combination of the two is even better, about as good a meal as you can provide. Mix it yourself or purchase a premixed product. Follow the package directions; even natural products can burn plant foliage if they are too strong. Any foliar feeding should be done on an overcast day when the temperature is below 80°F (leaf stomata, or pores, close at temperatures above 85°F, making foliar feeding ineffectual).

Over time plants can deplete the nutrients in the soil, but topdressing with compost every year should be enough to keep most flowers happy. If needed, the best time to fertilize is when plants have the greatest need: when growth starts in spring and just before flowering. A few species, including astilbes, chrysanthemums, dahlias, delphiniums, lilies, peonies, and phlox, have bigger appetites than most garden flowers, but if the soil is regularly enriched with organic matter, additional fertilizer is rarely necessary. Flowers growing in pots, window boxes, and other containers must be fed regularly because watering flushes nutrients out of the soil. Many gardeners add a small amount of soluble fertilizer to the watering can every time they fill it. Or feed with a diluted liquid fertilizer every week or two, something with a 1-2-1 ratio.

Just as the goal of fertilizing should be to feed the soil, the goal of watering should be getting moisture to the soil. "If gardeners will forget a little the phrase, 'watering the plants' and think of watering as a matter of 'watering the earth' under the plants . . . the garden will get along very well," Henry Beston wrote in the American classic *Herbs and the Earth* (1935).

Flowering plants especially need a steadfast supply of moisture; leaves and stems may recover from wilting, but blossoms rarely do. Moreover, most annuals either slow or stop flowering during extended drought. If the top few inches of soil feel dry, you probably need to water. Remember that seedlings and transplants are keenly sensitive to both overwatering and underwatering; they need careful attention. (For more information about watering, see "Water, Water Everywhere," page 52.)

WEEDS AND PESTS

Like flowers, weeds can be annuals, biennials, and perennials, and all of them can compete successfully with garden flowers for space, food, and moisture. Perennial species are the most difficult weeds to control, as humorist Dave Barry wrote about crabgrass, which, he claimed, "can grow on bowling balls in airless rooms, and there is no known way to kill it that does not involve nuclear weapons." Gardeners who find new shoots of crabgrass every time they inspect their beds and borders know that Dave Barry isn't altogether kidding. It's impossible to eliminate every weed, but gardeners can reduce their numbers to single digits. The secrets are good soil preparation, mulch, and eternal vigilance. Spacing flowers closely also helps keep weeds in check: Bare ground is an invitation for weeds to move into the neighborhood.

All the work involved in making new gardens weed-free *before* they are planted (for more about soil and weeds, see "Breaking Ground," page 80) pays dividends for the next 20 years, and probably longer. Likewise, it's important to remove as many weeds as possible *before* laying down mulch, which will help smother new weed growth. And it's crucial to keep after weeds. "One year's weed, 7 years' seed" is country wisdom at its best. Allow weeds to spread their seeds—or their roots—and the battle is lost. It's mano a mano with weeds: pulling, hoeing, and digging. And more pulling, hoeing, and digging. Little by little, though, the weeds become fewer and their control will become easier.

Plant pests and diseases are more problematic, although flowers are plagued with far fewer troubles than are vegetables and fruits. Cultural practices—how plants are grown—are half the answer. (For more about cultural practices in the flower garden, see "Making Soil Better," page 75.) A prompt reaction when problems appear is the other half.

The value of healthy soil can't be overestimated, either, and it isn't new data coming from research done by a PhD at a state agricultural college. Thomas Jefferson made the same case in a 1793 letter to his daughter: "When earth is rich it bids defiance to droughts, yields in abundance and of the best quality. I suspect that the insects which have harassed you have been encouraged by the feebleness of your plants and that has been produced by the lean state of your soil." Healthy soil promotes strong, healthy plants that can either put up with or outgrow many pests and diseases. If the site drains well and gets the appropriate amount of light—full sun for species like sunflowers and afternoon shade for impatiens—and if the soil contains the proper nutrients and has the right pH, chances are there will be few problems.

However good your soil, keep an eye out for signs of pests and diseases. Plant leaves, especially their undersides, are the place to start looking, and then react quickly. Chapter 7 (page 147) provides specific remedies as well as general methods designed to avoid and limit problems, but gardeners also should accept the possibility that removing a plant is the wisest and best response. If you don't want Japanese beetles, for example, you may have to give up flowers in the rose family, Rosaceae, which are magnets for these immigrant insects.

GOOD GROOMING

Weeding and mulching, which are discussed earlier in this chapter, are two important ways of keeping a flower bed tidy. So is edging (see "Boundaries," page 96). "A crisp edge between a flower bed and the lawn," Sydney Eddison asserted in *The Self-Taught Gardener*, "goes a long way toward making a garden look orderly." There are still other chores that will keep gardens looking spiffy.

Staking. Some gardeners would argue that when it comes to flowers, beauty isn't in the eyes of the beholder, it's in the plant that can stand up by itself. Tying and propping up plants is one of the garden jobs that most people despise. Making sure plants get the proper amount of light and aren't overfed helps keep them erect, but the truth is that some tall species and species with elephantine blossoms need help staying upright, especially when the wind blows. Yet who wants to give up growing delphiniums, lilies, peonies, hollyhock (*Alcea rosea*), perennial and annual sunflowers (*Helianthus* spp.), exhibition dahlias, and other flowers that need some help in the verticality department? If you can't live without 6-foot plants and blooms the size of basketballs, staking will be a necessary evil.

Don't wait until plants begin to teeter, either from their own weight or from fierce winds, to give them support. Applying twine and stakes to full-grown plants makes them look as if they are wearing a bathing suit three sizes too small. The same is true of climbing species, such as black-eyed Susan vine (*Thunbergia alata*), morning glories (*Ipomoea* spp.), and cup-and-saucer vine (*Cobaea scandens*). Once

Flower Garden Chores. *Deadheading a daylily like 'Lavinia Love' won't keep the plant flowering longer—as deadheading many annual flowers will—but it keeps the garden looking neat. Be sure to add the spent blooms to the compost pile.*

their stems are 3 or 4 feet long, threading them through trellises or training them around posts and wires is hopeless.

Garden stores, both local and mail order, are loaded with devices for keeping plants upstanding, devices that are easy to install and are less obtrusive than ever before. Be sure you've chosen the appropriate prop—round metal grow-through hoops with mesh grids for 'Chiffon Parfait' and other garden peonies with double blooms or single-stem wire supports with top loops for lilies. Then install them early, long before they're needed. Gardeners in hot climates should avoid metal supports (unless they are covered with plastic), which can heat up and burn plants.

Set supports, which should be shorter than the plants they're shoring up, deep enough to be sturdy and near the base of plants—but not so close that you pierce bulbs or damage roots. Ties should be loose and soft to prevent injuring stems. Rather than circle the support and the stem with a tie, which will allow the stem to sag to one side and become girdled, use a figure eight: one loop around the support and the other around the stem.

Deadheading. "Deadhead" was a common horticultural term long before Jerry Garcia became a musical pied piper. *Deadheads* are faded, or spent, blooms, and *deadheading* is removing those spent blooms. Deadheading is especially important with annual species, for once annuals start producing seeds, they slow or stop producing flowers. Deadheading keeps them blooming.

Some cultivars, such as the Wave and Fantasy Series petunias and all impatiens, are either self-cleaning—their blossoms quickly disappear on their own—or are sterile and don't make seeds. They don't need deadheading. The general rule, however, is to deadhead all annual species to keep them blooming. Either cut or pinch off the flower and any incipient seeds that are forming beneath it, but take care not to damage the plant. Deadheading individual flowers of plants that sport clusters of tiny blooms, such as sweet alyssum (*Lobularia maritima*), is difficult; rather than try, shear the entire plant back by one-third after the initial flowering is finished.

Most perennials—iris, daylilies, astilbes, purple coneflowers (*Echinacea purpurea*), hostas, and peonies immediately come to mind—look better if they are deadheaded regularly. How it's done depends on the perennial's habit. For plants like Siberian iris (*Iris sibirica*) that have many flowers atop a long stem, remove only the spent blossom. Once no buds remain, remove the entire stem. (Lilies are an exception—do not remove the stem.) Flowers like garden peonies and rudbeckias that have many leafy flower stems should be deadheaded back to a healthy leaf or lateral stem or bud.

For some perennial species, deadheading also prolongs their bloom period or promotes reblooming later in the season. The results aren't as dramatic with perennials as they are with annual flowers, but deadheading is worth trying with many perennials, including yarrows (*Achillea* spp.), hollyhock (*Alcea rosea*), golden Marguerite (*Anthemis tinctoria*), coreopsis, globe thistle (*Echinops ritro*), purple coneflower (*Echinacea purpurea*), sneezeweed (*Helenium autumnale*), gayfeathers (*Liatris* spp.), red hot pokers (*Kniphofia* spp.), lupines (*Lupinus* spp.), speedwells (*Veronica* spp.), and salvias, or sages (*Salvia* spp.). When deadheading perennials, be sure to remove the seedpod that is forming beneath the flower.

Pinching, thinning, and shearing. Pruning plants—either by pinching out new growth, by thinning, or by shearing back plants after they have flowered—has many effects. Like deadheading, it can extend the bloom season by encouraging the production of new buds or by staggering bud and flower production. It stimulates fresh vegetative growth, discourages diseases and pests by improving air circulation, and increases the number of flowers. And it can reduce plant height and size and extend plant life by redirecting resources from making seeds to replenishing the bulb or root system. Don't be too eager to whack off stems, but don't be afraid, either. Plants are amazingly accommodative, even when gardeners make mistakes.

Pinching, a common practice with seedlings and transplants to encourage good vegetative development, also can be used with established plants. Pinching—removing the growing tip of a stem, an inch at most, with your thumbnail and first finger—promotes thick, bushy growth, reduces plant height,

---

D **SO LONG, BUD**

isbudding, or *debudding*—removing some of a plant's flower buds—isn't necessary but is a standard practice by growers seeking to produce flowers huge enough to qualify for *The Guinness Book of World Records* or to win a blue ribbon at a garden club exhibition. Dahlias, peonies, and chrysanthemums are the usual subjects. To disbud, pinch off buds before they begin to develop, leaving only one or two buds on each stem. The bad news? Peonies the size of soccer balls require supports the size of fence posts.

A PLEA FOR UNTIDINESS

Good grooming is usually good practice but not always. Hardy spring bulbs—flowers such as tulips, daffodils, crocuses, and crown imperial (*Fritillaria imperialis*)—need to be left to their own devices. Don't cut off their leaves or stems when flowering ends; don't braid them or tie them with rubber bands. Bulbs gather the energy they need to produce next year's flowers through the photosynthesis that occurs in their leaves. Let them mature on the plant. Do remove seed pods, however, and you can remove plant leaves once they turn brown. Lilies also need time to recoup: Allow the *stems* to die back naturally, or there will be no blooms next year.

and encourages the production of more flowers, albeit smaller ones. Pinch just *above* an axil, the spot where a pair of leaves or a leaf is attached to the stem. Late spring is the time when most North American gardeners pinch back plants (earlier in warm regions). Pinching retards blooming, so don't wait so long—or repeat pinching so late—that the plant doesn't have time to flower. You can extend the flowering time of a clump of a particular plant, *Aster novi-belgii* 'White Lady', for example, by pinching some plants later than others or pinching some plants and not others.

Perennials that branch, such as garden chrysanthemums, asters, and golden Marguerite (*Anthemis tinctoria*), are among the usual subjects for pinching. Don't pinch flowers that have long, largely leafless flower stems, as do daylilies and iris; plants that grow from bulbs, corms, tubers, or rhizomes; or plants that grow from a basal rosette of leaves—a circle of leaves formed at the soil surface like a dandelion's. Remove the terminal buds from these plants and there are unlikely to be any flowers.

Thinning is nothing more than removing some stems so more light and air can reach the plant. Flowers that are susceptible to mildew, such as asters, bee balms (*Monarda* spp.), and garden phlox (*Phlox paniculata*), are helped by cutting out some of their stems; thinning also has the tendency to produce larger blooms. Cut the stems slightly above the soil surface in late spring.

Shearing, or *cutting plants back*, renews vegetative growth of perennials and annuals and sometimes produces a second flush of flowers. It can also be used to reduce a plant's mature height—and the need for staking—and to delay flowering. Shearing involves removing a goodly portion of the plant, sometimes leaving only an inch or two. Don't rush to cut plants back simply because flowering has stopped or foliage is tattered: Photosynthesis, which produces the sugars and other compounds that perennial plants need to sustain themselves, occurs in plant leaves. But if shearing is called for, use sharp pruning or hedge shears to make the cuts.

If you're shearing to limit plant height, as you might with chrysanthemums or asters, cut plants back in late spring or early summer, well before the plant blooms. If you're shearing for aesthetic reasons, wait until the plants finish flowering. Or when flowering slows, as it sometimes does in annuals such as petunias and snapdragon (*Antirrhinum majus*). Cut back low-growing, spring-flowering perennials, such as candytuft (*Iberis sempervirens*) and moss phlox (*Phlox subulata*), by one-half to stimulate new growth. Catmints (*Nepeta* spp.), thread-leaved coreopsis (*Coreopsis verticillata*), and baby's breaths (*Gypsophila* spp.) are three flowers that bloom a second time when sheared, but many flowers won't. Most will produce healthy new vegetative growth, however. Perennials that bloom in summer and fall are unlikely to rebloom after being cut back. The standard advice is that if you can see new growth at the base of a plant after it blooms, as you can with globe thistle (*Echinops ritro*), it's safe to cut its stems to the ground even though it may not flower again.

Dividing. When perennial plants outgrow their site, die out in the center of the clump, or lose vigor, they need to be divided, to be separated into pieces and replanted. (For how-to details, see "Spreading the Joy," page 139.) Each division, or piece, will produce a plant exactly like the one you divided, so in this process, division multiplies.

How often to divide depends on the garden and on the plant. A few species, peonies and bleeding hearts (*Dicentra* spp.) are two, almost never require dividing. Other perennials—those that spread with abandon as asters do, or species such as coreopsis that need to be divided to maintain vigorous health—may need attention every two or three years. Wait for the signals. If a plant is pushing out its neighbors, has dead or sickly growth at the center,

Keeping the Garden in Bounds. *Fast-growing perennials like Ozark sundrops (Oenothera macrocarpa) need to be divided every few years to keep them from overwhelming other, less aggressive plants.*

has flowers smaller than they used to be, or has bottom foliage that is increasingly sparse, it's probably time to pull out the spade and turn one into many.

Spreading the Joy

The English writer Beverly Nichols, whose sense of humor is never in doubt, is at his irrepressible best when writing about plant cuttings: "Do you not realize that the whole thing is miraculous? It is exactly as though your were to cut off your wife's leg, stick it in the lawn, and be greeted on the following day by an entirely new woman, sprung from the leg, advancing across the lawn to meet you. Surely, you would be surprised if, having snipped off your little finger, and pushed it into a flower pot, you were to find a miniature edition of yourself in the flower pot a day later."

Rooting cuttings, one way of propagating plants vegetatively, is as miraculous as growing plants from seeds. Vegetative propagation is necessary for flowers such as iris that have seeds that are highly dormant and take forever to germinate and for hybrid cultivars that don't *come true* from seed, meaning they don't produce plants with the same traits the parent plant has. Vegetative propagation ensures that the new plants will be exact copies of the old, and it is a cost-free way to multiply the flowers in your garden.

Many flowers are amenable to several vegetative propagation methods, but others are fussier, willing to put up with only one method, or, in the case of many annuals, are grown exclusively from seed. (The preferences of individual flowers are included in Plant Portraits beginning on page 213.) Whether saving seeds or propagating vegetatively, always begin with a healthy, vigorous plant.

CUTTINGS

Depending on the plant, it's possible to propagate from *leaf cuttings*, *stem cuttings*, and *root cuttings*. While the root cuttings method isn't difficult, don't expect 100 percent success. Use clean containers and a sterile medium for rooting, such as a 50-50 mixture of perlite and sphagnum peat moss or a mixture of perlite and vermiculite.

Leaf cuttings. These are most often used with houseplants—only a limited number of garden flowers can produce new plants from their leaves—but rex begonia (*Begonia rex*) is one flower than can be generated from a leaf. To root a leaf cutting, notch the veins of the leaf's underside with a knife, lay the leaf flat on a dampened rooting medium (notch side down), and pin the leaf so it stays in contact with the medium. New plants will emerge from the notches. Some lily species—*Lilium lancifolium* and *L. longiflorum* are two—also can be propagated from leaves. Choose mature leaves with *heels*, short bits of the plant stem, and insert them in a container of moist vermiculite; enclose the container in a plastic bag and set in a cool (65°F), well-lighted location. Roots should form in about six weeks.

Root cuttings. Many garden flowers can be propagated from root cuttings, including bergenias (*Bergenia* spp.), purple coneflower (*Echinacea purpurea*), globe thistles (*Echinops* spp.), sea hollies (*Eryngium*

spp.), meadowsweets (*Filipendula* spp.), blanket flowers (*Gaillardia* spp.), salvias, or sages (*Salvia* spp.), and mulleins (*Verbascum* spp.). With many of these species, root cuttings are so successful that accidentally severing bits of root in the garden produces new plants without any help from the gardener. Begin in late winter or early spring, when plants are still dormant or just beginning to grow, with 2-inch-long pieces of root. Small plants can be lifted to take cuttings, then reset in the garden; with larger species like purple coneflower (*Echinacea purpurea*), dig carefully around the plant's base to expose the roots and take cuttings (no more than four roots from any plant). The thickest roots normally are the best candidates.

Root cuttings should be set vertically in a premoistened planting medium (such as a mix of perlite and sphagnum peat moss) and must be orientated correctly: The end that was nearest the plant's crown goes up. Insert the cuttings in the medium (in containers with good drainage) and set them in a brightly lit, cool room or cold frame; keep the soil moist. (Lay very thin roots horizontally on the surface of the planting medium and cover them ½ inch deep.) Top growth will begin before root growth, so don't transplant cuttings until you're sure that new roots have developed; then move the small plants to individual containers or to the garden, and feed them with a half-strength soluble fertilizer that is high in phosphorus.

Stem cuttings. Also called "slips," stem cuttings are most often used to propagate perennial and annual flowers that have branching stems, including asters, begonias, chrysanthemums, impatiens, yarrows (*Achillea* spp.), pinks (*Dianthus* spp.), catmints (*Nepeta* spp.), and many more. Impatiens, coleus (*Solenostemon scuttellarioides*) and salvias, or sages (*Salvia* spp.) are so agreeable that they root in water, but most stem cuttings must be inserted, or *stuck*, in a rooting medium.

Midsummer is the usual time for making stem cuttings of perennials, late summer for annuals, but see the entries in Plant Portraits beginning on page 213 for specific recommendations. Have everything ready—containers with good drainage filled with premoistened mix—*before* you head to the garden because cuttings dry out quickly. Take cuttings in early morning, choosing vigorous terminal stems with leaves that are fully open (pinch off any flowers or flower buds). The stem cutting should be between 3 and 6 inches long and have at least two nodes, the joints along the stems where leaves and flowers are

Multiplication in the Garden. *Coleus* (Solenostemon scutellarioides) *is one of several common garden plants that are extremely easy to propagate from stem cuttings.*

attached. Cut just below a node and place the cutting in a plastic bag or in water to limit desiccation.

Remove any leaves from the portion of the stem that will be inserted into the rooting medium, and dust the cut with a *rooting hormone*, a powder containing grow regulators that stimulate the formation of roots. Rooting hormone powder comes with instructions and is sold at garden centers and by mail-order firms; Rootone, which also contains a fungicide, is a widely available brand. A 0.1 percent formula is the right strength for herbaceous stems.

Use a pencil to make a holes in premoistened rooting medium; insert the cuttings—half in, half out of the medium—then firm the medium around the stems. Set the container in a plastic bag (to keep the plastic off the cuttings, insert straws or small stakes in the medium to "tent" the bag), and seal it loosely. Place it in a warm location—air temperature between 65°F and 75°F is ideal and will speed rooting—where it will get good light but not direct sun. Open the bag daily to let fresh air reach the cuttings. Watering shouldn't be necessary, but check regularly to be sure the medium hasn't dried out or become too wet. Once the cuttings have developed healthy roots—it takes up to two months for some species—they can be transplanted to individual pots or to the garden and fed with a soluble, high-phosphorus fertilizer applied at half strength.

Layering. This technique—covering a portion of a stem with soil while it's still attached to the parent plant—is most often used to propagate woody plants, but it can be used with *Dianthus* and *Verbena* species and other deciduous plants that climb, trail, or creep; gardeners growing coleus (*Solenostemon scuttellarioides*) often discover the plants layer themselves, as do lavenders (*Lavandula* spp.) and candytuft (*Iberis sempervirens*). Think of layering as a stem cutting without the cutting. Once the buried section develops roots, make the cutting: Sever the new plant from its parent.

DIVISION

Division—separating a large plant into pieces—is the easiest, most common, and foolproof method of vegetative propagation. In addition to creating more plants, division solves the problems of plants outgrowing their location, center dieback, and general loss of vigor. The usual candidates for division are clumping plants with fleshy roots like daylilies and hostas and species with slender, spreading roots,

DO NOT DIG

Flowers that have taproots are not only difficult to divide, but they resent being disturbed. Perennials that have deep, wide-ranging roots or brittle roots that are easily broken are best left alone once they are planted. Unless there is an all-important reason to dig (and there aren't many), keep your shovel away from these flowers.

Anemones (*Anemone* spp.)

Baby's breaths (*Gypsophila* spp.)

Balloon flower (*Platycodon grandiflorus*)

Baptisias (*Baptisia* spp.)

Bleeding hearts (*Dicentra* spp.)

Bluebells (*Mertensia* spp.)

Butterfly weed (*Asclepias tuberosa*)

Gas plant (*Dictamnus albus*)

Hellebores (*Helleborus* spp.)

Lupines (*Lupinus* spp.)

Monkshoods (*Aconitum* spp.)

Peonies (*Paeonia* cvs.)

Poppies (*Papaver* spp.)

Poppy mallow (*Callirhoe involucrata*)

Sea hollies (*Eryngium* spp.)

Sea lavender (*Limonium latifolium*)

Sweet peas (*Lathyrus* spp.)

such as bee balms (*Monarda* spp.) and purple coneflower (*Echinacea purpurea*).

Old hands claim you can divide plants any day the ground isn't frozen. That's a bit of hyperbole, but it is safe to divide most plants after they stop flowering. Another general rule is that perennials that flower in spring should be divided in late summer; perennials that flower in summer and fall should be divided in early spring, just as they are beginning to grow. Whatever the season, water any plant thoroughly a couple of days before you divide it, cut it back to 6 or 8 inches, and do the dividing in the late afternoon, after the sun has gone down.

To divide a large perennial, spade around the plant on all sides and then lift it from its hole. If it's impossible to pull the clump apart, use a sharp knife or a spade (or even an axe or saw) to cut the clump into generous sections, each with at least two

Floral Math. *Dividing vigorous flowers like daylilies (Hemerocallis cvs.) provides new plants for your garden. Daylily clumps are tough and may have to be cut or sawed into sections.*

Flowering plants like bearded irises that grow from *rhizomes* should be divided after they finish flowering. Cut the rhizomes with a sharp knife, making sure that each division has at least one eye, or bud. Set the divisions at the same depth they were growing, and make sure the eye is pointed in the correct direction. *Stolons*, which are stems masquerading as roots, produce new plants as they travel along (or slightly under) the surface of the soil. Stoliferous flowers can spread too quickly—showy evening primrose (*Oenothera speciosa*) and gooseneck loosestrife (*Lysimachia clethroides*) are good examples—but they lend themselves to division. Either lift the clump and divide it into sections, or use a spade to cut portions from an existing plant, then replant them elsewhere and fill in the empty spot with compost.

Bulbous plants need only a slightly different approach. While specialists use more complicated techniques to propagate these species—scooping, scoring, coring, sectioning, and cutting—most home gardeners stick with division. True bulb species, both tunicate and nontunicate, produce *bulblets*, or *offsets*, alongside the main bulb; they are easy to pull loose and can be replanted to produce new plants. Tulips, daffodils, hyacinths, and ornamental onions (*Allium* spp.) grow from tunicate bulbs—each has a dry protective *tunic*, or cover—and all produce bulblets.

Fritillarias (*Fritillaria* spp.) and lilies are nontunicate, or scaly, bulbs; they lack a protective tunic and are easily damaged, so dig and handle carefully. Lilies can be propagated by scaling. Pull off several outer scales—each scale is a modified leaf able to sprout shoots and roots—and replant them. Some lily species also produce *bulbils*, small aboveground bulbs, along the stem at the base, or *axil*, of a leaf. Once they ripen, collect the bulbils and press them into the soil where you want them to grow. Or allow them to drop and sprout on their own. Gladioli and other flowers that grow from *corms* produce a new corm each year, and they form *cormels* around the top of the new corm. Like bulblets, cormels can be detached and replanted. One warning: Bulblets, bulbils, cormels, and scales need several years to grow before they produce flowers.

The best time to harvest offsets and scales is after the plants have flowered and their leaves begin to yellow. Propagating bulbous plants is rife with tales of spreading diseases, so most gardeners dust any offsets and especially scales with a fungicide—sulfur dust is an organic option—before replanting them.

or three shoots and a good supply of healthy roots. Many perennials, such as meadowsweet (*Filipendula ulmaria*) and yarrows (*Achillea* spp.), die out in the center over time; discard this old, woody growth. Don't let the divided sections dry out. Replant them immediately at the same depth they were growing, water and feed with a balanced liquid fertilizer at half strength. Pot up extras to share with friends. If you plant in the same site, be sure to enrich the soil before you reset a division.

SAVING SEEDS

Saving seeds from plants growing in the garden is another propagation route. Before heading for the zinnias with paper bag in hand, remember that flowers in the home garden have been pollinated willynilly. Their seeds may or may not—and probably not—yield plants and flowers exactly like the ones you're growing. Hybrid cultivars in particular do not breed true, and some hybrids don't produce any seeds at all.

With that in mind, don't hesitate to save seeds of species and nonhybrid cultivars, especially varieties that have been around for many years. Always harvest from healthy plants, waiting until the seed is *almost* ripe. (Wait until it is fully ripe and many seedpods split and spread their treasure before you can collect it.) Place the seeds in a paper bag and store in a warm, dry location until the seeds ripen completely. Once seeds are fully dry, place them (in the pods or out) in a sealed glass jar (don't forget to label and date the jar) and store it in a location with low humidity and temperatures between 35°F and 40°F. In other words, in the refrigerator. (To ensure low humidity, wrap ½ cup powdered milk in a tissue or cloth bag and place it at the bottom of the jar.) Although many seeds remain viable for years, it's a good idea to use home-collected seeds within one year. And to be on the safe side, do a germination test on a few seeds before sowing in the garden.

Time for Bed

Fall is the melancholic season, as the 19th-century poet Thomas Hood wrote in "The Departure of Summer":

> *Summer is gone on swallow's wings,*
> *And Earth has buried all her flowers:*
> *No more the lark, the linnet sings,*
> *But Silence sits in faded bowers:*
> *There is a shadow on the plain*
> *Of Winter ere he comes again.*

Despite Hood and scores of other poets, fall has a perversely happy aspect for gardeners: It marks a pause in most garden work. *Most.* Veterans don't walk away once blossoms begin to succumb to the cold. Fall is a good time both to plant and to divide perennials in North American gardens (spring is safer in regions with a truncated growing season).

Planting in autumn translates into larger plants in spring as long as it is done early enough to give plants at least a month to establish their roots before the ground freezes.

Tulips, daffodils, crocuses, and other hardy bulbs must be planted in autumn. (Don't forget to mark where you put them.) And tender flower species, such as dahlias, gladioli, cannas, and caladiums (*Caladium* spp.), have to be dug and stored a dark, dry, and cool place that is safe from rodents. Check Plant Portraits (page 213) for specific recommendations.

There are housekeeping chores as well. Plant foliage with signs of disease or pests should be cut down and discarded, not composted. Most annuals should be pulled and composted (for exceptions, see "Partly for the Birds," page 145). There are opposing sentiments about cutting back all deciduous plants after their foliage withers. One side insists that foliage left to die back on its own provides winter protection for the plants, winter interest for gardeners, and shelter and food for birds, butterflies, and other wildlife. If you choose the leave-it-be approach in fall, be sure to remove any remaining debris in early spring, before plants begin growing.

Harvesting Tomorrow's Plants. *It's wise to save seeds from perennial plants like wild senna (Cassia marilandica) that have long taproots and are difficult to divide or transplant.*

Winter Beauty. *Ornamental grasses are almost as beautiful in winter as they are in summer. Not cutting back plants in fall can be a visual windfall for the housebound gardener as well as a source of food and shelter for wildlife.*

It's hard to argue against aiding and abetting the animal world, but the opposing notion on garden cleanup has far more converts because removing spent stems and leaves reduces the chances that disease organisms and pests will overwinter in the beds and borders. And you don't have to chop down every plant in the garden; leave a few stems for the birds and for your own visual pleasure.

If you side with the Prevent-Problems School of Garden Cleanup, wait until the top growth of perennials has dried and browned, then cut it back severely, between 2 to 4 inches from the ground. (Cutting closer to the soil can damage crowns.) Don't compost any debris that shows signs of disease or insect infestation; *never* compost peony foliage, no matter how healthy it looks, as it almost always carries botrytis, a mold that overwinters in the soil. With flowers that sprout new growth at their base in late summer and fall, as do some beardtongues (*Penstemon* spp.) and hardy geraniums or cranesbills (*Geranium* spp.), cut back the old, dead stalks; but don't harm the new foliage even though it may be killed back during the winter.

Clean out beds and borders: Pull any weeds, rough up the old mulch, and loosen the soil between plants. If rain has been sparse and the ground isn't frozen, water the garden thoroughly. And if you don't have a map of what your garden contains, this is an opportune time to make one. *But don't fertilize.* Feeding plants in autumn encourages tender new growth that will be killed when the mercury falls.

Gardeners in cold regions often lay down mulch in autumn. (See "Much Ado About Mulch," page 131.) The mulch isn't to keep the soil from freezing but to keep the soil frozen so that perennials don't *heave*, or uproot, from the ground's alternately freezing and thawing. If you live in a region blessed with oaks, maples, sycamores, and other shade trees, take advantage of their bounty. Shred leaves first—a lawn mower does a good job, especially if it has a mulching blade—then spread them between plants at a depth of 2 inches. Don't cover plant crowns, which encourages rotting. Other good mulch materials are pine boughs, pine needles, and compost. If you already have problems with voles, mice, and other rodents, fall mulching is likely to make things worse. The good news is that materials not used to mulch the garden can be added to the compost pile.

Garden containers should be emptied and stored upside-down; terra-cotta pots should be stored

PARTLY FOR THE BIRDS

Don't race out to take down your feeders if you plant garden flowers that yield seeds to supplement the diets of wild birds. Some of the best do-not-cut candidates are members of the aster family, Asteraceae, especially sunflower (*Helianthus annuus*). Here are more flower heads you may want to leave standing once Jack Frost ends the garden season.

Asters (*Aster* spp.)
Bachelor's button (*Centaurea cyanus*)
Bee balms (*Monarda* spp.)
Cockscomb (*Celosia argentea*)
Coreopsis (*Coreopsis* spp.)
Cosmos (*Cosmos* spp.)
Four-o'clock (*Mirabilis jalapa*)
Gayfeathers (*Liatris* spp.)
Globe thistles (*Echinops* spp.)
Goldenrods (*Solidago* spp.)
Larkspur (*Consolida ajacis*)
Marigolds (*Tagetes* spp.)
Orange coneflowers (*Rudbeckia* spp.)
Perennial and annual sunflowers (*Helianthus* spp.)
Pot marigold (*Calendula officinalis*)
Purple coneflower (*Echinacea purpurea*)
Spider flower (*Cleome hassleriana*)
Verbenas (*Verbena* spp.)
Zinnias (*Zinnia* spp.)

indoors where temperatures are above freezing, as terra-cotta is water absorbent and freezing causes *spalling*, or surface flaking. Drain garden hoses and store them indoors. Take time to clean, sharpen, and oil garden tools. Use a wire brush to remove any dirt, then wash tools with water, dry them, and wipe metal surfaces with an oily rag or spray them with WD-40. Sand and then wipe wood parts with tung or linseed oil. (For more about maintaining tools, see Chapter 9, page 195.)

Then lean back in a comfortable chair, put your feet up, and think about the year. What flowers did well? What flowers were failures? Update your garden diary. Begin perusing seed and plant catalogs. Sketch new beds and borders. Make plant lists. Dream.

Resolute Flowers. *If not allowed to dry out, spring-flowering primulas are among the perennial flowers least bothered by diseases and insects. Ensuring that plants get the cultural conditions they prefer is essential to reducing problems in the garden.*

CHAPTER SEVEN

Bugs and Other Bothers: Handling Problems in the Flower Garden

*W*ith heedful eye;
Quick as a hatching bird, the gardener roves
Precautionary, nipping mischief's bud.

Vita Sackville-West, *The Garden,* 1946

APPARENTLY ADAM, WHO GETS THE CREDIT FOR being the world's first gardener, was not as "quick as a hatching bird." His heedful eye overlooked the serpent, the first garden pest on record, which went on to do its mischief and, as Countess von Arnim observed in *Elizabeth and Her German Garden* (1898), produced "all that sad business of the apple."

147

Most long-ago gardeners were adamant about removing serpents from their beds and borders. Their methods included planting mugwort, burying eagle dung, watering the soil with powdered goat's hoof infused in vinegar, and fumigating plants with the smoke from burning old shoes. The last method may not have kept snakes away, but surely it kept passersby from nicking flowers.

Snakes weren't the only garden enemy our predecessors identified: "Scorpions, Todes, Gardenmise, Weasels, and all other Greater Beasts," as well as "Moles, Ants, Gnats, Flies, Frogges, Snailes, and Earth wormes" were candidates for elimination. Anything that flew, walked, crawled, or slithered was fair game. Crimes varied but punishment was inexorable. "Frogges," Thomas Hill wrote in *The Gardener's Labyrinth* (1577), should be purged because they were "wont to be disquieters to the wearied Husbandmen . . . by chirping and loud noise making."

Eradicating horticultural adversaries was a transcendent concern in garden literature well before the Englishman Thomas Hill. The Greek philosopher Democritus, the first to contend that the Milky Way was a conglomeration of stars, recommended soaking dead crayfish in water, then sprinkling plants with the water to "find yourself freed from all Sorts of Insects, whatsoever." The Roman historian Pliny the Elder advised wetting plants with "the mother of oyle Olive" to drive away pests. Other ancients advocated drying seeds in the "skinne of the Tortuise" to make them pestproof, and dusting plants with chimney soot to repel bugs.

Clearly not all ancient wisdom was wise. Nor is all modern wisdom. Scientists have excelled in discovering which pests and diseases cause trouble in the garden, but their solutions haven't been 100 percent desirable. Synthetic chemical solutions, which became commonplace in the 1940s, were lavishly applied without a full understanding of their side effects. Not until 1962, when Rachael Carson alerted the world to the negatives of DDT in *Silent Spring*, did the public begin to recognize the perils of the new sprays and dusts.

Although many horticultural chemicals have been banished, even legal products can be dangerous to your health, to the health of your family, your friends, your pets, and other living creatures—to anyone who ventures near your garden. And not so near your garden, for these toxins make their way into the groundwater, streams, lakes, oceans, and the air. Applying synthetic chemicals to control flea

beetles or powdery mildew does more damage than the beetles or mildew ever could. That said, when the hollyhocks (*Alcea* spp.) are being devoured by a platoon of Japanese beetles or the delphiniums begin wilting, even the most "green" of gardeners is tempted to reach for a sprayer filled with a high-powered, long-lasting, all-purpose poison that someone somewhere has guaranteed will kill anything and everything in 24 hours.

But think again. You don't want a chemically dependent flower garden. There are less-toxic alternatives to coping with difficulties—*coping*, not eliminating. Remember that no matter how potent the poisons, no matter how faithfully applied, nothing can permanently expunge all pests and diseases from your garden. If the first lesson about garden troubles is to prevent rather than to rectify, the second lesson is to forbear. As Hugh Johnson expressed it in *Principles of Gardening* (1996), "Gardeners must be philosophers, accepting that they and theirs have a place in the cycle of life which nothing, or very little, can alter."

Environmentally responsible gardeners reconcile themselves to a few chewed or yellow leaves, a few damaged flowers, a few dead plants. They even may choose to stop growing certain flowers for a year or two to discourage the problems they attract, or choose to bar them permanently. Henry Mitchell, the late garden columnist for the *Washington Post* did: "I do not grow anything that has to be sprayed," he wrote in 1997.

Gardening in an environmentally safe way isn't just for vegetable and fruit growers. Who wants a small child sniffing a lily that has been doused with chlordane, a popular pesticide that was shown to cause cancer and was banned only a few years ago? The list of prohibited chemicals grows each year, a reminder that what we don't know *can* hurt us. Learning to meet horticultural vicissitudes without using dangerous, destructive chemical poisons is one way gardeners help protect the earth not just for plants but for themselves and for those who will follow.

Preventing Calamity

Some plants have their own methods of protecting themselves. Orchids, for example, produce crystals of calcium oxalate, which make them taste bad to insects and other animals, and some *Tanacetum*

Certitude with Snowdrops. *Diminutive snowdrops (Galanthus nivalis) have no serious disease or pest problems. Like most members of the Amaryllis family, they have little appeal to deer and rodents but great appeal to gardeners.*

species contain terpenes in their leaves and flowers, which are lethal to pests.

Skunk cabbage (*Symplocarpus foetidus*) uses both bad flavor and an atrocious odor to discourage predators. Thorns, spines, and stinging hairs are obvious defenses against some foes, as are leaves with heavy waxy coatings, slippery surfaces, or other repelling attributes. Insectivorous plants—pitcher plants, sundews, Venus' flytraps, and other botanical carnivores—don't repel insects, they catch and digest them. But few plants can fend off all enemies and catastrophes. Gardeners must do their part. Begin with Henry de Bracton's axiom, "An ounce

of prevention is worth a pound of cure," which has been around since the 13th century. While it wasn't written for gardeners, it could have been, since prevention is as much a cardinal virtue in the garden as elsewhere. A good deal of grief can be avoided by following these "precautionary" rules.

Grow appropriate plants. Every flower has limits. Sun-loving species, such as zinnias and sunflowers (*Helianthus* spp.), won't flourish in the shade; impatiens, although they are perennials, won't survive winters in the North, whereas most daffodils require

GARDENER BEWARE

Plants' built-in defenses can pose a danger to gardeners as well as insects and other pests. This list of familiar garden flowers, culled from many sources, includes *some* of the plants known to be hazardous if ingested (many more plants are skin and eye irritants). While adults understand that the flower garden is not meant for grazing, children and pets are less cautious. Castor bean, especially, should never be grown in gardens where children play.

Autumn crocus/meadow saffron (*Colchicum autumnale*); all parts

Belladonna lily (*Amaryllis belladonna*); bulb

Bleeding hearts (*Dicentra* spp.); all parts

Castor bean (*Ricinus communis*); seeds

Chinese lanterns (*Physalis* spp.); seeds

Daffodils (*Narcissus* spp.); bulb

Delphiniums (*Delphinium* spp.); all parts

Four-o'clock (*Mirabilis jalapa*); seeds

Foxglove (*Digitalis purpurea*); all parts

Glory lily (*Gloriosa superba*); bulb

Hellebores (*Helleborus* spp.); all parts

Hyacinth (*Hyacinthus orientalis*); bulb

Lily-of-the-valley (*Convallaria majalis*); all parts

Lupines (*Lupinus* spp.); all parts

Monkshoods (*Aconitum* spp.); all parts

Morning glories (*Ipomoea* spp.); seeds

Periwinkles (*Vinca* spp.); all parts

Snowdrop (*Galanthus nivalis*); bulb

Squills (*Scilla* spp.); bulb

Stars-of-Bethlehem (*Ornithogalum* spp.); all parts

Tree tobacco (*Nicotiana glauca*); leaves

a cold season to rebloom. Trying to cultivate plants that don't like the conditions your garden offers is as productive as milking a he-goat, as old-time farmers like to say.

Choose resistant or tolerant plants. Some flowers are either naturally resistant or tolerant or have been bred to resist or to tolerate certain pests or diseases. (*Resistant* means a plant has some ability to repel a disease or pest; *tolerant* means the plant will prosper despite a disease or pest.) For example, 'Marshall's Delight' and 'Violet Queen' are bee balms (*Monarda didyma*) bred to have good resistance to powdery mildew.

Keep the garden clean. Good housekeeping won't create a Maginot Line around your garden, but it will slow—and sometimes halt—invaders. The basics begin with removing weeds and plant debris that provide shelter and sustenance to bugs and diseases. Badly diseased and infested plants should be eliminated the minute you spot them. And destroy them—don't add them to the compost pile.

Keep the soil healthy. Healthy soil leads to healthy plants. It's that simple.

Keep plants healthy. Diseases and pests make a beeline to weak and stressed plants, so do everything you can to keep your flowers healthy. Give them the right location and soil and the proper amounts of space, water, and fertilizer.

Don't make things worse. This would seem to be a no-brainer, but the devil is in the details. Some of those details? Water in the morning, not the evening; don't wet plant foliage; don't work among wet plants; don't introduce diseased or pest-ridden plants, bulbs, or seeds to your garden; keep tools clean; don't smoke in the garden; don't overfeed; handle plants gently. As they say in medicine, "First, do no harm."

Problems Great and Small

If you've spent immoderate amounts of energy, time, and money creating a flower garden—or even moderate amounts—the last thing you want are plants nibbled by deer, roots consumed by voles, leaves embellished with yellow spots, or buds swarming with insects. There are scores of calamities that *can* strike a flower garden, but most of those calamities *don't* strike. However, no garden makes a clean getaway.

CULTURAL PROBLEMS

Not every discolored leaf, limp stem, and blasted bud is the result of an animal, a bug, or a disease. Some plant difficulties—known as *cultural*, or *physiological*, *disorders*—are caused by the conditions in your garden. The most common sign of cultural disorders is yellow foliage, or *chlorosis*. It can appear on individual leaves or on all leaves. Look, too, for wilted leaves or leaf drop; brown leaf margins, or edges; irregular or dead spots on leaves; and for leaf malformations.

Poor plant basics—too little or too much light, moisture, space, and nutrition—are the usual causes of cultural disorders, along with problematic soil, air pollution, and physical injuries. Chlorosis of leaf margins and tips, for example, often points to soil that lacks potassium; dead leaf margins and tips can indicate a potassium deficiency, excesses of boron or fluoride, or underwatering; wilted leaves can signal both under- and overwatering. Because cultural disorders weaken plants, they also make them more susceptible to diseases and pests.

Before assuming that plant problems are the result of pests or diseases, make sure the cause isn't physiological. One clue: If the symptom is garden-wide rather than random or limited to one plant, it's likely to be cultural. (For more information about creating a healthy environment for growing flowers, see Chapters 2 through 4.)

WILDLIFE PROBLEMS

No matter where you live, you share your space with wildlife. Moreover, beautiful blooms and succulent plants are siren songs to all sorts of animals. Wildlife problems may be fewer in urban settings, but even Manhattan gardeners must deal with animals, especially *Homo sapiens*. As if finding a place to get a plant into the ground weren't difficult enough in cities, many residents also are forced to plant under wire covers, to cement planters to the sidewalk, and to install alarms and cameras.

Before you dismiss human vandals as a 21st-century phenomenon created by the media, drugs, and working mothers, take a look at *Rural Hours* (1876), a journal by Susan Fenimore Cooper, daughter of the American novelist James Fenimore Cooper. Flora filching, she wrote, was not only a widespread crime of mischievous boys but of full-grown men, including one "who having selected the flowers most to his fancy, he arranged them tastefully and then walked off with a free and jaunty air." Nor was it an exclusively male misdeed. Even young girls "help themselves . . . to their neighbor's prettiest flowers."

Bipedal primates of the human kind may require the most cunning responses, but other wildlife—deer, raccoons, rabbits, mice, birds, woodchucks, voles, dogs, cats, and more—are challenging. And damaging. One night a bed is blanketed with giant hosta leaves; the next morning it is a sprawl of leafless stems sticking up like stalks of celery. As the saying goes, animals like gardens as much a gardeners do, and they're much better at harvesting them.

Remember that elimination of wildlife is not necessary, not advisable, not possible—and probably not legal. Success in preventing wildlife from looting the flower garden first requires your naming the culprit. There's no sense hanging out bars of soap, which are supposed to repel deer, when it's rabbits that are eating your seedlings. Timing also is important. Anticipate animal invaders and take action *before* they overrun your plants, or respond the minute you see damage. Some wildlife, such as deer, aren't a one-night-only event. There will be return raids on your garden. Finally, realize that one size doesn't fit all. You'll need more than one strategy to keep your flowers safe from two- and four-legged pirates. Defenses against wildlife can be reduced to habitat modifying, repelling, fencing, and trapping. (For practical ways to deal with wildlife, see "Wildlife," page 173.)

BUG PROBLEMS

Aphids, spider mites, Japanese beetles, and caterpillars are just a few of the small pests that damage plants by feeding on them or by transmitting diseases to them. Most insects and other bugs are beneficial or at least harmless, and even the destructive types are normally a threat only when they occur in huge numbers. As Vermont garden writer Ruth Page pointed out, "Whoever taught youngsters to chant, 'ladybug, ladybug, fly away home,' was definitely not a gardener."

The first step in dealing with garden bugs is to identify the culprit. An inexpensive 10× hand lens and an insect handbook will help with differentiating the good from the bad, as will the descriptions of the most common garden pests that begin on page 162.

Most of the bad are true insects—small invertebrates with three body segments, six legs, and wings—although they take different forms during their life cycle, a process biologists call *metamorphosis*. While the forms they pass through can differ, the process itself is either simple or complete. With simple metamorphosis, the eggs of insects such as aphids, leafhoppers, thrips, and scale hatch immature insects called nymphs, which molt (shed their skin) several times until they reach the adult stage. Nymphs and adults look alike, and both feed on plants.

Lacewings, leaf miners, and beetles are among the insects that undergo the four-stage complete metamorphosis. Adults lay eggs that hatch into worm-like larvae (called caterpillars, grubs, or maggots

Good Old *Bufo Americanus.* *The American toad eats insects, slugs, almost anything it can snag with its sticky tongue and get in its mouth. All toads have warts. Have warts—not cause warts, so gentle handling is safe.*

depending on the insect). When the larvae are ready to mature, they pupate, a nonfeeding phase during which they are encased in a cocoon or other shell; last, they emerge as adult insects. Larvae and adults look nothing alike and have different feeding habits. Larvae ordinarily are more destructive to plants than adults.

Insects leave a basketful of calling cards, including yellow or stippled foliage, leaf spots and holes, leaf drop, slime trails and honeydew, even plant wilt. Because insects go through different stages, timing is significant in curbing garden pests. Insects that undergo complete metamorphosis, for instance, are most easily dealt with as pupae, when they can't move. Before you decide on a control, know which stage of the insect threatens your flowers.

DISEASE PROBLEMS

The great majority of *microorganisms*—organisms so small they require a microscope to be seen—that inhabit gardens are beneficial. They help break down organic matter in the soil, convert nitrogen from the air into ammonia in the soil, release hormones that can stimulate plant growth, even kill garden pests. Some microorganisms, however, are pathogenic and cause destructive diseases. Gardeners who eschew synthetic chemicals have fewer weapons for coping with diseases than with insect pests. As a result, disease prevention becomes paramount, because the options are limited once plants are affected. In many cases, the wisest, if not the only, recourse is to remove and destroy diseased plants.

Gardeners not only need to recognize what pathogen is attacking their plants but to know when and under what conditions plants are likely to be infected and which plants are most likely to be affected. Garden books sometimes refer to these three—pathogen, host plant, and conducive conditions—as *the disease triangle*, the three elements that are necessary for a disease to occur. Knowing that snapdragons (*Antirrhinum majus*) are susceptible to gray mold in damp, crowded conditions, for instance, warns a gardener to plant them in soil that drains well and in a sunny, well-ventilated location.

Garden plant diseases are caused primarily by bacteria, fungi, and viruses. *Bacteria*, which usually are transmitted in soil and water, typically enter plants through natural openings or wounds. Look for wilted foliage, galls on stems, and rotted leaves, stems, roots, bulbs, or other underground organs. Bacterial diseases thrive in warm, moist conditions; they cannot be cured. *Fungi* are responsible for 75 percent of the diseases in the flower garden. They like warm, humid conditions and are spread by wind and water. Fungi cause galls, leaf yellowing, leaf spotting, wilting, and the sudden death of seedlings. Some plants will be too diseased to save, but others can be treated with organic fungicides, including antitranspirants, baking soda, Bordeaux mixtures, copper mixtures, fungicidal soaps, and sulfur mixtures. *Viruses* are typically carried by insects and by gardeners—on our hands, feet, and tools—and on infected plants and seeds. Stunted, yellowed, puckered, and rolled leaves are the common signs of viral infections. Viral diseases cannot be cured.

Plant Rx

Gardeners have a hierarchy of recourses at their disposal when troubles appear: cultural, physical, biological, and chemical. Cultural measures are the most environment-friendly, chemical measures the least, even if you're using organic chemicals. Begin with responses that are the least toxic and least damaging. Flower gardeners are the last people who should be spewing poisons into the landscape.

CULTURAL CONTROLS

Cultural controls—changes in the way gardeners grow plants—are often old fashioned but *not* outmoded practices. While they are long-term solutions, not magic bullets for immediate results, they still should be your first response to signs of diseases and pests. (Some cultural controls overlap with strategies to avoid problems; see "Preventing Calamity," page 148.)

Maintain healthy soil. Healthy soil—soil that contains plenty of organic matter has a pH near 6.5 and harbors lots of earthworms—helps prevent diseases by sustaining a balance between beneficial microorganisms and pathogens. (For more about maintaining healthy soil, see Chapter 4, page 63.) If you don't remember anything else, remember that adding organic matter to the soil is *always* a good thing to do.

Plant at the right time. Cold, damp soil and low air temperatures inhibit seed germination and transplants, opening them to diseases and pests. Early bird gardeners often *don't* get the worm. Similarly, you may escape some bugs by careful timing. A delay in moving transplants to the garden can reduce damage from leafhoppers, leaf miners, and other pests that are active in early spring.

Provide appropriate conditions. No plant will thrive unless it has the right amounts of sun, water, food, space, and healthy soil. Plants stressed because of poor habitat are more susceptible to pests and diseases.

Choose tolerant and resistant cultivars. Flowers with built-in tolerance and resistance do the work for you—look for them in seed and plant catalogs.

Switch plant locations. Growing the same flower in the same spot year after year can be an invitation for pests and diseases to take up permanent residence in the garden. If the problem is soilborne, replace your problematic flowers with flowers from a different plant family.

Water properly. In addition to seeing that plants get the right amount of moisture, remember that many diseases are spread by water. Avoid wetting plant leaves, and water in the morning so that plants will dry before nightfall. (For more about watering, see Chapter 6, page 116.)

Use mulches. Mulches not only discourage weeds and conserve moisture, but they act as a barrier against water splash, a primary carrier of pathogens. Organic mulches also encourage the presence of beneficial microorganisms. (For more about mulches, see "Much Ado About Mulch," page 131.)

Practice good hygiene. Many insect and disease hassles are eliminated by removing weeds and by a thorough garden cleanup at the end of the garden year. Good hygiene also means keeping tools clean.

Encourage natural predators. There is a host of beneficial organisms, insects, and animals that can help in the garden. Do all you can to promote and sustain them—ladybugs, beneficial nematodes, toads, birds, and more—in your garden.

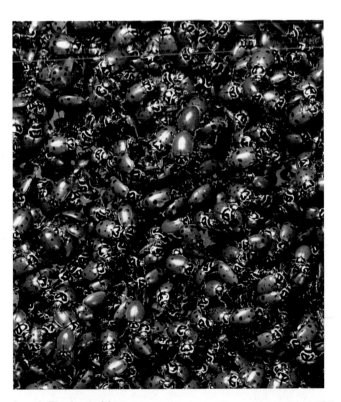

Don't Fly Away Home. *Ladybugs can help control aphids and other slow-moving pests. Growing yarrows (Achillea spp.), other flowers with umbrella-shaped blooms, and culinary herbs like dill and fennel will help keep ladybugs in your garden.*

FOR THE BIRDS

*W*hile it's true that birds eat beneficial bugs as well as pests, the good they do far outweighs the bad. Some birds that don't typically eat insects as adults do feed them to their young. (A house wren, which does eat insects, may snare up to 500 insects per day for its offspring.) In addition to planting trees and shrubs and installing houses, you can encourage insect-eating birds by providing suet. Another high-protein food source for insect-eating avians is Bird Grub, a product made from dehydrated caterpillars.

Don't make things worse. Some diseases and pests inevitably will find their way to your flowers, but be sure you aren't the vector. Buy bulbs, seeds, and planting stock that are certified disease-free; inspect transplants for signs of diseases and pests; stay out of the garden when plants are wet; and keep your tools clean.

Keep your eyes open. You can't fix what you don't see: Look for signs of pests and diseases and act quickly, before problems spread throughout the garden. As Vita Sackville-West expressed it, have a "heedful eye."

PHYSICAL CONTROLS

Physical controls are practices that require the gardener's direct involvement: manual removal, setting up physical barriers, and more. Most are simple and obvious, sometimes so simple and obvious that gardeners overlook them.

Remove the problem. With garden centers constantly touting the merits of pesticides, don't forget that handpicking slow-moving bugs and doing away with diseased plants are among the easiest methods of control. Squeamish gardeners can drop or shake pests into a jar of soapy water. (Bolder growers may enjoy smashing them between their thumb and index finger—the "seize and squeeze" approach.) Infected leaves, stems, or entire plants should be removed and destroyed, not composted. And keep the garden weed-free. Not only do weeds compete for food, water, and light, they harbor pests and diseases.

Erect barriers. One of the best garden inventions of late 20th century was the *row cover*, a spunbonded fabric so light that it can be laid directly on plants to exclude flea beetles and other pests while letting in light and water. Row covers, which were originally intended as season extenders, are most at home in vegetable gardens, but they can be used by flower growers, especially in cutting gardens. Seal the edges by burying them with soil so that insects can't sneak under the cover. Once the threat is past—for example, after the insect has stopped laying eggs—remove the cover.

To keep cutworms from dining on tender young plant stems, fashion a *plant collar* out of a paper-towel or toilet-paper tube. The collar need be only 3 or 4 inches high. Encircle each new plant stem with a collar, burying it 2 inches deep. The collars can be removed once the stems become sturdier. Shields made from heavy black plastic—use small pieces of trash bags—and laid on the soil around seedlings will stop female pests from laying their eggs at the base of plants.

Many crawling pests are discouraged by spreading *abrasive materials* such as wood ashes, crushed eggshells, and diatomaceous earth around the base of plants. (*Diatomaceous earth*, or *DE*, is a rough powder made from microscopic ocean animals.)

Use repellents. Start with water to rebuff insects—a forceful spray can dislodge aphids, mites, and other pests. If water isn't enough, try *insecticidal soaps*, which are sold by garden centers and mail-order suppliers. (For more information, see "Insecticidal Soaps," page 161.) Organic gardeners have traditionally used garlic to discourage insects, and there is limited evidence that garlic may have fungicidal properties as well. Garlic Barrier is a commercial product, but you can make your own spray (soak 10 to 20 pureed garlic cloves in 2 cups vegetable oil, strain, and add 2 teaspoons to a quart

HOT STUFF

*P*epper sprays are not only murder on pests, but they can be murder on gardeners. When working with chilies, wear gloves and keep fumes and your hands away from your face. To make a spray, combine 1/2 cup pureed hot peppers (including the seeds and membrane, which is where the "heat" lies) with 2 cups water. Strain. Add 1 teaspoon liquid soap to the strained liquid and mix well. Apply as needed; reapply after rainfall.

Hands On. *Squishing beetles and other plant pests between your fingers is pure pleasure for some, distasteful to others. Fastidious gardeners can deposit their victims in a jar of soapy water.*

of an insecticidal soap). Some gardeners add garlic plants—or chives, garlic chives, or other alliums—to the flower border, a safe option that may repel aphids and Japanese beetles. Or concoct your own spray from hot peppers or other natural repellants. There's evidence that sprays made from seaweed extract or compost have disease-resistant qualities as well as nutrient value.

Organically acceptable fungicides, including Bordeaux mix and sulfur and copper solutions, are available at garden centers and from mail-order catalogs and online stores. They are modestly effective in preventing diseases from spreading, but to protect they must be applied *before* pathogens enter plants. Horticultural oils also help safeguard plants by repelling water and the fungi it carries, and there is evidence that *antitranspirants* can prevent some fungal diseases. (For more information, see "Chemical Controls," page 159.)

Finally, some flowers—including asters, pot marigold (*Calendula officinalis*), geraniums (*Pelargonium* spp.), marigolds, and nasturtium (*Tropaeolum majus*)—may be *natural repellants*. Adding herbs to the flower bed also may discourage pests. The evidence is largely anecdotal, but borage (*Borago officinalis*), catnip (*Nepeta cataria*), garlic (*Allium sativum*), mints (*Mentha* spp.), rosemary (*Rosmarinus officinalis*), rue (*Ruta graveolens*), sage (*Salvia officinalis*), tansy (*Tanacetum vulgare*), and thymes (*Thymus* spp.) are among the herbs that have insect-rebuffing reputations. And they're ornamental to boot.

Install traps. Luring pests to their demise is less violent than squishing caterpillars between your fingers and less fun than whooshing plants with the garden hose, but it is still effective. Just don't forget that the good guys are also attracted to traps, and monitor your results: If you catch more ladybugs than leafhoppers, take the trap down.

Sticky traps use gluelike substances to catch small, fast-moving bugs like aphids, flea beetles, and thrips. You can purchase sticky traps or make your own by painting a 12 × 12–inch square of wood bright yellow (the color that attracts the most pests). Nail the board to a stake, coat with a sticky compound, such as Tangle-Trap Insect Trap Coating, and place it plant-high near the flowers under siege. Scrape the board and reapply the sticky compound as needed.

Pheromone traps use chemicals secreted by females to entice others of their kind. The jury's still out on their overall effect. Once highly recommended for controlling Japanese beetles, follow-up research discounts their value except when used throughout a large area: USDA entomologist Michael Klein has determined that traps only lure Japanese beetles from 200 yards or less—in other words, beetles that are already present. He recommends not using traps if you live adjoining a golf course or other large expanse of turf and not positioning a trap close to target plants, such as hollyhocks (*Alcea* spp.) and bee balms (*Monarda* spp.). Instead, locate the trap at least 30 feet away and near a nonflowering plant, such as a conifer, and encourage neighbors to set out traps too.

Food traps—especially those baited with fermenting foods—draw many bugs. Slugs and snails are suckers for beer or baker's yeast dissolved in water (1 teaspoon per 3 ounces water). Use shallow containers set to the brim in the soil, or purchase a commercial trap. Check the traps each morning, remove the victims, and replenish the bait.

Shade traps can be made from anything that creates a cool, shady place for slugs and other pests to hide: pieces of board, carpet, stone, overturned flowerpots, upside-down grapefruit rinds, and more. Lift traps often, and remove and dispose of their inhabitants.

Plant traps, or *trap crops*, are decoy plants grown to appeal to particular pests. Japanese beetles, for example, are attracted to borage (*Borago officinalis*), flea beetles and leaf miners to radishes (*Raphanus sativus*), aphids to nasturtium (*Tropaeolum majus*). Grow trap plants in pots set at least 25 feet from flower beds. Once the trap plants are infested, hand-pick the pests or remove and destroy the plants.

Solarize the soil. If the fault is not in your stars but in the soil—gangs of dirt-dwelling fungi or Japanese beetle larvae—try solarizing. It won't kill all soilborne vectors, but it will reduce them. You'll probably want to approach your garden piecemeal, beginning with one bed or small parts of beds that are most affected. (For more information, see "Death by Sun," page 81.)

Biological Controls

Using biological controls is like setting backfires, using fire to fight fire. In the garden it's using diseases, bugs, and animals to stop diseases, bugs, and animals. Eleanor Perényi put it nicely in *Green Thoughts* (1981): "Cultivate that enemy and he will do your work for you."

The scores of natural helpers include everything from spiders and toads to flower beetles and lizards. Toads—there are species throughout North America—are so adept at snagging slugs, caterpillars, flies, cutworms, and other live game with their sticky tongues that they were once routinely kept in greenhouses. One estimate is that a single toad eats as many as 10,000 pests in a garden season. It's a bill of fare that may explain why the American writer Charles Dudley Warner went so far as to say that no garden was complete without a toad.

There are beneficial microorganisms as well, bacteria, fungi, nematodes, protozoa, and viruses that infect garden pests with fatal diseases. These benefactors will make your garden theirs with a little encouragement. Even the family dog or cat can be a biological control, keeping deer, rabbits, and other animals at bay. (Keeping the dog and cat out of the garden is another pest problem.)

Toads, midges, assassin bugs, spined soldier bugs, and all sorts of soil-dwelling microorganisms are a few of the beneficials that are natives. They're *already* in your garden. Your job is to keep them there and to lure their comrades. To do that, you must provide a diverse, chemical-free environment that includes fresh water, shelter, and food. If there

---

BENEFICIAL FOR BENEFICIALS

*M*any beneficial insects feed on flower nectar and pollen. Common herbs such as parsley, mint, dill, rue (*Ruta graveolens*), and borage (*Borago officinalis*) are good food sources, as are the flowers listed below. Add some of these blooms to your garden to sustain scores of natural allies.

Asters (*Aster* spp.)

Baby's breaths (*Gypsophila* spp.)

Bachelor's button (*Centaurea cyanus*)

Bee balms (*Monarda* spp.)

Butterfly weed (*Asclepias tuberosa*)

California poppy (*Eschscholzia californica*)

Candytufts (*Iberis* spp.)

Catnips (*Nepeta* spp.)

China aster (*Callistephus chinensis*)

Cosmos (*Cosmos* spp.)

Farewell-to-spring (*Clarkia* spp.)

Feverfew (*Tanacetum parthenium*)

Flowering tobaccos (*Nicotiana* spp.)

Gayfeathers (*Liatris* spp.)

Globe thistles (*Echinops* spp.)

Goldenrods (*Solidago* spp.)

Heliotrope (*Heliotropium arborescens*)

Hollyhock, single flowered (*Alcea rosea*)

Lavenders (*Lavandula* spp.)

Leopard's bane (*Doronicum* spp.)

Marigolds (*Tagetes* spp.)

Mexican sunflower (*Tithonia rotundifolia*)

Milkweeds (*Asclepias* spp.)

Money plant (*Lunaria annua*)

Orange coneflowers (*Rudbeckia* spp.)

Ox-eye daisy (*Leucanthemum vulgare*)

Pot marigold (*Calendula officinalis*)

Salvias and sages (*Salvia* spp.)

Sea pink/common thrift (*Armeria maritima*)

Siberian squill (*Scilla siberica*)

Sunflowers (*Helianthus* spp.)

Sweet alyssum (*Lobularia maritima*)

Winter aconite (*Eranthis hyemalis*)

Yarrows (*Achillea* spp.)

Zinnias (*Zinnia* spp.)

Food for Garden Helpers. *This showy bee balm* (Monarda *'Cambridge Scarlet') is as appealing to hummingbirds as it is to bees, an ideal perennial for luring beneficials to your garden.*

enough, however; there needs to be a small pest population to keep beneficials in residence. (That's one of the reasons that the liquidation of all bugs should never be a gardener's goal.)

In addition to doing all you can to tempt native allies into your garden, you can purchase them from mail-order and online sources. (Local garden centers rarely sell beneficial insects because of their short shelf life.) Identify your pest before you take out your credit card, or you may end up purchasing a beneficial that is little or no help. Keep in mind, too, that beneficials aren't chemical pesticides. They aren't an immediate fix. Often they must be released repeatedly, and they are unlikely to be 100 percent beneficial. Trichogramma wasps, for example, parasitize butterfly eggs as well as those of aphids and thrips; the parasitic bacterium *Bacillus thuringiensis* (Bt) kills *all* caterpillars, including those that produce black swallowtail butterflies and monarchs. That said, many of these commercially available beneficials will help keep some garden problems at bay.

Bacillus popilliae (Bp). Pathogenic bacteria used to control Japanese beetle larvae. Also known as milky spore disease.

Bacillus thuringiensis (Bt). Parasitic soil bacterium that preys on caterpillar larvae and some beetles.

Beneficial nematodes. Tiny pathogenic and parasitic beneficials that attack armyworms, rootworms, fleas, fungus gnats, stem borers, root weevil, cutworms, and billbugs.

Convergent lady beetles, or ladybugs. Adults and larvae feed on aphids, mealybugs, scale insects, spider mites, whiteflies, and other soft-bodied pests.

Decollate snails. Feed on brown garden snails and slugs.

isn't a natural water source, add some sort of water feature. At the least, fill several shallow pans with water and place them in and near the garden; be sure to empty the pans weekly to prevent mosquito larvae from maturing. (Set rocks in the pans so that insects have a place to perch.) Use organic mulches in which beneficials can hide and lay eggs.

Many adult beneficial insects are nectar- and pollen-feeders. In North American gardens, members of two plant families especially are attractive to these insects: the aster family, Asteraceae, and the mint family, Lamiaceae. Nectar and pollen aren't

DUCK, DUCK, GOOSE, GOOSE

*M*arie Antoinette enjoyed a rustic Viennese retreat where she kept perfumed sheep and goats and used domestic fowl for pest control. You may not want ducks and geese picking their way through your flowers; although they are great bug and slug eaters, they also are great seedling eaters. (Using your—or a loved one's—breasts as molds to make porcelain bowls for watering and feeding the poultry, as Marie did, is optional.)

The Good Serpent in the Garden. *Garter, or gardener, snakes, are harmless to humans but lethal to insects, slugs, snails, and small rodents. They are the most widely distributed reptile species in North America and the only snake found in Alaska, a "rare visitor from Canada."*

Entomopathogenic and other fungi. Infect and kill a range of pests; some microbials work as fungicides.

Green lacewings. Larvae feed on aphids, mites, scales, mealy bugs, whiteflies, thrips, leafhoppers, and other small insects and insect eggs.

Parasitic wasps. Parasitize many pests and their larvae, including aphids, caterpillars, cutworms, borers, thrips, hornworms, bean beetles, scale insects, and whiteflies.

Praying mantises. Feed on most insects, including beetles, flies, caterpillars, grasshoppers, as well as beneficials.

Predatory mites. Feed on pest mites, such as spider mites.

Soldier beetles and spined soldier beetles. Adults and larvae feed on aphids, various caterpillars, and insect eggs and larvae.

There's little argument over the effectiveness of applying beneficial microorganisms like Bt outdoors or loosing beneficial insects into a greenhouse, but the reviews are mixed on releasing beneficial insects into a garden. A pint of ladybugs—about 9,000—are likely to disperse within 24 hours if conditions aren't right. (Some experts claim that 90 percent will disperse no matter what the conditions.) If you purchase beneficials, follow the instructions that come with them to the letter. All in all, the best tack for most gardeners is to conserve and encourage the beneficials already in residence.

Chemical Controls

Chemical controls are the last recourse for environmentally responsible gardeners. If chemicals become necessary in your flower garden, look for *biorational chemicals*. These are botanical or mineral pesticides and other "cides" that occur naturally, not highly synthesized commercial products such as carbaryl (marketed as Sevin). Biorationals aren't harmless, however. Some are even more toxic than synthetic products. (Nicotine sulfate, for example, is so dangerous that it is prohibited by most organic certification programs.) Most are nonselective; they can kill beneficial bugs and pose dangers to humans, pets, and wildlife. Because they are less persistent, they must be timed precisely and may need to be reapplied several times to be effective. Most are also slower to act. As a group, however, biorationals are less harmful to the environment because they are less toxic and less persistent—they are broken down rapidly by light or microbes.

What follows are some of the biorational chemicals you'll find in garden catalogs and in local stores and nurseries. Read the fine print because many products contain more than one substance. Pyola Insecticidal Spray, for example, combines canola oil with pyrethrins. Then choose carefully and apply with moderation.

Antitranspirants such as Wilt Pruf were created to reduce moisture loss in plants but can do double duty by protecting against fungus diseases, such as powdery and downy mildews. Do not treat drought-stressed plants when temperatures are above 85°F. Because they reduce photosynthesis, antitranspirants should not be used in regions where sunlight is low. Antitranspirants are nontoxic.

Azadirachtin, or neem, comes from the neem tree (*Azadirachta indica*) and is one of the safest botanicals. Applied as a liquid spray, it repels or kills a wide range of pests, especially leaf eaters and immature pests, and it also has fungicidal properties. Because it coats plant surfaces, azadirachtin is most effective as a fungicide when used before problems occur. Relatively nontoxic to bees and other beneficials, birds, earthworms, and mammals, neem is toxic to fish and aquatic invertebrates. It biodegrades rapidly in sunlight and does not persist in the soil. Commercial products such as Neem-Away, BioNeem, and Dyna-Gro Pure Neem Oil can vary in the percentage of azadirachtin they contain as well as other pesticides that have been added. Neem products are labeled for either pest or fungus control.

Bicarbonate sprays that help prevent powdery mildew and other fungal diseases include baking soda (sodium bicarbonate), an old-time remedy available commercially as Bonide Remedy, and newer products like Kaligreen, which contain potassium

Reading the Fine Print. *Garden products are labeled for contents and safety. Remember that "organic" is not synonymous with "safe"; even biorational controls, such as pyrethrins, pose dangers to the environment and should be used with restraint.*

READING THE WARNINGS

Garden chemicals, including biorational products, are rated by the Environmental Protection Agency (EPA) for "acute toxicity values." Test results—rats are the usual subjects—are expressed by the LD_{50} number, the median lethal dose that kills half of the subjects through oral, dermal, or inhalation exposure. The *lower* the LD_{50} number, the greater the toxicity. (LD_{50} ratings do not reflect a substance's long-term effects or its persistence in the environment.) Once tested, substances are grouped in four categories: Category I includes the most toxic and carries a skull and crossbones and the signal words DANGER POISON; Category II is designated by WARNING; Category III carries a CAUTION admonition, as does Category IV, the least toxic group.

In addition to "warning" and other signal words, labels sometimes detail products' dangers. When you see statements such as "Do not breathe spray mist" or "Causes irreversible eye damage," take them seriously.

bicarbonate. Biocarbonates work best when combined with a horticultural oil and when applied before any infection occurs. To make your own baking soda spray, combine 4 teaspoons of baking soda, 2½ tablespoons horticultural oil in 1 gallon of water. Biocarbonates have very low toxicity but can accumulate in the soil; do not overuse.

Citrus oils, such as Orange Guard for Ornamental Plants, are both fungicides and contact pesticides, effective against aphids, mites, and other soft-bodied pests. They are relatively nontoxic.

Copper and copper formulations are preventive fungicides and bactericides. The best known compound is Bordeaux mixture, a combination of copper sulfate and lime named for the French region where it was first used to discourage people from stealing grapes. More toxic than sulfur, copper-based substances are nonspecific, indefinitely persistent in soils, and harmful to soil microorganisms and beneficial insects. They are highly toxic to aquatic life and should not be used near water. Available as powders or liquids, repeated applications of copper can stunt plant growth. Toxicity varies depending of the formulation—two widely available products are Acme Bordeaux Mixture and Bonide Liquid Copper.

Horticultural oils include a range of insecticidal petroleum sprays that suffocate aphids, mites, scales, caterpillars, and other pests and their eggs on contact. (Newer to the market are oil sprays that are also fungicidal, such as Organocide and Sporan, and vegetable-oil products like Oil-Away.) Look for summer, or superior, oils such as SunSpray Ultra-Fine Year-Round Pesticidal Oil, which

Bee Candy. *Flowers like showy stonecrop (Sedum spectabile) attract bees, butterflies, and other beneficials. Stonecrops thrive in poor soil, even on old window frames if we are to believe William Wordsworth's poem "The Excursion" (1814).*

are intended for actively growing plants, or read the label of dormant oils carefully and weaken them to a growing-season dilution before applying. Although they degrade rapidly through evaporation, oil sprays can damage leaves if applied when plants are water-stressed and temperatures are high. A homebrew of 2 percent vegetable oil and 98 percent water has been shown to be as effective as many commercial products. Oils are safe for mammals but are toxic to many beneficials and to aquatic life. To increase efficacy, add isopropyl alcohol to the mix: 1 cup alcohol, ½ teaspoon summer oil, and 4 cups water.

Insecticidal soaps like Safer Insect Killing Soap are formulations of plant or animal fatty acids that smother and kill slow-moving, soft-shelled, and sucking insects on contact. Since they have no residual effect once they dry, use them only when pests appear, not as a preventative measure. Most insecticidal soaps—there are also soap-based fungicides and herbicides—are relatively specific and virtually nontoxic to humans, but they can harm beneficial insects and aquatic life. Some flowers, including bleeding hearts (*Dicentra* spp.) and sweet pea (*Lathyrus odoratus*), are sensitive to insecticidal soaps; test a few leaves before spraying an entire plant. Do not apply when plants are in full sun or in temperatures above 85°F. Insecticidal soaps are not compatible with rotenone- or copper-based pesticides. Many soap products, such as Organica K+Neem and Soap-Shield, contain additional substances that raise their toxicity.

Iron phosphate is used in molluscicides, products such as Sluggo and Escar-Go!, that are designed to control slugs and snails. Its toxicity is low, and it is safe to use where there are pets; do not apply near ponds or other water sources.

Pyrethrins are contact poisons made from pyrethrum daisies. (*Pyrethrins* are the natural products derived from flowers; *pyrethroids* are synthetic chemicals that resemble pyrethrins but are more toxic and persistent; and *pyrethrum* is the general term for both compounds.) Known for their ability to kill or stun pests, pyrethrins persist only a few hours in sunlight when temperatures are above 50°F. They are one of the environmentally safer botanicals. Safer but not harmless: More persistent in damp conditions, pyrethrins are nonspecific and extremely toxic to aquatic life and moderately toxic to beneficial insects. Pyrethrins—look for

names like Garden Safe Rose & Flower Insect Spray—often are combined with other pesticides or a synergist, a substance such as piperonyl butoxide (PBO), that boosts effectiveness. Avoid aerosol products, which are more persistent.

Rotenone is a slow-acting contact and stomach poison. Made primarily from the roots of tropical leguminous plants, rotenone has been used for more than 150 years. It is still widely sold despite being one of the most potent natural insecticides—one considerably more toxic than many synthetic products. (Rotenone has an LD50 of 132, while the LD50 of Malathion, a widely used synthetic, is 1,375.) In addition to killing aphids, mites, thrips, caterpillars, beetles, and other hard-shelled pests, rotenone is lethal to fish and aquatic invertebrates.

SAFETY FIRST

*U*sing any pesticide can harm the gardener and other organisms as well as the garden. Apply pesticides sparingly and with care. Purchase only as much as you need.

- Read the label. Establish that the product will control your problem and mix and apply it at recommended rates.
- Treat individual plants rather than the entire garden.
- Spray or dust plants in the early morning or evening, when beneficial insects are less active. Do not apply pesticides on windy days or near water.
- Protect yourself with appropriate clothing and equipment. Wash hands and face after handling pesticides.
- Keep pesticides in their original containers and store them out of the reach of children.
- Check pesticide labels for shelf-life information and dispose of them properly. Never dump pesticides on the ground, pour them down the drain, or put them in the trash. For disposal help, look for "Hazardous Materials" under your town, county, or state's listings in the telephone directory, or go to the Earth 911 site, www.earth911.org (800-CLEANUP). Never reuse a pesticide container.

(It is the poison of choice to kill "trash" fish during restocking projects.) Rotenone is also lethal to some beneficial insects and birds and mildly toxic to mammals. More deadly when inhaled than ingested, rotenone persists about five days in the garden when temperatures are above 75°F (much longer when temperatures are below 50°F). Products' makeup and strength vary, so look for the toxicity rating. As one major organic seller warns, rotenone is "an absolutely last resort."

Sulfur has been used as a fungicide for at least 3,000 years and can be applied as either a dust or a spray in its elemental form (Bonide Sulfur Plant Fungicide) or in combination with other natural substances (Hi-Yield Lime Sulfur Solution). It is most effective as a preventative for plants that are highly susceptible to powdery mildew, rusts, and other fungus diseases. While only mildly toxic to mammals, sulfur can kill beneficial soil microorganisms and insects, and can damage plants if applied in temperatures above 90°F. Do not use sulfur in combination with horticultural oils.

You may want to start with homemade remedies, such as sprays made from hot peppers and garlic, rather than with a commercial product. Many pests can be controlled by a simple oil and soap spray. Combine 1 teaspoon light vegetable oil, such as canola or corn oil, and 1 teaspoon liquid dish soap (use a soap without dyes or fragrances) in 1 gallon water; substituting chamomile or compost tea for a portion of the water may give the concoction even more punch. Even homemade mixtures can be harmful, so make test applications before you drench your plants. Some species, especially those with fuzzy foliage like lamb's ear (*Stachys byzantina*), are sensitive to even relatively benign sprays.

Garden Foes

Before you can stop your adversary, you must identify it. A Chinese proverb says, "Know your enemy as you know yourself and you can fight a hundred battles with no danger of defeat." Sadly, that's not entirely true for the gardener—who *will* face defeats—but "know your enemy" is the starting point for any battle. This is the ID section, the horticultural equivalent of the "wanted" posters hanging in the Post Office.

Garden Plagues. *Grasshopper populations tend to fluctuate in cycles, high for two or three years, then moderate or low for several years. Adult grasshoppers are always moving, which makes sprays largely ineffective.*

COMMON PESTS

There are thousands of insects and other small creatures sharing your yard and garden. Since most of them are beneficial, not harmful, don't rush for the sprayer. Examine plants, especially leaf undersides. To identify the opposition, start with its feeding form, or forms. And what does it eat? Does it chew holes in the leaves, suck juices out of the plant, or bore into stems and leaves? Use the descriptions and the "Prime targets" information that follow to determine who is causing the trouble; then use the "Prevention" and "Control" information to keep the troublemakers in check. Remember that all toxic controls, *even organic ones*, are deadly and often unselective.

Aphids

Aphids, which mass on leaf tips and undersides, are soft-bodied, pear-shaped insects the size of a pinhead, variously colored green, pink, brown, yellow, or black. They suck juices from all parts of plants, often spreading diseases as they feed. Yellow, curled foliage, damaged flower buds, and distorted flowers are signs of infestation, as is a sooty mold on leaves that grows on the honeydew aphids excrete. Eggs laid in fall overwinter on plant debris. Aphids undergo simple metamorphosis and occur primarily in spring and early summer throughout North America.

Prime targets. There are well over 1,000 aphid species, which attack scores of flowers, including asters, astilbes, bellflowers (*Campanula* spp.), blanket flowers (*Gaillardia* spp.), chrysanthemums, columbines (*Aquilegia* spp.), coreopsis, cosmos, dahlias, delphiniums, foxgloves (*Digitalis* spp.), geraniums (*Pelargonium* spp.), gladioli, hyacinths, impatiens, larkspur (*Consolida ajacis*), lilies, marigolds, milkweeds (*Asclepias* spp.), nasturtium (*Tropaeolum majus*), pinks (*Dianthus* spp.), poppies (*Papaver* spp.), salvias, sunflowers, tulips, and verbenias.

Prevention. Avoid high-nitrogen fertilizers, especially soluble fertilizers. Encourage ladybugs, lacewings, aphid midges, parasitic wasps, and other natural predators. Clean up plant debris in fall.

Control. Hose plants daily with a strong stream of water to dislodge aphids. Spray with insecticidal soap, citrus oil, or horticultural oil, making sure to wet leaf undersides, every three days until pests are controlled. Use neem, pyrethrin, or rotenone as a last resort.

Beetles

While the number of different beetles is enormous, only a few are serious pests in the flower garden. Among those are tan-colored rose chafers, which feed on hollyhock (*Alcea rosea*), peonies, and poppies; blister beetles, which prefer asters, chrysanthemums, phlox, and zinnias, and should be handled with gloves; and Asiatic garden beetles, a nocturnal species that attacks annual and perennial asters, cannas, chrysanthemums, cosmos, delphiniums, petunias, phlox, and zinnias. Other potential foes are snout, cucumber, and June beetles. The most common beetle problems in flower gardens come from pinhead-size flea and metallic green Japanese beetles. All beetles undergo complete metamorphosis and damage plants with their chewing mouthparts. (See page 164 for more on flea beetles and page 165 for more on Japanese beetles.)

Borers

Borers, the larvae of various beetles and miller moths, drill into plant stems to feed. Sudden stem wilt or water-soaked leaves standing at odd angles are a sign of borers, as are small, round holes in stems and scarred foliage. Some borers damage roots and plant crowns. Eggs overwinter in plant debris.

Borers are most problematic in late spring and early summer in central and eastern North America. Bacterial soft rot often invades rhizomes damaged by borers.

Prime targets. Irises are susceptible to iris borers. Other borers, such as stalk borers, attack asters, bee balms (*Monarda* spp.), dahlias, delphiniums, centaureas (*Centaurea* spp.), chrysanthemums, columbines (*Aquilegia* spp.), cosmos, hollyhock (*Alcea rosea*), marigolds, peonies, phlox, orange coneflowers (*Rudbeckia* spp.), salvias, snapdragon (*Antirrhinum majus*), and zinnias.

Prevention. Remove and burn garden debris in fall; clean up again in early spring. Introduce parasitic nematodes in early spring before borers emerge; treat soil repeatedly with Bt in early spring.

Control. Slit affected stems and kill the grub. Dig and destroy badly infested plants. Dust the soil around the base of plants with pyrethrin in early spring to kill newly hatched grubs. Because borers feed inside the plant, contact sprays are ineffective.

Caterpillars

Caterpillars are the larvae of scores of moth and butterfly species; they range from smooth to fuzzy, large to small. Many are strikingly colored and marked, and are clearly visible. Caterpillars dine on plant leaves and buds, but only a few are serious pests in the garden. Watch for holes and jagged edges in foliage and for rolled leaves or buds tied shut with silk. Caterpillars are one stage in a complete metamorphosis; they occur throughout North America, primarily from early spring to early summer.

Prime targets. Caterpillars feed on ageratums, cannas, catmints (*Nepeta* spp.), columbines (*Aquilegia* spp.), daffodils, mignonette (*Reseda odorata*), nasturtium (*Tropaeolum majus*), peonies, pinks (*Dianthus* spp.), statice (*Limonium* spp.), annual and perennial sunflowers, verbenas, and other flowers.

Prevention. Encourage natural enemies, including parasitic wasps, spined soldier bugs, and toads; plant trap plants, such as parsley, then handpick.

Control. Handpick. Apply Bt to leaves if handpicking is inadequate; spray with a horticultural oil or an insecticidal soap. Avoid indiscriminate spraying, which will kill desirable butterflies and nocturnal moths. Use neem, pyrethrin, or rotenone as a last resort.

Cutworms

Cutworms, the plump, naked larvae of moths, are largely ground dwellers. They get their name from the damage they do: cut off young, tender plants at the soil line, typically leaving the tops on the ground. Up to 1½ inches long and colored gray or dull brown—sometimes with stripes or mottling—most cutworms are nocturnal and hide under plant debris (or just below the soil surface) during the day, often curling up like the letter C. They occur throughout North America, especially in spring.

Prime targets. Most seedlings and transplants.

Prevention. Remove plant debris where cutworms hide during the day. Use collars around the stems of transplants and seedlings. Spread wood ashes, cornmeal, or diatomaceous earth around the base of young plants. Encourage braconid and trichogramma wasps and beneficial nematodes, which are natural predators, as are toads and birds.

Control. Handpick at night. Cultivate around plants to kill eggs and larvae. Soak the soil around plants with an insecticidal soap. Dust vulnerable plants with Bt or spray with a horticultural oil or an insecticidal soap.

Flea Beetles

Shiny black or brown flea beetles are pinhead-sized and jump when disturbed. They chew tiny holes in new foliage, causing the leaves to brown or wilt, and they can spread viral diseases. Adults overwinter underground and emerge in spring to lay eggs in the soil. After they hatch, the larvae—thin white grubs with brown heads—live in the soil and feed on plant roots, then pupate and finally emerge as adults. Flea beetles occur throughout North America and are especially active when the weather is hot and dry.

Prime targets. Flea beetles are most problematic in vegetable gardens, but they also feed on asters, forget-me-nots (*Myosotis* spp.), nasturtium (*Tropaeolum majus*), petunias, phlox, and sunflowers.

Prevention. Destroy eggs and larvae by cultivating the soil regularly. Cover seedlings with floating row covers in spring if practicable. Spread diatomaceous earth around and on susceptible plants. Encourage beneficial nematodes, which will kill the larvae, and toads and songbirds, which eat adult beetles.

Control. Plant radishes as a trap crop, then spray plants with pyrethrin, rotenone, or neem. Use white sticky traps; hose plants with water at noontime. Spray severe infestations with neem, pyrethrin, or rotenone as a last resort.

Grasshoppers

It's difficult to sympathize with essayist Verlyn Klinkenborg's description of the grasshopper as having a "muted, almost Italianate beauty" once your garden has been invaded. Yet only a few species pose real problems to flowers, including migratory, differential, two-striped, and red-legged grasshoppers. There are three stages in the grasshopper's simple metamorphosis. Adults lay eggs in the soil in autumn. The wingless nymphs, which hatch in spring and early summer, begin feeding immediately on flower foliage (look for damage on leaf margins). Nymphs reach the adult—and flying—stage in about 60 days. Adults are variously colored brown, gray, or green (and sometimes marked with yellow), have wings, and measure between ¾ and 2 inches long. Grasshoppers are a summer problem throughout North America but are most destructive in the Midwest and West, especially in areas that get less than 25 inches of rainfall a year.

Prime targets. Grasshoppers chew leaves, and no plant is safe. Favorites are asters, columbines (*Aquilegia* spp.), dahlias, marigolds, pinks (*Dianthus* spp.), and zinnias. Populations are affected by environmental factors and are largest when a dry, warm summer is followed by a wet spring. In high-population years, grasshoppers will eat almost anything, including wood and plastic window screens.

Prevention. Row covers, where they can be used, will protect young plants. Plant "barrier plants" around gardens to prevent grasshoppers from migrating in. Cultivate garden soil in fall and spring to expose egg pods. Encourage natural predators, including robber flies, spiders, praying mantises, paper wasps, tachinid flies, parasitic wasps, and blister beetle larvae. Frogs, lizards, and birds are good grasshopper predators.

Control. Chickens and other poultry love eating grasshoppers but are impractical for most home gardeners. Handpick in early morning when grasshoppers are sluggish; install yellow sticky traps. Make small traps out of jars (buried to their rim) filled with water and a 10 percent molasses solution topped with a film of canola oil. Treat plants with a pepper or neem spray. There is no effective or safe spray for adults, as they move constantly.

Japanese Beetles

Shiny, handsome, and highly visible, ½-inch long Japanese beetles are metallic green with bronze wing covers. Female beetles burrow into the ground and lay eggs in late summer. The dirty white grubs, which often curl into a C-shape, have brown heads and overwinter in the soil, where they eat plant roots; adults emerge in late spring. Japanese beetles occur primarily in eastern North America and devour leaves, buds, and blossoms from early summer through midfall.

Prime targets. Many flowers, including asters, astilbes, cannas, cosmos, daylilies, delphiniums, evening primroses (*Oenothera* spp.), foxgloves (*Digitalis* spp.), hardy geraniums (*Geranium* spp.), gladioli, globe thistles (*Echinops* spp.), hollyhock (*Alcea rosea*), leopard's banes (*Doronicum* spp.), marigolds, morning glories (*Ipomoea* spp.), peonies, coneflowers (*Echinacea* spp.), rose mallows (*Hibiscus* spp.), and zinnias.

Prevention. Treat lawns with Bt, milky spore disease, on a neighborhood-wide basis to control grub populations. Introduce beneficial nematodes. Spray plants with neem to repel adult beetles. Plant borage, hollyhock, and other trap crops well away from your flower gardens, then handpick beetles that feed on those plants.

The Asian Invasion. *Accidently imported to North America a century ago, Japanese beetles feed on more than 400 plant species. Lacking the natural enemies of their native habitats, they have become serious garden pests, especially in the East.*

Control. Handpick beetles. Trap adults in pheromone traps on a neighborhood-wide basis (traps in one garden are ineffective). Treat serious infestations of adults with pyrethrin or rotenone.

Leafhoppers

Most leafhoppers are small—less than ½ inch long—wedge-shaped, winged insects that are variously colored green, brown, or yellow, sometimes with mottling or bright markings; they jump wildly when they're disturbed. Both nymphs and adults suck juices from plant stems, leaves, and buds, injecting a toxin as they feed, and transmit diseases. Look for small white specks or stippling, the telltale sheen of honeydew (which fosters the growth of fungi), leaf tip and edge burn, and curled or crinkled leaves. Leafhoppers undergo simple metamorphosis and occur throughout North America; they are most active from midspring to midfall.

Prime targets. Asters, astilbes, blanket flowers (*Gaillardia* spp.), catmints (*Nepeta* spp.), dahlias, hardy geraniums (*Pelargonium* spp.), hollyhock (*Alcea rosea*), lupines (*Lupinus* spp.), marigolds, primroses (*Primula* spp.), statice (*Limonium* spp.), and flowering tobaccos (*Nicotiana* spp.). The aster leafhopper is the primary agent of aster yellows disease.

Prevention. Keep gardens weed-free and remove plant debris. Cover plants with floating row covers in early spring if practicable. Encourage natural predators such as assassin bugs, damsel bugs, lacewings, and parasitic wasps; songbirds also prey on leafhoppers.

Control. Spray foliage with a strong stream of water; apply an insecticidal soap or pepper spray; dust plants with diatomaceous earth. Use neem, pyrethrin, or rotenone only for severe infestations.

Leaf Miners

Leaf miners, the translucent larvae of various moths, flies, or beetles, get their name from the way they feed: They tunnel, or mine, through leaf tissue. Tan or white serpentine trails on leaf surfaces indicate their presence. Their damage is unsightly but rarely fatal. Leaf miners undergo complete metamorphosis; they occur throughout North America, especially in spring and early summer.

Prime targets. Ageratums, asters, baby's breaths (*Gypsophila* spp.), blanket flowers (*Gaillardia* spp.), chrysanthemums, columbines (*Aquilegia* spp.), coreopsis, dahlias, delphiniums, hardy geraniums (*Geranium* spp.), Joe-Pye weeds (*Eupatorium* spp.), pinks (*Dianthus* spp.), pot marigolds (*Calendula* spp.), salvias, Transvaal daisy (*Gerbera jamesonii*), verbenas, and zinnias.

Prevention. Encourage parasitic wasps, which destroy the larvae. Keep the garden free of lamb's-quarters, dock, and other host plants; remove plant debris. Destroy the white, cylindrical eggs that adults lay on leaf undersides. Encourage parasitic wasps, which are natural predators. Apply an insecticidal soap or pepper spray. Use neem to deter adult flies.

Control. Once larvae enter the leaves, sprays are ineffective. Remove infested leaves.

Mites

Often called spider mites, these minute, spiderlike pests are pale green, yellow, or red and suck plant juices, usually feeding on leaf undersides. They cause yellow stippling or speckles on leaf tops and leaf curling; severe infestations weaken and stunt plants. Mites are hard to see, so look for their tell-tale white webs. Adults overwinter in organic matter in the soil. Spider mites are present throughout North America, and most are especially damaging during hot, dry weather. They undergo simple metamorphosis.

Prime targets. Many flower species, including ageratums, begonias, bellflowers (*Campanula* spp.), blanket flowers (*Gaillardia* spp.), cannas, chrysanthemums, columbines (*Aquilegia* spp.), coreopsis, crocuses, dahlias, delphiniums, gladioli, hyacinths, impatiens, larkspur (*Consolida ajacis*), lilies, marigolds, nasturtium (*Tropaeolum majus*), pansies, petunias, phlox, pinks (*Dianthus* spp.), salvias, snapdragon (*Antirrhinum majus*), spider flower (*Cleome hassleriana*), violets, and zinnias.

Prevention. Spray plants with water to discourage mites. Remove and destroy all yellowed foliage; remove plant debris in autumn. Allow plants room to spread. Encourage natural enemies, such as damsel bugs, lacewings, ladybugs, pirate bugs, and predatory midges and thrips.

Control. Apply insecticidal soap, pepper spray, citrus oil, or a horticultural oil. Use neem or pyrethrin only for severe, damaging infestations: The same controls that destroy mites kill their natural enemies. Dig and destroy bulbs that are infested with mites.

Disguise Artist. *Some species of flower, or crab, spiders have the ability to change color—white, yellow, green—as they wait to ambush their prey. Bees, unfortunately, are common victims.*

Nematodes

Nematodes, which are microscopic, translucent worms, come in two classes: beneficial and harmful. Most harmful nematodes live in the soil and don't directly injure plants: They spread viral diseases that damage and kill plants. Plants that are inexplicably sickly, weak, or stunted—with yellow or bronze foliage—may be the victims of nematodes. Most active in summer and fall, nematodes occur throughout North America and overwinter in soil and in plant tissue.

Prime targets. Anemones (*Anemone* spp.), astilbes, bearded irises, bellflowers (*Campanula* spp.), coreopsis, delphiniums, hardy geraniums (*Geranium* spp.), hostas, lavenders (*Lavandula* spp.), lilies, lobelias (*Lobelia* spp.), ox-eye (*Heliopsis helianthoides*), pincushion flowers (*Scabiosa* spp.), Russian sage (*Perovskia atriplicifolia*), snakeroots (*Cimicifuga* spp.), speedwells (*Veronica* spp.), tulips, and violets (*Viola* spp.).

Prevention. Keep soil rich in organic matter by adding compost regularly; cultivate soil frequently to expose root-knot nematodes to sun. Plant marigolds throughout the garden, especially 'Tangerine' or 'Petite Gold'. Mulch with pine needles. Plant nematode-resistant cultivars. Alter the location of susceptible flower species. Encourage predatory mites, springtails, and other natural enemies.

Control. Solarize the soil. Remove and destroy infected plants. Apply Clandosan, a nematocide made from ground shellfish, to the soil.

Scales

Scales are second cousins of aphids, whiteflies, and other sucking insects. Look for small white, yellow, brown, or black flattened bumps, especially on new foliage and stems, which are the shells that protect the insect and its eggs. Some species excrete honeydew, which encourages the growth of sooty molds on leaf surfaces. Severe infestations cause leaf yellowing and leaf drop. Scale insects undergo simple metamorphosis. They occur throughout North America, but are most severe in late spring and early summer and in warm climates.

Prime targets. Primarily an indoor problem. Begonias, cannas, hardy geraniums (*Geranium* spp.), and peonies can be attacked.

Prevention. Avoid high-nitrogen fertilizer. Encourage lacewings, parasitic wasps, predatory beetles, and other natural predators, such as chickadees and other insect-eating birds. Remove plant debris from garden in fall.

Control. Remove and destroy scale-infested stems and leaves. For small infestations wipe stems and leaves with a cloth dipped in isopropyl alcohol. Spray plants with insecticidal soap or horticultural oil to suffocate scales. Use pyrethrin or rotenone as a last resort.

Slugs and Snails

Land-dwelling mollusks, snails and slugs (which are snails minus their shells) eat seedlings and plant leaves. Slimy trails on foliage or the ground are evidence of their presence, as are big, ragged holes in leaves and damage along leaf margins; rather than damage plants by chewing, slugs and snails eat with a radula, a toothed ribbon that draws food into their mouths. Most active at night, they rest during the day in moist, dark places. Slugs and snails undergo simple metamorphosis and occur throughout North America from spring until midfall.

Prime targets. Many, many flowers are attacked, and seedlings are especially vulnerable. Bellflowers (*Campanula* spp.), delphiniums, hostas, lilies, nasturtium (*Tropaeolum majus*), snapdragon (*Antirrhinum majus*), and sweet peas (*Lathyrus* spp.) are some of the prime targets.

Prevention. Surround plants with barriers, such as wood ashes, sand, eggshells, diatomaceous earth, or a commercial snail and slug product made from iron phosphate. Keep garden free of debris; remove mulches. Encourage birds, toads, fireflies, soldier beetles, and other natural predators. Avoid watering late in the day. Cultivate soil to expose adults and eggs to the sun.

Control. Handpick, especially at night. Set out traps—shallow containers of beer, wide boards, carpet pieces, stone pavers, or ceramic pots and grapefruit rinds turned upside-down—and empty them daily.

Spittle Bugs

Spittle bugs are easy to identify: Look for masses of saliva-like bubbly foam on plants. The foam hides and protects the larvae; the winged adults are variously colored depending on the species and damage flowers by piercing stems and sucking plant juices. Serious infestations may stunt plant growth and flower development, but spittle bugs are more unsightly than destructive.

Prime targets. Many flowers, including chrysanthemums and most daisylike flowers.

Prevention. Weed frequently; remove plant debris in fall.

Control. Spray with a strong stream of water to dislodge the spittle masses.

Thrips

Thrips, which undergo simple metamorphosis, are barely visible, 1/5-inch-long sucking insects that move in a flash and scrape leaves and flowers looking for food. Distorted and oddly colored flowers are a sign of thrips, as are discolored or sooty leaves. Thrips occur throughout North America from summer until fall, especially during hot weather.

Prime targets. Asters, beardtongues (*Penstemon* spp.), begonias, bellflowers (*Campanula* spp.), chrysanthemums, coreopsis, dahlias, foxgloves (*Digitalis* spp.), hardy geraniums (*Pelargonium* spp.), gladioli, irises, lilies, lupines (*Lupinus* spp.), orange coneflowers (*Rudbeckia* spp.), peonies, red-hot poker (*Kniphofia uvaria*), and Transvaal daisy (*Gerbera jamesonii*).

Prevention. Remove plant debris in fall. Mulch heavily to prevent adults from emerging from the ground in spring. Do not water plant foliage in the evening. Spread diatomaceous earth around plants. Encourage natural enemies—damsel bugs, lacewings, predatory mites, lady beetles, and nematodes. Cultivate around plants in autumn.

Control. Remove and destroy affected flowers. Wash thrips off with a strong spray of water. Install blue or yellow traps to catch adults. Spray plants with an insecticidal soap, horticultural oil, or neem; dust leaves with diatomaceous earth. For severe infestations, apply neem or pyrethrin.

Whiteflies

Whiteflies are tiny, winged insects that gather on leaf undersides. The white adults suck juice from plants, causing leaves to yellow, wilt, and drop, and their feeding stunts growth. They also excrete honeydew, which fosters the growth of black fungus on leaves. Brush plant leaves with your hand for the telltale cloud of white these insects produce when they are disturbed. Whiteflies undergo simple metamorphosis; they occur throughout North America in greenhouses and outdoors in warm, humid climates.

Prime targets. Many common flowers, including ageratums, asters, begonias, chrysanthemums, dahlias, hardy geraniums (*Pelargonium* spp.), petunias, salvias, and spider flower (*Cleome hassleriana*).

Prevention. Most whiteflies originate with nursery transplants: Check leaf undersides carefully before purchasing stock. Encourage natural predators such as parasitic wasps, lacewings, pirate bugs, and songbirds.

Control. Install yellow sticky traps. Spray plants with a hard stream of water. Spray with neem or a solution of insecticidal soap and isopropyl alcohol (concentrate on leaf undersides). Spray plants with horticultural oil or an insecticidal soap. Use pyrethrin or rotenone as a last resort.

Floating Row Covers. *Permeable to water, air, and sunlight, spunbond polypropylene covers can protect plants from many pests as well as from the cold. They are most useful in cutting gardens.*

Wireworms

Adult wireworms, which are brownish-black hard-shelled click beetles about ¾ inch long, overwinter in the soil, where they lay eggs. The larvae hatch within weeks but often don't pupate for a year or more. Wireworms are ¾ inch long, slender, and shiny reddish or yellowish brown; they do all their eating underground, burrowing into seeds, roots, and other underground organs. Adults feed on flowers and foliage but do little damage. Wireworms undergo complete metamorphosis; they occur throughout North America but are found most commonly in warm, damp soil.

Prime targets. Flowers with fleshy or tuberous roots, such as tuberous begonias, dahlias, and gladioli. Also asters, lobelias (*Lobelia* spp.), and phlox.

Prevention. Do not plant in areas where turf was recently growing. Cultivate soil often from summer until fall to disturb the larvae and expose them to birds and other natural enemies. Move susceptible plants to a different location.

Control. Make a trap from a stick attached to a piece of potato buried in the soil 1 inch deep; inspect the potato periodically and destroy any wireworms it attracts. Plant French marigolds (*Tagetes patula*), which may discourage wireworms. Apply beneficial nematodes.

COMMON DISEASES

Flowers are less susceptible to disease than are edible crops, but they aren't immune. Moreover, plant diseases—bacterial, fungal, or viral—often are difficult to identify. The list that follows includes some of the most common diseases that afflict garden flowers. Use the descriptions and "Prime targets" information to establish what your problem is, then use the "Prevention" and "Control" recommendations to cope with it.

One reminder: Preventing diseases is much easier than curing them. In many cases, infected plants should be removed and destroyed, not pruned or sprayed. (Destroy infected plant material—don't compost it.) Most ailments can be spread by contact, especially when plants are wet, so don't make things worse by working among wet plants. Wash your hands and disinfect tools before moving from infected plants to healthy ones.

Blights

Blight diseases, caused by both bacteria and fungi, occur throughout North American but are most troublesome in humid areas east of the Rockies. Southern blight, which is caused by the *Sclerotium rolfsii* fungus, is a particular problem in the southern United States. Blights, which also are ruinous in vegetable gardens, overwinter in plant debris and are spread by wind, water, and infected plants and seeds. Signs differ depending on the specific pathogen. Look for wilting and for lower leaves marked with brown and black blotches; eventually the leaves brown completely and die.

Prime targets. African daisies (*Arctotis* spp. and *Osteospermum* spp.), ageratums, anemones (*Anemone* spp.), begonias, bee balms (*Monarda* spp.), cannas, chrysanthemums, columbines (*Aquilegia* spp.), coneflowers (*Echinacea* spp.), daffodils, dahlias, delphiniums, hardy geraniums (*Geranium* spp.), gladioli, hollyhock (*Alcea rosea*), impatiens, irises, marigolds, pansies, peonies, salvias, snapdragon (*Antirrhinum majus*), sweet peas (*Lathyrus* spp.), tulips, and zinnias.

Prevention. Purchase resistant cultivars and certified seeds. Avoid working among wet plants; rotate location of susceptible flowers. Mulch plants to prevent splash. Spray plants with a fungicide before signs occur. Clean up and destroy plant debris in fall.

Control. Most blights cannot be cured; remove and destroy infected plants. Solarize the soil.

Damping-Off

Any flower seedling can fall victim, especially those grown indoors, to damping-off, a soilborne fungal disease. Damping-off can rot seeds before they germinate, but the most common sign is a flat of seedlings that have rotted at the soil line and collapsed—often overnight.

Prime targets. Seedlings growing indoors.

Prevention. Sterilize containers with a solution of 1 part chlorine bleach and 9 parts water and use a sterile, soil-free planting medium when sowing seeds indoors. Dust soil surfaces with milled sphagnum moss, and water from below. Make sure containers drain quickly and that seedlings are not crowded and have good air circulation. Supply seedlings with plenty of heat and light.

Control. Once seedlings have been affected they cannot be saved. Destroy them and the medium in which they were growing, and sterilize any containers.

Leaf Spot Diseases

Leaf spots are a symptom rather than a disease and can be caused by an assortment of bacteria and fungi. Whatever the cause, the typical result is brown or purple spots on leaf tops. Among the most common leaf spot diseases that occur throughout North America are anthracnose, which attacks flowers but is most destructive in the vegetable garden; bacterial leaf spot, which is most common in spring when conditions are warm and humid; cercospora leaf spot, a fungus disease that thrives in wet conditions; and peony leaf spot, a fungus that attacks when humidity is high. Leaf spot diseases overwinter in plant tissue, plant debris, and the soil; they are spread during the growing season by wind, water, and contact and through infected seed.

Prime targets. Many flowers are susceptible to leaf spot diseases, including asters, balloon flower (*Platycodon grandiflorus*), black-eyed Susan (*Rudbeckia*

PLAYING THE ODDS

No plant is 100 percent disease-free; but these flowers are among the least troubled by rots, mildews, wilts, and other infections, making them especially good plants for beds or borders that have been plagued by diseases in the previous seasons.

Cup-and-saucer vine (*Cobaea scandens*)

Daffodils (*Narcissus* cvs.)

Daylilies (*Hemerocallis* cvs.)

Feverfew (*Tanacetum parthenium*)

Gas plant (*Dictamnus albus*)

Globe thistles (*Echinops* spp.)

Glory-of-the-snow (*Chionodoxa* spp.)

Goat's beard (*Aruncus dioicus*)

Golden Marguerite (*Anthemis tinctoria*)

Leopard's banes (*Doronicum* spp.)

Lily-of-the-valley (*Convallaria majalis*)

Love-in-a-mist (*Nigella damascena*)

Mexican sunflower (*Tithonia rotundifolia*)

Pasque flower (*Pulsatilla vulgaris*)

Russian sage (*Perovskia atriplicifolia*)

Sea pink/common thrift (*America maritima*)

Siberian bugloss (*Brunnera macrophylla*)

Siberian iris (*Iris sibirica*)

Snowdrop (*Galanthus nivalis*)

Soapworts (*Saponaria* spp.)

Spider flower (*Cleome hassleriana*)

Snow-in-summer (*Cerastium tomentosum*)

Swan River daisy (*Brachyscome iberidifolia*)

Winter aconite (*Eranthis hyemalis*)

Avoiding Problems. Hemerocallis *cultivars are flowers for gardeners who want to sidestep diseases and pests. The handsome old timer 'Frans Hals' is a tough, long-blooming, bicolor daylily that flowers in midsummer.*

hirta), begonias, chrysanthemums, columbines (*Aquilegia* spp.), coral bells or heucheras (*Heuchera* spp.), coreopsis, cosmos, daffodils, daylilies, delphiniums, flowering tobaccos (*Nicotiana* spp.), hardy geraniums (*Geranium* spp.), hollyhock (*Alcea rosea*), hostas, hyacinths, impatiens, irises, lobelias (*Lobelia* spp.), marigolds, monkshoods (*Aconitum* spp.), nasturtium (*Tropaeolum majus*), pansies, peonies, phlox, salvias, snapdragon (*Antirrhinum majus*), sunflowers, violets, and zinnias.

Prevention. Choose resistant cultivars and buy certified seeds. Give plants good ventilation and drainage. Mulch garden beds to prevent water splash. Avoid working in the garden when plants are wet. Apply fungicidal soap, neem, or antitranspirant sprays early in the season, before the diseases appear. Rotate plant locations. Clean up the garden in autumn.

Control. Pick off and destroy infected leaves. Remove and destroy badly infected plants. Use a sulfur-based fungicide or a Bordeaux mix to slow severe infections.

Mildews

The two most troublesome mildews for home gardeners, downy and powdery, are fungal diseases caused by different classes of fungi. Signs of downy mildew—gray-white patches on leaf undersides and pale green or yellow splotches on leaf tops—usually appear first on older foliage. Powdery mildew, which is more common than downy, produces whitish patches on both sides of leaves. Mildews are rarely fatal but are unsightly. Most powdery mildews thrive in dry as well as humid conditions and in warm temperatures and low light; they are most common in late summer and fall. Downy mildews, which are most often found in greenhouses, flourish when humidity is high and temperatures are cool. All mildews are spread by wind, water, and contact; they occur throughout North America. Mildews overwinter on infected plants and plant debris.

Prime targets. The most common host plants for mildews are asters, bee balms (*Monarda* spp.), begonias, chrysanthemums, columbines (*Aquilegia* spp.), cosmos, dahlias, delphiniums, geum, or avens (*Geum* spp.), goldenrods (*Solidago* spp.), hollyhock (*Alcea rosea*), leopard's banes (*Doronicum* spp.), lungworts (*Pulmonaria* spp.), mallows (*Hibiscus* spp.), monkshoods (*Aconitum* spp.), mulleins (*Verbascum* spp.), orange coneflowers (*Rudbeckia* spp.), phlox, pot marigold (*Calendula officinalis*), salvias, snapdragon (*Antirrhinum majus*), spider flower (*Cleome hassleriana*), sunflowers, Transvaal daisy (*Gerbera jamesonii*), turtleheads (*Cleome* spp.), violets and pansies, yarrows (*Achillea* spp.), and zinnias.

Prevention. Plant resistant cultivars, and inspect new plants to ensure you're not introducing mildew to your garden. Do not crowd plants—allow for good air circulation and adequate sun. Don't overfeed plants, especially with high-nitrogen fertilizers. Prune stems on flowers with dense growth. Water in the morning; avoid wetting plant foliage. Don't work among plants when they are wet. Apply fungicidal soap, biocarbonate sprays, neem, or antitranspirant sprays early in the season, before the diseases appear. Clean up and destroy infected debris in fall.

Control. Remove and destroy affected leaves; remove and destroy badly infested plants.

Mold Diseases

Botrytis gray and white mold are two of the most common of the many mold strains that can damage flowers. All molds are fungal diseases and occur throughout North America. Gray mold, or botrytis blight, thrives in cool, wet weather and overwinters in the soil; it is spread by water and wind, and produces brown spots on foliage, bud blast, damaged flowers, and stem and crown rot. White mold fungi can persist in the soil for many years and attack plants above and below ground, especially in humid conditions. Telltale signs are wilting and white cottonlike growths at stem bases. (Sooty mold, a third common mold, grows on the honeydew excretions left by sucking insects, such as aphids, mealybugs,

and scale. Wash off foliage and treat plants with insecticidal soaps to control insect populations.)

Prime targets. Many flowers, including begonias, bleeding hearts (*Dicentra* spp.), China aster (*Callistephus chinensis*), chrysanthemums, coral bells or heucheras (*Heuchera* spp.), cosmos, daffodils, dahlias, delphiniums, forget-me-nots (*Myosotis* spp.), foxgloves (*Digitalis* spp.), hardy geraniums (*Geranium* spp.), hollyhock (*Alcea rosea*), impatiens, irises, marigolds, pansies, peonies, petunias, poppies (*Papaver* spp.), primroses (*Primula* spp.), Shasta daisy (*Leucanthemum* × *superbum*), snapdragon (*Antirrhinum majus*), sunflowers, sweet pea (*Lathyrus odorata*), Transvaal daisy (*Gerbera jamesonii*), and zinnias.

Prevention. Keep plants vigorous by giving them good light and ventilation, room to grow, and fertile, well-drained soil. Keep soil pH near neutral; apply mulch. Avoid overhead watering; reduce watering. Deadhead plants and clean up garden refuse in fall. Soil where molds have occurred should be cultivated deeply—inverting the soil will discourage the fungi from germinating. Apply fungicidal soap, biocarbonate sprays, neem, or antitranspirant sprays early in the season, before the diseases appear. Keep garden weeded; many common weeds are host plants.

Control. Spray target plants weekly with a sulfur or Bordeaux mix as soon as molds appear to slow their development. Remove infected buds, flowers, or leaves; always dig and destroy badly infected plants.

Rot Diseases

Bacterial and fungal rots, which attack plant stems, roots, and crowns, occur throughout North America, especially in regions with high humidity, and cause leaves to be stunted or discolored, stems and roots to develop brown or black lesions, and plants to wilt and die. Rots are spread by specific pathogens, but good culture can prevent most rot-disease outbreaks. Stem, root, and crown rot are most common. Stem and root rots typically begin with an injury to stems and roots; crown rot is encouraged by plant crowns being covered by too much soil or mulch, especially during winter months. Most rot diseases are soil- or waterborne, or they are introduced to the garden by infected plants.

Prime targets. Ageratums, asters, begonias, bleeding hearts (*Dicentra* spp.), chrysanthemums, columbines (*Aquilegia* spp.), cosmos, daffodils, dahlias, delphiniums, hardy geraniums (*Geranium* spp.), hostas, impatiens, irises, larkspur (*Consolida ajacis*), lungworts (*Pulmonaria* spp.), marigolds, pansies, peonies, petunias, phlox, salvias, snapdragon (*Antirrhinum majus*), strawflower (*Bracteantha bracteata*), sunflowers, tulips, verbenas, yarrows (*Achillea* spp.), and zinnias.

Prevention. Buy disease-free plants. Provide organically rich soil that drains well. Don't transplant seedlings until the soil has warmed. Keep soil pH close to neutral. Set plant crowns higher than the soil surface, and don't cover susceptible plants with mulch in winter. Cultivate around plants regularly but take care not to damage roots. Reduce watering. Plants that are overly succulent are more susceptible to attack—don't overfeed with high-nitrogen fertilizers.

Control. Remove and destroy affected plants.

Rust Diseases

Rust diseases are caused by fungi and are among the easiest ailments to identify. Look on leaves surfaces for small yellow spots and for orange, yellow, or brown powderlike spores; severe infections can cause leaves to shrivel or yellow. Rusts occur throughout North America but are most common in the West, especially in humid weather. Rust spores are spread by wind and rain.

Prime targets. Ageratums, asters, bachelor's button (*Centaurea cyanus*), bellflowers (*Campanula* spp.), cannas, chrysanthemums, fuchsias (*Fuchsia* spp.), hardy geraniums (*Geranium* spp.), hollyhock (*Alcea rosea*), lilies, pansies, pinks (*Dianthus* spp.), salvias, snapdragon (*Antirrhinum majus*), sunflowers, and yarrows (*Achillea* spp.).

Prevention. Grow resistant cultivars. Use disease-free cuttings and transplants. Provide plants with good light and air circulation. Increase the distance between plants to ensure ventilation; avoid wetting foliage and working among wet plants. Mulch plants to prevent water splash. Remove weeds, which may harbor rust fungi. Clean up plant debris in fall. Apply fungicidal soap, biocarbonate sprays, neem, or antitranspirant sprays early in the season, before the diseases appear.

Control. Remove infected leaves and stems to slow spread. Treat with sulfur or Bordeaux mix. Remove and destroy badly infected plants.

Viral Diseases

Plants with viral diseases like aster yellows, mosaic, and beet curly top, may have abnormally small or distorted leaves; yellowing leaves, yellow mottling, and yellow spots on leaves; leaf puckering and rolling; and stunted growth. Viruses are present throughout North America and are spread by insects—aphids, whiteflies, leafhoppers, and others—by gardeners and tools, by cigarette smoke, and by infected plants, bulbs, and seeds. Many viruses overwinter in plant debris.

Prime targets. Many annual and perennial flowers, including asters, balloon flower (*Platycodon grandiflorus*), bellflowers (*Campanula* spp.), cannas, centaureas (*Centaurea* spp.), China aster (*Callistephus chinensis*), chrysanthemums, cockscomb (*Celosia argentea*), coneflowers (*Echinacea* spp.), coreopsis, cosmos, crocuses, daffodils, dahlias, delphiniums, gladioli, hardy geraniums (*Geranium* spp.), hollyhock (*Alcea rosea*), irises, marigolds, nasturtium (*Tropaeolum majus*), peonies, petunias, pinks (*Dianthus* spp.), poppies, statice (*Limonium sinuatum*), sunflowers, tulips, and zinnias.

Prevention. Grow resistant cultivars. Plant disease-free seeds, cuttings, and transplants. Use row covers if practical to protect plants from insects. Remove chicory, dandelions, knotweed, lamb's-quarters, quack grass, plantain, ragweed, and other host weeds. Keep hands and tools clean. Remove and destroy plant debris in fall.

Control. Once plants are infected, there is no cure—remove and destroy them.

Wilts

Wilts are fungal or bacterial diseases that shut off the movement of water and nutrients in plants. The three most common wilts in flower gardens are verticillium wilt, a fungal disease that occurs through North America; bacterial wilt, which is most common in northern gardens east of the Rockies; and fusarium wilt, a fungus that plagues plants in warm, humid regions. All three cause leaves to turn yellow and wilt, with bottom leaves usually affected first. Verticillium wilt fungi overwinter in the soil and infect flowers through their roots, and it can also be spread through water and on tools, shoes, and hands. Bacterial wilt is spread by flea beetles, grasshoppers, cucumber beetles, and other pests, and it is as well soilborne. Fusarium wilt spores overwinter in the soil.

Home Remedies. *Spraying* Monarda *cultivars with a baking soda solution can help prevent powdery mildew and other fungal diseases that scourge many common garden flowers.*

Prime targets. Primarily perennial flowers (but some annuals, too), including asters, astilbes, bleeding hearts (*Dicentra* spp.), centaureas (*Centaurea* spp.), chrysanthemums, cosmos, dahlias, flaxes (*Linum* spp.), forget-me-nots (*Myosotis* spp.), fuchsias (*Fuchsia* spp.), impatiens, monkshoods (*Aconitum* spp.), peonies, pinks (*Dianthus* spp.), salvias, sunflowers, sweet alyssum (*Lobularia maritima*), sweet pea (*Lathyrus odorata*), and verbena.

Prevention. Use resistant cultivars when possible. Keep plants vigorous and healthy, especially during hot weather; don't allow soil pH to become too acid, lower than 6.0, or soil to dry out completely. Mulch soil to keep it cool. Solarize affected soil. For verticillium wilt, avoid growing flowers where vegetables or berries were growing without solarizing the soil. For bacterial wilt, use row covers if practicable to exclude carriers. Apply fungicidal soap, neem, bicarbonate sprays, or antitranspirant sprays early in the season, before the diseases appear.

Control. There are no safe, effective controls for wilts once plants are infected. Remove and destroy infected plants.

WILDLIFE

Changing the habitat so that your garden is less inviting to nuisance wildlife means eliminating one or more of their basic requirements: food, water, and shelter. Some modifications—such as sealing building foundations so that animals can't take up residence, moving pet food indoors, and removing plant debris and weeds—have few negative effects. But taking down the bird feeders that lure raccoons also means fewer finches, cardinals, and woodpeckers.

DEERPROOF, MAYBE

*I*f deer are stressed—without their usual food sources—they will eat anything. *Anything.* No plant is entirely safe, but these common flowers are usually Bambi's second choice, not his first.

Ageratum (*Ageratum houstonianum*)	Lily-of-the-valley (*Convallaria majalis*)	Spider flower (*Cleome hassleriana*)
Bergenias (*Bergenia* spp.)	Marigolds (*Tagetes* spp.)	Spotted deadnettle (*Lamium maculatum*)
Black snakeroot (*Cimicifuga racemosa*)	Monkshoods (*Aconitum* spp.)	Spurges (*Euphorbia* spp.)
Bleeding heart (*Dicentra spectabilis*)	Nasturtium (*Tropaeolum majus*)	Sweet alyssum (*Lobularia maritima*)
Columbines (*Aquilegia* spp.)	Orange coneflowers (*Rudbeckia* spp.)	Sweet woodruff (*Galium odoratum*)
Cosmos (*Cosmos* spp.)	Oriental poppy (*Papaver orientale*)	Thread-leaved coreopsis (*Coreopsis verticillata*)
Flowering tobaccos (*Nicotiana* spp.)	Purple coneflower (*Echinacea purpurea*)	Verbenas (*Verbena* spp.)
Forget-me-nots (*Myosotis* spp.)	Rock cresses (*Arabis* spp.)	Yarrows (*Achillea* spp.)
Foxgloves (*Digitalis* spp.)	Russian sage (*Perovskia atriplicifolia*)	Zinnias (*Zinnia* spp.)
Lavenders (*Lavandula* spp.)	Salvias/sages (*Salvia* spp.)	

Food for Bambi. *Annual sunflowers* (Helianthus annuus), *especially when still small, are as popular with deer as their seedheads will be with birds at the end of the season.*

If animals are devastating your garden—as deer do in parts of North America—you may need to rethink what flowers you grow. Tulips, lilies, and hostas are deer candy. Consider replacing them with less appetizing species.

Repelling. Repellents are available by the dozens, both commercial products and homegrown concoctions. Claims and promises are huge but results are mixed. For every gardener who swears by Shot-Gun Deer & Rabbit Repellent, bags of human hair, sprays made from putrefied eggs, urine (coyote, bobcat, fox, wolf, mountain lion, and more), or dried blood or by planting mint and garlic, there is a gardener who found these repellents to

be useless. If you want to try a commercial olfactory product—bulb experts Brent and Becky Heath recommend Ropel—make sure its ingredients are environmentally safe. And be prepared to reapply or replace it often.

Many gardeners insist that seeing and hearing, not smelling or tasting, are the keys to keeping wildlife out of beds and borders. Their gardens are bedecked with scarecrows, bells, whirligigs, blaring radios, pie plates, wind chimes, Mylar scare tapes, inflated owls and snakes, colored balloons, mirrors, and reflective sheets of aluminum foil. (The ultimate repellers are propane cannons, which produce an ear-shattering boom every few minutes; ceramic speakers, such as the Victor Mini Ultrasonic PestChasers, that produce "a non-repeating continuous concert of sound . . . a three-octave spectrum of high-low sound complexity that prevents rodent conditioning"; and a smart scarecrow water sprinkler that is triggered by a motion sensor and "fires up to 5,000 times on one 9-volt battery.")

Natural Security. *Spider flower* (Cleome hassleriana) *has spiny stems that makes it pretty close to deerproof. When food is scarce, however, no flower is safe from deer.*

Most visual and aural devices are more at home in the vegetable than the flower garden. Moreover, animals are canny and quickly catch on to movements and sounds. Even if you're prepared to move the devices daily, these repellants usually fall short of adequate.

Fencing. Fences are the best and most permanent protection against many wild animals, such as rabbits and deer, and the best fences are electric. Alas, electric fences aren't suitable for most ornamental gardens, unless they surround an entire property. If your animal problems are severe enough to require jolting garden raiders into going elsewhere, choose a system with a "low impedance" control, which sends current pulses that last only a few ten-thousandths of a second. That's not enough to start a fire if the line is touching dry debris, but it's plenty enough to discourage animals.

Fences can be handsome assets to any garden. Home-building companies offer prefab wood models that you can install—everything from stockade to picket—or you can start from scratch. Squirrels and other agile climbers won't be deterred, but a fence should slow if not eliminate rabbits, raccoons, skunks, deer, and the neighbors' dogs. Choose a fence with closely spaced pales so that small animals can't slip in. For deer, the fence must be at least 8 feet high; to discourage burrowing animals, such as groundhogs, dig a 1-foot-deep trench at the base of the fence and line it with chicken wire or hardware cloth.

Trapping. Trapping is normally a last resort, and it's a hodgepodge solution at best. On the bright side, trapping is safer than poisoning and shooting. It does remove animals from your garden. But traps that kill are distasteful, especially when the prey is cuddly and cute or larger than a vole. Using a live trap is an alternative to dispatching animals, but it isn't without its liabilities. By moving a pest elsewhere, you're creating problems for someone else. Some states and communities have prohibitions against relocating animals, so check with a local wildlife officer before shopping for a trap.

Understand, too, that live trapping may not be all that humane. Research now suggests that many animals are unable to adapt after having been trapped and relocated, and they quickly die or are killed. If you still want to use a live trap, handle your captives with care. Most wildlife that loiter around yards and gardens are susceptible to zoonoses, diseases like rabies that can be transmitted from animals to people. Always wear gloves. To reduce stress on the captive, cover the trap with a cloth and move it gently.

So that your captives don't find their way back to your garden—many wild animals are wide-ranging—choose a new home that is far enough away from yours. Experts recommend 10 miles for raccoons, 5 miles for skunks and squirrels, and 3 miles for rabbits, woodchucks, small mammals, and rodents.

If you don't have the stomach for trapping wildlife, there are professionals who can do the deed for you. Look under "Animal Removal" in the Yellow Pages.

UNBOTHERED BULBS

This list from the experts at the Netherlands Flower Bulb Information Center contains their recommendations for bulbous flowers "high on beauty and low on pest-appeal." Nothing is guaranteed in the garden, but these flowers have a good chance of surviving, even where squirrels, deer, and other wildlife are grazing.

Autumn crocuses/meadow saffrons
  (*Colchicum* spp.)

Camassias/quamashes (*Camassia* spp.)

Crocuses (*Crocus* spp.)

Crown imperial (*Fritillaria imperialis*)

Daffodils (*Narcissus* cvs.)

Glory-of-the-snow (*Chionodoxa luciliae*)

Grape hyacinths (*Muscari* spp.)

Hyacinth (*Hyacinthus orientalis*)

Snowdrop (*Galanthus nivalis*)

Snowflakes (*Leucojum* spp.)

Spanish bluebell (*Hyacinthoides hispanica*)

Spring star flower (*Ipheion uniflorum*)

Squills (*Scilla* spp.)

Stars-of-Bethlehem (*Ornithogalum* spp.)

Winter aconite (*Eranthis hyemalis*)

A River Runs through It. *Not that lucky? Create a water garden. Even a small water feature, a modest pool, or two or three aquatic plants growing in a container placed on a deck or patio can add new delights to any home landscape.*

CHAPTER EIGHT

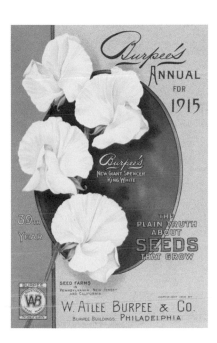

Being Single-Minded: Creating Gardens of Special Delight

A garden is like those pernicious machineries we read of, every month, in the newspapers, which catch a man's coat-skirt or his hand, and draw in his arm, his leg, and his whole body to irresistible destruction.

Ralph Waldo Emerson, *Conduct of Life: Wealth*, 1860

SOME OF THE MOST IRRESISTIBLE GARDENS ARE those created with one purpose in mind. A garden filled only with fragrant flowers, for example, or one filled with flowers that are

177

still beautiful after the sun sets. A garden for attracting wildlife or for enchanting children. A garden in which all the flowers are edible or one filled with herbs that have beautiful flowers. A water garden. A cutting garden, one planted to bring indoors. Even a one-note garden filled with nothing but daylilies. Or nothing but yellow flowers. The possibilities are unlimited. What follows are a few suggestions for getting started. Remember that the lists are just a place to begin—hundreds of other plants could be added if there were room. You'll have the same problem in the garden—how to find room for everything you want to grow.

Marigolds (*Tagetes* spp.)

Meadow rues (*Thalictrum* spp.)

Narrow-leaved zinnia/Mexican zinnia (*Zinnia haageana*)

Orange coneflowers (*Rudbeckia* spp.)

Phlox (*Phlox* spp.)

Purple coneflower (*Echinacea purpurea*)

Sea pink/common thrift (*Armeria maritima*)

Shasta daisy (*Leucanthemum* × *superbum*)

Sweet alyssum (*Lobularia maritima*)

Yarrows (*Achillea* spp.)

A Butterfly Garden

Giant swallowtail. Monarch. Grayling. Buckeye. Great spangled fritillary. Mourning cloak. Painted lady. Red admiral. Spring azure. West Coast lady. Who wouldn't want these butterflies in his or her garden, if only for their evocative names? Flowers will bring these and more, especially fragrant species with clustered blossoms that provide a place for butterflies to perch. Include some native flowers; a local entomologist or butterfly organization will have suggestions for specific plants for the butterfly species endemic to your region. You can guess that butterfly weed is a good choice. So are these flowers, all appealing to a wide range of butterflies.

Asters (*Aster* spp.)

Astilbes (*Astilbe* cvs.)

Basket-of-gold (*Aurinia saxatilis*)

Bee balms (*Monarda* spp.)

Blanket flower (*Gaillardia* × *grandiflora*)

Butterfly weed (*Asclepias tuberosa*)

Candytuft (*Iberis sempervirens*)

Coreopsis (*Coreopsis* spp.)

Cosmos (*Cosmos* spp.)

Cottage pinks (*Dianthus plumarius*)

Gayfeathers (*Liatris* spp.)

Heliotrope (*Heliotropium arborescens*)

Hollyhock (*Alcea rosea*)

Joe-Pye weeds (*Eupatorium* spp.)

Lavenders (*Lavandula* spp.)

A Child's Garden

Think quick, think spectacular, think unusual. The attention span of young children is short, and their gardens need to be filled with plants that appeal to more than sight—to sound, smell, taste, and touch. Grow a few annuals from seeds, such as sunflowers, but buy some annual and perennial plants to reduce the wait. Consider creating a "secret hideout" by covering a frame with a mix of flowering vines (see "Climb High," page 49). Add a couple of food plants to the flower garden, such as cherry tomatoes and peas, so that your children can graze. Or plant a pumpkin for Halloween carving. Be sure to exclude any species, however interesting, that have toxic parts, such as bleeding heart (*Dicentra spectabilis*) or Jack-in-the-pulpit (*Arisaema triphylla*). A partial list of common plants that are potentially dangerous can be found at www.akca.org/library/poison.htm.

Bee balm (*Monarda didyma*); for its fragrance and for attracting hummingbirds

Canterbury bells (*Campanula medium*); for its bell shape

Cockscomb (*Celosia argentea* Cristata Group); for its fuzzy, rooster-comb flowers

Lady's mantle (*Alchemilla mollis*); for its ability to turn water drops into diamonds

Lamb's ear (*Stachys byzantina*); for its furry foliage

Love-in-a-mist (*Nigella damascena*); for its rattling seed heads

GROWING GARDENERS

*C*hildren are like their elders when it comes to gardening: Enthusiasm is unbounded in spring, and it wanes when nothing is going on and weeds and pests are thick. Moreover, children are not adults. Their initial excitement is greater, their boredom quicker to develop and longer to last, and their ability to see ahead more limited. In a nutshell, don't preach, teach; don't show, share. Above all, remember that gardening is not like learning to cross the street safely. It is not mandatory, no matter how much *you* love it.

Allow children to have their own space. It need not be large—4 × 4 feet is plenty for a small child—but locate it centrally. Don't exile children to the completely shaded back of the yard where nothing will grow, including their interest.

Share your own garden. Children delight in working side by side, but they are not fools. They will want to do the same jobs you enjoy—planting, watering, harvesting—and will be as impatient with pulling weeds as you are.

Don't grade on tidiness. Harping about weeds in the garden will kill children's interest before the bindweed climbs and smothers the sunflowers.

Be inventive. Plant a red-flower garden, a picking garden, or re-create Mr. McGregor's garden. Design and make fancy plant labels. Put up a scarecrow.

A Place of Their Own. *Give children their own plot for growing flowers and edibles if you want to encourage a new generation of gardeners. And don't forget: It's their garden.*

Money plant (*Lunaria annua*); for its coinlike seedpods

Nasturtium (*Tropaeolum majus*); for its spicy flavor

Pansy (*Viola × wittrockiana*); for its cheerful faces

Shasta daisy (*Leucanthemum × superbum*); for determining if you are loved

Snapdragon (*Antirrhinum majus*); for its snapping mouths

Sunflower (*Helianthus annuus*); for its size and seeds

Touch-me-nots/jewelweeds (*Impatiens capensis, I. pallida*); for their exploding seedpods

A Fragrant Garden

"A garden full of sweet odours is a garden full of charm," American writer Louise Beebe Wilder wrote in *The Fragrant Garden* (1932). "Fragrance speaks to many to whom color and form say little." Color and form (and size) have been the passions of flower breeders for the last 50 years, resulting in sweet peas (*Lathyrus odoratus*) with no fragrance and other misdeeds—but recently fragrance has reemerged as a worthy breeding goal. This list includes flowers with fragrant blossoms. Don't forget that there are many plants, such as Palm Springs daisy (*Cladanthus arabicus*), scented geraniums (*Geranium* spp.), and bee balms (*Monarda* spp.), that have scent in their foliage rather than their flowers. And check the fine print—or sniff before you buy—for not all cultivars that *ought* to be fragrant *are* fragrant.

> August lily (*Hosta plantaginea*)
> Bearded irises (*Iris* Bearded Hybrids)
> Dame's rocket/sweet rocket (*Hesperis matronalis*)
> Garden phlox (*Phlox paniculata*)
> Evening primroses (*Oenothera deltoides, O. pallida*)
> Flowering tobaccos (*Nicotiana alata, N. sylvestris*)
> Four-o'clock (*Mirabilis jalapa*)
> Heliotrope (*Heliotropium arborescens*)
> Hyacinth (*Hyacinthus orientalis*)
> Lily-of-the-valley (*Convallaria majalis*)
> Mignonette (*Reseda odorata*)
> Moonflower (*Ipomoea alba*)
> Oriental lilies (*Lilium* Oriental Hybrids); also many Trumpet and Aurelian Hybrids
> Peonies (*Paeonia* cvs.)
> Petunia (*Petunia* × *hybrida*)
> Pinks (*Dianthus* spp.)
> Poet's narcissus (*Narcissus poeticus*)
> Regal lily (*Lilium regale*)
> Stocks (*Matthiola longipetala, M. incana*)
> Sweet alyssum (*Lobularia maritima*)
> Sweet pea (*Lathyrus odoratus*)
> Sweet violet (*Viola odorata*)
> Sweet William (*Dianthus barbatus*)
> Wallflower (*Erysimum cheiri*)

An Under-a-Tree Garden

Mature oaks, maples, beeches, ornamental crabs, and other large trees are valuable additions to any home landscape. Rather than remove them in order to grow flowers, consider *underplanting* them (see "Underplanting," page 107). Removing a few low limbs will let in more sun and adding compost and

The Arcadian Garden. *Shade-loving, shallow-rooted species, such as these heart-leaved bergenias* (Berginia cordifolia), *are ideal residents for a spot under the trees. Flowers set under trees may need extra fertilizer and water.*

other organic matter will improve the soil. Be ready to water and feed this garden regularly, as the flowers' roots must compete with the trees'. Don't remove or completely cover any surface tree roots, and don't raise the grade under the tree more than 4 inches. Choose flowers that are shallow-rooted and shade and drought tolerant. In addition to the flowers listed, good candidates for this site are small spring bulbs that flower before tree leaves appear, such as glory-of-the-snow (*Chionodoxa* spp.), species tulips, crocuses, grape hyacinths (*Muscari* spp.), and winter aconite (*Eranthis hyemalis*).

Browallias/bush violets (*Browallia* spp.)
Bugleweeds (*Ajuga* spp.) 'Bronze Beauty',
  'Burgundy Glow', 'Silver Beauty', and others

Celandine poppy (*Stylophorum diphyllum*)

Columbines (*Aquilegia formosa, A. canadensis*)

Coral bells/heucheras (*Heuchera* cvs.)

Epimediums/barrenworts (*Epimedium* spp.)

Greater celandine (*Chelidonium majus*)

Green-and-gold/golden star (*Chrysogonum virginicum*)

Hardy geraniums, or cranesbills (*Geranium macrorrhizum, G. × oxonianum, G. phaeum*)

Hellebores (*Helleborus* spp.)

Hostas (*Hosta* cvs.) 'Baby Bunting', 'Cameo', 'Green Eyes', 'Pandora's Box', and others

Lily-of-the-valley (*Convallaria majus*)

Lilyturfs (*Liriope* spp.)

Periwinkles/myrtle (*Vinca* spp.)

Solomon's seals (*Polygonatum* spp.)

Spotted deadnettles (*Lamium maculatum*) 'Beacon Silver', 'White Nancy', and others

Sweet woodruff (*Galium odoratum*)

Valerian (*Centranthus ruber*)

Wild gingers (*Asarum* spp.)

Wood aster (*Aster divaricatus*)

An Edible Garden

Flowers are for more than looking and smelling: they're also for eating or, at least, gracing the plate. Not all flowers, however: Daffodils, foxgloves (*Digitalis* spp.), and morning glory (*Ipomoea purpurea*) are three flowers that don't belong on the dinner table. Never munch on a blossom unless you know for sure that it's edible—and that it hasn't been sprayed with insecticides. That said, here are some blooms that are safe to use at mealtime. In addition to the flowers listed below, herb blooms also make tasty additions to dinner, so consider serving chives, garlics, and garlic chives (*Allium schoenoprasum, A. sativum, A. tuberosum*), basil (*Ocimum basilicum*), mints (*Mentha* spp.), Roman chamomile (*Chamaemelum nobile*), rosemary (*Rosmarinus officinalis*), sage (*Salvia officinalis*), and dill (*Anethum graveolens*).

Anise hyssop (*Agastache foeniculum*)

Bee balm (*Monarda didyma*)

Daylilies (*Hemerocallis* cvs.)

English daisy (*Bellis perennis*)

Marigolds (*Tagetes* spp.)

Nasturtium (*Tropaeolum majus*)

Pinks (*Dianthus* spp.)

Pot marigold (*Calendula officinalis*)

Scarlet runner bean (*Phaseolus coccineus*)

Sweet woodruff (*Galium odoratum*)

Violets/pansies/Johnny-jump-ups (*Viola* spp.)

A Hillside Garden

Growing flowers on a hillside, even a small one, is an exciting opportunity: No garden is more visible than one on a slope. The ultimate in hillside gardening—and hillside urban planning—is the city of Macchu Picchu in Peru, which is built on an Andean mountainside that descends some 2,000 feet. Home gardeners don't face quite those challenges, but growing flowers on a hillside, even a small one, is still a challenge. Depending on the grade, it's not always easy to tend a hillside garden, so good soil preparation is essential. Add generous amounts of organic matter and mulch to discourage erosion. Avoid very tall plants, which will fall over; instead, choose either *ground covers*, low-growing plants that spread, or plants that grow in clumps and have good root systems. Shaded slopes might be covered with a collection of hostas and ferns or by shade-tolerant ground covers, such as bugleweeds (*Ajuga* spp.), forget-me-not (*Myosotis sylvatica*), lesser periwinkle (*Vinca minor*), lily-of-the-valley (*Convallaria majalis*), sweet woodruff (*Galium odoratum*), spotted deadnettle (*Lamium maculatum*), and others. This list is for a sunny slope. Start here, then add annuals for more color.

California poppy (*Eschscholzia californica*)

Catmints (*Nepeta* spp.)

Cypress spurge (*Euphorbia cyparissias*)

Daffodils (*Narcissus* cvs.)

Daylilies (*Hemerocallis* cvs.)

Golden Marguerite (*Anthemis tinctoria*) 'Moonlight'

Goldenrod (*Solidago sphacelata*) 'Golden Fleece'

Hardy geraniums/cranesbills (*Geranium* spp.)

Harebell speedwell (*Veronica prostrata*)

Native Delights. *You don't have to live in California to grow its official flower, the California poppy (Eschscholzia californica). Major-league sun lovers, the colorful blooms demand bright light: They close at sundown and refuse to open on cloudy days.*

Lavenders (*Lavandula* spp.)
Lilyturfs (*Liriope* spp.)
Lupines (*Lupinus* spp.)
Moss phlox (*Phlox subulata*)
Sedums/stonecrops (*Sedum* spp.)
Showy evening primrose (*Oenothera speciosa*)
Siberian iris (*Iris sibirica*)
Thread-leaved coreopsis (*Coreopsis verticillata*)
Valerian (*Centranthus ruber*)

Petunia (*Petunia* × *hybrida*)
Pot marigold (*Calendula officinalis*)
Scarlet sage (*Salvia splendens*)
Snapdragon (*Antirrhinum majus*)
Spider flower (*Cleome hassleriana*)
Swan River daisy (*Brachyscome iberidifolia*)
Sweet alyssum (*Lobularia maritima*)
Wax begonia (*Begonia semperflorens*)
Zinnia (*Zinnia elegans*)
Zonal geranium (*Pelargonium* × *hortorum*)

A Season-Long Garden

No one denies the merits of perennials, but if you're looking for flowers that bloom from spring until fall—the botanical equivalents of the Energizer bunny—plant annuals. The undisputed champion of staying in flower is impatiens, which are blooming in spring when you buy them at the garden center and are still blooming when the first frost hits. Zonal geraniums (*Pelargonium* × *hortorum*) run a close second, and there are superb new geranium cultivars, such as 'Crystal Palace Gem', 'Happy Thought', and 'Vancouver Centennial', that have leaves nearly as colorful as their blossoms. Be sure to feed and deadhead annuals to keep the flowers coming. Horticultural snobs may call these flowers "common," but remember that they are common because they are wonderfully reliable.

Ageratum (*Ageratum houstonianum*)
Annual phlox (*Phlox drummondii*)
Blanket flower (*Gaillardia pulchella*)
Browallias (*Browallia* spp.)
Cosmos (*Cosmos bipinnatus, C. sulphureus*)
Fibrous begonia (*Begonia semperflorens*)
Garden verbena (*Verbena* × *hybrida*)
Gomphrena/globe amaranth (*Gomphrena globosa*)
Impatiens (*Impatiens walleriana*)
Marigolds (*Tagetes* spp.)
Mealy-cup sage (*Salvia farinacea*)
Morning glories (*Ipomoea* spp.)
Narrow-leaved zinnia/Mexican zinnia (*Zinnia haageana*)
New Guinea impatiens (*Impatiens*) New Guinea Hybrids

A Path Garden

Paths and walkways provide a chance to create small border gardens filled with low-growing perennials and annuals. Most plants on this list have pretty flowers, and all have interesting foliage that remains attractive from spring though autumn. Included among the flowers are several plants, with aromatic foliage, that are more at home in herb gardens than in perennial borders. Brushing against fragrant plants gives another dimension to a walkway, one so appealing that you may find yourself adding more herbs to your path garden.

Artemisias (*Artemisia* spp.) 'Powis Castle'; silvermound artemisia (*A. schmidtiana* 'Nana')
Astilbes (*Astilbe* cvs.)
Bergenias (*Bergenia* spp.)
Bloody cranesbill (*Geranium sanguineum*)
Candytuft (*Iberis sempervirens*)
Catmints (*Nepeta* spp.)
Coral bells/heucheras (*Heuchera* cvs.)
Heron's bills (*Erodium* spp.)
Hybrid sage (*Salvia* × *sylvestris*)
Lady's mantles (*Alchemilla* spp.)
Lamb's ear (*Stachys byzantina*)
Lavenders (*Lavandula* spp.)
Lesser periwinkle (*Vinca minor*)
Phlox (*Phlox subulata, P. divaricata*)
Pinks (*Dianthus deltoides, D. gratianopolitanus, D. plumarius*)
Plumbago/leadwort (*Ceratostigma plumbaginoides*)

Sea pink/common thrift (*Armeria maritima*)

Spotted deadnettle (*Lamium maculatum*)

Strawberry begonia (*Saxifraga stolonifera*)

Sweet woodruff (*Galium odoratum*)

Thymes (*Thymus* spp.)

An Herb Garden for Flower Lovers

The word *herb* comes from "herbaceous," and it is often used to refer to plants that have culinary or medicinal uses. The blooms of many herbs are non-descript, but some have stunning flowers—so lovely, in fact, that they are completely at home in flower gardens. Grow these plants and your flower bed will also be an herb garden.

All heal/valerian (*Valeriana officinalis*)

Anise hyssop (*Agastache foeniculum*)

Bee balm (*Monarda didyma*)

Borage (*Borago officinalis*)

Chives (*Allium schoenoprasum*)

Dill (*Anethum graveolens*)

Elecampane (*Inula helenium*)

Feverfew (*Tanacetum parthenium*)

Hyssop (*Hyssopus officinalis*)

Lavenders (*Lavandula* spp.)

Marsh mallow (*Althaea officinalis*)

Meadowsweet (*Filipendula ulmaria*)

Nasturtium (*Tropaeolum majus*)

Flowers and then Some. *Many herbs are first-class additions to ornamental beds and borders. Borage (*Borago officinalis*) is presumed to "revive the hypochrondriac and cheer the hard student." Even better, it adds blue flowers to the garden.*

Pot marigold (*Calendula officinalis*)
Roman chamomile (*Chamaemelum nobile*)
Rue (*Ruta graveolens*)
Sage (*Salvia officinalis*)
Scented geraniums (*Pelargonium* spp.)
Sweet woodruff (*Galium odoratum*)
Tansy (*Tanacetum vulgare*)
Violet (*Viola odorata*)
Yarrow (*Achillea millefolium*)

An Old-Fashioned Garden

Gardeners wanting to recreate their great-grandmother's garden have lots of choices. Interest in old-fashioned, or *heirloom*, flowers has been growing for the past two decades, so much so that there now are nurseries selling nothing but plants that have been around for at least 50 years. Old House Gardens is the mother lode for bulbous species, offering daffodil cultivars dating from before 1600 and much more. A good source of both seeds and plants for annual, biennial, and perennial heirlooms is Perennial Pleasures Nursery. (For more sources of heirloom seeds and plants, see Appendix, page 457; for a list of cultivated heirloom plants, see "Heirloom Beauties," page 27.) The backbones of our ancestors' gardens, however, were "unimproved" species. These are some of their favorites.

Batchelor's button (*Centaurea cyanus*)
Bee balm (*Monarda didyma*)
Bellflowers (*Campanula* spp.)
Bleeding heart (*Dicentra spectabilis*)
Bouncing Bet (*Saponaria officinalis*)
China aster (*Callistephus chinensis*)
Columbines (*Aquilegia* spp.)
English primrose (*Primula vulgaris*)
Feverfew (*Tanacetum parthenium*)
Forget-me-nots (*Myosotis* spp.)
Foxglove (*Dicentra purpurea*)
Garden phlox (*Phlox paniculata*)
Gas plant (*Dictamnus albus*)
Golden Marguerite (*Anthemis tinctoria*)
Hollyhock (*Alcea rosea*)
Jacob's ladder (*Polemonium caeruleum*)

Lady's mantle (*Alchemilla mollis*)
Lemon lily (*Hemerocallis lilioasphodelus*)
Lily-of-the-valley (*Convallaria majalis*)
Love-lies-bleeding (*Amaranthus caudatus*)
Maltese cross (*Lychnis chalcedonica*)
Marsh mallow (*Althaea officinalis*)
Morning glory (*Ipomoea purpurea*)
Nasturtium (*Tropaeolum majus*)
Oriental poppy (*Papaver orientale*)
Peonies (*Paeonia* cvs.)
Pinks (*Dianthus* spp.)
Pot marigold (*Calendula officinalis*)
Sea pink/common thrift (*Armeria maritima*)
Snowdrops (*Galanthus nivalis*)
Sweet violet (*Viola odorata*)

An Everlasting Garden

Almost any flower or leaf is a candidate for a dried arrangement, but the best choices are referred to as *everlastings*, plants with little moisture in their blooms that hold their color well when dried. Flowers intended for drying should be picked in the morning *after* the dew has dried and when they are only partially open, or immature. Air-drying is the easiest technique: Gather flowers in small bunches and hang them upside down in a warm, dark location. But there are other techniques, all of which are detailed in *Dried Flowers: A Complete Guide* by Lindy Bird (2003). Or enter "how to dry flowers" in www.google.com and peruse the 12,700,000 hits that are supplied in only 0.12 seconds.

Agapanthus/African lily (*Agapanthus campanulatus*)
Ageratum (*Ageratum houstonianum*)
Baby's breath (*Gypsophila paniculata*)
Bells-of-Ireland (*Molucella laevis*)
Candytuft (*Iberis sempervirens*)
Celosia (*Celosia argentea*)
Common stock (*Matthiola incana*)
Feverfew (*Tanacetum parthenium*)
Globe thistles (*Echinops* spp.)
Gomphrena/globe amaranth (*Gomphrena globosa*)
Immortelle (*Xeranthemum annuum*)

Flower Garden Harvest. *Drying flowers that hold their color, like these blue salvias (Salvia spp.), globe amaranth (Gomphrena globosa), tricolor sage (Salvia officinalis 'Tricolor'), and celosia (Celosia argentea) do is straightforward and easy.*

Larkspur (*Consolida ajacis*)
Lavenders (*Lavandula* spp.)
Love-in-a-mist (*Nigella damascena*)
Mealy-cup sage (*Salvia farinacea*)
Money plant (*Lunaria annua*)
Pearly everlasting (*Anaphalis margaritacea*)
Pincushion flower (*Scabiosa stellata*)
Sea hollies (*Eryngium* spp.)
Sea pink/common thrift (*Armeria maritima*)
Snow-on-the-mountain (*Euphorbia marginata*)
Statice (*Limonium sinuatum*)
Strawflower (*Bracteantha bracteata*)
Winged everlasting (*Ammobium alatum*)
Yarrows (*Achillea* spp.)
Zinnia (*Zinnia elegans*)

A Woodland Garden

The essence of a woodland garden is its graceful naturalness. Native plants are the typical residents, and many of the plants listed here are native. For information on creating a purely native plant garden, a specialty that's outside the scope of this book, consult Vicki Ferreniea's *Wildflowers in Your Garden* (1991) and *The New England Wild Flower Society Guide to Growing and Propagating Wildflowers of the United States and Canada* (2000) by Bill Cullina. If you have a shady corner, try planting any of these informal plants. Don't forget that ferns are good additions. And remember, too, that even these shade-tolerant plants need some sun, preferably in the morning, or bright, dappled all-day shade.

Astilbes (*Astilbe* cvs.)

Bergenias (*Bergenia* spp.)

Columbines (*Aquilegia* spp.)

Coral bells/heucheras (*Heuchera* cvs.)

Corydalis (*Corydalis* spp.)

Epimediums/barrenworts (*Epimedium* spp.)

Fairy bells (*Disporum* spp.)

Foam flowers (*Tiarella* spp.)

Foxgloves (*Digitalis* spp.)

Fringed bleeding heart (*Dicentra eximia*)

Hostas (*Hosta* cvs.)

Lady's mantle (*Alchemilla mollis*)

Lenten rose (*Helleborus* × *hybridus*)

Ligularias (*Ligularia* spp.)

Lily-of-the-valley (*Convallaria majalis*)

Lungworts (*Pulmonaria* spp.)

Phlox (*Phlox divaricata, P. stolonifera*)

Primroses (*Primula* spp.)

Rodgersias (*Rodgersia* spp.)

Snakeroots (*Cimicifuga* spp.)

Solomon's seals (*Polygonatum* spp.)

Sweet woodruff (*Galium odoratum*)

Toad lilies (*Tricyrtis* spp.)

Violets (*Viola* spp.)

Yellow wax bells (*Kirengeshoma palmata*)

A Hanging Garden

A lush basket of flowers suspended overhead may not be one of the Seven Wonders of the World, but it's darn nice. (And it turns out that the Hanging Gardens of Babylon weren't "hanging" in the modern sense of the word, but were an overhanging series of terraces.) All the flowers on this list—a mix of annuals and tender perennials—have a cascading form, perfect for hanging baskets (and window boxes), and all can tolerate the cramped quarters that containers offer. Because there are lots of roots using the same soil, hanging baskets should be fed every few weeks with a balanced, liquid fertilizer. Baskets dry out quickly, especially those in sunny sites, so check the soil often.

To slow drying, use a coir or sphagnum peat moss–lined container rather than a plastic one. To encourage branching, pinch back plants that grow too enthusiastically.

Baby blue-eyes (*Nemophila menziesii* var. *atomaria*) 'Snowstorm'

Chilean bellflower (*Nolana paradoxa*)

Dwarf morning glory (*Convolvulus tricolor*) Enchantment Series

Edging lobelia (*Lobelia erinus*) Cascade Series

Garden verbena (*Verbena* × *hybrida*) 'Quartz Waterfall Mix'

Heliotrope (*Heliotropium arborescens*)

Impatiens (*Impatiens walleriana*) Mosaic Series, Super Elfin Series

Ivy-leaved geranium (*Pelargonium peltatum*) Cascade Series, Minicascade Series

Madagascar periwinkle (*Catharanthus roseus*) 'Mediterranean Lilac'

Monkey flower (*Mimulus* × *hybridus*)

Moss rose (*Portulaca grandiflora*)

Narrow-leaved zinnia/Mexican zinnia (*Zinnia haageana*) Star Series

Nasturtium (*Tropaeolum majus*) 'Tom Thumb Mixed'

Petunia (*Petunia* × *hybrida*) Wave series, Cascade Series

Snapdragon (*Antirrhinum majus*) 'Floral Showers', 'Lampion Mix"

Swan River daisy (*Brachyscome iberidifolia*) Splendor Series

Sweet alyssum (*Lobularia maritima*)

Tuberous begonia (*Begonia* × *tuberhybrida*) pendant forms including Dragon Wings Series, Illumination Series

Tweedia/Southern star (*Tweedia caerulea*)

Twining snapdragons (*Maurandya* spp.)

A Hummingbird Garden

Hummingbirds in the garden are a treat whether you live east of the Mississippi River, where only one hummingbird is native, or in the West, where there are dozens of species. One or many, you can guarantee that these avian jewels will come to your house by planting some of the 150 flowers that supply the nectar they seek. Many of these plants have the typical "hummer qualities," including tube-shaped red blooms spaced far enough apart to leave room for the birds' whirling wings. Be a good citizen and add a hummingbird feeder to your garden for times when flowers are scarce and install a water source for dry days. These common flowers are a good place to begin.

Beard-tongues (*Penstemon* spp.)

Bee balms (*Monarda* spp.)

Cannas (*Canna* cvs.)

Cardinal flower (*Lobelia cardinalis*)

Columbines (*Aquilegia* spp.)

Coral bells (*Heuchera* × *brizoides*, *H. sanguinea*)

Cosmos (*Cosmos* spp.)

Cypress vine (*Ipomoea quamoclit*)

Daylilies (*Hemerocallis* cvs.)

Firecracker plant (*Cuphea* × *purpurea*)

Flowering tobacco (*Nicotiana alata*)

Four-o'clock (*Mirabilis jalapa*)

Foxglove (*Digitalis purpurea*)

Fuchsias (*Fuchsia* cvs.)

Geraniums (*Pelargonium* spp.)

Gladioli (*Gladiolus* cvs.)

Hollyhock (*Alcea rosea*)

Lilies (*Lilium* cvs.)

Monkey flowers (*Mimulus* spp.)

Mountain garland (*Clarkia unguiculata*)

Salvias/sages (*Salvia* spp.)

Scarlet runner bean (*Phaseolus coccineus*)

Spider flower (*Cleome hassleriana*)

Torch lily (*Kniphofia uvaria*)

A Perennial Cutting Garden

Every perennial is worth bringing indoors, even daylilies, which have individual flowers that last only a day (new buds continue to open after the stem is cut). Some perennials, such as those listed here, excel in the vase because they remain fresh for many days, or they have long stems, rich fragrance, or other irresistible qualities. Most cut-flower gardeners,

since they're growing a crop to be harvested, plant in rows like vegetable gardeners do. Choose a sunny site with soil that drains well for a cutting garden—and, because all the flowers will be picked, locate it somewhat out of sight, as you might a vegetable garden. Annuals are the meat-and-potatoes of cutting gardens, but why not try a perennial cutting? Some genera, such as *Lilium*, have species that flower at different times in the garden calendar; bloom times may be slightly different in your location.

SPRING–EARLY SUMMER

Bellflowers (*Campanula* spp.)

Columbines (*Aquilegia* spp.)

Coreopsis (*Coreopsis* spp.)

Daffodils (*Narcissus* cvs.)

Foxglove (*Digitalis purpurea*)

Globeflowers (*Trollius* spp.)

Iris (*Iris* spp.)

Lupines (*Lupinus* spp.)

Peonies (*Paeonia* cvs.)

Sweet William (*Dianthus barbatus*)

Tulips (*Tulipa* cvs.)

Wild blue phlox (*Phlox divaricata*)

(continues on next page)

KEEPING THEM FRESH

*A*ll cut flowers have a preordained shelf life—or, more accurately, vase life—but they will last longer if you handle them properly.

- Cut flowers in the morning and place them in warm water immediately, while you're still in the garden.
- Before placing them in a vase, recut the stems *under water* on a slant; don't crush the stem.
- Remove all extra foliage; don't submerge leaves in the water.
- Don't set the vase in the sun, in a hot location, in a draft, or near fresh fruit; do change the water often.
- Recut the stems every three or four days.
- Remove spent blossoms.
- Mist the flowers occasionally.

SUMMER

Astilbes (*Astilbe* cvs.)

Baby's breath (*Gypsophila paniculata*)

Balloon flower (*Platycodon grandiflorus*)

Beardtongues (*Penstemon* spp.)

Bee balm (*Monarda didyma*)

Blanket flower (*Gaillardia aristata*)

Canterbury bells (*Campanula medium*)

Crocosmias (*Crocosmia* cvs.)

Delphiniums (*Delphinium* spp.)

Feverfew (*Tanacetum parthenium*)

Lavenders (*Lavandula* spp.)

Lilies (*Lilium* cvs.)

Pinks (*Dianthus* spp.)

Purple coneflower (*Echinacea purpurea*)

Sea lavender (*Limonium latifolium*)

Shasta daisy (*Leucanthemum* × *superbum*)

Speedwell (*Veronica spicata*)

Torch lily (*Kniphofia uvaria*)

Yarrows (*Achillea* spp.)

LATE SUMMER–FALL

Asters (*Aster* spp.)

Black-eyed Susan (*Rudbeckia hirta*)

Chrysanthemum (*Chrysanthemum* × *morifolium*)

Fall-blooming Japanese anemones (*Anemone hupehensis*, A. × *hybrida*, A. *tomentosa*)

Garden phlox (*Phlox paniculata*)

Gayfeathers (*Liatris* spp.)

Globe thistle (*Echinops ritro*)

Goldenrods (*Solidago* spp.)

Monkshoods (*Aconitum* spp.)

Orange coneflower (*Rudbeckia fulgida*)

Ox-eye (*Heliopsis helianthoides*)

Perennial sunflowers (*Helianthus* spp.)

Sneezeweed (*Helenium autumnale*)

Flowers for the Vase. *Purple coneflower* (Echinacea purpurea) *is one of many perennials that are suited for bouquets. When the petals fade, many gardeners preserve their decorative centers, or cones, for dried arrangements.*

Yellows, Golds, and Oranges. *Vibrant marigold blooms like these award-winning French marigolds (Tagetes patula 'Bonanza Bolero') are among the common garden flowers most often used for dyeing yarn and other fibers.*

A Dyer's Garden

Whether you want to learn how to dye fabric or just love the idea of collecting flowers with a purpose, plants used for dyeing are an interesting lot. There isn't always a one to one connection when using plants as dyes: Blue flowers don't necessarily turn the yarn or cloth blue. Beginners will want to consult Rita Buchanan's *A Weaver's Garden: Growing Plants for Natural Dyes and Fibers* (1999), which presents the ins and outs of dye plants and details how to grow them. These common dye plants are handsome as well as practical, so your garden also will be one to die for.

Black-eyed Susan (*Rudbeckia hirta*)
Bloodroot (*Sanguinaria canadensis*)
Catnip (*Nepeta cataria*)
Common mullein (*Verbascum thapsus*)
Coreopsis (*Coreopsis* spp.)
Cosmos (*Cosmos sulphureus*)
Elecampane (*Inula helenium*)
Foxglove (*Digitalis purpurea*)
Golden Marguerite/dyer's chamomile (*Anthemis tinctoria*)
Hollyhock (*Alcea rosea*)
Joe-Pye weeds (*Eupatorium* spp.)
Marigolds (*Tagetes* spp.)
Roman chamomile (*Chamaemelum nobile*)
Sunflower (*Helianthus annuus*)
Sweet woodruff (*Galium odoratum*)
Tansy (*Tanacetum vulgare*)
Wood betony/bishop's wort (*Stachys officinalis*)
Yarrow (*Achillea millefolium*)

A Moon Garden

"Nighttime sharpens, heightens each sensation / Darkness wakes and stirs imagination," sings the disfigured phantom who lives in the catacombs of the opera house. Night is also magical in the garden. Moon gardens were popular with 19th-century gardeners, who filled them with a mix of white and fragrant flowers that either opened or stayed open at night. Not only magnets for human lovers of the night, moon gardens are captivating to moths and other pollinating creatures who work the late shift. A first-rate book about after-dark gardens is *The Evening Garden* by Peter Loewer (1993). The definitive after-dark flower is the tender night-blooming cereus (*Cereus peruvianus*), which waits until night to bloom. All these flowers are suited for viewing by moonlight; those marked with an asterisk are fragrant.

Angel's trumpets (*Datura innoxia, Brugmansia* spp.)★

Balloon flower (*Platycodon grandiflorus*) 'Albus'

Bleeding heart (*Dicentra spectabilis*) 'Alba', 'Pantaloons'

Cosmos (*Cosmos bipinnatus*) 'Purity', 'Sonata White'

Dame's sweet, rocket (*Hesperis matronalis* var. *albiflora*)★

Ever-flowering gladiolus (*Gladiolus tristis*)★

Flowering tobacco (*Nicotiana alata*) 'Grandiflora'★, 'Evening Fragrance'★, 'Sensation Mixed'★; *N. noctiflora*★, *N. sylvestris*★

Four-o'clock (*Mirabilis jalapa*) 'Baywatch'★

Foxglove (*Digitalis purpurea*) 'Alba'

Garden phlox (*Phlox paniculata*) 'David'★

Heliotrope (*Heliotropium arborescens*) 'Alba'★

Love-in-a-mist (*Nigella damascena*) 'Miss Jekyll', 'Cramers' Plum'

Madonna lilies (*Lilium* Candidum Hybrids)★

Mignonette (*Reseda odorata*)★

Moonflower (*Ipomoea alba*)★

Night-scented stock (*Matthiola longipetala* spp. *bicornis*)★

Obedient plant (*Physostegia virginiana*) 'Summer Snow'

Oriental Hybrid lilies (*Lilium* Oriental Hybrids) 'Casa Blanca'★

Peonies (*Paeonia* cvs.) 'Miss America'★, 'Moonrise'★, 'Charlie's White', 'Cheddar Cheese'★

Petunia (*Petunia* × *hybrida*) 'White Cascade', 'White Wave', 'Primetime White'

Purple coneflower (*Echinacea purpurea*) 'White Swan', 'White Lustre'

Snowdrops (*Galanthus* spp.)

Snow-on-the-mountain (*Euphorbia marginata*)

Spider flower (*Cleome hassleriana*) 'Helen Campbell'★

Tuberose (*Polianthes tuberosa*)★

A Container Garden

Container gardening's popularity is easily explained by its instant gratification, its adaptability to the smallest spaces, and its modest costs. Make sure your container has good drainage, fill it with a commercial potting soil, not soil from the garden, and expect to fertilize often with a balanced, soluble fertilizer. A superb guide filled with new and different ideas is *Gardens to Go: Creating and Designing a Container Garden* (2005) by Sydney Eddison. Take a careful look at what's new, but don't overlook the tried-and-true and consider adding plants with handsome foliage, such as dwarf cannas, coleus (*Solenostemon scutellarioides*), and ornamental sweet potatoes (*Ipomoea batatas*). This list is limited to slightly out of the ordinary annuals and to species typically grown as annuals.

African daisies (*Arctotis* spp., *Osteospermum* spp.)

Annual phlox (*Phlox drummondii*)

Browallias/bush violets (*Browallia* spp.)

Celosia (*Celosia argentea*)

Cigar plant (*Cuphea* spp.) 'David Verity'

Cupflower (*Nierembergia caerulea*)

Dahlberg daisy (*Thymophylla tenuiloba*)

Edging lobelia (*Lobelia erinus*)

Fan flower (*Scaevola aemula*)

Flowering tobaccos (*Nicotiana* cvs.) Merlin Series, Starship Series, 'Domino Mix'

Gomphrena/globe amaranth (*Gomphrena globosa*) 'Buddy', Gnome Series

Heliotrope (*Heliotropium arborescens*) 'Marine'

Melampodium (*Leucanthemum paludosum*)

The Contained Garden. *This colorful pot created at the Brooklyn Botanic Garden contains white-leaved* Caladium *'Candidum' and pink-and-green C. 'Funny Munson', dark purple and pink leaved* Alternanthera dentante *'Purpurea', pink and white leaved* Fuschia *'Firecracker', and* Begonia *'Sophia Irene', green with white speckles.*

Million bells (*Petunia* Hybrids) 'Million Bells'

Narrow-leaved zinnia/Mexican zinnia (*Zinnia haageana*)

Orange cosmos (*Cosmos sulphureus*) Ladybird Series

Prairie gentian (*Eustoma grandiflorum*) 'Forever Blue', Mermaid Series

Summer snapdragon (*Angelonia angustifolia*)

Treasure flowers (*Gazania* Hybrids)

Wishbone flower (*Torenia fournieri*) 'Clown Mix'

Flower Garden Equipment. *Clay pots, spades, hoes, watering cans, wheelbarrows, compost bins, gloves, hats—the possible accouterments of growing flowers are almost infinite. New gardeners should take their time when buying equipment. Despite the ads, every task does not require its own tool. Start with the basics: shovel, rake, hoe, and trowel.*

CHAPTER NINE

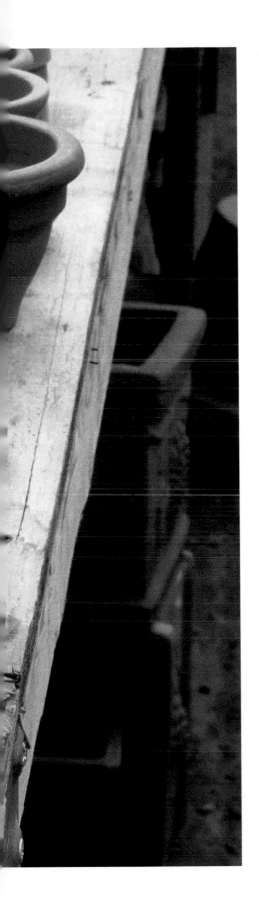

Tool Talk: Equipping the Flower Gardener

I wish with all my heart I were a man,
for of course the first things I should do would
be to buy a spade and go and garden.

Countess von Arnim,
Elizabeth and Her German Garden, 1898

IT'S BEEN MORE THAN A CENTURY SINCE THE
Countess von Arnim not only felt she couldn't buy garden tools
but couldn't write under her own name, publishing instead as
"Elizabeth." While much has changed for women since 1898,
garden spades haven't evolved a great deal. In fact, the designs
for most basic horticultural implements—spade, hoe, rake,
trowel, watering can—have been around for more than 2,000
years. It was the original tool man Archimedes, after all, who

said that with a lever and a place to stand, "I can move the earth."

There have been many inventions since the Greeks and Romans, as well as new materials that have made garden tools and equipment stronger, lighter, and longer-lasting. The result is a mishmash of things to buy. Horticulture is a shopper's paradise—or hell, depending on your point of view. Garden centers, nurseries, hardware stores, and big-box stores are bulging with equipment and supplies. If there is no well-stocked store near you, all the things you could need or want—and lots that you neither need nor want—are available by mail. (For mail-order and online equipment sources, see Appendix, page 457.)

Look at the beautiful things in stores or glossy catalogs—hand-forged steel shovels with wood D-handles, wrought-iron trellises and arches, polished brass thermometers, plantation-farmed teak benches—and it's easy to believe that one of everything is essential to growing flowers. But before reaching for your wallet, realize that there is an inverse relationship between the number of years spent gardening and the number of tools used: the greater the years, the fewer the tools.

Depleting your assets is not necessary to grow flowers. If your garden consists of only a couple of large pots or a 2-foot-long window box, then a trowel, a bucket for carrying, and a watering can may be the only tools you need (and you probably can get by without those if you don't mind abusing your serving spoons and forks and have a large pitcher). But for anything more ambitious, you'll need the basic implements.

Like the size of your garden, where you garden also affects what equipment is required. Gardeners in North America's frosty spots use cold frames to give plants a head start in spring and floating row covers and cloches to protect them from early frosts in autumn, whereas gardeners in hot, arid regions are more interested in hoses, sprinklers, and irrigation systems. Land-challenged city gardeners rely on clay pots and other containers to grow flowers, and they do their composting in polyethylene barrels made for that job. Country gardeners battling with wildlife look for humane equipment to prevent Bambi and friends from eating their lilies and tulips.

To avoid wasting money with thingamabobs that will do nothing but gather dust, begin with the essential tools: shovel, rake, hoe, and trowel. Gardening is an addiction: You'll have a lifetime to fill your tool shed. (For the record, prefab sheds are available at lumberyards, garden centers, big-box stores, and even by mail, $2,500 and up for an 8×8–foot model.) There will be plenty of time to furnish your garden with a three-orb copper birdbath ($165) or cast-iron tortoise stepping-stones ($28 each), or whatever catches your fancy. But that comes later. Trust the experts: Start slow.

Quality Counts

It doesn't take many tools to create and maintain a small flower garden, so don't skimp on quality. You want to purchase well-made shovels, rakes, garden carts, and other equipment that will be worth passing down to the next generation. European garden tools are among the best, but there's no need to limit yourself to implements made by British firms with an appointment to Her Majesty the Queen.

Equipment manufactured in this country and sold at garden centers, nurseries, hardware and farm stores, and even at some national chains is second to none. There also is a handful of down to earth mail-order and online companies that specialize in basic garden tools and equipment, not titanium spades with teak handles and Victorian hose carts listed at $250 plus shipping. Prices for the same tool made by the same firm can differ rather shockingly, so it's worth checking around before you buy.

WHAT'S YOUR SIZE?

Tools should be easy to manage and not feel heavy when you first pick them up. Fortunately, almost every garden tool—shovel, rake, hoe, trowel, even mechanical equipment—comes in different sizes. If you're not built like King Kong, buy a smaller or lighter version of the tool you need. Just make sure it has the same quality its bigger brother (or sister) has. Smaller models are sometimes marketed as "lady's" tools, but don't let patronizing labels put you off. Try different models and sizes, and pick the tool that best fits you.

In addition to topnotch garden tools and equipment, there is an exhaustive supply of third-rate merchandise for sale. Price isn't always a giveaway, so knowing a little about materials and construction methods will help you avoid bad choices. Watch for model terms such as "professional," often an indication of high caliber. Look for these qualities:

High-carbon steel heads. Spades, shovels, rakes, forks, and other hand tools should be made of high-carbon steel, not stamped steel or cast aluminum, which bends easily. The terms *forged* and *tempered* indicate that the metal part of the tool is made from one piece of steel. Stainless steel blades are strong and rustproof but are the devil to sharpen. They also are more expensive than tools with carbon-steel blades but not better enough to justify the extra money.

Hardwood handles. Tool handles should be made of hardwoods, such as hickory or ash. Look for knot-free handles with a straight grain that runs lengthwise, and don't buy tools with painted handles: It's a manufacturer's trick for disguising softwood. Some high-end tools are fitted with stainless steel and fiberglass handles. They are expensive and strong but overkill for most home gardeners.

Solid-socket connection. Where the metal meets the wood, "Ay, there's the rub." Hamlet wasn't referring to the gravedigger's spade, but he could have been. The connection between a tool's head and handle is its Achilles' heel. Avoid tools with an open-socket connection (the handle is fitted in a short metal collar that is open in the back). Less problematic but a clear second choice is a tang-and-ferrule connection (the head has a tang, or prong, that is driven into the handle and the connection is wrapped with a small metal ferrule, or collar). In contrast, a solid-socket, or solid-strap, connection unites the head and handle with a long metal collar secured with pins. It's heavier than other designs, but the disadvantage of the extra weight is offset by greater strength.

Digging, Raking, and Hoeing

The best digging tool is a *shovel*, not a *spade*. (Shovel blades, or heads, are slightly concave and have an angled edge, while spade blades are nearly flat and straight-edged.) Spades are the tool of choice in England, where people have been turning the same soil for tens of centuries, but not in North America. As the American writer Charles Eliot expressed it in *The Transplanted Gardener* (1995), "No Englishman would dig with a shovel. By preference I wouldn't dig with anything else. And I also use a shovel to shovel with."

Turning the Soil. *A traditional garden fork is an ideal tool for loosening and aerating the soil of a flower bed or border, and the Wellington boots are perfect for keeping the gardener's feet dry.*

SHOVELS, SPADES, AND FORKS

Shovels are ideal for digging as well as for scooping and moving soil, compost, and other materials. You can choose from many models, each of which is available in various sizes and weights, but a standard *common*, or *round-point*, *shovel* weighs between 5 and 6 pounds and has a head that measures about 8 × 12 inches. Be sure to buy a shovel with a footrest on the top of its blade. And try it out: If it feels too heavy, opt for a smaller version. Don't forget that you not only have to lift the shovel, you have to lift what's on the shovel.

Many flower gardeners, including those endowed with muscles a body builder would covet, prefer working with a smaller *floral shovel*. It has a head measuring about 7 × 10 inches, which makes it plenty big enough for digging but small enough to maneuver between plants. (Even smaller is the *border shovel*; it has a 6 × 8–inch head and also is useful for working in established gardens.)

Those who champion the *spade* over the shovel tout their straight (or near-straight) bottom edge for removing sod, cutting through roots, edging, and trenching. Standard models have blades that measure about 7 × 11 inches. There also are spades with smaller heads (5½ × 9 inches) for smaller hands and muscles that are known as *border spades*. Large or downsized, a spade needs a foot tread, or lip, and it should be made of heavy, tempered steel, and fitted with a hardwood handle at least 28 inches long.

If you are constantly creating new beds and borders or separating and moving large plants, consider purchasing a *garden fork*, the ideal tool for turning cultivated soil and for digging up plants and bulbs. Garden forks are nothing more than short-handled shovels with tines rather than a blade. Most have four 12-inch flat tines and weigh about 5 pounds. (Much heavier is the square-tined English pattern fork; it's *not* what you want to buy.)

RAKES AND HOES

A *common garden rake* is the best tool for smoothing dug ground. It can break clods, remove stones and debris, level, spread and mix in compost and other soil amendments, cover seeds, and more. Good garden rakes have long handles—the tip of the handle should come up to your ear when the hoe is vertical—and one-piece forged-steel metal heads fitted with 14 to 18 curved 3-inch-long teeth. The design can be either flathead or bowhead—the difference between the two is in how the head is attached to the handle and isn't very important—but stay with a head that is no more than 18 inches wide.

The *hoe* is a versatile tool, good for weeding and cultivating, making planting holes, and discouraging dogs and cats that venture into the garden. There is a herd of hoes for sale, and new designs appear every year. As Tyler Whittle remarked in *Some Ancient Gentlemen* (1965), "A good deal of heat is generated by the devotees of each particular kind [of hoe]. They try to convert each other and argue with the passion of a Jehovah's Witness who has his foot in the door." Flower gardeners don't spend as much time with a hoe as vegetable gardeners do, but it's still basic equipment for people who grow more zinnias than zucchinis.

The long-handled *common*, or *garden*, *hoe* is the place to start. It has a broad, flat blade, or head, that measures about 6 × 4 inches and is sharpened on the outside of the bottom edge. A standard garden hoe weighs between 2 and 3 pounds and has a long handle that attaches to the blade at a 70-degree angle. It's also called a *draw hoe* because of the way it is used: drawn toward the gardener.

Look for a common hoe that has a head and neck made from a single piece of forged steel, not one that is welded. The head should be attached to the handle with a socket, and the handle should be long enough so it's unnecessary to bend your back when you work.

The *floral hoe* is a pocket-sized version of the garden hoe. Despite its name, it isn't a tool for

HANDLE HORSE SENSE

*D*igging tools—shovels, spades, and forks—are available with either long handles or short handles capped by a D- or T-shaped grip. If you choose a short-handle model—which is easier to control—make sure that the grip reaches your waist when the blade is sunk in the ground. All digging tools should have a flat lip, or tread, on the top of the blade to protect your feet. To reduce strain on your back, keep the handle of your shovel, spade, or fork perpendicular to the ground. Place your foot on the tread and let your weight push the blade into the ground; bend slightly at the waist and knees to pull the spade backward, then straighten up and lift the load.

A FINE EDGE

*W*hile not a digging tool in the same way a shovel or fork is, most ornamental gardeners wouldn't do without an *edger*, a tool made for cutting through turf and creating tidy margins for beds and borders. Edgers have a long handle and a sharp blade in the shape of a half-circle. Make sure the model you buy has a lip on the top edge to protect the sole of your foot.

SHARPENING UP

Tools work best when they're sharp. To sharpen them, use a flat or half-round coarse file with a double-cut tooth pattern. Digging tools, such as shovels, should be honed at a sharp angle on the inside edge; hoes and most other weeding tools should be filed at a shallower angle, typically on the outside edge. Always sharpen the beveled edge of a tool blade, never the flat edge. Use the flat side of the file for flat edges, the half-round side for curved edges. Sharpening is made easier if you can clamp the tool in a vise. File on the forward stroke, pushing away from the blade of the tool.

flower gardeners: It's too light to deal with anything but the smallest weeds. Wider isn't better either, so avoid *onion* and *collinear hoes*. Similarly, the triangle-shaped *Warren hoe*, an American-designed tool first sold in the 1870s, is better suited for vegetable gardeners than flower growers.

Two other hoes are at home in flower gardens. One is the *oscillating hoe*, which has a stirruplike head that is hinged to a long handle. The 1-inch wide blade is sharpened on both sides and cuts on both pull and push strokes. Oscillating hoes aren't good for some jobs, but they are superb at cutting off weeds at the soil surface. The other hoe worth considering is a *tined hoe*, which has from three to five curved tines rather than a blade and is superb for aerating the soil between plants.

Short-Handled Tools

In addition to shovels, hoes, and rakes, you'll want to have tools for small jobs—on-your-knees work such as weeding, planting bulbs, and filling pots and window boxes. These short-handled tools are often sold in sets: a *trowel* and *hand fork* for digging and a *claw* for weeding and opening the soil surface. The fork and claw are useful, but the trowel is the essential member of the trio.

Set or single tool, you don't want aluminum heads, which bend easily: Choose tools made of high-carbon or stainless steel. And you do want tools with strong handles and hardwood or a cushioned grip to reduce hand fatigue. Standard trowels with blades about 3½ inches across are most helpful, but if most of your flower growing is done in containers, choose a narrow-bladed model. Wider and longer is not better in trowels—if you need to dig a foot-deep hole, you need to use a shovel.

Help with Handwork. *Narrow trowels are designed for digging in small spaces, as in this flat of carpet bugleweed (Ajuga reptans 'Burgundy Glow') seedlings. Ajuga is a fast-spreading, perennial groundcover, good in sun or shade.*

Hand weeders—claws, miniature hoes, hooks, and more—are for working in close quarters. Most are designed to cut weeds off at the soil surface, not dig out their roots. While these are praised by many, gardeners are probably better off trying to pull weeds, which takes no tools at all.

Our oldest ancestors used a sharpened stick to make holes for seeds and transplants. Over the centuries that stick metamorphosed into a *dibble*, a pointed tool usually fitted with a metal point and a T-grip. Dibbles, or *dibbers*, are traditionally made of hardwood and are so handsome, so aesthetically pleasing to eye and hand, that it seems necessary to have one. It isn't, of course, unless you set out hundreds of seedlings every spring, which is known as *dibbering in* seedlings.

Carrying

Gardeners always have something that needs to be moved from one place to another: tools, a load of compost, two flats of marigold seedlings, a clump of daylilies that has outgrown its space, a bale of straw, and much more. Despite the wheel being mightier than the back, some carrying is done easily by hand. A 5-gallon plastic *bucket* recycled from a construction site isn't a certified garden tool, but it's perfect for carrying small loads back and forth—or buy a galvanized steel bucket.

Another choice for toting lightweight debris is a *collapsible garden bucket*—the original is the Kangaroo Gardening Bucket, made from reinforced vinyl. It measures 15 inches in diameter, 18 inches tall, and is tear resistant and collapsible, making it easy to store. New are Flexitubs, containers made of lightweight but tough recycled polyethylene. They can bear heavier loads than most gardeners can and are available in different sizes. Or, for light loads, use a tarpaulin, old sheet, or bedspread. Lay it down where you're working, toss the rubbish on it, grab the four corners, and drag it to the compost pile.

Unless your garden is very small, you'll want something beyond a bucket for carrying. *Wheelbarrows* have long been the garden vehicle of choice, but many flower gardeners are better off with a *garden cart.* (Wheelbarrows are less expensive than carts, easier to maneuver in small spaces, and can turn on a dime, but they are tricky to balance.) Garden carts—wood boxes mounted on two large wheels—don't require balancing and are easy to push or pull. They can carry extremely heavy and large loads—up to 500 pounds for large models.

Pick a plywood cart that is at least 4 feet wide, has a steel frame, inflatable bicycle tires, and a hinged front panel, which lets you dump loose matter like compost or mulch. Garden carts aren't cheap—$300 or more, depending on the size—but

Horticultural Hauling. *The wheelbarrow was invented in China in the 1st century B.C., not for toting garden debris but for carrying military supplies. It takes advantage of two world-changing inventions: the wheel and the lever.*

if they are stored in a protected place, they will last indefinitely. Don't be temped by molded plastic two-wheeled wheelbarrows or any wheeled vehicle with a canvas bed.

Watering

A handful of lucky gardeners in North America can depend entirely on rain for wetting flowers, but most gardeners need some watering equipment. If your garden is small, you won't need more than a *watering can*. Choose the largest size you can carry easily when filled (and that will fit under your faucet). Look for one made by Haws, which has an extra-long spout that makes it easy to supply water exactly where it's needed, is well-balanced, and has a spill shield that keeps water from sloshing out of the can.

Standard cans made of either galvanized steel, steel that has been treated with zinc to make it weatherproof, or polyethylene, which is lighter than steel, longer-lasting, and less expensive, are fine. Make sure that the sprinkling head, or *rose*, is detachable for cleaning. Brass and copper watering cans are handsome but impractical for outdoor use.

HOSES

A *hose*, which humorists Henry Beard and Roy McKie (*Gardening: A Gardener's Dictionary*, 1982) described as a "crude but effective . . . type of scythe towed through gardens to flatten flower beds," is a necessary purchase for most gardeners whose flower beds aren't set 10 feet from a faucet. Hoses are sold in increments of 25 or 50 feet; the longer the hose, the less water pressure, so don't buy a hose that is longer than you need.

Choose a hose that has at least a ⅝-inch diameter and a PSI, or pounds per square inch, rating of 500. (A ⅝-inch hose delivers about 17 gallons per minute.) Full-flow brass couplings signal quality, but if your hand strength is limited, you may want to buy a hose with ergonomically designed plastic couplings. When looking at hoses you'll also run into the term "ply," which means "layer." The more plies the better, with six being the cream of the crop.

Rubber, the traditional hose material, is strong, durable, and doesn't kink, but rubber hoses are also expensive and very heavy. A good choice for most flower gardeners is a high-quality rubber vinyl hose.

A step down is a reinforced vinyl hose. Reinforced vinyl hoses are strong, durable, and largely kink-proof, while cheaper and lighter than rubber models. Inexpensive nonreinforced vinyl hoses are a nightmare: They kink, they burst, they leak.

A reinforced Flexogen hose manufactured by Gilmour is the best of the bunch, and it comes with a full lifetime replacement guarantee. To extend any hose's life, work kinks out by hand—don't pull or yank. Make sure it is coiled without sharp bends or kinks when it's not being used and stored out of the sun. (Never hang a hose on a nail or a hook.) When the garden season is over, drain the hose and keep it indoors.

There are two hoses you don't want. *Flat hoses* are designed to save space when not in use. The catch is that they must be fully extended before water will pass from tap to nozzle, and they must be drained every time they are stored. *Coiled hoses* sound and look wonderful in the ads, one of which claims "each coil has a memory molded into its molecular structure, so no matter how hard you stretch the hose during use, it retracts on its own . . . without acquiring any of those annoying kinks of standard garden hoses." Trust gardeners who have tried them: They do not have a molecular memory. They twist and tangle, and their small diameter means it takes forever to water.

A water-conserving hose worth buying, especially in regions where it's necessary to water several times a week, is a *soaker hose*. Soaker hoses, which can be kept in place throughout the garden season, are dotted with holes and are meant to be laid on the ground, even buried under a layer of mulch. Drip-irrigation systems, another water-saving technique, are beyond the scope of this book but are covered in detail in Robert Kourik's *Drip Irrigation for Every Landscape and All Climates* (1993).

SAFETY NOTE

Gardeners who routinely drink from their garden hose should use a model designated "recreational," "boat," or "marine." These hoses have plastic linings that make the water that passes through them safe for ingestion; the lining of standard garden hoses is not guaranteed safe for transmitting drinking water.

Watering 101. *Don't overlook watering cans for getting moisture to flowers like these 'Sheffield Pink' chrysanthemums. Once called "watering pots" and "watering pails," this piece of garden equipment became a can about 1886 when Englishman John Haws patented the teapotlike design we use today. Haws cans are still manufactured in England and sold worldwide.*

WATERING EXTRAS

A watering can or a hose and *spray nozzle* (choose a standard adjustable nozzle made of brass) are all the watering equipment most home gardeners need, but there are devices that are worth investing in if watering is an everyday task.

Watering wands. These are rigid metal or plastic tubes that attach to the end of a hose to extend gardeners' reach. You can choose from several models, including the 30-inch-long standard wand, good for all kinds of watering; a 16-inch patio wand, made for watering container plants; and a hanging-basket wand, designed for overhead watering.

Timers. There are both simple and complicated timers, but all can turn a hose on and off, saving gardeners' time and water. Computer models can be programmed to operate at regular intervals, week in and out.

On/off valves. These are simple ball valves that attach between the end of the hose and a nozzle, wand, or sprinkler. They are not expensive and will save trips to the faucet when you want to change implements.

Sprinklers. While sprinklers aren't water-efficient, they cut down on time spent holding a hose. *Oscillating sprinklers*, which water in a rectangular pattern, are suitable for most flower gardens.

Seed Starting

The British writer Vita Sackville-West once marveled at a neighbor who made do with what she had—cardboard boxes, syrup cans, and baskets—for starting seeds: "I verily believe that she would use an old shoe if it came in handy." Contemporary gardeners are more likely to use yogurt containers, plastic milk jugs, and Styrofoam coffee cups, but the message is clear: Anything that will hold a soil mixture and has drainage holes will serve.

In addition to recycled containers, there is a conglomeration of equipment designed just for starting seeds, five-star ways of growing all the flowers a gardener could possibly want. (For information about sowing seeds and caring for seedlings, see "Starting from Seed," page 119.) All seeds need to sprout are a medium to grow in, a container to hold the medium, warmth, and moisture.

SOIL MEDIA

Starting seeds indoors is different from starting them outdoors, where they are perfectly content with garden soil. The villain inside is damping-off, a fungal infection that can topple a flat of seedlings overnight. (For more information about this disease, see "Damping-Off," page 169.) When sowing seeds indoors, always use a sterile *seed-starting medium*. There are plenty of inexpensive sterile mixes for sale—their ingredients vary—but most contain neither soil nor nutrients, which means that seedlings must be fertilized as soon as they emerge. In contrast, most *potting soils* do contain plant nutrients. Recent research has confirmed that the chemical and physical properties of commercial soil mixes change over time, however, so don't buy more than you can use in six months.

If you want to make your own sterile seed-starting medium, which contains no nutrients, combine equal parts perlite, vermiculite, milled sphagnum peat moss, and sharp, or builders', sand. Another formula is a mix of equal parts of milled sphagnum peat moss and vermiculite or perlite, plus 1 tablespoon of ground limestone. Or substitute coir for the sphagnum peat moss. All these ingredients are available at garden centers. (For recipes for

---

SEED STARTING HELPERS

Starting seeds indoors requires a planting medium that contains no diseases, pests, or weed seeds. Recipes differ, but most mixes are made up primarily of a combination of these five components.

Coir, or coco peat, which is the coarse fiber harvested from the husk of the coconut palm seed, serves the same role as sphagnum peat moss: to improve soil structure. It has a pH that ranges from 5.7 to 6.3 and is increasingly popular because it is a renewable product.

Perlite comes from volcanic rock that has been heated and crushed. It's sterile, light, and has a neutral pH, but contains no nutrients. A renewable material, perlite is used both to increase aeration and to retain moisture.

Sand that is added to a soil mix should be builders', or sharp, sand, not beach sand or the sand you buy for a backyard sandbox.

Sphagnum peat moss and **sphagnum moss** aren't the same thing. The latter is the living moss that grows on top of a sphagnum bog; sphagnum peat moss is the dead material mined from bogs and milled to make the dry product used in seedling mixes and as a soil additive. Same plant but different stages. Peat moss contains no nutrients and is not renewable (except in geologic time).

Vermiculite is derived from mica that has been heated to 2,000°F so that it breaks into small particles. Like perlite, it is sterile, contains no nutrients, and is a useful additive both to aerate and to retain moisture. Recent studies indicate that vermiculite products contain low levels of asbestos, but the risk to consumers is very small. The EPA, however, recommends that gardeners use premixed potting soils, which ordinarily contain less vermiculite, not pure vermiculite products.

Sowing Seeds. *Mix very small seeds, like those of nicotiana and petunia, with sand to help distribute them evenly. After sowing, gently press the seeds into the planting medium, mist the container, and set it in a warm location.*

potting mixes—media for growing-on seedlings—see "Mobile Homes," page 125.)

You also can purchase planting media that don't require a container. The most familiar are compressed *peat pellets*, which look like thick 50-cent pieces. Soaked in water, they expand to form small pots that are ready for sowing seeds. Two caveats: First, peat pellets retain water too well—be careful that your seeds and seedlings don't drown—and second, remove the mesh that holds the pellet together when you transplant the seedling. Less well known are Oasis Rootcubes, which are small biodegradable squares manufactured in sheets. The cubes, which contain fertilizer to get seedlings going, are available in different sizes with prepunched holes for sowing seeds and are meant as a first step: Once the seedling is transplant size, it—cube and all—must be reset in bigger quarters.

Or consider an ingenious device that makes containers unnecessary. *Soil blockers* are metal tools from England—now widely sold in North America—that compress a moistened planting medium into little blocks. The blocker sizes range from ½ inch square to 4 inches square. A 2-inch model is ideal for a home growers and costs about $25. Freestanding blocks of soil sound too good to be true but work extremely well. Because there are no container walls, plant roots don't circle inside the pot; instead, they grow to the edge of the soil block and stop.

Ordinary seed-starting mixes won't form freestanding blocks, but you can purchase mixes made specifically for making soil blocks. (DirtWorks is one source; see Appendix, page 457, for more information.) Or you can make your own by combining 2 parts coco peat or sphagnum peat moss, 2 parts black peat (sometimes sold as Michigan peat or *terre noire*), 2 parts worm castings or compost, ½ part sharp sand, and a handful of wood ashes or lime.

CONTAINERS

You can use an old shoe to plant seeds like Sackville-West's neighbor might have done, but likely you'll be happier using containers that are made for the job. Inexpensive *plastic containers* are widely available in different sizes and configurations, including individual pots, open flats, and celled flats. You may want to buy a large tray, either mesh or solid plastic, to hold them. It's better to start with small containers and then transplant seedlings to larger quarters as they grow, a process known as *potting on*. Using containers with individual cells will mean that you won't have to disturb plant roots when you pot on or transplant to the garden. Plastic containers can be reused after being cleaned thoroughly.

Peat and fiber containers are inexpensive and biodegradable, made either from sphagnum moss and wool fiber or recycled cardboard. Both individual pots and celled flats are for sale, and when it's time for the seedlings to go into the garden, their containers can go as well, keeping plant roots intact.

A *pot maker* is a clever and handsome wood tool—it looks like a pepper mill—that transforms strips of newsprint into small pots. No taping, gluing, or tying required, and when the seedling is ready for larger quarters, the pot, which will decompose, can go too, leaving plant roots intact. Or improvise with a small glass jar or can (one that is between 2 and 3 inches in diameter). Here are the directions.

1. Open one full sheet of newspaper, then fold in half lengthwise.
2. Cut a strip lengthwise, about 5 inches wide.
3. Wrap or roll the doubled newspaper strip around the jar, leaving about 1 inch of newspaper below the bottom of the jar.
4. Fold the overhanging inch of paper against the bottom of the jar to form the bottom of your paper pot.
5. Gently pull out the jar; place the pot in a flat and fill it with a seed-starting mix.
6. Set additional pots closely together in the flat.

MORE SEED-STARTING HELPERS

Germinating seeds on the top of a radiator and growing the seedlings on a windowsill are chancy arrangements. To provide the bottom warmth seeds need to spout well, use a *propagation*, or *heat*, *mat*, a waterproof rubber sheet that contains a heating element. Available in different measurements that coincide with the measurements of common trays and flats, mats provide even heat, about 74°F. *Heating cables*, waterproof cables sold in different lengths, are another option for providing bottom warmth. They can be laid under flats but usually are buried in the planting medium itself, making them especially useful for starting seeds outdoors in a cold frame.

Sprouting seeds indoors is easier than keeping the new plants healthy. Seedlings need at least 16 hours of light each day; without a greenhouse or a cold frame, it's nearly impossible to provide enough natural light to keep young plants from becoming tall and thin, or *leggy*. Garden stores sell well-designed but expensive multilayer floor and tabletop light stands, but if you're growing only a few seedlings, a clamp-on fixture fitted with a fluorescent bulb is all you need. If you want to start several flats of flowers indoors, buy one or more inexpensive workshop light fixture at the hardware store and fit them with fluorescent bulbs.

A *cold frame*, which is nothing more than a small unheated greenhouse, is usually considered a place to harden-off and overwinter plants. It is also useful for setting out sown pots of seed that need cold treatment in order to germinate. Add heat cables to boost the soil's temperature, and it becomes a *hot bed*, an ideal place to germinate seeds weeks before they can be sown in the garden. Traditional cold frames were made of wood, sunk slightly below ground level, and covered by recycled window sashes set on a pitch.

Today you can buy prefab cold frames, including pricey models with automatic vents that keep plants from overheating on sunny days—or you can construct your own. (Detailed plans can be downloaded from the web; enter "cold frame plans" in a search engine.) Or make a recyclable cold frame from bales of hay covered with old windows or corrugated polyethylene. Simple or complicated, cold frames need to be located on well-drained soil, have a southern exposure, and be near an electrical outlet if you want to turn them into hot beds.

Composting

The how-to of composting, including suggestions on building compost bins, is contained in Chapter 4, page 63. Gardeners with more enthusiasm than space may want to use a commercial composter to alchemize their garbage and yard waste into black gold. Most models are made of recycled polyethylene and come in different sizes. There are two basic types:

Continuous composters are prefab containers to which you add debris gradually just as you would with a homebuilt compost bin. Sizes range from small tubs that hold about 35 gallons of debris to large models that hold 77 gallons. All have vents to control temperature and are lidded. Expandable wire bins made from coated heavy-gauge steel are also sold. A 3-foot square bin holds 20 cubic feet (150 dry gallons) of yard debris and kitchen scraps.

Batch composters, or *tumblers*, are meant to be filled all at once and do their magic in a hurry, a few weeks at most according to the manufacturers. (One company calls batch composters the "sports cars of composting.") Most are barrel shaped or octagonal and are mounted on stands to make turning easy (or designed to be rolled on the ground). Capacity ranges from 40 to 70 gallons. The catch is that you must have room to save the raw ingredients—in separate piles, green and brown—until you have enough for a batch. And to speed the process, you need to shred everything that goes into the composter.

Continuous Composting. *Small stationary bins are for gardeners who are willing to wait for compost to "happen." This model has a top lid for filling, adjustable side air vents, and a sliding door on the bottom for removing the finished compost.*

Essential Others

There is a raft of other equipment that flower gardeners *may* need. To paraphrase the diarist Samuel Pepys, it's pretty to see what money will buy. If money's no object, go hog wild; otherwise, begin with these items:

Hand pruners. Pruners, also known as *secateurs*, are good for cutting flowers in spring and summer and shearing back stems in fall. Choose bypass pruners, which have a curved blade designed to cut cleanly, not anvil pruners. Make sure to buy a model that has blades made from high-carbon-steel and that can be taken apart to be sharpened. (If your flower garden is primarily a cutting garden, buy a pair of *garden scissors*.)

Pocket knife. Don't overcomplicate: A single 2- to 3-inch carbon-steel blade is all you need for the dozens of cutting jobs that will come up.

File. Keeping tools sharp requires a file. An inexpensive bastard file with a double-cut tooth pattern works fine. It can be either flat or a half-round model (flat on one side, round on the other), but make sure it's at least 10 inches long.

Plant labels. You'll know it's an aster and not a tulip, but is it *Aster novae-angliae* 'Ernest Ballard' or 'Ada Ballard'? Plant labels are a must for identifying what you've planted and where. There are scores of choices, from wood, which is unobtrusive but impermanent, to plastic, which lasts forever but can be eye-jarring. To write on either, you'll need an indelible marker or pencil. (For real permanence, buy a paint pen—Markal is one brand—with the smallest tip available.) Also permanent are metal labels, aluminum, zinc, or copper, which are likely to outlast the plant they identify. Most gardeners are happy with plain-Jane labels, but there are plenty of ornamental models on the market, and some resourceful growers paint names on rocks and set them next to the plant.

Plant supports. Tall flowers, such as lilies and asters, and plants like peonies and giant dahlias with huge blooms have a tendency to fall over, especially when the wind blows. Stakes and twine will do the job, but better—and far easier to install—are metal supports, including hoops, "grow-through" grids, single-stem supports, Y-stakes, and other devices that keep big and top-heavy species upright. They are available at good garden centers and from mail-order firms. Flowering vines will require trellises or netting.

Weather instruments. Three items are *sine qua non.* First, a reliable outdoor thermometer, preferably one with a maximum-minimum feature, will keep track of when tender plants can go outdoors or need to come inside, and provide weather data for your garden notebook. Oregon Scientific manufactures a wide selection of wireless models. Second, seeds and plants are sensitive to soil as well as air temperature; a *soil thermometer* will keep you from planting too soon. And third, buy a rain gauge. There are battery-controlled and self-emptying models, but a simple plastic model is sufficient.

Notebook. Knowing the details of your microclimate and garden is a good way to avoid making the same mistakes again and again. Buy a sturdy notebook and write down what you've planted and when, what did well and what didn't, what color combinations you liked and didn't like; record the weather—temperatures, first

Weatherwise Gardeners. *A simple rain gauge helps gardeners know if their flowers need to be watered. Set it in an open area, away from buildings and trees.*

and last-frost dates, rainfall, snowfall—and bloom dates; set down the length of plants' flowering, their heights and widths, anything that might be helpful another season. And take the notebook along when you visit other gardens or the local nursery and attend horticultural lectures and meetings. In time, it will be a passport to gardening successfully as well as an interesting record of what's gone before.

Adorning the Garden

Garden ornaments are a subject of lively debate—and of individual taste. The English garden writer Beverley Nichols, an avowed ornament hater who once described a stone cupid as looking like "a very horrible baby that has been petrified just as it was having an acute attack of wind," allowed that he was overcome while looking for a sundial. Instead of a garden timepiece, Nichols returned home with 60 yards of 18th-century stone balustrade, which he topped off with 9-foot Doric pillars.

Doric pillars are overmuch for average home gardeners, but a sculpture by a local artist or a statue of Saint Fiacre, the gardener's patron and, coincidentally, of Paris cab drivers—might be a graceful addition to a flower border, as a sundial would be. Sundials are established gardenware, even if, as Hilaire Belloc penned in *Complete Verse* (1954), "I am a sundial, and I make a botch / Of what is done far better by a watch."

Ornaments can create focus in a garden and help establish mood. A garden is an opportunity to express yourself—and a place to have some fun—and ornament choices are infinite. Wherever your taste runs—gnomes, pink flamingoes, stone toads, wind chimes, whirligigs, gazing globes—go ahead and indulge. If you want friends to visit, however, take a pass on the 71-inch-long copper snake with "with bronze bands and tongue" offered by a Georgia firm.

More practical but still ornamental are garden benches, especially those made from natural materials. Also in the practical-and-ornamental department are bee skeps, birdbaths and feeders, fountains, and many weather instruments. There are interesting and handsome copper sprinklers that rotate when you turn on the water and a rash of ornamental stepping-stones and plant labels, even downspouts and hose caddies. And give thought to a doorway boot brush (hedgehog models are popular, but other animals are available). No gardener wants to bring all of the garden indoors.

Horticultural Haute Couture

Henry David Thoreau warned in *Walden* (1854) to "beware of all enterprises that require new clothes." Fortunately—or unfortunately, if you're a clothes horse—gardening doesn't require a new wardrobe. Most gardeners don't give a hang about how they look as they plant dahlia tubers or remove Japanese beetles from the hollyhocks. Anything comfortable will serve: clothes that are loose enough to let you bend and kneel, things you don't mind getting dirty and stained.

For gardeners who do give a hang about how they look, there is more than one garden-supply company offering Japanese farmer's pants, imported rubber boots, silk-screened bandannas, elbow-high goatskin gloves, and hand-woven palm hats. If your garden is located on Beacon Hill or Pacific Heights, you may not want to be seen in patched pants and a threadbare T-shirt your son discarded in 1987; otherwise, wear what feels good, with these admonishments.

Protect your hands. Many gardeners prefer to work barehanded, but with thorny plants or plants that cause rashes, even diehards use gloves. There are scores to choose from, and good choices include the inexpensive cotton gloves available at hardware stores and garden shops. Heavy leather gloves are first-class protection against thorns, but animal hide is hot and becomes stiff if it gets wet and dries out. A better choice are Mud Gloves. Manufactured by Little's Good Gloves, a family company in Arizona; Mud Gloves are made from cotton that's been dipped in rubber. The gloves come in purple, red, royal blue,

and other bright colors, and are sold at garden stores and online (www.mudglove.com) about $8 a pair, in sizes XXS to XL.

Protect your skin. Dermatologists aren't blowing smoke: Prolonged exposure to the sun causes not just wrinkles but skin cancers. Gardeners should use sunscreens that are rated SPF 15 or higher and reapply them often. If possible, wear protective clothing as well: long-sleeved shirts, long pants, broad-brimmed hats, and UV-protective sunglasses. Little's Good Gloves makes a lightweight, broad-brimmed hat that is water-repellent, machine-washable, and has a chin draw cord to keep it on when the wind blows. (In *Gardening for Women*, 1908, Frances Garnet Wolseley suggested, "The old-fashioned plan of putting a couple of cabbage leaves in the crown of the hat is not to be despised, should the heat be felt very much.")

Protect your feet. Steel-toed leather shoes aren't necessary unless you're running power equipment, such as a rototiller, or your aim with a hoe is very poor, but you'll feel better after several hours in the garden if you wear what are euphemistically referred to as "sensible shoes." Whatever your taste in footwear, in the garden you'll want shoes that are sturdy and comfortable, that give your feet good support, and that are water-resistant and easy to clean. With rubber shoes, Louisa Johnson declared in *Every Lady Her Own Flower Gardener* (1840), "a lady may indulge her passion for flowers for all seasons, without risk of rheumatism or chills."

There are few shoes, rubber or otherwise, designed just for flower gardening, but there are some possibilities. Choose shoes—you may want more than one pair—that fit how you garden. If you don't do much more than picking flowers, clogs are all you'll need, but if your garden work includes lots of digging and tilling and other toe-threatening tasks, look for more substantial shoes.

Work boots are overkill for most flower gardeners, even though Mother Goose's Old Woman lived in one, but they are an excellent choice if you're doing jobs in the garden that involve hazardous power equipment and tools with sharp blades.

Rubber boots are known as Wellingtons and Wellies on the other side of the Atlantic, where they are knee-high, Kermit-green, and *de rigueur* for serious gardeners. (Wellies are named after Arthur, the first Duke of Wellington, who was such a fashion plate that coats, trousers, and hats also bear his name.)

Protecting the Gardener. *Wearing a hat and using sunscreen are good defenses against skin carcinomas, which are caused by prolonged exposure to the sun. Watering by hand is not the most environmentally efficient approach, but it is good for the soul.*

Waterproof and easy to clean, yes, but Wellingtons aren't comfortable enough to wear all day.

Gumboots, created by L. L. Bean himself in 1912, are a marriage of rubber shoes with leather uppers. This union, invented for hunters but valuable for gardeners, keeps feet dry and provides reasonable support and comfort. Both shoe and moccasin models make good garden shoes, and liners are available for when the mercury drops.

Garden clogs, made of hard, lightweight polyurethane, are deservedly popular. They are durable, waterproof, comfortable, and easy to slip on and off at the back door. Both open- and closed-heeled models are available. Be sure to choose clogs that have good arch support and do not have heels, such as those made by Birkenstock.

Floral Timepiece. *Flowers aren't weather instruments, but some have been used to tell time. Portulaca grandiflora 'Sundial Gold', a hybrid moss rose, opens its petals about 8 o'clock each day—if the sun is shining—then closes them when the light fades.*

Tools for the Brain

Not all garden tools are made of wood, metal, and plastic: Accurate information is crucial to successful gardening, and most garden writing is all about being "communicative," about sharing ideas and experiences, and collaborating. "I merely wish to talk to you on paper," Mrs. E. W. Earle begins *Pot-Pourri from a Surrey Garden* (1897).

For the latest news, consider subscribing to a garden magazine. *Horticulture, Fine Gardening, Canadian Gardening,* and *American Gardener* are all worthy titles, and there are also many specialized and regional horticultural periodicals, such as *Garden Design, Northern Gardener, Pacific Horticulture,* and *Mississippi Gardener.* There also are scores of garden newsletters published by commercial seed and plant companies, local horticultural organizations, botanical gardens and arboretums, plant societies, and avid individuals. A web search using a search engine—be as specific as possible—will produce many choices.

You'll also want to fill a shelf or two with books. Most large bookstores carry garden titles, as do online stores such as Amazon.com. A fine source for both new and used garden books is Powell's City of Books (www.powells.com), a mammoth store located in Portland, Oregon. Mail-order service is excellent, and it's a superb place to find out-of-print titles.

Joining plant and horticultural organizations, national or local, is another way to discover the very best garden information. Many groups publish magazines or newsletters, have seed and plant exchanges, sponsor flower shows, *and* provide a chance to meet and talk to other gardeners. If you want to help preserve old-time flowers, spend a few dollars and join the nonprofit Flower and Herb Exchange (FHE), an offspring of the Seed Savers Exchange. The FHE annual yearbook contains a list of 2,000 heirloom cultivars, the seeds of which FHE members make available

GARDENING FOR ALL

The 19th-century American author Charles Dudley Warner observed, "What a man needs in gardening is a cast-iron back, with a hinge in it." Back and joint pain sometimes come with gardening, but they don't have to. There now are more and more ergonomic tools—products designed to reduce stress and strain on the body—to choose from, everything from stools on wheels and knee pads to trowels with arm-support cuffs and gel-filled "anti-vibe" gloves. Also available are adaptive devices that can be fitted to standard garden tools, such as handle extensions and special grips. Look for tools manufactured by Good Grips, Peta Easi-Grip, GT, Fist Grip, and Wrist-Easy. Fiskars is among the traditional tool manufacturers that has developed a line of ergonomic hand tools. For additional information about ergonomic tools, contact the American Horticultural Therapy Association, 909 York Street, Denver, CO 80206; www.ahta.org. (See Appendix, page 457, for mail-order sources of ergonomic tools.)

to others. Joining is a good deal and a good deed. (See Appendix, page 457, for more information.)

As Katharine S. White demonstrated 40 years ago in her essays in *The New Yorker*, seed and plant catalogs are more than inventories of things to buy: "Whatever may be said about the seedsmen's and nurserymen's methods, their catalogue writers are my favorite authors and produce my favorite reading material." Not a bad recommendation, coming from the wife of E. B. White. Today's catalogs aren't as newsy as they were in White's day, but many still make good reading. You'll find companies large and small, national and local, general and specialized, everything from established firms like Burpee that sell a wide range of seeds and plants to companies with a precise focus, such as Brent & Becky's Bulbs, Schreiner's Iris Gardens, or Cricket Hill Garden, a Connecticut nursery that specializes in Chinese tree peonies. Get your name on mailing lists; there are hundreds of firms to choose from, and most catalogs are free or cost only a dollar or two.

Finally, don't forget to pick the brains of the experts. That group includes local gardeners, garden club and plant society members (who are a goldmine of reliable advice), and local professionals at newspapers, garden centers, botanical gardens, state universities, and Cooperative Extension Services.

You can query gardeners on the web by joining garden forums, which allow you to post specific questions, or by searching the enormous Cooperative Extension Service database. The site—webgarden.osu.edu—is maintained by Ohio State University and provides access to every state Cooperative Extension Service, to "Plant Facts,"

to an Internet search engine that focuses on plants and horticulture, to photographic databases, and more. Some government web sites, like the one sponsored by the Texas Cooperative Extension (aggie-horticulture.tamu.edu/plantanswers), will answer questions online. Web sites come and go at sonic speed, so don't be discouraged if you can't find a site that you used a month ago—just search for a new one.

Gardeners are a generous tribe. Face to face, telephone to telephone, mailbox to mailbox, or computer to computer, they willingly share their knowledge and their enthusiasm. "No one can garden alone," Elizabeth Lawrence observed. Her *Gardening for Love*, published posthumously in 1987, celebrates the connections made by "hard-working farm women who are never too tired . . . to gather seeds, to dig and pack plants, and to send them off with friendly letters." *The Little Bulbs: A Tale of Two Gardens* (1957), another Lawrence book, is not just a jubilation of spring's small bulbs, it is an account of a decade-long correspondence between two gardeners. We are, she wrote of herself and her friend Mr. Krippendorf, "an antiphonal chorus, like two frogs in neighboring ponds: What do you have in bloom, I ask, and he answers from Ohio that there are hellebores in the woods. . . . Then I tell him that in North Carolina the early daffodils are out."

Garden interchanges aren't new, of course. In 1735, the Englishman Peter Collinson wrote to his Virginia friend John Custis, "I think there is no Greater pleasure than to be Communicative and oblige others. . . . Wee Brothers of the Spade find it very necessary to share." Wee Sisters do too. Brother or sister, so will you.

PART II

Plant Portraits

Reasonably fertile soil, adequate light, moderate rainfall, and an attentive gardener are enough to make most flowers bloom, but not always to bloom well. Although some plants are more demanding than others, every plant has idiosyncrasies, or at least preferences. This Plant Portraits section lays out the individual needs of many common—and some not-so-common—garden flowers.

Each entry provides basic information about the plant: what its leaves and flowers look like, when it blooms, how large it gets. The How to Grow section details what conditions the plant needs to thrive. The What to Grow section lists recommendations of the best species and cultivars. The "Other Choices" sidebar offers names and descriptions of similar other flowers worth growing. The In the Garden section gives advice on the plant's uses.

And just in case the aphorism is as true for books as it is for Jack—that all work makes for dullness—entries also contain a bit of plant history and lore. Knowing that smoking the flower petals of California poppies (*Eschscholzia californica*) can "calm the nerves" isn't essential to growing or enjoying the flower, but it might come in handy after a hard day. Gardening, after all, should be fun.

While attempting to be as complete as possible, Plant Portraits is a place to begin. Flower growers forced to cope with extreme conditions, such as those with a tropical address or a site where the sun hardly shines, must go beyond these pages. They and readers with special interests—wildflowers, for examples, or Asiatic lilies—will need to consult more specialized or definitive resources. (See the Appendix, page 457, for suggestions for further reading.)

General how-to information—directions on sowing seeds, making stem cuttings, dealing with Japanese beetles and powdery mildew, deadheading or disbudding, raising or lowering soil pH, and much more—is contained in Chapters 1 through 9.

Achillea

(ah-KILL-ee-ah)

Yarrows

Aster family, Asteraceae. Hardy perennials.

○

In times past, some species of yarrow—there are more than 85—were important medicinal herbs. Linnaeus chose the genus name from the legend of Homer's hero Achilles, who gave pieces of the plant to his soldiers to stop their wounds from bleeding. Common yarrow, or milfoil (*Achillea millefolium*) apparently does have chemicals that help to clot blood, justifying its country names: nosebleed, woundwort, bloodwort, and staunchgrass.

Yarrow also has been prescribed for headaches, toothaches, consumption, bronchitis, and colds, but its most popular use was for matters of the heart: A piece under the pillow was said to make the sleeper dream of the person he or she would wed. The herbalist John Gerard recommended a mixture of yarrow and hogs grease "applied warme into the privie parts" to cure men's sexual ailments. Modern Casanovas should take care, as yarrow can cause minor skin irritations.

Common yarrow shouldn't be your first choice for the garden. Summer-blooming fernleaf yarrow (*A. filipendulina*) is a far better plant. (Renowned horticulturist Allan Armitage calls it one of "the most welcome of all plants for spring and summer gardens.") Its aromatic, elegant, fernlike foliage is topped by 3- to 6-inch flower heads held on long, stiff stems, each made up of a dense flat or slightly domed cluster of tiny mustard-yellow blooms.

HOW TO GROW

Fernleaf yarrow is easy to cultivate. It wants full sun and average, even infertile, soil that drains well, which makes it a good choice for a dry, semi-sandy location. (Rich

Yarrow, Achillea *'Coronation Gold'*

HORTICULTURAL SHORTHAND

These symbols are used throughout Plant Portraits to highlight important growing conditions for each plant. Keep in mind that flowers that require full sun in northern gardens may prefer partial sun in southern beds and borders and that different species of the same plant may need different conditions.

○ Full sun (more than six hours of sun per day; ideally, sun all day)

◑ Partial sun (some direct sun but less than six hours per day)

● Shade (dappled or low light but no direct sun)

▼ Grows well in containers

soil will produce weak, floppy growth.) New plants need regular watering, but once established they require little care. Yarrow spreads quickly and may require dividing every three or four years, either in spring or early fall.

Plants grown in full sun and thin soil won't need staking and will bloom a second time if deadheaded or cut back after the first flowers fade. Begin with nursery plants, plant divisions, root cuttings, or seeds. Growing from seed is easy, although many cultivars must be propagated by division or other vegetative means. Seeds need light to sprout, which takes about 12 days in 70°F temperatures; plants will bloom about a year from sowing. Set plants at least 18 inches apart.

Yarrow has few insect enemies, but powdery mildew can be a problem if plants are crowded.

WHAT TO GROW

Look for *A. filipendulina* hybrids 'Gold Plate' (4 feet tall, 5-inch gold flower clusters); midsummer-flowering 'Cloth of Gold' (3–4 feet, mustard yellow); 'Parker's Variety' (3 feet, yellow); 'Moonshine' (2 feet, lemon yellow); and 'Anthea' (2 feet, pale yellow). 'Coronation Gold', which has *A. filipendulina* as one of its parents, is 3 feet tall and has bright yellow 3-inch flower clusters and gray-green foliage. It was released in 1953 to mark Queen Elizabeth's coronation and is still one of the best. All are hardy in Zones 3 to 9. Plants tend to be spindly in the warmest zones.

A. millefolium 'Citronella', which may be the best of the common yarrows, is pale yellow, 30 inches tall, strong stemmed, long-flowering, and boasts fair repeat blooms. S. 'Colorado' is vigorous and long-flowering in shades of red, pink, terra-cotta, and yellow, as well as white; it's popular with cut-flower growers. Two-foot 'Lilac Beauty' has strong stems and received four stars in a Chicago Botanic Garden trial; 'Fanal', one of the Galaxy Hybrid Series, has large crimson flower heads and stout stems; 'Cassis', a Fleuroselect winner, has cherry red flowers. Other popular cultivars are 'Fire King' and 'Summer Pastels'. All are hardy in Zones 3 to 9.

IN THE GARDEN

Yarrows are handsome, versatile additions to sunny gardens—especially those that have somewhat dry,

well-drained soil. Plant them with hardy geraniums, or cranesbills (*Geranium* spp.); daylilies; purple coneflower (*Echinacea purpurea*); salvias, or sages (*Salvia* spp.); ornamental grasses; and yuccas (*Yucca* spp.). The flowers are excellent for cutting for fresh bouquets and also make stunning dried flowers. Pick blooms once they have full, rich color and before they turn brown. Hang blooms in small bunches in a warm, dry spot for drying.

Aconitum

(ak-oh-NIE-tum)

Monkshoods, aconites, wolfsbanes

Buttercup family, Ranunculaceae.
Hardy perennials.

Striking and long-lived, monkshoods are invaluable perennials for the rich colors they add to the garden from midsummer to fall. Most come in shades of blue and violet, sometimes combined with white, but there also are species with yellow flowers. The showy parts of the flowers aren't real petals but petal-like sepals. The uppermost sepal is enlarged and hood shaped, thus the common name monk's hood or monkshood. And that's just the beginning. Aconitums are also called auld wife's huid, friar's cap, and helmet flower, all allusions to their flowers. Individual blossoms are usually 1 to 2 inches long and are carried in large, showy, branched clusters. Like other members of the buttercup family, monkshood foliage is fernlike, a nice enhancement to the flowers.

If yours is a garden frequented by small children apt to stick plant parts in their mouths, be aware of another, more sinister, aspect of monkshoods that is hinted at in common names such as wolfsbane and mousebane. These plants contain aconitine, a toxic alkaloid and one of the most poisonous plant compounds known. Highest concentrations are found in the carrotlike roots, but the compound is present in all plant parts. *Aconitum ferox*, which is not grown in gardens, has the highest concentration, but the garden plant *Aconitum napellus* contains the second-highest concentrations. Medicinal uses date at least to A.D. 200, when aconites were mentioned

---

OTHER CHOICES

Woolly yarrow (*Achillea tomentosa*) has creeping stems and yellow flowers borne on 10-inch stalks. 'Moonlight' has pale yellow blooms. It spreads quickly but requires sun and well-drained soil, exactly the conditions that rock gardens provide. Plants are hardy in Zones 4 to 8, but don't like humidity or high heat.

in Chinese herbals. The root was once prepared as a restorative, but dosage was crucial: Over the centuries, monkshoods have also been used to make a decoction for poisoning wolves—and criminals. Shakespeare, who knew garden plants well, was aware of its potency—as strong as "rash gunpowder," he wrote in *King Henry VI*.

HOW TO GROW

With their rich color and mid- to late-season bloom, it's a wonder that monkshoods aren't found in more flower gardens. Add to that their appreciation of a spot in partial or dappled shade, and you have a perennial to treasure. Monkshoods also grow in full sun, but they struggle with heat and don't thrive where nighttime temperatures stay above 70°F. Give plants rich, evenly moist soil away from damp spots, and water deeply during dry spells. Since monkshoods have tall, brittle stems that carry heavy loads of flowers, their only other site requirement is a spot protected from wind.

Start with plants in spring or fall—monkshoods are tough to grow from seeds. Since they resent transplanting, dig a good-size planting hole and work in plenty of organic matter. Once planted they'll thrive *in situ* for many years. If the clumps do outgrow their location, they can be divided in spring or fall. Handle the tuberlike roots carefully, as they break easily.

Monkshoods may need staking. Deadhead back to lateral stems to promote a second round of flowers. Plants are sometimes attacked by mildews, and crown rot will attack the roots if the soil is too wet. Remember their sinister nature whenever you handle them: Wear rubber gloves, especially when handling the roots, since sap on skin will cause tingling and numbness, and be sure to keep your hands away from your face, especially your eyes and mouth.

WHAT TO GROW

Popular blue- and purple-flowered monkshoods are similar in appearance, but it still pays to plant several different species or cultivars since they bloom at slightly different times. Azure monkshood (*A. carmichaelii*), hardy in Zones 3 to 8 and usually 2 to 3 feet tall, produces violet-blue blooms from late summer through fall. 'Arendsii' and 'Pink Sensation' are good cultivars. Common monkshood (*A. napellus*),

Common monkshood, Aconitum napellus

Zones 3 to 7 and 3 to 4 feet tall, bears blue-violet flowers in mid- to late summer. A. × *cammarum* (formerly A. × *bicolor*), hardy in Zones 4 to 8, is also 3 to 4 feet tall. Its blue, violet, purple, or bicolor flowers appear from mid- to late summer. Available cultivars include 'Blue Sceptre' and 'Bressingham Spire', which reach only 3 feet and need no staking. For yellow flowers, consider wolfsbane (*A. lycoctonum* spp. *vulparia*), hardy in Zones 4 through 8 and 2 to 6 feet tall. It blooms from midsummer to early fall. A. 'Ivorine' bears pale ivory-yellow flowers on 3-foot plants that don't need staking.

IN THE GARDEN

Handsome wherever they're grown, monkshoods are best planted toward the back of a perennial border or near the center of a flower bed. Otherwise they look tall and ungainly. Shorter selections are compact enough for a front-of-the-border spot. Monkshoods also make lovely cut flowers. Combine them with perennials such as snakeroots (*Cimicifuga* spp.), Solomon's seals (*Polygonatum* spp.), turtleheads (*Chelone* spp.), asters, chrysanthemums, fall-blooming anemones (*Anemone hupehensis*, *A.* × *hybrida*, *A. tomentosa*), and sneezeweed (*Helenium autumnale*).

Ageratum houstonianum

(ah-jer-RAY-tum hoo-sto-nee-AN-um)

Floss flower

Aster family, Asteraceae. Annual.

Ageratum's popularity as a bedding plant is not simply because it offers a range of blue flowers (Blue ageratums photograph horribly, but they are lovely in person.) Its popularity is also due to its tidy mounding habit, its easy culture, and its willingness to flower from late spring until the first frost.

Ageratum flower clusters are made up of tiny fluffy blooms, explaining the common name blue puffs. Colors are various and include lavender, lilac, pink, and white, as well as blue. A native of Mexico and Central America—another common name is Mexican ageratum—floss flowers range from 5 to 24 inches tall and spread from 5 to 18 inches. Their opposite, rough, green leaves are ovate, or egg-shaped, with rounded teeth, and they have a textured look.

The long life of each flower cluster, another ageratum trait, is embedded in its name: *Geras* means "old " in Greek, and the *a* that precedes it changes the meaning to "not old." The flowers retain their color for weeks, one reason they are prized by the cut-flower industry. The species name honors William Houstoun, an 18th-century Scottish plant collector.

Despite its tidy habit, ageratum is a noxious weed in some tropical settings, giving rise to the common names of goat weed, Todd's curse, and blue billygoat weed. Most North American gardeners have nothing to fear, however, and can use a gentler nickname, pussy-foots.

HOW TO GROW

Ageratums like average, moist but well-drained soil and full sun. (In regions with torrid summers, give plants afternoon shade and don't let them dry out.) Set plants 6 to 12 inches apart, depending on the cultivar. You can begin with seeds, which are tiny and need a head start of at least eight weeks as well as light to germinate. It's easier to take advantage

Floss flower, Ageratum houstonianum *'Fine Wine'*

of the market packs of live plants that every garden center offers in early spring. Set plants out after the danger of frost has passed.

You must deadhead faithfully to keep flowers coming; if plants begin to falter in midsummer, cut them back 2 or 3 inches to stimulate new growth. Like most annuals, ageratums resent too much fertilizer, so feed them sparingly if at all. Ageratums have few pest or disease problems, but planting too early in spring when the ground is still cold and wet can cause root rot, which is signaled by wilted or yellowing plants. Overwatering encourages powdery mildew.

WHAT TO GROW

Among the short varieties, 'Blue Mink' is the old standby, but there are new and better cultivars including 'Blue Blazer' (5 inches tall, deep blue); Royal Horticultural Society winner 'Blue Danube' (a.k.a. 'Blue Puffs', lavender-blue, 6 inches); 'Purple Fields', a violet-blue Fleuroselect F₁ hybrid winner that spreads to 15 inches and grows 8 to 10 inches tall; 'Southern Cross' (blue-white bicolor, 12 inches); and 'Shell Pink Hawaii', another F₁ hybrid with double flowers, 7 inches tall and 7 inches across. If you want every ageratum color, try 'Hawaii Mixed', a collection of pinks, blues, and white, all 6 to 8 inches tall. The flowers of white cultivars, such as the 12-inch 'Silver Pearl', turn brown as they age.

For cut flowers or fillers in the herbaceous border, pick taller ageratums, which have more open blooms. Good choices are 'Blue Bouquet', which grows to 2 feet; 'Florist's White', which has sturdy 2-foot stems; and 'Blue Horizon', a vigorous, branching triploid with stiff stems that grows to 30 inches and bears 3-inch mid-blue flower clusters.

IN THE GARDEN

Ageratum is a traditional edging and pattern plant, but it deserves more. Include small cultivars in flower boxes and containers; taller cultivars can add color to the middle of borders and beds. An all-season bloomer, ageratums combine nicely with sweet alyssum (*Lobularia maritima*), marigolds, pink petunias, lobelias, verbenas, dusty miller (*Senecio cineraria*), feverfew (*Tanacetum parthenium*), salvias or sages (*Salvia* spp.), impatiens, Madagascar periwinkle (*Catharanthus roseus*), and many other flowers.

Alcea rosea

(AL-see-ah ROSE-ee-ah)

Hollyhock

Mallow family, Malvaceae. Hardy perennial.

○

This grand dame of cottage gardens—"barn flowers" to those who remember them growing untended at the base of farm buildings—usually is treated as a biennial or annual. Its former moniker was *Althaea rosea*, that genus name means "heal." The common name also tells a story: It was once known as holy-hock because one source of the plant was the Holy Lands. The "hock" part of the name refers to the leaf's supposed power to cure swelling of horses' hocks.

In 1631, John Winthrop Jr., sent to England for a half-ounce of "hollihock" seeds. Perhaps he believed the herbalists who claimed that the plant could "mollifie hard tumours," for his large seed order included few ornamentals. Certainly a Puritan like Winthrop didn't subscribe to this ancient hollyhock recipe:

> Buds of hollihocke
> Topes of Thyme
> Flowers of Hazel
> In Rose-water brime
> Steeped in the sun
> Rubbed on the eye
> On a moonlight midnight
> A Fairie ye'll spy.

There are many modern cultivars—towering and dwarf; single, semidouble, and double forms; and every color except true blue—but the plant's basic

OTHER CHOICES

If you love ageratums and want to add a perennial with fluffy blue flowers to a shade or wildflower garden, consider hardy ageratum (*Eupatorium coelestinum*). Also called mistflower, it is a native wildflower and hardy in Zones 5 to 9. See *Eupatorium* on page 306 for more information.

Hollyhock, Alcea rosea *'Indian Spring'*

nature hasn't really changed. "Hollihocks," John Parkinson wrote 400 years ago, "both single and double, of many and sundry colours, yeeld out their flowers like roses on their tall branches, like Trees." If you have a historical bent, you may want to grow 'Nigra', a purple-black single. Thomas Jefferson did.

Hardy in Zones 3 to 9, hollyhocks have large, coarsely lobed leaves and are sharply vertical plants, taller than broad; their 2- to 4-inch flowers appear atop the stems, which can stretch to 10 feet, half of which will be covered in blooms. Single types have five petals; double blooms resemble double peony flowers. Hollyhocks bloom in summer, beginning at the bottom of the spire.

HOW TO GROW

Garden centers sell seedlings in spring that will bloom by summer, but hollyhocks are simple to grow from seeds. Germination takes two weeks at 65°F. Most old-fashioned single types must be treated as biennials: Sow seeds shallowly in individual pots in midsummer and transplant to the garden a month before the first-frost date. Modern cultivars will flower the first year like annuals do if they are begun indoors at least eight weeks before the frost-free date. Transplant outdoors once the soil has warmed.

Hollyhocks want moderately rich, moist soil that drains well, full sun, and room to grow. Plants will flower in partial shade, but tall cultivars, which should be staked before their flowers open, are even less likely to stay upright if not grown in full sun. (Tall cultivars can be cut back in spring to limit their height.) Mature plants resent having their roots disturbed and are nearly impossible to transplant. Deadhead regularly. To promote a second bloom, cut plants back severely once flowering has ended. In the language of flowers, hollyhocks signify fruitfulness—and for good reason, as they self-seed capably. To save seeds, allow the seedpods, which look like miniature cheese wheels, to dry on the plant.

Hollyhocks are susceptible to rust, which begins on the bottom leaves and moves up. Remove and destroy yellowing and rust-infected leaves. Plants are beloved by Japanese beetles and sometimes troubled by spider mites.

OTHER CHOICES

Fig-leaved hollyhock (*Alcea ficifolia*) is worth looking for. It has pale yellow single flowers and grows to 6 feet. 'Happy Lights Mix', a blend of 3-inch white, pink, red, purple, and yellow flowers, has excellent rust resistance. It can be grown as an annual or biennial.

Perennial mallows, or malvas, are hollyhock cousins—and hollyhock look-alikes. Look for cultivars of tree mallow (*Malva sylvestris*). Drought-tolerant dwarf 'Zebra' has pale pink flowers striped with purple; the blooms of 'Mystic Merlin' range from purple to mauve to violet; plants grow to 4 feet. Hollyhock mallow (*M. alcea* var. *fastigiata*) bears 2-inch cupped rose-pink flowers on its many 3-foot stems. Musk mallow (*M. moschata*), which has naturalized in the Northeast, has 2-inch pink flowers. All like sun and well-drained soil and do better in the North than in warmer climates. Malvas flower in summer and are self-seeding. Musk mallow is hardy to Zone 3, the others to Zone 4; all can be grown south to Zone 8.

Annual mallow (*Lavatera trimestris*) is a bushy annual that is covered with 2-inch hollyhock-like flowers throughout summer. Three good cultivars are the white 'Mont Blanc', 'Pink Beauty', which is pale pink with purple veins, and the bright rose-pink 'Silver Cup'.

Annual mallow, Lavatera trimestris *'Pink Beauty'*

WHAT TO GROW

It's hard to understand why anyone would want a short hollyhock, but if you do, 'Majorette', a semi-double, is under 3 feet. It and 'Summer Carnival', a 5-footer, are bred to flower in their first year. Both are All-America Selections winners. A good double is 'Chater's Double', which comes in a mix of colors. The classic single hollyhock is harder to find in garden centers. Look for 'Country Garden', 'Indian Spring', or 'Old Barnyard'; all are mixes. 'Crème de Cassis' has both single and double 3-inch flowers, wine purple with white edges—an eye-catcher at 6 feet.

IN THE GARDEN

Hollyhocks by the doorway or along a fence are garden clichés but appealing all the same. Ideal flowers for cottage or casual gardens, they belong in the back of borders, planted in numbers rather than singly. Combine them with baby's breaths (*gypsophila* spp.) and phlox. Hollyhocks also are dependable seashore plants, and they attract beneficial insects. Mix them with lupines, columbines (*Aquilegia* spp.), pinks (*Dianthus* spp.), and bee balms (*Monarda* spp.) to guarantee a charm of hummingbirds.

Alchemilla mollis

(al-kuh-MIL-lah MOL-iss)

Lady's mantle

Rose family, Rosaceae. Hardy perennial.

Dainty pleated leaves and soft-textured clusters of chartreuse flowers make this perennial a subtle garden resident that grows on you. Both scientific and common names have interesting origins: In the Middle Ages, the pleated and scalloped leaves were thought to resemble headdresses worn by the Virgin Mary, thus the name lady's mantle. The name *Alchemilla* came from the Arabic name for the plant and refers to its use in alchemy. One expert states that *Alchemilla* means "little magical one," and says this phrase refers to another one of this plant's charms—water or dew beads up on the leaves and decorates them like glistening jewels. Alchemists

Lady's mantle, Alchemilla mollis

called the dewdrops that collected on the leaves "water from heaven" and gathered them for experiments.

Lady's mantle, native to the Carpathians, Caucasus, and Turkey, is a mounding perennial, with rounded leaves that have 9 to 11 lobes and sprawling stems that spill over pathways and blend with nearby bed companions. Loose clusters of tiny, star-shaped flowers appear from early summer to early fall, and plants range from about 15 to 24 inches tall. Plants are hardy from Zones 3 through 7.

HOW TO GROW

Buying a plant or two is the easiest way to add lady's mantle to your garden, and since plants self-sow, you'll soon have plenty to move around the garden or share with friends. Give plants a spot that's sunny or partially shaded. Rich, moist, but well-drained soil is a must if plants are to thrive, and in areas with hot summers, consistent moisture and shade during the hottest part of the day are essential to success.

Strangely enough, alchemilla are what botanists call *apomicts*, meaning plants set seeds without pollination and yield seedlings that are identical to their parents. Deadhead plants to curtail seed production, and in spring or early summer either move seedlings that appear or pull them up. Clumps also can be divided in spring or fall. Fussy gardeners prop up the sprawling stems with twiggy brush, but most gardeners enjoy seeing plants sprawl and blend. If plants get messy-looking in midsummer, cut them down and keep them evenly moist; they'll reward this care with a new flush of leaves for fall. Plantings also can be mown down or cut back in late winter to neaten them. Plants have no serious pest or disease problems.

WHAT TO GROW

A few cultivars of A. *mollis* are offered in the trade—including 'Auslese' and 'Robusta'—but they differ little from the species. 'Thriller' does sport larger leaves and flowers than the species.

IN THE GARDEN

Use lady's mantle as an edging, allowing it to add casual charm to pathways and patios with its sprawling stems. It is handsome in perennial beds and borders, where it combines well with other front-edge residents such as small- and medium-size hostas, Siberian iris (*Iris sibirica*), astilbes, and ferns. Or use it as a ground cover under shrubs such as rhododendrons, azaleas, and lilacs.

Allium

(AL-ee-um)

Ornamental onions, alliums

Lily family, Liliaceae. Hardy bulbs.

Both cooks and vegetable gardeners are familiar with onions and their kin—garlic, chives, shallots, and leeks—and anyone who has weeded a lawn or a garden bed has done battle with another pesky onion cousin, field garlic (A. *vineale*). Alas, flower gardeners too often overlook alliums entirely, yet this genus of about 700 species deserves the ornamental part of its ornamental onion moniker. Better still, most are as easy to grow as daffodils are.

Ancient gardeners certainly recognized the value of alliums, although not always for their horticultural merits. A. *moly*—also known as leek lily and golden garlic—was reputed to have magical qualities in Greek mythology: Odysseus escaped being turned into a swine because of golden garlic, which was an antidote to the sorceress Circe's

Persian onion, Allium aflatunense

poison. In southern Europe, growing golden garlic was believed to bring good luck and protection from demons. The English were more suspicious. "As for repeating of foolish and vaine figments," the herbalist John Gerard wrote at the end of the 16th century, "I leave them to such as had rather plaie with shadowes than bestow their wits about profitable and serious matters."

All alliums are bulbs, ranging from small to large. In some cases the bulbs are barely developed and may be connected by short rhizomes so the plants form clumps over time. Dig up a clump of chives (A. *schoenoprasum*), and you'll find a tight clump of bulbs that really look more like fleshy stems with hairlike roots attached at the bottom.

The genus contains garden-worthy plants that bloom in spring, summer, and fall. Leaves range from cylindrical to strap-shaped and usually have a characteristic onion aroma when bruised or broken. While the individual flowers are small—they're bell, cup, or star shaped—they're carried in showy clusters called *umbels* atop hollow, unbranched stems. The individual blooms may be loosely arranged in graceful clusters or densely packed to form ball-like heads. Size ranges from dainty 1-inch pom-poms to huge 5-inch globes.

HOW TO GROW

Not surprisingly in a group as large as this one, there are alliums to fit a wide variety of garden sites; hardiness varies as well. In general, a spot in full sun with well-drained soil keeps most alliums happy. They'll grow in poor soil or rich, and they also perform well in soil that stays on the dry side. One thing to keep in mind when planting alliums is that the leaves of most species die back just before or after the plants flower. To avoid having an empty hole in the garden, plan on pairing them with perennials, annuals, or low-growing shrubs that can hide the leaves as they die back and fill the empty spot once they're gone. Do not cut the foliage back before it yellows completely—it's making food for next year's flowers.

Plant dormant bulbs, pointed end up, in fall, setting the top of the bulb at a depth about three times the diameter of the bulb. Plant potted alliums in spring or fall, setting them at the same depth they were growing in the pot. Once they're in the ground, alliums need little care. Deadhead species that self-sow too vigorously, such as garlic chives (*A. tuberosum*). Common chives (*A. schoenoprasum*), an edible family member that also deserves a spot in the flower garden, benefits from a postblooming haircut: Shear the clumps, foliage and all, to about 2 inches, and they'll produce new leaves.

You can propagate alliums by digging and dividing the clumps just after flowering, by removing offsets from the parent bulb or by planting the tiny bulbils in the flower heads produced by some species. To start from seeds, sow in pots and set them in a protected spot outdoors in summer or fall. Dig seedlings produced by species that self-sow, such as *A. christophii* and *A. tuberosum*, and move them to other locations in the garden.

Allium bulbs can rot in wet sites, but they are seldom bothered by pests or diseases.

WHAT TO GROW

By planting early, midseason, and late species, you can enjoy alliums' showy blooms from spring to fall.

Early blooming alliums flower from spring to early summer, starting with Persian onion (*A. aflatunense*). It produces dense, 4-inch, red-violet balls on 2- to 3-foot plants. Hardy in Zones 4 to 8, it resembles *A. giganteum*, but the bulbs are less expensive, and the plants last longer in the garden. Blue globe onion (*A. caeruleum*) features dark blue, 2-inch clusters and ranges from 1 to 2 feet tall. Hardy from Zones 3 to 8, it likes a warm spot and needs very well-drained soil. Star of Persia (*A. christophii*), which makes an especially handsome dried flower, has loose, open silver-purple clusters, 8 to 12 inches across. Plants reach 1 to 2 feet and are hardy in Zones 4 to 8. Giant onion (*A. giganteum*) has 4-inch rosy-purple globes on 3- to 5-foot stems. Plants are hardy from Zones 4 to 8 but tend to be short-lived. Low-growing lily leek (*A. moly*) produces loose, 2-inch clusters of yellow flowers on foot-tall plants. Hardy in Zones 3 to 9, it grows in sun or partial shade. Plants need soil

Leek lily, Allium moly

Common chives, Allium schoenoprasum

3-inch umbels in rich violet-purple; and 'Mount Everest', with white, 6-inch blooms. All are hardy in Zones 4 or 5 to 8.

Two popular species add color to the summer garden. Both are clump formers, and *A. senescens,* or German garlic, features attractive leaves that stay green all summer. It produces round, inch-wide, mauve-pink clusters on foot-tall plants, and it is hardy in Zones 3 to 9. *A. senescens* var. *glaucum* has attractive, twisted, silver-blue leaves. Nodding onion (*A. cernuum*), which grows in shade, has clusters of nodding, rose-purple or pink flowers on 1½- to 2-foot plants. A North American native that naturalizes easily, it is hardy in Zones 4 to 9.

Of the alliums that flower from late summer to fall, garlic chives (*A. tuberosum*) is the best known. It produces rounded, 2-inch clusters of starry white flowers on 2-foot plants. Hardy in Zones 4 to 8, it's happiest in rich, evenly moist soil and needs regular deadheading to prevent excessive self-seeding. Finally, two other fall bloomers will add cheer to your late-season garden if you can find them. Look for *A. thunbergii,* or October onion, and *A. virgunculae.* Both feature rose-purple flowers, reach about 8 inches, spread to form nice clumps, and are hardy in Zones 4 to 8.

IN THE GARDEN

Combine alliums with other perennials that thrive in well-drained soil, including daylilies, coreopsis, yarrows (*Achillea* spp.), catmints (*Nepeta* spp.), lamb's-ears (*Stachys* spp.), and ornamental grasses. The blooms also are handsome punctuation marks in beds filled with shorter annuals and perennials, and springing up through ground covers. Alliums make pretty cut flowers. Cut the blooms (choose heads that have only half their florets open) the day before you need them and place them in water overnight to reduce the onion odor. Most species also make handsome dried flowers.

that is well drained and after flowering, nearly dry conditions. Chives (*A. schoenoprasum*) has cheerful, rosy pink blooms. Plants are hardy in Zones 3 to 9, and both foliage and flowers are edible.

A few hybrids are worth planting as well. Look for statuesque 'Globemaster', with 6- to 8-inch purple blooms; 'Lucy Ball', with 5-inch heads of dark purple; 'Purple Sensation', with dense,

Amsonia tabernaemontana

(am-SO-nee-ah tah-ber-nae-mon-TAH-nah)

Willow blue star, amsonia

Dogbane family, Apocynaceae.
Hardy perennial.

○ ◑

Willow blue star, Amsonia tabernaemontana

Also called blue star flower, eastern blue star, and blue dogbane, this native wildflower is named for Dr. Charles Amson, an 18th-century Virginia physician and traveler. (Its species name honors a German herbalist J. T. Tabernaemontanus.) A handsome, clump-forming perennial—established clumps actually look more like shrubs than perennials—it has narrow, alternate, willowlike leaves and produces rounded clusters of ½- to ¾-inch flowers in spring or early summer.

Each pale blue flower has a tubular, funnel-shaped base and a flared, starry face with five lobes. In addition to bringing truly blue flowers to the garden, willow blue star also features colorful yellow to orange fall foliage. (British plantsman Christopher Lloyd once described their blue as "wishy washy," but he is alone in that judgment.) Plants range from 1 to about 3 feet in height—they're taller and lankier in shade than sun—and form clumps that can spread 2 or 3 feet.

HOW TO GROW

Hardy in Zones 3 to 9, willow blue star is easy to grow and will pay big dividends if just given a spot in sun or partial shade with average, moist but well-drained soil. While established plants tolerate some drought, they are happiest with even moisture. They bloom best in full sun.

Once planted, they need little care to look their best. Most willow blue stars benefit from a post-blooming haircut, so cut them back to 6 or 8 inches to keep them from flopping and promote compact growth. Growing clumps through circular supports—like the hoops used to contain peonies—also helps keep them erect if you want to skip the pruning.

To propagate amsonias, divide the clumps in spring or fall or propagate by stem cuttings taken in early summer. Plants also self-sow, and seedlings are easy to dig up and move. To start seeds, soak them

OTHER CHOICES

Other species of amsonia make nice additions to the garden. *Amsonia hubrechtii* is a shrub-size native perennial, 2 to 3 feet tall, with pale blue flowers and narrow leaves. Its best season is fall, when the clumps turn a spectacular golden yellow. Downy blue star (*A. ciliata*) is a Southeast native. Plants reach 1 to 3 feet, produce pale blue flowers, and have threadlike leaves that turn yellow in fall. Both species are hardy in Zones 5 to 9.

overnight in warm water, then sow in pots—don't cover the seeds, as they need light to sprout. Set the pots outside in a cold frame or a protected spot for germination the following spring. Plants are rarely bothered by pests or diseases.

WHAT TO GROW

While the species is most commonly grown in gardens, two variants are available—*A. tabernaemontana* var. *salicifolia*, which has narrower leaves and looser flower clusters, and *A. tabernaemontana* var. *montana*, dwarf willow blue star, which is a compact form that only reaches about 1½ feet. Both are hardy in Zones 3 to 9.

IN THE GARDEN

Use amsonias with other native wildflowers, especially meadow plants like asters, Joe-Pye weeds (*Eupatorium* spp.), and meadow rues (*Thalictrum* spp.). They also make a handsome addition to perennial gardens in dappled shade or sun, where they can be combined nicely with ferns, coreopsis, lady's mantle (*Alchemilla mollis*), hardy geraniums, or cranesbills (*Geranium* spp.), bellflowers (*Campanula* spp.), cornflower (*Centaurea montana*), and Siberian iris (*Iris sibirica*).

Anemone

(ah-NEM-oh-nee)

Anemones, windflowers

Buttercup family, Ranunculaceae.
Hardy perennials, bulbs.

Grecian windflower, Anemone blanda

Anemones light up gardens at both ends of the season with their saucer-shaped blooms, each graced with a showy central cluster of golden-yellow stamens. Popular late summer and fall-blooming anemones carry their flowers in loose, branched clusters atop wiry stems that wave in the breeze. Spring- and early summer-blooming types tend to be lower growing and bear flowers in clusters or one bloom per stem. While classic anemones are single, they come in semidouble and double flowers as well. Blooms—which may be white, pink, rose-red, scarlet, yellow, lavender, or violet-blue—have showy petal-like sepals instead of true petals. Anemones feature attractive, deeply cut to almost fernlike leaves that are borne at the base of the plant. Some species also have leaves on their wiry flower stems. Root systems are diverse too: Anemones can have rhizomes, fleshy or fibrous roots, or woody tubers.

The name *Anemone* is from the Greek for "wind" and has obvious connections to the flower's common name, windflower. Pronunciation of the genus name differs slightly from the classical ah-nem-OH-nee; ah-NEM-oh-nee is more often used today. One Greek myth has it that the nymph Anemone was turned into a flower by the jealous Flora, the goddess of flowers and spring. Another version is that the anemone sprang from the tears of Venus: "And catching life from ev'ry falling tear, / Their azured heads anemones shall rear."

While members of this diverse genus look delicate enough to have sprung from tears, their appearance is deceptive, for many are tough, undemanding plants. There are about 120 species in all, plants for sun or shade as well as ones that can be used in perennial borders, as cut flowers, and in woodland gardens.

HOW TO GROW

Culturally, anemones can be divided into two groups: spring and early summer bloomers and late summer to fall flowering species. For the most part, spring-blooming anemones—A. *blanda*, A. *canadensis*, A. *nemorosa*, and A. *sylvestris*—need partial shade and rich, moist soil. A. *blanda* and A. *nemorosa* go dormant after flowering and are best combined with other low-growing perennials that will hide the hole they leave in the garden. Fall-blooming anemones grow in sun to partial shade and also need rich, moist, well-drained soil. A site protected from wind and afternoon sun is best, especially in areas with hot summers.

Pot-grown spring-blooming anemones can be planted in spring or fall. A. *blanda* grows from woody tubers that should be soaked overnight and planted in fall. Plant 2 inches deep and set the tubers on their sides, since it's hard to tell top from bottom. Fall-blooming anemones are best planted in spring.

Most anemones thrive for years without needing to be disturbed, but they can be dug and divided every four or five years for propagation or to keep the clumps from spreading too far. Add plenty of compost to the soil at planting time, and keep clumps well watered for the first season so plants put down healthy roots. Fall-bloomers should be mulched regularly.

Slugs and other leaf-eating pests attack anemones, as do deer, and they are subject to root decay and rust.

WHAT TO GROW

Spring-Blooming Anemones. Of these, Grecian windflower (A. *blanda*) is perhaps the best-known garden plant. It bears daisylike white, pink, or blue flowers that are 2 inches across. Various cultivars are available, including 'Blue Star', 'Pink Star', and 'White Star'. 'White Splendour' has creamy white flowers, and 'Charmer' features rosy pink ones. Plants are 6 to 8 inches tall, go dormant after flowering, and are hardy in Zones 4 to 8. Meadow anemone (A. *canadensis*), a native wildflower, is a vigorous species that spreads by rhizomes—it can be invasive—and produces single, white, 2-inch flowers on 6- to 8-inch plants. Use it as a ground cover in a wildflower garden. It needs moist soil and grows in sun or shade in Zones 3 to 7. Wood anemone (A. *nemorosa*) produces white, pale pink, or lavender-blue, ½- to ¾-inch flowers on plants that can reach 10 inches.

It spreads slowly by rhizomes and goes dormant after flowering, Zones 4 to 8. Snowdrop anemone (A. *sylvestris*) produces single, white, 2-inch flowers on 1- to 1½-foot plants. It spreads moderately fast and is hardy in Zones 3 to 8.

Fall-Blooming Anemones. Collectively called Japanese anemones, these include A. *hupehensis*, A. × *hybrida*, A. *tomentosa* (sometimes sold as A. *vitifolia* 'Robustissima'), and their cultivars. All have fibrous roots and bear loose clusters of 2- to 3-inch flowers on wiry stems that wave a foot or more above the foliage. The flowers, produced from late summer to fall, can be single, semidouble, or double

Japanese anemone, Anemone × hybrida *'Honorine Jobert'*

Grape-leaf anemone, Anemone tomentosa

and come in a range of pastels from pale to deep pink and white. Height ranges from 2 to 5 feet, and plants are hardy in Zones 4 to 8; *A. tomentosa* can be grown in Zone 3 with winter protection.

Many cultivars are available. If you tend to classics, consider 'Honorine Jobert', a pure-white single discovered in France in 1858. 'Whirlwind', a semidouble white, has 4-inch flowers compared to Honorine's 2- to 3-inch ones. Other selections include 'September Charm', which has pink flowers; 'Hadspen Abundance', deep pink single blooms; 'Margarete', a semidouble to double deep pink; and 'Queen Charlotte', which has 4-inch semidouble pink flowers.

Florist's Anemones. Also called poppy anemones (*A. coronaria*), these produce showy single or double blooms in scarlet, violet, or white. 'De Caen', a single-flowered type, and 'St. Brigid', a double, are most popular. Unlike most commonly grown anemones, these are neither hardy nor particularly long-lived. Where hardy—they're only reliable in Zones 8 to 10—they can be planted outdoors in fall. Give them sun or partial shade and well-drained, rich soil. In the North, grow them as annuals: Plant tubers in spring, or for better flowering, plant in

8-inch pots in fall, and overwinter them in a cool, frost-free place. Water sparingly until leaves appear, then keep the soil evenly moist.

IN THE GARDEN

Combine spring-blooming anemones with shade-loving plants, such as ferns. They're lovely planted with small bulbs, including species tulips, grape hyacinths (*Muscari* spp.), and daffodils. Other good perennial companions include smaller hostas, primroses (*Primula* spp.), columbines (*Aquilegia* spp.), fringed bleeding heart (*Dicentra eximia*), lungworts (*Pulmonaria* spp.), and foam flowers (*Tiarella* spp.). Both *A. canadensis* and *A. sylvestris* can be used as ground covers.

Fall-blooming anemones make handsome additions to perennial beds and borders, where they can be combined with asters, ornamental grasses, snakeroots (*Cimicifuga* spp.), monkshoods (*Aconitum* spp.), boltonia (*Boltonia asteroides*), and ornamental grasses.

Anthemis tinctoria

(an-THEE-mus tink-TOR-ee-ah)

Golden Marguerite

Aster family, Asteraceae. Hardy perennial.

Native from the Mediterranean to Iran, golden, or hardy, Marguerites produce an abundance of cheerful daisylike flowers throughout summer. One of the scores of plants that are recognized as "chamomile," the plant is also called ox-eye chamomile, yellow chamomile, and dyer's chamomile, because its blooms have long been used to dye wool and other fabrics (the *tinctoria* in *Anthemis tinctoria* means "dye plant"). Widely grown in New England before 1800 for this practical quality, the jaunty flowers, which are about 1½ inches across, come in a range of colors from creamy yellow to gold and bright orange.

Golden Marguerite plants have aromatic leaves that are deeply cut and somewhat resemble flat-leaved parsley; plants form 2- to 3-foot-wide clumps that reach about 3 feet high. While this free-flowering plant is a perennial, it is a short-lived one. Plants need proper culture and regular propagation to persevere in the garden.

HOW TO GROW

Golden Marguerites are sun-lovers that grow and bloom best in poor but well-drained soil. Hardy in Zones 3 to 8 and among the flowers that thrive at high altitudes, they are drought tolerant once established. In rich soil, plants will be taller but tend to flop over if not staked. Remove blossoms as they fade; after the clumps come to the end of their blooming cycle, cut them back hard to encourage branching and basal growth.

To keep golden Marguerites healthy and vigorous, dig and divide the clumps every two or three years, either in spring or fall. Discard older portions of the clumps and replant the younger, healthier growth. Plants can be propagated by division, by stem cuttings taken in spring or early summer, or by seeds. Sow seeds in pots in spring and set them in a protected location outdoors. Or let the plants do it for you: Golden Marguerites reseed with enthusiasm.

Golden Marguerites are only occasionally bothered by pests or diseases. And, according to many gardeners, they're rarely bothered by deer.

WHAT TO GROW

Perhaps the most popular cultivar of A. *tinctoria* is 'E. C. Buxton', with 2-inch flowers sporting creamy white petals and lemon centers. 'Kelwayi' bears bright yellow flowers on 2-foot plants. 'Moonlight', 18 inches tall, features pale yellow flowers with deeper yellow centers. A. *sancti-johannis* is a similar species and has been widely crossed with A. *tinctoria* to produce many available cultivars. Hardy from Zones 4 to 9, it bears orange-yellow flowers on 2- to 3-foot plants.

IN THE GARDEN

Golden Marguerites are perfect for adding summer color to perennial beds and borders, especially ones that don't have the best of soils. Combine them with

Golden Marguerite, Anthemis tinctoria *'E. C. Buxton'*

oman chamomile (*Chamaemelum nobile*) was formerly an *Anthemis* (*A. nobilis*) and is grown much like Marguerites. It, too, bears daisylike flowers and has aromatic foliage that's deeply cut and theadlike.

It is most commonly grown in the herb garden, but there is every reason to add it to flower beds and borders, especially as it is reputedly a "plant doctor"—able to cure problems of any ailing plant growing next to it.

Roman chamomile is the iconic plant of fragrant lawns. As Shakespeare's Falstaff observed, "the more it is trodden on the faster it grows." Plants reach 12 inches and are hardy in Zones 6 to 9.

Roman chamomile, Chamaemelum nobile

ornamental grasses like blue fescues (*Festuca* spp.), daylilies, salvias or sages (*Salvia* spp.), hardy geraniums or cranesbills (*Geranium* spp.), and yarrows (*Achillea* spp.). Like many aster-family plants, the blooms of golden Marguerites attract butterflies and beneficial insects. They also make fine cut flowers.

Antirrhinum majus

(an-tir-RHY-num MAY-jus)

Snapdragon

Scrophulariacae, Figwort family.
Tender perennial grown as an annual.

Snapdragons, short-lived perennials that most gardeners grow as annuals, produce two-lipped flowers, singles and doubles, in nearly every hue except blue. (You may want to avoid the azalea, butterfly, and bell types. As Katharine White declared decades ago in *The New Yorker*, the snapdragon is a complicated flower. "Fuss it up, and it becomes overdressed.") Traditionally sown on thatched roofs to discourage fire, the snapdragon is also known as lion mouth, toad mouth, and dog's mouth.

This oral fixation comes from the flower's form. Turn a blossom upside down, and it looks like an

Snapdragon, Antirrhinum majus 'Rocket Pink'

animal face; pull open the "mouth" and it snaps shut—one of those botanical tricks that children love. (The fancied-up cultivars have lost their snap, but the blooms of open-throat cultivars like 'Madame Butterfly' last much longer than the traditional snapping forms.) Snapdragon's scientific name comes from the Greek *anti*, meaning "opposite," and *rihn*, meaning "snout." One Roman writer described the bloom as "the stern and furious lion's gapping mouth." The species name, *majus*, means "large."

Although ancient herbalists considered it to have no useful properties—"They are seldome or never used in physicke by any in our dayes," the herbalist John Parkinson wrote—early gardeners wisely recognized the snapdragon's merits, among which is a vigorous and hardy constitution. Plants have glossy, dark green, lance-shaped leaves and bear upright stalks topped with blooms; some cultivars have a spicy fragrance. Snapdragons begin flowering in late spring and continue through summer in regions with cool temperatures; in tropical regions, gardeners can plant them in autumn for winter bloom.

HOW TO GROW

Snapdragons prefer cool conditions, full sun, and organically rich, slightly acid soil that drains well. Be sure to set tall cultivars out of the wind and stake if necessary; avoid overhead watering, which encourages the fungal diseases snapdragons are prone to. Deadhead to promote the growth of new flower stems. If flowering wanes in midsummer, cut plants back hard, water, and fertilize to promote new growth and a second wave of blooms (which will be smaller than the first).

Most gardeners purchase transplants, but if you want to start from seed, do so eight to ten weeks before the frost-free date. Sow seeds—do not cover them with soil—in a sterile medium (snapdragons are prone to damping-off); for sturdy seedlings, keep temperatures cool, about 55°F. Pinch stem tips to encourage branching; set outdoors when the danger of frost has passed. In warm climates snapdragons will self-sow.

Plant disease-resistant cultivars, such as the Monarch Series, to avoid rust and other fungus

OTHER CHOICES

*A*nother two-lipped flower and snapdragon relative is nemesia (*Nemesia strumosa*), a cool-weather annual native to South Africa that produces showy racemes of flowers in mid- and late summer. The individual flowers are 1 inch wide and have a large, flaring lower petal with two lobes and a somewhat smaller upper petal that has four lobes. Blooms come in shades of pink, red, blue, purple, yellow, and white, and may be solid or have upper and lower petals in two different colors. Give nemesias full sun and average to rich, moist, well-drained soil. They are best in areas with mild summers: They need cool nighttime temperatures to bloom well. Start with plants or sow seed just as you would for snapdragons.

Monkey flower (*Mimulus* × *hybridus*) is yet another member of the figwort family grown for its two-lipped, tubular flowers in yellow, red, or orange-red. Blooms are often spotted with a contrasting color. Like nemesia, it does best in areas with cool, wet summers. It grows in constantly moist to wet soil. Monkey flowers are tender perennials (hardy from Zone 7 south) commonly grown as cool-weather annuals. Start with plants or sow seeds indoors about 15 weeks before the last spring frost date.

Cape jewels, Nemesia strumosa '*Carnival Mix*'

diseases that can be problematic, especially in over-wet soil and humid conditions. Snapdragons are rarely troubled by insects, although aphids are occasionally a problem.

WHAT TO GROW

There are scores of cultivars, grouped in three classes: tall (2 to 4 feet), intermediate or semidwarf (1 to 2 feet), and dwarf (to 1 foot). Dwarf types spread 6 to 8 inches, intermediates up to 12 inches, and talls, 18 inches or more. Tall snapdragons are good cut flowers but need staking in the garden. Good dwarf cultivars include 'Royal Carpet Mixed', an F_1 hybrid with rust resistance; 'Floral Carpet Mixed'; All-America Selections winner 'Floral Showers'; and 'Kim Mix', which received a Royal Horticultural Society award. Worthy intermediates are the Sonnet and Liberty Series and the fragrant 'First Ladies Mix', 'Snap Happy Mix', 'Cinderella', 'Giant Rust Resistant', and 'Monarch Mix'. Tall cultivars worth trying are Rocket Strain, 'Topper Mix', and 'Giant Tetra'. 'Lampion Mix' is a cascading snapdragon, bred for containers and ideal for hanging baskets and window boxes. Its flowers—in white, yellow, pink, violet, and bicolors—have a fruity fragrance and are self-branching.

If you love snapdragons, try *Antirrhinum braunblanquettii*, a perennial snapdragon, hardy in Zones 6 to 10, that produces spikes of creamy white flowers with yellow throats. Plants bloom from spring to fall with deadheading, and they also self-sow.

IN THE GARDEN

Gertrude Jekyll, the English garden-design maven, called snapdragons "one of the best and most interesting and admirable of garden plants." They are great flowers for beds and borders, talls in the back, dwarfs as edging plants. Small cultivars also do well in containers and rock gardens; intermediate and tall cultivars make fine vertical accents along with delphiniums, phlox, daylilies, purple coneflower (*Echinacea purpurea*), lamb's-ear (*Stachys byzantina*), hostas, feverfew (*Tanacetum parthenium*), hardy geraniums or cranesbills (*Geranium* spp.), pinks (*Dianthus* spp.), and thread-leaved coreopsis (*Coreopsis verticillata*). Snapdragons are relatively resistant to deer, and they also can be used as dye plants.

Intermediate and tall cultivars are admirable plants for the vase, too (cut when about half the blooms have opened, and keep the cut stems upright). Since their flower spikes open from the bottom, they just get better and better.

Aquilegia

(ack-will-EE-gee-ah)

Columbines

Buttercup family, Ranunculaceae.
Hardy perennials.

The uniquely shaped blooms of columbines have provided the inspiration for a variety of names, both scientific and common. The flowers have five petals, each of which forms a cuplike shape below the stamens, then narrows to form a hollow spur that juts out behind the bloom. Five showy, petal-like sepals are attached behind the true petals. In bicolored columbines, petals and sepals are generally different colors.

The genus name, *Aquilegia*, is thought to derive from *aquila*, Latin for "eagle"—*Aquila chrysaetos* is

Columbine, Aquilegia *'Songbird Bunting'*

the scientific name for our native golden eagle—and refers to the flower's talonlike spurs. Fanciful common names abound, too. Columbine comes from the Latin *columbinus*, meaning "dove" or "like a dove." From above, the petals of short-spurred types resemble doves with their tails in the air, hence the common names doves-in-a-ring and doves-round-a-dish. Granny's bonnet, another common name for *Aquilegia vulgaris*, refers to its flaring, bonnetlike petals.

While European columbine (*A. vulgaris*) long ago was naturalized in North America, our native wild columbine (*A. canadensis*) also was noticed and collected early—one of the first records dates from 1635, when it appeared in Jacques Philippe Cornut's *Canadensium plantarum*. Jesuits had transported it—no doubt by seed—from Canada to France. It has been called meetinghouses because the spurs suggested a circle of people with their heads bent together, but the Iroquois had a different slant. The five petals, the legend goes, were five Indian chiefs who had neglected their people and lands in order to seek a sky maiden. As punishment, the Great Spirit turned them into a flower. Thomas Jefferson reported growing columbine at Monticello, although whether he crushed the plant's seeds to make perfume, as some Indian tribes did, is unrecorded.

Columbines bloom from late spring into summer and come in a wide range of colors, including shades of true blue and violet as well as white, yellow, maroon, pink, lavender, red, and bicolors. There are double-flowered columbines as well. Blooms are carried on wiry stems atop mounds of handsome, rounded leaflets, usually carried in sets of three. Leaves range from green to silvery or blue-green and often have silver-colored undersides. The plants grow from long, carrotlike taproots and, as a result, are fairly drought tolerant. "Rock-loving columbine," was Ralph Waldo Emerson's description in the poem "Musketaquid," a reference to the plant's ability to thrive without great amounts of water.

HOW TO GROW

Give columbines a spot in sun or partial shade with moderate moisture and rich, average to light soil that is well drained. While flowers last longer in partial shade, plants bloom better and are more vigorous in full sun. A site with afternoon shade is best where summers are hot. Most columbines are hardy in Zones 3 to 8; a few, including *A. chrysantha* and *A. longissima*, are more heat tolerant and can be grown into Zone 9.

Golden columbine, Aquilegia chrysantha

OTHER CHOICES

Several popular *Aquilegia* species, native to North America, are good additions to wildflower as well as conventional gardens. Rocky mountain columbine (*A. caerulea*) bears 2-inch blue-and-white flowers from late spring to midsummer on 1½- to 3-foot plants. Wild columbine (*A. canadensis*) has dainty, nodding, red and yellow flowers on 1- to 2-foot plants. 'Corbett' is a fine yellow-flowered cultivar. Golden, or yellow, columbine (*A. chrysantha*) is a heat-tolerant southwestern native with pale to golden yellow flowers on 3- to 4-foot plants. 'Texas Gold' is especially heat tolerant. Another heat tolerant Southwest native is long-spurred columbine (*A. longissima*), which grows from 2 to 3 feet tall; it and its cultivar 'Maxistar' bear yellow flowers that sport 6-inch-long spurs.

Starting with plants provides instant gratification, but columbines are easy from seeds, too. Because the plants have taproots, purchase small plants; older plants in containers are likely to be pot bound. Sow seeds outdoors where the plants are to grow from early spring up to two months before the first fall frost. Or sow them in containers in early winter and set the containers outside in a protected spot to germinate. Do not cover the seed, as light speeds germination. Once you have columbines in your garden, you'll find that self-sown seedlings pop up everywhere. Columbines are a promiscuous bunch and cross readily with one another, so seedlings won't necessarily resemble their parents.

Columbines need minimal care through the seasons. Deadheading prolongs bloom and curtails self-sowing. Cut the foliage back at the end of summer after it turns yellow. New foliage will appear in fall when cool temperatures arrive. Established clumps don't like being disturbed, although you can dig them in early spring and cut off offsets with a sharp knife to propagate.

The most common pest that attacks columbines is leaf miners, which make the leaves unattractive but rarely affect the health of the plant. Aphids sometimes cluster on stem tips but do little damage; plants are subject to crown rot.

WHAT TO GROW

The most popular columbines today are hybrids, with the large-flowered, long-spurred McKana Hybrids—sometimes called McKana Giants—the best known. Awarded an All-America Selections award in 1955, these hybrids bear solid or bicolored flowers in shades of blue, yellow, and red on 2-foot plants. Other hybrid strains that come in a mix of colors include the Dragonfly Series, Song Bird Series (also called Dynasty Series), and Musik Series. All range from 2 to 3 feet in height. Dwarf hybrids also make a nice addition to gardens, where they add color to the front of beds and borders. Dwarf Fantasy Series plants are about 4 inches tall.

European columbine (*A. vulgaris*) is another heavily hybridized species. Plants range from 1½ to 3 feet and have short-spurred flowers in a range of colors, including deep violet-blue, pink, and white. The most popular are doubles, which fall into the "love-'em-or-hate-'em" category with many gardeners. 'Magpie' bears purple-black flowers marked with white; 'William Guinness' produces double flowers on 2-foot plants; and 'Nora Barlow Mix' produces plants with double flowers in pink, purple, lavender, and white.

IN THE GARDEN

Columbines make charming additions to perennial gardens, especially when planted in lavish drifts of color and set around other spring and early summer bloomers, such as irises, peonies, and hardy geraniums, or cranesbills (*Geranium* spp.). Dwarf types are good for the front of the garden but can become tatty looking by midsummer, so place them just behind lower-growing edgers like dwarf blue fescue (*Festuca glauca*), germander (*Teucrium chamaedrys*), or dwarf shrubs. Columbines make handsome cut flowers, although cut stems last only about a week. Columbines are also must-have plants for hummingbird gardens. Fortunately for color-conscious gardeners, hummers don't visit only red flowers. They'll sip from any color columbine they see, so plant away!

Aruncus

(*ah-RUN-kus*)

Goat's beards

Rose family, Rosaceae. Hardy perennials.

Although their lacy clusters of creamy white flowers resemble astilbes, goat's beards are actually more closely related to meadowsweets (*Filipendula* spp.). Plants produce plumelike panicles of tiny, creamy white flowers atop mounds of pinnately compound, or fernlike, leaves. Examine the tiny flowers with a hand lens, and you'll discover the plants are *polygamo-dioecious*, meaning they bear a few perfect, or bisexual, flowers, but most of the tiny blooms are unisexual, and male and female flowers are generally borne on separate plants.

The genus name *Aruncus* literally means "goat's beard" and according to most sources, the name originates with the Roman scholar Pliny. The plant is also known as bride's feathers. Both common names allude to the plant's flowers. *Aruncus dioicus* was recorded as being grown in Britain in 1633 by

Goat's beard, Aruncus dioicus

the Tradescants, the famous father and son gardeners and collectors of plants and curiosities (such as the mantle of Powhatan, the father of Pocahontas). Poultices made from the roots of goat's beard once were used to treat bug bites and stings, and a tea made from the root was prescribed to stop bleeding in childbirth.

HOW TO GROW

Goat's beards need partial shade and rich soil that stays evenly moist. They can grow in full sun in areas with cool summers provided the soil stays moist. In the South, pick a spot that gets shade during the hottest part of the day and water regularly.

Goat's beards are tough, vigorous plants that grow from short, sturdy rhizomes and form large clumps in time; once established, they need little care and can go a decade before dividing is called for. Water regularly in sites where the soil is apt to dry out; the leaves turn brown and crispy around the edges if moisture is lacking. To propagate, divide clumps in spring. Be warned that established plants have deep, woody roots and are difficult to dig. Or sow seeds in pots in fall, and set them outdoors in a protected location or in a cold frame. Plants also self-sow and have almost no disease or pest problems.

WHAT TO GROW

Two species of goat's beard are grown in gardens, and both bloom from early to midsummer. Goat's beard (A. *dioicus*) is a shrub-size plant ranging from 3 to 6 feet tall and bearing plumelike 1- to 2-foot clusters of creamy white flowers. A native North American wildflower, it spreads to 4 feet and is hardy from Zones 3 to 7. 'Zweiweltenkind', a German hybrid, is shorter and sturdier than the species, better for windy sites but hardy only to Zone 5. Dwarf goat's beard (A. *aethusifolius*), hardy in Zones 4 to 8 and a Korean native, is an 8- to 12-inch species topped by 2- to 6-inch-long clusters of creamy white flowers.

IN THE GARDEN

Plant goat's beards along woodland edges, in shade gardens, and near ponds or other water features. Larger A. *dioicus* can be used along the front of a shrub border; it forms large, dense drifts with time. Combine both species with hostas, ferns, primroses (*Primula* spp.), and other moisture-loving plants. When planting along a stream or pond, set plants so the crowns are a foot or so above the water table. Goat's beard blooms also make fine cut flowers.

Asclepias tuberosa

(*ah-SKLEE-pee-ass too-ber-OH-sah*)

Butterfly weed

Milkweed family, Asclepiadaceae.
Hardy perennial.

Also called pleurisy root, this showy native wildflower was once grown for its roots, which were made into a bitter, nutty-tasting tonic prescribed for a variety of ailments, including pleurisy, bronchitis, pneumonia, and influenza. Native Americans used the orange flowers as a dye as well as a medicine; according to Mrs. William Starr Dana (*How to Know*

Butterfly weed, Asclepias tuberosa

flowers are followed by seedpods filled with flat seeds, each attached to a tuft of silky hair. The pods open when ripe, allowing the silky parachutes to carry the seeds far and wide. Leaves are lance-shaped, and the plants grow from deep, fleshy taproots.

HOW TO GROW

Give butterfly weed full sun and average, slightly acid garden soil that drains well. A prairie native, plants also tolerate thin, dry sandy soils. Established plants are very drought tolerant. Because their taproots are brittle, plants are difficult to move and are best left undisturbed once established. Deadhead to promote reblooming. Propagate by cuttings taken from shoots at the base of the plant in late spring or early summer, by root cuttings taken in fall, or by seeds sown in early spring, and set in a cold frame or protected location outdoors. Plants have no serious pest or disease problems.

WHAT TO GROW

Butterfly weed (*A. tuberosa*) is a shrubby, 2- to 3-foot perennial native to dry fields from Minnesota to Maine and south. Hardy in Zones 3 to 9, established clumps can exceed 2 feet, and plants bear rounded clusters of bright orange, orange-red, or occasionally yellow flowers in midsummer. 'Gay Butterflies' is a strain that can be grown from seeds and produces plants with orange, yellow, or red flowers.

IN THE GARDEN

Use butterfly weed in perennial and wildflower gardens, combining it with coreopsis, daylilies, yarrows (*Achillea* spp.), and ornamental grasses. It is a must for any garden designed to attract butterflies.

the Wild Flowers, 1893), they also boiled the seedpods "and ate [them] with buffalo-meat." A display of butterfly weed made a huge splash at the 1876 Centennial Exhibition in Philadelphia, Pennsylvania, Dana observed, noting that the plants had been brought from Holland. "Truly, flowers, like profits, are not without honor save in their own country."

Today, butterfly weed is primarily prized as a plant for sunny flower beds and meadow and butterfly gardens. It is an important food source for monarch butterfly larvae (caterpillars), and milkweed flowers of all species are popular with adult monarchs, other species of butterflies, and bees. Although butterfly weed lacks obvious milky sap, the common name milkweed refers to the fact that most *Asclepias* species have milky sap in their stems and leaves.

Plants bear rounded clusters of small flowers that have reflexed petals and five hoodlike lobes. The

OTHER CHOICES

*A*sclepias contains in all about 110 species. In addition to *A. tuberosa*, consider adding swamp milkweed (*A. incarnata*) to your garden. Another native wildflower, it is rhizomatous and ranges from 3 to 5 feet tall, is hardy in Zones 3 to 8, and spreads slowly to form clumps. It does best in best in rich, evenly moist to wet conditions; its flat-topped, pale pink to rose-pink flower clusters are produced in midsummer and early fall. 'Ice Ballet' has white flowers.

Aster

(AS-ter)

Asters

Aster family, Asteraceae. Hardy perennials.

Few flowers are as closely connected with autumn as are asters. While the asters that line roadsides in the East are primarily New England or New York asters (*A. novi-belgii* or *A. novae-angliae*), asters of all sorts decorate wild areas throughout North America. "Never has the world seen so many asters as we produced in North America," Ann Leighton wrote in *American Gardens in the Eighteenth Century* (1976). Take one glance at Roger Tory Peterson and Margaret McKenny's *A Field Guide to Wildflowers* (1968) and you'll see the riches: 37 species in northeastern and north-central regions alone. The genus contains about 250 species in all and hundreds more cultivars. As with many of our native plants, North American asters were cultivated and hybridized in Europe—the first to reach England were taken there by the younger John Tradescant in 1637—long before improved cultivars were sent back to this side of the Atlantic to become staples of our gardens. Many of our native species are still not commonly grown.

Aster is the ancient Greek word for "star" and refers to the starry blooms that characterize all the members of this genus. Know as starworts in England, asters have a legend as lovely as their flowers: Asterea, the Greek goddess of the sky, wept when she saw there were no stars on earth, and asters sprouted where her tears fell.

Whether described as starry or daisylike, the flowers are actually a short, dense cluster of flowers called a *head*, or *capitulum*, that consists of petal-like ray florets surrounding dense buttonlike centers of *disk florets*. Aster flowers are typically yellow in the center and have rays in shades purple, violet, lavender, blue, pink, ruby-red, and white. They can be single, semidouble, or double and are produced in loose, showy clusters. Plants form spreading clumps and range from 6 inches to 8 feet tall; leaves are usually lance-shaped.

HOW TO GROW

The most commonly grown asters want full sun and rich, well-drained, evenly moist soil, but New England and New York asters will bloom in light shade and tolerate dry soil. For best results, start with pot-grown plants. To keep them looking their best, feed plants in spring by topdressing with compost, well-rotted manure, or a balanced organic fertilizer.

Most gardeners pinch out stem tips in spring and again in early summer to encourage branching, more flowers, and less staking due to the shorter, sturdier growth pinched plants produce. Don't pinch after about June 15 (July 1 from Zone 7 south) or you will remove the emerging flower buds. Tall asters should be staked early, in spring or very early summer, and all asters appreciate being mulched to help hold moisture in the soil. Deadhead regularly or cut the stems back immediately after flowering to prevent cultivars from self-sowing. Cultivars won't come true from seed, and the self-sown seedlings will out-compete cultivated forms.

New York aster, Aster novi-belgii *'Patricia Ballard'*

New England aster, Aster novae-angliae *'Alma Potschke'*

At the same time, remember that birds eat aster seeds and consider leaving a few seed heads, then cut the stems back in spring.

Most asters need dividing every two or three years because the clumps die out in the center. Dig them in spring, discard the woody portions from the clumps' center, and replant the vigorous growth. Division is the easiest way to propagate asters, but species can also be grown from seed. Sow in fall or early spring in pots and set them outdoors in a protected location or in a cold frame. Cuttings are another propagation option: Make them in spring or early summer and root in a mix of half sand and half perlite.

Powdery mildew can disfigure aster leaves and their flowers; plants are subject to aster wilt, verticillium wilt, and rust. Aphids and Japanese beetles sometimes infest asters.

WHAT TO GROW

New England asters (A. *novae-angliae*) and New York asters (A. *novi-belgii*) are sometimes called Michaelmas daisies, a name that comes from England, where they bloom at the same time as St. Michael's Day is celebrated. Hardy in Zones 3 to 8, they are far and away the most popular members of this clan. Both bloom in late summer and produce large, showy clusters of 2- to 2½-inch flowers. While the two species have distinct characteristics, they have been heavily hybridized—with each other and with other species. Classic New England asters include rose-pink 'Alma Potschke' (to 4 feet); salmon-pink

Tartarian aster, Aster tataricus *'Jindai'*

OTHER CHOICES

It's just not possible to have too many flowers in fall, and boltonia (*Boltonia asteroides*) is another native fall-blooming Aster-family plant that makes a fine addition to the flower or wildflower garden. The species is grown far less than the cultivar 'Snowbank', a 5-foot plant covered with small, white, 3/4-inch, daisies in fall. 'Pink Beauty' bears pink flowers. Both are hardy in Zones 3 to 9, tolerate drought, and generally stand without staking.

Goldenrods (*Solidago* spp.) are also outstanding perennials for adding late summer to fall color in beds, borders, and wildflower gardens. They also belong to the Aster family, and most are native to North America. Unlike asters, goldenrods don't have daisylike flowers. Instead they bear tiny golden yellow flower heads that are carried in broad, showy, plumelike clusters. Most golden-rods need full sun (wreath goldenrod, *S. caesia*, which grows in partial to full shade, is the exception) and poor to average soil that is moist but well drained. European goldenrod (*S. virgaurea*) and its cultivars 'Cloth of Gold' and 'Crown of Rays' need even moisture, but most other species also tolerate dry conditions. Choose carefully for spots in beds and borders, since some goldenrods spread vigorously by rhizomes and can become invasive. Good choices for flower gardens include sweet golden-rod (*S. odora*), hardy in Zones 3 to 9; dwarf goldenrod (*S. sphacelata*) and its cultivar 'Golden Fleece', Zones 4 to 9; and seaside goldenrod (*S. sempervirens*), Zones 4 to 9. All three of these species also grow in poor and sandy soil and are good choices for seaside gardens. 'Fireworks', a cultivar of rough-leaved goldenrod (*S. rugosa*), is a 3- or 4-foot species with lacy, arching flowers that are stunning in perennial gardens.

Goldenrod, Solidago cultivar

'Harrington's Pink' (to 5 feet); violet-blue 'Hella Lacy' (to 4 feet); and white-flowered 'Wedding Lace' (to 4 feet). 'Purple Dome' is a dense, 1½- to 2-foot-tall selection with violet flowers. Classic New York asters that range from 3 to 4 feet tall include double-flowered lavender-blue 'Ada Ballard'; 'Eventide', a semidouble with violet flowers; 'Crimson Brocade', with semidouble red flowers; and 'Arctic', with double white blooms. There also are dwarf New York aster cultivars, all less than 15 inches tall: 'Lady in Blue'; semidouble 'Little Pink Beauty'; white 'Niobe'; and lavender-blue 'Professor Kippenburg'.

Frikart's aster (*A. × frikartii*), which is hardy in Zones 5 to 8, produces loose sprays of lavender-blue flowers from midsummer through fall on 2- to 3-foot plants. 'Monch' and 'Wonder of Staffa', both lavender-blue, are the most popular cultivars.

The giant of the lot is Tartarian aster (*A. tataricus*), hardy in Zones 2 to 8. This aster produces large clusters of lavender-blue flowers in mid- to late fall on plants that range from 5 to 8 feet. Despite their height, plants are strong-stemmed and generally do not require staking. The cultivar 'Jindai' is smaller, 4 to 5 feet tall.

For a shade or wildflower garden, consider planting one of our native shade-loving asters. Blue wood aster (*A. cordifolius*) is a 2- to 5-foot plant with pale lavender or white flowers from late summer to fall; white wood aster (*A. divaricatus*) bears clusters of small white flowers from midsummer through fall on 1- to 1½-foot plants. Both are hardy in Zones 4 to 8.

There even are asters for gardens with very poor soil; here again, native asters are the best choices. Look for heath aster (*A. ericoides*) with sprays of white flowers from late summer to fall on 1- to 3-foot plants; calico, or starved, aster (*A. lateriflorus*) bears starry white to pale lavender flowers from midsummer to fall on 2- to 4-foot plants. Both stay compact in poor soil, and both are hardy in Zones 3 to 8.

IN THE GARDEN

Plant asters in perennial borders, meadows, and wild gardens designed for late-season color. They combine well with boltonia (*Boltonia asteroides*), goldenrods (*Solidago* spp.), *Sedum* 'Autumn Joy', monkshoods (*Aconitum* spp.), and ornamental grasses. Dwarf asters are handsome along the front of a bed or border and can be used as a low hedge in the right spot. Asters make lovely cut flowers, too. Cut the stems when about three-quarters of the flowers have opened; split the stems under water if they are woody to encourage water uptake.

Astilbe

(uh-STILL-be)

Astilbes

Saxifrage family, Saxifragaceae.
Hardy perennials.

Although called by common names such as spirea, false spirea, and false goat's beard, astilbes are not related to plants in the true genus *Spiraea* or to seemingly similar plants like goat's beards (*Aruncus* spp.) and meadowsweets (*Filipendula* spp.). Botanists classify astilbes, with their plumy, soft-textured blooms, as saxifrages because they have eight or ten (sometimes fewer) stamens and usually two or three pistils that may be united or separate. Blooms of *Aruncus* and *Filipendula*, both rose-family members, have numerous stamens and many separate pistils. You'll need a hand lens to see the difference for yourself, though.

The genus name *Astilbe* comes from two Greek words: *a*, which means "without," and *stable*, which

Chinese astilbe, Astilbe chinensis *var.* pumila

means "brilliance" and, depending on the source, refers either to the dull leaves of many species or to their inconspicuous individual flowers. Astilbes don't have a long garden history in North America and weren't widely grown until the arrival of the first hybrids bred by George Arends, a nurseryman from Rondsdorf, Germany. Arends died in 1952, but his nursery is still in business, run by his granddaughter, and is the source of nearly all the lovely hybrid astilbes sold today.

The feathery spikes of astilbes add color and elegance to gardens from late spring to summer. Plants produce mounds of attractive, fernlike leaves, and flowers are carried well above the foliage. When in bloom, plants range from about 1 foot in height to 3 feet and more. Where happy, plants spread steadily to form dense, broad clumps. The blooms come in white, shades of pink, ruby-red to crimson, and rosy purple. They are actually branched clusters, called *panicles*, that are packed with tiny individual blooms. The shape of the panicles varies: Popular cultivars tend to have roughly pyramidal plumes, but others bear weeping flowers. You may want to remove spent plumes for aesthetic reasons, but dead-heading won't produce a second crop of flowers.

HOW TO GROW

To grow successfully, astilbes need moist soil that is rich in organic matter but well drained. Wet soil in winter spells certain death. A spot that receives morning sun and afternoon shade is ideal. In the North, where summers remain relatively cool, astilbes grow well in full sun as long as the soil stays moist. In the South, partial shade to full shade is a must. Plants bloom less in full shade, however. Curled-up leaves with crispy brown leaf edges develop whenever a plant receives too little moisture or too much sun. Astilbes are hardy in Zones 4 to 8 or 9, but will survive Zone 3 winters with protection.

Buy plants—or beg divisions from a friend—to add astilbes to your garden. Plant in spring or fall and dig plenty of compost or other organic matter into the soil at planting time. Water regularly in summer to keep the soil evenly moist. Astilbes are shallow rooted and tend to dry out before the plants around them do—allowing them to dry out can be fatal. Mulching with chopped leaves or compost helps keep the soil moist and cool, plus it adds essential organic matter to the soil and keeps down weeds. Feed plants in spring with a topdressing of compost or a balanced organic fertilizer.

If the woody crowns grow above the soil surface, either topdress them with loose soil or compost or

Ostrich plume astilbe, Astilbe thunbergii *'Straussenfeder'*

divide the plants and replant them slightly below the soil surface. Divide astilbes every three to four years in spring or early fall to keep plants vigorous. When digging the clumps, discard the old, woody portions at the center of the clump and replant the younger, more vigorous portions around the outside. Division is the best way to propagate astilbes, since cultivars do not come true from seed. Fresh seed can be sown outdoors in summer or early fall, however.

If their need for moist soil is attended to, astilbes have few other problems. In constantly wet soil, they can develop root and crown rot.

WHAT TO GROW

Nearly all of the astilbes grown in gardens are hybrids—only a few astilbe species are grown, and they are hard to come by. Start by choosing flower colors you like, but also pay attention to bloom season. Cultivars flower at slightly different times; even though each plant only blooms for a few weeks, by planting early, midseason, and late-blossoming astilbes, you can stretch out the bloom season. White-flowered cultivars include late spring-blooming 'Deutschland' and 'Irrlicht', which flowers in early summer just before 'Bridal Veil'. 'White Gloria', blooms in midsummer. Pink-flowered cultivars include 'Europa' (late spring and early summer); and 'Rhineland', 'Cattleya', and 'Peach Blossom', all of which bloom in summer. 'Fanal', 'Federsee', and 'Red Sentinel' are red- to carmine-flowered astilbes and blossom in summer. All are cultivars of either *A.* × *arendsii* or *A. japonica*.

Cultivars of *A. thunbergii*, ostrich plume astilbes, are grown in gardens where they can be appreciated for their size—most grow as tall as 3 or 4 feet if they are given rich, moist soil. 'Ostrich Plume' produces pink flowers in late summer, and 'Professor van der Weilen' features graceful white flowers in midsummer.

Chinese astilbe (*A. chinensis*) and its cultivars are tougher than most other astilbes and make fine ground covers for moist shade. All produce narrow, upright panicles of flowers in late summer. *A. chinensis* var. *pumila*, the most widely grown, bears reddish pink flowers. Height varies according to the amount of moisture and shade the plants get. Plants average about 10 inches tall, but they can reach 2½ feet. 'Visions' bears pinkish purple flowers; 'Veronica Klose' has rose-purple flowers. *A. chinensis* var. *taquetti*, commonly called fall astilbe, and its cultivar 'Superba' tolerate drier soil and more sun than most

astilbes. They only reach their full height of 4 feet in rich soil, however.

Star astilbe (*A. simplicifolia*) is another late-blooming selection with handsome glossy, dark green leaves. 'Sprite' is best known: It bears pale pink flowers on 14-inch plants. Other cultivars include 'Hennie Graafland', which has pale pink blooms on 16-inch plants, and 'Gnom', with pink flowers on 6-inch plants. Star astilbes take more time than most astilbes to become established, about three seasons to reach full size.

IN THE GARDEN

Plant astilbes in shaded gardens where they are perfect neighbors for other perennials that thrive in moist, rich soil: hostas, ferns, lady's mantle (*Alchemilla* spp.), lungworts (*Pulmonaria* spp.), barrenworts (*Epimedium* spp.), and bleeding hearts (*Dicentra* spp.). They also are lovely when planted with shade-loving annuals, such as impatiens and wax begonias, and can be underplanted with daffodils or other hardy spring bulbs. Sites along ponds and streams also can be ideal, because the plants benefit from constant soil moisture. Be sure to set them above the water line; otherwise, root and crown rot can become a problem.

Astilbes make attractive but not long-lived cut flowers. Cut the stems when about half the individual flowers are open. They dry nicely, too: Hang them in a warm, dry, and dark place.

Baptisia australis

(bap-TEES-ee-ah aw-STRAL-iss)

Blue false indigo, baptisia

Pea family, Fabaceae. Hardy perennial.

Grown for its handsome dark blue flowers, blue false indigo, or blue wild indigo, is a shrub-size perennial native to eastern North America. The botanical name *Baptisia*—from the Greek *baptizen*, "to dye"—alludes to the fact that members of this genus, especially *B. tinctoria*, are traditional dye plants. Various Native American tribes, including the Mohicans and Meskwaki, also used *B. tinctoria*,

Blue false indigo, Baptisia australis

Gardeners prize the plant for its many racemes of pea-shaped flowers, which are borne in early summer. Blooms are set off against blue-green leaves, and they are followed by curious black seedpods that are woody and bladderlike. When the pods dry, their seeds rattle "like a small Indian's calabash [gourd]," according to Thoreau. Plants reach about 5 feet in height and spread to form clumps 2 feet or more across.

HOW TO GROW

Grow blue false indigo in full sun and rich, evenly moist but well-drained soil. Plants will tolerate light shade but will bloom less. All baptisias tolerate drought once established, because they have deep taproots. Since plants grow slowly and are difficult to transplant, select a site with care and work plenty of organic matter into the soil. Once planted, baptisias can be left undisturbed for years. Clumps may need staking, especially if they do not receive full sun, if the soil is overly rich, or if they are growing on an exposed, windy site. Some gardeners remove the flowers as they fade to keep seeds from forming; others let them develop and harvest the pods for arrangements. Shearing back plants after flowering ends keeps them tidy but will not produce more flowers. Cut the plants to the ground after a hard

which has a wagonload of names, including yellow broom, rattlebush, clover broom, and indigo weed, to make an antiseptic wash for gangrenous wounds. Henry David Thoreau wrote of another use: "I do not know whether the practice of putting indigo-weed about horse's tackling to keep off flies is well founded, but I hope it is, for I have been pleased to notice that whenever I have occasion to tie a horse I am sure to find indigo-weed not far off." Efficacious or not, *B. tinctoria* is also known as horse fleaweed, horsefly weed, and shoofly.

OTHER CHOICES

Hybridizers have become interested in baptisias in recent years, and new hybrids are being introduced regularly. Four native species, all suitable for sites with dry, poor soil, are much more available than they once were. White wild indigo (*B. alba*), hardy in Zones 5 to 8, produces its white flowers on 2- to 3-foot plants. Prairie wild indigo (*B. lactea*, formerly *B. leucantha*), Zones 4 to 8, is a 3 to 5 foot tall with white flowers. Plains wild indigo (*B. bracteata*), hardy in Zones 3 to 9, is a spreading, 1- to 2-foot-tall plant with creamy yellow flowers in drooping clusters. Yellow false indigo (*B. sphaerocarpa*) and its cultivar 'Screaming Yellow', hardy in Zones 5 to 9, bear yellow flowers on 5-foot plants. Two good hybrids are 'Carolina Moonlight', with butter yellow blooms, and 'Purple Smoke', with blue flowers; both reach 3 feet and are hardy in Zones 3 or 4 to 9.

freeze, and rake any mulch off them after the ground freezes to prevent mice and voles from moving in and dining on the crowns and roots over winter.

Divide baptisias in spring or fall only if you need more plants or if they've outgrown their site. Dig deeply to get as many roots as possible, then use a sharp knife to cut the crowns apart. Growing from seed is slow. Scarify seeds, then sow in pots and set them outdoors in a protected location; or sow them indoors. Seeds should germinate in about two weeks at temperatures of 70°F. Seedlings take two to three years to bloom. Plants have no disease or pest problems.

WHAT TO GROW

Blue false indigo (*B. australis*), hardy in Zones 3 to 9, has blue-green leaves and erect, showy clusters of dark blue flowers that bloom in early summer on 3- to 5-foot plants. Cut the spikes of inflated blue-black seedpods midsummer for dried arrangements or leave them to add winter interest in the garden.

IN THE GARDEN

Think shrub when you look for a spot to plant any of the baptisias. They're perfect for the back of a perennial border, a wildflower meadow, or even as foundation or specimen plants. Combine blue false indigo with other perennials that thrive in rich, moist, well-drained soil, including daylilies, peonies, columbines (*Aquilegia* spp.), Siberian iris (*Iris sibirica*), and yarrows (*Achillea* spp.). They're also large enough to grow with shrub roses, ornamental grasses, and other large perennials in beds and borders.

Begonia

(bih-GOAN-yah)

Begonias

Begonia family, Begoniaceae. Tender perennials grown as annuals, hardy perennials.

Named for the French naval officer, diplomat, and amateur botanist Michel Bégon (1683–1710), the vast begonia clan contains a wealth of colorful members primarily grown as house and greenhouse plants. Bégon, with the help of another Frenchman—the

Tuberous begonia, Begonia tuberhybridacultorum

renowned botanist Fr. Charles Plumier, who also was sent to Santo Domingo by King Louis XIV—collected hundreds of tropical plants throughout the French West Indies. Among them were begonias, which the two men sent back to France, where the the plants become hugely popular. So much so, in fact, that Britain soon began combing their colonies in the West Indies for begonias and other tropical species. Although an American plant, begonias didn't make it to the United States until the late 1800s, when they were imported by the Prince Nursery on Long Island in New York.

Despite being natives of equatorial regions, many begonias are perfectly at home in temperate zones during warm months. Outdoor gardeners have a particular interest in wax, tuberous, and hardy begonias. Most of the 1,300 species of *Begonia* have fleshy leaves that are asymmetrical and rounded or wing-shaped, although they vary in color, and plants grow from rhizomes, fibrous roots, or tubers.

Their flowers set begonias apart: Plants bear separate male and female blooms, usually on the same plant and often side by side in the same cluster. The

Tuberous begonias. As the name suggests, tuberous, or tuberous-rooted, begonias (B. *tuberhybridacultorum*) grow from tubers, which actually are modified stems. They're fussier than wax begonias but well worth the effort. They grow best where summer nighttime temperatures are cool (60°F to 65°F) and may disappoint where summers are hot and dry. Give them partial shade and loose, rich, and well-drained soil that is well protected from wind. You can find them in any garden center, but for a really wide selection, look to mail-order catalogs. Either way, buy only tubers that are firm and solid, with no soft or moist spots or cuts; they should not be shriveled or deformed. Small pink buds are fine, but avoid tubers that have already sprouted. Small transplants are available for sale as well.

Start tubers indoors eight to ten weeks before the last spring frost date by setting them in containers—concave-side up—filled with a loose, barely moist potting medium. Keep the medium barely moist until the buds start growing. Once tubers have inch-long sprouts, move them to pots, barely covering the tops of the tubers with premoistened potting medium. Give plants bright light but not direct sun. When the shoots are several inches tall, transplant the tubers to the containers or beds where they will bloom. Insert thin stakes—bamboo is good—next to tall cultivars at planting time, and use yarn to tie the stems loosely to the stakes as they grow, since the brittle stems break easily. Container-grown plants should be fed every two or three weeks with manure tea or a diluted, balanced liquid fertilizer. To keep plants

female flowers have a swollen, winged seed capsule directly behind the petals; male blooms have petals but lack the seed-bearing capsule. Flowers are often carried in clusters of three, with one male flower between two females.

HOW TO GROW

The different types of begonias grown in gardens need slightly different care to thrive.

Wax begonias. Give wax begonias (B. *semperflorens*) a spot in sun or shade, although they're actually happiest in partial shade, especially in the South. Average to rich well-drained soil is fine. These are tender perennials grown as annuals and must be planted outdoors only after all danger of frost has passed. Purchased plants are the easiest way to add these hardworking bloomers to your garden, but it's possible to grow them from seeds sown in early winter. The best way to propagate wax begonias—or bring plants indoors to overwinter them—is to take stem cuttings, which root in water or a mix of half perlite and half vermiculite. Once planted, they need almost no care beyond watering during dry weather.

Hardy begonia, Begonia grandis *spp.* evansiana

OTHER CHOICES

A few other begonias make nice additions to shady spots in the garden. Rex begonias (*B. rex*) are grown for their colorful leaves but are wonderful in containers and can be planted in beds anywhere that tuberous begonias would grow. Fibrous-rooted begonia hybrids that have wing-shaped leaves—Dragon Wing Series is one—are happy with the same easy culture that wax begonias are and also are handsome additions to shady beds and borders and to container gardens.

for another year, dig the tubers when frost threatens. Dry them in a protected, shady, well-ventilated spot, remove any excess soil, and store in boxes or shallow trays filled with dry peat moss at temperatures around 45°F. Check regularly for signs of rot.

Hardy begonias. Give hardy begonias (*B. grandis* spp. *evansiana*) partial to full shade and rich, moist, and well-drained soil. Hardy in Zones 6 to 10—or to Zone 5 with a mulched, protected site in winter. They grow from small tubers and are ideal additions to shade gardens, where they add color from late summer to fall. Although hardy begonias can be grown from seed, they're easiest to grow from the tiny bulbils produced in the leaf axils. Collect the bulbils in late summer or fall and treat them like large seeds. Plant them indoors in winter, or store the bulbils in a cool, dry place and plant them outdoors in spring where they are to grow. Either way, plant shallowly and barely cover them with loose soil.

All begonias have dustlike seeds, which can be sown in early winter. Sprinkle the seeds thinly on the surface of a moist, sterile seed-starting mix. Do not cover the seeds with soil—they need light to germinate—but cover the container with a pane of glass or a piece of plastic wrap. Seedlings appear in 15 to 20 days; keep wax begonias at 70°F, tuberous and hardy begonias at 60°F.

In addition to causing roots and tubers to rot, very wet soil also can lead to powdery mildew and other foliage diseases. Fluctuations in soil moisture and temperature can make flower buds drop, but plants will recover once growing conditions stabilize. Plants that are yellowed, stunted, sickly, or wilted despite soil that is evenly moist may be infested with nematodes. Discard them.

WHAT TO GROW

Wax begonias are sold everywhere in spring, from grocery stores to nurseries. Their flowers, singles and doubles, are borne in abundance from spring until frost and come in white as well as shades of red and pink, or bicolors. Their rounded succulent leaves may be green, maroon, or bronzy, and plants are compact, ranging from 8 to 15 inches tall. Any number of hybrid strains are available, including bronze-leaved Cocktail and Senator Series and green-leaved Ambassador and Varsity Series. 'President Mix' features flowers in all colors with both green and bronze foliage. Wax begonias are undemanding and dependable, rewarding even the most indifferent gardener with a colorful, summer-long display.

Tuberous begonias feature far showier blooms than wax types, flowering in a variety of shapes, sizes, and colors. They are divided by flower or plant

Wax begonia, Begonia semperflorens 'Olympia Salmon Scarlet'

type into 13 groups, including crested and camellia- and carnation-flowered types, picotees, and rose-buds. Colors, which are vivid and pure, include pale pink to dark red, yellow, orange, cream, white, and bicolors. Blackmore & Langdon Series Strains, the Non-Stop Series, and the bronze-leaved Ornament Series are among the tuberous begonias that can be grown from seeds. The relatively new Scentiment Series tuberous begonias are fragrant. Some of these cultivars can reach 2 feet, but there also are trailing forms, or *pendulas*, that are ideal for hanging baskets and window boxes. Pendulous types include the Illumination Series and 'Show Angel'. For big plants from the get-go, start with dormant tubers or from container-grown plants.

Hardy begonias feature airy sprays of pink flow-ers (there is also a white form) that add charm to shady beds and borders from late summer to fall. Plants have large, attractive wing-shaped leaves and grow about 2 feet tall.

IN THE GARDEN

Use wax begonias in containers and as edgings, as miniature temporary hedges, or in shade gardens to add summer long color. They make a great filler over daffodils or other spring bulbs. Tuberous begonias can be grown in containers alone or with other shade plants, such as impatiens, browallias, and lobelias. In the ground, they are lovely combined with ferns and other shade-loving perennials. Keep them set back from walkways, as the stems are brittle and easily broken. Plant hardy begonias in a shaded site with hostas, lungworts (*Pulmonaria* spp.), barrenworts (*Epimedium* spp.), hellebores (*Helleborus* spp.), and ferns.

Bergenia

(ber-GYN-ee-ah)

Bergenias

Saxifrage family, Saxifragaceae.
Hardy perennials.

While it is true that the leathery leaves of berge-nias emit a sound like a pig squeaking when rubbed between thumb and forefinger—thus the common name pigsqueak—this is not the characteristic that

Heart-leaved bergenia, Bergenia cordifolia *'Purpurea'*

has endeared the plants to gardeners. Bergenias are grown as much for their leaves as their spring flow-ers, and their foliage is responsible for a second com-mon name, elephant ears. Plants produce handsome clumps of rounded, cabbagelike leaves that turn from green to bronze-purple, reddish, or rich maroon in fall. The leaves are evergreen but are usually tattered and not very ornamental by spring. The plants are topped by rounded clusters of pink flowers in early spring and grow from thick, branching rhizomes that spread slowly to form broad clumps.

Two former botanical names for this genus still sometimes crop up: *Saxifraga* and *Megasea*. The botanical name *Bergenia* commemorates Karl August von Bergen, a German botanist and author of *Flora Francofurtana*, published in 1750. Heartleaf bergenia was discovered in Siberia and sent to England in 1779, where it was widely known as giant saxifrage. Don't agonize about which hybrid to plant. According to plantsman Allan Armitage, "If ever a genus had too many cultivars with too few differ-ences, this is the one."

HOW TO GROW

Give bergenias a spot in partial to dappled shade with rich, moist, well-drained soil. In the North, they can grow in full sun if the soil remains moist. In the South, a spot in shade is best or a site where plants are protected during the hottest part of the day. Since large, luxuriant leaves are the goal, set them in deeply prepared soil enriched with generous amounts of organic matter. Once established, plants can withstand short periods of drought.

Plant in spring, and mulch new plantings to keep the soil moist. Water during dry weather, and cut back flower stalks after blooms fade. Mulch plants again in fall where snow cover is inconsistent. Cut back tattered leaves in spring, not fall.

Although bergenias spread by rhizomes, they are not invasive and only need dividing when the clumps become too crowded or die out in their centers. Division, in spring or fall, is also the easiest way to propagate these plants. They also can be propagated by cuttings. Only determined seed-starters will want to try them from seeds, since seedlings will be variable. If you like a challenge, sow by spreading seeds on the surface of the medium (light aids germination) and germinate at 70°F.

Slugs love to feast on bergenia leaves, but otherwise the plants have few problems.

WHAT TO GROW

Heart-leaved bergenia (*Bergenia cordifolia*) is the most commonly available species, but hybrids have also become popular and more available in recent years. All are hardy in Zones 3 to 8. Heart-leaved bergenia has leathery, 10-inch-long leaves and produces clusters of nodding, funnel-shaped, ¼- to ½-inch-wide, rose-pink flowers on stout stems. Plants are 8 to 12 inches tall, to about 15 or 18 inches when in bloom.

Hybrids have been selected for flower color or for the color of their fall foliage. 'Bressingham White' has white flowers; 'Appleblossom' also has white flowers and is more heat tolerant than many bergenias. 'Bressingham Ruby' produces maroon-red flowers and leaves that turn maroon in fall; 'Sunningdale' sports lilac-magenta flowers and copper-red leaves in autumn; 'Abernet' has rich maroon fall foliage and deep pink flowers; and 'Ballawley' bears crimson flowers and bronzy red fall foliage.

IN THE GARDEN

Grow bergenias in perennial beds and borders or as ground covers. Long-lived and undemanding once established, they are vigorous enough to plant in masses for covering large areas and are able to tolerate the dry shade under trees although they won't be at their best. They're attractive in shady rock gardens, along stone walls, and as edging plants. A

pond- or streamside site is another option, provided the plants are located above the waterline so that the soil is not constantly wet. Keep in mind that the flowers don't last long and concentrate on using them in combinations that highlight the waxy foliage. They're stunning combined with other shade-loving perennials such as lungworts (*Pulmonaria* spp.), epimediums (*Epimedium* spp.), hostas, hellebores (*Helleborus* spp.), and ferns.

Brachyscome iberidifolia

(brah-key-SCO-me eye-ber-id-ih-FOE-lee-ah)

Swan River Daisy

Aster family, Asteraceae. Annual.

This native Western Australian annual brings masses of fragrant daisylike flowers to the garden. *Brachyscome*, also spelled *Brachycome*, has dainty individual blooms—they measure about 1½ inches across—but well-grown plants produce masses of flowers in summer, literally covering the mound-shaped plants. Each flower consists of petal-like ray florets that surround a dense cluster of disc florets, or the eye. Flowers are typically blue-purple with yellow eyes, but also come in shades of violet, pinkish purple, and white. The much-branched plants have deeply cut, fernlike gray-green leaves and grow to 1½ feet.

The common name Swan River daisy comes from the Swan, a river in southwest Australia. The genus name alludes to the hairs on each blossom's *calyx*, the collective term for a flower's sepals. A hairy pappus allows seeds to float on the wind once they ripen, an evolutionary strategy for making sure that there are Swan River daisies next year and every other year.

HOW TO GROW

A spot with full sun and rich, well-drained soil suits Swan River daisies, although plants grow in both sandy and clayey conditions. This is a cool-weather annual and is not a good choice for gardens where summers are hot and humid. Gardeners in Zones 9 to 11 can plant Swan River daisies in fall for winter bloom.

Plants are widely available in nurseries, or start from seed, either sown outdoors after danger of frost

Swan River daisy, Brachyscome iberidifolia

has passed or sown indoors four to six weeks before the frost-free date. Indoors, germinate the seed at temperatures between 60°F and 65°F. Pinch seedlings to encourage bushy growth. Seedlings can be fussy about being transplanted. Move them to the garden once the weather is settled, well after the danger of frost has passed. Unless seedlings are pinched back in spring, plants will need staking to keep them from flopping; twiggy brush is perfect for keeping plants upright. Install it around seedlings or young plants, then let them grow up into it. Deadhead to prolong flowering; plants affected by summer's heat can be rejuvenated by shearing them back by half.

Swan River daisies require little care once in the garden; water during dry weather, and be on the outlook for slugs and snails, which may be a problem.

WHAT TO GROW

A few cultivars are available, including the heavy blooming Splendour Series cultivars, which have black centers and white, purple, and lilac-pink flowers. 'Blue Star' reaches 12 inches and bears purple-blue flowers with pointed petals; 'Bravo' comes in white, blue, and violet; and 'Hot Candy' is a new, heat-resistant hybrid. Other cultivars include 'Blue Mist', 'Strawberry Mousse', and 'Mini Yellow'.

IN THE GARDEN

Grow Swan River daisies at the front of a bed or border—they grow in great masses in their native Australia—either in large drifts or with other annuals. They may be at their best in containers, however.

Bracteantha bracteata

(brack-tee-AN-tha brack-tee-AY-tah)

Strawflower

Aster family, Asteraceae. Annual.

Strawflowers are more often seen in dried flower bouquets than in gardens, since the blooms are offered everywhere from florists to craft stores. Amazingly long-lasting when dried, they represent "never-ceasing remembrance" in the Victorian language of flowers. At the same time, these natives of Australia—where they are larval food-hosts for the Australian painted lady butterfly—are easy to grow and undemanding, extremely good garden residents.

The strawflower is considered to be the first Australian daisy to be cultivated and hybridized. German breeders released it in the 1850s. Seeds were first brought to Europe by the British explorer-naturalist Sir Joseph Banks, a member of Captain James Cook's first voyage of discovery to the South Pacific in 1768. The plant gained popularity, especially with Victorians who decorated their dark, stuffy parlors with dried flowers.

Strawflowers are annuals or short-lived perennials producing showy blooms that resemble

Strawflower, Bracteantha bracteata, *Monstrosum Series*

double or semidouble daisies. Formerly classified as *Helichrysum bracteatum*, strawflowers' new scientific name, *Bracteantha bracteata*, is a double reference to their flowers, which lack true petals. Instead, each bloom is made up entirely of disk florets, and its showy "petals" are actually papery, petal-like bracts. Strawflowers come in bright shades of yellow, gold, red, orange-red, pink, and white; leaves are lance-shaped. And they may come with yet another a new name, as they have tentatively been reclassified as *Xerochrysum bracteatum*.

HOW TO GROW

Strawflowers require full sun and average soil that is well drained to grow well and thrive in areas with long, hot summers. You'll probably have to add them to your garden by sowing seeds, since they're not often sold as bedding plants. Sow seeds indoors six to eight weeks before the last spring frost date and germinate them at 65°F to 70°F. In areas where the growing season is long, strawflowers can be direct-sown outdoors in spring after the last-frost date. Indoors or out, be sure only to press the seeds onto the soil surface, as they need light to germinate. Transplant carefully—seedlings resent being moved—after danger of frost has passed and the soil has warmed.

Once in the garden, strawflowers require minimal care. Feed with compost tea monthly to encourage blooming. Plants have rigid stems, but tall cultivars may require staking.

WHAT TO GROW

Several mixes of strawflowers are available. 'Summer Solstice' produces flowers in pale yellow, white, gold, and rose on 3-foot plants. 'Finest Mix' yields extra-large flowers in colors from maroon and red to pink, white, and gold. It was developed for the cut-flower trade, and mail-order seed companies may offer 12 or more separate colors. 'Dwarf Spangle Mix' and the Bright Bikinis Series yield dwarf plants that reach only 12 inches and come in a range of colors. 'Porcelain Rose Shades' are 8-inch-tall plants in shades of pale pink to salmon.

IN THE GARDEN

Plant patches of strawflowers in sunny beds filled with other summer-blooming annuals such as marigolds or orange coneflowers (*Rudbeckia* spp.). Strawflowers are prime candidates for the cutting garden; dry them by hanging in small bunches in a warm, dark, dry place. The stems are very brittle, and flower arrangers often reinforce or replace the stems with florist wire. Make a tiny U at one end of the wire, then insert the other end through the flower, and pull down until the U is buried in the flower head.

Calendula officinalis

(cah-LEN-du-lah off-fish-in-NAL-iss)

Pot marigold

Aster family, Asteraceae. Annual.

Also called English marigold and field marigold, this popular garden annual has a nearly endless history of medicinal uses. It has been prescribed to combat ulcers, eczema, athlete's foot, and swollen glands—and that's just the beginning. (The 17th-century herbalist Nicholas Culpeper prescribed a paste of calendula blossoms, hog's grease, and turpentine applied to the chest to strengthen the heart.) The flowers also have been used to dye fabric and color foods and cosmetics.

In the garden, pot marigold is valued for its long bloom. The flowers are said to last a month, and the botanical name *Calendula* is from the Latin *calendae*, a reference to the first day of the month, the day when interest is paid. Linnaeus, the father of the plant-name system, noted that the blooms were open between 9 A.M. and 3 P.M., which would make the flower doubly appropriate for planting outside a bank. King Charles I of England observed the same characteristic of the flower from his prison at the Castle of Carisbrooke: "The marigold obeys the sun, / More than my subjects me have done." Shakespeare noted the same characteristic, calling the calendula "The marigold that goes to bed with the sun, / And with him rises weeping."

Pot marigold is a fast-growing plant with single or double daisylike flowers ranging from about 2 to 4 inches across. The flowers have petal-like ray florets in shades of yellow or orange, with centers (disk florets) in yellow, orange, purple, or brown. Leaves are spoon or lance shaped, softly hairy, and aromatic.

HOW TO GROW

Give pot marigolds a site in full sun or very light afternoon shade with average, well-drained soil. They'll grow just fine in poor, somewhat dry soil, too; in fact, rich soil yields weak, rangy plants. These are cool-weather annuals, and in areas that have cool summers they will bloom from summer to fall. Grow them for spring or fall bloom where summer temperatures routinely rise above about 80°F. In areas with hot summers but mild winters (Zone 8 and warmer) sow seeds in late summer for flowers from winter into spring.

Plants are available at garden centers in spring, but pot marigolds are a cinch to grow from seeds sown outdoors several weeks before the last spring frost date. Or sow indoors six to eight weeks before the last-frost date, then keep plants at 45° to 50°F at night and no more than 55° to 60°F during the daytime; seedlings grown at warmer temperatures will be floppy and weak. If sowing indoors, use sterile seed-starting medium and water from below to prevent damping-off, which can be a problem.

Pot marigolds die out in hot summer weather. If this happens, cut them back hard and water. They'll start growing again when cooler weather returns.

Regular deadheading keeps plants blooming. In additions to aphids, slugs, and snails, a few diseases attack pot marigolds. Powdery mildew, fungal leaf spots, and virus diseases, including aster yellows, can be problems. Pulling and destroying infected plants is the best response to most disease problems.

WHAT TO GROW

Pot marigolds range from 1 to 2½ feet tall. Use dwarf cultivars for bedding, including the 12-inch Bon Bon Series, which comes in shades of yellow, orange, apricot, and cream and produces 2½- to 3-inch flowers. 'Cheddar Dwarf Mix' grows from 12 to 14 inches tall and produces 2-inch, semidouble and double flowers in shades of yellow and orange with red-brown centers. 'Touch of Red Mix' yields 14-inch plants with 2-inch flowers that are bicolored—each petal has mahogany-red on the back. Taller selections, while still fine in the garden, make better cut flowers, another use for which this plant is ideal. Reaching a height of 2 feet, 'Pacific Beauty Mix' is a fine cut flower, and plants withstand summer heat. The 1½-inch flowers come in shades from creamy to bright yellow, ranging to deep orange. If you're planning to use your pot marigolds in herbal preparations, look for cultivars that have high resin content such as 'Resina' or 'Alpha'.

IN THE GARDEN

Pot marigolds are ideal for adding color to the herb garden and containers, and they also are at home with both annuals and perennials in flower beds and borders. Dwarf selections can be grown as edgings. The flowers are popular with butterflies and with chefs, who use the edible petals in salads, to brew tea, as a substitute for saffron, and to add color to cakes and other desserts. Before using petals fresh or in cooking, make sure they were grown organically and not exposed to any chemicals. For fresh arrangements, cut the flowers when they are about half open. They also can be used in dried arrangements: To dry, hang them in small bunches upside down in a warm, dry place.

Pot marigold, Calendula officinalis *'Bon Bon Mix'*

Campanula

(*cam-PAN-you-lah*)

Bellflowers

Bellflower family, Campanulaceae.
Hardy perennials, biennials, annuals.

Generations of gardeners have succumbed to the charms of bellflowers. Thomas Jefferson did, and he grew them with white poppies at Monticello in Virginia. His were probably Canterbury bells, or cup-and-saucer (*Campanula medium*), which still is one of the most popular bellflowers grown. The English Quaker Peter Collinson (1694–1768) wrote to fellow Quaker John Bartram, an American farmer, botanist, and plant collector, to thank him for the "charming Campanella in flower—six feet high." The plant in this case was probably our native *C. americana*, which Collinson introduced to England in 1763. Perhaps the most famous member of the genus—but a member that is short-lived and requires impeccable drainage and alpine conditions—is the bluebell of Scotland (*C. rotundifolia*). In that country, where it is also known as auld-man's-bells, legend has it that anyone who hears the bluebell ring on a stormy night will die within two weeks, a fortnight.

Most bellflowers are easily satisfied garden residents that bloom over a long season. The most popular are perennials, but old-fashioned Canterbury bells (*C. medium*) are biennials, and *C. americana* is one of the few annuals in the genus. Plants range in form, from mat-forming spreaders to stately, upright perennials suited for beds and borders. All have a mound or rosette of lower, or basal, leaves. Flowering stems, which have smaller leaves along their length, rise above the basal leaves.

Despite a genus name derived from *campana*, Latin for "bell," not all campanulas have bell-shaped flowers. There are species with narrow, tube-shaped blooms as well as ones with starry, cup-shaped flowers. While many species have nodding blooms, there also are bellflowers with flowers that face out or up. Blossoms are usually carried in branched clusters, or racemes.

Altogether there are somewhere around 300 species, and entire books have been written about this

Canterbury bells, Campanula medium

compelling clan. The best garden subjects, however, are not rare species but those with reliable blooms and easy culture. The plants themselves suggest one way to sort them out in the garden: Taller bellflowers are appropriate for beds and borders, and lower-growing species are suitable for planting in walls, rock gardens, and similar situations. Last, there are native American species for wildflower gardens. Unless otherwise noted below, bellflowers are hardy in Zones 3 to 7.

One species to avoid is creeping bellflower (*C. rapunculoides*), which bears violet-purple bells on 3-foot plants. "Creeping" is hardly the right word to describe this fast-spreading, invasive plant that travels both by rhizomes and by seeds. Once established, it is nearly impossible to eradicate.

HOW TO GROW

In general, bellflowers are not heat tolerant: They're happy where temperatures dip below 70°F at night in summer and fade where daytime temperatures rise above about 90°F. They grow in full sun or partial shade, depending on whether you live in an area with hot summers or cool ones. In the South, give them shade during the hottest part of the day, and expect to replace plants, because they will be short-lived.

Bellflowers typically grown in beds and borders—including *C. glomerata*, *C. lactiflora*, *C. latifolia*, *C. medium*, and *C. persicifolia*—want a spot in sun to light shade and soil that is rich and moist but well drained. Bellflowers that need well-drained, somewhat gritty soil that is moist and cool—including *C. carpatica*, *C. cochleariifolia*, *C. portenschlagiana*, *C. poscharskyana*, and *C. rotundifolia*—are suitable for sunny or lightly shaded for sites along pathways, in raised beds, along terraced beds, or at the front of a perennial border, as long as the soil is well drained.

Plant bellflowers in spring or fall, and work organic matter into the soil at planting time. To start bellflowers between rocks in a wall or rock garden, work compost into the crevice, then tuck small plants in with a narrow-bladed trowel. Once planted, campanulas need to be watered deeply during dry weather and mulched to keep the soil cool and moist. Deadhead plants to prolong flowering; ragged plants can be cut back to the basal foliage after flowering ends. Established clumps require dividing every three or four years, in spring or fall, sooner for fast-spreading species. Taller bellflowers need staking.

Division is an easy way to propagate campanulas. Cut clumps apart in spring, discard the old, less vigorous growth, and replant the healthy sections. Or take cuttings from shoots that arise at the base of plants in spring. Starting from seeds is also an option. Sow seeds indoors on the soil surface at least eight weeks before the last spring frost, then transplant hardened-off seedlings to the garden after the frost-free date.

Bellflowers have few disease problems, but slugs and snails sometimes feed on their flowers and foliage.

WHAT TO GROW

Canterbury bells (*C. medium*), a biennial, is a cottage-garden favorite that produces purple, lavender, white, or pink bell-like blooms from 1½ to 2 inches long. Flowers appear from late spring to midsummer on 1½- to 3-foot plants. While old-fashioned Canterbury bells are single, double-flowered cultivars are available. Dwarf types—such as 16- to 18-inch 'Bells of Holland'—don't need staking.

Clustered bellflower (*C. glomerata*), hardy in Zones 3 to 8, spreads by underground rhizomes and forms broad clumps topped by rounded clusters of violet or white flowers from early to midsummer.

Great bellflower, Campanula latifolia

Plants are 1 to 2 feet tall, don't need staking, and tolerate moderately wet soil. 'Joan Elliot' produces violet flowers in early summer. Violet-flowered 'Superba' is especially vigorous and more heat tolerant than the species. 'Alba' is a white-flowered selection; 'Nana' and 'Purple Pixie' are smaller cultivars with deep purple flowers.

Milky bellflower (*C. lactiflora*) is a stately 3- to 5-foot plant that produces showy branched clusters of white or lavender-blue flowers that are about 1 inch long. Plants bloom from early to late summer in Zones 5 to 9 and need evenly moist, well-drained soil and a spot in partial shade for best growth. Established plants do not transplant well. For best results, sow seeds where they are to grow.

Great, or giant, bellflower (*C. latifolia*), hardy in Zones 4 to 9, produces 2- to 3-inch-long bells in summer on 4- to 5-foot plants that spread by fast-growing rhizomes to form 3-foot-wide clumps. Blooms are pale lilac-blue, violet, or white and held on stiff, unbranched stems. 'Gloaming' bears pale blue flowers; 'Alba' has large white blossoms.

Peach-leaved, or willow, bellflower (*C. persicifolia*) is a graceful, 1- to 3-foot-tall species with bell- or saucer-shaped blooms that point out rather than hang down. Flowers are borne from early to midsummer and come in shades of pale blue, violet-blue, and white. This is a clump former, hardy in Zones 4 to 9, that spreads gradually but steadily. There are both single and double cultivars, including 'Chettle Charm' a single white with 1-inch flowers edged in pale blue; and 'Bennet's Blue' and 'Boule de Neige', pale blue and white doubles respectively. 'Planiflora' is a dwarf variety, 8 inches tall with medium-blue flowers.

Best known of the species suitable for rock gardens and other spots with gritty, well-drained soil is Carpathian harebell (*C. carpatica*). A 6- to 12-inch-tall mounding species hardy in Zones 3 to 9, it produces masses of blue,

Peach-leaved bellflower, Campanula persicifolia

Dalmatian bellflower, Campanula portenschlagiana

dry sites. Plants produce trailing panicles of starry, pale blue flowers in early summer and spread quickly by underground runners. Cut plants back after flowering for repeat bloom in late summer.

Scotch bluebell, or harebell (*C. rotundifolia*), is a dainty, 6- to 12-inch species hardy in Zones 2 to 8 and native to North America as well as Scotland. Plants bear nodding bells on slender stems in summer in typical bellflower colors of pale- to violet-blue or white. This clump-forming plant spreads by underground runners. The round basal leaves from which the species takes its name die away early in the season. Long-flowering 'Olympica' is the cultivar most often offered by nurseries and garden centers, but it is short-lived. All Scotch bluebells demand good drainage and alpine conditions.

IN THE GARDEN

Use bellflowers anywhere you need a touch of blue, purple, violet, or glistening white. They make fine additions to beds and borders. Use taller species toward the middle or back of plantings, shorter species as edgings or mixed with other perennials of similar height. Combine them astilbes, delphiniums, hardy geraniums or cranesbills (*Geranium* spp.), baby's breaths (*Gypsophila* spp.), columbines (*Aquilegia* spp.), pinks (*Dianthus* spp.), foxgloves (*Digitalis* spp.), lilies, and Siberian iris (*Iris sibirica*). They are also attractive with hostas and ferns in a lightly shaded spot. Low-growing bellflowers, such as Dalmatian bellflower (*C. portenschlagiana*) and Serbian bellflower (*C. poscharskyana*), are vigorous, fast-spreading ground covers.

violet, and white cup-shaped, up-facing flowers. Plants bloom from late spring through summer. Plants can be short-lived, but they self-sow. 'Blue Clips' and 'White Clips' are excellent, vigorous, and widely available cultivars. 'Chewton Joy' has light blue petals edged with dark blue.

Dalmatian bellflower (*C. portenschlagiana*), hardy in Zones 4 to 9, is a 4- to 6-inch alpine species with open bell-shaped, 1-inch-wide flowers that are violet-purple and borne from late spring to early summer. This vigorous bellflower from southern Europe spreads quickly via underground stems, sometimes reblooms in fall, and is fairly heat tolerant, making it a good choice for Southern gardens.

Serbian bellflower (*C. poscharskyana*), hardy in Zones 5 to 9, is a vigorous, almost invasive 6- to 12-inch-tall species that makes a good ground cover in

OTHER CHOICES

Common ladybell (*Adenophora confusa*), hardy in Zones 3 to 9, is a bellflower relative that produces panicles of bell-shaped blue flowers on 2- to 3-foot plants. Plants are more heat tolerant than the *Campanula* species, grow either in sun or part shade, and prefer moist, rich, well-drained soil. In ideal conditions, this ladybell is no lady, though, and reproduces to the point of becoming a weed. Even more heat tolerant is lilyleaf ladybell (*A. liliifolia*), a 18- to 24-inch plant with light blue, bell-shaped flowers. Cut both species down to their basal leaves when flowering stops.

Canna × generalis

(CAN-ah gen-er-AL-iss)

Canna

Canna family, Cannaceae. Tender perennial.

Cannas bring a taste of the tropics to the garden but have a checkered history as ornamentals. They traveled from the American tropics to England and Europe in the 16th century and reached their height of popularity in Victorian bedding schemes. In more recent years that use translated to cannas planted in whitewashed truck tires or in round beds, where they erupted from a ring of screaming red salvia. It pays to remember, however, that English garden designer Gertrude Jekyll used cannas to add color to her late-season gardens, as do contemporary American garden designers Wolfgang Oehme and James Van Sweden, none of whom would know a whitewashed truck tire if it rolled into their garden. Today, cannas are prized both for glowing flowers and colorful foliage, and they are found in beds, borders, and containers of gardens both naive and sophisticated.

Also called Indian shot because of their hard, pealike seeds—which colonial Spanish missionaries turned into rosary beads—cannas grow from thick, branching rhizomes. Today's hybrids range from 2-foot dwarfs to giants of 10 feet or more. Flowers look something like gladiolus blooms but exhibit a peculiar botanical structure: The showy "petals" are actually petal-like stamens, called *staminodes*, whereas the true petals are greenish and small. Individual flowers are 3 to 5 inches long and are carried in terminal clusters that can reach 1 foot in length. They come in shades of yellow, red-orange, red, salmon, rose-pink, and hot pink and bloom from summer through early fall.

Typically cannas have green leaves, but more recently cultivars with handsome bronzed or variegated leaves have become widely available, making the foliage rather than the flower the main attraction. The bold banana-like leaves are paddle-shaped and up to 2 feet long and 1 foot wide, with the lower part of each leaf sheathing the stem.

HOW TO GROW

Give cannas a spot in full sun with well-drained, evenly moist soil that is rich in organic matter.

Canna, Canna 'Phil's Scarlet Lady'

Provided the soil stays moist, they will thrive in the hottest summer weather. And while moist, well-drained soil is the norm for these plants, cannas also can be grown in containers set in water gardens. Either buy plants acclimated to growing in water or acclimate your own by keeping them moist and gradually increasing the water they receive. Plants can eventually grow with 1 to 6 inches of water covering the crowns.

Cannas are hardy in Zones 8 to 10 and may overwinter outdoors in Zone 7 with an extra layer of mulch for winter protection. In the North, replace them annually or dig up the clumps and overwinter the roots indoors. The plants are so fast-growing and easy to please that they produce a good show even in areas with short growing seasons.

To get cannas started quickly in your garden, buy plants or rhizomes. While there are good cannas that can be grown from seeds, rhizomes or plants are the only way to get most of the improved cultivars with variegated leaves. Look for thick, fleshy rhizomes that are firm to the touch and have no soft, rotted-looking spots. Add a good dose of well-rotted manure or compost to the soil at planting time. From Zone 7 south, plant the rhizomes directly outdoors. In the North, start rhizomes indoors four to six weeks before the last spring frost date in containers filled with fast-draining potting soil. Set the rhizomes barely under the soil surface with the pointed growing tips up. Keep them warm (75°F) and the soil barely moist. Once they begin to grow, move them to a sunny spot, keep the soil evenly moist, and feed weekly with a balanced liquid fertilizer at half strength. Don't move plants to the garden until the danger of frost has passed and the soil has warmed to about 65°F.

Keep the soil evenly moist to ensure good growth and lush leaves. Deadhead to encourage new flowers to form, and remove tattered leaves to keep plants looking their best. Dig and divide cannas every three years if they're grown outdoors year-round. Otherwise, dig them in fall after the first light frost and set the clumps of roots—with the soil attached—in boxes filled with barely damp vermiculite, peat, or sand. Store them in a cool (40° to 50°F), dry place. Keep the medium just moist enough so that the rhizomes don't shrivel. Divide the rhizomes in spring, not fall, because the cut surfaces tend to rot over winter. Be sure each section contains at least two buds.

Canna, Canna 'Tropicana'

To grow cannas from seed, start in midwinter, and nick the hard seed coats with a file, then soak them in warm water for 48 hours. Place the seeds in a plastic bag filled with moist sphagnum peat moss and set it in a warm (75°F) place. Inspect the bag every few days—germination can be uneven—and pot up seedlings as they appear. Seed-grown plants will produce rhizomes that can be overwintered in subsequent years.

Slugs and beetles are attracted to their leaves, but overall cannas are remarkably problem free.

WHAT TO GROW

Cannas have been heavily hybridized, and named cultivars are grown almost exclusively. Be forewarned: Once you've grown a canna or two, you'll be tempted to start a collection. Green-leaved cultivars include 'Cleopatra', a 3- to 4-foot heirloom with green leaves sometimes marked with a maroon stripe and yellow flowers spotted and striped with red; 'Endeavor', 5 to 6 feet, with red flowers; 'Lucifer', 3 to 4 feet, red flowers with petals edged in yellow; 'Picasso', a dwarf, 2- to 3-foot selection with yellow-and-white flowers spotted with red; 'President', an old-fashioned, 6- to 8-foot cultivar with scarlet flowers; and 'Richard Wallace', 3 to 4 feet tall, with yellow flowers.

Bronze- and maroon-leaved cultivars include 'Black Knight', 4 to 6 feet with red flowers; and 'Red King Humbert', 5 to 6 feet, with orange-red flowers.

Variegated cultivars include 'Durban', 4 to 7 feet tall, with orange-red flowers and new leaves striped with dark red, pink, bronze, and pale yellow that age to bronzy green with yellow stripes; 'Intrigue', 6 feet, with burgundy and green leaves and salmon orange flowers; 'Pretoria', 6 to 8 feet and also sold as 'Bengal Tiger', which has yellow and green striped leaves and orange flowers; 'Striped Beauty', a 2- to 3-foot selection with yellow-and-green leaves and red buds opening into white and yellow flowers; and 'Stuttgardt', 6 to 8 feet, with orange flowers and green leaves variously striped and splashed with white.

If you'd like to start cannas from seeds, consider 'Tropical Rose', a dwarf selection at 2½ to 3 feet with green leaves and rose-pink flowers, or Pfitzer Series plants, which come in a range of colors and reach about 3 feet.

IN THE GARDEN

Cannas can be combined with both annuals and perennials, and are ideal for adding color to beds and borders in mid- to late-summer, when other plants struggle with the heat. Plant them with large, bold plants or with masses of smaller perennials and annuals. Yarrows (*Achillea* spp.), sneezeweeds (*Helenium* spp.), daylilies, ornamental grasses, and dahlias are all good companions. They also can be used along foundations, as hedges, in shrub borders, or along walkways. Cannas make handsome container plants, especially dwarf types. Plant them in large containers and feed regularly through the summer to keep them blooming. They also are also attractive to hummingbirds, making them essential for wildlife gardens.

Catharanthus roseus

(cath-ah-RAN-thus ROE-see-us)

Madagascar periwinkle

Dogbane family, Apocynaceae.
Tender perennial grown as an annual.

This pretty and popular flower proves that powerful medicinal plants can come in the most unlikely packages. Historically, Madagascar periwinkle has been used to treat such maladies as hypertension, indigestion, and diabetes. Since the 1950s, alkaloids found in the plants have been found to reduce white blood cell counts, leading to treatments for leukemia, Hodgkin's disease, and other cancers.

Also called old maid, vinca, and rose periwinkle—the last a reference to the rosy pink flowers—this species is native to the island of Madagascar, off the coast of Africa, although it has naturalized in tropical regions around the world. Although grown as an annual, Madagascar periwinkle is actually a tender, evergreen perennial, hardy only in Zones 10 and 11; in frost-free climates it develops a woody stem and can grow to 3 feet. Formerly listed as *Vinca rosea*, plants bear charming, five-petaled flowers that look like those of lesser periwinkle (*Vinca minor*). Flowers are actually *salverform*, meaning they are tubular at the base and flair into flat 1½-inch-wide faces. Plants bear several solitary flowers from the leaf axils toward the tips of the shoots. In addition to rose-pink, blooms come in white, pale pink, lilac, and hot pink to red. Often they have an "eye" at their center in a contrasting color. The glossy leaves are opposite and narrowly oval in shape.

HOW TO GROW

Give Madagascar periwinkles full sun to light shade. They prefer average soil—rich soil will reduce flowering—that is well drained yet evenly moist. Since they need a long growing seasons and revel in heat

Madagascar periwinkle, Catharanthus roseus

months before the last spring frost date. Transplant after the weather is warm and settled. Pinch back young plants to encourage bushy growth. It's also possible to propagate Madagascar periwinkles from cuttings taken in spring or early summer, but the results are likely to be uneven.

WHAT TO GROW

Few gardeners plant the species, as there are many improved hybrids, and they are most commonly sold. Look for Cooler Series plants, which have broad petals that overlap and come in shades of pink and white. Pacific Series are heavily branched and come in pinks plus lavender pink and white; Pretty Series plants also come in shades of pink, white, and red. In most cases, plants in a Series are available in separate colors as well as in a mix of colors.

Hybrids also feature a more compact habit—generally less than 1 foot tall—than the species does. Plants in the Carpet Series top out at 4 inches. One exception is 'Parasol', which has 2-inch white flowers (with pink centers) and grows 2 feet tall. It was an All-America Selections winner, as are six other cultivars, including 'Pretty in Rose', 'Jaio Scarlet Eye', and 'Stardust Orchid'.

Madagascar periwinkles are seldom troubled by pests or diseases, but they can be attacked by various fungus diseases. Avoid wetting the leaves when watering.

IN THE GARDEN

Use Madagascar periwinkles as edging plants—they can be arranged along the front of borders to form a low, temporary hedge—and as ground covers. They are also handsome combined with other sun-loving annuals such as salvias or sages (*Salvia* spp.) and zonal geraniums (*Pelargonium* × *hortorum*) and are superb container plants. One warning: Plants are poisonous if ingested or smoked.

and humidity, they are perfect choices for southern gardens, where summer weather can strain many popular plants. If plants become ragged, cut them back to stimulate new growth. Once established, plants are moderately drought tolerant.

Start with plants purchased at the garden center, or sow seeds indoors in winter, three to four

Celosia argentea

(seh-LOW-see-ah are-JEN-tee-ah)

Cockscomb, feathered amaranth

Amaranth family, Amaranthaceae.
Tender perennial grown as an annual.

Despite their modern-looking, fiery-colored flowers colors and unusual forms, these easy to grow bedding plants have long been cultivated by gardeners. Introduced from Asia to England in the 1500s, where they were grown primarily as houseplants and called flower gentle, celosias were cultivated both by George Washington and Thomas Jefferson in the 18th century. Jefferson expressed his admiration for the oddly shaped blooms of the Cristata Group but also labeled them "a curiosity."

The name *Celosia* celebrates the fiery-hued flowers; the word is from the Greek *keleos*, for "burned." Blooms appear in brilliant orange, scarlet, yellow, and deep red, as well as shades of pink, salmon, and cream. In addition to referring to flower color, the name *Celosia* also alludes to the shape of one of the two types of celosias gardeners encounter: Plumosa Group cultivars, which produce clusters of upright, plume- or flame-shaped blooms, and they are often called feathered amaranths. The Cristata Group cultivars are responsible for the common name cockscomb. They bear tightly rounded and curled blooms that resemble a rooster's comb or a colorful head of cauliflower. The showy flowers actually are flower clusters consisting of hundreds of tiny, chaffy blossoms and the result of a mutant gene that causes *fasciation*, a fused, flattened appearance.

Celosia leaves are oval to lance-shaped and usually green in color, although some selections have bronze foliage. Cultivated celosias are grown as annuals, but the wild form of *Celosia argentea* is a short-lived perennial with silvery white plumes that grows as tall as 6 feet.

HOW TO GROW

Cockscombs thrive in full sun, although they'll tolerate very light afternoon shade. They also grow well in hot, humid weather. Give them a spot with rich, well-drained soil that stays evenly moist.

You can add cockscombs to your garden by purchasing plants—usually offered at garden centers in market packs. If possible, buy plants that are not yet in flower. For a better selection, however, begin with seeds, since most garden centers offer only a limited number of colors or types. Seed is also your best bet if you want to grow a particular color, since garden centers usually sell packs of mixed colors, not single hues. Sow seeds indoors six to eight weeks before the last spring frost. Sow in individual containers, as seedlings resent transplanting. Move plants to larger containers if necessary: Any interruption in steady growth, such as becoming pot bound, will stunt plants and affect flowering. Don't move plants into the garden until well past the last spring frost date; temperatures below 60°F (or nighttime temperatures below 50°F) will retard growth.

Rot root is problematic in soils that are too wet, but cockscombs have few other troubles.

WHAT TO GROW

When you select cockscombs, think about how you plan to use them in the garden. Dwarf cultivars are the best choices for edgings or using with other

Cockscomb, Celosia argentea *Cristata Group*

Feathered amaranth, Celosia argentea Plumosa Group *'Kewpie Mix'*

OTHER CHOICES

Wheat celosia (*C. spicata*) produces pretty flower heads that look something like feathery wheat on 2-foot plants. Flamingo Series plants, with their silvery cream and pink flower heads, are a good choice. Wheat celosias are especially good for drying, considerably better than plumed celosia. Chinese woolflowers (*C. argentea* Childsii Group) have globe-shaped terminal flowers—one description suggests that their "flower heads look like twisted and tangled balls of yarn"—but they're rarely found in commerce.

annuals, whereas you'll want taller cultivars if you plan on using them as cut or dried flowers. Cristata Group cultivars include 6- to 8-inch-tall 'Jewel Box Mix' and 'Amigo Mix', which are available in single colors as well as mixes. 'Big Chief Mix' produces 3-foot plants with 6-inch flowers; 'Prestige Scarlet', an All-America Selections winner, produces 3-inch red flowers on 18-inch plants.

Plumosa Group cultivars include the 8-inch-tall 'Kimono Mix', which comes in 10 individual colors as well as the mix. Century Series and Sparkler Series produce 12-inch-tall plants in a variety of

vivid colors. The 20-inch 'Apricot Brandy' bears apricot-orange flowers and is another All-America Selections award winner. Both 'Forest Fire' and 'New Look' have colorful leaves, maroon and purplish respectively, combined with red blooms.

IN THE GARDEN

Combine celosia with other annuals and perennials in sunny beds and borders. Also consider them for planting over bulbs or cool-weather annuals that finish blooming as soon as warm summer weather arrives. Low-growing cultivars can be used as edgings or in containers. Tall cultivars make fine cut and superb dried flowers. Pick them just as the blooms open fully. To dry, strip off the leaves and hang in small bunches in a warm, dry place. Colors last almost indefinitely.

Centaurea

(*sen-TOR-ee-ah*)

Cornflowers, knapweeds, bachelor's buttons

Aster family, Asteraceae.
Hardy perennials, annuals.

○

Also called hardheads, basket flowers, ragged sailors, caltrops, and star thistles, centaureas are common roadside flowers in North America. Most species found in this country were originally from Europe, botanical immigrants that have naturalized in every state but Alaska according to USDA maps. A few species—including American knapweed, or basket flower (*C. americana*)—are natives. The name *cornflower* comes from the plant being a common resident in grain fields (in Europe the term *corn* was once used to refer to all cereal grains). Herbalist John Gerard called *C. cyanus*—the species probably longest in cultivation—hurt-sickle because it dulled the blades of the corn reapers' scythes.

The name *Centaurea* has its origins in Greek mythology. A wise centaur, the half-man, half-horse Chiron, used the flowers to treat his wounds and thereby taught humankind the value of medicinal plants. *Centaurea* species continue to be traditional medicines used to reduce inflammation and to heal minor wounds and conjunctivitis. But the color of the cornflower is its chief attraction. In the 16th century it was called blewbottle, an allusion to the pure blue of its blooms, which artists used to create paints and writers used to make blue ink.

Centaureas bear charming, rounded, thistle-like blooms that add an informal, cottage-garden look to gardens. Each bloom is actually a cluster of flowers, much like a daisy, that consists of florets crowded together to from a head. Unlike the flat, unlobed petals of a daisy, however, cornflower florets are deeply cut, giving the blooms a ragged spidery appearance. Each flower head has a scaly, conelike base. Blooms come in violet-blue, mauve, pale to hot pink, white, and yellow, as well as pure blue. Plant leaves are deeply cut in a featherlike fashion or are lance-shaped.

HOW TO GROW

Give cornflowers a spot in full sun with average to rich soil that is moist but well drained. One species, mountain bluet (*C. montana*), also grows in partial shade. Cornflowers tolerate dry soil but bloom and grow best if watered regularly when there is no rain.

Purchased plants are the easiest way to add perennial cornflowers to your garden, but seed is easiest for the annuals, including bachelor's button (*C. cyanus*) and basket flower (*C. americana*). Perennial cornflowers can be grown from seed, too. Sow seeds outdoors where the plants are to grow on or slightly before the last spring frost date. In southern gardens, try sowing seeds of annual species outdoors in fall for bloom the following spring. Or sow seed indoors, four to six weeks before the last spring frost date; move plants to the garden on the last-frost date. For best results, sow in individual pots to reduce root disturbance at transplanting.

Regular deadheading encourages new buds to form, and plants may need staking to keep them from flopping. Cut perennial types to within a few inches of the ground when they stop blooming to encourage repeat bloom in fall. Pull up annuals after they have finished flowering. Flowers left to set seeds will self-sow.

Propagate perennial cornflowers by division. Mountain bluet (*C. montana*) needs dividing every two to three years in spring or fall to keep it contained and vigorous. Other perennial species need

Bachelor's button, Centaurea cyanus

OTHER CHOICES

Stokes' aster (*Stokesia laevis*), also called cornflower aster, is a perennial native to the southeastern United States and is hardy in Zones 5 to 9. Plants are from 1 to 2 feet tall and produce rosettes of rounded, lance-shaped, evergreen leaves topped by shaggy, 2- to 3-inch-wide cornflower- or asterlike blooms from midsummer to early fall in shades of violet-blue, pink, or white. 'Klaus Jelitto' bears very large purple flowers; 'Mary Gregory', soft yellow blooms; 'Blue Danube' has 4-inch-wide lavender-blue flowers; and 'Alba', white flowers. Give Stokes' aster a site in full sun or light shade with rich, acid, well-drained soil. Plants grow in somewhat dry to evenly moist soils, but it can't stand heavy clays or poorly drained soil. They make excellent cut flowers.

Cupid's dart (*Catananche caerulea*) is a Mediterranean native that also belongs to the aster family and makes a nice cut flower. Plants reach about 2 feet, are hardy in Zones 3 to 8, and produce clumps of grassy leaves topped by 1- to 2-inch-wide lilac blue flower heads that have a collar of papery bracts beneath the flowers. Grow them as you would Stokes' aster, and divide clumps every year or two to keep them vigorous.

Cornflower aster, Stokesia laevis

dividing every three to four years. Plants are subject to few pest or disease problems.

WHAT TO GROW

Two species of cornflowers are easy to grow, cool-weather annuals. Of these, old-fashioned bachelor's button (*C. cyanus*) is perhaps the best known and most widely planted. It bears 1- to 1½-inch flowers in dark blue, mauve, pink, rosy-red, or white flower heads. Plants range from 6 inches to 2½ feet tall and flower from spring to early summer. For continued bloom, sow new crops of seeds every two to three weeks. Taller strains—36-inch 'Frosted Queen Mix' is one—are best for cut flowers or mixing in with taller perennials. Dwarf strains such as 'Polka Dot Mix' or 'Florence Mix', which grow to 14 or 16 inches, need less staking and are better for bedding.

Basket flower, or American knapweed (*C. americana*) is a native North American wildflower with 4- to 6-inch-wide flowers in pink, pinkish lavender, or white in summer. Plants are 3 to 5 feet tall.

Of the perennial cornflowers, mountain bluet (*C. montana*) is by far the most popular. This is a vigorous perennial, bordering on weedy, that produces deep blue, 2-inch flower heads on 1½- to 2-foot plants. Hardy in Zones 3 to 8, it prefers cool temperatures and spreads less vigorously in the South. Summer-blooming Persian centaurea (*C. dealbata*) produces pink, 1½-inch flowers on 2- to 3-foot plants and is hardy in Zones 4 to 8. Hardy in Zones 3 to 7, globe centaurea (*C. macrocephala*) bears yellow, 1½- to 2-inch-wide flower heads on 3- to 5-foot plants.

IN THE GARDEN

Use annual and perennial cornflowers in beds and borders where they can be allowed to mix with other perennials and flowering shrubs. Because of their charming, cottage-garden appearance, they are more suitable for informal gardens than formal ones. Combine them with peonies, foxgloves (*Digitalis* spp.), or other late spring to early summer perennials. Use annual cornflowers to fill in empty space in the garden—just sow a patch of seeds. All make fine cut flowers and can be dried. For cutting or drying, harvest when the flowers have expanded fully. The petals of bachelor's button (*C. cyanus*) also can be added fresh to salads.

Centranthus ruber

(cen-TRAN-thus RUE-ber)

Valerian, red valerian

Valerian family, Valerianaceae.
Hardy perennial.

Valerian, Centranthus ruber 'Albus'

Also called Jupiter's beard, fox's brush, red spur, Mercury's blood, setwall, and keys of heaven, *Centranthus ruber* is a perennial native to the Mediterranean region, from southern Europe and northwestern Africa to Turkey. When it got to England is unclear, but the 16th-century herbalists John Gerard and John Parkinson both grew it. Its flowers, Parkinson observed, were "of a fine red colour very pleasant to behold." The name *Centranthus* is from the Greek *kentron*, "spur," and *anthos*, "flower," and refers to the spurred shape of the small, tubular, ½-inch-long flowers, which have star-shaped faces and make up each cluster. Flowers come in shades of pink to reddish pink, plus white; plants bloom from late spring through summer. The flowers are followed by dandelion-like seed heads that release seeds on the wind to travel to other parts of the garden and beyond.

Plants are clump forming, 1 to 3 feet tall, and have woody bases with somewhat fleshy blue-green, lance-shaped to rounded leaves. They're grown for their fragrant flowers, which are crowded in clusters at the ends of the stems. Don't confuse red valerian with common valerian (*Valeriana officinalis*), also called garden heliotrope, another European native with pinkish-lavender or pinkish-white flowers that has escaped cultivation and is naturalized in North America. While common valerian has been used medicinally for centuries, *Centranthus ruber* has not, despite the fact that it has been listed at one time or another as *Valeriana ruber*, *V. rosea*, and *V. coccinea*.

HOW TO GROW

Valerians thrive in full sun and grow best in poor or average, alkaline soil that is well drained—they blanket England's White Cliffs of Dover, which offers exactly those conditions—but don't do well in excessive heat and high humidity. Deadhead regularly, as valerians self-sow vigorously and can be invasive in some regions. Cut plants back by half if they stop flowering in summer's heat or if they become floppy; shearing will encourage a second wave of flowers. Cut plants to 6 inches.

Valerians are not long-lived, so plan on starting new plants from seeds or let self-sown seedlings take over every three or four years. Established plants have deep roots and are difficult to move, although they can be propagated by division in early spring, provided you dig deeply and handle the plants carefully. Seedlings are easy to move and will flower in their first year. Plants are seldom troubled by pests or diseases.

WHAT TO GROW

Valerian is hardy in Zones 4 to 8. Several cultivars are available, including 'Albus' and 'Snowcloud', which bear white flowers; 'Coccineus', which produces carmine-red blooms; and 'Roseus', which has rose-pink flowers. 'Star Ruber Mix' yields plants in a range of colors, including pink, maroon, and white.

IN THE GARDEN

Combine valerians with other perennials that tolerate poor soil, including yarrows (*Achillea* spp.), asters, salvias or sages (*Salvia* spp.), coreopsis, and lavenders (*Lavandula* spp.). They are at their best when used in raised beds, where drainage is excellent, and they also are suitable for rock gardens. Red valerian makes an excellent cut flower.

Chrysanthemum × morifolium

(kris-AN-theh-mum more-ih-FOE-lee-um)

Mum, garden mum, florist's mum

Aster family, Asteraceae. Hardy perennial.

Whether they're filling a container, edging a walkway, or mixing with other fall-blooming perennials in a bed or border, few autumn gardens are without a clump or two of chrysanthemum. Their showy flowers in shades of yellow, maroon, rust, bronze, mauve, purple, red, and white are a joy at the end of the garden season. Once available only in late summer and fall, it's now possible to pick up pots of mums any time of year. That's because commercial growers know how to manipulate the plants' bloom time. Chrysanthemums are short-day plants, which means they need long periods of uninterrupted darkness at night to flower. Growers now use black shade cloth to cover mums for the requisite ten or 11 hours it takes to force them into bloom.

With the onset of year-round availability, mums are now treated like annuals: Gardeners buy them at garden centers and grocery stores and plop them in the garden for instant color. Instant is the operative word, for these plants are usually transient. One reason is that many of the cultivars sold today aren't hardy; moreover, most fall-planted mums don't have enough time to establish themselves in order to overwinter in cold climates. Depending on the cultivar, fall mums are hardy in Zones 4 or 5 to 9.

While the availability of instant color is a boon to gardeners, becoming a throwaway plant is a sad fate for a flower with such a noble and ancient history. Confucius wrote about mums 2,500 years ago, and Imperial Chrysanthemum exhibits were common in Japan—where the flower is sacred and symbolizes happiness and longevity—by the 5th century. Despite being an Asian plant, the name *Chrysanthemum* is from the Greek *chrysos*, "gold," and *anthemon*, for "flower." A few species were imported to Europe in the 17th century, but mums didn't catch on in the West until 1843, when Robert Fortune brought the fall-flowering species back to England.

Garden mums flower heads consist of petal-like ray florets surrounding a densely packed center of disc florets. Flower forms vary—and breeders are forever inventing new ones—and include singles, semidoubles, doubles, and much more. Both buds and flowers can withstand light frosts, and new buds continue to open long after annuals have been blackened by the cold. Plants range from 1-foot cushion types to 2 feet tall or more; their attractive, lobed leaves are aromatic when bruised.

Garden chrysanthemum, Chrysanthemum × morifolium *'Bold Christine'*

OTHER CHOICES

Plants were scattered far and wide when botanists broke up the genus *Chrysanthemum*. See *Leucanthemum* for information about the popular Shasta and ox-eye daisies. Painted daisy (*Tanacetum coccineum*, a.k.a. *C. coccineum*, and *Pyrethrum coccineum*) is another popular garden plant grown for its 3-inch daisylike flowers, yellow centers, and petals in shades from pale to hot pink, red, or white. Hardy in Zones 3 to 7, they bloom from early to midsummer on 1- to 3-foot plants that have pretty, fernlike leaves. They bloom best in light shade and tolerate a wide range of soils, from dry and sandy to rich. Cut plants back hard after flowering to encourage a second flush of bloom. Propagate by seed,

division, or cuttings of spring shoots taken from the base of the plant.

Despite the extreme nomenclatural confusion surrounding feverfew (now *Tanacetum parthenium*, but formerly *C. parthenium*, *Matricaria parthenium*, and *Pyrethrum parthenium*), it is another plant very worthy of a place in home gardens. It bears tiny, ¾-inch daisies with white petals and yellow centers. Foliage is aromatic, and the 1- to 3-foot plants bloom from summer to fall. Hardy in Zones 4 to 8, feverfew is a short-lived perennial. Plants thrive in sun or afternoon shade, and they need well-drained soil. Cut plants back hard after flowering to encourage repeat bloom. Propagate from seed or by cuttings.

Painted diasy, Tanacetum coccineum 'E. M. Robinson'

HOW TO GROW

Give mums a spot in full sun, although if plants are being grown as annuals to be discarded after flowering, exposure doesn't matter all that much. Average to rich, well-drained soil is best for hardy cultivars, and good drainage is crucial over winter, when water collecting around the crowns causes rot.

To grow chrysanthemums as perennials, start in spring with rooted cuttings or small, starter plants of hardy cultivars. Pinch off any flower buds and cover cutting-grown plants with bushel baskets or burlap for a day or so. Keep the soil evenly moist—mums are shallow rooted and shouldn't be allowed to dry out—and feed plants twice, in early spring and again in midsummer. Pinch the stem tips about two weeks after planting and again each time the stems produce another 6 inches of new growth.

Stop pinching in early July in the North, mid-July in the South, to allow plants to form flower buds. Cultivars take different amounts of time to flower. If you order by mail, you'll find notations about whether cultivars are early-, mid-, or late-blooming plants. Early-blooming mums are the best choice in areas with very short seasons. In areas where killing frosts don't come until late October or November, plant a mix of early, midseason, and late cultivars to lengthen the bloom season.

Deadheading extends bloom time; after flowering ceases, cut hardy cultivars back hard, to 4 or 5 inches, and cover them with straw or evergreen branches once the ground has frozen. Dig and divide plants annually in spring, discarding any woody growth and replanting only young, healthy growth. Mums also are easy to root from basal cuttings taken in early spring; cuttings will produce blooming plants by fall.

Mums can be attacked by aphids and spider mites; virus diseases and nematodes are sometimes problematic.

Garden chrysanthemum, Chrysanthemum × morifolium *'Golden Regards'*

WHAT TO GROW

With hundreds of nonhardy cultivars, it makes sense to choose mums by flower and plant type. There are more than a dozen classes based on flower form, everything from charming daisies to quilled cultivars to gigantic football mums. Plants range from compact cushion types—16 to 24 inches tall—to plants that reach 3 or 4 feet at blooming time. Local nurseries will have a wide range of choices. 'Sheffield Pink' is an outstanding perennial cultivar with soft pink daisylike flowers with yellow centers. Cultivars in the Firecracker Series, bred by Jefferies Nurseries, Ltd., in Canada—including 'Dreamweaver' (mauve), 'Suncatcher' (yellow), and 'Firestorm' (red)—are reliably hardy to Zone 3.

IN THE GARDEN

Set mums wherever summer-blooming annuals have petered out, add them to containers, or plant them as edgings: In beds and borders, they can be combined with daylilies, sneezeweeds (*Helenium* spp.), asters, ornamental grasses, or goldenrods (*Solidago* spp.). They make excellent vase flowers; cut them while the blossom centers are still tight for longest vase life.

Garden chrysanthemum, Chrysanthemum × morifolium *'Bordeaux'*

Cimicifuga

(sim-ih-sih-FEW-gah)

Snakeroots, bugbanes, black cohosh

Buttercup family, Ranunculaceae.
Hardy perennials.

The botanical name for this genus of late-blooming perennials is derived from the Latin, *cimex*, for "bug," and *fugare*, "to drive away," and it refers to the use of an Asian species as a bug repellant. Common names abound and include snakeroot, bugbane, fleabane, black cohosh, fairy candles, squawroot, and rattle-top. Some names allude to medicinal uses for the plants—various species have been used in preparations to lower fevers, soothe aches and pains, control coughing, and treat various other ailments.

Gardeners value these large perennials, native to moist, shady areas in North America, Europe, and Asia for their airy, bottlebrush-shaped flowers and handsome, shrub-size mounds of compound leaves. "The great stout stems, large divided leaves and slender spikes of the feathery flowers render this the most conspicuous wood-plant of the season," Frances Theodora Parsons wrote in *According to the Seasons* (1902), although she contended that the flowers' "rank odor" was a detraction from the plant's beauty. Most bugbane growers would disagree.

While the individual white or cream-colored flowers are tiny and lack petals, they are borne in dense, graceful terminal wands from midsummer to fall, and they are carried far above the foliage. Leaves are usually green, but there are newer introductions that feature bronze- to maroon-colored foliage.

HOW TO GROW

Plant snakeroots where they will receive partial to dappled shade and rich, evenly moist soil. In the North, a spot in full sun is fine provided the soil is moist and rich. In the South, select a site with moist soil and shade during the hottest part of the day. For best results, choose a permanent location from the start, as snakeroots are slow to establish and are happiest if left undisturbed once they are planted. Very tall plants may need staking. Seedheads are an attractive addition to the winter landscape, so allow them to remain once flowering ends.

Snakeroot clumps almost never need dividing. To propagate, which is tricky at best, dig and divide clumps in spring in cold climates or fall in warm regions, or try slicing a small plant off the edge of an established clump. Plants self-sow in the garden, and they also can be started from seed sown in pots and overwintered outdoors. They may take two years to germinate, so be patient. Bugbanes are seldom troubled by pests or diseases.

WHAT TO GROW

Two native bugbanes are hardy in Zones 3 to 8. American bugbane (*C. americana*) is a 2- to 4-foot-tall species that can reach 8 feet in bloom. Its

Black cohosh, Cimicifuga racemosa

racemes are 2 feet long and are composed of creamy white, ¼- to ½-inch-long flowers from midsummer to fall. Black snakeroot, or black cohosh (C. *racemosa*), produces foliage mounds that are 2 to 3 feet tall; but plants stretch as high as 7 feet when they bear their fluffy, branched racemes of small creamy white flowers in midsummer.

Kamchatka bugbane, or autumn snakeroot (C. *simplex*), hardy in Zones 4 to 8, forms mounds of foliage from 2 to 3 feet tall. Plants bear arching 3- to 12-inch-long racemes of fragrant, ¾-inch-long flowers in early fall. Cultivars include 'Brunette', which has brown-purple foliage, purple stems, and 8-inch-long racemes of white flowers with a purple cast; the 2- to 3-foot 'White Pearl', which requires no staking; and 'Pritchard's Giant', which grows 4 to 5 feet tall and bears white flowers. Dark-leaved cultivars include 'Hillside Black Beauty' and 'Black Negligee'.

IN THE GARDEN

Few perennials add such handsome, late-summer appeal to the garden. Grow snakeroots in shady perennial beds and borders, and combine them with hostas, Solomon seals (*Polygonatum* spp.), monkshoods (*Aconitum* spp.), ferns, and shade-loving annuals. Native species are also excellent subjects for shady wildflower gardens or woodlands.

Cleome hassleriana

(*klee-OH-me hass-ler-ee-AH-nah*)

Spider flower, cleome

Caper family, Capparidaceae. Annual.

Spider flower, Cleome hassleriana *'Purple Queen'*

Cleome hassleriana is native to South America, although it has naturalized in some portions of the southeastern United States. Plants produce large terminal racemes of small, strongly scented, four-petaled flowers from summer until frost. Blooms come in white, shades of pink, and pinkish purple and have amazingly long stamens, which are responsible for the common names spider flower and cat's whiskers.

Each plant produces a main flower cluster with smaller side branches, and the clusters continue to lengthen as new flowers open from the top. As the flowers fade, long, narrow seedpods form along the stems. Leaves are compound, with leaflets arranged in a palmate fashion, like fingers on a hand. The stems are sticky and hairy, and there are short spines at the base of the leaf stalks. Plants reach 5 feet or more by the end of the season and are a look-alike for marijuana (*Cannabis* spp.).

Breeders argue that cleome, which was highly popular in the 1800s, would be equally popular today if plants could be manipulated to bloom while still in the garden-center cell-pack. Dwarf cultivars do, but the tall forms—the cultivars worth growing—need time to reach their full height before they flower. There's no need to stake these tall annuals, for their woody stems keep them upright in all but gale winds.

HOW TO GROW

Spider flowers like heat. Give them a site in full sun with organically rich, well-drained soil—pretty much anything but soggy conditions—and space plants at least 2 feet. You can start with small transplants from the garden center or start from seed. Either sow seeds indoors six to eight weeks before the last-frost date, or seed them directly in the garden once nighttime temperatures remain above 40°F and the danger of frost has passed. (To speed germination, refrigerate seeds for two weeks before sowing.)

Established plants will grow and bloom in dry soil, but for the most flowers, keep the soil evenly moist. Plants self-sow—wantonly in warm climates—but seedlings are easy to pull up where they are not wanted. Deadheading, which also prevents excess self-sowing, is a tedious task, but fortunately it's almost impossible to have too many spider flowers in the garden. Or spiders, for that matter. Plants are sometimes attacked by aphids but are generally trouble-free.

WHAT TO GROW

The most widely grown spider flowers belong to the Queen Series, which is available as a mix or in individual colors, including 'Rose Queen', 'Cherry Queen', 'Purple Queen', 'Pink Queen', and 'White Queen'. These are tall plants that will self-sow and yield offspring that are fairly true to their parent's color. 'Color Fountain Mix' is another tall selection with a full range of colors. If you want to maintain a self-sowing, solid-color population in your garden, pull up any plants exhibiting colors that aren't consistent with your scheme when they first bloom—well before they set seed.

Hybridizers also have introduced semidwarf spider flowers. Sparkler Series plants are about 3 feet tall and are bushier than old-fashioned spider flowers. ('Sparkler Blush', with pink-and-white flowers, won an All-America Selections award in 2002; 'Pink Queen' won in 1942.) Sparkler Series plants are F_1 hybrids and won't come true from seed. 'Solo' is another new dwarf cultivar that grows to 16 inches and bears pink and white blooms. It also features spineless stems and is open pollinated, which means it will come true from seed.

IN THE GARDEN

Although a favorite target of night-flying moths, grow cleomes where you—and the hummingbirds and bees—can enjoy them by day, then watch their flowers change color: They open rose and magenta in the afternoon and fade to white. (This characteristic, alas, has been bred out of most new cultivars.)

Spider flowers are in their element when planted in large drifts along the back of a perennial border along with asters, monkshoods (Aconitum spp.), and other fall-flowering plants. Use them to fill in between clumps of perennials—they're ideal for giving a new garden a mature look while perennials are still small. They also are large enough to combine with many shrubs. To grow tall, more slender plants—ideal if you've planted in drifts—remove side branches. For shorter plants that are bushier, pinch out the main flower cluster when it is about 1 foot long, which will encourage side branches to form. Dwarf cultivars make good container plants.

Convallaria majalis

(con-vah-LAIR-ee-ah mah-JAY-liss)

Lily-of-the-valley

Lily family, Liliaceae. Hardy perennial.

Take one whiff of the sweetly scented blooms of lily-of-the-valley, and it isn't hard to understand why forced crowns of these dainty perennials were popular winter decorations during the Victorian era. In the language of flowers, the arching stem of dangling, bell-shaped flowers symbolizes the return of happiness. Folk tradition, however, warns that taking lily-of-the-valley indoors may bring misfortune.

While the flowers are tiny—from ¼ to ½ inch—their aroma is huge. In A Modern Herbal (1931), Mrs. M. Grieve includes the legend that the flower's fragrance was so sweet that it "draws the nightingale from hedge and bush, and leads him to choose his mate in the recesses of the glade." No surprise, then, that the perfume industry extracts a volatile oil from the flowers to make scents for similar ends.

Lily-of-the-valley also has been used medicinally since at least the 2nd century A.D., primarily as a diuretic. John Gerard, who called the flower May lily, prescribed lily-of-the-valley water for "griefe of the gout." The plant is also known as glovewort, because of its reputed power to cure chapped hands.

Lily-of-the-valley, Convallaria majalis

leafless stems in late spring and are followed by sprays of small, round red berries. Plants, which are hardy in Zones 2 to 8, are from 6 to 9 inches tall and can spread indefinitely.

HOW TO GROW

Plant lily-of-the-valley in partial shade and evenly moist, rich soil. Plants will grow in full sun, provided they have adequate moisture, as well as in full shade. Established clumps can grow in dry shade, but plants will not survive in a wet, poorly drained site. In the South, where plants struggle with heat, plant them in partial to full shade, although flowering will be less in a sunless location. In cooler zones, plants will quickly form a dense ground cover. Keep these vigorous plants away from other perennials, or divide clumps after they flower to keep them in check. Water during excessively dry spells to keep the foliage attractive or simply let the plants die back— once the leaves turn yellow they can be cut to the ground.

To add lily-of-the-valley to your garden, start with potted plants or, better yet, with *pips*, which are bare-root pieces of fleshy rhizome that have both growing buds and roots. Gardening friends who have this old-fashioned plant are likely to have divisions to share. Plant pips in fall, late winter, or in early spring, ideally before the leaves emerge.

WHAT TO GROW

There are cultivars to consider planting, but don't overlook the charming white-flowered species, which is as fragrant as any of them. *C. majalis* var.

Convallaria majalis is moderately toxic, especially to cats. Keep small children away from its seductive red berries to be safe.

The plant's somewhat rounded, lance-shaped leaves are produced above freely branching rhizomes that form dense mats with time. Blooms appear on

rosea bears very pale mauve-pink blooms. 'Fortin's Giant' and 'Giant Bells' are vigorous, 1-foot--tall selections with larger flowers. Foliage fanatics will want to search for pips of either 'Albostriata', with white-striped leaves, or 'Aureovariegata', which has yellow-striped ones.

OTHER CHOICES

Several other perennials can be grown as ground covers in the same conditions that satisfy lily-of-the-valley. Consider some of the following:

Bugleweeds (*Ajuga* spp.). These produce rosettes of spoon-shaped leaves topped by spikes of densely packed purple-blue flowers. Common bugleweed (*A. reptans*), from 4 to 6 inches tall and hardy in Zones 3 to 9, spreads very fast. Cultivars include large-leaved 'Catlin's Giant' and variegated 'Burgundy Glow', which spreads slowly. Blue bugleweed (*A. genevensis*), from 6 to 12 inches tall, and

Spotted deadnettle, Lamium maculatum *'White Nancy'*

pyramid bugleweed (*A. pyramidalis*), 6 to 10 inches, also spread more slowly and are hardy in Zones 3 or 4 to 8.

Green-and-gold (*Chrysogonum virginianum*). A 6- to 8-inch-tall native wildflower, this species is also called goldenstar. Hardy in Zones 5 to 8, it bears 1½-inch single yellow flowers and heart-shaped leaves.

Plumbago (*Ceratostigma plumbaginoides*). Hardy in Zones 5 to 9 and also called leadwort, this is a semiwoody, 6- to 12-inch-tall perennial that can spread quickly and will overwhelm less vigorous neighbors. Plants are grown for their rich, brilliant blue ¾-inch flowers, borne from summer to fall, and for their orange or red fall foliage.

Spotted deadnettle (*Lamium maculatum*). Hardy in Zones 3 to 8, this is an 8- to 10-inch perennial grown for its whorls of ¾-inch-long, two-lipped flowers in summer as well as its handsome variegated leaves. Cultivars are the story here—look for 'Beedham's White' with chartreuse leaves and white flowers or 'Beacon Silver' with green-edged silver leaves and pink flowers. Don't plant closely related yellow archangel (*L. galeobdolon*), which is an invasive spreader with whorls of ¾-inch yellow leaves. Its cultivar 'Herman's Pride' with silver-streaked leaves is somewhat less invasive, however.

IN THE GARDEN

Lily-of-the-valley is best used as a ground cover in shaded locations. Plant it under and around trees and shrubs, along shady walkways, or in drifts near terraces. In all but the hottest zones, it may be too vigorous to combine with other perennials.

Coreopsis

(*core-ee-OP-sis*)

Coreopsis, tickseeds

Aster family, Asteraceae. Hardy perennials, tender perennials, annuals.

The brightly colored flowers of coreopsis are cheerful additions to any garden, and the fact that they're

easy to grow, long-blooming, basically undemanding plants makes them even more valuable. Despite their virtues, their garden history isn't as long or rich as you might expect. All species are native Americans, ranging from the United States and Canada to Central America, and their ubiquity is probably one reason they weren't used in gardens more often, along with their lack of medicinal qualities. Only a few made their way to England before 1700, but once there they grew in popularity. The beauty of golden-flowered annual calliopsis, or plains coreopsis (*C. tinctoria*), a 19th-century observer noted, had "secured it a passport to almost every respectable garden in the kingdom."

The name *Coreopsis*, bestowed by Linnaeus, is from the Greek for "like a bug" and refers to the plants' dark seeds. The seeds also explain the common name tickseed. The origin of other names—lady's breast pin, wild flax—is murky, although the name dye-flowers is easily explained:

Calliopsis, Coreopsis tinctoria 'Mardi Gras'

The petals of some species can be used to dye cloth red. No state chose coreopsis as its official flower, but Mississippi and Florida have designated it as their "official wildflower."

Coreopsis produce daisylike flowers that can be single, semidouble, or double. Single-flowered types have a row of petal-like ray florets surrounding a solid center of smaller disk florets. Semidouble and double-flowered types have more ray florets, so many that the central disk may not be visible. The flowers usually are bright gold to yellow-orange in color, although there are selections with pale yellow, pink, and bicolored blooms. Leaves range from simple to deeply lobed or divided in a palmate fashion, with narrow leaflets arranged like fingers on a hand. Flowers are produced on upright stems that may be branched or unbranched.

HOW TO GROW

Coreopsis need full sun and well-drained soil to flourish. Average garden soil is fine—it's no accident that coreopsis are roadside regulars—and plants grown in rich soil tend to be overly tall and will need to be staked. These are flowers that thrive in heat, so a spot that gets some morning shade but is exposed to full sun all afternoon is fine. *C. auriculata* and *C. rosea* are the best choices for partial shade. Plants are happiest in soil that is evenly moist but once established will withstand considerable drought. Set large species at least 1 foot apart.

Add both annual and perennial coreopsis to your garden by purchasing plants. Many selections

are also easy from seed. Sow seeds indoors six to eight weeks before the last-frost date; start seeds eight to ten weeks before the frost date if you are growing *C. grandiflora* as an annual. Don't cover seeds, as light helps germination.

Once in the garden, coreopsis need minimal care. Excessive fertilizing is likely to reduce flowering rather than increase it. Deadheading is a necessary chore, however, for it greatly lengthens the flowering season by directing plants' energy into producing more flowers rather than producing seeds. Divide perennial coreopsis every two to three years after they finish blooming: Discard the old, woody portions at the center of the clump and replant the rest. Division is the easiest option for propagation, but rooting cuttings works as well. Take cuttings from the new shoots at base of the plant in spring, or take stem cuttings of shoots in summer.

Coreopsis are astonishingly resistant to diseases and pests, although crown rot can be a problem in soil that does not drain well.

WHAT TO GROW

Fortunately for gardeners, it's hard to go wrong when it comes to choosing among these tough, reliable plants. As one wildflower expert observed: "Anyone seeking a clear-cut path through the jungle of Coreopsis history could be pardoned for giving up the task." Calliopsis, or plains coreopsis (*C. tinctoria*, formerly *Calliopsis tinctoria*), is an annual 4-foot native that bears yellow, daisylike flowers marked with maroon or brown in summer. Calliopsis cultivars come true from seed, so enjoy the species or look for selections

Pink coreopsis, Coreopsis rosea

like the foot-tall 'Mahogany Midget', with blooms that have maroon-red petals and yellow centers.

Large-flowered coreopsis (*C. grandiflora*) and lance-leaved coreopsis (*C. lanceolata*) are similar species that bear yellow or orangish, 1- to 2½-inch flowers on 1- to 2-foot plants. Hardy in zones 3 or 4 to 9, both are good cut flowers and bloom from spring to late summer if plants are deadheaded regularly. If the plants become ungainly in late summer, cut them to the ground, which will encourage fresh foliage to appear. *C. grandiflora* is a short-lived perennial that lasts two to three years in the South, slightly longer in the North. *C. lanceolata* is longer-lived but blooms less freely. Frequent division keeps both species vigorous, and both are easy to start from seeds. There are single-, semidouble-, and double-flowered cultivars of *C. grandiflora* that can be grown from seeds (many cultivars actually are crosses between the two species). All-America Selections winner 'Early Sunrise' will bloom the first year from seeds sown indoors in midwinter. Plants reach 18 inches

and produce double, bright yellow blooms. 'Sunray' produces double golden yellow flowers on 16-inch plants; 'Mayfield Giant' has showy single yellow flowers with a dark red-brown eye. *C. lanceolata* cultivars include 12- to 18-inch 'Baby Sun', with yellow-orange flowers; and the 9-inch 'Goldfink', with single, 2-inch yellow flowers.

Mouse-ear coreopsis (*C. auriculata*) is a 1- to 2-foot species that bears yellow-orange, 2-inch flowers from late spring to summer. Hardy in Zones 4 to 9, it is often used as a ground cover or edging, since plants spread steadily via stolons but are not invasive. The foliage remains attractive all season if the soil is kept evenly moist. 'Nana', more popular than the species, is a dwarf, 8-inch-tall selection.

Not surprisingly, pink coreopsis (*C. rosea*) bears rosy pink, 1-inch daisies with yellow centers. Hardy in Zones 4 to 8, plants bloom from summer to early fall, covering the 1- to 2-foot mounds of needlelike leaves. Unlike most coreopsis, *C. rosea* tolerates either moist or dry soil and spreads vigorously in fertile, moist soil.

Thread-leaved (*C. verticillata*), which is also known as fernleaf and whorled coreopsis, may be the pick of the litter. This species bears narrow, threadlike leaves and 1- to 2-inch daisies that range from pale to golden yellow. Hardy in Zones 3 to 9, plants range from 1 to 3 feet tall, spread slowly, and rarely need staking. After the first main flush of flowers is finished, cut plants back to encourage a second flush of blooms in fall. Pale yellow 'Moonbeam' is the most popular selection—it was the 1992 Perennial Plant of the Year—but it is less hardy than other selections or the species. It reblooms without deadheading and flowers from early summer to fall. 'Zagreb' boasts golden-yellow blooms on 12- to 18-inch plants and is particularly drought tolerant. 'Grandiflora' or 'Golden Showers'—bright yellow daisy-like flowers with darker yellow centers—can reach 2½ feet and may need support to stay upright;

Large-flowered coreopsis, Coreopsis grandiflora

Thread-leaved coreopsis, Coreopsis verticillata

it was a 1993 Royal Horticultural Society Award of Garden Merit winner.

IN THE GARDEN

Combine coreopsis with any sun-loving, summer-blooming perennial, including lavender (*Lavandula angustifolia*), daylilies, bellflowers (*Campanula* spp.), hardy geraniums or cranesbills (*Geranium* spp.), yarrows (*Achillea* spp.), balloon flower (*Platycodon grandiflorus*), purple coneflower (*Echinacea purpurea*), and ornamental grasses. They also are handsome with annuals, and most are superb choices for the cutting garden. Smaller cultivars make excellent container plants; all cultivars are at home in a butterfly garden.

Corydalis

(*coe-RID-ah-liss*)

Corydalis

Poppy family, Papavaraceae.
Hardy perennials.

Corydalis are grown for their delicate tubular, spurred flowers, which are carried above handsome mounds of fernlike, blue-green foliage. The small blooms—from ½ to 1 inch long, depending on the species—resemble the flowers of their better-known cousins, the bleeding hearts (*Dicentra* spp.). Close comparison reveals that while bleeding hearts have two spurs per flower, corydalis blooms have only one. Long ago corydalis was classified with the bleeding hearts in the fumitory family and was known as *yellow fumiterre*, and it was recommended as "a very proper Plant to grow in Rockwork, or upon old Walls or Buildings, to hide their Deformity."

The botanical name *Corydalis* is a reference to the flowers and comes from the Greek *korydallis*, for "crested lark"—in this case, a lark's head. Yellow corydalis is the only common name for the most-grown species, C. *lutea*, but gardeners who grow the plant—it's been rock-gardeners' well-kept secret for years and only recently has appeared in mainstream plant catalogs—are tempted to call it "that great little flower that never stops blooming." For it hardly does, producing lovely yellow blossoms in regions with cool summers from early spring until the first (or second) fall frost.

HOW TO GROW

Most corydalis need a spot in dappled sun to partial shade—morning sun and afternoon shade is ideal—and soil that is well-drained and has a neutral pH. Well-drained is the operative word. Wet soil almost guarantees plants won't survive winter's cold. Rock garden conditions, as long as summer heat is moderate, are ideal.

Start with container-grown plants. It's possible to grow corydalis from seeds, but seeds must be absolutely fresh and treated to warmth, cold, and warmth

Yellow corydalis, Corydalis lutea

again, or the result will be disappointing. Despite gardeners' problems with growing from seeds, corydalis self-sows with enthusiasm. Established plants resent being transplanted, but seedlings are easy to move: Lift them with a trowel and replant. Plants grow slowly and rarely require division. Corydalis are sometimes attacked by slugs in damp settings but otherwise are problem free.

WHAT TO GROW

Once you've tried one corydalis, you'll want to grow others. The easiest and most adaptable—the absolute first choice—is yellow corydalis (*C. lutea*), which produces foot-tall mounds of ferny, blue-green leaves that stay attractive from early spring through late fall, and even into winter in mild climates. Plants, which grow from rhizomes, are hardy in Zones 4 to 8 and bear an abundance of yellow flowers from early spring until frost.

Ferny corydalis (*C. cheilanthifolia*) is slightly smaller than *C. lutea*—it produces 1-foot-tall mounds of very lacy leaves and dense racemes of bright yellow flowers in spring and summer. A native of China, it is hardy in Zones 3 to 6. *C. ochroleuca*, or white corydalis, is also 1 foot tall and bears racemes of yellow-throated white flowers from spring to summer. It is hardy in Zones 5 to 8.

Blue corydalis (*C. flexuosa*) produces gorgeous light blue flowers atop 1-foot mounds of blue-green leaves from spring to summer. While fairly easy to grow in areas with cool summers, it rarely survives in gardens where summers are hot and humid. Hardy in Zones 5 to 8, plants go dormant after flowering. 'Blue Panda' has sky blue flowers, and 'Pere David' lavender ones.

C. solida (also listed as *C. halleri* and *C. transsylvanica*) is a tuberous species. The tubers are available from bulb dealers in fall. *C. solida* produces 6-inch mounds of ferny, gray-green leaves topped by racemes of mauve-pink tubular flowers in late spring. Hardy in Zones 5 to 8, it is a spring ephemeral, meaning the foliage dies down after the plants flower.

IN THE GARDEN

Use corydalis along shaded walkways and toward the front of garden beds and borders that are protected from hot afternoon sun. They're stunning combined with small hostas, lungworts (*Pulmonaria* spp.), primroses (*Primula* spp.), violets, species iris, wild blue phlox (*Phlox divaricata*), spring bulbs, and ferns.

Cosmos

(*COZ-mose*)

Cosmos

Aster family, Asteraceae. Annuals.

While there are perennial species of cosmos, the plants most often grown by gardeners are annuals native to Mexico—*C. bipinnatus* and *C. sulphureus*. Along with gold, silver, and other riches, 16th-century Spanish explorers also helped themselves to the country's natural treasures, sending hundreds of plants back to Madrid. Cosmos wasn't collected until the late 1700s, however, and from Spain made its way to England in 1789, thanks to the wife of the English ambassador to Spain, the Marchioness of Bute.

It was at least another 50 years until cosmos got to the United States, indirectly from England and Spain and more directly from Mexico. This late start in British and American gardens probably accounts for the plant having no widely used common name, answering instead to its genus name, *Cosmos*, which comes from the Greek word *kosmos*, meaning "beautiful." The names xeric daisy and Mexican aster sometimes crop up, but even longtime flower growers are unlikely to recognize or use them.

Cosmos are prized for their abundant, silky, daisylike flowers and their unflappable, easy-care nature in the garden. The blossoms of these aster-family plants consist of showy petal-like ray florets surrounding a dense center button of disk florets. Depending on the species, blooms may be pink, carmine-red, red, white, yellow, or orange. Plant leaves are delicate, deeply divided, and threadlike.

HOW TO GROW

Plant cosmos in full sun—in very hot regions they can take afternoon shade—and give them protection from strong winds. They need light soil with average to poor fertility that has a neutral or slightly alkaline pH and is well drained. Plants need even moisture to get started, but mature cosmos are drought tolerant; plants produce more and larger flowers, however, if they are watered regularly. Soil that is too rich yields weak-stemmed, sparsely flowered plants that bloom

Cosmos, Cosmos bipinnatus 'Sonata Pink'

late and flop over, so avoid soil that has been heavily amended, and don't be tempted to feed plants.

While bedding plants are sold in spring, cosmos are simple and inexpensive to grow from seeds. Either sow outdoors after danger of frost has passed, or for an early start on summer blooms, sow seeds indoors four to five weeks before the last spring-frost date. Both germination and growth are fast, but plants are frost tender, so don't be in a rush. Cosmos are light sensitive and don't bloom their best until late summer, when the days grow shorter. Move these heat-loving annuals to the garden after danger of frost has passed and the soil has warmed. Pinching stem tips can reduce height and encourage branching but isn't necessary.

Tall cosmos sometimes need to be staked—giving them full sun will help keep them upright—but a better approach than staking is to space plants more closely than the recommended 2 feet and let them support each other. Deadheading is worth the extra effort, as it lengthens the bloom season. Plants that aren't deadheaded will self-sow in warm regions.

WHAT TO GROW

Flower color is the main reason for choosing between the two commonly grown annual species. Cultivars of *C. bipinnatus* bloom in modest, soft shades of pink, maroon, crimson, and white with yellow centers; plants range from 1 to 5 feet tall. Some of the unfussed-up cultivars, such as 'Sensation', which is a tall plant with simple, daisylike flowers, are still the best according to cosmos connoisseurs. It won an All-America Selections award in 1936. 'Purity' is a white cultivar, 4 feet tall.

If you want to see what breeders can do to an unassuming flower, try some of the newer cultivars.

'Seashell Mix' cultivars bear flowers in a full range of pink and rose colors and have petals that are rolled to form shell-like tubes on 3- to 4-foot plants. 'Sonata Mix' and 'Gazebo Mixed' have simple flowers but are dwarf, 3 feet at most; 'Versailles Mix' plants were bred for the cutting garden. 'Picotee' bears white blooms with pink edges; 'Daydream', another bicolor, has white flowers that fade to pink in their centers.

If you like strong hues, sulphur cosmos (*C. sulphureus*), which bears single or double flowers on 1- to 4-foot plants, is the species to grow. Its blooms come in shades of bright yellow, orange-red, and orange. 'Cosmic Orange', a 2000 All-America Selections winner, suggests the intensity of colors. Other choices include the Klondike and Ladybird Series, both dwarf types, and 'Polidor', which bears semidouble flowers.

IN THE GARDEN

Cosmos deserve a place in every sunny garden. They're traditional cottage garden plants and perfect for all manner of informal plantings. Use taller cultivars in the back of the border and to fill in around clumps of perennials like lilies, irises, and ornamental grasses. They're also stunning combined with annuals, such as cleome, and tender perennials like cannas and dahlias. Dwarf and semidwarf plants can be used toward the front of beds and borders and in containers. All cosmos attract butterflies and make outstanding cut flowers.

Sulphur cosmos, Cosmos sulphureus 'Sunny Orange'

OTHER CHOICES

Chocolate cosmos (*C. atrosanguineus*, formerly *Bidens atrosanguinea*) is also called black cosmos. It's a tender, tuberous-rooted perennial that can be grown as a perennial in Zones 7 to 10 or as an annual in colder locations. Mature plants reach 3 feet and bear deep maroon, 3/4-inch daisylike flowers with dark red-brown centers—and, as their common name suggests, have a slight chocolate fragrance.

Crocus

(KROE-kus)

Crocuses

Iris family, Iridaceae. Hardy bulbs.

The spring crocus (*C. vernus*) traveled from the Middle East to England in the 16th century and was an immediate hit—Shakespeare and Francis Bacon knew it, the herbalist John Gerard grew it. It is the best-known garden species, but this genus of 80 species has much more to offer than the violet, lavender, white, and yellow cultivars that are inevitably described as "harbingers of spring." Perhaps the biggest departure from these popular flowers are crocuses that bloom in fall. Plant some along a pathway and startle garden visitors who will insist on knowing exactly what you're growing.

The genus name *Crocus* celebrates an important economic use for one species in the genus, the fall-blooming saffron crocus (*C. sativus*). The name is from the Greek *krokos*, for "saffron," a medicinal herb and spice that has been prized for over 4,000 years. It is also the world's most expensive spice, because it takes the stigmas from 150,000 flowers and countless work hours to make just over a pound of dried saffron. Saffron can be grown in the home garden—you won't need anywhere near a pound of it to flavor sauces, stews, soups, and cakes—and is also prized as a dye. In 2005, the color was immortalized—at least for 16 days—when the artists Christo and Jeanne-Claude erected "The Gates," 7,500 saffron-colored cloth-draped gates in Central Park, one gate every 12 feet along 23 miles of walkways, the largest public arts project in New York City's history.

Whether they bloom in spring or fall, crocuses produce cup-shaped blooms and grow from corms, which look like—and often are called—bulbs but actually are swollen underground stems covered with a papery tunic. Each corm produces from one to four or five flowers and grassy leaves that appear with or just after the flowers. The blooms lack true above-ground stems and grow from the base of the corolla that arises directly from the ground. Flowers consist of six petals, which are more correctly called *tepals* because three actually are true petals and three are petal-like sepals. Spring crocuses belong to the iris family, and are different from autumn crocuses (*Colchicum* spp.), which are members of the lily family.

HOW TO GROW

Crocuses need full sun for best performance and like poor to average soil that is sandy or gritty and well drained. Spring-blooming crocuses can be planted under deciduous trees, where they will be in full sun in spring while they are growing actively, and are tolerant of the dry soil once they are dormant. Avoid sites with heavy clay or wet soil, because the corms will rot.

Spring crocus, Crocus vernus

OTHER CHOICES

Hardy bulbs are among the easiest flowers to grow, and they're inexpensive, too. In addition to crocuses, daffodils, and tulips, plant buckets of these so-called "little bulbs." All thrive in basically the same conditions required by crocuses, and the bulbs are easy to slip in anywhere. They are, as the housemaid explains in *The Secret Garden*, "things as helps themselves. That's why poor folk can afford to have 'em." (For more bulbs that bloom in summer, see the Gladiolus and Lilium entries on pages 324 and 366 respectively.)

Winter aconite, Eranthis hyemalis

LITTLE BULBS FOR SPRING

Glory-of-the-snow (*Chionodoxa luciliae*). Hardy in Zones 3 to 9, this 4- to 6-inch species bears racemes of clear blue, star-shaped flowers with white eyes in very early spring. Plants produce an abundance of offsets and self-sown seedlings.

Winter aconite (*Eranthis hyemalis*). Usually the first bulb to bloom in late winter, winter aconites bear yellow, cup-shaped flowers with a ruff of green leaves beneath the blooms. Hardy in Zones 4 to 9, plants are 3 to 6 inches tall and are not true bulbs; rather, they grow from knobby tubers that should be soaked overnight in warm water before planting. Plants self-sow and prefer rich, well-drained soil that remains evenly moist in summer.

Dogtooth violets, trout lilies (*Erythronium* spp.). These delicate-looking bulbous plants, most of which are native wildflowers, bloom in spring to early summer, and produce dainty, nodding, lilylike flowers that come in pink, purple, yellow, cream, and white. Unlike many spring-blooming bulbs, erythroniums have attractive leaves often mottled with purplish-brown or cream. Plants grow from tooth- or fang-shaped bulbs and thrive in partial or dappled shade with rich, moist soil. Species include European dogtooth violet (*E. dens-canis*) with solitary pink, lilac, or white flowers; yellow adder's tongue, or trout lily (*E. americanum*), with solitary yellow flowers; the yellow glacier lily (*E. grandiflorum*), native to western North America; and fawn lily (*E. californicum*) a California native that bears creamy white flowers. All three species bloom in spring and are hardy in Zones 3 to 9.

Snowdrops (*Galanthus* spp.). These bear small pendant white or green-and-white flowers with teardrop-shaped petals in late winter or very early spring. Plants range from

Yellow glacier lily, Erythronium grandiflorum

4 to 8 inches and are happiest in partial shade and rich soil that remains evenly moist but not wet in summer. The bulbs produce abundant offsets and self sow. Clumps left undisturbed will become large. Two species are commonly available: Common snowdrop (*G. nivalis*) is hardy in Zones 3 to 9 and giant snowdrop (*G. elwesii*) in Zones 3 to 9.

Bluebells (*Hyacinthoides* spp.). Several species of *Hyacinthoides* are grown for their erect, midspring spikes of bell-shaped blue, white, or pink flowers. All self-sown species produce abundant offsets and form large, handsome clumps. Botanists have reclassified plants in this genus numerous times. *H. hispanica*, Spanish bluebell, is

Spanish bluebell, Hyacinthoides hispanica

also listed as *Endymion hispanicus, Scilla campanulata,* and *S. hispanica. H. non-scripta,* the English bluebell, is listed as *E. non-scriptus, S. non-scripta,* and *S. nutans.* Both species are hardy in Zones 4 to 9.

Spring starflower (*Ipheion uniflorum*). These produce small, starry, lilac-blue flowers in late winter or early spring on 6- to 8-inch plants. Plants produce abundant offsets, and clumps can be left undisturbed for years until flowering diminishes. The foliage appears in fall and persists over winter. Spring starflowers can be grown in Zones 6 to 9, but mulch the plants with evergreen boughs to protect plants over winter in colder parts of Zone 7 and in Zone 6.

Snowflakes (*Leucojum* spp.). Hardy in Zones 4 to 8, snowflakes produce nodding, white, bell-shaped blooms dotted with green in mid- to late spring. Plants do best in moist, humus-rich soil. Summer snowflake (*L. aestivum*) is 1½ to 2 feet tall and hardy in Zones 4 to 9. Spring snowflake (*L. vernum*) is 8 to 12 inches tall and hardy in Zones 4 to 8.

Grape hyacinths (*Muscari* spp.). Grown for their fragrant, grapelike clusters of early- to midspring flowers,

grape hyacinths are long-flowering and come in shades of violet, purplish blue, pale blue, and white. Plants are 4 to 10 inches tall and produce offsets and self-sown seedlings in abundance. *M. armeniacum* and *M. latifolium* are hardy in Zones 4 to 8; *M. botryoides,* common grape hyacinth, is hardy in Zones 2 to 8.

Stars-of-Bethlehem (*Ornithogalum* spp.). These members of the lily family produce erect, late-spring spikes

Grape hyacinth, Muscari armeniacum *'Blue Spike'*

Star-of-Bethlehem, Ornithogalum umbellatum

OTHER CHOICES (*continued*)

of starry, white flowers that are often striped with green on the outside. Two hardy species of *Ornithogalum* are *O. nutans*, hardy in Zones 6 to 10 and 8 to 18 inches tall, and *O. umbellatum*, hardy in Zones 3 to 9 and 6 to 12 inches tall. Both produce abundant offsets and seedlings and can become invasive. Plant them along the base of a shrub border or naturalize them in a lawn.

Striped squill (*Puschkinia scilloides*). The small, bell-shaped flowers of striped squills are carried in hyacinthlike clusters from early to midspring. Blooms are bluish white with dark blue stripes and plants range from 6 to 8 inches. Plants, hardy in Zones 3 to 9, produce both seedlings and offsets and will form good-size clumps in time.

Squill (*Scilla* spp.). Several species of squill are planted for their early spring clusters of starry or bell-shaped flowers in rich blue, purple, white, or pink. Most species are 4 to 8 inches tall. Siberian squill (*S. siberica*) bears deep blue nodding bells and is hardy in Zones 2 to 8. Twin-leaf squill (*S. bifolia*) bears starry, purple-blue flowers and is hardy in Zones 3 to 8. Over time, both form good-size clumps, which can be left undisturbed for years.

LITTLE BULBS FOR FALL

Autumn crocuses (*Colchicum* spp.). These produce showy, crocuslike flowers in shades of pink or rose-purple in fall, although their strap-shaped leaves appear in spring. *C. autumnale*, 4 to 6 inches tall, and *C. speciosum*, 6 to 7 inches tall, both hardy in Zones 4 to 9, are most commonly grown. Plant the corms as soon as they are available in late summer or very early fall. The corms are more expensive than those of true crocuses but are poisonous and not bothered by rodents. With time, they produce large clumps.

Autumn daffodil, lily of the field (*Sternbergia lutea*). The golden yellow, goblet-shaped flowers of *Sternbergia* are always a welcome sight in fall. Plants reach about 6 inches and need very well drained, somewhat fertile soil. They are hardy in Zones 6 to 9.

Autumn crocus, Colchicum autumnale

Striped squill, Puschkinia scilloides

Autumn daffodil, Sternbergia lutea

Buy corms at garden centers or look for mail-order bulb specialists to see the full range of cultivars and species available. Plant corms 3 to 4 inches deep; plant spring-blooming crocuses in late fall, and fall-blooming selections as soon as they are available in late summer or very early fall. Propagate by separating the offsets just as the leaves turn yellow and the corms go dormant. Most crocuses self-sow and produce abundant offsets where happy. Unless otherwise noted, crocuses are hardy in Zones 3 to 8.

Mice, voles, chipmunks, and squirrels will eat crocus corms. Lay hardware cloth down on top of new plantings to keep critters at bay. Since the corms are quite inexpensive, another option is just to plant so many of them that you have a few to spare.

Hybrid crocus, Crocus × luteus '*Dutch Yellow*'

WHAT TO GROW

Spring, or Dutch, crocuses (C. *vernus*) reach 4 to 5-inches and bear white, pale lilac, to rich purple flowers. Among the many cultivars are 'Flower Record', with dark purple blooms; 'Jeanne d'Arc', white with a purple base; 'Pickwick', white striped with purple; 'Mammoth Yellow'; and 'Remembrance', with violet-purple blooms. All of the Dutch crocuses are vigorous and good for naturalizing.

Scotch crocus (C. *biflorus*) blooms somewhat earlier—from late winter to early spring—but also is vigorous and excellent for naturalizing. Despite its common name, this species is native to Italy, the Balkans, and southern Ukraine to Iran, not Scotland. The 2- to 2½-inch plants bear yellow-throated flowers in white or lilac-blue with outer petals that are sometimes striped with brown-purple. 'Miss Vain' bears fragrant white flowers with pale lilac-blue bases and showy orange styles.

Snow crocus (C. *chrysanthus*) is one of the first crocuses to bloom. The 2-inch plants open their lightly fragrant flowers from late winter to early spring. The species has golden yellow flowers, often marked with maroon on the outside, with showy orange stamens. Cultivars include 'Advance', with pale peach yellow flowers that are white and bluish violet on the outside and have orange stamens; 'Blue Bird', creamy white inside and violet blue outside; 'Blue Pearl', soft blue on the outside with a bronze yellow base and a yellow throat; 'Cream Beauty', creamy yellow; 'E. P. Bowles', lemon yellow with bronze-yellow at the base; 'Ladykiller', white striped with purple; and 'Snow Bunting', with white flowers streaked with lilac on the outside.

Other spring-blooming crocuses include the 4-inch-tall Italian Crocus (C. *imperati*), a late winter to early spring bloomer hardy in Zones 5 to 8 with purple flowers striped with yellow on the outside. C. *tommasinianus*, another 3- to 4-inch species that's vigorous and good for naturalizing, blooms from late winter to early spring and bears pale lilac to red-purple blooms.

Fall-blooming crocuses include the saffron crocus (C. *sativus*), a 2-inch-tall species with lilac-purple flowers veined in dark purple. Plants do not flower well in areas with cool, wet summers, and are hardy in Zones 5 to 8. Other fall-blooming species include *C. laevigatus*, 1½ to 3 inches tall with white or lilac flowers and hardy in Zones 5 to 8; *C. medius*, a 3-inch species hardy in Zones 3 to 8 and bearing dark purple flowers with brilliant orange styles; *C. ochroleucus*, a 2-inch species hardy in Zones 5 to 8 with creamy white flowers that have yellow throats; and *C. speciosus*, a vigorous 4- to 6-inch species with violet-blue flowers hardy in Zones 3 to 8.

IN THE GARDEN

The more the merrier should be your guideline for planting crocuses or any of the little bulbs. Although their flowers are small when compared to summer-blooming perennials, they pack a punch early in the season—or in the fall—when flowers and color are at a premium in the garden. So plant them by the hundreds if you can. For the longest display of bloom, plant several species and cultivars. The earliest-blooming crocuses include snow crocuses (*C. chrysanthus*) and *C. tommasinianus*, which flower from late winter into early spring. Scotch crocuses (*C. biflorus*) and Dutch crocuses (*C. vernus*) bloom slightly later. Dutch crocuses are one of the best species for naturalizing in a lawn but tend to die out after several years. Other species suitable for naturalizing in a lawn include *C. biflorus* and *S. tommasinianus*. Do not mow the lawn until after the crocus foliage turns yellow and dies back. Naturalized crocuses planted in wild gardens as well as en masse in beds and borders will be longer lived than ones planted in lawns.

Formal decorative dahlia, Dahlia 'Hulin's Carnival'

Dahlia

(DAHL-ee-ah)

Dahlias

Aster family, Asteraceae. Tender perennials.

Few flowers add as much color to the garden as modern dahlias do. The plants grown today are all hybrid descendents of species native to Mexico and Central America. The Aztecs were the first people to record growing dahlias—they were included in a medicinal record dating to 1582—and the tree dahlia, a 20-foot cultivar (*Dahlia imperialis*), was an early immigrant to Spain. It took several centuries before other species—all with single daisylike flowers—made their way across the Atlantic, where they were crossed and recrossed. And named after the Swedish botanist Andreas Dahl, who was a pupil of Linnaeus. By 1850 several thousand double and bicolored dahlias had been created, followed in the next 75 years by many new flower shapes. Although the hybridizing frenzy has quieted somewhat, dahlia devotees continue to seek a trinity of goals: a blue dahlia, a fragrant dahlia, and a hardy dahlia.

Gardeners have a staggering array of shapes and sizes to choose among, from enormous double blooms that measure 1 foot across to petite pompons. Flowers come in all colors except the elusive blue: mahogany, scarlet, magenta, pink, orange, yellow, cream, and white, plus scores of bicolors. There are dwarf, 12- to 15-inch-tall, cultivars for bedding, but most dahlias are tall plants, ranging from 3 to 6 feet. Green leaves are typical, but some plants

for a site that is protected from wind but receives good air circulation. Rich, deeply dug soil and even moisture are musts, too, as is good drainage, for the tuberous roots will rot in wet soil. Work plenty of compost or humus into the soil before planting.

The best way to add dahlias to your garden—and the only way to acquire most of the improved cultivars—is to buy tubers, pot-grown plants, or small bedding plants. The thick, fleshy tuberous roots should be firm to the touch, have no soft or rotted-looking spots, and each should have a piece of stem attached. (The eyes, or growing buds, are on the main stem where it is attached to the tuber, not on the tuber itself.)

Plant the tubers in the garden (2 inches deep in soil that has been dug to 8 inches with the buds pointed up) after the last-frost date and the soil has warmed. Wait if the weather has been unusually cold or wet, since tubers rot in cold, wet conditions, and plants are frost tender. If you're growing tall dahlias—anything taller than 3 feet—install a stake *before* you plant to avoid injuring the tubers. Some gardeners give dahlias a head start by potting up the tubers indoors four to six weeks before the frost-free date. Set the buds just above the surface of the soil, and keep the soil moist and the containers in a warm, bright spot. Set the plants in the garden—at the same depth they were growing—after the last spring frost date *and* after hardening them off. When plants have two to three sets of leaves, pinch back the shoot tips to encourage branching.

To bloom well, dahlias must grow steadily and quickly, so keep plants watered and feed them with compost tea or a diluted, low-nitrogen liquid fertilizer when they go into the garden, when the first flower buds appear, and again about a month later. Remove spent flowers to encourage new buds to form. Gardeners after large flowers rather than many flowers should *disbud* their plants.

When flowering ceases in Zone 8 and south, cut the plants to 6 inches and mulch them. Dig and divide clumps every two to three years to keep them vigorous. In cold regions, cut plants back to 6 inches as soon as they are blackened by frost. Dig the clumps and store them over winter in paper bags filled with slightly moistened vermiculite in a well-ventilated location where temperatures remain between 36° and 45°F. The objective is to keep the tubers from either drying out or rotting—check them periodically and mist them if they appear shriveled. If there is any rot, trim it off.

have handsome bronzed or maroon foliage; leaves are divided with leaflets arranged in a featherlike fashion.

Dahlias bloom from midsummer until frost, growing from tuberous roots that are hardy from Zone 8 or 9 south, where they can be cultivated outdoors year-round (with protection in Zone 8). In northern gardens they either are treated like annuals and replaced each year or the tuberous roots are overwintered indoors and replanted in spring. Fast growing and easy to please, dahlias produce a floral show even where the garden season is abbreviated.

HOW TO GROW

Plant dahlias in full sun. The more sun they receive, the more flowers you get: It's that simple. In torrid climates, a bit of shade during the hottest part of the day will protect plants from heat, however. Look

Cactus-flowered dahlia, Dahlia 'Connie'

(www.dahlia.org) often hold spring and fall plant sales and exchanges. There are 18 official flower forms, 15 official colors and color combinations, and nine official flower sizes, so making a choice isn't easy. Flower forms, for example, offer everything from dahlias that look like peonies, cactuses, anemones, and water lilies, to ball-shaped, pompon-shaped, and daisy-shaped cultivars.

For dahlias that produce the most blooms per plant, pick cultivars with uncomplicated flowers less than 3 inches across and plants under 3 feet tall,

Semicactus dahlia, Dahlia 'Amy K'

Propagate dahlias by dividing the tuberous roots in spring or by taking cuttings from shoots that sprout from the roots in spring. (Don't divide them in fall before overwintering, because the cut roots tend to rot over winter.) Dahlias also can be grown from seeds, sown indoors four to six weeks before the last spring frost date.

Cutworms, stalk borers, spider mites, and aphids can attack dahlias but are rarely major problems. Good air circulation and thinning out stems help prevent powdery mildew.

WHAT TO GROW

While most well-stocked garden centers may offer a dozen dahlia cultivars, there are thousands available, and more are introduced every year. If you're growing dahlias for the first time, stick with tubers and plants from your garden center and choose on the basis of color and size. For exhibition-quality plants, you'll need to order by mail or find a dahlia enthusiast. Local chapters of the American Dahlia Society

free-flowering cultivars informally known as "garden dahlias." Look for 'Santa Claus' (red and white bicolor), 'Blue Bell' (lavender), 'Fire Mountain' (red), 'Diamond Rose', 'G. F. Hemerik' (salmon orange), 'Yellow Sneezy', 'Hartenaas' (pink), 'Honey' (yellow blend), 'Red Riding Hood', and 'Sunny Glow' (yellow). Bedding dahlias, which commercial growers typically start from seed to produce small nursery plants, also are fine garden plants. Three widely available series are Diablo, Figaro, and Sunny. Cultivars with striking maroon or bronze foliage include 'Bishop of Llandaff' (red flowers), 'Classic Summertime' (yellow flowers), 'Roxy' (rose-pink flowers), and 'Ellen Houston' (orange-red flowers). Cultivars in the Gallery Series are good choices for containers.

IN THE GARDEN

Dwarf dahlias excel as edging plants along walkways or at the front of sunny beds and borders; small cultivars do well in containers. Plant taller dahlias at the center of island beds or toward the back of borders and combine them with annuals like sunflower (*Helianthus annuus*), Mexican sunflower (*Tithonia rotundifolia*), and salvias or sages (*Salvia* spp.). Cultivars with smaller flowers (under 6 inches) generally are more effective for combining with other plants.

If cut or exhibition flowers are your goal, plant dahlias in a cutting garden where they can grow without having to compete with other plants. Cut dahlias when the flowers are nearly open but still firm in the center. Cut just above a leaf node, and recut stems under water.

Delphinium

(del-FIN-ee-um)

Delphiniums

Buttercup family, Ranunculaceae.
Hardy perennials.

If there's one perennial that gardeners dream about, it's the delphinium. And when they dream, they dream about its color. As the American poet Louise Driscoll wrote in "My Garden is a Pleasant Place,"

There is no blue like the blue cup
The tall delphinium holds up,
Not sky, nor distant hill, nor sea,
Sapphire, nor lapis lazuli.

Delphiniums' stately spires appear in summer and come in all the hard to find blues—pure blue, sky blue, royal blue, and more—as well as violet, lavender, pink, mauve, and white. The only thing delphiniums lack is fragrance. And adaptability: Alas, delphiniums are not plants that can be grown everywhere. They're staples of English gardens in summer, where cool, rainy conditions prevail; in North America, delphiniums thrive in the Pacific Northwest, northern and coastal New England, and much of Canada. As one nursery web site put it, delphiniums "get bad press in Texas and no press in Florida."

Delphiniums are short-lived perennials, hardy from Zones 3 to 7, that frequently are grown as biennials or even annuals in regions without cool summers. Plants produce clumps of palmately lobed leaves, with lobes arranged like fingers on a hand, topped by wiry, branched stems of single, semidouble, or double flowers that are ¾ to 2½ inches across.

But technical descriptions don't do this flower justice. *D. elatum*, the ancestor of most of today's hybrids, was the first perennial delphinium grown in English gardens; by the mid-1800s, British and European breeders were working their magic on delphiniums, turning them into floral towers worthy of the common name candlestick larkspur. Early in the 20th century, Frank Reinelt, once a gardener to Queen Marie of Romania, immigrated to California, established a nursery, and created the famous Pacific Giant hybrids, which are still the most widely grown delphinium cultivars in North America.

HOW TO GROW

Cool summer weather and very rich, deeply prepared, well-drained soil are what delphiniums need to thrive. Extra attention, however, will mean the difference between a nice display of delphiniums and a spectacular one.

In areas with cool summers, plant delphiniums in full sun; in warmer regions, choose a site that receives morning sun and shade during the afternoon. Good air circulation helps prevent disease problems, but stay away from a windy location. Add plenty of compost, leaf mold, or well-rotted manure to the soil before you plant, and dig it in to a depth of a foot or more. Delphiniums are happiest with

Bee delphinium, Delphinium × elatum *'Blue Bird'*

two-year-old plants; thin to five or six strong shoots on mature clumps. Thinning improves air circulation and helps direct the plant's energy into producing fewer but larger bloom spikes.

All but the shortest delphiniums need support. Begin staking when the hollow stems are about 1 foot tall; many gardeners install a stake for each stem (bamboo and plastic-covered steel are two options). Remove the main flower stalks after blooms fade, cutting just above the basal mound of foliage, and fertilize to encourage a second flush of flower spikes in late summer or fall. After the first frost, remove all stalks. Divide clumps in spring every four years to maintain vigor.

Many experts contend that the strongest plants are those grown from seeds rather than from divisions or cuttings. To start delphiniums from seeds, sow indoors in February; after hardening-off, move plants to the garden in early spring, on or slightly before the frost-free date. Or sow seeds outdoors in pots in July; transplant seedlings to the garden once their true leaves begin to develop and cover them with loose mulch over winter. Delphinium seeds loose viability quickly, so be sure seeds are fresh, and give them five days in the freezer before you sow them.

Delphiniums have more than their share of disease problems. Powdery mildew is disfiguring and delphinium blight is lethal; crown wilt and stem and root rot are common in soil that doesn't drain well. Slugs sometimes dine on the foliage, and mites, aphids, and beetles can infest plants. Despite this litany of woes, gardeners still dream of delphiniums.

neutral to slightly alkaline pH. The plants need soil that stays evenly moist, but sodden soil encourages crown rot, so avoid spots where water collects.

Mulch in spring to keep the soil cool, and feed plants with a balanced organic fertilizer when plants are about 6 inches tall and again when flower buds appear. Water deeply every week if there is no soaking rain; keep water off the leaves to prevent foliage diseases. Once the plants are established and growing, remove all but the three strongest shoots on

WHAT TO GROW

Hybrids are the most popular delphiniums grown in gardens, although exactly who fathered whom is less than crystal clear. These, however, are the two names you're likely to encounter in catalogs and at the nursery.

OTHER CHOICES

For rich delphinium colors—blues, violets, lavenders, magenta, pink, and white—without all the trouble, consider planting larkspur (*Consolida ajacis*), a super easy to grow annual also called annual delphinium. Once classified as *Delphinium consolida* and *D. ajacis*, plants have deeply cut, lacy leaves and single or double, 1½-inch blooms carried on spikes that can reach 2 feet in length. Depending on the cultivar planted, the spikes may be loose and open or densely packed with blossoms; plants, which range from 1 to 3 or 4 feet tall, also may be sparsely or well branched. Give larkspurs full sun or very light afternoon shade and average to rich soil that is well drained. In areas with cool summers, they bloom from late spring to summer, but in the South they die out once summer heat and humidity arrive. To add larkspurs to your garden, purchase transplants or sow seed outdoors in late fall (South) or in early spring (North) where the plants are to grow. There are dwarf cultivars for the front of the border and full-size ones, which make ideal cut flowers. Plant a mix of colors or buy from a supplier who sells the colors separately. Larkspurs also are superb dried flowers.

Larkspur, *Consolida ajacis*

Elatum Group hybrids. Also called *D. × elatum* hybrids, these plants produce dense spikes of flat, single, semidouble, or double flowers held on 4- to 8-foot-tall plants and are known as bee delphiniums. There are several Elatum strains, including the new Mid-Century Hybrids, the Giant Imperial Series, and the popular Pacific Hybrids. Also known as Pacific Giants, these delphiniums often are grown as annuals, but in cold regions they can live for many seasons. Cultivars in the Round Table Series have Arthurian names, including 'King Arthur' (dark blue), 'Guinevere' (lavender), and 'Galahad' (white). 'Blue Bird' is another superb cultivar, blue with a white center. Pacific Giants are typically grown from seed, so colors can vary.

One other Elatum strain that deserves to be mentioned is the Connecticut Yankee Series. It blooms in blue shades (and an occasional white) and produces heavily branched spikes from 2 to 3 feet tall that are covered with 2½-inch flowers. Despite its New England roots—it was developed by the acclaimed photographer Edward Steichen in his Connecticut garden and won an All-America Selections award in 1963—many Connecticut Yankee cultivars do well as far south as Zone 7.

Belladonna Group hybrids. Also called *D. × belladonna* hybrids, these plants grow to 3 or 4 feet and bear loosely branched spikes of flowers that bloom from midsummer to fall. Names to look for are 'Bonita' (gentian blue), 'Bellamosa' (deep blue), 'Casa Blanca' (white), and 'World Peace' (deep blue). The flowers of most cultivars are typically cup-shaped and usually sterile.

IN THE GARDEN

Few plants are more spectacular in garden beds and borders. "What's not to like?" is the standard comment. Try to grow drifts of delphiniums, three plants at least, more if there is room. Taller cultivars are stunning against a wall or board fence, which provides a backdrop and also protects plants from wind. Combine delphiniums with peonies, iris, poppies (*Papaver* spp.), and daylilies. Delphinium flowers begin opening at the bottom of the spike. For cut flowers or drying, cut the spike when it is about half open. To dry, hang stems upside-down in a warm dry place.

Dianthus

(*die-AN-thuss*)

Pinks, dianthus

Pink family, Caryophyllaceae.
Perennials, biennials, annuals.

○

The genus *Dianthus* is a vast clan of charming, old-fashioned flowers that have been grown in gardens almost since Eden. The genus name *Dianthus*, which is from the Greek for "Zeus's flower" or "divine flower," dates to the 4th century A.D., but the Roman historian Pliny was writing about clove carnations in the 1st century A.D., and Asian herbalists were describing members of the genus well before Pliny. As the authority Allan Armitage explained in *Herbaceous Perennial Plants* (1997), dianthus "have been in gardens as long as there have been gardens."

Not surprisingly, it didn't take long for dianthus to make their way across the Atlantic. Thomas Jefferson was among the many colonial gardeners who grew them, including China pink (*D. chinensis*), seeds for which he obtained from the Philadelphia nurseryman Bernard McMahon in 1807. The New England poets Henry Wadsworth Longfellow and Emily Dickinson were among the many 19th-century gardeners who grew pinks. By then sweet William

Allwood pink, Dianthus × allwoodii *'Essex Witch'*

(*D. barbatus*), which was one of the first dianthus immigrants to North America, had naturalized so successfully that most Americans thought of it as a native wildflower. "To praise this flower would be like gilding refined gold," another writer of that century observed.

The common name pinks may refer to the color of the flowers; to *pinksten* or *pfingsten*, German for "flowers that bloomed at Pentecost"; or to their fringed or ragged edges, which look as if there were trimmed with pinking shears. Pinks is the usual common name, but *Dianthus* also are known as carnations, gillyflowers, sweet William, colminiers, sops in wine, horse-flesh, blunkets, cloves, and more. "The fairest flowers o' the season / Are Carnations and streak'd Gillyflowers," Perdita says in *A Winter's Tale*.

Even if the name pinks doesn't refer to color, there are plenty of pink pinks, as well as red, rose, salmon, cerise, purple, magenta, maroon, and white pinks. Many cultivars—and there are more than

Cheddar pink, Dianthus gratianopolitanus *'Bath's Pink'*

30,000 of them—feature two or more colors. The petals of all pinks can be used fresh in salads and also are dried for use in potpourris. Alas, many modern cultivars no longer have spicy-scented blooms since hybridizers have focused on other features of the flowers in their breeding programs. The plants are generally low-growing and mound-shaped, with attractive blue- or gray-green leaves, often evergreen in moderate climates, that are lance-shaped to grasslike.

HOW TO GROW

Site selection is the key to growing pinks: They are happiest in full sun and well-drained soil. Pinks also prefer cool weather, so morning sun and afternoon shade is better in areas with hot summers. As long as it is well drained, soil can be moist or dry; a slightly alkaline or neutral pH is ideal, but most dianthus will tolerate moderately acid conditions. A wet location, however, is lethal, as plants will rot during the winter.

Container-grown pinks are readily available at garden centers in spring and need little care once planted. They appreciate a spring dose of water-soluble fertilizer that is high in phosphorus. If their shallow feeder roots become exposed, cover them up with loose soil mixed with compost or leaf mold, but don't mulch plants. Deadheading prolongs the blooming season, but most pinks stop flowering in summer heat. Shearing back to 2 or 3 inches stimulates new foliage and helps prolong the life of some species, but it doesn't guarantee a second round of flowers. Divide clumps every two to three years to maintain vigor; replant the healthy outer growth and discard the dead center portions.

China pink, Dianthus chinensis 'Telstar Picotee'

Allwood pink, Dianthus × allwoodii *'Doris'*

'Zing Rose' blooms from late spring to fall; 'Bright Eyes' has white flowers with red centers; 'Rosea' flowers in shades of pink.

Cheddar pinks (*D. gratianopolitanus*) feature fragrant, single or double, 1-inch flowers in late spring on dense, 4- to 12-inch mats of foliage, and they are hardy in Zones 3 to 8. Shearing encourages plants to continue blooming. 'Tiny Rubies' bears fragrant, double ½-inch flowers on 4-inch plants; other fragrant cultivars are 'Bath's Pink' and 'Karlik' (pink). 'Firewitch' (magenta) and 'Bath's Pink' are especially heat tolerant.

Cottage pinks (*D. plumarius*), which are also known as border, grass, and old-fashioned pinks, produce fragrant, 1-inch single, semidouble, or double flowers on plants 1 to 2 feet tall. 'Spring Beauty' (pink), 'White Ladies', and 'Musgrave's White' are three fragrant cultivars.

To start plants from seeds, sow indoors six to ten weeks before the last spring frost date, depending on the species. Or sow outdoors in midspring, just before the last-frost date, in pots and set the pots in a protected spot outdoors. Pinks are promiscuous, and seeds saved from garden plants may not produce plants that resemble their parents. For progeny that's identical to the parent plants, propagate by division or by taking cuttings in summer.

Plants are subject to crown and root rot and to rust in humid weather; aphids, mites, and beetles can be a problem.

WHAT TO GROW

Hardy pinks are perennials that start flowering just as the main flush of spring bulbs are finishing up, adding color to the garden from late spring into summer. Most have evergreen leaves. Exact parentage of the cultivars can be confusing, and you may just want to buy pinks at a local garden center on the basis of which flowers are most appealing. Hardiness varies, too, depending on a cultivar's parentage, but most perennial pinks are hardy from Zones 3 to 8, although they tend to be short-lived wherever they are grown.

Hardy species to look for include maiden pinks (*D. deltoides*), which bear single, 1- to 1½-inch flowers above low, spreading mats of foliage, 6 to 12 inches tall. Maiden pinks are vigorous plants, hardy from Zone 3 into Zone 9, that self-sow with enthusiasm; cut plants back after the main flush of bloom to encourage rebloom in fall. The deep red cultivar

China pink, Dianthus chinensis *'Ideal Violet'*

Allwood, or modern, pinks (D. × *allwoodii*) are hybrids, hardy in Zones 4 or 5 to 8. They bear 2-inch, usually double flowers on 12- to 20-inch, compact plants for up to eight weeks, but most have only modest fragrance. Recommended cultivars that are fragrant include 'Baby Treasure' (pink with red center), 'Aqua' (white), 'Doris' (salmon-pink with a pink center), and 'Rachel' (pink).

Sweet William (D. *barbatus*), a short-lived perennial often treated as a biennial, is an old-fashioned plant, perfectly at home in a cottage garden. Plants range from dwarfs to 2 feet and most self-sow with abandon, making propagation work-free. Most flower clusters lack fragrance despite the "sweet" in the common name; they bloom in colors that range from pink to scarlet as well as white and bicolors, usually with a contrasting center, or eye. Many of the new cultivars are annuals. Old-timer 'Wee Willie' is an open-pollinated, long-flowering 6-inch selection; 'Hollandia Mix' is a newer, annual hybrid; hybrid 'Cinderella Mix' was bred for the cutting garden; 'Excelsior Mix' plants reach 18 inches and bear fragrant flowers.

Also called rainbow and Indian pink, China pink (D. *chinensis*) is hardy only to Zone 7. Most of the cultivars now sold either are annuals or can be treated like annuals. Flowers are typically single with fringed petals, come in a variety of colors and patterns, and are carried on 6- to 12-inch plants from midsummer to fall. Look for Ideal, Festival, and Melody Series, which are especially free flowering. Hybrids 'Snowfire', 'Magic Charms', and 'Corona Cherry Magic' are All-America Selections winners.

IN THE GARDEN

Combine pinks with other perennials that appreciate well-drained soil, including thread-leaved coreopsis (*Coreopsis verticillata*), columbines (*Aquilegia* spp.), bellflowers (*Campanula* spp.), speedwells (*Veronica* spp.), hardy geraniums or cranesbills (*Geranium* spp.), sedums or stonecrops (*Sedum* spp.), and thymes. They are superb plants for rock gardens and are excellent cut flowers.

Dicentra

(*die-CEN-trah*)

Bleeding hearts, dicentras

Fumitory family, Fumariaceae.
Hardy perennials.

Named for their inflated, pendant, heart-shaped, two-spurred flowers, the name *Dicentra* is derived from the Greek word *dis*, "two," and *kentron*, "spurred." These hardy perennials are easily grown and much-loved garden plants. The flower form is most obvious in the common bleeding heart (D. *spectabilis*), an old-fashioned plant whose species name *spectabilis*, says it all: "spectacular." While bleeding heart is the most common name for the garden species, it and other *Dicentras* are known as Chinamen's breeches, turkey corn, staggerseed, lady's locket, our Lady in a boat, lyre flower, seal flower, lady's heart, squirrel corn,

Common bleeding heart, Dicentra spectabilis

best when given the heat protection that a somewhat shady spot provides. To encourage *D. eximia* and *D. formosa* to bloom all summer, look for a spot where they will receive morning sun and afternoon shade. Protecting bleeding hearts from hot afternoon sun is essential in southern gardens.

Container plants are available at garden centers in spring. Work generous amounts of compost into the soil when planting. Be sure to handle plants carefully, as their brittle roots and rhizomes break easily. Mulch plants to retain moisture, and water if rain is sparse. Deadhead *D. eximia* and *D. formosa* as the flowers fade to encourage new blooms to form. Common bleeding heart dies back after it flowers; its foliage can be cut to the ground once it yellows.

Unlike many perennials, bleeding hearts don't need to be divided regularly, and established plants

Dutchman's breeches, soldier's cap, white hearts, eardrops, kitten breeches, and more.

Apparently *D. spectabilis* was brought to England early in the 19th century but died out and didn't become widely grown until the plant hunter Robert Fortune reintroduced it in 1846. Having found it on an island off the coast of China, he brought it back in a Wardian case, a travel-friendly terrarium invented in 1829 by the London physician Dr. Nathaniel Ward. Three decades later bleeding heart was so popular in England that it had moved indoors to become a popular wallpaper pattern.

Common bleeding heart found its way to North America in the mid-1800s, an instant hit with flower-loving pioneers who carried it west. While coddling this Chinese-via-England import, those same gardeners ignored native bleeding hearts. In a bit of botanical irony, cultivars of the American species *D. eximia* are now more widely grown in England than is *D. spectabilis*.

Most garden bleeding hearts bear their blooms in racemes or panicles on plants with deeply divided and fernlike leaves. Plants grow from rhizomes or fleshy taproots.

HOW TO GROW

Bleeding hearts are shade-lovers for the most part, hardy from Zones 3 to 9, and are happiest when given a spot that has rich, moist, well-drained soil. Damp, poorly drained soil spells root rot and death when winter comes. While common bleeding heart will survive in full sun in cool climates, plants grow

Common bleeding heart, Dicentra spectabilis *'Alba'*

OTHER CHOICES

Although seldom seen in gardens, two native wild-flowers also belong to this family—Dutchman's breeches (*D. cucullaria*) and squirrel corn (*D. canadensis*). Both produce dainty white flowers in spring and die back after flowering. You may be able to find plants of these species at native plant sales held by botanical gardens or at nurseries specializing in natives. Collecting *Dicentras* from the wild is illegal in many states; for environmental reasons, it's better not to collect plants from the wild or purchase plants that may have been collected from the wild.

resent being moved. Plants can be propagated from seeds sown in pots in late summer and set outdoors in a protected location, from divisions, and from root cuttings in summer or fall. Plants are subject to stem rot.

WHAT TO GROW

Old-fashioned common bleeding heart (*D. spectabilis*) is the best known of the dicentras. It is a bushy 1½- to 2½-foot perennial with arching racemes of pendant, heart-shaped, pink-and-white flowers. Hardy in Zones 2 to 9, it blooms for a few weeks in spring, then dies back. Plants linger if the soil stays evenly moist. In addition to the species, white-flowered cultivars—'Pantaloons' is one—are available but tend to be less vigorous. 'Gold Heart' has gold foliage.

Two native bleeding hearts, both hardy in Zones 3 to 9, are garden-worthy plants: fringed bleeding heart (*D. eximia*) and Western bleeding heart (*D. formosa*). They grow from 10 to about 18 inches tall and have delicate, lacy foliage. Both send up spikes of pendant, heart-shaped flowers, which are carried above the foliage. Better still, both bloom from spring to fall—as long as the soil stays evenly moist and temperatures are moderate. 'Stuart Boothman' has blue-gray leaves and rich pink flowers; 'Luxuriant' bears red-pink flowers over blue-green leaves; 'Snowdrift' bears white flowers.

IN THE GARDEN

Common bleeding heart and its North American cousins add both color and wonderful foliage to shady beds and borders and wildflower gardens.

Combine them with other natives such as wild columbine (*Aquilegia canadensis*), foam flowers (*Tiarella* spp.), and wild blue phlox (*Phlox divaricata*); in shade gardens that include non-native plants, consider planting them with hostas, astilbes, epimediums, or barrenworts (*Epimedium* spp.), ferns, and spring bulbs.

Dictamnus albus

(dick-TAM-nus AL-bus)

Gas plant

Rue Family, Rutaceae. Hardy Perennial.

There's little doubt that flower growers with patience—plus sun and well-drained soil—will be rewarded by adding a gas plant or three to their gardens. Patience is important, because these tough, long-lived perennials take a few years to get established, so they're not for anyone who moves plants around on a regular basis. Given a permanent home in the garden, though, gas plants will bloom for years without further care. Fifty-year-old clumps that still bloom generously aren't unusual.

Also called dittany, fraxinella, and burning bush, gas plants are shrublike perennials, 3 to 4½ feet tall, that produce a handsome clump of glossy, dark green, pinnately compound leaves. The foliage is citrus-scented when bruised, and the plants' spikes of flowers are also fragrant. Both flowers and leaves emit a volatile oil, and common names like gas plant and burning bush refer to the fact that on a sultry, windless evening, the volatile oil can be ignited for a split second. Some sources say the leaves themselves ignite; others that it's the perfume given off by the older flowers. Although plant-savvy gardeners discount their ability to flame, try holding a match under a flower, watch closely, and see what happens.

One thing to keep in mind regarding gas plant's oils is that they cause a blistering, poison-ivylike rash in some gardeners, especially in hot weather.

HOW TO GROW

For best performance, set gas plants in full sun, although they will tolerate light shade, in soil that

Gas plant, Dictamnus albus '*Ruber*'

drains well and stays on the dry side. Wet or poorly drained conditions lead to root rot. Two-year old plants, the usual size sold at nurseries, will need another two years to become established. Work the soil deeply and incorporate compost or well-rotted manure to enrich the soil before you plant. Handle plants carefully during transplanting, as both roots and stems are brittle and easily broken. Give each plant at least 3 feet to spread. Water during very dry weather, and topdress annually with compost or well-rotted mature.

If you absolutely must transplant a clump, disturb the roots as little as possible and replant immediately. Plants can be propagated by division—use a sharp spade to cut cleanly through the crown and the roots and replant the divisions immediately—although the divisions often have difficulty reestablishing themselves. Growing plants from seed is also problematic, as germination is uneven. If you try, start with fresh seeds gathered in late summer and sow in individual pots. Set the pots in a cold frame or

a protected location outdoors; plants will bloom in three to four years. All in all, propagating gas plants is as difficult as growing them is easy. If you need more plants, head for the garden center.

Gas plants are seldom bothered by pests or diseases.

WHAT TO GROW

There are only two forms of gas plants, but if you love these old-fashioned perennials, you'll want to grow both. First is the species (*D. albus*), which boasts white, 1-inch flowers on 3-foot-tall plants. Each bloom has five showy petals and long, curled stamens that give them a spidery appearance. *D. albus* var. *purpurascens* (also listed as '*Purpureus*') has purple-mauve flowers that have darker veins. Flower color varies somewhat from plant to plant. The duration of bloom is brief, but established plants are well worth the space they occupy in the garden. The handsome foliage is an added bonus and stays attractive all season long. Plants flower in late spring to early summer and are hardy in Zones 3 to 7, but they are at their best in areas with where nighttime temperatures are cool.

IN THE GARDEN

Combine gas plants with other perennials that bloom in early summer such as baby's breaths (*Gypsophila* spp.), coreopsis, hardy geraniums, or cranesbills (*Geranium* spp.), flax (*Linum* spp.), daylilies, penstemons (*Penstemon* spp.), and yarrows (*Achillea*). The flowers are lures for butterflies, and the foliage is an attractive backdrop for summer-blooming annuals or smaller perennials.

Digitalis

(dih-gih-TAL-iss)

Foxgloves

Figwort Family, Scrophulariaceae.
Hardy perennials, biennials.

Grown for their erect racemes packed with tubular, somewhat two-lipped flowers, foxgloves are biennials or short-lived perennials native to Europe, northwestern Africa, and central Asia. The botanical name

Digitalis is from the Latin for "finger," *digitus*, and refers to the shape of the flowers as well as explains the common name finger flower. Other common names—fox-bell, for one—allude to the flowers' bell-like shape. "And the stately foxglove / Hangs silent its exquisite bells," the poet Christina Rossetti wrote in "Bride Song." Blooms come in shades of pink and purple as well as white and yellow and often are speckled on the inside. The plants produce rosettes of large basal leaves; lance-shaped smaller leaves are produced along the flower stems.

While foxgloves are the quintessential old-fashioned cottage garden plant, they also are important medicinal plants. Plants contain a variety of cardioactive glycosides, including digitoxin, and in pharmaceutical circles, the term *digitalis* refers to the powdered leaves of common foxglove (*D. purpurea*). All parts of foxglove plants are poisonous. Contact with the foliage can irritate skin.

Common, or purple, foxglove (*D. purpurea*) is an English wildflower. Although both English gardeners and English herbalists grew it in their gardens, it wasn't until the late 1700s that it was recorded as growing in North America. Once here, however, it jumped the garden fence and naturalized in moist locations. As many authorities have observed, foxgloves were designed for colonizing new places, for their tiny seeds—it takes more than 4.5 million to weigh a pound—are easily spread and germinate in high numbers.

HOW TO GROW

Select a site that has rich, evenly moist, well-drained soil and is in full sun or partial shade. In areas with hot summers, afternoon shade helps protect plants from heat.

To add foxgloves to your garden, start with purchased plants or grow your own from seeds. Sow seeds outdoors in spring or summer up to two months before the first fall frost, either in a prepared seedbed or in pots set in a protected location. Or sow indoors in individual pots six to eight weeks before plants are scheduled to go into the garden. Whether you sow outdoors or in, you want to have plants that are ready to move to the garden by early fall, which is the classic schedule for growing common foxglove (*D. purpurea*) as a biennial, or in early spring. Arrange plants in drifts of three, five, or more for the best effect, and keep them evenly moist until established.

Once planted, foxgloves need very little care. They'll stand without staking, and they need only to be watered during dry weather and mulched to help keep the soil cool and prevent heaving in winter. If you are growing them as biennials, pull up two-year-old plants after they bloom and replace them with new seedlings. All foxgloves self-sow. Leave some flowers on the plants to set seed, then collect and spread them wherever you want new plants. Volunteer seedlings are easy to move with a trowel. Perennial foxgloves also can be propagated by division in early spring or fall.

Too-wet soil can cause root and stem rot; plants are sometimes troubled by mildew and by aphids and Japanese beetles.

Common foxglove, Digitalis purpurea

WHAT TO GROW

Biennial common foxglove (D. *purpurea*) is by far the most popular member of this clan. Hardy in Zones 3 through 9, it produces a rosette of leaves—up to 10 inches long—the first year and showy 3- to 5-foot spikes of flowers the following year. Plants sometimes bloom for a second or third season as short-lived perennials, but for the most dramatic show from these plants, pull them up and replace them after they bloom the first time. The species produces flowers in shades of purple, pink, and white, but many cultivars are available. 'Excelsior Hybrids' are among the best known and yield showy spikes of large flowers that are mottled on the inside and come in pastel pinks and purples, creamy yellow, and white; 'Glittering Prizes Mix' is similar, flowering in a wide range of colors with darkly marked throats. Individual colors, such as

'Primrose Carousel' (yellow) and 'Alba' (white), are available as well. 'Foxy Hybrids' are fast-blooming, 2- to 3-foot-tall plants that flower the first year from seed. They can be grown as an annual if seeds are sown indoors in late winter. Where happy, common foxglove self-sows generously.

Yellow foxglove (D. *grandiflora*, also listed as D. *ambigua* and D. *orientalis*) is a perennial species with loose racemes of pale yellow flowers on 2- to 3-foot plants. It is hardy in Zones 3 to 8. Strawberry foxglove (D. × *mertonensis*), another perennial, bears pink or white flowers on 3- to 4-foot plants. Hardy in Zones 3 through 8, this hybrid comes true from seeds. Rusty foxglove (D. *ferruginea*) is a 3- to 4-foot species, hardy in Zones 4 to 7, that can be grown as a biennial or a perennial. It produces racemes of golden brown flowers in summer.

IN THE GARDEN

Foxgloves are classic late-spring plants for cottage gardens and other informal plantings. Use them in beds and borders combined with bleeding hearts (*Dicentra* spp.), hardy geraniums or cranesbills (*Geranium* spp.), astilbes, catmints (*Nepeta* spp.), and bellflowers (*Campanula* spp.). They are especially effective at the edge of a woodland in dappled shade, where they can be planted with hostas, ferns, and wild blue phlox (*Phlox divaricata*).

Echinacea purpurea

(eck-in-AY-see-ah pur-PUR-ee-ah)

Purple coneflower

Aster family, Asteraceae. Hardy perennial.

These days, this native North American plant is almost as well known as a medicinal as it is a garden plant. First used by Native Americans to treat wounds and as a cure-all, purple coneflower is now a staple anywhere health food products are sold. For medicinal purposes, plants are grown for the roots, which are used to treat skin diseases, fungal infections, slow-healing wounds, and other complaints. Gardeners grow the plants for entirely different reasons—most notably for their easy-care nature and showy flowers. Plants produce an abundance of

Common foxglove, Digitalis purpurea *'Foxy Mixed'*

Purple coneflower, Echinacea purpurea

daisylike flowers with drooping, purple-pink petals surrounding orange to golden-brown centers.

The botanical name *Echinacea* celebrates the spiny, conelike centers of the flowers. It's from the Greek *echinos*, meaning "hedgehog." Over time the plant has collected a barnful of common names, including black-Sampson, black-Susan, comb-flower, droops, Indian-head, snakeroot, rattlesnake weed, and scurvy-root. While a few allude to the plant's flowers, most refer to its powers as a medicinal herb. In the 17th century, a Reverend Banister reputedly was the first to take this native flower to England, according to Roy Genders (*The Cottage Garden and the Old-Fashioned Flowers*, 1984), where it "came to be planted in every cottage garden . . . [and] took kindly to all soil types and flowered in autumn when colour in the garden was much needed."

Hardy in Zones 3 to 9, purple coneflower usually ranges from 2 to 4 feet, although plants can grow to 5 or 6 feet. They produce ovate, toothed leaves that are roughly hairy and red-tinged stems. Plants begin blooming in midsummer and continue until frost if deadheaded.

HOW TO GROW

To keep coneflowers happy, give them a spot in full sun with average, well-drained soil. They'll tolerate a range of soil types, but richly organic soil will cause lanky plants that flop over. Although prairie natives, they are sometimes found in open woodlands and will grow and bloom in dappled shade. Plants in even light shade tend to get lanky, however, so pinch them back in spring to encourage compact growth, or stake them.

Buy plants at your local garden center or grow from seed. Several popular cultivars come reasonably true from seeds, including 'Magnus', 'Leuchtstern', and 'White Swan'. Sow seeds indoors about eight weeks before the frost-free date. (If you've saved seeds, place them in the refrigerator for at least a

Purple coneflower, Echinacea purpurea 'White Swan'

Several other interesting coneflowers make good garden plants. Pale coneflower (*E. pallida*) bears pale pink, drooping flower heads on 3- to 4-foot plants and is hardy in Zones 4 to 8. Narrow-leaved coneflower (*E. paradoxa*) produces yellow-petaled daisies on 32-inch plants and is hardy in Zones 3 to 8. Tennessee coneflower (*E. tennesseensis*) is an endangered wildflower that was brought into cultivation and is now available as a nursery-propagated plant. This species reaches 3 feet and bears flowers with narrow mauve ray florets and greenish-pink centers.

month before sowing.) Or sow in late winter and set the pots outdoors in a protected spot. Purple coneflowers also self-sow, and seedlings are easy to move.

After planting, purple coneflowers need little in the way of care. They're drought tolerant but bloom best if watered deeply during dry weather and if topdressed with compost in spring. Deadheading prolongs bloom—and prevents excessive self-sowing—and cutting back plants after the main flush of flowers has finished will encourage new buds to form.

Plants can go for years without needing division, but if you want to propagate a particular plant—or if it outgrows its space in the garden—divide in spring (or autumn in warm regions). Purple coneflowers also can be propagated by stem cuttings and from root cuttings. Plants are attractive to Japanese beetles but overall have few problems with diseases or insects.

WHAT TO GROW

While the species is a perfect choice for wildflower meadows and other naturalized plantings, consider one or more of the improved cultivars for beds and borders. 'Magnus' produces large, purple-pink flowers on compact, 3- to 4-foot plants; 'Bright Star' bears 3-inch flowers on 18-inch plants. 'Kim's Knee High' is another dwarf selection that bears clear pink flowers on 1½- to 2-foot plants. 'Little Giant', to 16 inches, has fragrant, 5-inch-wide flowers; 'Ruby Giant' is a 3-foot-tall selection with 5- to 7-inch rosy pink blooms; and 'Doppelganger' bears double-decker flowers: A second bloom forms on top of the first. 'Prairie Frost' is a new cultivar, the first with variegated foliage.

There also are white-flowered cultivars, including 'White Swan', 2 to 3 feet tall, and 'White Lustre', 3 feet. White-flowered cultivars tend to be more sensitive to poor drainage than the purple-flowered plants and can be short-lived.

IN THE GARDEN

Purple coneflowers are must-have perennials for sunny beds and borders. In meadows and other naturalized plantings, combine them with other native wildflowers, such as asters, goldenrods (*Solidago* spp.), and butterfly weed (*Asclepias tuberosa*). They also are excellent companions for a range of other popular perennials, including daylilies, yarrows (*Achillea* spp.), catmints (*Nepeta* spp.), and Russian sage (*Perovskia atriplicifolia*). The flowers are excellent for cutting. For gardeners who enjoy wildlife, purple coneflowers are perfect additions to butterfly gardens, and the seed heads help feed overwintering birds.

Echinops

(ECH-in-ops REE-tro)

Globe thistles

Aster family, Asteraceae. Hardy perennials.

For this perennial, the common name says it all. Globe thistle is a prickly-looking plant with deeply cut, thistlelike leaves and spiny round flower heads. While the leaves of some species of *Echinops* can do serious damage, the leaves of *E. ritro* are spinier looking than they are, and far less spiny than most true thistles. The round, silvery to steely blue flower heads are produced above the foliage in mid- to late summer. The flowers range from 1 to 2 inches across and have bristly bracts beneath, and these warrant the use of gloves when handling plants.

Echinops shares the origins of its name with purple coneflower, *Echinacea*, as well as with several cacti. All their names are derived from the Greek word *echinos*, "hedgehog." To make the name *Echinops*, botanists added *ops*, "appearance," a reference to the spiny blooms. The 2- to 4-foot plants have deep taproots and are hardy in Zones 3 to 9.

and well-drained soil that is not overly rich, which will cause plants to be floppy. Poor drainage, especially in winter, leads to crown and root rot. Plants are drought tolerant and do not need staking or feeding, except perhaps for a spring topdressing of compost. They're best left undivided, as digging disturbs their deep taproots. Deadheading encourages new flowers to form. Once flowering ends and new basal growth appears, cut the stems to the ground to produce a second round of blooms.

If you start with container-grown plants, loosen the soil deeply to ensure good drainage. To grow plants from seed, surface sow, as light aids germination. Plants bloom the second year from seeds, but take up to three years to become established. Or propagate globe thistles by cutting off some of the small rosettes that grow up around the main clump. Pot them up and set them in a protected location until they are established. Globe thistles also can be propagated by root cuttings.

Plants have few pest or disease troubles.

WHAT TO GROW

E. ritro is the most commonly grown species, although some popular cultivars have recently been moved to *E. bannaticus*, a similar species. Look for 'Veitch's Blue', which is a 3-foot plant that reblooms and produces dark steel-blue flowers. The widely sold 'Taplow Blue' bears bright blue flower heads. Neither of these cultivars comes true from seeds. 'Arctic Glow' is a 32-inch-tall selection with silver-white flowers and coarse, silver-gray foliage.

Globe thistle, Echinops bannaticus *'Blue Glow'*

Perhaps it is because it resembles the weedy roadside thistles that are the bane of farmers that *E. ritro* seems to have a relatively short history as a garden plant. Once established in the garden, however, no one will mistake globe thistle for a weed.

HOW TO GROW

In the right site, globe thistles are as tough and undemanding as plants come. They need full sun

IN THE GARDEN

Combine globe thistles with other perennials that thrive in sun and well-drained, average soil, including yarrows (*Achillea* spp.), purple coneflower (*Echinacea purpurea*), orange coneflowers (*Rudbeckia* spp.), rose campion (*Lychnis coronaria*), daylilies, Russian sage (*Perovskia atriplicifolia*), and herbs such as lavender. The flower heads are excellent for cutting and also dry well. They're attractive to birds in winter, too.

Epimedium

(eh-pih-MEE-dee-um)

Epimediums, barrenworts, bishop's caps

Barberry Family, Berberidaceae.
Hardy perennials.

Epimediums are tough-as-nails perennials that flower in early spring and have handsome foliage that lasts to autumn and beyond. Plants prefer light shade and thrive with no more than an annual haircut. What more could a gardener demand? Magazines and catalogs that feature epimediums are likely to focus only on the delicate sprays of small spring flowers, but experienced gardeners also prize these hardworking garden plants because of their handsome foliage. Established clumps look good through fall, long after their flowers fade.

Flowers appear before the leaves, at about the time daffodils are at their peak. Blooms are ½- to 1-inch-wide and borne on wiry stems in loose, airy racemes or panicles. The flowers are cup or saucer shaped, often have spurs, and come in shades of yellow, white, red, pink, and purple, as well as bicolors. The divided, heart-shaped to somewhat-triangular leaves appear while or immediately after the plants are blooming, and often are bronze-tinted when they emerge. Many species are semi-evergreen or evergreen in warmer regions, and several have good autumn color. Plants range from 6 to 16 inches tall and spread by rhizomes. Most are hardy in Zones 5 to 8, but many will survive into Zone 4 with winter protection.

Epimediums have become increasingly popular as garden flowers in the last 25 years. With the opening of China to the West, the number of species has doubled and botanists expect that there still are more to be discovered.

HOW TO GROW

Plant epimediums in partial shade; for the most luxuriant foliage, give them rich, evenly moist soil. They also will grow in full shade, even dry shade, and in full sun in regions with cool summers. If planted in full sun, even moisture is critical.

Purchase container-grown plants or beg divisions from a gardener who has established plants. Plant in spring after the last frost or in early fall, digging a shovelful of compost into the soil at planting time. Spacing depends on the species, since some spread more quickly than others. *E. alpinum, E. × rubrum, E. × warleyense,* and especially *E. × versicolor* all spread with ease, although they are not invasive, so space plants at about twice their height. Keep the soil evenly moist until plants are established, and mulch with compost or chopped leaves. Established epimediums need little care. Cut back old foliage in late winter, before the flowers begin to emerge.

The easiest way to propagate epimediums is by division in early spring or late summer. You can also root individual sections of rhizome. Only determined gardeners will want to try epimediums from seeds. If you do, be sure to use absolutely fresh seeds and sow in fall in pots to be left outdoors in a protected location, as seeds need cold to germinate.

Plants are subject to no serious pest or disease problems.

WHAT TO GROW

If you want epimediums that will cover the ground or make large drifts in the garden, choose spreaders such as *E. ×*

Yellow epimedium, Epimedium × perralchicum *'Fröhnleiten'*

perralderianum, an especially vigorous 10- to 12-inch species that spreads to 2 feet and bears yellow flowers on evergreen to semi-evergreen plants. *E.* × *perralchicum*, also evergreen to semi-evergreen, is another good spreader, 12- to 16 inches tall, with bright yellow flowers. Its cultivar 'Fröhnleiten' produces 1-inch-wide blooms. Warley epimedium (*E.* × *warleyense*), which will spread to about 3 feet, has showy, brick- to orange-red flowers on 8- to 12-inch plants.

Bicolor epimedium (*E.* × *versicolor*), 10 to 12 inches tall, bears red-and-yellow flowers on plants that spread to about 18 inches. Cultivars 'Neosulfureum', with pale yellow flowers, and the darker yellow 'Sulfureum' are available. All are evergreen to semi-evergreen. Alpine epimedium (*E. alpinum*), hardy in Zones 3 to 8, bears red flowers on 6- to 9-inch plants; clumps spread to about 1 foot. Longspurred epimedium (*E. grandiflorum*), also spreading to about 1 foot, bears 1- to 1½-inch flowers. Cultivars include 'Lilafee' (violet-purple), 'Rose Queen', 'Orange Queen', and 'White Queen'.

IN THE GARDEN

Grow epimediums in shady beds and borders, along woodland edges or shady paths, and as ground covers. They are most effective when allowed to form broad drifts. Combine them with spring bulbs like daffodils, tulips, grape hyacinths (*Muscari* spp.), snowdrops (*Galanthus* spp.), and Spanish bluebell (*Hyacinthoides hispanica*). They make fine companions for hostas, ferns, hellebores (*Helleborus* spp.), lungworts (*Pulmonaria* spp.), and other shade-loving plants.

Eryngium

(eh-RIN-gee-um)

Sea hollies

Carrot Family, Apiaceae.
Hardy perennials, biennials.

○

Many different species of sea holly—there are several hundred—have been used medicinally, most notably in eastern Europe, England, and in North America. Perhaps the most interesting use was in England

Miss Wilmott's ghost, Eryngium giganteum

during the 17th and 18th centuries, when the roots of *Eryngium maritimum* were harvested and made into sweet lozenges, which were considered a restorative and an aphrodisiac. *E. maritimum* roots also have been used medicinally to treat urinary-tract complaints and are sometimes made into a conserve or used as a flavoring for jelly and toffee. Herbalist John Gerard recommended the roots candied with sugar for "nourishing and restoring the aged."

Native Americans used both button snakeroot (*E. aquaticum*) and rattlesnake master (*E. yuccifolium*) medicinally, as well as *E. foetidum*, a species that is not often grown in gardens and is commonly called thorny or perennial coriander. Its flavor is similar to but stronger than coriander (*Coriandrum sativum*), and it is used in Latin American and Southeast Asian cuisines. While most sea hollies are native to dry, sandy, or rocky soils, primarily in the

Mediterranean, there also are sea hollies native to North America.

As their common name suggests, sea hollies are spiny-leaved plants with leathery, oval-, heart-, or sword-shaped leaves that often are deeply divided. Their tiny flowers are carried in dense, rounded, thistlelike cones. The individual flowers are small—from ½ to 1¼ inches—but they are borne in branched clusters, and each has a ruff of showy, stiff, spiny bracts at its base.

The 2- to 3-foot plants have an otherworldly look to them, with leaves in shades of steely blue-gray, gray-green, or silver-green. Flowers are spectral looking as well and bloom in metallic shades of purple-blue, blue-gray, or whitish green.

HOW TO GROW

Give sea hollies a spot in full sun with average, well-drained soil. They tolerate heat, drought, and poor soil—most tolerate high salt levels as well—but some species, those with fibrous roots, including *E. agavifolium*, *E. eburneum*, and *E. yuccifolium*, thrive in rich, evenly moist, well-drained soil. All require good soil drainage, especially in winter.

Buy container-grown plants to begin, and select a permanent location for sea hollies species with taproots, because established plants resent being disturbed. Once in the ground, sea hollies ask for little. Deadheading doesn't prolong flowering, but it does curtail self-sowing; feed plants in spring to encourage vigorous growth. Flower stems can be cut to the ground in late summer, but take care not to disturb the basal growth.

If you have sea hollies in your garden, the easiest way to propagate them is by moving the self-sown seedlings around. They also can be propagated from seeds and root cuttings and by severing and digging the small plantlets that arise at the base of the clump.

Plants are largely free of pests and diseases but may be troubled by slugs and snails when conditions are damp.

WHAT TO GROW

Alpine sea holly (*E. alpinum*), hardy in Zones 5 to 8 and growing to about 2 feet, produces a rosette of spiny, heart-shaped leaves and branched stalks of metallic blue-gray flowers from midsummer to fall. Amethyst sea holly (*E. amethystinum*), 2 feet and hardy in Zones 3 to 8, grows from a taproot and

forms rosettes of rounded, spiny leaves with metallic blue and silver-gray blooms, mid- to late summer. Flat sea holly (*E. planum*) is an evergreen, 3-foot-tall species hardy in Zones 5 to 9. Plants grow from taproots and bear rounded leaves that are toothed and lobed; they produce steely blue flowers with blue-green bracts from midsummer to fall. Rattlesnake master (*E. yuccifolium*) is a North American species hardy in Zones 4 to 8 that grows from a taproot. Plants have rosettes of semi-evergreen, spiny-margined, sword-shaped leaves that are blue-gray. From midsummer to fall, they bear branched, 4-foot-tall stalks of round, greenish white and gray-green flowers.

Miss Wilmott's ghost (*E. giganteum*) is a fibrous-rooted biennial or short-lived perennial that produces a rosette of heart-shaped green leaves topped by branched stems of spiny leaves and rounded, 2½-inch steely blue flowers that have ruffs of showy, prickly, silver bracts.

IN THE GARDEN

Sea hollies are outstanding plants for perennial beds and borders and are especially useful when combined with other species that like well-drained to dry soil, such as yarrows (*Achillea* spp.), lavenders, catmints (*Nepeta* spp.), and flax (*Linum* spp.). Rattlesnake master can be used in meadow and sunny wildflower plantings, as well as prairie plantings. All make superb—if spiny—cut flowers, and they are perennial favorites in dried arrangements.

Eschscholzia californica

(eh-SCHOLT-zee-ah cal-ih-FOR-nih-kah)

California poppy

Poppy family, Papaveraceae. Tender perennial grown as an annual.

Treasured for its showy, brilliantly colored flowers, California poppy is a popular native of western North America. Plants have finely divided fernlike leaves and produce cup-shaped, poppylike flowers with silky-textured petals. Typically, the flowers are yellow-orange to orange and measure about 3 inches across; plants grow about 12 inches tall.

California poppy, Eschscholzia californica

for calming the nerves and relaxing the spirit. Makes an intriguing smoke." Adding that Dr. James Duke, former USDA eth-nobotanist, has confirmed that California poppy is sometimes smoked "as a safe and pleasant *Cannabis* substitute," the web site nevertheless concludes, "we prefer it as an evening tea mixed with mint and honey."

HOW TO GROW

All California poppies need to grow is a site in full sun and light or sandy, poor to average well-drained soil. Soil that is too rich yields plants with lush foliage and few flowers.

Add these easy to grow, cool-weather flowers to your garden by sowing seeds outdoors where the plants are to grow after the last spring frost date (or in fall in mild-winter areas, from Zone 6 south). Indoor sowing is an option in regions with short seasons, but like many poppy-family plants, these flowers resent transplant-ing and roots are easy to damage. If you sow indoors, do so two to three weeks before the last-frost date and use in indi-vidual pots to minimize transplant shock. California poppies are sometimes offered in spring at garden centers in nursery packs, but direct-sown seedlings usually are more successful and vigorous than transplanted ones.

Once planted, California poppies need little care and have few disease or pest problems. Deadheading increases flower production, but leave some flowers so that plants can self-sow. Technically peren-nials, most gardeners outside California treat this flower as if it were an annual.

WHAT TO GROW

While many gardeners happily grow the orange- and yellow-flowered species, many good cul-tivars are available. Thai Silk Series produces wavy-edged single or double flowers in shades of orange, red, and pink on compact plants, 8 to 10 inches. Also look for 'Apricot Flambeau', creamy yellow flowers with fluted edges tinged with coral orange; 'Champagne & Roses', rose flowers with fluted pet-als; and 'Mission Bells Mix', semidouble flowers in

The botanical name *Eschscholzia* commemorates Dr. Johann Friedrich Eschscholz (1793–1831), a German naturalist and physician who participated in explorations of North America's Pacific Coast. The official state flower of California, California poppies are touted for more than their lovely flowers. One "botanicals" web site offers "organic-biodynamically grown" flower petals as "a gentle sedative, excellent

shades of cream, orange, pink, and red. The Sunset Series has single flowers, in various colors.

IN THE GARDEN

Plant California poppies in sunny beds and borders, where they can be left to mingle with other low-growing annuals. They also can be sown in sunny wildflower meadows, provided the soil is poor and well drained, and they are a good choice for seaside plantings, hillsides, and where they naturally thrive, vacant lots and parking strips. They are good in containers and rock gardens. Although short-lived, they make pretty cut flowers.

Eupatorium

(you-pah-TORE-ee-um)

Joe-Pye weeds, hardy ageratums, eupatoriums

Aster Family, Asteraceae. Hardy perennials.

Hardy ageratum, Eupatorium coelestinum

Joe-Pye weed is a recent "discovery" of sophisticated perennial gardeners and plant breeders, but people who love butterflies have been growing it for years. And no one, flower or wildlife lover, should be without at least one of these sturdy perennials. While there are eupatoriums native to other continents, the species most grown in gardens are native wildflowers that thrive from Canada to Florida. They are valued for their showy clusters of small, fuzzy flowers, which are rich in nectar and attract bees and a host of beneficial insects and butterflies from summer into fall.

The genus name honors Mithridates Eupator (120–63 B.C.) of the ancient kingdom of Pontus. A fractious leader, he fought against the Romans and is credited with discovering that one species of eupatorium is an antidote for poison. Several species have medicinal uses. The rhizomes and roots of Joe-Pye weed (*E. purpureum*) are used to treat urinary tract disorders, whereas boneset (*E. perfoliatum*) is used to make an infusion to treat fevers, congestion, constipation, and to stimulate the immune system. Tradition has it that if you put a Joe-Pye weed leaf in your mouth while making advances to the opposite sex you will be successful. Ignore tradition,

however, and take heed of an American Herbal Products Association warning that the plant should be labeled "For external use only."

Despite belonging to the aster family, Asteraceae, eupatoriums don't bear the typical daisy-shaped flowers characteristic of many asters. Individual blooms are small and buttonlike—the flower heads have all disk florets, no showy ray florets, or petals. They are carried in large, branched, rounded or flat-topped clusters and come in white, mauve, pink,

rosy purple, and blue. Leaves are usually opposite or whirled.

HOW TO GROW

Give eupatoriums full sun or partial shade, moist soil, and stand back They grow better in organically rich ground that is well drained but can tolerate wet conditions. In fact moist soil yields the largest plants—eupatoriums are one of the summer- to fall-blooming wildflowers that happily inhabit roadside ditches. Acid to neutral pH is best, but *E. purpureum* and *E. rugosum* also grow well in alkaline soils. Joe-Pye is an undemanding fellow. As to his identity, the record is murky. The most common version is that Joe Pye was a Native American who used eupatorium to help New England colonists suffering from typhus.

Plant eupatoriums in spring or fall by purchasing plants; most improved cultivars do not come true from seeds. Once in the ground, plants don't require regular care. They are slow to become established and take a couple of seasons to put roots down and really begin to grow. Mulch to retain moisture, and cut stalks to the ground at the end of the garden season. If you want to restrict height of taller selections, cut them back once or twice in early summer to encourage branching and bushier growth. Hardy ageratum (*E. coelestinum*) does best if cut back, which reduces flopping and encourages more flowering. Most species do not require regular dividing and can be left undisturbed for years.

Propagate eupatoriums by division in spring, by slicing off small plants that arise around the outside edge of the clumps, or by taking stem cuttings in early summer. Most species self-sow or can be grown from seeds. Sow seeds in pots in fall, as soon as the seeds are available; set pots outside in a protected location to overwinter.

Eupatoriums are occasionally troubled by crown rot and mildews.

WHAT TO GROW

Hollow Joe-Pye weed (*E. fistulosum*) is one of the giant species designed for adding drama to late summer plantings. This native can grow to 10 feet tall, is hardy in Zones 3 to 8, and features wine-purple stems topped by rounded, 6- to 10-inch-wide clusters of mauve-pink flower in midsummer. Spotted Joe-Pye weed (*E. maculatum*), another native giant at 4 to 7 feet, is hardy in Zones 3 to 7 and bears purple-spotted stems and flat-topped, 4- to 6-inch-wide clusters of pale to dark purple flowers from midsummer to fall. 'Gateway' produces pink flowers on 5-foot, black-stemmed plants; 'Bartered Bride' has white flowers; 'Atropurpureum' bears dark purple stems and flowers in late summer.

Joe-pye weed (*E. purpureum*), another native hardy in Zones 3 to 8, ranges from 3 to 7 feet tall. It produces rounded 4- to 6-inch-wide clusters of pale rose-pink or purplish flowers from midsummer to fall. Finally, hardy ageratum, or mistflower (*E. coelestinum*) is a native wildflower that reaches 2 to 3 feet tall and is hardy in Zones 5 to 9. It produces fluffy, flat-topped, 2- to 4-inch-wide clusters of lilac-blue flowers from late summer to fall. Plants tend to spread.

IN THE GARDEN

Eupatoriums are a must for butterfly gardens, and if the stalks are left standing over the winter, the seed heads will provide a feast for birds. Plant larger species in beds, borders, and sunny wildflower gardens. Combine them with ornamental grasses, purple coneflower (*Echinacea purpurea*), orange coneflowers

---

OTHER CHOICES

Vernonia is another native genus in the aster family that blooms from late summer to fall. Commonly called ironweeds, *Vernonia* species are prized for their rich, deep, reddish-purple blooms, which are fluffy and rounded. *V. noveboracensis*, hardy in Zones 5 to 9 and ranging from 3 to 7 feet tall, is most often cultivated. Grow ironweeds as you would Joe-Pye weeds.

(*Rudbeckia* spp.), ox-eyes (*Heliopsis* spp.), asters, and common rose mallow (*Hibiscus moscheutos*). Use hardy ageratum (*E. coelestinum*) and white snakeroot (*E. rugosum*) in smaller plantings of wildflowers and informal gardens.

Euphorbia

(*you-FOR-bee-ah*)

Euphorbias, spurges

Spurge family, Euphorbiaceae.
Hardy perennials, biennials, annuals.

Cushion spurge, Euphorbia polychroma

The spurge family is a big clan that includes everything from poinsettias (*Euphorbia pulcherrima*) and tender cactuslike succulents to popular hardy perennials and annuals. There are about 2,000 species of euphorbias in all, and every one exudes a milky latex when its stems or leaves are cut or damaged, even the 70-foot tree species. The genus name honors a first-century physician to the king of Mauretania, Euphorbus, who used the plant for medicinal purposes. Despite its reputed healing powers, euphorbia sap can cause skin and eye irritation—"so acid," herbalist Mrs. M. Grieve wrote in 1931, "that it burns the fingers"—and the internal use of euphorbias has been largely abandoned.

Although the history of this genus is most often found in herbals and medical tracts, euphorbias are not without poetic connections—most famously in poet Dante Gabriel Rossetti's often-quoted line, "The woodspurge hath a cup of three" ("The Woodspurge," 1856).

What poinsettias have in common with popular annuals like snow-on-the-mountain (*E. marginata*) and some of the perennial spurges are their insignificant flowers, which are surrounded by petal-like bracts that are *not* insignificant and are commonly thought to be the flowers. Whatever you call them—available in shades of yellow, red, green, purple, pink, brown, or white—they are lovely.

HOW TO GROW

Most garden euphorbias prefer full sun and require loose, well-drained, poor to average soil. Once established, they are extremely drought tolerant and need little care to look their best. Removing the flowering shoots at the base of the plant after they have bloomed isn't necessary but does control self-sowing, especially on annual species. Divide perennial species in spring as needed to control their spread or if the clumps die out in the center.

Propagate perennial spurges by dividing the clumps in spring, or fall in the South. Or propagate from stem cuttings taken from shoots that arise at the base of the plant in spring or early summer or from plant stems after flowering. Annual and biennial species grow easily from fresh seeds; seeds saved from perennial species should be refrigerated for eight weeks, then soaked in water for several hours before they're sown. Sow indoors six to eight weeks before the last frost, outdoors after the frost-free date.

Plants may attract mealybugs, aphids, and mites and are occasionally bothered by fungal and viral diseases.

WHAT TO GROW

Perennial euphorbias are primarily grown for their spring to summer flowers, but some also feature handsome foliage. Perhaps the most popular is cushion spurge (*E. polychroma*), a mounding, 1- to 2-foot perennial with yellow-green flowers in spring. Plants grow in full sun or partial shade and are hardy in Zones 4 to 9. A spot with afternoon shade is best in Southern gardens.

Other perennial spurges include Griffith's spurge (*E. griffithii*), which is grown for its orange-red flower clusters, borne over deep green leaves that turn red in fall. Myrtle euphorbia (*E. myrsinites*), Zones 5 to 9, bears yellow flowers in spring over blue-gray, evergreen leaves. Plants are 6 to 10 inches tall and have trailing, prostrate stems. Wood spurge (*E. amygdaloides* var. *robbiae*) is an excellent choice for a spot in evenly moist, rich soil in partial to full shade. Hardy in Zones 6 to 9, this species has greenish yellow flowers from midspring to early summer, but it is mostly appreciated for its shiny, handsome evergreen leaves. The 1½- to 2-foot plants can spread vigorously and may become invasive in some gardens.

E. dulcis bears greenish yellow, early summer flowers on foot-tall plants that have handsome dark green or bronze leaves. Hardy in Zones 4 to 9, it prefers evenly moist, rich soil and light shade but also will grow in dry shade. 'Chameleon' has purple-maroon foliage. Both self-sow.

There are two easy to grow, warm-weather annual euphorbias that thrive in full sun and well-drained soil. Snow-on-the-mountain (*E. marginata*), with white-edged bracts, or flowers on 2- to 4-foot plants is best known. Annual poinsettia

Snow-on-the-mountain, Euphorbia marginata '*Snowtop*'

(*E. cyathophora*) has small red bracts. Both can be grown from seed.

IN THE GARDEN

Use euphorbias to add color and unusual form to beds and borders. Sun-lovers can be planted with daylilies, columbines (*Aquilegia* spp.), lamb's ear (*Stachys byzantina*), catmints (*Nepeta* spp.), hardy geraniums or cranesbills (*Geranium* spp.), and evening primroses (*Oenothera* spp.). Shade-lovers are ideal with hostas, coral bells or heucheras (*Heuchera* spp.), lungworts (*Pulmonaria* spp.), hellebores, and ferns. *E. polychroma* and *E. myrsinites* are fine additions to rock gardens. Most euphorbias also make handsome cut flowers.

Filipendula

(fill-ih-PEN-due-lah)

Queens-of-the-prairie

Rose family, Rosaceae. Hardy perennials.

These sturdy perennials are found throughout the north temperate region—in Europe, Russia, China, Japan, and North America. *Filipendula ulmaria*, commonly called meadowsweet, sweet-hay, and queen-of-the-meadow, was considered to be one of the most sacred herbs of the Druids. The blooms and leaves do smell sweet, "so pleasing a sweet scent," John Parkinson wrote in 1629, that "Queen Elizabeth, of famous memory, did more desire it than any sweet herb to strew her chambers withall."

Used as a strewing herb during medieval times, filipendula also has a history as a medicinal plant with aromatic, astringent, and antacid properties. The oil distilled from the flower buds, which is sometimes used in potpourri, smells like wintergreen. Dried plants are used in tablets, infusions, and other preparations to treat various gastric ailments such as heartburn and gastritis and joint pain. In 1838, salicylic acid, later synthesized as aspirin, was first isolated from this species.

Blooms are borne above mounds of large, handsome, featherlike leaves. While the individual flowers are tiny, they are carried in large plumy clusters

Queen of the meadow, Filipendula ulmaria

that resemble the blooms of astilbes, goat's beards (*Aruncus* spp.), and spiraeas (*Spiraea* spp.). The individual flowers have five petals and come shades of pink as well as white.

HOW TO GROW

Plant filipendulas in full sun or light shade. They prefer rich, moist, well-drained soil that contains good amounts of organic matter. Both *F. rubra* and *F. ulmaria* will grow in boggy soil, but *F. vulgaris* prefers a site with full sun and dry, alkaline soil. Once in the ground, filipendulas require little care. Mulch to keep soil moist and protect the roots. If plants become tattered looking after flowering ends, cut them to the ground and keep the soil moist until new shoots emerge. Clumps that become too crowded and lose vigor or outgrow their space should be divided in early spring, fall in warm regions.

Propagate by division in early spring (fall in hot regions), by root cuttings taken in late winter or early spring, or by sowing seeds in pots and setting them outside either in fall or in late winter. Plants grown from seed normally take two years to bloom.

Filipendulas are rarely bothered by diseases or pests, although mildews can develop in shaded locations.

WHAT TO GROW

Gardeners interested in native wildflowers will want to try queen-of-the-prairie (*F. rubra*) a native of moist soils from New York to Minnesota and south to Kentucky and North Carolina. Plants range from 6 to 8 feet tall, spread to 4 feet or more, and are topped in midsummer by fluffy, 5- to 6-inch clusters of fragrant pink flowers. 'Venusta', which also is sold as 'Venusta Magnifica' and 'Magnifica', bears rose-pink flowers; 'Albicans' has white blooms. All are hardy in Zones 3 to 9.

Meadowsweet, or queen-of-the-meadow (*F. ulmaria*), hardy in Zones 3 to 9, grows from 3 to 6 feet tall and produces 5-inch clusters of white flowers in early summer. 'Variegata' has variegated foliage. Siberian Meadowsweet (*F. palmata*), hardy in Zones 3 to 8, is a 3- to 4-foot-tall species with 8-inch plumes of pink flowers in midsummer. 'Rubra' has reddish pink blooms. Japanese Meadowsweet (*F. purpurea*), hardy in Zones 4 to 9, produces mounds of 10-inch-wide leaves, reaches 3 to 4 feet, and bears 2-inch clusters of bright pink flowers in mid- and late summer.

OTHER CHOICES

Turtleheads (*Chelone* spp.) are native North American wildflowers enjoying similar conditions to filipendulas. Give them full sun or partial shade and moist, rich soil. They'll also grow in bog gardens, where the soil stays wet, as well as in heavy clay. Plants bear showy clusters of unusual, tubular, two-lipped flowers in shades of pink, purple, and white, and they spread to form 2-foot clumps and range from 2 to 4 feet, depending on the species. Hardiness varies slightly: *C. glabra*, also called snakeshead, is hardy in Zones 4 to 9; *C. lyonii*, Zones 3 to 8; and *C. obliqua*, Zones 5 to 9.

Dropwort (*F. vulgaris*) is the munchkin of the genus at a compact 2 feet. Hardy in Zones 4 to 9, plants produce a mound of ferny leaves and loose, 4- to 6-inch clusters of creamy white flowers in early and midsummer. 'Kohome' has light rose flowers.

IN THE GARDEN

Use filipendulas in informal beds, borders, and other plantings where they can be combined with irises, daylilies, turtleheads (*Chelone* spp.), larger bellflowers (*Campanula* spp.), common rose mallow (*Hibiscus moscheutos*), and bee balms (*Monarda* spp.). Compact *F. vulgaris* can be used as an edging along walkways.

Fritillaria

(fri-tih-LAIR-ee-ah)

Fritillaries

Lily family, Liliaceae. Hardy bulbs.

About a hundred species belong to this genus of charming bulbs. The name *Fritillaria* is from the Latin, *fritillus*, for "checkerboard" or "dicebox," and is a reference to the checkered color patterns—botanists call them *tessellate*—on the blooms of many species. The common name guinea hen also stems from the spotted markings. Species range from commanding, stately bulbs for beds and borders to tiny rock garden plants.

Most fritillaries have pendant flowers that are bell-shaped, tubular, or saucer-shaped and are solitary or borne in clusters in spring or early summer. Each flower has six tepals; three are true petals and three petal-like sepals. Plant leaves are lance-shaped to grassy. Fritillary bulbs are constructed in one of two ways. They either consist of fleshy scales that fit closely together and are sometimes covered with a papery tunic, or they are made up of separate, overlapping scales like a lily bulb's.

The genus has a long history in the garden, but no species more so than crown imperial (*F. imperialis*), which was cultivated in the Middle East for centuries before it was brought to Europe and England. One Christian legend has it that the flower, once white, was the only plant not to bow

Crown imperial, Fritillaria imperialis

at first and try them in a site that seems suitable. Once you've experimented and found a site where they will thrive, add more bulbs.

A few fritillary bulbs will be available in the fall at local garden centers; but for more unusual species, you'll have to buy from mail-order bulb specialists. Keep in mind that all fritillary bulbs are very fragile and should never be allowed to dry out before planting. Examine bulbs carefully for signs of shriveling or other damage, because dried-out bulbs will not grow. If you can't plant right away, store the bulbs in barely moist vermiculite or peat moss.

Before planting fritillary bulbs, dig the soil deeply and incorporate organic matter several inches *below* where the bulbs will sit. Plant at a depth of four times the bulb's height, about 5 inches deep for most species. Experts recommend placing 2 or 3 inches of builders' sand under *Fritillaria* species, such as crown imperial, that have open-crowned, scaly bulbs; the sand helps improve drainage and prevents moisture from being caught in the top of the bulb. Also, set the bulbs *on their sides* when planting to prevent moisture from pooling on the bulb and rotting it.

down as Jesus prayed in the Garden of Gethsemane, and ever since the flower has been red and hung its head in shame. The name *crown imperial* apparently comes from the fact that one of the first European gardens to grow it was the Imperial Gardens in Vienna. Or perhaps it is simply because the crown imperial looks regal enough to be monarch's crown.

HOW TO GROW

Fritillaries range from bulbs that are quite easy to grow to plants that can be fussy and difficult. Most want a spot in full sun or light shade that has rich, moist, but well-drained soil. If you're not sure you have the right spot to grow fritillaries, buy a few bulbs

Most fritillaries benefit from compost mulch and a spring feeding of well-rotted manure or organic fertilizer. Species that prefer dry conditions when dormant—including *F. michailovskyi* and *F. persica*—don't require mulching. Fritillaries can be left in place for years without needing to be divided. Dig them only if they become too crowded and begin to bloom less. If you must divide, dig plants in early summer after the foliage has ripened but before it disappears completely. Propagate plants by division, from bulblets, or—a last choice because germination is erratic—sow seeds in pots in fall and set them in a protected location outdoors over winter.

Like most hardy bulbs, fritillaries have few pest or disease problems.

WHAT TO GROW

By far the best known of the fritillaries is crown imperial (*F. imperialis*), an old-fashioned plant hardy in Zones 4 to 8 that originally came from Asia. Plants grow to 2 or 4 feet and produce showy umbels of up to eight flowers that are 2½ inches long. The cluster of pendant flowers is topped by a sheaf of upright, leaflike bracts, and all parts of the plant have a musky odor. While the species bears orange flowers, 'Lutea Maxima' has yellow flowers; 'Aurora' bears burnt orange blooms; 'Rubra Maxima' produces bright orange flowers; and 'Prolifera' bears double orange-red blooms.

Commonly called checkered lily, guinea-hen flower, or snake's-head fritillary, *F. meleagris* bears flowers in the checkered pattern characteristic of many members of this genus. Hardy in Zones 3 to 8, plants are about 12 inches tall and bear nodding, bell-shaped flowers in spring that are 1¾ inches long, carried singly or in pairs, and checked with purple and white; 'Alba' bears white flowers. Checkered lilies, which rot easily in wet winters, are good choices for rock gardens.

Another intriguing fritillary that is easy to grow is *F. pallidiflora*, a ½- to 2-foot species with clusters of creamy yellow flowers blushed with green in late spring and early summer. Best in partial shade, it is hardy in Zones 3 to 8. Hardy in Zones 5 or 6 to 8, *F. pontica* is a spring-blooming, 6- to 8-inch species with green, 1¾-inch flowers mottled with brown or maroon.

F. michailovskyi, hardy in Zones 5 to 8, is a rock-garden species that needs rich but very well-drained soil and dry conditions when dormant. Plants are 4 to 8 inches tall and bear purple-brown, bell-shaped flowers edged in yellow in late spring or

Checkered lily, Fritillaria meleagris

early summer. The flowers are solitary or carried in clusters of up to four. *F. persica* is a 1- to 3-foot species that produces racemes of 20 to 30 or more mauve-purple ¾-inch flowers. It is best grown in a hot, sun-baked site and is hardy in Zones 5 to 8. This species is endangered so be sure you purchase nursery-propagated plants.

IN THE GARDEN

Plant fritillaries in beds and borders along with other spring bulbs. Larger species are effective planted among larger perennials that will fill in after they have finished blooming. Smaller species are perfect for planting under ground covers or in rock gardens or raised beds.

Fuchsia

(FEW-shah)

Fuchsias

Evening primrose family, Onagraceae.
Tender perennials.

The first European to discover a fuchsia was Fr. Charles Plumier, a missionary to Santo Domingo. While discovered in 1703 and named by Fr. Plumier after Leonhart Fuch (1501–1566), a German physician and botanist, fuchsias took another 75 years to reach England, where they quickly gained popularity for their showy, pendant flowers. Since the genus name honors a German, it probably should be pronounced FOOKS-ee-ah. FEW-shah prevails, however, for this lovely flower, which is most often grown in greenhouses and containers and as an annual bedding plant—and where hardy, as a perennial.

Fuchsias are primarily tender shrubs and small trees, most usually grown as container plants. Although about 100 species exist—all come from Central and South America, New Zealand, and Tahiti—hybrid cultivars are far and away the most popular as garden plants. Most have been produced in the United States in the last 50 years, and there now are literally thousands available. Don't let this bounty keep you from taking a close look at a fuchsia blossom. The poet Robert Browing did, as he wrote to a friend: "Do look at a fuchsia in full bloom and notice the clear little honey-drop depending from every flower. I have just found it out to my no small satisfaction—a bee's breakfast."

All cultivars bear entire leaves and showy, usually pendulous, flowers commonly—and appropriately—known as lady's eardrops. The tubular blooms have four colorful, wide-spreading sepals at the end of the tube along with four petals. Blooms may be single, semidouble, or double. Petals and sepals are often different colors, and flowers are carried either singly or in clusters. Fuchsias come in many shades and combinations of pink, purple, red, and cream. Size varies, too, and individual flowers can range from ½ inch to as much as 2½ inches.

HOW TO GROW

Fuchsias require a spot that receives partial shade, or morning sun and afternoon shade, along with soil that is rich, evenly moist, yet well drained. They can be a challenge to grow in areas with hot summers, where they require shade and regular, even daily, watering. Single-flowered cultivars tend to be the most heat tolerant. Container-grown plants—fuchsias are standard residents of hanging pots—are especially susceptible to drying out.

Add fuchsias to your garden by purchasing plants—they're commonly sold in good-size containers for holidays like Mother's Day, but smaller plants intended for use in beds and borders also are available. Once plants are in the ground, be sure to water deeply and regularly, as the soil must stay

Fuchsia, Fuchsia × hybrida *'Lord Beaconsfield'*

evenly moist. Drying out causes buds to drop from the plants. However, it is equally important not to drown them. Feed pot-grown plants weekly during the summer with a balanced fertilizer.

Fuchsias are most often propagated by cuttings, and this is the only way to propagate cultivars, which will not come true from seeds. Take stem cuttings in spring or late summer. To overwinter fuchsias, pot up entire plants or move containers to a bright, cool (40°F to 45°F) spot before the first fall frost. Cut plants back to 2 or 3 inches in late winter to promote new growth.

Watch for whiteflies, aphids, scale, and mites; plants are susceptible to blight and wilt diseases.

WHAT TO GROW

Fuchsia hybrids (*F.* × *hybrida*) come in a staggering array of colors and flower forms, and it's best to choose on the basis of what appeals to you. All are tender shrubs, hardy only in frost-free areas, and range from 1 to 2 feet tall. If you are just getting started growing fuchsias, pick a popular, readily available cultivar—'Swingtime', with pink-and-white-flowers is one example—and see how easy they are for you to grow. There are upright, shrubby cultivars that are most appropriate for beds and borders or large pots, as well as the better-known trailers, which are ideal for hanging baskets.

IN THE GARDEN

Fuchsias can be grown as shrubs in frost-free areas, from Zone 9 south; however, they rarely grow well in the frost-free parts of the Southeast because of high temperatures in summer. Use them as bedding plants or plant them in containers. The flowers attract hummingbirds.

Gaillardia

(*gah-LAIR-dee-ah*)

Gaillardias, blanket flowers

Aster family, Asteraceae.
Hardy perennials, annuals.

All members of the genus *Gaillardia*—30 species in all—are native to North, Central, or South

Blanket flower, Gaillardia × grandiflora

America. The species commonly grown in gardens today are either native wildflowers or hybrids: *G. aristata* is native to the Canadian and American West, and *G. pulchella* is native to the southern United States, Mexico, and Central America. *G.* × *grandiflora*, the most popular of all, is a cross between these two species.

Despite several origins, the genus name commemorates an 18th-century French patron of botany Gaillard de Charentonneau. The common names blanket flower and Indian blanket allude to the colors of the flowers, which are often similar to the colors found in the blankets made by Native Americans. As several have observed, gaillardias mix blood with their gold. Novelist Willa Cather described the profusion of gaillardias on her Nebraska prairie, where they "matted over the ground with the deep velvety red that is in Bokhara carpets."

Gaillardias have showy, daisylike flower heads that feature dense, colorful, buttonlike centers surrounded by showy petal-like ray florets. The centers, which produce the seeds, are red-orange, red-brown, purple-red, red, or yellow. Ray florets come in shades of yellow, orange, red, and maroon and are often bicolored—for example, predominately red with yellow tips. Plants produce a mound of leaves topped by flowers on long stems. Plants bloom over a long season.

HOW TO GROW

All gaillardias demand is a spot in full sun. They will thrive in poor, dry soil as well as sandy soil and are extremely drought tolerant. They also tolerate salt and are an excellent choice for seaside gardens. What they don't tolerate is heavy clay soil that is not well drained, which leads to root and crown rot. Soil that is highly fertile produces leggy, short-lived plants.

To add gaillardias to your garden, either purchase plants or start your own from seeds. Perennials—G. *aristata* and G. × *grandiflora*—can be planted in spring in pots set outdoors and transplanted to the garden in autumn. Sow seeds of annual G. *pulchella* in spring, either outdoors after the last frost or indoors, four to six weeks before the last frost. Seeds need light to germinate.

Watering during extremely dry weather helps keep plants looking their best. They continue blooming without deadheading, but removing the faded flowers helps keep the plants neat looking. Most gaillardias stand without staking. Divide perennial gaillardias in spring or early fall every two to three years; otherwise, the centers of the clumps die out and plants lose their vigor. Division is the easiest way to propagate, but plants also can be grown from stem cuttings made in early summer or from root cuttings. Perennial gaillardias are easy to start from seed—they often self-seed—but seed-grown strains produce plants that are variable.

Plants are subject to powdery mildew and aster yellows, and sometimes they are bothered by Japanese beetles and leafhoppers.

WHAT TO GROW

Most gardeners grow hybrid blanket flower (G. × *grandiflora*), which is a short-lived, 2- to 3-foot-tall perennial with lance-shaped or lobed leaves and 3- to 5½-inch flower heads. Hardy in Zones 3 or 4 to 8, it blooms from early summer to fall, with heaviest flowering from early to midsummer. Many cultivars are available, and most feature brilliant, bicolored flowers in shades of red, maroon, orange, and yellow. Dwarf cultivars include 8-inch-tall 'Baby Cole', with red ray florets tipped in yellow that surround maroon-red centers. 'Goblin', which reaches 12 inches, has red flowers with a yellow band, and 'Golden

Goblin' produces yellow flowers on 12-inch plants. 'Arizona Sun', also 12 inches, bears 3-inch-wide flowers that are red-orange with yellow petal tips.

Common blanket flower (G. *aristata*), hardy in Zones 3 to 8, is a 2- to 2½-foot perennial with yellow flowers with red-orange centers. The ray florets are lobed at the tips, giving the flowers a somewhat shaggy appearance. Plants bloom from summer to fall.

G. *pulchella* is a 1- to 1½-foot-tall warm-weather annual that blooms from summer to fall. Flowers are 2 inches wide and come in red, yellow, or red with yellow tips. Disk florets are dark purple. Double-flowered cultivars—such as Plume Series in red or yellow—are available.

IN THE GARDEN

Gaillardias are perfect for adding dependable color to beds and borders during hot summer weather. Combine them with summer-blooming perennials such as coreopsis, daylilies, yarrows (*Achillea* spp.), red-hot pokers (*Kniphofia* spp.), and salvias or sages (*Salvia* spp.). Dwarf selections make stunning edging plants and are good in containers. All are excellent for combining with sun-loving annuals such as marigolds (*Tagetes* spp.), orange cosmos (*Cosmos sulphureus*), and coxcombs (*Celosia* spp.). Full-size gaillardias also make outstanding cut flowers, and all types are attractive to butterflies.

Galium odoratum

(GAL-ee-um oh-dor-AY-tum)

Sweet woodruff

Madder family, Rubiaceae. Hardy perennial.

Formerly known as *Asperula odorata*, sweet woodruff is a charming ground cover that thrives in shade. These low-growing plants bear unbranched stems topped by whorls of linear leaves. From late spring to midsummer, they produce dainty clusters of small, star-shaped, tubular white flowers. While even the clusters are small—about 3 inches wide—a fragrant drift of sweet woodruff in bloom is still a lovely sight.

The genus name *Galium* comes from the Greek for "milk," and it probably alludes to the use of yellow

Sweet woodruff, Galium odoratum

bedstraw (G. *verum*) to curdle milk in cheese making. *Odoratum*, of course, means "fragrant." When dried, the stems and leaves turn black but have the sweet aroma of fresh-mown hay, and the plant was often stuffed into mattresses to mask less pleasant odors, as was its cousin, lady's bedstraw (G. *aparine*).

Sweet woodruff has long been used as an herb. Dried leaves can be added to potpourri, and they also are used fresh to flavor wine drunk on May 1—called *Maibowle* in Germany—to mark the start of spring. Sweet woodruff is used traditionally as a tonic, a diuretic, and as a sedative, although modern research shows that it causes liver damage in laboratory animals. A few springs in a bowl of Rhine wine won't harm you, however. Happy spring.

HOW TO GROW

Select a spot in partial to deep shade for sweet woodruff, although plants also will grow in full sun provided the soil is kept moist and temperatures don't go too high. Ideally, give plants soil, either light or heavy, that is rich and moist but well drained. Once planted, sweet woodruff needs little care and spreads at a moderate speed.

Dig plants as necessary in spring or fall to keep them in bounds. Propagate sweet woodruff by division—make sure each division has both roots and a piece of the plant crown—or propagate from stem cuttings. Sweet woodruff seeds must be fresh to germinate, so sow them as soon as they ripen, in late summer. Plant in pots and set them outdoors in a protected location over the winter.

Sweet woodruff is rarely bothered by disease or insects.

WHAT TO GROW

You won't find cultivars of sweet woodruff at the garden center, but the white-flowered, 6- to 8-inch- tall species is all you need; it is hardy in Zones 4 to 8.

IN THE GARDEN

Plant sweet woodruff in drifts—at least three or five plants if the area you want to cover is small, more if you are covering a larger area. Consider growing it as a ground cover under trees, shrubs, and larger shade-loving plants, such as hostas, or the larger spring bulbs, such as tulips and daffodils. Keep sweet woodruff away from small, less-vigorous plants, though, as it may overrun them.

Gazania ringens

(gah-ZAY-nee-uh RIN-genz)

Gazania, treasure flower

Aster family, Asteraceae.
Tender perennial grown as an annual.

These sun-loving natives of tropical Africa are grown for their brilliantly colored, daisylike flowers. And brilliantly colored is no exaggeration. Blooms come in an array of hot hues—including gold, orange, orange-red, red, rose-pink—but that's only half their appeal. The showy blooms usually are striped or banded with contrasting colors and feature eyes that are darker than the petal-like ray florets, two features that make them even more eye-catching.

While the flowers blaze away during sunny weather, they close at night and remain closed on cloudy days, and they do not make a good cut flower. Most plants produce two types of leaves: Some are narrow and entire, the others are deeply lobed. All leaves are glaucus, or grayish, on their undersides and turn upward at night. Sixteen species belong to the

OTHER CHOICES

*P*lants in several genera are commonly called African daisies, including *Arctotis* spp., *Dimorphotheca* spp., and *Osteospermum* spp. All prefer growing conditions similar to gazanias; give them sun and well-drained average soil.

Arctotis species. These bear 3- to 4-inch-wide daisy flowers that resemble tall gazanias. Tender perennials usually grown as annuals, they bloom from midsummer to early fall. Monarch of the veldt (*A. fastuosa*) ranges from 1 to 2 feet and bears 4-inch daisies with orange petals and deep purple to black eyes. 'Zulu Prince' produces flowers with creamy white petals that are marked with black and orange at the base. 'Harlequin' hybrids bear dark-centered 3-inch flowers on 18- to 20-inch plants and come in shades of orange, pink, white, apricot-yellow, and red. Blue-eyed African daisy (*A. venusta*), to 2 feet tall, has white-petaled, 3-inch-wide daisies with dark blue centers, or eyes.

African daisy, Arctotis × hybrida

Dimorphotheca species. The two most popular species—rain daisy (*D. pluvialis*) and star of the veldt (*D. sinuata*)—are warm-weather annuals native to dry, mostly sandy areas of South Africa. They bear showy, daisylike flower heads from midsummer to fall over mounds of coarsely toothed, aromatic foliage. Rain daisy, or weather prophet (*D. pluvialis*), is 1 to 1½ feet tall and bears 2½-inch daisies with dark eyes and white petals that have a ring of purple around the center disk. The backs of the petals also are purple. The common names—rain daisy and weather

prophet—stem from the fact that the flowers close in rainy and cool weather and also at night. Star of the veldt (*D. sinuata*) reaches about 1 foot and bears 1½-inch daisies that sport purple-brown centers and white, yellow, orange, or pink petals. 'Pastel Silks' produces flowers in shades of cream, soft orange, pale yellow, and buff.

Star of the veldt, Dimorphotheca sinuata

Osteospermum species. These are tender perennials or subshrubs grown as warm-weather annuals. Look for *O. ecklonis*, which ranges from 2 to 5 feet tall and boasts gray-green leaves and 2- to 3-inch daisies, borne from early summer until frost, that have dark violet-blue centers and white petals that are blue on the back. *O. jucundum*, a tender perennial grown as an annual, has gray-green leaves and 2-inch mauve to magenta-pink flowers.

genus *Gazania*, but most of the garden plants grown today are hybrids of G. *ringens* and G. *linearis*.

The botanical name *Gazania* commemorates Theodore of Gaza, a 15th-century scholar who translated the botanical writing of the Greek Theophrastus into Latin. As for the common name treasure flower, you only have to grow a golden strain of these tropical sunflowers to understand its origins. Rainbow daisy is another common name you may encounter and is equally well deserved.

HOW TO GROW

Plant gazanias in full sun and give them poor to average soil that is light, very well drained, and has a neutral or slightly sweet pH. These are plants that thrive in both heat and, once established, in dry soil. They also tolerate salt spray, making them suitable subjects for a seaside garden, but tend to rot in areas with humid, wet summers or when planted in soil that remains constantly moist.

Gazanias do not bloom well in rich soil, but plants, particularly those growing in containers, will flower better and longer if fed once a month with a diluted, balanced soluble fertilizer. Deadheading also prolongs the bloom season. If you live anywhere from Zones 8 or 9 or warmer, grow gazanias as perennials; elsewhere, either buy new plants each spring or start your own from seeds. Sow indoors six to eight weeks before the frost-free date; transplant seedlings outdoors once the soil warms, no earlier than two weeks after the frost-free date. To overwinter plants, dig and pot them up before the first hard fall frost. During the winter, give plants bright light but keep them cool and barely moist.

Aphids, mealybugs, and spider mites can be trouble if left unchecked; molds and stem and root rots are problematic if plants are overwatered or the soil doesn't drain adequately.

WHAT TO GROW

Gazania hybrids, tender perennials usually grown as annuals, range from 8 to 12 inches tall. Flowers are 3 to 4 inches wide and appear from summer to fall. While some gazanias bear solid-color flowers, plants with blooms banded, striped, or spotted in contrasting colors are most common. Daybreak Series plants reach 8 inches and spread to 10 inches, and yield both bicolored blooms and flowers in single colors. 'Mini-Star Mix' plants are 6 inches tall; the Kiss Series produces 8-inch plants in various colors. All

Treasure flower, Gazania ringens *'Chansonette Mix'*

are F$_1$ hybrids so seed collected from plants you grow won't come true.

G. *krebsiana* 'Tanager', a recent 4-inch-tall introduction, is hardy from Zone 6 and warmer; it has fluorescent orange flowers and is self-seeding.

IN THE GARDEN

Plant gazanias along the front edge of beds and borders, or use them to edge a walkway or patio, where they'll add color from midsummer to fall. Gazanias also can be used to add summer color to rock gardens, and they thrive in containers. They are ideal for seaside gardens and for xeriscaping, and if that weren't enough, they also attract butterflies.

Geranium

(*jer-AY-nee-um*)

Hardy geraniums, cranesbills

Geranium family, Geraniaceae.
Hardy perennials.

These versatile, handsome perennials are not to be confused with the ever-popular, round-leaved plants commonly called annual, or zonal, geraniums. Those ubiquitous plants, botanically speaking, are members of the genus *Pelargonium*, as are scented geraniums, and are tender perennials grown as annuals in all but the warmest regions of North

Purple hardy geranium, Geranium × magnificum

America. True geraniums—also known as English geraniums—are hardy, primarily mounding plants that feature pretty, five-petaled flowers and attractive deeply lobed, often lacy-looking foliage. Plants are herbaceous in cold regions, but in areas with mild winters, many can boast of semi-evergreen or evergreen leaves. Several hardy geraniums have colorful foliage in fall.

The cup- or saucer-shaped flowers come in shades from palest pink to screaming magenta as well as lavender, violet, violet-blue, purple, and white. Most hardy geraniums bloom in late spring or early summer. The genus name *Geranium* comes from *geranion*, the Greek name for the plant, but it is also related to *geranos*, the Greek word for "crane." The reference is not to the geranium flower but to its seedpods, which have tiny bill-like projections.

In addition to their legacy as beautiful perennials for bed and border, hardy geraniums also have a history as medicinal plants, especially noted for their ability to heal wounds. "It likewise profiteth much those what are wounded into the body," the herbalist John Gerard wrote, "as my selfe have likewise proved." The plants have a high tannin content and have been used as astringents in traditional medicine. Native North Americans used American, or wild, cranesbill (*G. maculatum*), which is also commonly called alumroot, to stop bleeding and as an antiseptic. That species has yet other names: old-maid's nightcap—from the shape of the flower—and shameface, from the rose color of the flower.

HOW TO GROW

The site and soil conditions for hardy geraniums depend on the species. There are hardy geraniums both for full sun and for partial shade. Most bloom best in moderately rich soil that is well drained but evenly moist. In areas with hot summers, plant geraniums in a spot that receives afternoon shade.

Start with purchased plants, setting them out in spring in Zones 6 and north so they have time to become established before winter; in warmer regions, plant in spring or fall. Dig the soil deeply before planting, and work in plenty of organic matter to promote good drainage.

Once they're in the ground, hardy geraniums are easy to care for. Topdress plants with well-rotted manure or compost in spring to keep them growing vigorously. Taller species may flop in the garden, and gardeners approach this tendency in two different ways. They either prop the plants up with twiggy-brush, or let the plants flop and mingle with their

Grayleaf cranesbill, Geranium cinereum '*Ballerina*'

neighbors. Either way, after the plants finish blooming, cut them back to a height of about 1 inch, and they'll produce a mound of new leaves within a few weeks. Some species will rebloom.

Divide hardy geraniums regularly to keep them looking and blooming their best. While this chore can be avoided with some species—provided they are still blooming well and have not outgrown their site—G. *endressii*, G. *himalayense*, G. *sanguineum*, and G. *sylvaticum* all need to be divided every two to three years for best performance. Dig clumps in spring in the North, spring or fall in the South, and discard the old, woody portion at the center of the plant. Most geraniums can be pulled apart with fingers, but a few species have thicker rhizomes and must be cut apart with a knife.

Propagate geraniums by division, as popular cultivars do not come true from seed, or from root cuttings taken after flowering ends. If you are growing species geraniums, sow seeds in pots and set them outdoors in a protected location over winter.

A few pests and diseases, including slugs and mildews, can trouble geraniums, but generally they are problem free.

WHAT TO GROW

One of the best ways to decide which geraniums to grow is to match them to site—there are species for sun or semishade, for beds and borders, for rock gardens, and even geraniums that can be used as ground covers. You may want to avoid planting herb Robert (G. *robertianum*), a weedy annual or biennial that self-sows with abandon but does have the merit of being easy to pull out. It bears ½-inch pink flowers from early summer to late fall and has lacy, aromatic leaves.

The largest number of geraniums are suitable for sunny beds and borders with rich, moist, well-drained soil. Clark's geranium (G. *clarkei*) bears ¾-inch violet-purple or white flowers with lilac veins from late spring into early summer. Hardy in Zones 4 to 8, it is a mounding 15- to 20-inch-tall species. Lilac cranesbill (G. *himalayense*) bears violet-blue flowers, 2 inches wide, on 12- to 15-inch-tall plants in early summer. Hardy in Zones 4 to 8, this species also boasts handsome orange-red fall foliage and makes a good ground cover. 'Plenum', or 'Birch's Double', has double, violet-blue flowers.

Hybridizers have produced scores of outstanding geraniums for beds and borders. 'Johnson's

Lilac cranesbill, Geranium himalayense

Blue', with lavender-blue, 1½- to 2-inch flowers in early summer, is best known. Plants grow in full sun but also tolerate light shade; they are hardy in Zones 4 to 8. 'Brookside', which has sapphire flowers on 20-inch plants, is an improved, easier to grow version of 'Johnson's Blue' and hardy in Zones 4 to 8. 'Anne Folkard' features 1½-inch magenta-pink blooms with dark centers from midsummer to fall. The 2-foot plants, hardy in Zones 5 to 9, have yellow-green leaves and scrambling stems that spread to about 3 feet. 'Anne Thomson also features gold leaves and violet flowers from spring to midsummer. Hardy in Zones 4 to 8, it is more heat tolerant than 'Anne Folkard'. 'Rozanne', hardy in Zones 5 to 8, bears blue-violet flowers atop 18-inch plants and blooms from early summer until frost.

Meadow cranesbill (G. *pratense*) produces blue-violet, 1½-inch flowers in late spring and early summer. These are 2- to 3-foot plants, hardy in Zones 2 or 3 to 8, that need evenly moist soil; they self-sow with enthusiasm. Armenian cranesbill (G. *psilostemon*) is a stunning, 2- to 3-foot-tall, shrub-size geranium that needs staking along with evenly moist soil and shade during the hottest part of the day. Hardy in Zones 5 to 8, plants also boast bright red fall foliage.

Bloody cranesbill (G. *sanguineum*) is an adaptable species that can be grown in full sun or partial shade and produces 8- to 12-inch mounds of lacy, deeply cut leaves topped by 1- to 1½-inch pink flowers from spring to summer. Hardy in Zones 3 to 8, this species bears red fall foliage, tolerates heat and drought, and self-sows. 'Shepherd's Warning' is

Bloody cranesbill, Geranium sanguineum

chocolate brown foliage and lavender flowers. Dusky cranesbill (G. *phaeum*), hardy in Zones 5 to 7, produces black-purple, maroon, violet, or white 1-inch flowers with reflexed petals. This is a clump-forming species, 1½ to 2½ feet tall, that has thick rhizomes and grows in partial shade and evenly moist soil but also tolerates full shade and dry soil. Finally, woody cranesbill (G. *sylvaticum*), hardy in Zones 3 to 8, bears violet-blue, 1-inch flowers in spring on 2½- to 3-foot plants. It self-sows.

Geraniums that are vigorous enough to use as ground covers and that generally spread too quickly for most beds and borders include Endress cranesbill (G. *endressii*), which is hardy in Zones 4 to 8 and is best for areas with cool summers. Plants bear pale pink flowers in spring on 15- to 18-inch plants. Bigroot geranium (G. *macrorrhizum*) is an adaptable species for sun or partial shade that tolerates heat and drought because of its fleshy, deep roots. Hardy in Zones 3 to 8, it bears pink to purplish-pink flowers in spring and 1½-foot mounds of aromatic leaves that are evergreen in mild climates. Hybrid G. × *oxonianum* produces pink 1½-inch flowers from spring to fall on 1½- to 3-foot plants. Hardy in Zones 4 to 8, it is a vigorous clump former that does best in dappled shade. 'Claridge Druce' is a good cultivar with rose-pink flowers, as is 'Wargrave Pink'.

While a great many gardeners lack traditional rock gardens, geraniums that thrive in rock gardens are also suited for planting along the edges of raised beds or at the top of walls, where drainage is good. These are not plants for moist soil or heavy clay. Grayleaf cranesbill (G. *cinereum*), hardy in Zones 5 to 8, bears purplish pink flowers on 6- to 12-inch plants. 'Ballerina' is a 4- to 6-inch-tall cultivar that produces pink flowers throughout the summer. Dalmatian cranesbill (G. *dalmaticum*) and bloody cranesbill (G. *sanguineum*) are two more excellent choices for rock-garden conditions.

IN THE GARDEN

Hardy geraniums are ideal plants for adding color to the front of a bed or border—or for planting just behind very low-growing edging plants. Combine them with bellflowers (*Campanula* spp.), coral bells (*Heuchera* spp.), Siberian iris (*Iris sibirica*), Shasta daisy (*Leucanthemum* × *superbum*), salvias or sages (*Salvia* spp.), and columbines (*Aquilegia* spp.). Combine shade-loving geraniums with hostas, astilbes, ferns, epimediums, and hellebores.

4 to 6 inches tall with pink flowers. G. *sanguineum* var. *striatum* ranges from 6 to 8 inches tall and also has pink flowers. Many other cultivars are available, including 'New Hampshire Purple', 'Album' (white), 'Elsbeth' (pink), 'Alpenglow' (rose-red), and the compact 'Max Frei' (reddish purple).

Hardy geraniums for partial shade include Dalmatian cranesbill (G. *dalmaticum*), which has pale pink, 1-inch blooms and is hardy in Zones 4 to 8. This species spreads vigorously, but it is generally not invasive and also features red-orange fall foliage that remains attractive well into the fall. Plants are evergreen in mild climates. Wild cranesbill (G. *maculatum*) is another species for a spot in partial shade with moist, well-drained soil. It ranges from 1 to 2 feet and bears pink, 1¼-inch flowers in late spring to midsummer. Cultivar 'Patricia' sports magenta pink flowers over a long season and grows from 2 to 3 feet; 'Expresso' features 15-inch mounds of

Geum

(GEE-um)

Geums, avens

Rose family, Rosaceae. Hardy perennials.

○

Although known by a few gardeners as avens, geums, one British writer explained, "arrived too recently in this country to have equipped themselves with an English name." Late comer or not, geums are herbaceous perennials grown for their saucer- to bowl-shaped flowers. Blooms, which look something like potentilla flowers, usually have five petals and come in shades of orange, red, and yellow plus cream and pink. Double-flowered forms also are available. Flowers are borne singly or in small clusters from late spring to early summer.

Most garden plants are cultivars of G. *chiloense*, the most famous of which is 'Mrs. J. Bradshaw', in whose English garden it appeared as a chance seedling. *Chiloense* is a giveaway for the species' origin, Chile and the Chilean island Chiloe. *Geum* comes from the Greek *geno*, meaning "to give off." Many geum species have aromatic roots that give off scents and were once used to ward off moths. Herbalist John Gerard prescribed the roots and leaves for healing those who "have fallen from some high place," although whether he had ladder climbers or politicians in mind is unrecorded.

Avens, Geum chiloense 'Mrs. J. Bradshaw'

OTHER CHOICES

Two species of geum are commonly overlooked by gardeners, and both can be grown from seed. Water avens, or Indian chocolate (G. *rivale*), is a ½- to 2-foot-tall species hardy in Zones 3 to 8. It prefers moist or even boggy soil and bears small, pendant, bell-shaped, purple-pink flowers from late spring to midsummer. Prairie smoke, or purple avens (G. *triflorum*), is a native North American wildflower hardy in Zones 1 to 7. It has ferny, gray-green leaves and creamy-colored, 1½-inch flowers with long purple bracts. The flowers are followed by silvery pink seedpods that have a fuzzy, smokelike appearance.

HOW TO GROW

Give geums a spot in full sun and average to rich soil that is evenly moist but well drained. Since plants don't tolerate heat well, gardeners south of Zone 6 should select a site that is shaded during the afternoon. Good soil drainage is especially important in winter, when wet conditions can lead to crown rot.

Water geums regularly in dry weather. Plants also appreciate a spring topdressing of well-rotted manure or compost. Deadheading will extend the bloom period. Once flowering stops, plants can be cut back to the new basal foliage. Geums tend to be short lived and need to be divided every two to four years to stay vigorous. Discard old, woody growth and replant the plantlets that grow at the edges.

Dividing the clumps in spring is the best way to propagate geums, as plants hybridize in the garden and seeds don't come true. Two cultivars to start from seeds are 'Lady Stratheden', a semidouble yellow, and the scarlet 'Mrs. J. Bradshaw'. Sow seeds in pots in fall and set them outdoors in a protected location.

Geums can have problems with mildews, spider mites, and caterpillars.

WHAT TO GROW

The most commonly grown geum is G. *chiloense*. It is a clump-forming plant, hardy in Zones 4 to 7 or 8, that ranges from 1½ to 2 feet tall and produces a mound of deeply lobed, toothed leaves. Plants bear loose clusters of saucer-shaped, 1½-inch red flowers in summer. Good cultivars, in addition to 'Lady Stratheden' and 'Mrs. J. Bradshaw', include 'Fire

Opal' (semidouble red-orange blooms) and 'Double Bloody Mary' (double red-orange flowers). G. *coccineum* features orange-yellow flowers with bright yellow stamens from late spring to midsummer and grows 12 to 20 inches tall; it is hardy in Zones 5 to 8.

IN THE GARDEN

Add geum to beds and borders, planting it toward the front and combining it with other summer-blooming perennials such as coreopsis, hardy geraniums or cranesbills (*Geranium* spp.), and smaller ornamental grasses. Geums make pretty cut flowers and last about a week in water. Pick flowers when they are about three-quarters open, as tight buds won't open in water.

Gladiolus × hortulanus

(*glad-ee-OH-lus hor-tew-LAY-nus*)
Common gladiolus, garden glad
Iris family, Iridaceae. Tender bulb.

Bold, colorful glads are a familiar sight in cut flower arrangements—especially large arrangements created for hotel lobbies and big events. They're also popular in gardens, where they are not only easy to grow but come in a seemingly endless array of colors. While the genus contains about 180 species, summer-blooming hybrids are by far the most popular garden plants. These are tender perennials, hardy in Zones 8 to 10 only, or possibly in Zone 7 with a thick wintertime mulch. Wild, or hardy, gladiolus (*Gladiolus communis* spp. *byzantinus*) were once called whistling Jacks and squeakers in England, where children used the leaves as reeds to whistle.

Whether tender or hardy, all glads produce showy spikes of funnel-shaped flowers. Each bloom has six tepals: three petal-like sepals and three true petals. The flowers usually are arranged on one side of the spike, and they open in progression starting from the bottom. Glads come in shades of pink, magenta, yellow, red, white, orange, lavender, violet, maroon, green, and purple. There are selections with both solid-color and bicolor blooms.

Glads grow from corms, each of which produces a sheaf of sword-shaped leaves arranged in fans and

Garden gladiolus, Gladiolus × hortulanus 'Flevo Junior'

one flower spike. The official plural of gladiolus is gladioli, but most gardeners use gladiolus for one plant or many plants. The botanical name, *Gladiolus*, is from the Latin *gladius* and means "little sword," a reference to the plant's foliage. Also known as the sword lily, European species were growing in English gardens as early as the late 1500s, and new species and cultivars just kept coming. Americans were less receptive, and there are few records of gladiolus being cultivated here until the late 19th century, when Luther Burbank and other breeders became interested in the plant. Interest hasn't waned since, and the hybrids just keep coming.

HOW TO GROW

Gladiolus are easy and inexpensive to add to the garden—a dozen or so corms purchased at the local garden center is a good place to begin. Most well-stocked retailers will offer glads in a range of colors for spring

> ### OTHER CHOICES
>
> *H*ardy gladiolus (*G. communis* spp. *byzantinus*) is a 2- to 3-foot-tall species that produces graceful spikes of 10 to 20 flowers in late spring and early summer. The 2-inch-wide flowers are magenta-pink striped with white or pale pink on the lower tepals that form the lip. This species is hardy in Zones 5 to 10 and spreads freely by cormlets.

planting, but for the full component of colors—or if you're looking for a shade or combination that's unusual—you'll have to order from a mail-order nursery. All glads need to succeed is a spot in full sun with light, evenly moist soil that is rich in organic matter.

Plant tender glad corms in spring, after the danger of frost has passed. Many gardeners grow gladiolus in cutting gardens by digging a shallow trench, setting the corms in place, and then filling the trench in with soil as the plants grow. Standard-size corms (ones that are more 1 inch in diameter) can be set 6 inches deep; set medium-size corms (½- to 1-inch in diameter) at a depth of 4 to 5 inches; and set small corms (½ inch or less in diameter) 3 inches deep. In general, close spacing is best, 2 to 6 inches apart. Planting the corms deeply helps reduce the need to stake plants. In beds and borders, interplant glads with annuals and perennials that can help support the stems. For a progression of color and a continuous supply of flowers for cutting, plant corms at two- to three-week intervals from spring to midsummer.

In areas where glads are not hardy, they can be grown as annuals or dug, overwintered, and replanted in spring. To overwinter glads, let the foliage ripen for six weeks after flowering stops, then dig the corms, cut off the tops, and set the corms in a warm, dry place for a few hours to dry. Separate the new corms and small cormels from the old withered one, which will not bloom again and should be discarded. Dust the corms with sulfur or another fungicide and store them in a cool (40°F to 50°F), dry place over winter.

Watch for signs of scab, blight, and yellows; thrips, aphids, and Japanese beetles can also be troublesome.

WHAT TO GROW

Common gladiolus, or garden glads, are usually listed as G. × *hortulanus*. These 3- to 4-foot plants produce 1- to 3-foot spikes that can contain as many as 28 flowers. There are tens of hundreds of cultivars available in all colors except true blue. Exactly what you plant will depend on your gardening style. Select glads in shades that blend with or accent your other plantings, or plant a mix of colors and scatter them throughout your garden. Catalogs often divide garden glads into three groups: grandiflora types, which bloom from late spring to fall depending on when they are planted; nanus types, which bloom in early summer; and primulinus types, which flower throughout the summer.

IN THE GARDEN

Use glads to add color to plantings of sun-loving annuals or perennials. Keep in mind that these are tall, narrow plants, and it's very easy to end up with a flower bed that seems punctuated by exclamation points. They are most effective when planted closely together, because they'll form larger drifts of color. Close planting also encourages plants to lean on

Hardy gladiolus, Gladiolus communis *spp.* byzantinus

one another and reduces the need to stake. If you are growing glads as cut flowers, consider devoting a row of your vegetable garden to their cultivation or creating a cutting garden. In these cases, run strings along either side of the row to keep the plants upright. Glads also can be added to containers filled with other sun-loving annuals and perennials.

Gomphrena

(gum-FREE-nah)

Gomphrenas, globe amaranths

Amaranth family, Amaranthaceae. Annuals.

Grown for their round, colorful blooms, gomphrenas somewhat resemble clover, but the texture of the buttonlike flowers is decidedly prickly—more like a pot scrubber than a soft flower one might use to make a floral necklace for a child. The blossoms are composed of tiny, densely packed flowers, each borne above a stiff, showy bract. The clusters of blossoms and bracts look like tiny colored hedgehogs. Flowers, which have no scent, are about 1½ inches in diameter and appear from summer to early fall. The plants are fairly low-growing and bushy, with lance-shaped to ovate leaves that are softly hairy.

Most garden-grown gomphrenas are hybrids or cultivars of species native to Central and South America. The botanical name Gomphrena is derived from an ancient name for amaranth (Amaranthus), a closely related but entirely different plant. The most common species, G. globosa, describes the flowers in its species name, globosa, or "globelike." Gomphrenas are often used in making herb wreaths; for obvious reasons it, as well as several other very different flowers, is sometimes referred to as bachelor's button.

OTHER CHOICES

While gomphrenas are worth growing simply to enjoy their flowers in the summer garden, they also are outstanding dried flowers. Here are some other annuals that make fine additions to dried bouquets. All need growing conditions that are similar to gomphrena's.

Pearly, or winged, everlasting (*Ammobium alatum*). This species bears daisylike, 1-inch flowers with papery white "petals" and orange or yellow centers.

Rose everlastings, or strawflowers (*Rhodanthe* spp.). Both *R. chlorocephala* spp. *rosea* and *R. manglesii* are grown as everlastings—you may still find them listed as *Helipterum* species. They produce papery-textured daisylike flowers with white or pink petal-like bracts and yellow centers.

Yellow ageratum (*Lonas annua*). Also called African daisy, this species bears rounded, 3- to 5-inch clusters of buttonlike yellow flowers.

Rattail, or Russian, statice (*Psylliostachys suworowii* formerly *Limonium suworowii*). Also called pink poker, rattail statice bears showy, narrow, cylindrical spikes of rose-pink flowers.

Several other annuals make great additions to a dried flower garden, including strawflower (*Bracteantha bracteata*), statice (*Limonium sinuatum*), and star flower (*Scabiosa stellata*).

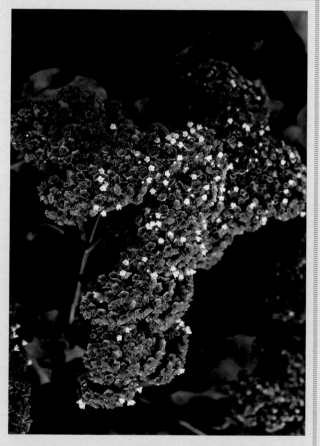

Sea lavender, Limonium sinuatum *Fortress Series*

cultivars that flower on 6-inch-tall plants. Gnome Series plants are 6 inches tall and come in pink, white, and shades of purple. 'Woodstock Mix' yields 18-inch plants with orange, white, pink, or purple flowers. *G. haageana* is a 2-foot-tall annual with flower heads in shades of pale red to reddish orange. Cultivars include 'Lavender Lady' and the red-flowered 'Strawberry Fields'.

IN THE GARDEN

Use gomphrenas to edge beds and borders that contain flowers that thrive in full sun and well-drained soil. They are handsome with a wide range of plants, including perennials like yarrows (*Achillea* spp.) and coreopsis, annuals like salvias or sages (*Salvia* spp.), and herbs like lavender (*Lavandula angustifolia*). Gomphrenas are fine container and cut-flower plants, and they also attract butterflies. Last, gomphrenas are staples of dried-flower arrangements: Cut stems just as the blooms open fully and hang in bunches in a warm, dry, dark place.

Globe amaranth, Gomphrena globosa 'Gnome Pink'

HOW TO GROW

Gomphrenas need full sun and average, well-drained soil. This is an annual that thrives in hot weather and also tolerates dry soil. It does less well where summers are humid. Add gomphrenas to your garden by purchasing them as bedding plants, if you can find them, or by starting plants from seeds. Gomphrena seeds, one dealer put it, "have a limited shelf life," so make sure you have fresh seeds and soak them for 24 hours before sowing. Sow indoors six to eight weeks before the last spring frost, moving seedlings outdoors after the danger of frost has passed, or sow outdoors after the last spring frost. While most how-to books recommend pinching back seedlings to encourage bushy growth, James Crockett, the original Victory Garden television gardener, advised growers to keep their hands off: Pinching interferes with the plant's natural shape.

Root rot can be a problem in wet soil, but gomphrenas are rarely bothered by diseases or pests.

WHAT TO GROW

Gardeners will find two species of gomphrena offered for sale. *G. globosa* is a 1- to 2-foot-tall annual that bears flowers in shades of pink, purple, or white. 'Buddy Purple' and 'Buddy Rose' are compact

Gypsophila

(jip-SOF-ih-lah)

Baby's breaths

Pink family, Caryophyllaceae.
Hardy perennials, annuals.

Despite these plants' evocative common name, baby's breath, the botanical name of this familiar group of garden flowers is pure practicality. *Gypsophila* alludes to the plants' soil preference; it is from the Greek *gypsos*, for "gypsum," and *philos*, for "loving," a clear indication that this genus wants alkaline soil. Fittingly, another common name is chalk plant. Baby's breath is a staple of florists' bouquets, especially for weddings, where it is traditionally included in the hope that the marriage will be fruitful. It also symbolizes a pure heart, festivity, and gaiety, but without comment on the possible conflicts between these sentiments.

Although the individual flowers are tiny, they are borne in abundance in loose, branched panicles. Most are single and star-shaped, and come in white or pink, but there are cultivars with double flowers as well.

Annual baby's breath, Gypsophila elegans

Gypsophila adds airy elegance to gardens just as it does to flower arrangements and bouquets, and it is especially effective when used to fill in among other plants. Plant leaves, commonly linear to lance-shaped in popular garden-grown species, are blue- to gray-green.

HOW TO GROW

Both annual and perennial baby's breaths need full sun or light afternoon shade in hot regions and rich soil that is evenly moist yet well drained. They prefer neutral to alkaline soil—pH 7.0 to 7.5. Perennial baby's breath (G. *paniculata*) and creeping baby's breath (G. *repens*) tolerate slightly acid soil, only to pH 6.5, and plants growing in less-than-neutral soil tend to be short lived. If you want to grow baby's breath, test the soil pH the fall before you plant, so you have time to sweeten it if necessary.

To grow perennial baby's breath, start in spring with plants because the best cultivars do not come true from seeds. Plants have roots that delve far into the ground, so dig deeply at planting time, and work in a few shovels of compost to ensure well-drained soil. Move plants in spring but only if absolutely necessary. Until recently, cultivars of G. *paniculata* were sold as grafted plants, but now plants propagated by tissue culture or cuttings and grown on their own roots are more common. If you are planting a grafted plant, set the graft union 1 inch below the soil surface, which encourages the grafted plant to develop its own roots.

Annual baby's breath (G. *elegans*) is easy and fast from seeds sown outdoors where the plants are to grow, or it can be sown indoors six weeks before the frost-free date. To keep the flowers coming, sow new crops of seeds every two to three weeks until midsummer. Perennial baby's breaths can be sown in pots in fall or early spring and set outdoors in a protected place. Divide G. *repens* plants in early spring or in midsummer, after flowering ends, if the clumps spread too far or if the plants die out in the center.

Annual baby's breath is drought tolerant, but perennial types do best if they are watered during dry spells. Full-size plants of G. *paniculata* also need staking to look their best. Deadhead plants, then cut stalks to the ground when flowering ends—you

OTHER CHOICES

Sea kales (*Crambe* spp.) somewhat resemble baby's breath in the garden. They produce mounds of tiny white flowers and can be grown in much the same conditions that suit baby's breath—full sun to very light shade and rich, moist, deeply dug soil that is well drained. *C. cordifolia* bears airy mounds of tiny white flowers and can reach 5 feet across and 8 feet in height. *C. maritima* bears denser clusters of flowers that reach about 2½ feet in height. Both are hardy in Zones 6 to 9, and both tolerate poor soil, need neutral pH, and can be grown in seaside gardens, although they do best when they are protected from strong winds.

Sea lavender (*Limonium latifolium*) is another perennial that resembles baby's breath. (See the *Limonium* entry on page 370.)

can shear G. *repens* to encourage plants to rebloom. Expect to replace G. *paniculata* every few years, since plants become woody and stop blooming.

Leafhoppers can be problematic, and plants are sometimes subject to botrytis and yellows.

WHAT TO GROW

For the perennial gardener, *Gypsophila paniculata*, hardy in Zones 3 to 9, is by far the most popular plant. When in bloom, the standard-size plants are 3 to 4 feet tall and wide, dwarf cultivars about 2 feet tall. 'Bristol Fairy' bears double white flowers and reaches about 3 feet; 'Pink Fairy' is slightly shorter, 2½ feet. 'Compacta Plena' is a double, white dwarf cultivar, 1½ feet; 'Pink Star' is another 1½-foot-tall selection with double flowers. Plants bloom from mid- to late summer, and all rebloom into fall if they are deadheaded and cut back.

Creeping baby's breath (G. *repens*), hardy in Zones 4 to 8, is a mat-forming perennial that grows only 4 to 8 inches tall. Its bluish to gray-green leaves are semi-evergreen, and plants bear loose clusters of ½-inch pink or white flowers from early to midsummer. Good cultivars include the white 'Alba' and 'Dorothy Teacher', which has pink flowers.

Annual baby's breath (G. *elegans*), a cool-weather annual, ranges from 1 to 2 feet tall and produces loose panicles of ½-inch white or pink flowers. It is a superb cut flower—most of the baby's breath used by florists is G. *elegans*—but it doesn't dry well. Available cultivars include the white-blooming 'Covent Garden', 18 inches tall and developed for use as a cut flower; 'Early Summer Lace', with flowers in white and shades of pink; 'Gypsy', a light pink, double-flowered form; and 'Garden Bride', a single pale pink.

IN THE GARDEN

Use baby's breath as a filler in plantings of perennials or annuals. It's good combined with bellflowers (*Campanula* spp.), purple coneflower (*Echinacea purpurea*), and daylilies, and it is useful for filling in under lilies or taking the space left by perennials that bloom early in the season, then disappear, such as common bleeding heart (*Dicentra spectabilis*). Use creeping baby's breath (G. *repens*) in rock gardens, to fill in between paving stones, as an edger, or as a ground cover. Taller baby's breaths are essential fillers for fresh flower arrangements, and perennial baby's breath (G. *paniculata*) is an excellent dried flower.

Helenium autumnale

(hel-EE-nee-um aw-tum-NAL-ee)

Helenium, sneezeweed

Aster family, Asteraceae. Hardy perennial.

This handsome perennial is treasured for the glowing, daisylike blooms it brings to beds, borders, and meadow gardens from summer to early fall. Don't for a minute worry that the showy blooms cause sneezing; they don't, despite the unfortunate common name sneezeweed, which may have been assigned because heleniums bloom at the same time as ragweed. Although sneezing isn't a helenium-related problem, contact with the foliage can cause allergic skin reactions. Also, all parts of the plants are poisonous if eaten.

The genus name *Helenium* is just as unfortunate. It is from *helenion*, the Greek name for another plant, and honors Helen of Troy. For this reason, heleniums are sometimes called Helen's flower, although Helen of Troy never saw one since all *Helenium* species are native to either North or Central America. Other common names are false sunflower, ox-eye, staggerwort, swamp sunflower, and yellow star.

Nomenclature aside, helenium flowers will fill your garden with brilliant late-season color, as blooms come in shades of rich mahogany, burnt orange, orange-yellow, gold, red, and yellow. Flower

Common sneezeweed, Helenium autumnale

heads consist of showy petal-like ray florets that surround a raised, buttonlike center of disk florets, that produces the seeds. The ray florets are wedge-shaped, and the widest part of the petal is toothed to give the blooms a ragged yet somewhat lacy appearance. Plants have branched, winged stems and lance-shaped, toothed leaves.

HOW TO GROW

Add heleniums to your garden in spring or early fall by starting with purchased plants. Give them a site in full sun with rich, evenly moist, well-drained soil. Plants also will grow in moist to wet soil. Add a few shovels of compost or some well-rotted manure to the soil at planting. Cut new plants back by one half after they are planted.

Heleniums benefit from a spring feeding with a balanced organic fertilizer or a topdressing of compost, and they need to be watered during dry weather. If clumps produce a dense tangle of stems that seem too close together, thin stems so they are from 3 to 5 inches apart. Tall cultivars will need support: Install stakes early, when plants are a foot tall, or let them sprawl over their neighbors—a solution that looks charming in informal plantings. Pinching stem tips several times in spring and early summer produces more compact plants (and more flowers)

and may eliminate the need to stake. After flowering, leave the seed heads for birds to enjoy, or cut plants back by half if they look too untidy.

To keep heleniums healthy and vigorous, divide them every three to four years in spring, discarding the woody center section. Division is the easiest way to propagate these plants, or grow from seeds. Sow seed in pots and set them outdoors in a protected spot to overwinter, or sow indoors eight to ten weeks before the last spring frost date.

Plants are susceptible to mildews in humid conditions.

WHAT TO GROW

Common sneezeweed (*H. autumnale*) is hardy in Zones 3 to 8 or 9 and produces yellow flowers with brown centers from late summer to fall. This species grows naturally in areas with moist soil, but cultivars are a better choice for most gardens. These range from 2 to 5 feet tall and often are hybrids of mixed parentage and must be purchased as plants. Dwarf cultivars—those that stay under 3 feet—need no staking and can be used toward the middle of flower borders. Dwarf cultivars include 'Butterpat' (yellow), 'Crimson Beauty' (bronze-red), early blooming 'Moerheim Beauty' (bronze- to copper-red), 'Rubinzwerg' (red and yellow), and 'Wyndley'

OTHER CHOICES

Ox-eye (*Heliopsis helianthoides*) is another garden-worthy member of the aster family. Also called sunflower heliopsis and false sunflower, this is a 3- to 6-foot-tall perennial that is native to North America and bears golden yellow, 1½- to 3-inch-wide daisylike flower heads from midsummer to early fall. Ox-eyes grow in full sun or partial shade and in average to rich, evenly moist, well-drained soil. They need to be divided regularly, as sneezeweeds do. *H. helianthoides* spp. *scabra* is a subspecies that has hairy leaves (the species has smooth leaves) and remains more compact than the species—it reaches about 3 feet. Many of the best ox-eye cultivars are cultivars of this subspecies. Its cultivars 'Gold Greenheart' (also sold as 'Goldgrünherz'), with lemon yellow flowers, bright yellow 'Light of Loddon', and golden yellow 'Summersonne', or 'Summer Sun', are all good choices. All have semidouble or double flowers and are hardy in Zones 4 to 9.

Ox-eye, Heliopsis helianthoides

(bronze-copper and yellow). Full-size heleniums for the back of the garden include 'Kugelsonne' (yellow) and 'Flammenspiel' (brown-yellow). 'Sunshine Hybrids', 2 to 4 feet tall, yield red, orange, yellow, gold, and mahogany blooms from seed.

If you have a spot where the soil tends to be on the dry side, consider another native helenium, orange sneezeweed (*H. hoopesii*). Hardy in Zones 3 to 7, it is native to the Western United States and bears yellow to orange, 3-inch flowers in early to midsummer on 2- to 3-foot plants.

IN THE GARDEN

Combine heleniums with asters, perennial sunflowers (*Helianthus* spp.), boltonia (*Boltonia asteroides*), goldenrods (*Solidago* spp.), lilies, obedient plant (*Physostegia virginiana*), and ornamental grasses. They are invaluable because of their extended bloom time in mid- to late summer or early fall. Also consider using them in the moist soil around ponds and other low-lying areas or in sunny wildflower plantings. Plants attract butterflies and other beneficial insects.

Helianthus

(hee-lee-AN-thuss)

Sunflowers

Aster family, Asteraceae.
Hardy perennials, annuals.

Today, the huge, gold-and-brown blooms of annual sunflowers are familiar to gardeners and nongardeners alike. They're so commonly offered at street flower stands that city dwellers may see them as often as dedicated country gardeners do. The perennial species of sunflower are less well known, however, despite the fact that they are easy to grow natives with showy flowers. One challenge with many of these perennials is that most of them are very large plants that take up considerable room. Used effectively, though—essentially like flowering shrubs that die to the ground each winter—they make stunning additions to the summer garden.

All sunflowers bear flower heads with petal-like florets surrounding dense, rounded centers of disk

Annual sunflower, Helianthus annuus

florets that produce the seeds. Annual sunflowers (*Helianthus annuus*) are grown specifically for their oil-rich seeds, which are used in breads and other baked goods, eaten toasted or raw, and are used for feeding birds. The seeds also are pressed for their oil, which is used in cooking and in the manufacture of margarine and other products. Sunflowers—either whole plants or seeds—also have been used to treat bronchial infections and to lower cholesterol.

Spanish, English, and French explorers sent sunflowers back to their homelands, where their colors and size dazzled gardeners. Height was crucial to popularity, and Old World gardeners were quick to measure, probably fisherman style: In the early 1600s, the 14-foot sunflower described by one English herbalist was dwarfed by Spanish claims of a 24-foot plant in the Royal Garden in Madrid,

Spain, which was surpassed by reports of a 40-foot sunflower in Italy.

Both the common name, sunflower, and botanical name suggest that these are plants for full sun—*Helianthus* is from the Greek *helios*, "sun," and *anthos*, "flower"—although a few species are suitable for shady sites. Both names could refer to the sunny colors of the flowers as well, since bright yellows and golds are the standard hues.

HOW TO GROW

Add annual sunflowers to your garden by starting seeds or buying them as bedding plants. Perennial sunflowers can be started from seed, but purchased plants provide more immediate gratification. Cultivars of perennial species must be asexually propagated plants, as seeds will not come true. Most sunflowers want full sun and average soil that is moist but well drained; tall cultivars will need protection from strong winds.

Sow annual sunflowers outdoors after danger of frost has passed, or start them indoors in individual pots four to six weeks before the last spring frost date. Once in the garden, topdress young plants with compost. Plants grown in a cutting garden can be spaced more closely than normal to reduce the flower size slightly.

Once planted, feed perennial species annually in early spring with a topdressing of compost or well-rotted manure. Pinch the stem tips in spring, in early summer and again in midsummer, if you want to encourage branching and curtail height. Most sunflowers stand without staking if they get full sun. Removing spent flowers, or picking them regularly for bouquets, will extend the bloom season on plants.

Perennial sunflowers may need to be divided every three or four years, either in early spring or in fall after flowering, and division is the best way to propagate them. Plants also can be propagated from cuttings taken from stems at the base of the plant in early spring. Or grow from seeds sown in containers and set outdoors after the last frost; transplant to the garden in fall.

Sunflowers are sometimes troubled by leaf spot and mildews; pests include aphids and beetles.

WHAT TO GROW

Annual, or common, sunflowers (*H. annuus*) are vigorous and fast-growing, making them great choices for children's gardens. These warm-weather plants

MOTHER CHOICES

*M*exican sunflower (*Tithonia rotundifolia*) is a native from Mexico through Central America and has sunflower or daisylike blossoms borne from late summer to frost in shades of yellow, orange, or red. It is an easy-care annual that thrives in heat and just needs full sun and poor to average, well-drained soil. Give plants soil that is too rich—or too much fertilizer—and they reward you with loads of foliage but few flowers. To grow Mexican sunflowers, start with seeds, either sown indoors six to eight weeks before the last spring frost date or outdoors after the last-frost date. Deadhead plants regularly to encourage new flowers to form, and water plants during dry weather. If your garden is in a windy site, you may need to stake the 3- to 6-foot-tall plants to keep them from toppling over. The species bears 3-inch-wide orange or orange-red daisy flowers, but cultivar 'Torch' produces 4-inch-wide orange-red flowers. 'Goldfinger' bears burnt orange flowers on compact, 30-inch-tall plants.

Mexican sunflower, Tithonia rotundifolia *'Fiesta Del Sol'*

bear flowers that are single, semidouble, or double and range from 4 inches to 1 foot or more across. Leaves and stems are roughly hairy, and the leaves are large (from 4 to as much as 16 inches across) and broadly oval or heart-shaped. Standard-size cultivars, including those that are grown for seed production, reach 6 to 12 feet. Both 6-foot-tall 'Mammoth Russian' and 11-foot 'Russian Giant' bear 10- to 12-inch-wide yellow flowers and produce a good crop of seeds. Annual sunflowers now come in a range of colors. 'Velvet Queen', 'Prado Red', and 'Moulin Rouge' all bear maroon-red petals and dark centers; 'Moonshadow' and 'Italian White' have white petals and dark centers; 'Valentine' produces pale yellow blooms; 'Moonwalker', pale lemon yellow ones; 'Ring of Fire' yields orange-yellow flowers with petals marked with maroon; 'Soraya' boasts golden orange flowers with dark centers.

Sterile hybrids that do not shed pollen and do not set seeds are another recent development in annual sunflowers. Look for Sun Series plants—'Sunbright Supreme', 'Moonbright', or 'Sunbright'. A number of cultivars bear somewhat smaller flowers in branched clusters and are better for cutting. These include Prado Series plants 'Autumn Time' (yellow and orange) and 'Cutting Gold' (yellow). Finally, dwarf cultivars range from 10 inches to about 3 feet in height. These include 'Big Smile', 'Sunspot', and 'Pachino', with yellow flowers and dark centers; the 3-foot-tall 'Teddy Bear' has double, golden flowers. The jury is still out on dwarf sunflowers.

Perennial sunflowers to consider include Maximillian sunflower (*H. maximilianii*), which is hardy in Zones 3 to 8 and bears clusters of 2- to 3-inch yellow flowers with brown centers from late summer to fall. Plants range from 4 to 10 feet tall and grow in regular garden soil as well as wet soil.

Willow-leaved sunflower (*H. salicifolius*) produces clusters of golden yellow, 2- to 3-inch flowers from early to midfall on 3- to 7-foot plants. It is hardy in Zones 3 or 4 to 8.

Swamp sunflower (*H. angustifolius*) thrives in ordinary garden soil as well as wet soil and tolerates partial shade. Hardy in Zones 6 to 9, it produces branched clusters of golden-yellow, 3-inch flowers with purple to brown centers from early to midfall on 4- to 8-foot plants. 'Low Down' is a dwarf cultivar with yellow daisies on mounding, 20-inch-tall plants. 'Gold Lace' is less vigorous than the giant-size species and produces golden yellow flowers on 5- to 6-foot plants; 'Mellow Yellow' produces soft, pastel yellow flowers on 8- to 10-foot plants .

Many-flowered hybrid sunflower (*H. × multiflorus*), hardy in Zones 5 to 9, bears golden yellow, 5-inch flowers from late summer to midfall on 3- to 5-foot plants. Cultivars include 'Loddon Gold' and 'Flore Pleno', both with double yellow flowers. *H.* 'Lemon Queen' is an outstanding hybrid of unknown parentage that bears abundant crops of pale yellow flowers on 4½-foot plants.

If you have a shady garden, but still want to grow sunflowers, look for thin-leaved sunflower (*H. decapetalus*), woodland sunflower (*H. divaricatus*), or pale-leaved wood sunflower (*H. strumosus*)—in addition to the swamp sunflower. All produce yellow flowers on plants that can reach 6 feet. They need some sun to bloom, so give them a spot that is shaded only part of the day.

IN THE GARDEN

For bold, sunny summer color, add both annual and perennial sunflowers to beds and borders. The perennial species are big, vigorous plants best used in large plantings—the large clumps are stunning planted along the back edge of a border or along a fence or foundation. Keep them away from less vigorous perennials, however, since they are overpowering. Combine them with asters, goldenrods (*Solidago* spp.), Joe-Pye weeds (*Eupatorium* spp.), and ornamental grasses. They also are ideal for meadow gardens and semiwild areas; the flowers attract butterflies, beneficial insects, and birds.

Annual sunflower, Helianthus annuus *'Velvet Queen'*

Helleborus

(hell-eh-BORE-us)

Hellebores, Lenten roses

Buttercup family, Ranunculaceae.
Hardy perennials.

Hellebores are treasured not only for their showy, if subtle, flowers but also for their longevity, for their shade-tolerance, for their foliage, which is evergreen in warmer parts of North America, and for the earliness of their blooms. Add to that an undemanding nature plus an amazingly long bloom season, and you have a garden gem.

Hellebores come into flower at a time when few plants in the garden are showing signs of life. Flowers usually range from 2 to 3 inches across, are mostly cup- or saucer-shaped, and are borne singly or in small clusters. Colors include shades of cream, green, white, mauve, pink, and purple—a limited palette, to be sure, but handsome nonetheless. The showy parts of the flower are actually petal-like sepals, which remain attractive for as many as four months in spring while the seed capsules form. Plants grow about 2 feet tall and have leathery, dark green leaves that are divided into lobes or leaflets and often are toothed.

Although sometimes called Christmas, or Lenten, roses, hellebores are not related to roses. They do have scores of Christian connections, however, including the legend of Madelon, a shepherd girl who went to Bethlehem without a gift. Seeing her tears, the angle Gabriel appeared and where he touched the frozen ground around the young girl, white flowers sprang up. And when the Christ child touched the blooms, they turned pink.

Despite their many religious associations, hellebores also have a more sinister side, a toxic one: All parts of the plants are poisonous if ingested, and the sap from bruised leaves causes skin rashes. The genus name *Helleborus* is a warning, as it stems from two Greek words, *helein*, meaning "to kill," and *bora*, "food." Christmas rose (*H. niger*) is also known as black hellebore, the English garden author Reginald Farrer wrote in 1922, "because its heart, or root, is black, while its face shines with a blazing white innocence." Whether it was for its black heart or its white face is unknown, but in earlier centuries plants were used to ward off witches, evil spirits, and spells, and to cure madness.

HOW TO GROW

To add hellebores to your garden, start with purchased plants. Set plants in light to full shade in rich, evenly moist soil that is well drained. A spot under trimmed-up deciduous trees is perfect because plants will receive full sun during the winter and shade or bright, indirect light from midspring to fall.

Lenten rose, Helleborus × hybridus *'Tom Wilson'*

Don't try to grow hellebores in sites that receive deep year-round shade or full sun in summer. For extra-early bloom, choose a spot that is protected from wind with a southern exposure. Since plants happily bloom for years without needing to be divided, take care in picking a site.

Most hellebores prefer a pH that is neutral to slightly alkaline, although Lenten rose (*H. × hybridus*) tolerates slightly acid soil. If you suspect your soil is acid, test and adjust it before setting out plants, and work compost or leaf mold into the soil at planting time.

Established hellebores don't need much in the way of regular care, but they appreciate a spring top-dressing of compost. Keep leaves and mulch off the plants in fall if they are in danger of being smothered. Cut off the leaves of clump-forming species like Lenten rose in midwinter when they begin to look tattered. On shrubby species, like stinking hellebore (*H. foetidus*), cut stems to the ground when they finish flowering to promote new growth.

In theory, hellebores can be divided, but doing so is often fatal—and divisions that survive often take several years before they bloom. The clumps are showiest (and happiest) if allowed to grow undisturbed. Plants do self-seed with enthusiasm, however, providing dozens of seedlings that can be transplanted. Growing plants from seeds is rated by many gardeners as "difficult to impossible." Intrepid seed-starters with great patience should sow seeds in pots in fall and overwinter them outdoors in a protected location.

Hellebores are susceptible to mildews in warm, humid regions, and slugs are fond of their foliage.

WHAT TO GROW

Christmas rose (*H. niger*) and Lenten rose (*H. × hybridus*, often sold as *H. orientalis*) are the most popular plants of hellebore. Both are clump-forming species with evergreen foliage in warmer regions. Christmas rose bears saucer-shaped, 2- to 3-inch flowers that are white or white flushed with pink from early winter to early spring on 12- to 15-inch plants. Flowers are borne one per stem or occasionally in clusters of two or three. Usually blooming in early spring, Christmas roses may bloom in winter in a very protected location or in warmer regions. They are hardy in Zones 4 to 8.

Lenten rose also bears its 2- to 3-inch flowers in clusters in late winter to early spring. The saucer-shaped blooms face down or out and come in shades of cream, greenish white, white, purple, and mauve. Hardy in Zones 5 or 6 to 9, Lenten rose is easier to grow than Christmas rose and tolerates dry to evenly moist soils that are well drained as well as acid to alkaline pH.

Stinking hellebore (*H. foetidus*) produces large, showy clusters of nodding, green flowers from midwinter to early spring that range from ½ to 1 inch across. This is a shrubby species and flowering stems are biennial—cut them to the ground when they've finished blooming. Hardy in Zones 6 to 9 and to Zone 5 with winter protection, stinking hellebore has narrow, deeply cut leaves that have an unpleasant scent when crushed and give rise to the plant's common name.

IN THE GARDEN

Hellebores add welcome color to spring shade gardens and make fine companions for hostas, ferns, lungworts (*Pulmonaria* spp.), epimediums (*Epimedium* spp.), wild blue phlox (*Phlox divaricata*), and other shade lovers. They're also good companions for drifts of little bulbs like snowdrops (*Galanthus* spp.). Site them along pathways or outside windows so you can enjoy the flowers when if it is too early to work in the garden. Plants also can be combined with larger spring bulbs such as daffodils or tulips.

Hemerocallis

(*hem-er-oh-CAL-iss*)

Daylillies

Lily family, Liliaceae. Hardy perennials.

Daylilies bring showy color plus an admirably tough constitution to gardens. Not only can these easy to grow perennials be used in a variety of garden situations and soils but they bloom despite drought and survive extremes of heat and cold. There's little wonder that they are one of America's favorite plants. Daylilies are not American natives but plants that arrived with the early colonists and, like the human immigrants, began making their way west. Before long, commercial and amateur breeders were—and still are—producing cultivars by the truckload.

Daylily, Hemerocallis 'Stella de Oro'

That wasn't always the case, although daylilies have been grown in Asia as long as there have been gardens, for the beauty of their flowers but also for the flavor of their buds and for their medicinal powers. Known as the plant of forgetfulness in China, it was prescribed to cure sadness (by forgetting it). Plants made their way to Europe and England in the 16th century but didn't attract a great deal of attention or a raft of common names. Perhaps that's because the common name daylily, or lily for a day, says it all: The flowers are fleeting, open only one day. The genus name *Hemerocallis* alludes to the same characteristic: *hemera*, Greek for "day," and *kallos*, which means "beauty."

Well, they used to be open for only a day, but there are now cultivars that like Orphan Annie's sun, "will come out tomorrow." Or at least stay open for somewhat more than one day. Reblooming cultivars, which have a main flush of bloom, then produce a second flush of flowers later in the season, are now available as well, and only the blue daylily has eluded the enormous crowd of enthusiastic amateur and commercial hybridizers. The blooms of most daylilies still open for only a day, but that brevity is made up for by stalks with scores of buds, so plants bloom over a long season. A good-size clump—standard clumps can spread from 2 to 4 feet, dwarf plants, 1 to 2 feet—will produce over 300 flowers in one season.

Daylily flowers are carried in clusters atop erect stalks, or *scapes*, which arise out of 1- to 2-foot-tall clumps of long, arching, sword-shaped fanned leaves. Flower scapes can be as short as 10 to 12 inches tall, but most plants bear their flowers on 2½- to 3½-foot scapes. There are a few towering cultivars whose scapes reach 6 feet. Flowers are trumpet-shaped and typically have six petal-like tepals, three true petals and three sepals.

HOW TO GROW

You'll want to start with purchased plants to add daylilies to your garden. Garden centers usually offer container-grown specimens. Bare-root plants are less expensive, just as easy, and the standard for mail-order companies. Both bare-root and container-grown plants should have at least two fans of leaves.

Plant daylilies in full sun or sun with light afternoon shade in the hottest regions. Plants will bloom with less than eight hours of sun, but they won't bloom as well. Daylilies grow well in a range of soil types, but they are happiest in average to rich soil that is well drained, evenly moist, and has a near-neutral pH. Daylilies also grow in poor soil and survive drought but won't bloom as well as plants in more comfortable conditions. Plants growing in overfertilized soil tend to produce foliage at the expense of flowers.

Dig compost or other organic matter into the soil when planting to encourage moisture retention and good drainage. Container-grown daylilies are best planted in spring but can be set out almost

Daylily, Hemerocallis 'Cool Jazz'

Daylily, Hemerocallis *'Hot Lips'*

any time the ground is not frozen; place plants at the same depth they were growing in the container. Soak bare-root daylilies in water for an hour or two before planting in spring or fall; in fall, get them in the ground at least a month before the first frost, especially in Zones 2 to 4, so they can begin growing roots before the ground freezes. Make sure the crown of the plant—the point where the roots meet the leaves—is at or just below the soil surface. Water thoroughly after planting, and keep the soil slightly moist until plants become established.

Daylilies benefit from an annual spring topdressing of well-rotted manure or a balanced organic fertilizer; mulching helps keep the soil moist and weeds down and eventually adds organic matter to the soil. Most cultivars need to be watered only during extended droughts. Water is especially important when flower buds are forming and plants are flowering, so those are times to supplement Mother Nature.

Removing spent flowers is a necessary chore but only for aesthetic reasons, as spent blooms have been described as looking like "limp toilet paper hanging from the plants." What is more important is to pick off any seedpods, as few cultivars come true from seed and making seed takes energy away from the plant.

Daylilies need to be divided when they become too crowded, outgrow their space, or begin to bloom less. Spring and fall are the typical times to divide, but clumps can be dug almost any time. Cut the foliage back to 2 to 3 inches after dividing. If you can't pull apart a division, use a knife or saw to cut segments. Don't be skimpy—aim for segments with three- or four-fans each. Division is also the easiest way to propagate daylilies.

WHAT TO GROW

There are tens of thousands of daylily cultivars from which to choose, and deciding which ones to grow can be overwhelming. Most daylilies are hardy from Zones 3 to 9, but hardiness varies, and some cultivars are more suitable for gardens in the North, others for southern gardens.

Daylilies come in a staggering array of colors. Orange is probably best known, but there are selections with flowers in yellow, peach, apricot, yellow-orange, orange-red, red, pinkish lavender, plum, and nearly white. Flowers can be a single color or can feature one or more contrasting colors. Daylilies that have one main color with a contrasting throat are popular, as are bicolored cultivars, cultivars with a band, a halo, or a watermark. Shapes vary, too, and flowers may be a classic trumpet shape or have either a somewhat triangular or circular face. There are daylilies with narrow petals that form star-shaped or spidery blooms. Petal edges can also be ruffled or crimped.

It helps if you have an understanding of basic daylily terminology. Diploid daylilies have two sets of chromosomes, while tetraploids have four sets, or twice the normal number. Tetraploids usually are larger plants than diploids and have larger, more brightly colored flowers. Tetraploids also often have ruffled or frilled petal edges.

A daylily described as a miniature bears flowers that are under 3 inches across, but it isn't necessarily a small plant. If you want small plants, look for terms like "dwarf" or look for plant heights. 'Mini Pearl' is both a miniature and a dwarf, for example, because it bears 3-inch flowers on 16-inch plants.

Look, too, for an indication of bloom season in catalog descriptions or the information on labels. If you select daylilies in several different standard bloom-season categories, you can extend the flowering season in your garden and plan color combinations for plants that will bloom together. Standard categories are extra early (EE), early (E), early midseason (EM), midseason (M), late midseason (LM), late (L), and very late (VL) cultivars.

Daylily, Hemerocallis *'Irish Glory'*

your area. When you are looking at daylily plants, take note of flower color, to be sure, but also look to see if the flower scapes are well branched and are producing a generous number of buds, as well as whether or not the plants themselves look healthy and attractive.

If you are just beginning with daylilies, consider starting out with a collection of classic cultivars that have won awards. Look for plants that have been given awards such as the Stout Silver Medal from the American Hemerocallis Society—'Frances Fay', 'Ed Murray', 'Mary Todd', 'Ruffled Apricot', 'Always Afternoon', and 'Betty Woods'—as well as classic daylilies that have been around for years, such as fragrant-flowered 'Hyperion', 'Catherine Woodbury', and 'Joan Senior'. Plants that have won the All-American Daylilies award also are worthy selections. These include 'Judith', 'Orange Crush', 'Bitsy', 'Frankly Scarlet', 'Plum Perfect', and 'Black-eyed Stella'.

Two other terms you should be aware of are "reblooming" and "everblooming." Reblooming daylilies produce a main flush of bloom followed by additional spikes later in the season. They're a good choice for getting the most color in a limited amount of space. Everbloomers produce flowering spikes continuously provided the soil remains evenly moist. Rebloomers include 'Barbara Mitchell', 'Mary Todd', 'Happy Returns', 'Pardon Me', 'Little Grapette', and 'Eenie Weenie'. 'Stella de Oro' is an everbloomer.

Daylilies also are classified according to foliage type; leaves can be deciduous (also called dormant), semi-evergreen, or evergreen. Evergreen types only remain green in the South and are best mulched with salt hay or conifer branches over winter in Zone 6 and the northern part of Zone 7. Semi-evergreen daylilies are deciduous in the North, but stay green only at the base of the leaves in the South, deciduous types go dormant in fall and return in spring wherever they are grown. Deciduous cultivars are the best choice for the northernmost zones, although there are some evergreens that are hardy to Zone 3.

One of the best ways to select daylilies for your climate is to visit displays and see what daylilies thrive at garden centers and in public plantings in

There are also species daylilies. Tawny daylily (*Hemerocallis fulva*) is the orange-flowered species that lines roadsides in early summer. Despite the widespread distribution, it is not a native wildflower. Fragrant, yellow-flowered lemon lily (*H. lilio-asphodelus*) and Middendorff's daylily (*H. middendorfii*) with yellow-orange flowers are both hardy in Zones 3 to 9. Citron daylily (*H. citrina*), hardy in Zones 5 to 9, bears fragrant, lemon-yellow trumpets on 3-foot stalks that open in the evening and remain open until about noon the following day.

IN THE GARDEN

Use daylilies in sunny beds and borders, where they can be combined with purple coneflower (*Echinacea purpurea*), perennial sunflowers (*Helianthus* spp.), yarrows (*Achillea* spp.), ornamental grasses, and all manner of sun-loving perennials. They are also wonderful when used as ground covers or in huge drifts or mass plantings along shrub borders, fences, or walkways. Many daylilies can be grown along streams and ponds and will survive periodic spring floods. Smaller cultivars are fine container plants. If you can bear to spare the flowers, daylily flower buds are edible and make interesting additions to stir-fry dishes.

Heuchera

(YOU-ker-ah)

Heucheras, coral bells, alumroots

Saxifrage family, Saxifragaceae.
Hardy perennials.

||||||||||||||||||||||||||||||||||||||||||||||||||||||||||||||||||||

The genus *Heuchera* contains about 55 species, all natives of North America and most from the Rocky Mountains. Nevertheless, the botanical name honors German botanist Johann Heinrich von Heucher (1677–1747), a professor of medicine at Wittenberg University. Native North Americans used the roots of alumroot (*H. americana*) to control bleeding and treat sores and wounds. The roots are a bitter astringent. Dr. Benjamin Smith Bargon, an 18th-century physician and naturalist from Philadelphia, believed they had even more promise; they were, he wrote, "the basis of a powder which has lately acquired some reputation in the cure of cancer."

In gardens, heucheras once were grown primarily for their flowers. All bear airy sprays of tiny, tubular flowers on erect stems high above the mounds of boldly veined semi-evergreen or evergreen leaves. Leaves are rounded to heart-shaped and often toothed or lobed. Today, however, heucheras are just as likely to be grown for their foliage than their flowers, since hybridizers like Dan Heims at Terra

Small-flowered alumroot, Heuchera micrantha *var.* diversifolia *'Palace Purple'*

Nova Nursery in Oregon have introduced an array of cultivars with colorful, boldly patterned leaves—and coauthored a book on the genus: *Heucheras and Heucherellas: Coral Bells and Foamy Bells* (2005).

Heucheras cultivated for flowers bear colorful bell- or funnel-shaped blooms, but foliage heucheras tend to have less conspicuous blossoms, and many gardeners cut them off because they detract from the leaves. Common names reflect this distinction: Heucheras grown for their flowers are commonly called coral, or matin, bells, while those grown for their foliage are typically referred to as alumroots or simply as heucheras.

HOW TO GROW

Start with container-grown plants when adding heucheras to your garden. Give them a spot that has rich, evenly moist but well-drained soil. For best results, look for a site that receives morning sun and afternoon shade. In areas with cool summers, coral bells (*H.* × *brizoides* and *H. sanguinea*) may tolerate all-day sun; elsewhere, they are best in a spot that

Foamy bell, × Heucherella *'Pink Frost'*

is shaded during the hottest part of the day. Foliage heucheras tolerate more shade than cultivars grown for their flowers, and a spot that is shaded in the afternoon will keep the leaves from bleaching out; deep shade will result in leggy plants and foliage that is less brightly colored, however.

Plant heucheras in spring. Dig a good dose of compost into the soil at planting time, which will improve drainage in clay soil and help hold moisture in sandy soil. Set plants with the crowns at the soil surface; water thoroughly; and mulch to keep the soil cool, moist, and weed free. Heucheras sometimes take a season or two to settle in after planting, so don't expect a spectacular show until the plants are established.

Feed heucheras in spring with a topdressing of compost or a balanced organic fertilizer. Renew the mulch around the plants as needed, and water during very dry weather. Remove spent flowers on coral bells to encourage more blooms, and remove tattered leaves to expose the new foliage growing below. Mulch heucheras—around, not over, the plants—after the ground freezes to prevent their heaving out of the soil. Gently press plants that do heave back into the ground and use mulch to cover their roots. Wait until spring to prune off damaged leaves.

Divide heucheras only to keep them vigorous—plants with crowns that are congested, woody, or have risen above the soil surface need to be divided—or to propagate. Divide in spring, discarding the old, woody growth at the center of the plant. It takes several years to produce a flowering plant from seeds.

Heucheras growing in well-drained soil have few problems.

WHAT TO GROW

Gardeners rarely grow species *Heuchera*, and in this heavily hybridized genus plant, names can be a bit confusing. You'll undoubtedly find cultivars listed

OTHER CHOICES

Foam flowers (*Tiarella* spp.) are another genus of heavily hybridized perennials native to North America. Allegheny foam flower (*T. cordifolia*) reaches 6 to 10 inches and forms 1- to 2-foot-wide clumps. It produces fluffy, white, spike-like racemes of flowers in spring that are held above the plant's attractive maplelike leaves. Cultivars include 'Brandywine', with red-veined leaves; 'Tiger Stripe', with red-veined leaves sporting a prominent central stripe; and 'Slickrock', with very deeply cut, dark green leaves. Wherry's foam flower (*T. wherryi*), also ranging from 6 to 10 inches tall, forms 6- to 10-inch-wide clumps with time. It, too, bears spikelike racemes of white or pink-tinged flowers in spring above clumps of attractive maplelike leaves. Cultivars include 'Oakleaf', with oakleaf-shaped leaves and pink flowers, and 'Dunvegan', with deeply lobed leaves topped by pink flowers. There also are loads of hybrids of unknown parentage to look for, including 'Butterfly Wings', with white flowers and lacy leaves veined with maroon; 'Iron Butterfly', with pink flowers and deeply lobed leaves marked with chocolate-maroon color; and 'Pirate's Patch', a long-blooming selection with white flowers and broad, maple-shaped leaves. Foam flowers are hardy in Zones 3 to 8. Plant them in a spot with partial to full shade and rich, evenly moist, well-drained soil.

Allegheny foam flower, Tiarella cordifolia *'Dark Star'*

under different species in different sources and will also see them listed without any species name at all. Don't worry about nomenclature; just pick the plants that appeal to you the most.

Coral bells produce an abundance of tiny ⅜- to ½-inch flowers that are showy despite their small size. Flowers are carried from late spring into early summer on 1- to 2½-foot stems above a 6-inch-tall mound of boldly veined, evergreen leaves, and come in shades of pink, coral, red, rose-red, and white. Cultivars are listed under two different species: *Heuchera sanguinea* and *H. × brizoides*. Cultivars currently thought to belong to *H. × brizoides* include 'Chatterbox', 'Firefly', 'June Bride', 'Mt. St. Helens', 'Raspberry Regal', and 'Rosamundi'. Better-known cultivars of *H. sanguinea* include 'Cherry Splash', 'Coral Cloud', 'Pluie de Feu', 'Splendens', and 'White Cloud'. All are hardy in Zones 4 to 8 and possibly to Zone 3 with winter protection.

Heucheras grown for foliage are listed under their cultivar names alone or as cultivars of American alumroot (*H. americana*) and small-flowered alumroot (*H. micrantha*). Hardy in Zones 4 to 8, these heucheras have leaves that are larger than those of coral bells—3 to 6 inches long—and are often shaped something like maple leaves. Plants form 1- to 1½-foot-tall mounds of leaves in a wide array of colors that includes green with gray and silver overtones and veins; purple-brown with metallic mottling; rose-burgundy with silver overtones and purple veins; and green with purple-red mottling. Plants continue producing new leaves all season. Color may fade during the heat of summer, but rich colors return when cool fall temperatures spark a new flush of growth. Foliage heucheras bear sprays of white, greenish white, or pinkish flowers in early summer. Cultivars include 'Palace Purple', 'Amber Waves', 'Amethyst Mist', 'Chocolate Veil', 'Chocolate Ruffles', 'Cappuccino', 'Frosted Violet', 'Ruby Veil', 'Dale's Strain', 'Garnet', 'Persian Carpet', 'Pewter Veil', 'Ruby Ruffles', and 'Velvet Knight'. And new cultivars just keep coming.

IN THE GARDEN

Use coral bells, or heucheras, to edge beds and walkways or arrange them in clumps or drifts at the front edge of a bed or border. Although coral bells are fairly tall in bloom, the flower stalks are airy and don't cover up plants that may be growing behind them. They are attractive additions for shaded rock gardens.

Combine foliage heucheras with ferns, yellow corydalis (*Corydalis lutea*), hostas, foam flowers (*Tiarella* spp.), lungworts (*Pulmonaria* spp.), hellebores, bleeding hearts (*Dicentra* spp.), and spring bulbs.

Hibiscus moscheutos

(hi-BISS-kus moe-SHOO-tos)

Common rose mallow

Mallow family, Malvaceae. Hardy perennial.

Also called swamp rose mallow, *Hibiscus moscheutos*, or common rose mallow, is a native North American wildflower that inhabits marshes and other areas with wet soil from Massachusetts, Michigan, and Ohio south. Fortunately for gardeners, these plants also thrive in ordinary, well-drained garden soil, and are among the largest-flowered perennials you can grow. While each flower opens for only one day, each stem produces an abundance of buds, and plants

Common rose mallow, Hibiscus moscheutos *'Intense Pink'*

OTHER CHOICES

Sunset hibiscus (*Abelmoschus manihot*) and annual musk mallow (*A. moschatus*) are tender perennials grown as annuals that are close relatives of perennial rose mallows. Both require full sun and rich, well-drained soil. Sunset hibiscus is 5 to 6 feet tall and bears pale yellow 5- to 6-inch-wide flowers with burgundy centers. Annual musk mallow reaches about 2 feet in the north, but it grows to 4 feet or more in areas with long, hot summers. Plants bear 3-inch-wide flowers in shades of pink, orange-red, and red. In areas with long growing seasons, roughly from Zone 5 north, sow them outdoors where the plants will bloom. (They take about three months to bloom from seeds.) Elsewhere, sow seeds in peat pots indoors eight to ten weeks before the last spring frost date.

bloom for a month or more. Flowers are funnel-shaped with five large, broad petals and a prominent central column consisting of the stamens and pistil. Blooms are borne singly or in clusters in early to midsummer, and the leaves of these shrub-size perennials are entirely to palmately lobed.

Robert Lemmon, remembering the plant from his childhood, put it more poetically in *Wildflowers of North America* (1961): "Imagine if you will, a vast sea of green marsh grass and Cat-tails rippling in a fresh August breeze. Floating a little above it is a second sea of pink—the untold millions of the Mallows. And infinitely far above all this the deep blue arch of the sky and a white fleet of slowly drifting clouds."

The genus was classified by Linnaeus and contains over 200 species. Linnaeus believed the plant to be of European origin and so used the name *moscheutos*, which he had learned from the writings of the Roman historian Pliny. The species was later changed to *H. oculiroseus* by Nathaniel Lord Britton, director of the New York Botanical Garden, but eventually it was returned to Linnaeus' classification.

HOW TO GROW

If you only want a plant or two—or one of the new cultivars—start with container-grown plants. Locate them in full sun, although they'll also grow in very light shade. Soil that is rich and evenly moist is ideal. Set the roots at least 3 inches below the soil surface so plants won't emerge too early in spring and

be killed by late frosts. Mulch to retain moisture and to protect roots over winter. Deadhead plants to prolong blooming, but wait until spring to cut back old stems. Prune plants in late spring to reduce height.

Established plants should be left in place to form broad clumps. They can be divided in spring if necessary, but they form tough, woody crowns with deep roots that are tough to dig. Sowing seeds is a safer option for propagating for the species and the strains that come true from seeds. Seeds sown indoors at least 12 weeks before the frost-free date should flower in their first year.

Japanese beetles can be a serious problem with rose mallow.

WHAT TO GROW

Common rose mallow ranges from 4 to 8 feet in height and forms clumps that are 3 feet or more across. Hardy in Zones 4 or 5 to 10, the species bears 8-inch-wide flowers that are white or pale pink with a ring of deep pink or purple at the base of the petals. Gardeners usually grow cultivars, which bloom in summer and come in shades of red, pink, or white. Disco Bell Series plants bear 9-inch-wide flowers on compact, 2- to 2½-foot-tall plants. 'Lady Baltimore' produces pink flowers, and 'Lord Baltimore' bears scarlet blooms. Both are 4-foot-tall plants and have 10-inch-wide flowers. Disco Bell Series cultivars and 'Lady Baltimore' cultivars come true from seed. Hybridizers have recently introduced a number of stunning new cultivars, including 4-foot-tall 'Kopper King', with foot-wide light pink flowers veined in red, each with a dark eye and dark purple foliage. 'Moy Grande' produces 1-foot-wide rosy red flowers on 5-foot plants, and 'Fantasia' bears 9-inch-wide rose-pink flowers on 3-foot plants.

Scarlet rose mallow (*H. coccineus*) is another North American native perennial that ranges from 5 to 10 feet in height and features lacy, deeply cut leaves with linear leaflets. It bears 6-inch-wide scarlet-red flowers from summer to fall and is hardy in Zones 6 to 11.

IN THE GARDEN

Use mallows in perennial gardens, where their giant-size flowers will add stunning summer color. They can also be planted in shrub borders, since established plants are shrub size, and are effective when used as accent plants against fences or hedges. The flowers are so large they almost seem artificial, but for eye-catching color, they're hard to beat.

Hosta

(*HOSS-tah*)

Hostas, plantain lilies

Lily family, Liliaceae. Hardy perennials.

Also sometimes called *funkia,* a word that reflects a previous botanical name for the genus, hostas hail from China, Japan, Korea, and eastern Russia. Some 70 species are found growing in woodlands, along streams, in mountain meadows, and even on rocky cliffs. In gardens today, hosta cultivars—thousands of them—plus the adaptable, easy-care nature of the plants themselves make these perennials hugely popular. That wasn't always the case. Hostas were known in Europe by the late 1700s but attracted little attention. Perhaps, some have suggested, it was because gardeners felt that any plant so easy to grow wasn't really worth growing.

The botanical name *Hosta* commemorates Nicholaus Thomas Host (1761–1834), an Austrian botanist and physician to the Emperor Frances II. Many new species began to reach Europe in the 1800s, including species found by the famed plant hunter Robert Fortune, and discoveries in the wild continue to be made. Breeders have been equally busy, especially the American Paul Aden who is responsible for many of the hostas we now grow. The garden value of hostas, he wrote in *The Hosta Book*

Hosta, Hosta *'Captain Kirk'*

(1990), "can be summed up with three words: foliage, useful and reliable."

True that is, for gardeners prize hostas more for their leaves than their flowers. Plants produce lush mounds of foliage that can be green, chartreuse, gray-green, blue-gray, or variegated. Clumps range from as small as 2 inches tall to more than 3 feet in height, and clumps of large cultivars can spread 5 feet. The individual leaves can be lance or heart shaped, ovate, or nearly round. Variegated hostas come in an amazing variety of patterns. Leaves may be green with white or yellow-green edges, chartreuse with dark green edges, or irregularly blotched with a

Hosta, Hosta *'Francee'*

Hosta, Hosta 'Brim Cup'

mix of white, cream, and dark green, for example. Leaf texture varies, too, and leaves may be smooth, deeply veined, heavily ribbed, or deeply puckered and corrugated.

Hostas bear trumpet-shaped flowers in white and shades of pale lavender, pinkish purple, or deep purple. Blooms are 1 to 6 inches long or longer and are borne in erect racemes that usually rise well above the mounds of foliage. Most are lovely, some fragrant, but with hostas, it's all about the leaves.

HOW TO GROW

Add hostas to your garden by purchasing plants, as most cultivars don't come true from seed. The best site for a hosta is one with moderately fertile, evenly moist soil that contains plenty of organic matter. One with morning sun and dappled shade for the rest of the day is close to perfect. Keep blue-leaved cultivars out of direct sun, as sun causes bleached-out yellow or white leaf spots; conversely, gold cultivars develop their best color in strong light—but not all-day sun. Established hostas tolerate pretty much anything except full sun with temperatures in the 90s, but giving them a little help in the way of organically rich soil, afternoon shade, and protection from

strong winds will make a big difference in the size of your plants.

Hostas can be planted anytime the soil isn't frozen, but early spring is usually the best time to move them into your garden. Dig organic matter such as compost into the soil at planting time to encourage deep, wide-spreading roots. If the container-grown hostas you are planting are large, consider dividing them before you set them in the garden, spacing the sections to form a drift. Keep in mind that hostas take a few years to become established and reach full size.

Hostas are tough, low-maintenance plants once in the garden. Keep them mulched with compost or chopped leaves to control weeds and help retain soil moisture. If slugs are a serious problem, don't mulch. But do feed plants each spring—either with a topdressing of compost or well-rotted manure or with an organic fertilizer. Watering enough to keep the soil evenly moist promotes the best growth, although plants are remarkably drought-resistant. If the ground becomes sun-baked and temperatures run very high, however, water. Cut flower stalks back to below the foliage before they set seed unless you want plants to self-sow; be warned that the offspring are unlikely to resemble the parent.

Hosta clumps can grow well for years without being divided, and if large plants and giant-size leaves are your objective, leave your shovel in the

Hosta, Hosta 'Banyai's Dancing Girl'

OTHER CHOICES

*A*ll manner of shade plants grow happily with hostas, but for an interesting foliage contrast, consider planting them with Solomon's seals (*Polygonatum* spp.), which produce unbranched erect or arching stems of leaves that have a feather- or plumelike habit. Plants bear small, pendant, bell-shaped or tubular flowers beneath the leaves in spring that are creamy colored or white with green markings. Look for Solomon's seal (*P. biflorum*), a North American native wildflower; hardy in Zones 3 to 9, it ranges from 1½ to as much as 7 feet tall—taller forms were once classified as *P. commutatum* and commonly called great Solomon's seal. Fragrant Solomon's seal (*P. odoratum*), hardy in Zones 4 to 8, is another good choice. It is 2½ to 3 feet tall and bears pendant, white, 1¼-inch-long flowers. The variegated form—*P. odoratum* var. *thunbergii* 'Variegatum'—is more popular than the species. It features green leaves striped at the edges with white and yellow fall foliage. Give Solomon's seals partial to full shade and rich, moist, well-drained soil.

Toad lilies (*Tricyrtis* spp.) are another great hosta companion; they also thrive in light to full shade in a site that has rich, moist, well-drained soil. These plants produce unusual flowers from summer to late fall and clumps of handsome foliage that features leaflets arranged in a featherlike fashion. Toad lily (*T. hirta*), hardy in Zones 4 to 9, is the most widely planted of the species. It is a 2- to 3-foot-tall perennial with clusters of white flowers that are spotted with purple. Its cultivar 'Variegata' bears leaves with yellow margins. 'Miyazaki', 3 feet tall, produces white flowers with lilac-purple spots.

Fragrant Solomon's seal, Polygonatum odoratum *var.* thunbergii *'Variegatum'*

tool shed. However, if a plant outgrows its space or you want more plants, divide clumps in spring before the leaves unfurl. Dig up as many of the fleshy, white, ropelike roots as possible, and use a sharp knife, spade, or saw to cut through the thick rhizome. You can also take a plant or two from an existing clump for propagation by simply slicing it off with a sharp spade. If you want to grow hostas from seeds, sow seeds in pots and set them in a protected location outdoors to overwinter.

Slugs and snails chew holes in large leaves and can devour small plants altogether. Generally, hostas with leaves that have a thick, heavy substance are more resistant. Voles and other rodents like chomping on hosta crowns and roots over the winter. Not mulching may help reduce both problems, as will cutting back all the frost-killed leaves in fall.

WHAT TO GROW

When you are picking out hostas, it pays to read labels and look carefully at plants before you buy. Hostas are long-lived plants and good garden investments. Don't hesitate to pay a bit more for well-grown plants. They'll grow faster than sickly, poorly cared-for plants offered by bargain-basement outfits, and it's wise to invest a little extra to buy top-notch cultivars. When shopping, compare the size of the plants in the pots. Hostas differ in the speed at which they grow, and fast-growing cultivars will fill out pots more quickly and thus tend to be less expensive than slow-growing ones. A pot that contains two or more clumps is a better buy than one that contains a single clump.

Keep in mind that while hostas grow well in pots, foliage colors and patterns are rarely as attractive as they are when plants are grown in good garden soil. Large hostas, especially, don't produce full-size leaves when grown in containers. Read the descriptions on plant labels to determine the size at maturity. Nearly all hostas are hardy in Zones 3 to 7, but some also grow in Zones 8 and 9 if given adequate shade and plenty of water in the summer.

Giant-size hostas produce foliage mounds that reach 30 to 36 inches—taller in rich, moist soil—and make handsome, shrub-size statements in the garden. Established clumps are easily one-and-one-half to two times as wide as they are tall. Classic cultivars, which bear pale lavender flowers in summer unless otherwise noted, include 'Blue Angel', with blue-gray, corrugated leaves and white flowers in mid-summer; 'Blue Umbrellas', with puckered, blue to blue-green leaves that turn green by midsummer; 'Krossa Regal', with vase-shaped clumps of ribbed, powdery blue-gray to gray-green leaves that turn green by midsummer; 'Regal Splendor', with ribbed blue-gray leaves variegated with creamy white; 'Sagae' (formerly *H. fluctuans* 'Variegata'), with smooth, blue-gray leaves edged in creamy yellow and white flowers in mid- to late summer; *H. sieboldiana* 'Elegans', with puckered and corrugated, blue-gray-green leaves and white early summer flowers; and 'Sum and Substance', with yellow-green to yellow leaves.

There are loads of medium-size hostas—with foliage mounds from 1 to 2 feet tall—in all manner of colors and patterns and white or pale lavender flowers. Some of the best with blue-green leaves include 'Blue Cadet', 'Blue Wedgewood', 'Halcyon', and 'Love Pat'. Variegated cultivars include 'Brim Cup', with puckered, cupped dark green, white-margined leaves; 'Golden Tiara', with green leaves irregularly margined in gold and showy purple flowers; 'Gold Standard', with golden leaves edged in dark green; *H. montana* 'Aureomarginata', with ribbed, dark green leaves patterned with irregular yellow margins; and 'Wide Brim', with wide creamy white margins. 'Sun Power' and 'Zounds' feature yellow-green leaves. 'Great Expectations' is a fabulous cultivar with yellow leaves and wide blue-green edges. The centers of the leaves turn white by midsummer on this slow-growing cultivar. 'June', with creamy yellow leaves edged in green and blue-green, is another eye-catching cultivar.

Low-growing hostas with foliage that is under 1 foot in height are perfect for edging beds and walkways. Consider 2-inch-tall, green-leaved 'Tiny Tears'; 'Kabitan', with lance-shaped, yellow leaves edged in dark green; 'Ginkgo Craig', with lance-shaped, dark green leaves edged in white; 'Gold Edger', with heart-shaped, chartreuse leaves; and *H. venusta*, with green, heart-shaped leaves in 4-inch-tall clumps and pretty lavender flowers in summer.

There also are hostas that produce fragrant flowers, and these are wonderful grown along a pathway where their scent can be enjoyed. They also make outstanding cut flowers. Look for white-flowered *Hosta plantaginea*, sometimes called August lily, and its cultivars 'Aphrodite' and 'Royal Standard'. Other fragrant-flowered hybrids include 'Fragrant Bouquet', 'Honeybells', 'So Sweet', and 'Summer Fragrance'.

IN THE GARDEN

Hostas are handsome combined with nearly any shade plants. Consider joining them with ferns, bleeding hearts (*Dicentra* spp.), hellebores (*Helleborus* spp.), lungworts (*Pulmonaria* spp.), and epimediums. They also are effective when several cultivars with different foliage patterns are planted together—a blue-green-leaved selection with one that has yellow leaves with blue-green margins, for example. Plant daffodils and other hardy spring bulbs around hosta clumps. As the hosta foliage emerges, it will hide the unattractive ripening bulb foliage. Hostas also make excellent ground covers and specimen plants. Since they thrive in moist soil, they can be planted along stream banks, bogs, and ponds.

Hyacinthus orientalis

(hi-ah-SIN-thus or-ee-en-TALL-iss)

Common hyacinth, Dutch hyacinth

Lily family, Liliaceae. Hardy bulb.

Along with daffodils and tulips, hyacinths are a sign of spring whether the flowers are in gardens or forced indoors in pots. While the species *H. orientalis* bears loose racemes of very fragrant flowers, gardeners are more familiar with hybrid offerings that produce densely packed racemes of tubular- to bell-shaped flowers. Although they are commonly called Dutch hyacinths, these plants are native to the Middle East, not Holland. The botanical name is from a Greek name used by Homer. Classical mythology has it that hyacinths sprung from the blood of Hyacinthus, a youth accidentally killed by Apollo. John Milton repeated the myth in "On the Death of a Fair Infant Dying of a Cough" (1626), when he wrote that Apollo "transformed him into a purple flower."

The popularity of the hyacinth myth likely is responsible for the plant's representing sorrow in the

Dutch hyacinth, Hyacinthus orientalis *'Bismarck'*

Victorian language of flowers, but botanists have established that the legendary flower created by the boy's blood was probably a gladiolus, not a hyacinth. As the saying goes, however, never let the truth get in the way of a good story.

Dutch hyacinths, which were planted in the botanical garden at Padua, the first botanical garden in Europe (founded in 1543), are prized for their intensely fragrant blossoms. The familiar erect, football-shaped trusses of flowers come in shades of pink, lilac-blue, violet, yellow, and white. Blooms are carried on thick stalks, 8 to 12 inches tall, that emerge from strap-shaped basal leaves. The individual flowers have six petal-like tepals, three true petals and three sepals. The tepals form a tube that opens with flaring tips that curve backward.

Although the Dutch can't claim the hyacinth as a native, they can take the lion's share of credit for breeding new cultivars—2,000 varieties by 1733—and for their popularity throughout the world. Undoubtedly it was a Dutch cultivar that led poet Percy Bysshe Shelley to observe the flower "flung from its bells a sweet peal anew / Of music so delicate, soft, and intense, / It was felt like an odour within the sense."

HOW TO GROW

Purchase hyacinth bulbs in fall, either at your local garden center or by mail. Set the bulbs in full sun or light shade in a well-drained site with average to rich soil, and plant at a depth of 4 to 5 inches. Hyacinths are hardy in Zones 5 to 9, but they can be grown in Zones 3 and 4 if planted in well-drained soil at a depth of 6 to 8 inches and mulched heavily.

Hyacinths produce the largest flowers—the classic, dense, oval-shaped clusters of blooms—their first spring in the garden. In subsequent years, as the plants produce offsets, they will produce smaller, looser spikes of flowers. If you want formal, upright, oval clusters, replace bulbs annually. However, many gardeners prefer the looser, more natural looking flowers. A spring topdressing, just as the leaves emerge, with well-rotted manure or a balanced organic fertilizer helps keep next year's blooms large. Propagate hyacinths by digging and separating the offsets in summer, just as the leaves die down.

WHAT TO GROW

Hundreds of hyacinth cultivars are available, nearly all with extremely fragrant flowers. 'Blue Jacket' bears dark violet-blue blooms; 'Peter Stuyvesant', violet and violet-blue flowers; and 'Delft Blue', pale lilac-blue. 'Carnegie' has creamy white blooms and 'White Pearl', white ones. 'City of Haarlem' is primrose yellow turning to creamy white; 'Yellow Queen' is a darker butter yellow; 'Gipsy Queen' is coral with salmon and peach; 'Jan Bos' bears pinkish red flowers; the blooms of 'Woodstock' are beet red; 'Lady Derby' is pale pink; 'Pink Pearl' is deep pink with pale pink edges; and 'Rosette' is a double-flowered pink. The list goes on and on, with new names added every year.

IN THE GARDEN

In addition to enjoying forced plants indoors, use hyacinths to fill beds with color and fragrance in spring. They can be planted among hostas, low-growing perennials, and also cool-weather annuals like pansies. Be sure to use them along walkways and near sitting areas where their fragrance can be enjoyed. They also make good cut flowers. When the flowers are almost fully open, cut the stems with a sharp knife where they emerge from the ground. Split the base of the stem to maximize water uptake.

Candytuft, Iberis sempervirens

Iberis

(eye-BEER-iss)

Candytufts

Mustard family, Brassicaceae.
Hardy perennials, annuals.

Cross-shaped, four-petaled blooms mark *Iberis* species as members of the mustard family, making them kin to plants more commonly found in vegetable gardens, such as cabbage, brussels sprouts, and broccoli. Like all members of the mustard family, candytufts bear their tiny four-sepaled flowers in terminal clusters. Both the name *Iberis* and the common name Spanish tufts are recognition of the fact that most of the 20 species in the genus hail from Spain, or Iberia. Candytuft, its best-known common name, also refers to a place. The herbalist John Gerard, probably the first to grow candytuft in England, obtained seeds from plants growing along "the highwaie sides in Crete or Candia; in Spain and Italie." An explanation of the common name "Billy come home soon" has yet to be found.

Candytuft got to this continent in the late 1600s and, not surprisingly, started out as an edging plant. According to most authorities, the first planting was in the gardens of the Governor's Palace in Williamsburg, Virginia. Jean, Lady Skipwith, a southern Virginia gardener with resources as large as her enthusiasm for flowers, grew it at her plantation in the late 1700s, and soon after both perennial and annual candytufts became common fare in seed-sellers' inventories. It was the beginning of turning this dainty cousin of the brussels sprout into the flower that edges millions of American gardens.

HOW TO GROW

Candytufts do best in full sun and will grow in any average, well-drained soil. All species like evenly moist soil, but wet soil, especially in winter, spells root rot and death for perennial candytufts. Add perennial candytufts to your garden by purchasing plants. All you need to grow a crop of annual candytuft is a packet of seeds or purchase packs of plants in spring.

Perennial candytufts require little attention after they've been planted in either spring or fall. They form broad mounds, so space plants at least a foot apart. After plants flower in spring, cut them back by one-half to remove spent blooms and encourage new growth. (Hedge shears make the job go quickly.) Prune off any winter damage in early spring. Plants don't need dividing unless they overrun their space, but division is an easy way to propagate plants. Dig plants immediately after they finish flowering. You also can look for stems that have rooted where they touched the ground, then cut them off the parent plant. Or propagate from cuttings. Growing perennial candytuft from seed is extremely slow.

Annual candytufts like sun but need afternoon shade in regions where summers are hot. They also are best in soil with a neutral to alkaline pH and can be pruned back lightly after they flower to encourage new buds. Remove plants if their foliage begins to brown from summer's heat. To grow plants, sow seed in a prepared seedbed outdoors after danger of frost has passed. Or, since seedlings do not transplant

Globe candytuft, Iberis umbellata *'Fantasia'*

well, sow seeds indoors in individual pots six to eight weeks before the last spring frost date. For continuous bloom, sow new crops every two weeks until midsummer. Plants sometimes self-sow in mild climates.

Candytufts occasionally attract caterpillars.

WHAT TO GROW

Perennial candytuft (*I. sempervirens*) is the best-known member of this genus. Its flat-topped, brilliant white blooms are a sure a sign of spring. Also called evergreen candytuft, this species bears dark green, narrow, almost needlelike leaves that set off the clusters of flowers perfectly. Hardy from Zones 3 to 9, perennial candytuft is actually a subshrub that has woody stems and ranges from 6 to 12 inches tall and spreads to 2 feet or more across. 'Little Gem' is a dwarf cultivar from 5 to 8 inches tall. 'Autumn Beauty' and 'Autumn Snow' bloom in spring and again in fall on 8- to 10-inch plants. Rock candytuft (*I. saxatilis*), hardy from Zones 2 to 7, bears similar rounded clusters of flowers on 3- to 6-inch-tall plants that also are evergreen.

Rocket candytuft (*I. amara*) is a 6- to 18-inch-tall, branching annual with mildly fragrant, 4- to 6-inch-tall flower clusters in white to pale lilac-white. 'Giant White Hyacinth Flowered' features good fragrance and is an especially good cut flower. Annual globe candytuft (*I. umbellata*), from 6 to 12 inches tall, bears flattened, 2-inch-wide clusters of fragrant flowers in summer in shades of white, pink, lilac, purple, and red. 'Flash Mix' plants come in an especially wide range of colors.

IN THE GARDEN

Annual candytufts make attractive fillers when planted among perennials and annuals in beds and borders. They also can be added to containers and make fine cut flowers. Use perennial candytufts as edging plants along the front of beds or borders as well as along terraces and walkways.

They make good ground covers and are excellent additions to rock gardens or raised beds, where they can be allowed to cascade over rocks, low walls, or bed edges. Combine them with spring-blooming bulbs such as daffodils and tulips as well as moss phlox (*Phlox subulata*) and columbines (*Aquilegia* spp.). Repeat-blooming candytufts are handsome in the fall garden as well, and the evergreen foliage contributes winter color anywhere the plants are grown.

Impatiens

(im-PAY-shens)

Impatiens, garden balsam

Balsam family, Balsaminaceae.
Tender perennials, annuals.

Garden impatiens, Impatiens walleriana '*Accent Midnight Rose*'

These popular garden flowers are related to jewel-weed or touch-me-not (*I. capensis*), a native weed or wildflower, depending on how you look at it, that grows in damp, shady spots throughout much of North America. Like all impatiens, it bears spurred flowers followed by seed capsules that, once ripe, explode and fling their seeds in all directions at the slightest touch. The botanical name for this genus refers to that characteristic. It's from the Latin word *impatiens*, meaning "impatient." The characteristic also explains the common name touch-me-not.

Impatiens have brittle, succulent stems and fleshy leaves. The five-petaled flowers are asymmetrical: The uppermost petal is not attached to the other two, while the four lower petals are fused together to form two lobed pairs. Cultivated impatiens usually bear flat single blooms or rounded double ones, although breeders have now added roselike blossoms to the repertoire. Whatever their flower form, most gardeners would argue that their greatest virtue is the ability to stay in flower from spring until the first frost.

Three types of impatiens are popular in today's gardens: garden impatiens, busy Lizzie, or patience plant (*I. walleriana*); New Guinea impatiens; and garden balsam (*I. balsamina*). Garden balsam was the first of the three to be planted in North American gardens, arriving here in the 17th century but not widely grown until the 18th. Thomas Jefferson, who knew 'Double Balsam' from his childhood, ordered it from the Philadelphia nurseryman Bernard McMahon in 1812 to grow at Monticello. McMahon not only sent Jefferson seeds of 'Double Balsam', which is described as one of the "more valuable and curious sorts of tender annuals," but also sent detailed instructions on how to grow plants in a hot bed heated by decomposing manure.

HOW TO GROW

All impatiens prefer soil that is rich, evenly moist, and well drained. Give garden impatiens a spot in partial to full shade; New Guinea impatiens are best in full sun to very light shade; and garden balsam is best in light to partial shade.

Add impatiens to your garden by purchasing bedding or container-grown plants. They are easy from seeds as well, although many New Guinea impatiens hybrids must be propagated asexually by cuttings. Sow seeds indoors eight to ten weeks before the last spring frost date. Light aids germination, so just press the seeds onto the soil surface. Since damping-off can be a problem, water seedlings from below. Transplant these warm-weather flowers to the garden several weeks after the last spring frost date, once night temperatures remain above 50°F.

While garden balsam is a true annual, garden impatiens and New Guinea impatiens are both tender perennials that are easy to propagate from cuttings taken in spring or summer. Stem cuttings made in late summer are an easy way to bring plants indoors for overwintering. Garden impatiens often root in water.

Impatiens may be bothered by aphids and mites; poor growing conditions encourage mold and wilt diseases.

WHAT TO GROW

Best known as an annual bedding plant, garden impatiens (*I. walleriana*) is a tender perennial ranging from 6 inches to 2 feet tall. Plants have rounded to lance-shaped green leaves that may be flushed with bronze. Gardeners love them because they bear showy, flat-faced, single or double flowers that range from about 1 to 2½ inches across, and they bloom from summer to frost, even in full shade. Flowers come in a wide range of colors, including pale to rich magenta pink, lavender, rose, white, salmon, red, and orange-red. Bicolors also are available. 'Super Elfin Mix' plants are 10 to 12 inches tall; 'Dazzler Mix' plants reach about 6 inches. 'Fanciful Mix Improved' are 12-inch plants that produce flowers with an extra frill of petals in the center, making them look double. Mini-Hawaiian Series plants are dwarf, well-branched plants that reach about 6 inches and bear an abundance of small, 1-inch flowers. New cultivars appear every spring.

Garden balsam (*I. balsamina*), from 1 to 2½ feet tall, is an old-fashioned annual that produces single or double flowers in the leaf axils along the main stem of the plant from summer to early fall. Flowers come in shades of pink, white, red, and purple. 'Tom Thumb Mix' plants are 8 to 12 inches tall. 'Camellia Flowered Mix' yields 2-foot, double-flowered plants.

New Guinea hybrid impatiens were developed by crossing various species of impatiens from New Guinea, including *I. schlecteri*. They are 12- to 14-inch plants with lance-shaped leaves that can be green, bronze, or variegated with yellow or cream. Flat-faced, 2- to 2½-inch-wide flowers appear from summer to frost in shades of rose, red, salmon, lilac-pink, and white. Many cultivars are propagated from cuttings, but 'Jungle Rain Mix', 'Rainforest Exotic Mix', and 'Spectra Mix' are strains that come true from seeds.

IN THE GARDEN

Impatiens make handsome temporary ground covers in shade gardens. They also can be planted among shade-loving perennials such as hostas to bring summer-long color to shady flower beds. Plant them in large drifts and let them fill in, or use them as edging plants along walkways, terraces, or at the front of a bed or border. Impatiens—especially dwarf selections—also make handsome additions to container plantings. Some species, particularly garden balsam (*I. balsamma*), self-sow. Hummingbirds, butterflies, and other beneficials visit many species of impatiens.

Ipomoea

(eye-poe-MEE-ah)

Morning glories

Morning glory family, Convolvulaceae.
Tender perennials, annuals.

The best-known members of this genus are the tender twining vines commonly called morning glories. These old-fashioned plants produce trumpet-shaped blooms in shades of violet, purple, true blue, pink, red, and white, often with a contrasting-colored throat. Blooms may be solitary, but most morning glories produce clusters of flowers. A few plants belonging to *Ipomoea* have racemes of narrow, tubular blooms.

The common name morning glory refers to the fact that many of these popular plants produce flowers that are only open in the morning. Most are twining climbers—the botanical name is from the Greek *ips*, "worm," and *homoios*, "resembling"—but the genus also contains nonclimbing annuals and perennials along with a few shrubs and trees. One of the

OTHER CHOICES

*I*f you have a place in your garden for morning glories, you probably have room for other tender perennial or annual vines. The species listed here require growing conditions similar to those morning glories need to make them happy. They also need a trellis to climb on. Consider combining more than one species on a trellis or other support. You'll double the flowers and your enjoyment of them.

Balloon vine (*Cardiospermum halicacabum*). Also called love-in-a-puff, this tender perennial vine reaches about 12 feet in a single season and bears fernlike leaves and small, greenish white flowers. The flowers are followed by interesting inflated seedpods that ripen to brown.

Black-eyed Susan vine (*Thunbergia alata*). A tender perennial that grows to about 8 feet, this species bears heart-shaped to triangular leaves and 1½-inch trumpet-shaped flowers that are orange, orange-yellow, or creamy white with a dark eye.

Cup-and-saucer vine (*Cobaea scandens*). Also called cathedral bells, this tender perennial can climb to 40 feet in frost-free areas. It has feather-like leaves and fragrant, bell-shaped flowers. Each flower (the cup) has a ruffled

green calyx (the saucer) at the base. Flowers are greenish white, aging to purple. 'Alba' bears flowers that stay greenish white.

Hyacinth bean (*Lablab purpureus*). A tender perennial or annual, hyacinth bean reaches 6 to 20 feet and is grown for both flowers and fruit. The pinkish purple pealike flowers are ½ to 1 inch long and are followed by glossy, maroon-purple seedpods.

Purple bell vine (*Rhodochiton atrosanguineum*). Another tender perennial, this species reaches about 10 feet in a single season and produces maroon-purple flowers that are 1¾ inches long. Flowers are pendant and have a long tube, which is the "clapper" while a showy calyx in mauve-pink forms the bell.

Scarlet runner bean (*Phaseolus coccineus*). A tender perennial that grows to about 12 feet in a single season, scarlet runner bean bears loose racemes of scarlet flowers in summer, which are followed by edible beans. 'Alba' bears white flowers.

Sweet pea (*Lathyrus odoratus*). Climbing sweet peas are annuals that can reach 6 to 8 feet and bear showy 1½- to 2-inch flowers in shades of lavender, rose-pink, purple-pink, white, and purple. Blooms may or may not be fragrant—older cultivars are more likely to be scented, since in recent years hybridizers have concentrated on other characteristics, such as color and flower form. 'Old Spice Mix' and 'Painted Lady' are two older, fragrant cultivars that climb to about 6 feet.

Black-eyed Susan vine, Thunbergia alata

Hyacinth bean, Lablab purpureus

Sweet pea, Lathyrus odoratus 'Royal Navy Blue'

Blue dawn flower, Ipomoea indica

best-known plants that belongs here is sweet potato (*I. batatas*), a nutritious root crop that thrives in regions with long, hot summers. Flower gardeners have recently started growing cultivars of this popular vegetable garden plant in flower beds: Cultivars like 'Blackie', with purple-black leaves, and 'Margarita', with chartreuse foliage, are handsome in containers or scrambling among flowers in the garden.

Although many morning glories are natives of Mexico and Central America, most species traveled to Europe before they made their way to North America. Thomas Jefferson didn't record growing any of the annual morning glories, but he did send his daughters seeds for cypress vine (*I. quamoclit*), a morning glory cousin, with instructions that they be planted "in boxes in the window." Of course Jefferson lived too early to know the morning glories we grow today. Certainly he would have wanted to grow 'Heavenly Blue', of which the English garden authority Gertrude Jekyll wrote, "there is no lovelier or purer blue."

HOW TO GROW

Give morning glories a site in full sun—some shade during the hottest part of the day in the warmest regions—that has average, evenly moist, well-drained soil. A support such as strings or a trellis on which to climb is also a must. (Install supports before you sow seeds or set out plants.) Training plants to grow up and onto shrubs is another option, one that can turn an all-green shrub into a colorful focal point in summer. Morning glories grow more up than out, so you'll want to plant several in order to have a good show.

In most cases, you'll have to start your own seeds, although some garden centers now offer seedlings in pots or market packs. Either sow seeds outdoors after the last frost, or, for a head start, sow seeds indoors in individual pots six to eight weeks before the frost-free date. Even seedlings need something to climb, so insert a thin stake in each pot before you sow the seeds. Morning glory seeds are hard; soak them in water over night before planting. Once the seeds sprout, thin to one plant per pot to avoid plants becoming entangled. Move plants to the garden a couple of weeks after the danger of frost is past, when temperatures are reliably above 45°F and the ground has warmed.

Plants sometimes attract Japanese beetles.

WHAT TO GROW

Three species are commonly called morning glories—*I. purpurea*, *I. nil*, and *I. tricolor*—and for the most part gardeners grow cultivars or hybrids of these species. *I. purpurea* is a 6- to 10-foot annual that has broad, rounded to lobed leaves and trumpet-shaped, 2½-inch-wide, white-throated flowers in summer in shades of blue, purple-blue, pink, red, and white; white flowers with stripes of color also are available.

Japanese morning glory. *I. nil* is an annual or short-lived, tender perennial that can grow to 15 feet in a single season. It has ovate, sometimes lobed, leaves and bears 2- to 4-inch-wide, white-tubed flowers from midsummer to fall in shades of pale to deep blue, plus red, purple, or white. 'Early Call Mix' is fast from seeds and a good choice for areas with short growing seasons. Platycodon Series bears purple, red, or white single or semidouble flowers. 'Chocolate' bears pale red-brown flowers. 'Scarlett O'Hara', a long-time favorite, bears red flowers.

Morning glory. *I. tricolor* is a vigorous annual or short-lived tender perennial that reaches 10 to 12 feet in a season. It bears 3-inch-wide flowers with white throats in shades from pale blue to purple

Spanish flag, Ipomoea lobata

season. It has lacy, deeply cut leaves and scarlet, ¾-inch-wide flowers in summer.

One other morning glory isn't actually an *Ipomoea:* Dwarf morning glory (*Convolvulus tricolor*) is a closely related bushy annual or tender perennial that has funnel-shaped, morning-glory-type flowers. Plants range from 12 to 16 inches tall and produce funnel-shaped, 1½-inch-wide flowers that are deep blue with yellow and white in the centers.

IN THE GARDEN

Use *Ipomoea* species to climb trellises or deck railings, cover shrubs, or to create screens. Some species do well in containers and hanging baskets. Hummingbirds are attracted to the blooms, especially red-flowered species and cultivars.

in summer. Popular 'Heavenly Blue' bears sky blue flowers with white throats. 'Crimson Rambler' bears red flowers with white throats; 'Flying Saucers' produces flowers marked with blue and white; and 'Pearly Gates' has white flowers.

Blue dawn flower. *I. indica* is a tender perennial with trilobed, dark green leaves that produces clusters of five blue and purple-blue flowers that fade to pink; plants grow rapidly and can be invasive in wet sites. It's ideal for covering large areas and flowers the first year from seed. Blue dawn flower often is sold under its former name *I. acuminata.*

Moonflower. *I. alba* bears giant-size morning-glory-type trumpets with a twist. Not only do the flowers open at dusk instead of dawn, but they also are very fragrant. Moonflower is a tender perennial climber that can reach 15 feet in a single season and bears large, rounded leaves with heart-shaped bases. The lemony scented flowers are 5½ inches wide and appear from midsummer to frost.

Spanish flag or exotic love. *I. lobata* is a tender perennial that reaches 6 to 15 feet in a single summer. Plants bear lobed leaves and showy, one-sided racemes of narrow, tubular flowers that are ½ to ¾ inches long. The flower buds and flowers are red at first, but they turn orange, yellow, then cream as they age.

Cardinal climber. *I.* × *multifida* is a 3- to 6-foot annual climber with deeply lobed leaves and brilliant red 1-inch-wide flowers that have a slender tube with a flared and flattened face.

Cypress vine or star glory. (*I. quamoclit*) is an annual that ranges from 6 to 20 feet in a single

Iris

(EYE-riss)

Irises, flags

Iris family, Iridaceae. Hardy perennials, bulbs.

Vast and variable, this genus contains about 300 species and tens of thousands of cultivars—from dainty spring-blooming bulbs to the tough bearded irises that inhabit gardens across North America. A genus exclusively of the Northern Hemisphere, the botanical name honors the Greek goddess Iris, who created the rainbow bridge connecting heaven and earth. In thanks for the rainbow, she was given a magic potion that when poured on the earth would produce a flower that bloomed in all the colors of the rainbow. So eager to collect her reward, Iris left a few drops of potion in the vial. And that explains why there is an iris of every color but true red.

Irises have been cultivated for at least 4,000 years. They appear in Cretan art and were used by kings and priests of that ancient country. Egyptians, Greeks, and Romans used orris, the dried iris rhizome of several species, to treat coughs, wounds, fevers, chills, and other complaints, as did the English beginning in the Middle Ages. An oil made from rhizomes and flowers, herbalist John Gerard wrote, "profiteth much to strengthen the sinewes and joynts." Iris rhizomes also contain the volatile oil irone, which smells of violets and still is used in perfume-making. For Native North Americans, blue flag (*I. versicolor*) was a vital medicinal plant. Blue flag continues to be used in homeopathic medicine, although it now comes with the warning "considered poisonous."

Gardeners, of course, treasure irises for their showy flowers. These esteemed garden residents are easy to grow, too, and there are irises for nearly any spot in the garden, from sunny, sharply drained rock gardens to shaded boggy plantings and even standing water. All irises bear six-petaled flowers that have three standards, petals that point up or out, and three falls, petals that point out or down. The flowers are usually borne in small clusters and the buds open in succession. Plants grow from rhizomes or bulbs, and the foliage is sword-shaped, strap-shaped, or grassy. Iris leaves typically overlap at their base, then spread out like a fan.

HOW TO GROW

Nearly all irises need full sun to bloom well. Feed herbaceous perennial irises—those that do not grow from bulbs—with a liquid fertilizer that is not high in nitrogen in early spring as growth begins. Siberian and Japanese irises benefit from a second feeding just after they finish flowering. Feed bulbous species once a year as the flowers fade. Remove spent iris flowers to prevent seed production and keep the plants attractive.

Division is the easiest way to propagate most irises, and most irises that grow from rhizomes need to be divided regularly. Cut the foliage back by about

Orris, Iris × germanica *var.* florentina

Bearded iris, Iris 'Edith Wolford'

half when dividing clump formers like Siberian or Japanese irises so that you can see the crown of the plant clearly. Then dig the clumps, cut them apart with a knife or sharp spade, and replant. Divisions should have four to six fans of leaves each. Do not let the roots dry out before replanting, and set the rhizomes of clump formers about 1 inch under the soil surface.

Bearded irises need to be divided every three or four years to remain vigorous. Dig clumps after they flower, at least two months before the first frost date. Cut the rhizomes into pieces that have at least one fan of leaves. Discard spongy, old rhizomes along with any that are infested with borer larvae, or that smell or are slimy, two signs of bacterial soft rot. Replant healthy rhizomes immediately and keep watered for a week if there is no rain.

Japanese iris, Iris ensata *'Caprician Butterfly'*

Dutch iris, Iris *xiphium hybrid*

To propagate bulbous species, separate and replant the small bulblets. If you want to try growing iris from seeds—remember that cultivars do not come true—soak seeds in water for 24 hours before planting. Sow seeds in fall in pots and set them outdoors in a shady, protected location to overwinter. Growing iris from seeds is both difficult and slow.

Most iris are relatively immune from diseases and pests. Not the bearded iris. It is troubled often by borers and the bacterial soft rot that invades the rhizome damaged by the borers. Good site selection—full sun and well-drained soil—and shallow rhizome planting help prevent problems with bearded types, as does an annual fall cleanup.

WHAT TO GROW

In general, irises bloom for a relatively short time, but by planting several species, you can have them in flower from late winter through midsummer. Here's a rundown of major types you'll have to choose from.

Bearded irises. These are hybrids with *I. germanica* making a major contribution to the "bloodline." All bearded irises have fuzzy beards at the top of each fall. Although tall-bearded irises, which range from 1½ to nearly 3 feet, are the most popular, there also are dwarf types. Botanists and iris enthusiasts recognize six height categories. Flowers range from 1 to 3 inches for dwarf and miniature cultivars and 4 to 8 inches across for intermediate and tall beardeds. While tall beardeds are most commonly available, it's worth searching out cultivars of some of the smaller types, since they bloom at slightly different times. Miniature dwarf beardeds bloom first in spring, followed by standard dwarf bearded cultivars, then intermediate bearded irises, and finally tall bearded irises. There are thousands of cultivars from which to choose, and more are introduced every year. Flowers come in colors from white and pale yellow, through peach, pink, raspberry, bronze-red, lilac, purple, and violet-blue to chocolate brown and red-black. The falls and standards may be the same color, contrasting solid colors, or have margins or mottling in contrasting colors—in purple and white, for example. The beards can be the same color as the falls or a contrasting hue. Many cultivars are fragrant. Select colors you like, or look for award-winning cultivars. These winners of the American Iris Society's Dykes Medal are all good choices: 'Beverly Sills', 'Bride's Halo', 'Dusky Challenger', 'Edith Wolford', 'Honky Tonk Blues', 'Jessy's Song', 'Silverado', and 'Victoria Falls'.

Siberian iris, Iris sibirica 'Pink Haze'

Yellow flag, Iris pseudacorus

Bearded irises are plants for full sun and well-drained soil that has a near-neutral pH. Hardy in Zones 3 to 9, they sprout from thick, fleshy rhizomes that grow on or near the soil surface. Plant bearded irises in midsummer to early fall. Loosen the soil at planting time, and work in enough compost or other organic matter to ensure good drainage. Soil that is too rich, especially in nitrogen, produces lush foliage but few flowers. Set the rhizomes so their tops are just above the soil surface. Rhizomes planted too deeply are likely to rot. Water plants regularly until they become established. Established plants are quite drought tolerant and should not be mulched, as it encourages rot. Remove dead and dying leaves. Tall cultivars may need staking. To help control iris borers, cut back the old foliage and destroy it in late fall. Also rake up any debris around the plants that may harbor the overwintering pupae. Divide bearded irises after they finish flowering in midsummer.

There also are bearded irises that bloom twice, once in early summer and again in fall, and many are fragrant. Good cultivars include the fragrant purple 'Autumn Bugler'; yellow 'Baby Blessed'; yellow 'Corn Harvest'; fragrant white 'Immortality'; wine purple 'Mulberry'; and light blue 'Sugar Blues'. Water rebloomers deeply if the weather is dry in mid- to late summer, and feed them in spring and again in midsummer.

Irises for sun. In addition to bearded irises, several other species are ideal for spots in full sun. The species listed here also do well with afternoon shade and thrive in rich, well-drained soil that remains evenly moist.

Japanese iris (*I. ensata*), hardy in Zones 3 or 4 to 9, produces clumps of grasslike leaves topped by round, flattened 4- to 8-inch flowers in early to midsummer. Plants are 2 to 2½ feet tall. Flowers can be single or double. They have large, showy falls, with standards that point downward and come in violet-blue, purple, lavender-blue, white, rose-pink, and wine-red. Japanese irises need very rich acid soil—pH 5.5 to 6.5—that is constantly moist in spring and summer when they are in active growth but drier in winter. Divide Japanese irises in early spring or early fall every three or four years. Provide a winter mulch in Zones 3 and 4.

Siberian iris (*I. sibirica*), hardy in Zones 2 to 9, is another beardless iris with 3-inch flowers in white, yellow, and shades of blue and violet. Plants range from 1 to 3 feet and form handsome clumps of grassy leaves. They'll grow in full sun to light shade, although the foliage may be floppy in shade and flowering will be reduced. Siberian irises thrive in evenly moist, organically rich soil. They don't need to be divided until the clumps stop flowering or they die out in the center. Dig and divide in early spring or early fall. Both Japanese and Siberian iris are pest and disease resistant. Some good Siberians are 'Butter and Sugar' (yellow and white flowers), 'Caesar's Brother' (violet), 'Dewful' (blue), 'Baby Sister' (light blue and white), 'Eric the Red' (wine purple), 'Pink Haze', and 'Ruffled Velvet' (violet).

Roof iris (*I. tectorum*), hardy in Zones 5 to 9, is a 10- to 14-inch-tall species with 2- to 5-inch-wide flowers that have a raised crest or ridge on each fall instead of a beard. Flowers are lavender or white and appear in late spring to early summer. Plants grow from spreading, fleshy rhizomes and are best divided every three to five years. Give roof irises full sun or partial shade and soil that is rich, evenly moist, and well drained. They will tolerate dry soil in shade and can be used as a ground cover.

Irises for damp soil. A number of iris species can grow in soil that is moist to constantly wet and even in standing water. Of the species listed below, yellow flag (*I. pseudacorus*) and blue flag (*I. versicolor*) also can grow in rich, well-drained soil. Siberian irises (*I. sibirica*) and Japanese irises (*I. ensata*) can be grown in moist sites, too.

Louisiana irises are hybrids developed by crossing several native species and are grown much like Japanese iris. They bloom from late spring to early summer, range from 1½ to 5 feet, and have flowers in shades of purple, blue-black, blue, red, and violet. Give them full sun to partial shade and very rich, acid soil that is constantly moist to wet. Divide their widely spreading rhizomes in late summer or early fall every three or four years to keep them in bounds. Typically, Louisiana irises are hardy in Zones 6 to 11, but there are cultivars that are hardy to Zone 4 with winter protection.

Yellow flag (*I. pseudacorus*) bears yellow 2½-inch flowers in early summer on 3- to 4-foot plants. Plants spread to form broad clumps and will grow in evenly moist to wet soil as well as in water up to about 10 inches. They need sun or partial shade. Divide them if they spread too far or lose vigor. Hardy in Zones 3 to 9, yellow flags are long-lived and vigorous. Blue flag (*I. versicolor*) and Southern blue flag (*I. virginica*) bear blue-violet or purple flowers that are 2 to 3 inches wide and appear from early to midsummer. Plants are 2 to 2½ feet tall. Blue flag is hardy in Zones 2 to 9; Southern blue flag, Zones 7 to 9.

Bulbous irises. These iris species are offered for sale in fall bulb displays alongside daffodils and tulips. Plant the bulbs at a depth of 3 to 4 inches. All grow in average to rich, well-drained soil in full sun or in a site that is sunny in spring but shaded in summer by deciduous trees. Like other spring bulbs, they bloom and then die back after flowering. Most require a warm spot with dry soil during their summer dormancy. Many gardeners handle bulbous irises as annuals or short-lived perennials, especially in areas with wet summers, because they bloom best the first spring and are not reliable after that. Plant the bulbs in late summer to early fall in very well-drained soil— ideally with perennials that do not require watering

in summer. Feed them after flowering with bone meal or another fertilizer high in phosphorus. Let the foliage turn yellow naturally. Dig in fall to transplant or divide the clumps.

Dutch, English, and Spanish irises, which belong to a group called the xiphium irises, are all perennial bulbous species, but they are usually grown as annuals because they are not reliable bloomers after the first year. All are outstanding cut flowers. Dutch and Spanish irises produce white, yellow, or violet flowers in spring or early summer on 15- to 30-inch plants. They are hardy in Zones 6 to 9. English irises, hardy in Zones 5 to 8, bear 4- to 5-inch-wide flowers on 20-inch plants in midsummer. Flowers come in shades of violet-blue, purple, white, and lilac-rose.

Danford iris (*I. danfordiae*) bears fragrant, yellow, 2-inch-wide flowers with brown spots in late winter or early spring. Hardy in Zones 5 to 8, plants reach 3 to 6 inches. Reticulated iris (*I. reticulata*) is hardy in Zones 3 to 8 and produces its fragrant, 2-inch-wide flowers in late winter to early spring on 4- to 6-inch plants. Flowers have grasslike leaves and are good for naturalizing, except in areas with hot, wet

Crested iris, Iris cristata '*Alba*'

summers. Flowers are sky blue, violet-blue, or red-purple. There are a number of cultivars, including 'Harmony', which bears deep blue flowers with yellow blotches on the falls, and 'Cantab', which has pale blue flowers with yellow blotches.

Irises for shade. Crested iris (*I. cristata*) is a native North American wildflower that thrives in partial to full shade and rich, evenly moist, well-drained, acid soil. It bears lavender-blue or white flowers with raised crests on the falls in late spring. Hardy in Zones 3 to 9, plants have arching, straplike leaves and spread to form broad mounds with time. They're best planted in early spring, and can be divided at that time if plants outgrow their space.

IN THE GARDEN

Combine irises with other perennials that bloom in early summer. They're perfect with hardy geraniums or cranesbills (*Geranium* spp.), bellflowers (*Campanula* spp.), peonies, lavender (*Lavandula angustifolia*), and columbines (*Aquilegia* spp.). Use irises that grow in moist to wet soil in low marshy spots or grow them around ponds or along streams, or add them to bog gardens. Crested irises can be planted with hostas, lungworts (*Pulmonaria* spp.), and other shade-lovers, and they also make good edging or ground cover plants for shady areas. All of the taller irises are spectacular cut flowers, and new buds will continue to open on cut stems, just as they would in the garden.

Kniphofia uvaria

(nih-FOE-fee-ah you-VAR-ee-uh)

Torch lily, red-hot poker

Lily family, Liliaceae. Hardy perennial.

While common names such as torch lily, red-hot poker, and poker plant describe the erect spikelike racemes of *Kniphofia uvaria*, the botanical name honors German botanist Johann Hieronymus Kniphof, who published a 12-folio-volume herbal in 1764. (Its 12,000 illustrations were made by hand, dipping pressed plants in ink and pressing them on the pages, then hand coloring the print.) The genus contains about 70 species, but gardeners primarily grow cultivars of common torch lily (*K.*

Torch lily, Kniphofia uvaria *'Flamenco'*

uvaria) or closely related hybrids. Garden-grown torch lilies produce showy, erect clusters of flowers that resemble bottle brushes or lighted torches. Each cluster, or torch, consists of densely packed tubular flowers The flower clusters are two-toned because unopened buds at the top of each cluster are darker in color—usually deep orange-red or orange, but also yellow—while older, open flowers toward the base of the cluster turn to yellow, pale orange, or white. Blooms arise from clumps of grassy leaves from mid- to late summer.

Torch lilies are natives of South Africa, and in the late 1700s were imported to England, where they were believed so tender that they were grown solely in greenhouses. In the 1840s, some curious gardener planted *K. uvaria* outdoors and discovered it was hardy. Despite this newfound versatility, torch lilies got mixed reviews in the 19th century, with one influential gardener writer grumbling that there were "not many species, and the few there are, are more than are wanted, from the Gardener's point to view." If planted in masses, he continued, one must take "a little extra care to avoid a violation of good taste." Gardeners have loosened up since then, and torch lilies are welcome even in hoity-toity beds and borders.

HOW TO GROW

Plant torch lilies in full sun and give them average to rich, evenly moist soil that is well drained. Plants absolutely require well-drained soil in winter and grow best in light, organically rich soil. Start with purchased plants, since growing flowering plants from seeds takes several years and cultivars do not come true from seed. Plant in spring after digging organic matter 1 to 2 feet into the soil. Plants grow from thick rhizomes and have fleshy roots; the rhizomes should be set no more than 2 to 3 inches below the soil surface.

Hardy in Zones 5 to 9, torch lilies are not difficult to grow. Feed them in spring with a balanced organic fertilizer, and mulch clumps to keep the soil evenly moist. Cut flower stalks to the ground once the flowers fade to encourage reblooming. If the foliage looks too messy, you can cut it back by half in late summer, but do not cut down all the foliage until spring. In the northern parts of Zone 5, cover the plants with salt hay, straw, or evergreen branches for extra winter protection. Cultivar hardiness can vary, and plants are especially susceptible to winterkill when a wet fall is followed by cold winter weather.

Torch lilies don't need to be divided regularly and will thrive for years without being disturbed. Dig them only if they become crowded, outgrow their space, or for propagation. Divide in spring, and do not let the roots of divisions or offsets dry out before replanting them. Plants can suffer from crown rot if the soil is too wet.

WHAT TO GROW

Common torch lily (K. uvaria) has evergreen leaves and flower spikes that are red-orange on top and yellow on the bottom. Flowers are borne atop 1- to 4-foot stalks. Good cultivars include 'Flamenco', with red, orange, yellow, and cream flowers; 'Primrose Beauty', yellow blooms; and green and yellow 'Ice Queen'. 'Prince Igor' produces yellow and orange blooms. 'Little Maid' is a 2-foot cultivar with yellow flowers. 'Alcazar' (salmon) and 'Earliest of All' (coral-rose) are reblooming cultivars.

IN THE GARDEN

Combine torch lilies with summer-blooming perennials such as yarrows (Achillea spp.), common sneezeweed (Helenium autumnale), daylilies, phlox, and orange coneflowers (Rudbeckia spp.). They are beacons for hummingbirds and many beneficial insects.

Leucanthemum × superbum

(leu-CAN-thuh-mum sue-PUR-bum)

Shasta daisy

Aster family, Asteraceae. Hardy Perennial.

Perhaps better known under their former botanical moniker, Chrysanthemum × superbum, Shasta daisies are the legacy of pioneer plant breeder and American horticulturist Luther Burbank (1849–1926). Burbank worked with scores of plants, producing new cultivars of plums, raspberries, blackberries, apples, peaches, nectarines, potatoes, tomatoes, corn, squash, peas, and even a spineless cactus that could be used to feed cattle. The Burbank Russet potato, now called the Idaho potato, is credited with helping Ireland recover after the great famine.

Burbank created the popular, easy to grow Shasta daisy in 1890 by crossing the Pyrenees chrysanthemum (L. maximum) and the Portuguese daisy (L. lacustre). The result was the sturdy perennial we grow today. Burbank gave the plant the name Shasta daisy because the bright white petals reminded him of the snow on nearby Mount Shasta. Shasta daisies bear their solitary flower heads on stiff stems. Like other aster-family plants, their blooms consist of showy, white, petal-like ray florets surrounding a yellow center of densely packed disk florets. The leaves are coarsely toothed.

HOW TO GROW

Shasta daisies require full sun and well-drained soil that is average to rich in organic matter content. Well-drained soil is especially important in winter, because damp soil around the crowns of the plants

Shasta daisy, Leucanthemum × superbum

WHAT TO GROW

The Shasta daisy (now *L. × superbum*, but formerly *Chrysanthemum maximum* and *C. × superbum*), hardy from Zones 4 to 9, is a 1- to 4-foot-tall clump-forming perennial that produces single, semidouble, or double flowers on stiff stems in summer. Blooms range from 2 to 5 inches across. 'Alaska' is an excellent, extra-hardy older cultivar that grows to 28 inches tall. 'Becky' received the Perennial Plant Association Perennial Plant of the Year award for 2003. It bears single flowers over a long season and is especially heat tolerant, making this a good choice for southern gardens. 'Wirral Pride' bears white flowers with downward-pointing petals and showy eyes—like a white coneflower. 'Aglaia' produces semidouble flowers with fringed ray florets. Dwarf cultivar 'Little Miss Muffet' is about 12 inches tall and does not need staking, and 'Snowcap' reaches only 14 inches. 'Snow Lady' can be grown from seeds—it is an F_1 hybrid—and reaches only 10 inches. 'Crazy Daisy' is a 2-foot-tall cultivar with variable 2- to 3-inch flowers that are shaggy and double. It can be grown from seeds.

IN THE GARDEN

Plant Shasta daisies in sunny perennial gardens, and combine them with daylilies, iris, yarrows (*Achillea* spp.), bellflowers (*Campanula* spp.), and hardy geraniums or cranesbills (*Geranium* spp.). Shasta daisies

causes rot. Plants grow in light shade and also withstand somewhat dry, sandy soil and seaside conditions, but only in full sun with moist, organically rich soil will they do their best. Shasta daisies tend to be short-lived. One theory is that the plants simply bloom themselves to death.

Your best bet for instant gratification is to start with container-grown plants, although some Shasta daisy cultivars can be grown from seeds. Feed plants in spring with a balanced organic plant food, then a second time when flower buds form. Standard-size plants may need staking—or reduce their height by pinching stems back in spring—but dwarf types generally do not need support. Deadheading religiously will keep plants flowering until frost, especially young plants.

Divide Shasta daisies in spring or fall every two or three years to rejuvenate them. Discard the older, woody growth in the center of the clump and replant the rest. Division is the easy way to propagate Shastas, but you also can propagate by rooting shoots cut from the base of the plant in spring. Or sow seeds in early spring in containers set outdoors in a protected place; do not cover seeds, just press them onto the soil surface.

Good air circulation reduces mildew, which is sometimes a problem.

OTHER CHOICES

Ox-eye daisy (*L. vulgare*, formerly *Chrysanthemum vulgare*) is a weedy, vigorous species bearing yellow-centered white daisies in late spring and early summer. It has escaped cultivation and is spread widely in North America, where it grows in sunny meadows and waste places. These 2- to 3-foot plants, hardy in Zones 3 to 8, are too vigorous for most gardens, but they can be included in sunny wild gardens. Cut plants to the ground after flowering to encourage repeat bloom and discourage abundant self-seeding.

Nippon, or Montauk, daisy (*Nipponanthemum nipponicum*, formerly *Chrysanthemum nipponicum*) is a shrubby mounding perennial that reaches 2 feet and produces white, 2½-inch daisy flowers in fall. Hardy in Zones 5 to 9, it needs full sun and average, very well-drained soil. Plants thrive in sandy soil and are good for seaside gardens.

make top-notch cut flowers, and small cultivars do well in containers. For a bountiful supply, consider planting extra clumps of Shastas in a cutting garden or even a corner of the vegetable garden, where picking all the flowers will not affect the look of beds and borders.

Liatris

(lie-AH-triss)

Gayfeathers, blazing stars

Aster family, Asteraceae. Hardy perennials.

○

This North American genus contains about 40 species, all of which produce flowers that are unusual for the aster family to which they belong. Also called button snakeroots and prairie button, plants bear featherlike spikes that are densely packed with small flower heads. The buttonlike blooms consist of nothing but seed-producing disk florets—there are no petal-like ray florets, which are characteristic of most asters and daisies. Flowers come in shades of pinkish purple, purple, or white. Another unusual gayfeather characteristic is the fact that blooms open from the top of the spike down, instead of from bottom to top, which is much more common in the flower world. One advantage of this directional shift is that spent blooms can be removed from cut flowers or from flowers in the garden by whacking off the tops of the spikes with pruning shears.

While gardeners favor the blooms, anyone interested in herbal or medicinal uses focuses on the leaves and roots of these native plants. Gayfeathers produce clumps of linear to lance-shaped leaves, with smaller leaves forming up the flower stalks. They grow from thick roots with swollen, flattened stems that are tuberlike. Spike gayfeather (*Liatris spicata*) is one of the species that has been used as a diuretic and as a poultice for snakebites. Gayfeathers also have antibacterial effects and have been added to herbal insect repellants and potpourris. Since the plants contain the toxic compound coumarin, they were banned as a flavoring in the 1950s because of the possibility they could cause liver damage and reduce blood clotting.

Lewis and Clark collected two species of *Liatris* in 1804 along the banks of the Missouri River in what is now South Dakota. Perhaps because of its North American origins, there is no explanation for the genus name—"unknown derivation" is the standard entry in plant name dictionaries. Despite the lack of a rich garden history, gayfeathers found themselves in the spotlight in the 1980s, when they were "discovered" by the cut-flower industry.

HOW TO GROW

Give gayfeathers full sun and soil that is average to rich and well drained. Soil that is too rich leads to floppy plants that need staking to stay erect. As a rule, gayfeathers rot in soil that remains damp, especially in winter, but spike gayfeather (*L. spicata*) grows in evenly moist soil. Dotted blazing star (*L. punctata*) prefers in dry, well-drained soil. Add gayfeathers to your garden by purchasing plants or planting seeds. Gayfeathers also are sold as tubers, which can be purchased and planted in spring or fall. Plant the tubers just under the soil surface.

Established gayfeathers require little care. Deadhead flowers by cutting the spike down to the basal foliage. Once established, gayfeathers are quite drought tolerant and can remain undisturbed for years. Divide plants only if they spread too far or the clumps die out in the middle. Division also

Spike gayfeather, Liatris spicata *'Kobold'*

Spike gayfeather, Liatris spicata *'Floristan'*

is a good way to propagate the plants: Dig clumps in spring or fall. Or sow seeds in fall in pots and set them outdoors in a protected location to overwinter. Plants have few serious pest or disease problems.

WHAT TO GROW

Spike gayfeather (*L. spicata*) is best known and most widely grown. Hardy in Zones 3 to 9, plants grow from 2 to 5 feet tall and produce 2-foot spikes packed with ½-inch pinkish purple flower heads from mid- to late summer. 'Kobold', sometimes sold as 'Goblin', is a compact, 2½-foot cultivar with mauve-violet flowers. 'Floristan' produces white flowers on 3-foot plants. Dotted blazing star, or snakeroot (*L. punctata*), hardy in Zones 2 to 8, is a 2½-foot species with 6- to 12-inch spikes of ⅛-inch rosy purple flower heads in late summer. Kansas gayfeather (*L. pycnostachya*), also called prairie blazing star, is hardy in

Zones 3 to 9 and ranges from 3 to 5 feet tall. Plants bear 1- to 2-½ foot spikes of ½-inch, mauve-purple flower heads in midsummer.

IN THE GARDEN

Use gayfeathers in wildflower meadows with other sun-loving native plants such as perennial sunflowers (*Helianthus* spp.). They also are handsome with ornamental grasses and daylilies in borders or combined with lilies. Gayfeathers make superb cut flowers and are worth planting in a cutting garden just to ensure a steady supply. They are good flowers for drying, too, and like other aster family plants, they attract butterflies and beneficial insects.

Ligularia

(lig-you-LAIR-ee-ah)

Ligularias

Aster family, Asteraceae. Hardy perennials.

Large, bold, moisture-loving perennials, ligularias are grown for their showy clusters of golden-yellow to orange daisylike flowers as well as their very large leaves. Botanical and common names for the plant are derived from the shape of petal-like ray florets. It's from the Latin *ligula*, for "a strap." Ligularias produce 2- to 3-foot mounds of rounded to kidney-shaped leaves that can exceed 1 foot in length. In summer, erect spikes or rounded clusters of daisylike flowers emerge from the foliage.

Sometimes called leopard plants and once classified in the genus *Senecio*, ligularias have been, according to British plant authority Christopher Lloyd, "the plaything of the botanists, taking species out, putting others in. What a game." Most ligularias are native to central and eastern Asia, although a few species—there are 150 in all—are native to Europe. In the wild, they grow in wet grass- and woodlands as well as along streams, in bogs, and in ditches. In gardens, for obvious reasons, they are plants for bog gardens, streamsides, and other damp places.

HOW TO GROW

First and foremost, ligularias need a spot with very rich soil that remains constantly moist. And they need a spot in light to partial shade—especially one that is in the shade in the afternoon to protect plants from heat and help keep them from wilting. Otherwise, plants will droop dramatically during the heat of the day. A site that is protected from wind also helps keep plants from wilting in midafternoon, because it reduces moisture loss.

Add ligularias to your garden by purchasing container grown plants. Once they're in the ground, they need very little care. Water deeply in dry weather; you'll need to do this daily if you don't have a naturally wet spot to offer them. Plants don't need staking and can be left undisturbed for years without being divided. If you want to propagate them, or a clump has spread too far, dig and divide in spring or fall.

With such large, inviting leaves, ligularias are a goldmine for snails and slugs.

WHAT TO GROW

One of the biggest differences between the species is the shape of the flower clusters. Big-leaved ligularia (*L. dentata*), also known as golden groundsel, produces

Big-leaved ligularia, Ligularia dentata

flattened clusters of flowers, called *corymbs* by botanists. Individual flowers are 4 inches wide, orange-yellow in color, and appear from summer to early fall, and form interesting seed heads. The leaves are kidney- to heart-shaped and leaf and flower stalks are red. Hardy in Zones 3 or 4 to 8, plants are 3 to 5 feet tall in bloom. 'Desdemona' features orange flower heads and brown-green leaves that are purple and maroon underneath. 'Othello' bears purple-green leaves with purple-red undersides. Hybrid 'Gregynog Gold' has pyramidal clusters of orange-yellow flowers.

L. przewalskii produces clumps of irregularly cut palmate leaves and erect, lacy-textured, 6-foot-tall racemes of ¾-inch-wide flower heads from early to late summer. It is hardy in Zones 4 to 8. *L. stenocephala*, hardy in Zones 4 to 8, bears toothed, triangular leaves with heart-shaped bases, and plants are topped by erect, 5-foot racemes of 1½-inch-wide yellow flower heads in late summer. 'The Rocket' is a popular cultivar that reaches 6 feet and has lemon yellow flowers.

L. 'Little Lantern' is a new, 18-inch cultivar with racemes of gold daisylike flowers. Like its big siblings, it prefers wet soil but is also "container friendly," according to one seed company.

IN THE GARDEN

Ligularias are perfect plants for damp sites around ponds, streams, or any place that stays moist. If you don't have a damp spot that's suitable, either create one or don't try to grow this handsome perennial.

Ligularia, Ligularia stenocephala 'The Rocket'

Lilium

(LIL-ee-um)

Lilies

Lily family, Liliaceae. Hardy bulbs.

These summer-blooming bulbs are one of the glories of the flower garden. Anyone who has grown them may be surprised by the fact that they're menu items in some parts of the world, however: The bulbs of various species of lilies are eaten as vegetables in parts of China and Japan, and bulbs are grown especially for this use. Lilies also have been used medicinally. Pliny recorded that the Madonna lily (*L. candidum*) was used to treat foot and skin problems. Some argue that Madonna lily is the oldest domesticated flower. While that is unlikely, certainly it's one of the loveliest. Today, the Madonna lily is grown as a garden flower, but several Chinese species are still used in traditional medicine, including *L. concolor*.

It was regale lily (*L. regale*) that almost killed the plant hunter E. H. Wilson, who sent bulbs back to England from China in 1904. His leg was crushed while searching for new plants, an injury Wilson thereafter referred to as his "lily limp." Despite being maimed, Wilson wrote that he would "proudly rest his reputation with the Regal Lily," and he warned that gardeners "who possess this treasure not to ruin its constitution with rich food."

Gardeners value lilies for their showy summer blooms that come in a range of colors, from fiery oranges, reds, and yellows to hot pink, pastel pink, cream, and white. Most lilies bear their blooms in branched clusters held on an erect, unbranched stem that grows from a bulb. Individual flowers have six petal-like tepals and may be trumpet, funnel, bell, star, or bowl shaped. The flowers can point up, out, or down and have six prominent anthers surrounding the flower's pistil. Some species have tepals that are recurved or reflexed, and these curve back from the center of the flower toward the stem. Lily leaves are narrow and lance shaped or grassy, usually arranged in whorls.

If you've ever planted a lily bulb, you've undoubtedly noticed that they're not quite like daffodil, tulip, or onion bulbs, which are tunicate, meaning they are hard bulbs with tightly packed layers of scales and a papery covering over the whole bulb. Lily bulbs have fleshy scales that are attached only at the base of the bulb and are loose at the top. Members of the genus *Lilium* are often called true lilies, because they share their common name with hundreds of other plants that may or may not be closely related. Lily wannabes include daylilies (*Hemerocallis* spp.), magic lily (*Lycoris squamigera*), trout lilies (*Erythronium* spp.), and checkered lily (*Fritillaria meleagris*).

HOW TO GROW

Most lilies need light, slightly acid, moderately rich soil that is evenly moist and well drained. Good

Asiatic lily, Lilium *'Headlight'*

Trumpet lily, Lilium *'Golden Splendor'*

drainage is essential in winter, when plants are dormant. Preferred sun exposure varies by lily species, but the perfect location for the most popular types being grown would be full sun in the morning and light shade during the hottest part of the day. Look for a site that has good air circulation but is protected from the wind, since the plants are top-heavy when in bloom and blow over easily.

Add lilies to your garden by purchasing bulbs in spring or fall. Some garden centers also offer pots of lilies, which are nice for the instant color they add to the garden. When handling lily bulbs, be aware that they are easily bruised or damaged and dry out quickly. Bulbs should have plump, fleshy scales; ideally, they should have fleshy roots attached to the bottom of the bulb. Unlike tulip bulbs, lily bulbs never have a true dormant season and deteriorate when they're not in the ground, so plant them as soon as you get them. If you can't plant right away, store the bulbs in the refrigerator, but no longer than a few days.

Work organic matter such as compost into the soil to a depth of about 2 feet at planting time. Plant most lily bulbs with the tops at a depth of two to three times the height of the bulb—or about 5 to 8 inches deep. Madonna lily (*L. candidum*) is one species that's an exception: Plant Madonna lily bulbs with only 1 inch of soil over the bulb noses.

While lilies need regular attention to look their best, many thrive in the garden for years without much care. Feed plants in spring with a liquid organic fertilizer just as leaves begin to emerge, then feed again when flowering is over. Install stakes—take care not to puncture the bulbs—for taller lilies in spring when plants are still small. Use soft yarn to tie stems to stakes, or purchase wire supports that have a loop at the top. Mulch to control weeds and keep the soil moist and cool, but keep mulch away from the stems to avoid rotting. Water plants deeply during dry weather. Remove flowers as they fade, but don't cut down the stalk until fall, when the leaves have turned brown.

Divide clumps that begin to bloom less or outgrow their space by digging them in spring or early summer. Dig deeply some distance from the edges of the clumps so you don't cut into the bulbs. Separate the bulbs and replant immediately. Division is a good way to propagate lilies, but they also can be grown from the pea-size, purple-black bulbils that arise in the leaf axils of many species. Some lilies produce small bulblets near the base of the stems, just above the bulbs. Pot up bulblets or bulbils in pots put outside to overwinter, or in a nursery bed at a depth of two to three times their height. Scaling is another way to propagate lilies. Pull a few scales off the outside of a bulb, dust them with sulfur (also dust the parent bulb and replant it), then plant the scales, pointed end up, in pots or a flat filled with moist, soilless mix. Set in a shady, protected spot outdoors or a warm, bright place indoors out of direct light. Keep the medium moist but not wet. After about two months, pot up the small bulblets that appear at the base of the scales. Most lily cultivars don't come true from seed, but species lilies are fine to grow from seeds. Sow seeds in pots in late summer or fall, and set them in a protected place outdoors.

Lilies can be attacked by stem borers and are subject to virus diseases, which are carried from plant to plant by aphids and other pests. And they are among the plants most plagued by deer.

WHAT TO GROW

It is hard to pick which lilies to grow, since each one seems more beautiful than the one before. There are about a hundred species and hundreds more cultivars; by selecting carefully, you can have lilies in bloom from early summer into fall. Peak bloom is

Oriental lily, Lilium 'Aubade'

3 to 6 feet tall. Candidum Hybrids (Division III) bear clusters of 4- to 5-inch flowers on 3- to 4-foot plants and come in shades of deep red, yellow-orange, and pale yellow. Hardy in Zones 4 to 9, both *L. candidum* and Candidum hybrids are long-lived and easy to grow. Plant them with no more than 1 inch of soil over the tops of the bulbs and give them neutral to slightly alkaline soil. Fall-planted bulbs will produce a low clump of evergreen leaves before winter.

Turk's cap lily (*L. martagon*) bears racemes of 2-inch-wide, nodding, purple-pink flowers with recurved petals. Plants reach 3 to 6 feet. *L. martagon* var. *album* has white flowers. Martagon Hybrids (Division II) produce 3- to 4-inch flowers, also on 3- to 6-foot plants. Both are hardy in Zones 3 to 8. The species and many of the Martagon hybrids

in midsummer—July to August in most areas. The genus has been organized into nine divisions—you'll find that bulb suppliers refer to the divisions—and some of the most popular divisions and species (all species lilies are in Division IX) are listed below according to bloom season.

Lilies for early to midsummer bloom. The most popular of these early flowering lilies are the Asiatic Hybrid lilies (Division I). Hardy in Zones 3 to 8, they are 2- to 5-foot plants with 4- to 6-inch-wide flowers. Flowers, which are not fragrant, can point upward, outward, or down and come in a wide range of colors, including orange, yellow, red, pink, purple, cream, and white. Asiatic lilies need full sun and well-drained soil, rarely need staking, and are vigorous and long-lived in the right site. Good cultivars include 'Connecticut King', 'Citronella', 'Cote d'Azur', 'Montreux', 'Enchantment', 'Fire King', and 'Mont Blanc'.

Madonna lily (*L. candidum*) also blooms from early to midsummer and produces fragrant, white trumpets that are 2 to 3 inches long. Blooms are borne in clusters of 5 to 20, and plants range from

Turk's cap lily, Lilium martagon

HEIRLOOM BEAUTIES

Several other genera offer an excellent return for the little effort it takes to plant the bulbs. Consider adding some of the following to garden beds and borders.

Camass, or quamash (*Camassia* spp.). Members of this genus of native North American bulbs were once important food plants for native Americans. All bear showy, erect racemes of small (1 to 2 inches wide) starry, six-petaled flowers in shades of blue, violet, or white. Plants bloom in late spring or early summer and range from 2 to 4 feet tall. Look for *C. cusickii*, hardy in Zones 3 to 10, *C. quamash*, Zones 4 to 10, or any of the other species offered by bulb dealers. Camassias grow in well-drained, rich soil and quickly form large drifts. They are excellent bulbs for naturalizing.

Crocosmias (*Crocosmia* spp.). These showy perennials grow from corms and form handsome clumps of strap-shaped leaves topped by arching clusters of brightly colored, trumpet-shaped flowers in summer. Hybrids are grown more often than the species, and you are likely to see these plants sold in containers, like conventional perennials, or as corms. Most hybrids are hardy in Zones 6 to 9, but orange-red 'Lucifer' is hardy to Zone 5. Give *Crocosmia* species full sun and rich, evenly moist soil; partial shade is best in the South.

Foxtail lilies (*Eremurus* spp.). As their name suggests, these produce erect spikes of small, densely packed flowers that resemble fluffy fox tails. Plants bloom in early summer, and flowers come in shades of pink, white, or yellow. Hardy in Zones 5 to 8, foxtail lilies grow from brittle, fleshy roots that are planted in fall. They are 4 to 8 feet tall, depending on the species or cultivar, and flower spikes range from 6 inches to 2 feet. Select a spot with full sun and rich, well-drained soil. Set the roots on a mound of coarse sand in the bottom of the hole to ensure that moisture will drain away from them. If you haven't grown foxtail lilies before, look for hybrids— *E.* × *isabellinus* Reiter Hybrids, for example, which come in a wide range of colors.

Naked lady, or resurrection lily (*Lycoris squamigera*). This species produces strap-shaped leaves in spring and showy umbels of pink funnel-shaped flowers, from 3 to 4 inches wide, in summer. Hardy in Zones 6 to 9, it is a long-lived species. Plant the bulbs with the necks at the soil surface.

---

have an unpleasant scent. Martagon lilies include the Blackhouse hybrids, including 'Mrs. R. O. Blackhouse', and the Paisley and Marhan hybrids. All of these lilies thrive in full sun to partial shade and tolerate acid to slightly alkaline soils.

Easter lily (*L. longiflorum*) is a popular florist pot plant with fragrant, white, 7-inch-long trumpets produced on 1½- to 3½-foot plants. It is not usually grown as a garden plant because it is only hardy in Zones 7 to 9 and is easier in pots than in the garden. Longiflorum Hybrids (Division V) are more adaptable. 'Mount Everest' can be grown in Zones 5 to 8 and thrives in partial shade.

A cross between *L. longiflorum* and Asiatic hybrids is responsible for the popular new L.A. hybrid lilies, first introduced in 1992. They have fragrant, trumpet-shaped flowers that face upward, good disease resistance, and an extended vase life. Cultivars to look for include 'Clubhouse', 'Dani Arifin', 'Golden Tycoon', and 'Red Label'.

Lilies for midsummer bloom. Two divisions are the stars of the peak lily season—Oriental Hybrids and Trumpet and Aurelian Hybrids. Oriental Hybrids (Division VII) produce wonderfully fragrant flowers that usually are flat-faced or bowl-shaped and can reach 10 inches across. Flowers come in white, shades of pink, and dark maroon-red, and many cultivars are striped with yellow or spotted with red. Hardy in Zones 4 to 8, plants range from 2 to 8 feet tall; tall Orientals require staking. Cultivars include 'Black Beauty', 'Casa Blanca', and 'Early Rose'.

Many Trumpet and Aurelian Hybrids (Division VI) feature classic trumpet-shaped blooms, but there are also cultivars with bowl-shaped or flat-faced flowers. Flowers usually are fragrant, face out or down, and come in red, pink, gold, yellow, orange, and white; some cultivars are purple-red, brown, or green on the outside of the flower. Plants are hardy in Zones 4 to 8 and range from 4 to 8 feet tall. These lilies almost always need to be staked. Cultivars include 'Black Dragon', 'Copper King', 'African Queen', and the Golden Splendor Group.

Regal lily (*L. regale*) is another species that blooms in midseason. It bears fragrant, 6-inch-long trumpets that are white inside and purple to wine colored on the outside. Hardy in Zones 3 to 8, this species is 2 to 6 feet tall.

Japanese lily (*L. speciosum*) produces fragrant, pink or white flowers that are 7 inches wide, flat-faced with recurved petals. *L. speciosum* var. *rubrum* has deep pink flowers. This is a vigorous species, hardy in Zones 4 to 8.

Native lilies for midsummer bloom. Canada, or meadow, lily (*L. canadense*) is a North American wildflower, hardy in Zones 3 to 7, with yellow-orange, 3-inch-wide flowers that have slightly recurved petals and dark spots. Plants range from 3 to 6 feet tall and thrive in damp to evenly moist, acid soil in full sun or partial shade. Unlike many lilies, Canada lily spreads via rhizomatous bulbs.

American Turk's cap lily (*L. superbum*) is another North American wildflower. Hardy in Zones 4 to 9, it bears orange-red, 3-inch-wide flowers with recurved petals that have dark spots. Plants reach 4 to 8 feet. Grow this species in a spot with damp to evenly moist, acid soil in full sun or partial shade. It, too, spreads by rhizomatous bulbs.

Lilies for fall bloom. There aren't many fall-blooming lilies, but Formosa lily (*L. formosanum*) is well worth growing. Plants bear fragrant white, 3- to 8-inch-long trumpets in early to midfall on 4- to 7-foot plants. Hardy in Zones 5 to 9, this species needs evenly moist, acid soil and spreads via rhizomatous bulbs. Unlike many lilies, Formosa lily blooms very quickly from seed: Seed sown indoors in winter will bloom the first year.

IN THE GARDEN

Combine lilies with perennials and annuals in beds and borders. They're best planted behind lower-growing flowers, since once the lily plants are out of bloom, they are not very attractive but should not be cut back. Keep in mind that lilies do not compete well with other plants, so be sure to give them plenty of room. Combine them with summer-blooming perennials such as daylilies, Siberian iris (*Iris sibirica*), phlox, and Shasta daisy (*Leucanthemum* × *superbum*). Lilies that thrive in partial shade can be planted behind hostas and epimediums (*Epimedium* spp.). Lilies also make spectacular cut flowers. When

cutting, select stems that have at least two buds that are opening and cut as short a stem as possible to leave adequate foliage on the plants to support next year's flowers. Some gardeners remove the dangling anthers before bringing the flowers indoors, because the pollen stains fabric. The anthers add considerable charm to the flowers, however, so instead of removing them, consider placing arrangements on washable surfaces, such as glass. Brush pollen off fabric or other surfaces with a dry sponge.

Limonium

(lih-MOAN-ee-um)

Sea lavenders, statice

Plumbago family, Plumbaginaceae.
Hardy and tender perennials.

The genus name *Limonium* is from the Greek *leimon*, "meadow" and refers to the usual habitat of these plants: salt meadows. Seeing "a salt marsh covered with several acres of lavender-coloured *Limonium*, in bloom, is an unusual and moving experience," according to plant authority Christopher Lloyd.

Gardeners concentrate most of their efforts on two species of *Limonium* although some 150 species belong to this genus. Statice, the tender perennial *L. sinuatum*, is most often treated as an annual. A Mediterranean native, it is grown for its brightly colored blooms that are prized in bouquets of dried flowers. The common name is pronounced by most gardeners like the word "status," but Lloyd contends that "the final e should be spoken as a separate syllable."

The other well-known species is sea lavender (*L. latifolium*), a summer-flowering hardy perennial that also is used for drying or as a filler—somewhat like baby's breath (*Gypsophila paniculata*)—in beds and borders. Both species produce a rosette of leaves at the base of the plant topped by panicles of tiny flowers in summer and fall. The flowers are tubular to funnel-shaped and have a papery texture.

HOW TO GROW

Sea lavender and statice both prefer a spot in full sun that has average to rich, well-drained soil. They

Statice, Limonium sinuatum, *Petite Bouquet Series*

WHAT TO GROW

Statice (*L. sinuatum*), which is grown as a warm-weather annual north of Zone 8 and can be grown as an annual or a perennial in Zones 8 though 11, reaches about 2 feet and is prized for its branched clusters of ½-inch-long flowers. Although the individual flowers are small, they're borne in showy, dense clusters and are brightly colored: Blooms come in shades of violet, lavender, yellow, pink, orange, salmon, and white. Statice blossoms hold their color exceptionally well when dried, but they can also be used in fresh bouquets. Pacific Series plants, 18 to 36 inches, come in a mix or can be purchased in separate colors; Petite Bouquet Series plants are only a foot tall.

Sea lavender (*L. latifolium*), hardy in Zones 3 or 4 to 9, produces a rosette of spoon-shaped leaves topped by rounded, airy clusters of tiny, ¼-inch-long flowers. The flowers are pale lavender to bluish in color, and clusters are 2 to 2½ feet tall.

thrive in sandy soils and are good choices for seaside gardens. Water only if the soil becomes very dry.

Add perennial sea lavender (*L. latifolium*) to your garden by purchasing container-grown plants. This species grows from a woody crown that is deep rooted, so for best results look for a good spot and make it permanent. Plants are slow to establish and best left undisturbed once in the ground. Deadheading prolongs blooming. Cut back dead foliage in the spring. To propagate perennial sea lavender, sever small, new crowns that arise around the outside of the main plant in spring (be sure to get some roots), or sow seeds in pots in fall or winter and set them outside in a protected location to germinate. Sea lavender also can be propagated by root cuttings.

The best bet for growing statice (*L. sinuatum*) is to start plants from seed. Sow indoors six to eight weeks before the last spring frost date, or sow outdoors where the plants are to grow after the last-frost date.

Statices are occasionally troubled by leaf spot and by mites and aphids.

Seafoam statice, Limonium perezii

Similar to statice and sea lavender is seafoam statice (*L. perezii*), a tender woody-based perennial, 2 to 3 feet tall and hardy only to Zone 9. It flowers in summer in shades of deep purple with tiny white corollas. The huge flower clusters are held above the large, rich green leaves. Excellent for cutting or drying, it is a superb seaside plant and has naturalized along the southern California coast.

IN THE GARDEN

Add statice to beds and borders, where it can act as a filler among other annuals. Statice is also ideal for a cutting garden, and you'll want to pick and dry some indoors for winter bouquets. Cut statice when most of the flowers in the cluster have opened fully and hang them in small bunches in a warm, dark place to dry. Sea lavenders make handsome additions to sunny perennial gardens, where they are best planted near the front so their leaves are visible. Combine them with irises, lavender, yarrows (*Achillea* spp.), and balloon flower (*Platycodon grandiflorus*).

Linum

(LIE-num)

Flaxes

Flax family, Linaceae.
Hardy perennials, annuals.

"The carnation of our gardens is a plant of respectable antiquity," Alice Coats wrote in *Flowers and Their Histories* (1956), "the iris is older, the Madonna lily older than the iris; but none of them can compare with *Linum usitatissimum*, the fragile-looking flax, which shares with the poppy the distinction of being one of the first plants to be associated with man." As Coats claims, common flax has been cultivated since ancient times and is the source of the fibers from which linen is made. It also produces seeds that are pressed and used to make linseed oil. This relative of perennials and annuals that are now grown in beds and borders chiefly for their flowers was also used medicinally as a laxative, expectorant, pain reliever, and to control coughing. The botanical name *Linum* is the classical Latin word for the

Perennial flax, Linum perenne *spp.* lewisii

plant. And, deservedly, the species name *usitatissimum* means "most useful."

Farmers who planted *L. usitatissimum* were said to be "sowing shirts." Flower gardeners are sowing pure blue, the main attraction of the species regularly grown in ornamental beds and borders. In addition to pure blue, these species produce pretty clusters of five-petaled flowers in shades of lavender, white, yellow, red, and pink. The individual flowers, which may be funnel to saucer shaped, open for only a day—and close for the day in the afternoon—but plants bear them in abundance so clumps are colorful over a long season in summer. The leaves are usually narrow and linear to lance shaped.

HOW TO GROW

Give flax a site in full sun to partial shade with very well-drained soil that has an average to rich organic matter content. Excellent soil drainage is essential to success, especially in wintertime. Add flax to your garden by purchasing plants or starting your own from seed. While perennial flaxes tend to be short-lived, they self-sow and will scatter themselves politely through garden beds. Once in the garden, flax needs little care. Plants may need staking, especially if the soil is on the rich side.

Propagate perennial flax by dividing clumps in spring or fall, by taking cuttings in early summer and rooting them in a mixture of half vermiculite and half perlite, or start plants from seed. Ideally, sow seeds out in the garden where they are to grow. Sow perennials in spring or fall, annuals in spring a few weeks before the last spring frost date. Annual flax also can be started in individual pots six to eight weeks before the last-frost date, but outdoor sowing is generally best because plants resent transplanting. Where winters are mild—roughly Zone 7 south—sow outdoors in late summer or fall for bloom the following year.

Plants are sometimes bothered by slugs and snails and are susceptible to anthracnose, wilts, and rots.

WHAT TO GROW

Perennial flax (*L. perenne*) is a wiry-stemmed, 1- to 1½-foot-tall perennial with panicles of rich, pure blue flowers that are ¾- to 1-inch wide. Hardy in Zones 4 to 8, plants are heat tolerant and bloom from early to midsummer. 'Sapphire' reaches 16 inches and has sapphire blue flowers and an attractive mounding habit. Narbonne flax (*L. narbonense*) is a 1- to 2-foot-tall species with 1½-inch-wide flowers—larger than those of perennial flax—that are pure blue with white eyes. Hardy in Zones 6 to 9, and to Zones 4 or 5 with winter protection, narbonne flax blooms from early to midsummer. Wild blue flax (*L. lewisii*) is a hardy wildflower with light blue blossoms held on 2- to 3-foot stems.

Golden, or yellow, flax (*L. flavum*) is a woody-based perennial that reaches 1½ feet and bears 1-inch-wide yellow flowers in summer. It is hardy in Zones 4 to 7. 'Compactum' is 6 to 9 inches tall.

Annual, or flowering, flax (*L. grandiflorum*) is a 1½- to 3-foot annual with gray-green leaves and saucer-shaped 1½- to 2-inch-wide flowers. This species produces its showy flowers in shades of lilac-blue, red, white, and pink.

IN THE GARDEN

Plant flaxes with other summer-blooming flowers, including salvias or sages (*Salvia* spp.), lilies, irises, valerian (*Centranthus ruber*), and yarrows (*Achillea* spp.). Use them in drifts of several plants, since they are fine textured and planting *en masse* gives them added impact.

Liriope

(lih-RIE-oh-pee)

Lilyturfs, turf lilies, liriopes

Lily family, Liliaceae. Hardy perennials.

Liriope is a small genus of perennials—it contains only five or six species—all native to Asia. Plants produce clumps of grasslike to narrowly strap-shaped leaves. The botanical name was inspired by the arching shape of the leaves and the fountainlike clumps they create. They aren't terribly exciting plants—most are low growing and their flowers are small—but they are enormously useful in beds and borders.

Lilyturfs are named for a character in Greek mythology, Liriope, a nymph and the mother of Narcissus, the unfortunate young man who fell in love with himself and was turned into a flower. Or, as Ovid expressed it in the *Metamorphoses*, "Wave-blue water-nymph Liriope, whom once Cephisos in his sinuous flow embracing held and ravished. In due time the lovely Nymphe bore a fine infant boy, from birth adorable, and named her son Narcissus."

Big blue lilyturf, Liriope muscari 'Variegata'

The common names lilyturf and turf lily recognize the grasslike appearance of these lily-family plants. Lilyturfs grow from tuberous roots and spread by rhizomes. They spread vigorously—be warned. Their arching leaves are evergreen or semi-evergreen in warmer regions, and plants form dense, broad clumps. Spikes of small, ¼ to ⅜-inch flowers, reminiscent of grape hyacinth flowers (*Muscari* spp.), appear from late summer to fall and are followed by round black berries.

HOW TO GROW

In the wild, lilyturfs are found primarily in woodland areas, so ideally give them a spot in partial or even full shade with rich, well-drained soil. Plants that get plenty of moisture will grow in full sun as well, except in very hot regions. These are tough, easy to grow plants that tolerate heat, humidity, drought, competition from tree roots, salt spray, as well as near total shade.

Add lilyturfs to your garden by purchasing plants; while the species can be grown from seed, improved cultivars must be propagated by division. Water regularly to help get plants established, but after that lilyturfs can do it on their own. Cut plants to the ground in late winter or early spring to make room for the fresh new foliage. Divide plants in spring if they outgrow their space (and they will) or to propagate. Plants will self-sow, and can be grown from seeds sown in pots and set outdoors in a protected location. Soak seed overnight in water before sowing.

Lilyturfs have few problems once they are established in the garden.

WHAT TO GROW

Big blue lilyturf (*L. muscari*) has evergreen leaves and reaches from 1 to 1½ feet. Hardy in Zones 6 to 9, it bears dense spikes of lilac-purple or white flowers in fall on stalks tall enough to hold the flowers above the foliage. 'John Burch' bears variegated leaves edged in gold; 'Big Blue' produces violet-purple flowers on 10-inch plants; and 'Variegata' has green leaves edged in creamy white and spreads relatively slowly.

L. spicata is a semi-evergreen species that is hardy in Zones 4 to 10. It bears spikes of pale lavender flowers on 1- to 1½-foot plants and spreads fairly quickly by rhizomes. 'Silver Dragon' has variegated foliage.

IN THE GARDEN

Use lilyturfs as ground covers in dappled shade. Big blue lilyturf is a world-class edging plant to use in borders and beds and along walkways; *L spicata* may spread too rapidly to be used as an edger. Lilyturfs also are attractive when combined with larger hostas because they add interesting foliage texture and contrast to plantings. One warning: *L. spicata* is considered invasive in some states. Check with local authorities before you add it to your garden.

Lobelia

(loe-BEE-lee-ah)

Lobelias

Bellflower family, Campanulaceae.
Hardy perennials, annuals.

The lobelias are an intriguing genus, about 370 species in all, that contains a dainty popular annual grown as an edging and container plant, showy perennials that attract hummingbirds, and a 9-foot-tall tree with blue flowers from Kenya and Uganda. Lobelias are found the world over, although most are native to North, Central, and South America. Popular edging lobelia (*L. erinus*) is originally from South Africa, but the two most popular hardy perennials in this genus are native North Americans.

One of those species is cardinal flower (*L. cardinalis*), which got to England from Canada via France. According to one account, the French Queen Henrietta Maria commented that the color of the flowers reminded her of "the scarlet stockings of a Cardinal." North American gardeners assume the common name alludes to the familiar bird, but apparently it refers to ecclesiastical attire. In any case, the British liked cardinal flower, for one 18th-century writer described it as "A flower of the most handsome Appearance... [which] excells all other Flowers I ever knew, in the Richness of its Colour." Ornithologist Roger Tory Peterson called it "America's favorite."

Lobelias also have a rich history of use as medicinal plants: Many species contain compounds that stimulate breathing and cause vomiting. "If yer ever wants to get rid of what's inside yer," a 19th-century witness reported, "jist make a tea of lobelia leaves

Edging lobelia, Lobelia erinus

and I'll bet my team of hosses it'll accommodate you." Native Americans used Indian tobacco (*L. inflata*), also called asthma weed and pukeweed, to treat bronchitis and other ailments. Contact with the milky sap of lobelias can irritate skin. Lobelia flowers have tubular, two-lipped flowers and simple leaves. Blooms are borne singly or in erect racemes or panicles. They come in shades of blue, lilac, violet, red, pink, white, and yellow.

HOW TO GROW

Give tender edging lobelia (*L. erinus*) a site in full sun to partial shade. Plants need rich, evenly moist soil for best growth. For good results in the South, plant edging lobelia in a spot that is shaded during the hottest part of the day. Water regularly during dry weather and feed every two weeks. Begin with market packs purchased at a garden center in spring, or start your own plants from seeds, sown indoors at eight to ten weeks before the last spring frost date. Press seeds into the surface of a damp seed-starting medium but do not cover, as they need light to germinate. Damping-off can be a problem with lobelia seedlings, so water only from below. Don't transplant seedlings outdoors until a few weeks after the last-frost date once temperatures remain above 45°F.

Hardy perennial lobelias—specifically *L. cardinalis*, *L. siphilitica*, and related hybrids—need light to partial shade and constantly moist soil that is very rich in organic matter. Plants will grow in full sun in northern gardens if the soil is kept moist. Buy container-grown plants or start your own from seeds or stem cuttings. Perennial lobelias are short-lived plants but self-sow where happy. To keep the plants vigorous, dig the clumps every two or three years in spring and discard the old growth at the center of the clump, replanting only the new rosettes of leaves that grew around it. Start seeds indoors as you would for edging lobelia, or sow them in pots in fall or winter and set them in a protected location outdoors.

Lobelia seedlings are highly susceptible to damping-off. Garden plants can be bothered by a

Cardinal flower, Lobelia cardinalis

litany of pests and diseases, but they are far less susceptible if growing conditions are appropriate.

WHAT TO GROW

Edging lobelia (*L. erinus*) is a tender perennial grown as a warm-weather annual. Originally from South Africa, this 4- to 9-inch-tall species has linear leaves and small clusters of ½-inch flowers from early summer to frost. Edging lobelias have been heavily hybridized, and the species is seldom grown. Plants can have bushy or trailing habits. Rainbow Series plants reach 5 inches and offer cultivars in several separate colors including dark blue 'Crystal Palace', which sports bronze leaves; light blue 'Cambridge Blue'; 'Rosamond', which has wine red flowers with white eyes; and 'White Lady', with white flowers. Rivera Series plants are even shorter—only

4 inches—and come in a range of colors from dark to light blue, pink, and white. Color Cascade Series plants are trailers—they reach 8 inches in height, but their stems trail, making them perfect for baskets and window boxes. Color Cascades come in shades of blue, lavender, rose, white, and red.

Cardinal flower (*L. cardinalis*) is the best-known of the perennial lobelias. It is a native North American wildflower found along streams or marshes and in wet places. Hardy in Zones 2 to 9, plants are 2 to 4 feet tall and produce racemes of flaming scarlet, 2-inch-long flowers in summer and early fall. 'Ruby Slippers' bears ruby red flowers, and 'Rosea', rose-pink blooms. Great blue lobelia (*L. siphilitica*), another native wildflower found in swampy and wet places, is 2 to 4 feet tall and produces racemes of rich blue 1- to 1½-inch-long flowers in late summer to fall. It is hardy in Zones 4 to 8.

If you have a spot for perennial lobelias, also consider some of the hybrids (*L. × speciosa*). 'Bee's Flame' features red-purple leaves and crimson red flowers. 'Queen Victoria' bears bronze-red leaves and scarlet flowers. Hardiness varies here, but most are fine in Zones 5 to 9.

IN THE GARDEN

As their name implies, edging lobelias are good plants for edging a bed or border. Look for bushy, nontrailing cultivars for this purpose. They are also pretty in mixed plantings of shade-loving perennials and annuals such as miniature impatiens, small hostas, and lungworts (*Pulmonaria* spp). Plant trailing types in baskets, containers, and window boxes. Use perennial lobelias to add a bright spot of color to bog gardens and other damp places. They also are handsome planted along a stream or pond. Lobelia flowers attract butterflies.

Lobularia maritima

(lob-you-LAIR-ee-ah mah-RIT-ih-mah)

Sweet alyssum

Cabbage family, Brassicaceae. Annual.

In the wild, sweet, or seaside, alyssum is a plant of rocky, sandy sites, especially coastal regions in the Mediterranean and Canary Islands, where it is native. Despite the lacy, delicate appearance of these cool-weather annuals, they are tough plants well suited for sunny dry spots—and are fine choices for seaside gardens. Plants bear rounded clusters of fragrant, four-petaled flowers in summer, which are pollinated not only by butterflies but ants.

The genus name comes from the Latin *lobulus*, or "small pod," which refers to the small round seedpods that the flowers form, whereas the species name, *maritima* is an obvious reference to the flower's native seacoast habitat. As for the common name of this diminutive plant, "sweet" recognizes the honey scent of the flowers. Alyssum comes from the Greek *a*, meaning "not," and *lyssa*, "madness." The Greeks grew a plant called *Alysson*, or madwort, that was believed to cure the bites of mad dogs, but whether it was *L. maritima* is not known. Perhaps it is enough for these small flowers, as one writer put it, to be a favorite of man and bee.

HOW TO GROW

Sweet alyssum will grow in full sun or partial shade. Average, well-drained soil is fine, and plants will thrive in both evenly moist and dry soil. Market packs of sweet alyssum are readily available at garden centers in spring and everywhere else annuals are sold. Starting your own plants from seeds also is easy. Either sow seeds indoors six to eight weeks before the last spring frost date, or sow seeds several weeks before the last-frost date outdoors where the plants are to grow. In warmer regions, you also can start seeds outdoors in fall for blooms the following spring. Whatever schedule you use, just press the seeds onto the soil surface, as light is required for germination.

Sweet alyssum is nearly carefree once plants are in the garden. Water them regularly for best bloom, and shear the plants back by one-half after the first flush of flowers has ended to encourage new buds to form. Plants self-sow, so be sure to allow some to set seeds. Plants usually have pest and disease problems only because their growing conditions are unmet.

WHAT TO GROW

Sweet alyssum (*L. maritima*, formerly *Alyssum maritimum*) is a 2- to 12-inch-tall annual with a spreading, well-branched habit and linear, gray-green leaves. Plants bear 1- to 3-inch-wide clusters of tiny, four-petaled flowers from spring to fall in white plus shades of pink, rose-red, violet, and lavender. Many cultivars are available, including white-flowered, 3- to 4-inch-tall 'Snow Cloth' and 'Carpet of Snow'. 'Royal Carpet', an All-America Selections winner, is a 3-inch tall selection with violet-purple flowers. 'Easter Basket Mix' yields plants in white and pastel pink, rose, lavender, and violet.

IN THE GARDEN

Sweet alyssum makes a fine temporary ground cover and can be grown alone or sown among low-growing perennials like pinks (*Dianthus* spp.), violets (*Viola* spp.), and thymes (*Thymus* spp.). It is a good choice for planting between stepping stones or in paving cracks, and also it can be used in containers. It is a natural for seaside and butterfly gardens.

Sweet alyssum, Lobularia maritima

Lunaria annua

(loo-NAIR-ee-ah ANN-yew-ah)

Money plant, honesty, moneywort

Cabbage family, Brassicaceae. Biennial.

Money plants bear racemes of four-petaled flowers above mounds of toothed, triangular to heart-shaped leaves. The flowers are followed by round, flat seedpods that have a brown, papery covering, or valve, on each side. When the valves fall or are gently rubbed off, a silvery, translucent, moon-shaped partition appears. It is the seedpods that explain the genus name *Lunaria*, which comes from the Latin, *luna*, for "moon," and the common name moonwort.

Each round seedpod also has a thin edge like the rim of a coin, and that characteristic and the round shape explain a raft of other common names, including money plant, moneywort, silver dollars, money-in-both-pockets, pennieflower, Judas pence, Merlin's money, silver shillings, two-pennies-in-a-purse, and even more names that would set a numismatist's heart aflutter. The common name "honesty" apparently alludes to the transparency of the seedpod after the outer valves are removed. Not surprisingly, *L. annua* represents honesty in the Victorian language of flowers. And perhaps that name explains why the Puritans, a righteous group if ever there were one, took it with them when they sailed to Massachusetts in 1630.

HOW TO GROW

Money plant grows in full sun or light shade and needs soil that is rich, evenly moist, and well drained. Plants of this biennial are rarely offered in garden centers, but it is easy to grow from seeds. Sow seeds outdoors where the plants are to grow anytime from a few weeks before the last spring frost date to early fall. Outdoor sowing is generally best, as plants resent being disturbed, but you can sow indoors in individual containers six to eight weeks before the last frost. Money plant produces foliage the first year and makes money the second. While the seedpods are the main attraction, the flowers are nicely scented as well as pretty.

And once you have a money plant, you *have* money plants: Plants self-sow with enthusiasm. Cut off the stems of seedpods to keep the number of seedlings under control. Money plants have no serious disease or pest problems.

WHAT TO GROW

Money plant (*L. annua*) is a biennial that forms 6- to 12-inch-tall mounds of foliage the first year and 2½- to 3-foot-tall racemes of rose-purple flowers the second year. Plants are hardy in Zones 5 to 9, and branched clusters of seedpods follow the flowers. 'Variegata' bears white-edged, evergreen leaves; 'Alba Variegata' bears white flowers and white-edged leaves. Both come true from seed.

OTHER CHOICES

*P*erennial money plant (*L. rediviva*) is similar but not as showy as its annual cousin. It bears pale lilac-white flowers in late spring or early summer, followed by stems of ellipse-shaped seedpods. It is hardy in Zones 6 to 9.

Money plant, Lunaria annua

IN THE GARDEN

Grow money plant in wild gardens, along shrub borders, and in informal plantings where seedlings can grow where they may without affecting the design. They are nice fillers among hostas and other shade-loving perennials. To use the seedpods for dried arrangements, cut them once they have turned from green to brown, and hang them in a warm, dry spot to let seeds and valves fall. Use your fingers to gently loosen any valves that do not fall naturally.

Lupinus

(lu-PIE-nus)

Lupines

Pea family, Fabaceae.
Hardy perennials, annuals.

○

Lupines are grown for their erect clusters of densely packed, pealike flowers that come in an array of colors from violet and blue to red, pink, yellow, and white. The individual flowers have an upright petal, called a standard, with two side, or wing, petals on either side. Two more petals at the bottom of the flower are joined at the base to form a sheath. About 200 species belong to this genus, most of them native to North, Central, and South America as well as the Mediterranean and North Africa.

Supposedly it was because lupines can grow in poor soil that they earned their genus name *Lupinus*, the classical name for the plant and

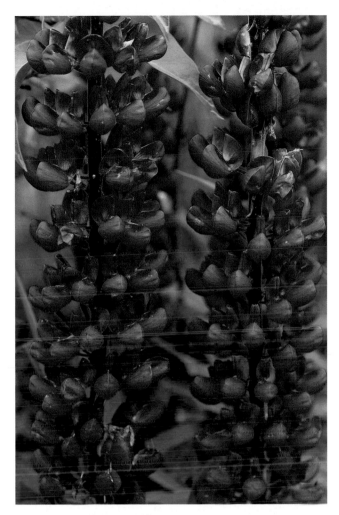

Lupine, Lupinus 'Red Flame'

thought to have derived from *lupinus*, or "wolf." The logic here was that the plants ate, or wolfed down, the nutrients in the soil, leaving it barren. Nothing could be further from the truth, for lupines are leguminous plants and among the very best green manures, plants grown to be turned under the soil in order to improve its fertility. Perhaps a better explanation is that *Lupinus* comes from the Greek *lupe*, which means "grief" and that Virgil's reference to "*tristis lupinus*" was an allusion to the bitterness of the plant's seeds, so terrible that they would make a strong man grimace or kill a hippopotamus, according to one 19th-century writer.

Somewhat nicer are the common names that refer to the flowers: monkey-faces, old-maid's-bonnets, babies' faces, Quaker bonnets, and wild-pea. Whatever the subtleties of its nomenclature, lupines are superb garden plants, but they may be at their best where they have jumped the garden gate and naturalized.

OTHER CHOICES

One lupine relative is a reliable perennial in gardens that have hot, humid summer weather: Carolina lupine (*Thermopsis villosa*, formerly *T. caroliniana*). This is a rhizomatous perennial native from North Carolina to Georgia, so it is adapted to hot, humid weather. It bears its ½-inch yellow flowers in erect, densely packed racemes in late spring and summer. Hardy in Zones 3 to 9, plants range from 3 to 5 feet tall and have attractive palmate leaves. Interesting seed heads follow the flowers.

Lupine, Lupinus *Russell Hybrid*

HOW TO GROW

Lupines need full sun and average to rich, slightly acid soil that is well drained. Most lupines also prefer cool, moist conditions, making them tough to grow in areas with even mildly hot summers. Most of the popular garden types thrive in the Pacific Northwest and in coastal and northern New England but often fail or are short-lived in areas with hot, humid summers. Even in the best of conditions, however, lupines aren't forever.

For first-class results with perennial lupines, start with purchased plants in spring or fall, and plant them in a permanent location, as they resent root disturbance. They can be started from seed in fall, sown in individual pots, and set in a cold frame or a protected location outdoors. Perennial species also can be propagated from cuttings taken from shoots at the base of the plant in spring. Root them in a mix of half perlite and half vermiculite. Plants self-seed but may not flower in the same colors as their parents did. Cutting back plants to about 6 inches after they stop blooming sometimes produces a second flush of flowers and also helps control aphids, which occasionally trouble plants.

Annual lupines can be started from seed: Sow seeds outdoors several weeks before the last spring frost date, or sow indoors in individual pots six to eight weeks before the last-frost date. Before you sow, chip the hard seed coats with a knife or file, or soak them in warm water for 24 hours. Transplant with care, as they resent root disturbance.

Blights and mildews sometimes trouble lupines, but well-grown plants are largely trouble-free.

WHAT TO GROW

Hybrid lupines—especially the popular Russell Hybrids—are probably the most popular of the perennials. These 3- to 5-foot-tall plants produce spikes of flowers in early and midsummer in purple, violet, yellow, pink, red, and white. While plants are hardy in Zones 3 or 4 to 8, they are best treated as annuals south of Zone 6 in eastern and central states.

Wild lupine (*L. perennis*) is a 2-foot-tall native species found from Florida to Maine. Hardy in Zones 4 to 9, plants bear 6- to 12-inch-long spikes of ½-inch blue flowers (or sometimes pink or white) in early summer.

Texas bluebonnet (*L. texensis*) is an iconic cool-weather annual species native to Texas that grows 10 to 12 inches tall and produces 3-inch-long racemes of blue to violet-blue and ½-inch-wide flowers in summer. 'Alamo Fire' bears spikes with buds that are rose pink and open into red flowers.

IN THE GARDEN

Use lupines in perennial beds and borders and in meadow gardens. Combine them with peonies, iris, lamb's ear (*Stachys byzantina*), phlox, and bellflowers (*Campanula* spp.). The flowers attract hummingbirds and beneficials.

Lychnis

(LICK-niss)

Lychnis, campions

Pink Family, Caryophyllaceae.
Hardy perennials, biennials.

Rose campion, Lychnis coronaria *'Angel's Blush'*

Lychnis has a name that harkens back to the days before electricity and light at the flick of a switch: It comes from the Greek *lychnos*, lamp, and refers to the fact that the woolly leaves of rose campion (*L. coronaria*) were once used as lamp wicks. (One common name is lamp flower.) Approximately 15 to 20 species belong here, both biennials and perennials, all of which produce five-petaled flowers that have tube-shaped bases and flattened faces. The petals—or, more accurately, petal lobes—are rounded, notched, or sometimes fringed at the tips. The flowers are borne on branched stems or in small, rounded clusters, and the plants have rounded, often hairy, leaves.

Lychnis species share common names with plants in the genus *Silene*—both are commonly referred to as campions and catchflies. The flowers are quite similar, so the confusion isn't a surprise. The two genera only differ in the number of styles (the stalk that joins the stigma and ovary of a pistil, the female part of a flower) in the flowers. *Lychnis*

species have five or sometimes four styles, whereas *Silene* species have three or four. *Saponaria*, another similar species commonly called soapwort, has flowers with two styles.

The origins of the common name "campion" is a little murky. Some argue that it is a form of champion, a name given because some species were used to make garlands for game winners. Catchfly belongs to the species that have sticky stems that trap insects.

HOW TO GROW

Plant lychnis in full sun or partial shade in a spot that has light, average to rich soil that is well drained. They're best grown where they'll receive shade during the hottest part of the day in areas with torrid summers. Jerusalem cross (*L. chalcedonica*) and German catchfly (*L. viscaria*) do best in rich soil that is slightly moist, while *L. × haageana* needs constantly moist soil. The silvery gray leaves of rose campion (*L. coronaria*) exhibit their best color in dry soil.

Add campions to your garden by purchasing plants or starting from seeds. Plants tend to be short-lived but self-sow and will replace themselves where happy. Tall species need staking; pinching stems in spring promotes bushy growth and may forestall having to prop up plants. Deadheading

OTHER CHOICES

Several lychnis look-alikes make fine garden plants and can be grown much like campions. Soapworts (*Saponaria* spp.) bear five-petaled flowers in shades of pink and thrive in sun and average, well-drained soil. Try bouncing bet, or soapwort (*S. officinalis*), which sports clusters of ¾-inch white, pink, or red flowers from summer to fall on 1- to 2½-foot plants. 'Alba Plena' bears double white flowers and 'Rosea Plena', fragrant pink ones. Hardy in Zones 3 to 9, all are vigorous plants that spread by rhizomes to form broad clumps. Royal catchfly (*Silene regia*), which grows in similar conditions, produces clusters of red, 1-inch flowers on 2- to 5-foot plants and is hardy in Zones 5 to 8.

prolongs bloom. Divide plants every two to three years in spring to keep the clumps vigorous.

Propagate plants by dividing them in spring (in fall in warm regions) or from seeds, which should be prechilled in the refrigerator for two weeks. Sow seeds in fall in pots and set them in a protected location outdoors, or sow directly in the garden in early spring. Campions are sometimes invaded by whiteflies but are trouble-free in the main.

WHAT TO GROW

Arkwright's campion (*L.* × *arkwrightii*) produces clusters of starry, 1½-inch flowers that are orange-red in color on 1½- to 2-foot plants. Plants bloom in early to midsummer and are hardy in Zones 4 to 8. 'Vesuvius' bears scarlet-orange flowers that are dramatically set off against dark brown-green leaves.

Jerusalem, or Maltese, cross (*L. chalcedonica*) is long lived and produces rounded clusters of brilliant red, star-shaped, ½-inch-wide flowers that have deeply notched petals. Hardy in Zones 4 to 8, plants bloom in early to midsummer and are 3 to 4 feet tall. 'Alba' has white flowers, and 'Rosea', pink blooms.

Rose campion (*L. coronaria*), also called mullein pink and dusty miller, is a biennial or short-lived perennial that features rosettes of woolly, silver-gray leaves. Branched clusters of 1- to 1¼-inch, magenta-pink flowers with notched petals in late summer. 'Alba' has white flowers; 'Angel's Blush' bears white flowers with bright pink eyes. Rose campion is hardy in Zones 4 to 8.

L. × *haageana* is a 1½- to 2-foot-tall hybrid species that produces loose clusters of brilliant red or orange-red flowers in summer, and it is hardy in Zones 4 to 8. German catchfly (*L. viscaria*), from 1 to 1½ feet tall, produces loose, spiky clusters of purplish-pink, ¾-inch-wide flowers in early and midsummer. 'Alba' bears white flowers. 'Fire' (also sold as 'Feuer') bears red, sometimes double, flowers. German catchfly is hardy in Zones 3 or 4 to 8.

IN THE GARDEN

Grow *Lychnis* species in perennial beds and borders and combine them with other plants that bloom at the same time. They're handsome with daylilies, bellflowers (*Campanula* spp.), yarrows (*Achillea* spp.), speedwells (*Veronica* spp.), and purple coneflower (*Echinacea purpurea*). Gray-leaved rose campion (*L. coronaria*) is handsome with catmints (*Nepeta* spp.), lavenders, and ornamental grasses.

Lysimachia

(lie-sih-MOCK-ee-ah)

Lysimachias, loosestrifes

Primrose family, Primulaceae.
Hardy perennials.

While gardeners are advised not to try this technique, legend has it that a lysimachia was once used by King Lysimachos of Thracia (360–281 B.C.) to pacify a bull. (Thracia was a kingdom on the northern shore of the Adriatic Sea, given to Lysimachos by Alexander the Great.) *Lysimachia* is from the Greek *lysis*, "releasing," and *mache*, "strife." Lysimachos had plenty of lysimachias to choose from, as there are about 150 species in the genus, and many are vigorous spreaders. If he pulled one stem, he would have gotten an armful, although there is no record of exactly how much lysimachia pacifying a bull requires.

Lysimachias bear five-petaled flowers, usually in shades of yellow or white, and blooms are starry to cup or saucer shaped. Depending on the species, they may be carried singly or in racemes or panicles. The leaves are simple. Despite the fact that loosestrife is a shared common name, *Lysimachia* species should not be confused with purple loosestrifes (*Lythrum* spp.),

Gooseneck loosestrife, Lysimachia clethroides

Whorled loosestrife, Lysimachia punctata

and spread with ease. Divide them in spring or fall as necessary to keep them in bounds. Division is both easy and frequently needed, making it the best way to propagate. Like many vigorous plants, they have few problems with pests and diseases.

WHAT TO GROW

Best known is gooseneck loosestrife (*L. clethroides*), a 3-foot-tall species that bears dense, curving clusters of ½-inch-wide white flowers from mid- to late summer. Hardy in Zones 3 to 9, plants are rhizomatous and spread vigorously to form broad clumps. Fringed loosestrife (*L. ciliata*) is also a rhizomatous spreader, hardy in Zones 3 to 9. It ranges from 1 to 3 feet tall and produces yellow, starry, 1-inch-wide flowers in midsummer. The flowers are solitary or carried in pairs in the leaf axils. 'Purpurea' bears purple-black leaves. Whorled loosestrife (*L. punctata*) produces whorls of 1 inch, cup-shaped, yellow flowers in summer. Plants reach 3 feet in height and, like their relatives, they spread, although less vigorously than gooseneck loosestrife. It is hardy in Zones 4 to 8.

Dense-flowered loosestrife (*L. congestiflora*) is a vigorous, mat-forming species that can be grown as a perennial from Zone 7 south; it is also sold as an annual for northern gardens. It bears clusters of ½- to ¾-inch-wide golden yellow flowers from summer to fall on 4-inch-tall plants. Plants can spread to 2 feet in a single season. 'Golden Harvest' and 'Outback Sunset' bear golden yellow flowers and handsome, yellow-variegated leaves.

IN THE GARDEN

Plant loosestrifes in beds and borders with other perennials that bloom in the summertime. Since they thrive in moist soil, consider combining them with bee balms (*Monarda* spp.), Siberian iris (*Iris sibirica*), ligularias (*Ligularia* spp.), perennial lobelias (*Lobelia cardinalis* and *L. siphilitica*), hostas, and ferns. Many loosestrifes aren't shy, especially gooseneck loosestrife, so don't plant them where they can overwhelm less aggressive neighbors.

which are perennials that have become noxious weeds in many areas of North America and should never be grown in gardens.

HOW TO GROW

Give lysimachias a spot in full sun or partial shade with rich, well-drained, evenly moist soil. Since they also tolerate constantly moist soil, consider them for a spot in a bog garden, moist border, or along a pond or stream, too. Plants wilt without adequate moisture, and dry soil slows their growth—not necessarily a bad thing for some of these vigorous colonizers, which spread by rhizomes and can become invasive. Cut plants to the ground in fall, after the foliage has been killed.

Add lysimachias to your garden by purchasing plants or begging divisions from other gardeners. Once in the ground, plants require little care

Malva

(MAL-vah)

Mallows, malvas

Mallow family, Malvaceae. Hardy perennials.

While *Malva* contains annuals, biennials, and perennials, gardeners commonly cultivate the perennials, which are grown for their showy clusters of five-petaled flowers. These have been used as medicinal plants since Roman times—the botanical name is the Latin name for the plant. Tree mallow (*M. sylvestris*) has been used to treat bronchitis, coughs, and throat infections, and it is also an expectorant. Fresh leaves can be used as a compress for insect bites. In addition, this plant has culinary uses. Flowers are used to brew teas, and young shoots and leaves are edible and can be added to salads, baked in quiches, and used to thicken soups as okra is. Other common names, cheeses and fairy cheeses, refer to the rounded seed capsules that follow the flowers, as does the name pancakes. The capsules, too, are edible and when still new and green can be added to salads.

Perennial mallows bear their cup- or saucer-shaped flowers in clusters in the leaf axils or in racemes—hollyhock mallow (*M. alcea*) produces them in both places. All mallows have petals that are somewhat squared-off at the ends, with notched tips. The flowers are roselike, which gives rise to common names like musk rose and skunk rose. Leaves are rounded or heart to kidney shaped and either entire or variously toothed and lobed.

Thomas Jefferson cultivated several mallows at Monticello, as well as a number of mallowlike flowers, including hollyhock (*Alcea rosea*) and *Lavatera*. Perhaps he liked the color mauve, which is most common in this family of plants. Gardeners less fond of the hue often refer to it as "pink trying to be purple."

HOW TO GROW

Plant mallows in full sun and give them average to moderately rich, well-drained soil and even moisture. They also will grow in partial shade, which is the best choice for warm-region gardeners. In general, mallows grow best in areas with cooler summers and struggle in the South, where heat and humidity are the norm.

Add mallows to your garden by purchasing plants. They're also fairly easy from seed. Since plants tend to be short-lived, plan to replace or propagate them regularly. Water plants often until they are established and during long droughts. Tall types may need staking if grown in rich soil. Pinching or cutting plants back in early spring encourages branching and limits height. Deadhead to extend the bloom season. Cut plants back to the new basal foliage once they are killed by frost or earlier if the leaves are tattered and unsightly.

Mallows self-sow, and self-sown seedlings can be a good source of new plants in the right site. Start seeds indoors in six to eight weeks before the last-frost date or sow outdoors, either in early spring in the garden, about the time of the last frost, or in

Tree mallow, Malva sylvestris *'Zebrina'*

fall in pots set outdoors to overwinter in a protected place. Mallows also can be propagated by division and from cuttings taken in spring from the shoots that grow from the base of the plant.

Mallows attract Japanese beetles and spider mites.

WHAT TO GROW

Hollyhock mallow (*M. alcea*) is a 2- to 4-foot-tall species with pink, 1½- to 2-inch flowers from early summer to fall. *M. alcea* var. *fastigiata*, also sold as 'Fastigiata', is more popular than the species. It bears 2-inch, rose-pink blooms on 2½- to 3-foot plants. Both are hardy in Zones 4 to 9.

Tree mallow (*M. sylvestris*) is a woody-based perennial, hardy in Zones 4 to 8. Sometimes grown as a biennial, it is 3 to 4 feet tall and bears clusters of 2½-inch pinkish purple flowers from late spring or early summer to fall. *M. sylvestris* f. *alba*, also sold as 'Alba', bears white flowers. 'Zebrina' bears white to pale pink flowers striped with dark pink on 2- to 3-foot plants.

IN THE GARDEN

Combine mallows with summer-blooming perennials such as daylilies, phlox, coreopsis, yarrows (*Achillea* spp.), feverfew (*Tanacetum parthenium*), gayfeathers (*Liatris* spp.), and valerian (*Centranthus ruber*).

Matthiola incana

(*mat-thee-OH-lah in-CAH-nah*)

Common stock

Cabbage family, Brassicaceae. Annual.

Also called gillyflower, common stock (*M. incana*) is grown for its sweetly scented flowers—both in gardens and as cut flowers. It is closely related to wallflowers (*Erysimum* spp.), which also are fragrant, and in its unhybridized form bears the four-petaled, cross-shaped flowers that mark it a relative of cabbage and broccoli. Garden-grown forms are more likely to bear double flowers than single ones.

Few flowers have a richer garden history than stocks. The Elizabethans grew them with relish, and new varieties were constantly being imported to England, most often from France. Early gardeners

Common stock, Matthiola incana 'Midget Rose'

had "precious Seacret" techniques for growing stocks successfully, including John Evelyn's instruction in *Directions for the Gardiner at Says Court* (1687) to "dig a Hole with a Spade about as broad and deep as a Hat" when setting out seedlings. Samuel Gilbert, in 1693, recommended transplanting seedlings "about the full Moon, into barren earth, or you may set them again in the same earth, after you have turned it and mixed sand with it to barren it, which must be done speedily upon their taking up."

The name *Matthiola* honors the 16th-century Italian botanist and physician Piesandrea Mattiolo; the species name *incana* alludes to the gray color of the leaves. They seem uninspired names for a plant treasured for its fragrance, although Mattiolo gets partial credit for prescribing stock medicinally, for "matters of love and lust."

HOW TO GROW

Give stocks a spot in full sun with average soil that is well drained; a pH that is neutral to slightly alkaline is ideal. These are plants that do best in areas that have cool summers, as they are intolerant of warm nighttime temperatures.

Either begin with market packs from a garden center in spring or start your own plants from seeds. For a longer bloom season, sow seed in individual pots indoors six to eight weeks before the frost-free date. Do not cover the seeds, just press them into

OTHER CHOICES

*I*f you love fragrant flowers, there are several other annuals you should try. All can be grown in much the way of common stock. Arrange them in drifts for the best fragrance effect, and keep clumps of different species somewhat separate so you can enjoy their individual aromas.

Night-scented stock (*Matthiola longipetala* spp. *bicornis*). A 1- to 1½-foot-tall, cool-weather annual, night-scented stock is grown for its loose racemes of fragrant pink, mauve, or purple flowers that release their strong, sweet fragrance at night. It is easier to grow and less fussy than common stock.

Virginia stock (*Malcolmia maritima*). Despite its common name this species is native to the Mediterranean. A cool-weather annual, it produces racemes of sweetly scented,

Four-o'clock, Mirabilis jalapa 'Red Glow'

four-petaled flowers in shades of pink, purple, white, and red from summer to fall on 8- to 16-inch plants.

Mignonette (*Reseda odorata*). This is a 1- to 2-foot-tall, cool-weather annual that has rounded spikes of small, yellowish green, white, or reddish green flowers. The flowers are intensely fragrant, but look for older cultivars with greenish flowers, as newer selections that feature brighter flowers tend to be less sweetly scented.

Four-o'clock (*Mirabilis jalapa*). This old-fashioned plant—a tender perennial grown as a warm-weather annual—is also called marvel-of-Peru. The fragrant flowers open on sunny days in late afternoon and last until early morning. Although each flower lasts for less than 24 hours, blossoms are produced in abundance, and plants bloom from midsummer until frost in shades of red, magenta, pink, yellow and white. Blooms may be a solid color or striped or spotted with a contrasting hue. Plants self-sow, and they also produce tuberous roots that can be dug in fall and overwintered indoors as you would dahlias.

Bells of Ireland (*Molucella laevis*). Also called shell flower, this cool-weather annual is grown for its showy, cup-shaped papery green calyxes more than its tiny, fragrant, white flowers. Plants reach 2 or 3 feet and bloom in late summer. They make excellent cut or dried flowers. For fresh use, cut the spikes once they have reached the desired length. For drying, cut them when the calyxes are still green or as they begin to turn beige.

the soil surface, use sterile containers and planting medium to avoid damping-off, and keep seeds and seedlings cool, about 50°F to 60°F. Let the medium dry out slightly between waterings. Seeds also can be sown outdoors after the last frost or in late summer or fall in Zones 9 and south.

Pinch seedlings to encourage branching. When hot weather arrives and the plants decline, pull them up and add them to the compost pile. Or let them linger a bit and self-sow. Stocks are susceptible to damping-off, powdery mildew, and to aphids.

WHAT TO GROW

Common stock (*M. incana*) is a ½- to 3-foot-tall tender perennial or subshrub that is grown as a cool-

weather annual. (Plants are hardy only in Zones 7 and 8.) Plants have feltlike, gray-green leaves and dense, erect clusters of spicy-scented, 1-inch-wide flowers in shades of pink, white, mauve, and purplish pink. Blooms may be single or double. 'Ten-Week Mix' is a commonly available selection, producing self-supporting 1-foot plants that are quicker to bloom than many cultivars and is a good choice for most North American gardens. 'Giant Column Mix' produces 2-foot stalks of mainly double flowers in a variety of colors and is an ideal cultivar for cutting.

IN THE GARDEN

Plant stocks in mixed beds and borders, especially along walkways and around patios, and in containers where their fragrance can be enjoyed. Combine them with other flowers for cutting, such as snapdragons (*Antirrhinum* spp.) and China aster (*Callistephus chinensis*). Or plant a patch in your cutting or vegetable garden to ensure a ready supply of scented blooms to add to bouquets. Stocks also are good choices for seaside gardens.

Monarda

(*moe-NAR-dah*)

Bee balms, monardas

Mint family, Lamiaceae. Hardy perennials.

Vigorous and versatile, these native North American wildflowers are both useful and handsome perennials, prized by gardeners who primarily grow two species—*Monarda didyma* and M. *fistulosa*. Bee balms were used by native North Americans to brew teas—thus the common name Oswego tea—and for medicinal purposes. M. *didyma* was prescribed as an expectorant, to lower fevers, and to treat minor digestive problems, whereas M. *fistulosa* was used to treat colds, sore throats, headaches, fevers, and gastric problems.

The name *Monarda* honors the 16th-century Spanish botanist and physician Nicholas Monardes, author of *Joyfull Newes of the Newe Founde Worlde* (1577), a treatise he wrote without ever visiting the Newe Founde Worlde. Monardes's "joyfull newes," which focused on the medicinal uses of North American plants, was positive about the curative potential of monardas but was downright gaga about tobacco, as the section entitled "Of the Tabaco and of His Greate Vertues" suggests. Gaga but not accurate, as he claimed that "in griefs of the breast it does make a marvelous effect, and in especially in those that do cast out matter and rottenness at the mouth, and in them that are short breathed."

Bee balms bring color to the garden in the form of rounded, ragged-looking clusters of two-lipped, tubular flowers. Clusters are 4 inches wide and have showy, colorful bracts beneath them. Blooms come in red, shades of pink, purple, violet, and white, and they are carried above erect stems of ovate to ovate-lance-shaped leaves. Square stems and aromatic

Bee balm, Monarda didyma '*Panorama Mix*'

(citruslike) leaves mark these plants as a relative of mints (*Mentha* spp.). Like mints, they spread by fast-creeping rhizomes to form broad clumps.

HOW TO GROW

Give bee balms a spot in full sun or light shade with evenly moist but well-drained soil—and good air circulation. To look its best, M. *didyma* needs fertile soil with good drainage but even moisture. Plants become ratty looking and are plagued by powdery mildew if the soil dries out during the growing season. M. *fistulosa* grows well in moist, average to rich soil but also tolerates drier conditions.

Start with plants when adding bee balms to your garden. Even one small plant will quickly spread to form a large clump. (Bee balms are vigorous in the North and can be invasive in the South.) Plant in spring or fall, and be sure to choose a location

Bee balm, Monarda didyma *'Cambridge Scarlet'*

resistant cultivars, including red-flowered 'Jacob Cline', pink 'Marshall's Delight', lilac-purple 'Prairie Night' (also sold as 'Prärienacht'), and 'Raspberry Wine', which has wine-red flowers. 'Petite Delight' is mildew resistant and reaches only 12 to 15 inches in height. Outstanding and popular 'Cambridge Scarlet' produces stunning red flowers but is not as mildew resistant as are some of the newer cultivars. 'Panorama Mix', which comes true from seeds, produces plants with a mix of red, pink, and salmon flowers. All are hardy in Zones 3 to 8.

Wild bergamot (M. *fistulosa*), also called wild bee balm and horsemint, is a 3- to 5-foot-tall species with rounder leaves that are less susceptible to mildew than those of M. *didyma*. Plants produce clusters of ¾-inch-long lavender-pink flowers from midsummer to fall and are hardy in Zones 3 to 9

IN THE GARDEN

Plant bee balms in informal or meadow gardens where their spreading growth habit will not be a major problem. They can be planted in beds and borders, but they will need regular attention to stay in bounds. Flowers of bee balm (M. *didyma*) can be added fresh to salads, and both species can be dried and added to potpourris. Combine them with garden phlox (*Phlox paniculata*), perennial sunflowers (*Helianthus* spp.), sneezeweeds (*Heliopsis* spp.), Joe-Pye weeds (*Eupatorium* spp.), and queens-of-the-prairie (*Filipendula* spp.). Monardas are absolutely, positively guaranteed to attract hummingbirds but, oddly enough, rarely attract bees, who are unable to reach the nectar in the blooms.

large enough to accommodate a clump that soon will be 2 feet and more in diameter. Pinching plants in early spring reduces height but also delays flowering.

Bee balms need minimal care once established. Removing spent flowers encourages plants to rebloom—look for blooms forming farther down the stem and cut just above them. Plants infected with mildew can be cut to the ground.

Dividing the clumps regularly is essential, as it keeps them vigorous and also helps control their spread. Dig clumps in spring or early fall, discard the old, woody growth at the center of the clump, and replant the newer shoots from the edges of the clump. Division is an easy way to propagate bee balms—even small pieces of the rhizomes sprout. To grow from seed, sow outdoors in early spring, about the time of the frost-free date, or in fall in pots that are set outside in a protected location to overwinter.

Plants are subject to powdery mildew and are beloved by Japanese beetles.

WHAT TO GROW

Bee balm (M. *didyma*), also commonly called bergamot and Oswego tea, is a 2- to 4-foot-tall perennial with aromatic leaves. From mid- to late summer, plants produce whorls of two-lipped flowers in shades of scarlet or pink with red-tinged bracts beneath them. For best results, plant mildew-

Myosotis sylvatica

(my-oh-SOE-tis syl-VAT-ih-cah)

Forget-me-not

Borage family, Boraginaceae.
Biennial/hardy perennial.

Forget-me-nots bring clusters of tiny, true blue flowers to the garden, as well as pink, violet, and white flowers. The small blooms are salverform, meaning they are trumpet-shaped with a flared and flattened face that has six petal-like lobes surrounding a yellow eye. Leaves are ovate to elliptical in shape and hairy, giving rise to the common name mouse ear. A biennial or short-lived perennial native to Europe, forget-me-not self-sows freely. "The blue and bright-eyed floweret of the brook, / Hope's gentle gem" was the 19th-century British poet Samuel Taylor Coleridge's description.

England's King Henry IV adopted forget-me-not as his personal emblem, believing that it would ensure he would never be forgotten. He hasn't been, of course, but probably for usurping the English crown from Richard II, starting the Lancastrian dynasty, and planting the seeds of the War of the Roses, not for wearing a forget-me-not on his shield.

One explanation for *Myosotis sylvatica's* most famous common name comes from the Christian myth that after God named all the plants, one small blue flower was unable to remember its name. So God gave it a new name, forget-me-not. It's a much sweeter tale than the legend that the name comes from the terrible flavor of the plant's leaves: If you taste them, you will never forget them.

HOW TO GROW

Plant forget-me-nots in full sun or light shade and in moist, well-drained soil. Shade during the hottest part of the day is necessary in hot climates. The only attention forget-me-nots require is a haircut after they've finished flowering if you want to prevent plants from self-sowing, which they do with vigor. (Don't cut them back if you want more plants.) Or pull plants when they finish flowering, treating them as if they were annuals.

To add forget-me-nots to your garden, start with container-grown plants or a packet of seed. Once you have them established, you probably won't need to plant them again. It's possible to begin seeds indoors, but seedlings are highly susceptible to damping-off, so it's wiser to sow outdoors where the plants are to grow several weeks before the last-frost date. From about Zone 6 south, sow in fall for bloom the following spring. Seedlings, yours or self-sown, are easy to transplant.

Forget-me-nots are sometimes troubled by powdery mildew.

WHAT TO GROW

Forget-me-not (M. *sylvatica*), also called woodland forget-me-not, is a 5- to 12-inch-tall biennial or short-lived perennial grown for its clusters of tiny, blue, white, or pink, ⅜-inch-wide flowers. Plants bloom in spring and early summer above clumps of gray-green leaves. They're hardy in Zones 3 or 4 to 9. Victoria Series plants reach 4 to 8 inches tall and come in white, blue, or pink.

IN THE GARDEN

Plant forget-me-nots in informal flowerbeds for an extra pick-me-up of spring color. They are pretty planted among emerging hostas, honesty (*Lunaria annua*), hardy geraniums or cranesbills (*Geranium* spp.), spring bulbs, and primroses (*Primula* spp.).

Forget-me-not, Myosotis sylvatica 'Blue Basket'

Narcissus

(nar-SIS-us)

Daffodils, jonquils, narcissus

Amaryllis family, Amaryllidaceae. Hardy bulbs.

Even nongardeners know a daffodil when they see one. These quintessential signs of spring show up in florist shops, flower stands, and grocery stores long before they could bloom in the garden, although daffodils show their faces—or their leaves—very early. In winter, the tips of their strap-shaped leaves poke above the soil surface after a spell of mild weather. Even though the leaves usually have to go back into winter's deep freeze before real daffodil days arrive, the flowers are not all that far behind: The earliest daffodils begin blooming in late winter, especially in protected sites. In the South, daffodils start blooming in late January or early February, several months before they flower in northern gardens.

The botanical name *Narcissus* is in honor of Narcissus of Greek mythology, the young man who was turned into a flower by the gods after he became entranced with his own reflection. Daffodils were in cultivation as early as 300 B.C., when the Greek Theophrastus, the father of botany, wrote about them. The Greek poet Homer called them "wondrously glittering, a noble sight for all, whether immortal gods or mortal men." The Roman Dioscoridis, a physician who served as a botanist in Nero's army, praised their medicinal value in his herbals, but recent findings don't support his beliefs. If eaten, daffodil bulbs cause violent vomiting and have other unpleasant side effects. Actually, that's good news for gardeners, since the poisonous nature of the plants isn't lost on rodents and deer: These are bulbs that won't be gobbled up by wildlife, however hungry.

Narcissus flowers have a unique construction. The bloom has six petal-like perianth segments that surround a corona, more often called a trumpet or a

Large cup daffodil, Narcissus 'Brighton'

Trumpet daffodil, Narcissus 'Mount Hood'

cup, in the center. (The corona is called a trumpet if it is long and a cup if it is short.) Most daffodils produce one flower per stem, but there are plants that produce clusters of up to 20 flowers on a single stem.

Daffodils come in many shapes and colors. The large yellow trumpets are most common—Wordsworth's "a crowd, / A host, of golden daffodils"—but narcissus also come in white, orange, pale yellow, and pink. Many narcissus have bicolor blooms—a deep orange cup surrounded by white petals, for example. There also are plants with double flowers and more. Bloom season varies, too, and cultivars are generally rated as early, midseason, or late blooming; planting a mix from different categories will extend the daffodil season. Most full-size blooms are 3½ to 4½ inches wide, but there are daffodils with 1½-inch blooms as well. Plant size varies, too: Daffodils usually are about 18 inches tall, but miniatures may only reach 4 or 6 inches. While all *Narcissus* species are commonly called daffodils, the term jonquil is often applied to dwarf plants with small-cupped flowers.

HOW TO GROW

Daffodils need full sun during their growing season, but are fine in a site shaded by deciduous trees, because they'll get ample light in spring when their leaves are out. They tolerate most soils as long as they have well-drained conditions; the bulbs of nearly all species rot in soggy soil. (*N. poeticus* and its cultivars tolerate moist to wet soil in winter and spring and fairly damp conditions in summer.) Keep bulbs above the water line if you plant them around

a pond or other water feature. The pH can be acid or alkaline—from pH 5.0 to 8.0. Ideally, give them evenly moist soil from fall to spring, with drier conditions in summer. If heavy, wet, clay soil is your lot in life, dig in plenty of compost or leaf mold to improve drainage, and plant bulbs on the shallow side. Planting in raised beds also is a good option for dealing with clay soil and poor drainage.

Plant daffodils in the fall. You'll find bulb displays everywhere, from garden centers to grocery stores. For the newest and best cultivars, stick to nurseries or mail-order suppliers. Look for firm, solid bulbs that seem heavy for their size. Reject any that have cuts, are shriveled, or have blackened or moldy spots. While you can put bulbs in the ground anytime before the soil freezes, early planting is best because it gives them time to grow roots before seriously cold weather arrives. Set the bulbs 2 to 3 times as deep as they are tall, generally with the shoulder of the bulb (the point where it swells out from the top) 4 to 6 inches below the soil surface—less for smaller bulbs.

Once planted, almost all you need to do is to enjoy these low-maintenance flowers. Let the leaves ripen for six to eight weeks after the plants finish blooming, then cut them back once they turn yellow or brown and topdress with compost. Don't braid or tie the foliage, as it restricts the leaves' access to sunlight and the renourishing of the bulb.

Propagate by digging and separating bulbs after their foliage has died back; replant immediately. Daffodils can be grown from seeds, but it's hardly worth the trouble. Several diseases and pests *can* trouble them, but they almost never do.

WHAT TO GROW

Deciding which daffodils to grow can be as fun as it is frustrating. There are about 50 species and thousands of cultivars to choose from, with cultivars being far more popular in gardens than the species. All have been organized into 12 divisions according to flower shape and origin, and you'll find that good garden centers and mail-order catalogs refer to these divisions. Don't worry about memorizing the names of the divisions; just knowing they exist helps you make good choices. In addition to lengthening the bloom season (plants in the different divisions tend to bloom at different times), planting daffodils from different divisions also ensures an interesting variety of flower shapes and sizes in the garden.

While most daffodils are hardy from Zones 3 or 4 to 8 (mulch in Zone 3 for winter protection),

Cyclamineus daffodils, Narcissus cyclamineus 'Tete-a-Tete'

or round, bulbs are a good buy; they're three years old and produce one or more flower stems the first year. Double-nose, or bedding-size bulbs, are four years old and usually produce two flower stems the first year. Exhibition-size, or triple-nose, bulbs are five years old and produce three or more flower stems. As with many things, when it comes to bulbs, cheap usually means cheap—make sure you are getting *at least* landscape-size bulbs when you buy. You can save a lot of money by buying in bulk or buying collections—look for special offers in catalogs from bulb specialists such as Brent and Becky's Bulbs (brentandbeckysbulbs.com).

Trumpet Cultivars, Division 1. Probably the best known daffodils, trumpets produce one flower per stem with a corona as long as or longer than the petals; they bloom in early to midspring. All-yellow 'King Alfred' introduced in 1899, belongs here, as do 'Arctic Gold', 'Dutch Master', 'Golden Harvest', and 'Unsurpassable', which also are all-yellow. White-flowered Division 1 cultivars include 'Beersheba', 'Empress of Ireland', and 'Mount Hood', which bears flowers slightly blushed in yellow when they open. Trumpet cultivars also can be bicolor—white and pale yellow 'Honeybird', yellow-and-white 'Las Vegas', or 'Spellbinder', with a yellow perianth and greenish yellow cup that matures to white. This division also contains miniatures, which are 6 to 8 inches tall when they bloom.

Large-Cupped Cultivars, Division 2. These cultivars also have one flower per stem, and flowers have a cup that is more than one-third the length of the petals. They bloom in midspring and come in a range of colors. Two-toned yellow, fragrant 'Carlton' belongs here, as does 'Camelot'. There also are all-white selections such as 'Easter Moon' and 'White Plume'. Bicolors include 'Fortissimo', with yellow petals and orange cup, and 'Ice Follies', with white petals and a yellow cup. There are

hardiness varies, too. Reputable firms will indicate the hardiness of their offerings; be suspicious of any sellers that say daffodils are all the same. (For example, paperwhites, *N. papyraceus*, which are commonly sold for forcing are only hardy in Zones 8 and 9. They can be forced into bloom in trays of pebbles and water, but if you live in the South and want to plant the bulbs outdoors after forcing, pot them in soil.)

When comparing prices, keep in mind that daffodil bulbs come in different sizes. Landscape-size,

Large-cupped daffodil, Narcissus 'Romance'

Triandrus Cultivars, Division 5. Triandrus daffodils produce clusters of two to six flowers with short cups and reflexed petals. They bloom in mid- to late spring, and plants are 12 to 14 inches tall. Cultivars include extremely fragrant, white-flowered 'Petrel', yellow 'Hawera', pink-and-white 'Katie Heath', and fragrant, white 'Thalia'.

Cyclamineus Cultivars, Division 6. These bear solitary flowers with a long trumpet and reflexed petals on 10- to 14-inch plants. Cultivars include 'Beryl', with yellow petals and a yellow cup banded in orange; 'Jetfire', which has yellow petals and an orange-red cup; 'Jack Snipe', with white petals and a yellow cup; and the all-yellow 'Rapture'.

Jonquilla Cultivars, Division 7. Jonquilla cultivars produce solitary or small clusters of small-cupped flowers with spreading petals and have grasslike leaves. These bloom in mid- to late spring, range from 12 to 16 inches tall, and often have

pink-flowered selections such as 'Peaches and Cream', with its white petals and a pale peach pink cup; 'Pink Charm', white petals and a white cup with a dark pink band; and 'Salomé', white petals with a pink cup rimmed with gold.

Small-Cupped Cultivars, Division 3. Also called short-cupped daffodils, these narcissus have cups that are only one-third the length of the petals. Good cultivars include 'Barrett Browning', with white petals and an orange-red cup; 'Sabine Hay', with gold petals and a brick-red cup; 'Verona', an all-white cultivar; and 'Sinopel', which has six petals instead of four and resembles a dogwood blossom.

Double Cultivars, Division 4. Division 4 daffodils bear flowers with doubled petals or a double cup. Flowers are solitary or there may be more than one flower per stem. 'Acropolis', bears single, fragrant white blooms. 'Flower Drift' is creamy white flecked with yellow-orange in the center; 'Tahiti' has yellow petals interspersed with bright orangey red segments; 'Cheerfulness', white, and 'Yellow Cheerfulness' are fragrant cultivars with two to three double blooms per stem.

Pheasant's eye, Narcissus poeticus *var.* recurvus

fragrant flowers. Cultivars include 8-inch miniature 'Baby Moon' with all-yellow flowers; 'Curlew', with clusters of fragrant white flowers that open creamy yellow; the all-yellow 'Quail, which bulb seller Brent Heath calls "one of the most floriferous daffodils on our farm"; and 'Sweetness', with fragrant golden yellow flowers produced one or two per stem.

Tazetta Cultivars, Division 8. These bear clusters of as many as 20 small flowers that are very fragrant but are less hardy than most daffodils—from Zones 5 or 6 to 9, depending on the cultivar. Good choices include 'Avalanche', with fragrant flowers that have white perianths and yellow cups; 'Geranium' with fragrant flowers that have white perianths and orange-red cups; and 'Aspasia', a fragrant, yellow heirloom cultivar.

Poeticus Cultivars, Division 9. These produce fragrant flowers with tiny, disc-shaped cups usually rimmed in red. Plants normally produce one flower per stem and bloom from mid- to late spring. They're hardy in Zones 3 to 7. 'Actaea', with white petals and a yellow cup edged in dark red, is best known. Other good cultivars are 'Angel Eyes', 'Felindre', and 'Milan'.

Other Divisions. You'll also see daffodils in three other divisions—Wild Species (Division 10); Split-Corona Cultivars (Division 11); and Miscellaneous Daffodils (Division 12). Commonly grown species include hoop petticoat daffodil (*N. bulbocodium*), which is 4 to 6 inches tall and bears grasslike leaves and 1½-inch-wide yellow flowers with megaphone-shaped trumpets surrounded by narrow petals. *N. bulbocodium* spp. *conspicuus* is a vigorous form with deep yellow flowers. Poet's narcissus (*N. poeticus*), and *N. poeticus* var. *recurvus*, commonly called pheasant's eye, have very fragrant flowers with white petals and small, yellow, red-rimmed cups. They are hardy in Zones 3 to 7.

IN THE GARDEN

Daffodils are an asset anywhere in any garden. Plant them in beds and borders, along walkways, or naturalize them in shade and woodland gardens. Hostas, which emerge and hide the ripening foliage, make effective companions, but daffodils also can be interplanted with pansies, forget-me-not (*Myosotis scorpioides*), grape hyacinths (*Muscari* spp.), and other early blooming annuals, biennials, and bulbs. They are excellent for naturalizing in woodlands or even the lawn, although if you grow them in lawn,

you must be prepared to leave the grass uncut for up to two months while the bulb foliage ripens.

Of course, daffodils also make excellent cut flowers. For the longest-lasting cut flowers, pull—do not cut—the stems, then slit the base of the stem and run it under warm water for a few minutes to reduce the amount of sap that flows out. Stand cut daffodils in water (up to their necks) for several hours before arranging.

Nepeta

(NEP-uh-tah)

Nepetas, catmints

Mint family, Lamiaceae. Hardy perennials.

Grown for their fragrant foliage and flowers, nepetas primarily bloom in shades of lavender, purple, violet, or white. Also called catmints, these are handsome, easy to grow perennials that are all too rarely planted. Catnip (*N. cataria*), named and known for its intoxicating effect on cats, belongs here—one *unreliable* garden adage says, "If you set it, the cats will get it; / If you sow it, the cats won't know it." Fortunately for gardeners, felines are indifferent to other members of the genus, the ones grown in flower gardens, such as *N. × faassenii*. That name replaced *N. mussinii*, although some very discerning gardeners believe that they are two slightly different plants, and you'll find both names in plant catalogs and garden centers. The species name *mussinii* was a major abbreviation of *Apollos Apollosovitch Mussin-Puschkin*, a Russian count and plant collector who lived two centuries ago. One plant or two, nepeta, as Alice Coats wrote in 1956, has "become practically indispensable to our borders, where it wears a deceptively 'old-fashioned' air, and is a very great favourite with bees."

Like catnip, ornamental catmints bear their small, two-lipped flowers in clusters—technically they are borne in spikelike cymes. They have square stems like other mint-family plants, and the species commonly grown in gardens have aromatic, gray-green leaves.

HOW TO GROW

Select a site in full sun or light shade. Catmints grow in average, well-drained soil and thrive in drier soil

Catmint, Nepeta × faassenii 'Six Hills Giant'

than many perennials will. Damp soil leads to crown rot. In the South, give catmints a spot that receives shade during the hottest part of the day.

Add catmints to your garden by purchasing plants in either spring or fall. They need to be watered regularly until they are established but are independent plants thereafter. Taller cultivars will flop if they're not staked, but they look fine flopping and mingling with their neighbors. After the main flush of flowers is over, cut plants back hard—by one-half. This encourages branching and new flowers.

If plants outgrow their space or begin to bloom less, divide the clumps in spring or fall. Division is also the easiest way to propagate. Dig plants in spring or fall and discard the old, woody growth, then replant the vigorous sections of the clump. Or propagate from stem or root cuttings. Ornamental catmints don't come true from seeds. Plants self-sow and become weedy if not cut back before seeds form.

Plants are sometimes bothered by stem rot and by leafhoppers and caterpillars.

WHAT TO GROW

For ornamental catmints, look to N. × *faassenii*. One to 2 feet tall and a clump former, it boasts silvery aromatic leaves and spikes of small, lavender-blue flowers from early summer to fall. 'Six Hills Giant' bears violet-purple flowers on 3-foot plants; 'Dropmore' also grows to 3 feet. 'Walker's Low' is 10 inches tall but spreads to 3 feet and bears lavender-blue flowers; 'White Wonder' bears white flowers. All are hardy in Zones 4 to 8, to Zone 3 with winter protection.

Siberian catnip (N. *sibirica*, formerly *Dracocephalum sibiricum* and *Nepeta macrantha*), hardy in Zones 3 to 9, is a 3-foot-tall species with dark green leaves and racemes of 1½-inch-long lavender-blue flowers in summer. Cut back hard in spring to encourage more compact growth.

If you have cats, you may want to include a patch of true catnip (N. *cataria*) somewhere in your garden. A 3-foot-tall perennial hardy in Zones 3 to 7, it has woolly, aromatic, gray-green leaves and insignificant white flowers.

IN THE GARDEN

Plant catmints in sunny, somewhat dry gardens, where they add cool color and lacy texture. They are effective combined with daylilies, coreopsis, scarlet sage (*Salvia splendens*), and purple coneflower (*Echinacea purpurea*). They are also effective as ground covers and often are used to underplant roses.

Nicotiana

(nih-koe-shee-AH-nah)

Flowering tobaccos, nicotianas

Nightshade family, Solanaceae.
Tender perennials, annuals.

Tobacco has its origins in pre-Columbian times: Archeologists have found relief carvings of the plant in Mexican temples that date to A.D. 100. The botanical name of this genus honors the Frenchman Jean Nicot, who introduced tobacco to the royal courts of France and Portugal in 1560—somewhat of a dubious honor if you consider the legacy of smoking since its introduction. Gardeners, however, celebrate Nicot's introduction—at least its unsmoked brethren, the ornamental flowering tobaccos. These are grown for their clusters of trumpet-shaped flowers that have narrow tubular bases and flaring, flat to cup-shaped faces. They bear undivided leaves that are often covered with sticky hairs and bloom from summer to frost.

Most nicotianas used to close up shop—their blossoms—about noon. (Some said that it was because they stayed open at night to perfume the air and attract moths and other pollinators.) Depending

Flowering tobacco, Nicotiana alata *'Starship Lemon-Lime'*

Zone 5 north. From Zone 6 south, the season is long enough to start them outdoors if you like. Just sow after the last-frost date. Either way, seeds need light to germinate: Press them onto the soil surface rather than cover them.

Flowering tobaccos need evenly moist soil, so water during dry weather. Removing spent flowers helps encourage new buds to form and also keeps plants neat looking. Some nicotianas self-sow, but to ensure a colorful patch of flowering tobaccos every year, you'll want to buy new plants or sow seeds each spring.

WHAT TO GROW

Several different species are commonly called flowering tobacco. These are annuals or short-lived, tender perennials (hardy only in Zones 10 and 11) that are grown as warm-weather annuals. Cultivars of N. *alata*, with spoon-shaped leaves and 4-inch-long flowers are common garden residents. While the 4- to 5-foot species bears very fragrant, greenish white or yellowish flowers that open at night, garden-grown cultivars are more compact—1½ to 2 feet usually—and bear flowers in shades of pink, red, white, and chartreuse; they remain open during the day. Most are not sweet-smelling, but Nicki Series plants bear fragrant flowers in a range of colors on 1½-foot plants. Domino Series plants, which belong to N. × *sanderae*, are heat resistant, 1- to 1½-foot plants with flowers in shades of red, pink, purple-pink, and white.

One other species to consider is stately N. *sylvestris*, a 5-footer that bears clusters of fragrant, white, 4-inch-long trumpets.

on what you're looking for, the fortunate or unfortunate result of this early to bed trait was a group of new hybrids that appeared around 1920, with day-blooming but largely fragrance-free flowers. Happily for gardeners, both types are available, the nicotiana "which wakes and utters her fragrance / In a garden sleeping," as poet Edna St. Vincent Millay wrote, and the more compact cultivars that have become staples of garden centers in spring.

HOW TO GROW

Give these warm-weather flowers a home in full sun or partial shade with rich, evenly moist, well-drained soil. In the South, a spot that is in dappled shade during the hottest part of the day helps protect plants from heat.

Flowering tobaccos are easy to find at any garden center, or you can start your own plants from seeds. Sow indoors six to eight weeks before the last spring frost date. Giving flowering tobaccos a head start indoors is a good idea in cooler regions—from about

Flowering tobacco, Nicotiana × sanderae *'Domino Mix'*

IN THE GARDEN

Large nicotianas are fine plants for the back of the garden; use dwarf flowering tobacco as edging plants, or grow them in mixed plantings of other sun-loving annuals such as petunias or combine them with perennials for an extra splash of color—they're fine with hardy geraniums, delphiniums, and dwarf asters, for example. Dwarf flowering tobaccos also make fine container plants. Nicotianas are excellent cut flowers, and all flowering tobaccos attract moths and hummingbirds.

Nigella damascena

(nye-JEL-ah dam-ah-SEEN-ah)

Love-in-a-mist

Buttercup family, Ranunculaceae. Annual.

Love-in-a-mist, Nigella damascena

Nigella damascena is a old-fashioned annual native to southern Europe and northern Africa. Plants have lacy, deeply cut leaves and flowers colored lavender-blue, purple, pink, and white. The blooms are saucer shaped, about 1¾-inches wide. They have a ruff of branched, threadlike, green bracts under the petals, a characteristic that led to the common name love-in-a-mist. The flowers, borne in summer, are followed by inflated seed capsules, which yield black seeds. The botanical name *Nigella* is from the Latin *niger*, "black," and refers to the seeds. (*Nigella* also refers to the black seeds of another species, *N. sativa*, commonly called black cumin, nutmeg flower, or Roman coriander. Those seeds, which have a spicy, fruity taste, were important in the spice trade until pepper was introduced to Europe. *N. sativa* is still used as a spice in India, Greece, Turkey, and the Middle East.)

N. *sativa* was the first nigella to reach England, but love-in-a-mist was being grown by the Elizabethan era. It appears in John Gerard's monumental herbal (1597), in which he called it gith and St. Katharine's flower and described it as "both faire and pleasant . . . [a flower] sowne in gardens: the wilde ones doe grow of themselves among corne and other graine, in divers countries beyond the seas." Other common names for this many-monikered plant are Persian jewels, devil-in-the-bush, fennel flower, love-in-a-puzzle, love-entangle, Jack-in-prison, and in France, *cheveux de Venus* and *barbe-bleu*.

HOW TO GROW

Give love-in-a-mist a spot in full sun or light shade and plant in well-drained, average garden soil that is slightly acid. These are cool-weather annuals and bloom best before summer heat arrives. Since plants are hard to find in garden centers, the easiest way to add them to your garden is to sow seeds outdoors where the plants will flower several weeks before the last-frost date; in warm regions, sow outdoors in fall for bloom the following spring. The plants resent transplanting, but they can be started indoors in individual pots six to eight weeks before the last-frost date. Outdoors or in pots, barely cover the seeds with soil. Sow new crops every four weeks to extend flowers in the garden.

Water plants during dry weather, and deadhead to keep plants blooming (keep in mind that deadheading eliminates the ornamental seedpods). Plants self-sow, often with abandon, but seedlings are easy to pull up if they take root where they're not wanted.

Nigella has no serious pest or disease problems.

WHAT TO GROW

Love-in-a-mist (*N. damascena*) ranges from 1½ to 2 feet tall. Plant the species or look for a mix like Persian Jewels Series, which yields 16-inch plants in an array of rich colors. 'Cramer's Plum' bears white flowers and purple pods. 'Miss Jekyll' has bright blue flowers; 'Blue Midget' grows only 10 inches tall; and 'Cambridge Blue' has double flowers.

IN THE GARDEN

Plant love-in-a-mist as a filler among clumps of perennials. They're handsome with coreopsis, dwarf daylilies, wormwood (*Artemisia absinthium*), and other sun-loving species. They are ideal cottage garden plants and lovely cut flowers. The pods are interesting in dried arrangements.

Oenothera

(ee-no-THEER-ah)

Evening primroses, sundrops

Evening primrose family, Onagraceae.
Hardy perennials, biennials, annuals.

Mrs. Grieve's *A Modern Herbal* (1931) reported that the leaves of *Oenothera biennis*, or common evening primrose, along with peelings from the stems were used to make treatments for asthma, whooping cough, and digestive disorders, among other things. The scientifically confirmed medicinal properties of the plant are a relatively recent discovery, however. In the 1980s, researchers discovered that evening primrose oil contains an unsaturated fatty acid that assists in the production of hormonelike substances. Today, the oil is used to treat everything from eczema and brittle nails to rheumatoid arthritis and hyperactivity. Evening primrose oil also is used in cosmetics.

O. biennis may have economic importance, but this common roadside weed is not generally grown in

Pink evening primrose, Oenothera speciosa *'Rosea'*

gardens. The cultivated *Oenothera* are normally divided by whether their blooms open in the morning, in which case they go by the common names sundrops, suncups, and golden eggs, or if they open in the afternoon or evening, in which case they're known as evening primroses. Both bear four-petaled, yellow flowers, shaped either like a cup or a saucer, that open over a long season in summer. Native species of *Oenothera* were among the first plants sent back to England from Virginia; gratefully received by gardeners and botanists, they were referred to as tree primroses of Virginia and have become naturalized in Britain.

The genus name *Oenothera* has several possible roots, but most dictionaries have settled on the Greek words *onos*, meaning "ass" or "beast," and *thera*, meaning "hunting." Neither of which, one authority has pointed out, has anything to do with the native American flowers that now bear the name *Oenothera*. Far more appropriate are the many common names the plants have acquired.

HOW TO GROW

Sundrops need full sun but are willing to put up with poor to average soil as long as it is well drained. Once established, plants tolerate drought. These are plants from mountain slopes and deserts—mostly in North America—and won't survive in wet soil, especially in winter. *O. fruticosa* and its cultivars do better in more fertile soil and can be planted in beds and borders that offer well drained, slightly moist conditions.

Start with container-grown plants, and get them into the garden in early spring. When planting, loosen the soil to a depth of 18 inches and work in some compost or other organic matter to improve drainage. Keep mulch away from the plant crowns to avoid crown rot.

Divide plants in early spring or late summer if they outgrow their space or begin to lose vigor or if you want to propagate them. When propagating, either dig the entire plant or use a trowel to remove some of the offsets that appear around the outside of the clump. Or propagate them from shoots that arise at the base of the plant in spring or early summer; root in a mixture of half perlite and half vermiculite. Or take root cuttings (roots tend to run along the soil surface, making them easily accessible). To grow from seed, sow indoors eight to ten weeks before the frost-free date or outdoors in early spring; seeds can be started in fall where winters are mild.

Plants are susceptible to powdery mildew as well as root rot in wet soil.

WHAT TO GROW

Common sundrops (O. fruticosa), a North American native hardy in Zones 4 to 8, is the most popular and showiest member of the genus. It bears clusters of deep yellow, 1- to 3-inch-wide flowers from late spring through summer on 1- to 3-foot plants. A number of compact, 1½- to 2-foot-tall cultivars are available and make outstanding garden plants. O. tetragona, now O. fruticosa spp. glauca, belongs here. Its cultivar 'Summer Solstice' blooms from early summer to fall on 12- to 16-inch plants and features maroon fall foliage. 'Youngii' is a 1½-foot species that blooms from early to midsummer and has scarlet autumn leaves.

Ozark sundrops (O. macrocarpa, formerly O. missouriensis) bears solitary, yellow, 5-inch-wide flowers from late spring to fall on 6-inch-tall plants. Also called Missouri evening primrose, this species grows in full sun or partial shade but demands well-drained or dry soil. It tends to be short-lived in rich, moist conditions. Hardy in Zones 5 to 8, plants self-sow and can be invasive in suitable sites.

Pink evening primrose (O. speciosa) also bears solitary, 1- to 2½-inch flowers on widely spreading, 1-foot-tall plants. This species, which is also called pink ladies, produces flowers in white and shades of pink. Pink-flowered cultivars such as 'Rosea' and 'Siskiyou Pink' are most often grown in gardens. Shear plants after the main flush of bloom in early summer to encourage repeat bloom. Hardy in Zones

5 to 8, these vigorously spreading perennials can be very invasive. Plant them in areas where their spreading won't pose a problem, such as around shrubs. Cultivars are somewhat less vigorous than the species.

If you want to try a night-blooming evening primrose, consider tufted evening primrose (O. caespitosa). A biennial or perennial hardy in Zones 4 to 8, it bears fragrant, white, 4-inch-wide flowers that open at sunset on 4- to 8-inch-tall plants. The following morning the flowers fade to pink and die. Plants bloom for four to six weeks in summer and are suitable for rock gardens or along rock walls.

IN THE GARDEN

Plant adaptable common sundrops (O. fruticosa) and its cultivars in perennial beds and borders with other summer-blooming perennials such as daylilies, yarrows (Achillea spp.), lavender (Lavandula angustifolia), catmints (Nepeta spp.), and ornamental grasses. Other species are suitable for raised beds, rock gardens, or sites where soil drainage is perfect.

Paeonia

(pay-OH-nee-ah)

Peonies

Peony family, Paeoniaceae. Hardy perennials.

Although primarily grown as garden flowers today, peonies have a history of use as medicinal plants that dates to A.D. 500. Both John Gerard and Nicholas Culpeper in their herbals (1597 and 1649 respectively) designated P. officinalis as a male peony and P. mascula as a female peony. Each peony was to be used to treat the complaints of its corresponding sex. It was a distinction that dates to Anglo-Saxon times, when seeds of the male peony were used as a charm against witchcraft and as a cure for nightmares, while female peony seeds were used for other ailments. Collecting seeds was not an easy task, for it was to be undertaken only at night. As Gerard explained, "for if any man shall pluck off the fruit in the day time, being seene of the Wood-pecker, he is in danger to lose his eies." Chinese herbals of the 12th century made a different distinction: by whether plants were wild or cultivated. Roots of wild plants were used to cool

Tree peony, Paeonia 'Mitama'

happily struggle with more demanding plants for lesser blooms, peonies flower every year with only minimal care. In fact, plants in abandoned gardens have been known to flower reliably for decades despite complete neglect. Planted in a good site and given regular attention, there's little doubt they are the glory of the spring to early summer garden.

The blooming period of herbaceous peonies translates into flowers as early as April in the South and from late May to early June in more northern gardens. Plants bear 5- to 8-inch-wide single and double blooms, often fragrant, on plants that range from 2½ to 3 feet tall. Once the flowers fade, gardeners are left with handsome green leaves that function as a backdrop for later-blooming flowers, much as small shrubs would.

HOW TO GROW

Long-lived and deep rooted, peonies will thrive in one spot for years, so chose sites carefully. It's not unusual for plants to remain for 20 years without being divided. Full sun is the first choice, but plants will flower—albeit less abundantly—in partial shade, although they cannot compete with tree roots. In Zone 7, and especially Zone 8, where summer heat and humidity take their toll, plant peonies where they will receive afternoon shade. As long as drainage is good, peonies tolerate a wide range of soils; a near-neutral pH is ideal. Look for a site that has good air circulation but is protected from wind, as the large blooms are easily damaged.

the blood, whereas roots of cultivated peonies were used in a tonic to treat liver and circulation problems.

Gardeners love peonies as ornamentals, however, and peonies have been in American gardens since the 1600s. The plantsman John Bartram recorded a shipment of peony roots to Charleston, South Carolina, in 1761, and both Jefferson and Washington grew them. Jefferson's "Calendar of the bloom of flowers" for 1782 records peonies flowering from mid-June through September, a bloom-season incredibly long for plants that normally blossom only a few weeks in late spring and early summer.

Peonies are no less popular today, beloved plants for the perennial garden, grown for their lavish, fragrant flowers in rich shades of pink, red, maroon, rose, white, and even yellow. And while gardeners

You'll find peonies offered as container-grown plants at garden centers for spring planting, but the main peony-planting season is in fall, from September to October, when bare-root plants are shipped from mail-order suppliers. Bare-root plants should have three to five red, healthy looking eyes, or buds. The fleshy roots should not be broken or diseased-looking. (If the roots look dried out, soak them in water for a few hours before planting. If you can't plant right away, repack the roots in moistened packing material and store them for no longer than a week in a dark, cool place.)

When planting, dig a large hole—18 inches *or more* deep and wide—that will accommodate all the roots. Since you won't need to plant again, work plenty of organic matter—several bucketsful—into the soil and add a handful or two of bonemeal. Space plants at least 4 feet apart, and set the roots with the red buds facing upward and *no more than* 2 inches below the soil surface. One of the most common reasons peonies fail to bloom is that they are planted too deeply. In the North, planting at two inches protects the buds in winter; in warmer regions, set the buds 1 inch deep so they will feel the slightest essential nip of winter cold. The soil and the roots will settle, so when in doubt, plant more shallowly. (Tree peonies—which are shrubs, not herbaceous plants—are grafted and should be set with the graft union 5 or 6 inches deep.) After planting, water thoroughly and mulch with evergreen branches, loose straw, or chopped leaves to prevent frost heaving over the first winter.

Feed peonies in spring with a topdressing of compost or a balanced organic plant food spread around but not on the emerging shoots. (Experts disagree about using manure on peonies, with some claiming that it encourages disease; others, equally qualified to speak, recommend manure as long as it is well-rotted.) Mulch to control weeds and keep the soil moist. Feed again in fall. Most peonies need

staking to keep the heavy flowers off the ground. Single-flowered cultivars are sometimes an exception, but if you are growing doubles install stakes or wire rings made for peony support shortly after the plants emerge in spring. If you seek mammoth blossoms, pinch off all but one bud per stem. Remove and discard spent flowers for cleanliness and neatness (however, deadheading will not promote new blooms). In late fall, cut peony foliage to about 3 inches from the ground. Do not compost the foliage, which often carries diseases, even if it appears to be healthy.

Divide peonies only if a clump has outgrown its site, has become too crowded to bloom well, or if you want to propagate. Dig clumps in late summer or early fall. Dig deeply to get as many roots as possible, wash the soil off the clumps with a hose, then use a knife to divide them into pieces with about five buds each. Discard old, woody portions of the crown, and replant the healthy sections. Seeds of cultivars don't come true; growing peonies from seeds is difficult and slow, making it a propagation approach undertaken by only the most enthusiastic hobbyist.

If flowers or flower buds turn brown and rot or fail to open entirely, the fungal disease botrytis may be the problem. Prune away any infected plant parts and discard them in the garbage. Rake off mulch and the top half-inch of soil as well. Peonies attract ants by the hundreds, but they do no damage.

WHAT TO GROW

Local garden centers generally offer a handful of peony cultivars—all are hardy in Zones 3 to 8—but specialist mail-order companies have a huge selection. There are hundreds of cultivars, and because these are long-lived plants that will only look better in your garden every year, it pays to search for top-quality cultivars in the colors and flower forms you want. Cultivars are rated as early, midseason, or late flowering, so select a mix for the longest bloom season. In Zone 8 and the warmer part of Zone 7, early blooming peonies are the best choice.

Garden peony, Paeonia 'Furnace'

Cultivars have a mix of flower forms: Single-flowered plants have a central cluster of showy, golden yellow stamens surrounded by a single row of petals. Semidoubles have two or more rows of petals surrounding a central boss of stamens. Double flowers have one or more rings of full-size petals surrounding a central cluster of smaller petaloids, modified stamens and carpels that look like petals. Japanese-type blooms have a ring or two of petals around a cluster of petaloids that are narrow and flat. Peonies that have flowers with a dense, rounded center are called "bombs" by some growers and "anemones" by others.

These are some classic, old cultivars along with some top-notch newer offerings to consider: 'America', early, red-flowered single; 'Bowl of Cream', white, midseason double; 'Bowl of Beauty', early, Japanese-type flowers with rose pink outer petals and creamy white centers; 'Festiva Maxima', early, very fragrant, white double with petals flecked occasionally with red, introduced in 1851 and good for southern gardens; 'Kansas', midseason, red double; 'Krinkled White', early, single white with crinkled petals introduced in 1928; 'Miss America', early, white semidouble, American Peony Society Gold Medal Winner; 'Monsieur Jules Elie', early, fragrant, rose-pink double with large outer petals and denser centers, introduced in 1888, good for southern gardens; 'Mrs. F. D. Roosevelt', midseason, fragrant, pale pink double introduced 1932; 'Paula Fay', early, magenta-pink semidouble, American Peony Society Gold Metal Selection; 'Pink Hawaiian Coral', early, fragrant, coral-pink semidouble, American Peony Society Gold Medal winner; 'Prairie Moon', early, single, pale butter yellow to white; 'Raspberry Sundae', midseason, pale-pink anemone with a dense central cluster of darker pink petals rimmed with creamy white petals; 'Sarah Bernhardt', late, fragrant, shell pink double with petals flecked occasionally with red introduced in 1906; Scarlett O'Hara', early, red single introduced 1958; and 'Seashell', midseason, shell-pink single introduced in 1937.

One of the early-flowering peony species that is sometimes grown in gardens is fernleaf peony (*P. tenuifolia*), which has finely divided, fernlike leaves and single, 3-inch-wide, ruby-red flowers. 'Rubra Plena' is a double cultivar. Both are hardy in Zones 3 to 8.

So-called Memorial day peonies are cultivars of *P. officinalis*, one of the parents of today's hybrids. (*P. lactiflora*, hardy in Zones 2 to 8 is another.) Both *P. officinalis* 'Rubra Plena', a double red, and 'Rosea

Superba', with double pink flowers, are Memorial Day peonies. They're hardy in Zones 3 to 8.

Tree peonies come in shades of pink from pastel to magenta as well as coral, cream, maroon, and pale to golden yellow. Blooms may be single, semidouble, or double and range from 6 to 10 inches or more across. They bloom about two weeks before herbaceous peonies, range from 3 to 5 feet tall, and are hardy in Zones 4 to 9. There are Japanese, Chinese, European, and American cultivars to choose from, and it pays to shop at a mail-order specialist so you can buy exactly the color and flower form that suits you.

IN THE GARDEN

Peonies are handsome additions in sunny beds and borders. Combine them with catmints (*Nepeta* spp.), Siberian iris (*Iris sibirica*), blue false indigo (*Baptisia australis*), candytuft (*Iberis sempervirens*), and other perennials that bloom in early summer. They also can be planted as a low hedge along a shrub border, provided they're located far enough away from the shrubs so root competition isn't a problem. Of course, they make superb cut flowers: Cut them when the buds are about half open and the first petals are beginning to unfurl. Leave two strong sets of leaves on the plant.

Papaver

(*PAH-pah-ver*)

Poppies

Poppy family, Papaveraceae.
Hardy perennials, annuals.

While many plants share the name poppy, members of the genus *Papaver* are the true poppies, grown for their delicate-looking blooms with silky, crepe-paper-textured petals. The genus contains one infamous member, opium poppy (*P. somniferum*), which has been cultivated for millennia. That poppy, according to the classical myth, was created by the god of sleep, Somnus, in order to help the goddess of agriculture, Ceres, rest, as she was so weary that she was neglecting her corn crop. After a good sleep, Ceres revived the corn, and to this day she is usually shown wearing a garland of corn and poppies.

Oriental poppy, Papaver orientale

Opium poppies—especially the round pods that follow the flowers—contain at least 25 alkaloids including codeine and morphine. For this reason, growing them is prohibited by law in the United States, but in a strange bit of logic, it is legal to sell the seeds. Many major seed companies have stopped doing so, however. Nevertheless, they remain popular cottage garden plants and seed is both sold commercially and traded over garden fences. Also known as bread-seed poppy, *P. somniferum* is the source of edible poppy seeds, which are used in baking. The seeds of corn poppy (*P. rhoeas*) also are tasty and can be used to flavor muffins and breads.

Poppies are prized for their bowl-, cup-, or saucer-shaped blooms, which come in brilliant shades of orange, orange-red, scarlet, hot pink, and yellow along with pastel pinks, pale yellow, and white. The flowers are followed by distinctive, rounded seed capsules, which make interesting additions to dried arrangements. The plants generally have toothed or deeply divided, almost fernlike leaves that disappear in midsummer in some species. Plant stems exude milky latex when cut.

Poppies are associated with a great assortment of things, but none is more poignant that the corn poppy's (*P. rhoeas*) identification with the carnage during World War I. The fields near Flanders beaten down and made barren by years of war, rebloomed with corn poppies when the fighting ended. The sea of red was seen as emblematic of the blood shed by soldiers, but also represented the healing of the land—and was immortalized in the poem "In Flanders Field" by John McCrae. Red corn, or Flanders, poppies are still sold and worn in England and North America on November 11, the day the war ended.

HOW TO GROW

Poppies are sun lovers, although in hot, humid southern gardens, a spot that receives morning sun and afternoon shade is better. All poppies need well-drained soil—especially alpine poppies (*P. alpinum*), which are fine plants for rock gardens—and do best in soil that is moderately rich. Since all poppies have large, delicate flowers, find a site that is protected from the wind.

To add Oriental poppies (*P. orientale*) to your garden, start with container-grown plants that have been vegetatively propagated. Most cultivars do not come true from seeds, and most seed-grown plants yield orange flowers. Since the plants spread, other gardeners may have divisions to share. Like all poppies, they also self-sow, so check during blooming season to see if the plants you are getting divisions of exhibit the lush hues of cultivated forms or the brilliant (and beautiful) orange of the species. The best time to plant Oriental poppies is in fall, although container-grown plants are available at garden centers in spring and can be planted then. When planting in fall, cover plants with straw, evergreen boughs, or another coarse mulch to discourage frost heaving during the first winter.

When planting, it also pays to remember that Oriental poppies bloom in late spring to summer, then go dormant in midsummer. For this reason, they're best located with other perennials, and not in solid drifts, because they leave an empty spot in the garden during summer. Oriental poppies generally take a season or two to become established and begin blooming well. Plants have deep roots and are happiest if they are left undisturbed. If you must divide, dig plants when they are emerging

Corn poppy, Papaver rhoeas *Shirley Series*

from summer dormancy, once the new shoots begin appearing. Discard old, woody growth and replant the vigorous sections of the clumps. Or propagate from root cuttings made either when you're dividing a plant or taken in spring by digging and removing a section of root without uprooting the main plant.

To grow other perennial and annual poppies, start your own plants from seeds. Poppies generally resent being transplanted, and sowing directly in the garden where the plants are to bloom is best. Sow annual poppies in early spring in cold regions, or start seeds indoors in individual containers six to eight weeks before the frost-free date. In Zones 8 and warmer, sow in fall. Perennial poppies can be started indoors or outdoors where they are to grow in early spring, about the time of the last frost.

Once planted, all you have to do with poppies is enjoy them. Remove all the seedpods from Oriental poppies to prevent self-sowing, but leave some pods on short-lived perennials and annuals and scatter them once the seeds are ripe so plants self-sow.

Poppies, in varying degrees, are subject to downy mildew and bacterial blight. Aphids are sometimes a problem.

WHAT TO GROW

Corn poppy (*P. rhoeas*), the red-flowered species found throughout Europe, is a 3-foot-tall cool-weather annual with 3-inch-wide flowers in red, orange, yellow, pink, or white with a black blotch at the base of the petals. Shirley Series plants yield single or double

flowers in a full range of colors without the black petal blotch.

Oriental poppy (*P. orientale*), hardy in Zones 3 to 7, bears brilliant red-orange flowers with purple-black centers on 2- to 4-foot-tall stems. The species bears 4- to 6-inch flowers, but blooms of cultivars can reach 8 inches. Plants go dormant by mid- to late summer, then reemerge about six weeks later. Plants spread by runners to form broad clumps; cultivars tend to spread more slowly than the species. Good cultivars include 'Helen Elizabeth', salmon pink; 'Cedric Morris', pale pink; 'Beauty of Livermore', deep red; 'Patty's Plum', red-purple; 'Perry's White', white; 'Prince of Orange', orange-red; and 'Raspberry Queen', raspberry pink. This is not a plant for gardens south of Zone 7.

Iceland poppy (*P. croceum*, formerly *P. nudicaule*), a short-lived perennial, dies out in hot weather in the South but is hardy in Zones 2 to 7. Plants bear showy, 3- to 5-inch-wide flowers on 1- to 2-foot-tall stems in spring and early summer in shades of orange, yellow, and white. Plants self-sow abundantly if a few seedpods are allowed to ripen. Iceland poppies are best in areas with cool nights and warm days, but even in those conditions are often treated as annuals as they bloom the first year from seeds.

Alpine poppy (*P. alpinum*), hardy in Zones 4 to 7, is another short-lived perennial that doesn't tolerate hot, humid weather and also self-sows abundantly. Plants bear cup-shaped, 1½-inch-wide flowers in early to midsummer on 6- to 10-inch-tall stems. Alpine poppies require very good drainage

Alpine poppy, Papaver alpinum

and are suitable for rock gardens or along the tops of low walls where perfect drainage is the norm.

IN THE GARDEN

Oriental poppies are handsome with other perennials that bloom in spring to early summer. Plant them with irises, bellflowers (*Campanula* spp.), blue false indigo (*Baptisia australis*), columbines (*Aquilegia* spp.), catmints (*Nepeta* spp.), and peonies. Use annuals or summer- to fall-blooming perennials to fill in after Oriental poppies go dormant in summer. Companions include asters, Russian sage (*Perovskia atriplicifolia*), baby's breath (*Gypsophila paniculata*), and Shasta daisies (*Leucanthemum × superbum*). Small poppies are ideal for the front of borders.

Most poppies make stunning cut flowers. Cut them when the buds begin to open, recut the stems once you're in the house, and dip the stem tips into an inch or two of boiling water for a few seconds. Or sear the ends with a match or the flame of a gas stove. Stand the flowers in cold water for several hours before arranging them.

Pelargonium

(pel-ar-GO-nee-um)

Geraniums

Geranium family, Geraniaceae.
Tender perennials usually grown as annuals.

These popular plants are a common sight in summer, as likely to be found growing in garden beds or containers in private gardens as they are window boxes at a bank. Although commonly called geraniums, *Pelargonium* species are not to be confused with hardy geraniums, or cranesbills (*Geranium* spp.). Tender perennials usually grown as annuals, most *Pelargonium* species are originally from South Africa. The genus name comes from the Greek *pelargos* for "stork," a reference to the stork's-bill-like fruits. Most cultivated geraniums fall into four horticultural groups, including zonal geraniums, ivy-leaved geraniums, scented-leaved geraniums, and regal, or Martha Washington, geraniums. All bear rounded to deeply cut or fernlike leaves that often are hairy and produce rounded clusters of five-petaled, star- or

Zonal geranium, Pelargonium × hortorum *'Pink Parfait'*

saucer-shaped flowers. Most bloom from spring to frost; in frost-free regions, many bloom year round.

Geraniums have been grown in North America since the colonial era. They have always been somewhat of a "woman's flower," perhaps because they often were overwintered on kitchen windowsills. The 20th-century British poet Laurie Lee described just such a scene in "Day of These Days": "Such a morning it is when love / leans through geranium windows." And in *Little Women* (1868), Louisa May Alcott wrote of "the green leaves, and the scarlet flowers of Amy's pet geranium." Despite the association with women, one of the most wonderful poems ever written about a geranium—or any flower—was by the American Theodore Roethke, and his geranium was a she but not at all genteel:

> . . . . she'd lived
> So long on gin, bobbie pins, half-smoked
> cigars, dead beer,
> Her shriveled petals falling
> On the faded carpet, the stale
> Steak grease stuck to her fuzzy leaves.
> (Dried-out, she creaked like a tulip.)

HOW TO GROW

Grow geraniums in a site with full sun that is protected from the wind, and give them moderately rich, well-drained soil with a near-neutral pH. In areas with very hot summers, set plants where they will receive dappled shade in the afternoon. Regal geraniums are an exception: They're best in areas with cool summers and happiest in partial shade. Geraniums can be grown outdoors as perennials in Zones 10 and 11, but in other zones they are either grown as annuals and discarded in the fall or are overwintered indoors.

You'll find geranium plants for sale everywhere, from garden centers to grocery stores, but mail-order specialists offer the best choice of colors—and there's lots to choose beyond run-of-the-mill red. Since geraniums are easy to propagate from cuttings—and plants can be overwintered indoors—it is worth it to look for and collect special cultivars. Or you can also start your own plants from seed sown indoors about 12 to 16 weeks before the spring frost-free date.

Transplant seed- or cutting-grown plants to the garden a week or so after all chance of frost has passed. Pinch plants to encourage branching and more flowers. Water plants—especially those in containers—when the soil becomes moderately dry. Deadheading keeps plants neat looking and directs plant energy into producing flowers rather than seeds. Geraniums grown in containers should be fed every six weeks with a balanced liquid fertilizer.

Zonal geranium, Pelargonium × hortorum '*Vancouver Centennial*'

It's possible to overwinter entire plants, but it's not always satisfactory as geraniums require strong light. By spring, plants are so leggy that they must be cut back drastically. A better approach is to take cuttings in late summer or early fall and root them. The usual approach is to root the cuttings, after allowing them to dry for six hours to seal the stem ends and applying rooting hormone, in damp perlite or vermiculite. Some geraniums, including zonals, will root in water. Pot on rooted cuttings and move to the garden—or the flowerbox, deck, or hanging basket—in spring.

Aphids and spider mites can troublesome when overwintering geraniums indoors, but plants are largely problem-free outdoors.

WHAT TO GROW

Bedding, or zonal, geraniums, commonly listed as *P. × hortorum*, are best known. These are fleshy-stemmed plants that actually are evergreen in frost-free regions. Where hardy, they're shrub size, but in northern gardens usually reach about 16 to 18 inches. They bear nearly round leaves that may or may not have the dark maroon band that gave the plants the common name zonal geranium. Plants produce showy, round, 3- to 5-inch-wide clusters of 1-inch red, pink, or white flowers from early summer to frost. Single-flowered types have five petals per flower and are most common. Rosebud geraniums bear double flowers, while Stellar geraniums have single, star-shaped flowers. In addition to the usual cultivars, more and more bedding geraniums with fancy foliage are being offered. 'Black Velvet Rose', an All-America Selections winner, features green leaves with chocolate brown centers and rose pink blooms; it can be grown from seed. Fancy-leaved geraniums are grown as much for their showy leaves their flowers: 'Mr. Henry Cox' has leaves marked with cream, yellow, green, purple-maroon, and red; 'Vancouver Centennial' has lobed, gold leaves with maroon-brown center splotches and red-orange, star-shaped flowers; and 'Bird Dancer' bears dark-zoned, maplelike leaves and 3-inch clusters of pink, star-shaped flowers.

Ivy geraniums (*P. peltatum*) bear trailing stems and fleshy, lobed, ivylike leaves. Plants bear 1½- to 2-inch-wide clusters of single or double flowers in shades of pink, mauve, lilac, and white, and they are ideal for hanging baskets and window boxes. Summer Showers Series can be grown from seeds and comes in a range of colors.

Ivy geranium, Pelargonium peltatum *'Solidor'*

Coconut-scented geranium (*P. grossularioides*) bears lobed, coconut-scented leaves, red stems, and small, star-shaped, magenta-pink flowers. Other scented geraniums featuring the fragrances that their names imply include apple geranium (*P. odoratissimum*), peppermint geranium (*P. tomentosum*), and rose geranium (*P. graveolens* or *P. 'Graveolens'*).

IN THE GARDEN

Geraniums make handsome additions to beds and borders, but they also are ideal plants for containers and window boxes. Grow them alone or combine them with other summer-blooming annuals such as scarlet sage (*Salvia splendens*), flowering tobaccos (*Nicotiana* spp.), verbena, and petunias. Scented types are appropriate additions to herb gardens and also handsome in containers. Hummingbirds and beneficials visit geranium flowers.

Penstemon

(PEN-steh-mon)

Beard-tongues, penstemons

Figwort family, Scrophulariaceae.
Hardy perennials.

Regal, or Martha Washington, geraniums (*P. × domesticum*) have rounded, sometimes lobed or toothed, leaves on 1- to 4-foot plants and 2- to 4-inch clusters of single and double flowers. Flowers come in solid colors or combinations of red, purple, pink, white, maroon, and orange and need cool nighttime temperatures (60°F or cooler) in order to keep blooming

Scented geraniums are grown for their pungent foliage rather than their small clusters of single, 1-inch-wide flowers. The leaves contain complex volatile oils and are used to make tea and to flavor sauces, sorbets, and vinegar. In addition to producing oils like lemon, peppermint, or nutmeg, several scented geraniums are used to produce geranium oil, which is used in perfumes and in aromatherapy. 'Mabel Grey' bears lemon-scented, deeply cut leaves and 2-inch-wide clusters of pale purple flowers. Nutmeg geranium, sold as *P. × fragrans* and *P. 'Fragrans'*, bears gray-green, nutmeg-scented leaves and 1- to 1¼-inch-wide clusters of white flowers.

Grown for their showy racemes or panicles of tubular- to bell-shaped flowers, beard-tongues are primarily native to North and Central America. The flowers have two lips, usually with three lobes on the bottom lip and two lobes on the top lip. Plants bloom in shades of lavender, purple, purple-blue, lilac-blue, pink, red, yellow, and white. Leaves are linear to lance shaped. The genus name *Penstemon* is pure botany: It means "five stamens." It is the fifth stamen that provides the common name beard-tongue: It is bearded.

Beard-tongues are found in a wide range of habitats, from the cool, moist, Western mountains to meadows in the Eastern half of the North America. There also are penstemons native to desert areas and woodlands. While the genus contains a wealth of showy plants, many do not grow well outside their native habitats. As a result, gardeners in the West can cultivate many more species—there are about 250 in the genus—than gardeners living elsewhere.

Richardson Wright, American author of the entertaining *The Gardener's Bed-Book* (1939), was an early penstemon fan. "Next year," he wrote, "I shall go exploring into the hinterlands of the Penstemon world, cross the civilized frontiers and push on into the wilderness. . . . I've no illusions about all the Penstemons being beauties, yet the experience will be worth the trouble."

Fortunately for today's gardeners, we don't have to cross any frontiers, civilized or otherwise, to find penstemons. Hybridizers have begun to develop cultivars for humid climates, and new ones are being introduced regularly—every one a beauty.

HOW TO GROW

The beard-tongues listed here need full sun to partial shade and rich, very well-drained, evenly moist soil. All grow best in areas with cool summers. In regions where heat and humidity are the summertime norm, select a site with afternoon shade. *P. digitalis* is more heat and humidity tolerant than most species. If you are growing penstemons native to your region, look for sites that are similar to those where they grow naturally. Otherwise, plants will be short-lived.

Hybrid beard-tongue, Penstemon *'Mother of Pearl'*

Foxglove penstemon, Penstemon digitalis *'Husker's Red'*

Add beard-tongues to your garden by purchasing container-grown plants in spring or begin from seeds. Water plants deeply at planting time and during dry weather. Pinching plants in spring when they are about 1 foot tall will encourage fuller growth and reduce height. Deadhead to prolong blooming, and cut declining, old stems to the ground. Where plants are marginally hardy or there is not a reliable snow cover, protect plants in late fall with a dry, loose mulch, such as evergreen boughs or straw.

For best results, divide beard-tongues every three to five years in spring to keep them vigorous. Division is also an easy way to propagate these plants, or take stem cuttings in summer. To grow beard-tongues from seed, sow in pots in fall and set them in a protected location outdoors to overwinter. Or sow indoors, eight to ten weeks before the frost-free date. Do not cover the seeds.

Plants without good drainage, especially in winter, are subject to crown rot; plants also are susceptible to several foliar diseases.

WHAT TO GROW

Common beard-tongue (*P. barbatus*), also called beardlip penstemon, is a 1½- to 5-foot-tall species from the western United States and Mexico. Hardy in Zones 4 to 9, it produces a mound of semi-evergreen leaves topped by panicles of pendant, tubular, 1½-inch-long flowers from early summer to fall. Blooms are red with tinges of pink. 'Elfin Pink' bears pink flowers on 1-foot-tall plants. 'Albus' bears white flowers, and 'Coccineus' bears red flowers. Rocky Mountain penstemon (*P. strictus*) is another western species; 2 feet tall, it has purple-blue flowers and is hardy in Zones 3 to 10.

Foxglove penstemon (*P. digitalis*) is native to the East and Southeast and makes a fine perennial for gardens in those parts of the country. Hardier— Zones 2 to 8—and longer-lived than common beard-tongue (and more tolerant of wet soil), it produces mounds of semi-evergreen leaves and panicles of 1-inch-long, white flowers that are tubular- to bell-shaped. 'Husker Red' has leaves that are maroon-red when young and white flowers tinged with pink. Another species native to the Northeast, *P. hirsutus*, is 1½ to 2½ feet tall and features evergreen leaves topped by loose racemes of tubular- to funnel-shaped, 1- to 2-inch-long flowers in summer. Flowers are pale lavender with white throats. *P. hirsutus* var. *pygmaeus* is a dwarf selection that reaches 4 inches in height, spreads from 4 to 6 inches, and bears maroon-purple-tinged leaves. Both are hardy in Zones 3 to 9. Small's penstemon (*P. smallii*), another wildflower native to the East, bears spikes of rose- to lilac-pink flowers in spring and is hardy in Zones 5 to 9.

Hybrid beard-tongues have become popular in recent years. Most are only hardy from Zone 7 south and best in Northwest Coastal gardens, because of their need for cool summer weather. In the East, they can be grown as biennials or short-lived perennials. Four cultivars hardy in Zones 3 to 8 are 'Prairie Fire', with bell-shaped, crimson flowers; 'Prairie Dusk', with purple blooms; 'Rose Elf', with rose-pink flowers; and 'Sour Grapes', with rose-purple flowers.

IN THE GARDEN

Use beard-tongues in beds and borders with perennials such as small daylilies, hardy geraniums, or cranesbills (*Geranium* spp.), sundrops (*Oenothera* spp.), and yarrows (*Achillea* spp.). They also are good choices for raised beds and rock gardens where soil drainage is excellent. Beard-tongues also make handsome cut flowers.

Perovskia atriplicifolia

(per-OFF-ski-ah ah-trih-plih-sih-FOE-lee-uh)

Russian sage, perovskia

Mint family, Lamiaceae. Hardy perennial.

Despite its common name, this species is not native to Russia; it's from Afghanistan and Pakistan. The Russian connection is in the genus name *Perovskia*, which honors the 19th-century Russian general V. A. Perovsky. Perovsky is remembered for leading the Russian campaign against Turkistan in the winter of 1839. He misjudged the weather, however, and lost two-thirds of his soldiers and all his pack camels and was forced to retreat. As one account stated succinctly, "Shortly thereafter, Perovsky was transferred."

Allan Armitage wrote in *Armitage's Garden Perennials* (2000) that he used to tell the story that Russian sage got its name from its leaves, "so pungent it was said to smell like the feet of marching Russian soldiers. But with the Cold War over . . . I apologize to all the Russian soldiers whose feet I maligned."

Whatever name you use and whatever story you tell, this is a striking, shrub-sized perennial that creates a long-lasting cloud of intense lavender-blue flowers in late summer. Like other mint-family relatives, plants bear two-lipped flowers. Despite their small size, the tiny blooms are borne in showy, branched, 12- to 15-inch-long panicles, and the overall effect is eye-catching, especially when combined with the plant's silvery foliage. Unlike other mint-family plants, Russian sages are not underground spreaders. Plants reach 3 to 5 feet and clumps grow to 3 or 4 feet wide. Not especially well known, perovskia got a public relations boost in 1995, when the Perennial Plant Association named it "Perennial of the Year."

HOW TO GROW

Plant perovskia in full sun. Poor to average soil is fine, but it must be very well-drained and not heavy. Plants tolerate dry, alkaline conditions and are a good choice for seaside gardens. If soil drainage is a problem, plant perovskia in a raised bed or on a mound of soil to ensure that the crowns remain dry when the ground freezes. Newly planted specimens take a year or two to become established but form substantial clumps with time, so space plants at least 3 feet apart.

To add perovskias to your garden, start with container-grown or bare-root plants in spring or fall, in warm regions. Work plenty of organic matter into the ground at planting time to ensure good drainage. Once established, perovskia needs little attention. To reduce height and encourage branching, pinch plants when they reach 1 foot. Prune plants in late fall (North) or spring (South) by cutting the stems down to 1 foot—the new growth originates from the old stems. Provide a winter mulch in colder regions, where plants will die back over winter.

Do not divide plants, because the woody crowns are hard to separate successfully. Propagate by taking cuttings in late spring or summer. Seed is rarely available. Russian sage has no serious pest or disease problems.

WHAT TO GROW

Most gardeners are happy growing the species, but 'Filagran' features very finely cut leaves, and 'Blue Spire' is a heavy flowering selection with violet blue flowers on 3-foot plants. 'Little Spire' bears lavender-blue flowers on plants that are just over 2 feet tall. Both species and cultivars are hardy in Zones 5 to 9 and to Zone 4 with winter protection.

OTHER CHOICES

*I*f plants with aromatic foliage are among your favorites, you won't want to be without lavender (*Lavandula angustifolia*), a 2- to 3-foot shrub commonly planted with herbaceous perennials and in herb gardens. The plants produce 3- to 4-foot-wide mounds of silvery-green, needlelike evergreen leaves and unbranched spikes of small, densely packed, two-lipped flowers that are pale lavender to deep purple in color. Both flowers and foliage carry the sweetly scented oil that has made lavender a beloved garden plant. Give lavender full sun and well-drained soil. Plants grow in soil that is rich in organic matter or poor, but they do not survive where the soil is poorly drained. The also will grow in very light shade, but will be leggy and bloom less. Plants are hardy in Zones 5 to 9, but in Zone 5 and colder parts of Zone 6, find a spot that is protected from wind to give the plants a bit of extra help in winter. Plant the species, or look for cultivars like dark purple-flowered 'Hidcote', a compact 1½- to 2-foot-tall selection, 1½-foot-tall 'Munstead' with lavender flowers, pale pink 'Jean Davis', or white-flowered, 1-foot-tall 'Nana Alba'.

Bluebeard (*Caryopteris* × *clandonensis*) is a mounding shrub or woody-based perennial grown for its showy clusters of blue flowers, which are borne in leaf axils and stem tips from late summer to early fall. Like perovskia and lavender, bluebeard also bears aromatic foliage. 'Dark Knight' features silvery leaves and violet-blue flowers, 'Worchester Gold' golden leaves and purple-blue flowers.

Plants are hardy from Zones 4 to 9; from Zone 6 north, they are routinely killed to the ground in winter and are grown as herbaceous perennials. In the South, cut plants back hard in spring.

Lavender, Lavandula angustifolia *'Munstead'*

Russian sage, Perovskia atriplicifolia

IN THE GARDEN

Plant perovskia in sunny beds and borders that have somewhat dry soil. They are handsome combined with purple coneflower (*Echinacea purpurea*), orange coneflowers (*Rudbeckia* spp.), coreopsis, mallows (*Malva* spp.), balloon flower (*Platycodon grandiflorus*), daylilies, and ornamental grasses.

Petunia

(peh-TUNE-yah)

Petunias

Nightshade family, Solanaceae.
Tender perennials usually grown as annuals.

This native of South America takes its botanical and common names from *petun*, a native Brazilian word for "tobacco" (*Nicotiana tabacum*). As members of the nightshade family, petunias count a number of vegetable-garden residents as kin, including tomatoes, potatoes, and peppers. In flower gardens, their relatives are less well known, but include *Salpiglossis, Browallia, Brugmansia* (angel's trumpets), and, of course flowering tobaccos (*Nicotiana* spp.). Of these, the trumpet-shaped blooms of petunias reign supreme in summertime flower gardens.

Nearly all the petunias gardeners now grow are hybrids, a testiment to plant breeders who have created countless offerings from which to choose. They are a long way from the first petunia, supposedly seen by Europeans about 1500, which was a scrubby, weedy plant with white flowers found growing in South America. Today, all petunias feature trumpet- to saucer-shaped blooms and ovate- to lance-shaped leaves that are sticky and hairy. Flowers are borne from summer to frost and come in shades of pink, salmon, red, rose-pink, burgundy, violet, lilac, yellow, and white. Blooms may be a single solid color or be marked with stripes, edges, or veins in contrasting colors.

Not all the breeding frenzy has been good, alas. Many cultivars have lost the fragrance that marked petunias 75 years ago, the characteristic scent that fragrance-maven Louise Beebe Wilder described as a "refined and delicious perfume" in *The Fragrant Garden* (1932). Fortunately for gardeners, many cultivars are still aromatic, especially those with white, mauve, and blue flowers. You may not notice, but night-flying moths will.

Some botanists believe that several of the species (not commonly grown until recently) should belong to the genus *Calibrachoa*; while others include them all in *Petunia*. Since all are cultivated in the same way, gardeners can continue enjoying these plants

Petunia, Petunia × hybrida *'Aladdin Sky Blue'*

last-frost date; petunias need light to sprout, so just press the dustlike seeds onto the soil surface. Water from below to avoid washing the seeds out of the pots. Once plants are up, pinch them to encourage branching and bushy growth. Don't move petunias to the garden until danger of frost has passed and the soil has warmed. Water regularly and deadhead to encourage new blooms to form; cut scraggly plants back by half in late summer to spur growth and encourage new flowers to form. Feed container-grown plants every three weeks with a balanced liquid fertilizer; petunias grown in good soil in the garden don't need feeding.

Plants sometimes self-sow, but hybrids do not come true from seeds. While it's easy to propagate from stem cuttings in late summer and from seeds, garden centers offer such an array of inexpensive plants that it's sensible to let others do the work. Petunias are relatively free of disease and insect pests.

WHAT TO GROW

Hybrid petunias (P. × *hybrida*) come in a few basic groups, all of which flower in the full range of petunia colors. Grandiflora petunias bear 4-inch-wide flowers. These are best for sheltered sites, since the flowers are easily damaged by rain and wind. Ultra and Storm Series grandifloras have improved resistance to weather. Multiflora petunias are bushier plants with 2-inch-wide flowers that are borne more abundantly than grandifloras. Wave Series multifloras, including popular 'Purple Wave', are vigorous, densely

while the cognomen debate rages. And enjoy we do, for commercial producers sell petunia seeds to growers by the ton. And there are between 285,000 and 300,000 seeds in an ounce!

HOW TO GROW

Plant petunias in a spot that receives full sun or light shade. Average to rich soil that is moist but well-drained is ideal, although petunias tolerate poor soil and are good choices for protected seaside gardens. They don't perform well in windy sites, however, or in wet conditions.

It's easy to pick up market packs of petunias in spring at garden centers or grocery stores, but it is a bit more difficult to start your own plants from seed. Sow them indoors ten to 12 weeks before the

Petunia, Petunia × hybrida *'Flash Pink'*

Million bells, Calibrachoa Million Bells 'Terra Cotta'

Heliotrope (*Heliotropium arborescens*) is another old-fashioned garden plant prized for its fragrance and long bloom. A tender perennial usually grown as an annual, it's perfect for adding to beds and borders as well as containers—with petunias or without them. Also commonly called cherry pie, plants bear dense, rounded flower heads consisting of many small, funnel-shaped flowers in rich lavender-purple or white. Give heliotropes full sun, or afternoon shade in warm regions, and rich, well-drained soil. When adding heliotropes to your garden, stick to cultivars selected for their sweet vanillalike perfume, since ones selected for flower color or size may not be fragrant. 'Fragrant Delight' and 'Marine Lemoine Strain' bear sweet-scented, purple blooms, and 'Alba' produces white, vanilla-scented flowers.

branched plants that can be used as ground covers. Celebrity Series and Primetime Series are two other popular Multiflora selections. Both Grandiflora and Multiflora plants grow 12 to 14 inches tall and can spread to about 3 feet. Fantasy Series plants, which are sold as Milliflora petunias, bear an abundance of 1- to 1½-inch-wide flowers on densely branching plants that spread to about 8 inches.

Million Bells, sold as a cultivated form of *Calibrachoa*, bears 1-inch flowers on 8-inch plants in shades of violet-blue, pink, magenta, and white. Plants have densely branching, trailing stems.

Gardeners may also see Supertunia and Surfinia Group petunias. These are compact, heavy blooming hybrids developed by crossing various cultivars with *P. integrifolia*, which is a petunia species grown for its magenta blooms. Supertunia and Surfinia petunias are propagated by cuttings and bear 2- to 3-inch-wide flowers in purple-blue, pink, white, fuchsia, lavender-blue, and purple-red. These vigorous growers need fertilizing every two weeks for best performance.

IN THE GARDEN

Petunias make handsome edging plants and also can be combined with other summer-blooming annuals in mixed plantings. They are superb in containers of all sizes and types, either alone or combined with other flowers. Their flowers attract both hummingbirds and moths.

Heliotrope, Heliotropium arborescens 'Black Beauty'

Phlox

(FLOCKS)

Phlox

Phlox family, Polemoniaceae.
Hardy perennials, annuals.

○ ◐ ● ▼

Creeping phlox, Phlox subulata *'Candy Stripe'*

Originally called bastard lychnis, phlox were one of the early floral exports from North America to Great Britain. Wild sweet William (*P. divaricata*) was known as flowering Lychnidea, as well as woods pink and trestle flower. English plantsman Peter Collinson, who grew several phlox species in his gardens in Peckham and Mill Hill, wrote to fellow Quaker and botanist John Bartram in 1765 that, "It is wonderful to see the fertility of your country in *Phlox*." Collinson, who died in 1777, wouldn't have known annual phlox, or pride of Texas (*P. drummondii*), however. It wasn't collected and sent abroad until 1835, the same year that Scotsman Thomas Drummond, the man who found it and whose name it bears, died while collecting plants in Cuba. The history of flowers, as many have observed, is also the history of flower collectors and growers.

North America is rich in phlox: All of the 70 species in the genus are native except one, Siberian phlox (*P. sibirica*). There are phlox suitable for sunny gardens and shady ones, as well as species for rock gardens. The earliest phlox to bloom are ground-hugging plants that thrive in sun and blanket themselves in color from midspring to early summer. Phlox light up shade gardens in spring and early summer as well, when foot-tall woodland species come into bloom. The season cumulates when the stately, summer-blooming phlox come into their own, including popular garden phlox (*Phlox paniculata*).

The botanical name *Phlox* is the same as the Greek word for "flame," a reference to the fact that species bear hot-colored flowers in shades of magenta and red. Phlox also come in softer colors, including white, pale pink, lavender, lavender-blue, and purple. Their flowers are what botanists call "salverform": a thin tube that opens into a flared and flattened face with five petal lobes. Most species produce their flowers in rounded clusters, although ground-hugging types like moss phlox (*P. subulata*) hold their flowers so close to the ground it's hard to

see the clusters. In 1883, William Robinson wrote in *The English Flower Garden*, "The annual phlox alone has produced distinct varieties enough to furnish a garden with almost every shade of color." With that sort of floral excess, phlox foliage—pairs of ovate leaves—is easy to overlook.

HOW TO GROW

With phlox, site and soil selection depends on the species you are growing. They can be planted in spring or fall; container-grown plants are the fastest way to have phlox up and blooming, and seeds are not available for most cultivars. Look for a site with good air circulation, which will help control powdery mildew, a problem for most phlox.

Once planted, low-growing phlox—*P. bifida,* *P. douglasii,* and *P. subulata*—along with shade-loving *P. divaricata* and *P. stolonifera* thrive with little care. They don't require annual feeding, staking, or regular dividing. They do require weeding, and the shade-loving species appreciate mulching and regular watering to keep the soil evenly moist, as they don't tolerate drought.

Topdress sun-loving, summer-blooming *P. paniculata*, *P. carolina*, and *P. maculata* in spring with compost or well-rotted manure. All three species are susceptible to mildew, so space them generously and thin stems in early spring by cutting out the smallest ones in order to leave 3 inches between those that remain. Water the plants regularly in dry weather, but keep water off the leaves. To keep plants compact and eliminate the need to stake, pinch out the tips of the stems once or twice from spring to early summer. This delays bloom and also reduces the size of the individual flower clusters. Deadheading plants greatly extends the bloom season and curtails self-sowing; remove seedlings that do appear, as they won't come true.

Annual phlox (*P. drummondii*) is a cool-weather annual that needs full sun and average to rich, moist, well-drained soil. Plants tend to die out by midsummer in hot, humid conditions. To grow from seeds, sow outdoors where the plants will grow several weeks before the last spring frost date, or sow indoors in individual pots six to eight weeks before the last-frost date. Where winter is mild, sow seeds in fall. Pinch seedlings to encourage branching. Feed garden plants monthly with a balanced liquid fertilizer and water regularly. Deadhead to prolong bloom; if plants become leggy, cut them back to 2 inches.

Propagate phlox by division in fall or in spring: Discard old, woody parts of the clump and replant the rest, or take nonflowering shoots that arise from the base of the plant in spring and root them in a mix of half sharp sand or vermiculite and half perlite. Many species, including moss pink (*P. subulata*) and other ground-hugging types, produce trailing shoots that spread out from the main plant, that can be rooted.

Phlox are more susceptible to problems than many garden perennials; in addition to powdery mildew, phlox are especially subject to infestations of spider mites. Look for disease-resistant cultivars.

WHAT TO GROW

Annual phlox. Annual, or drummond, phlox (*P. drummondii*) is a cool-weather annual that has been heavily hybridized. Plants are 4 to 18 inches tall and bear clusters of purple, lavender, salmon, pink, or red flowers in spring. Blooms are single or double, and the individual flowers are 1 inch wide. Dwarf Beauty Series plants are 8 inches tall; 'Globe Mix', 6 inches; 'Dolly Mix', 4 inches tall. 'Diamond Mix' plants are F_1 hybrids. All come in a full range of colors. If you want flowers for cutting, look for taller selections like 18- to 24-inch 'Tapestry' or 12- to 18-inch 'Twinkle Mix'.

Ground-hugging, spring-blooming species. *P. subulata* along with *P. bifida* and *P. douglasii* are plants for full sun with average to rich, well-drained soil. They require little care to thrive but appreciate dappled shade in the afternoon in areas with hot, dry summers. Space plants about 10 inches apart and shear them after they flower. To encourage the stems to root, gently lift up the edges of the clumps in late winter, remove any dead leaves, and carefully loosen the soil under the plants. All can be grown for years without being divided, but dig them in fall if they outgrow their space, die out in the centers of the clumps, or for propagation.

Whether it's called moss phlox, creeping phlox, or moss pink, *P. subulata* is the most widely grown of the ground-hugging species. Plants produce a blanket of ½- to 1-inch flowers in mid- to late spring in shades of lavender, purple, pink, or white. The 2- to 6-inch plants have dense, needlelike evergreen leaves and are hardy in Zones 2 to 9. Cultivars include 'Candy Stripe', with white flowers striped pink; 'Scarlet Flame', with rich reddish pink blooms;

Garden phlox, Phlox paniculata *'Harmony'*

'Snowflake', with white flowers; 'Blue Hills', which has purple-blue blooms; and 'Keryl', with lavender-blue blooms.

Cleft, or sand, phlox (*P. bifida*) bears fragrant, ¾-inch, lavender to white flowers in spring that have deeply notched petals. Hardy in Zones 4 to 8, it will grow in poor soil as long as it's well drained. Douglas's phlox (*P. douglasii*) produces white, lavender, or pink, ½-inch flowers from late spring to early summer. Blooms are borne singly or in small clusters on mounding 3- to 8-inch plants that are hardy in Zones 4 to 8.

Phlox for shade. Two species excel in shade gardens—*P. divaricata* and *P. stolonifera*. Give them light to full shade and rich, evenly moist, well-drained soil. Propagate either species by digging and dividing plants in spring after the flowers fade. Both need dividing only if they outgrow their space or for propagation. Digging up rooted plantlets is another easy propagation option, or take cuttings in spring or early summer.

Wild blue, or woodland, phlox (*P. divaricata*) bears clusters of fragrant flowers in spring on 10- to 14-inch plants that have semi-evergreen leaves. Blooms come in lavender, pale violet, or white. Cut

Annual phlox, Phlox drummondii *'Palona Mix'*

back spent flower stalks after they fade to curtail self-sowing, if it is a problem, and also to keep plants neat looking. Wild blue phlox is hardy in Zones 3 to 9. Creeping phlox (*P. stolonifera*), another woodland native, spreads more quickly and widely than *P. divaricata* and produces loose clusters of pink, lilac-blue, or white flowers in spring on 4- to 6-inch-tall plants. This species is hardy in Zones 3 to 8.

Phlox for summer bloom. Phlox that bloom in summer and thrive in sun are probably the best known. These include garden phlox (*P. paniculata*), Carolina phlox (*P. carolina*), and wild sweet William (*P. maculata*). Grow all of these species in full sun or partial shade and rich, moist, deeply dug soil. None tolerates drought, and all are happiest in areas with relatively cool summers. In the South, a site that receives shade during the hottest part of the day is best. Of these species, *P. paniculata*, especially, needs staking. Ideally, divide all three species every two or three years in spring or fall to keep the clumps vigorous and healthy. Discard older, woody portions at the center of the clump, dig compost or well-rotted manure into the soil, then replant. All of these phlox also require deadheading, since named cultivars do not come true from seeds, and self-sown seedlings will overwhelm improved cultivars. Remove seedlings that do appear. Dividing is the easiest way to propagate, or take cuttings in spring or early summer.

Garden phlox (*P. paniculata*) bears showy, rounded clusters of fragrant, ½- to 1-inch flowers from summer to early fall on 3- to 4-foot plants. This is a heavily hybridized species and many cultivars are available. Flowers come in shades of pale to rose-pink, orange-red, crimson, purple, lilac, and white, and

Wild blue phlox, Phlox divaricata

disease-resistant cultivars are the best choice. Look for 'David', with white flowers; 'Eva Cullum', rich pink; 'Starfire', red; and 'Katherine', with bluish pink flowers. All are hardy in Zones 3 to 8.

Carolina, or thick-leaved, phlox (*P. carolina*) is a disease-resistant selection with clusters of purple to pink, ¾-inch-wide flowers in summer. Plants range from 3 to 4 feet and are hardy in Zones 4 to 9. Wild sweet William (*P. maculata*), another disease-resistant species, bears clusters of fragrant, ¾- to 1-inch-wide, mauve-pink flowers in early to midsummer. Also called meadow phlox, it is hardy in Zones 4 to 8; plants range from 2 to 3 feet. 'Miss Lingard' (sometimes listed under *P. carolina*) has white flowers; 'Omega' is white with a lilac eye; 'Rosalinde' is rose pink; and 'Natascha' bears pink and white trusses.

IN THE GARDEN

Plant low-growing, spring-blooming phlox in rock gardens, or use them as edging plants or ground covers. They can be combined with spring bulbs, candytuft (*Iberis sempervirens*), rock rose (*Helianthemum nummularium*), lavenders, and thymes. Shade-loving phlox are handsome planted with hostas, ferns, lungworts (*Pulmonaria* spp.), bleeding hearts (*Dicentra* spp.), and spring bulbs. Combine the summer-blooming border phlox with hardy geraniums or cranesbills (*Geranium* spp.), astilbes, daylilies, obedient plant (*Physostegia virginiana*), and Shasta daisy (*Leucanthemum* × *superbum*). Annual phlox are pretty in containers and mixed plantings. All except the ground-hugging species make very nice cut flowers, and phlox flowers attract hummingbirds and beneficials.

Obedient plant, Physostegia virginiana *'Variegata'*

Physostegia virginiana

(phy-so-STEED-jah vir-jin-ee-AH-nuh)

Obedient plant, physostegia

Mint family, Lamiaceae. Hardy perennial.

○ ◑

Ahh, if only every flower in the garden were obedient. At least there is obedient plant, an eastern North America native that grows wild in thickets and along stream banks from Minnesota and Missouri east to Quebec and North Carolina. (A similar variety, *P. virginiana* var. *arenaria*, is a "dry prairie ecotype,"

native to Iowa and other plains states.) The common name obedient plant comes from a characteristic endearing to children and flower arrangers alike: Each bloom has a uniquely jointed base that allows it to be moved on the main stalk. Once moved, blooms obediently remain pointed in the direction they've been turned. Stay-in-place is another name that alludes to the unusual trait of the flowers.

False dragonhead, yet another common name, refers to the tubular, two-lipped flowers, and while they somewhat resemble snapdragons and their relatives, *Physostegia* species have the square stems that put them squarely in the mint family. They also share spreading rhizomes with mints. These are good garden plants, but they warrant watching or they will overspread their welcome. In this department, obedient plants are rarely obedient: They won't stay put for long.

The genus name *Physostegia* derives from the Greek words *physa*, "bladder," and *stege*, "roof covering," and refers to the plant's fruits. Physostegia was taken from Virginia to England in the early 1600s, where it adapted well but wasn't overwhelmed by enthusiastic growers. It has been enthusiastically welcomed by flower arrangers, however, who love the flower's long straight stems and spikes of flowers.

HOW TO GROW

Plant physostegias in full sun or partial shade. They grow well in average, evenly moist soil, but also tolerate wet conditions—and even dry soil, although they won't grow as tall or flower as well. In very rich, fertile soil, plants tend to flop, so don't overfeed. Plants are tolerant of a wide range of climates, from cool summers to hot. Add cultivars to your garden by planting container-grown plants, since physostegia cultivars do not come true from seeds.

Standard-size plants may need staking, especially in rich soil, but compact cultivars, which range from 2 to 3 feet tall, usually stand without help. Pinching taller cultivars back by half in spring may eliminate the need to stake. Deadhead to keep plants tidy and possibly to produce new flowers. When flowering is over, cut the stalks back to the new basal foliage.

Division, which is a good way to propagate, is necessary every two to three years to keep plants from spreading. Or propagate by stem cuttings taken in early summer or from seed sown in containers in fall, and set outdoors in a protected location to overwinter. Physostegias are sometimes bothered by rust.

WHAT TO GROW

Obedient plant (*P. virginiana*) is a rhizomatous, 3- to 4-foot-tall native wildflower that produces dense spikes of 1-inch-long, lavender- to rose-pink flowers from midsummer to early fall. 'Miss Manners' is a clump former that spreads much less aggressively than the species. 'Bouquet Rose' bears rose-pink flowers; 'Summer Snow', has white flowers and spreads somewhat less vigorously than the species; and 'Vivid' is a late-blooming selection with very bright rose-pink flowers. 'Variegata' has white-edged leaves and magenta flowers. All are hardy in Zones 3 to 9.

IN THE GARDEN

Obedient plants are perennials for moist, sunny borders, where they are handsome with asters, Joe-Pye weeds (*Eupatorium* spp.), perennial sunflowers (*Helianthus* spp.), and sneezeweed (*Helenium autumnale*). Physostegia flowers are attractive to hummingbirds, butterflies, and beneficial insects, and are good candidates for a cutting garden.

Platycodon grandiflorus

(plat-ee-COE-don gran-dih-FLOOR-us)

Balloon flower

Bellflower Family, Campanulaceae.
Hardy perennial.

Dependable balloon flowers are showy, summer-blooming perennials from Asia. They're grown for their inflated flower buds, which resemble balloons. The buds split open into broad, 3-inch-wide, five-lobed flowers. While the common name refers to the balloonlike buds, the botanical name refers to the broad, bell-shaped flowers. *Platycodon* is from the Greek *platys*, "broad," and *kodon*, "bell," and explains the less used common names Chinese bellflower and Japanese bellflower.

Although balloon flowers aren't hard to grow, the Victorian garden writer Shirley Hibberd in *Familiar Garden Flowers* (1898) declared that "the lover of hardy plants should give no rest to the soles of his feet or the palms of his hands till he has mastered every detail of their cultivation." One assumes Hibberd was interested in *P. grandiflorus* for its ornamental value and not for its roots, which sometimes were sold—fraudulently—as ginseng.

There's no long list of confusing species names to remember with *Platycodon*. The genus contains only a single species, *grandiflorus*, which clearly tells gardeners to expect big flowers; they bloom in purple, blue-violet, lilac-blue, pink, or white from early to midsummer. The plants have blue-green, oval- to lance-shaped leaves that turn nicely yellow in fall.

HOW TO GROW

Plant balloon flowers where they will have average to rich, light, well-drained soil and full sun; in southern zones, light or dappled shade in the afternoon is better. Start with nursery plants, setting them out in spring or fall. Choose the location

Balloon flower, Platycodon grandiflorus *'Sentimental Blue'*

carefully, because balloon flowers do not transplant well. Dig plenty of organic matter into the soil at planting time and handle plants carefully, as their long, fleshy roots break easily. Be sure to mark the location of plants with stakes or labels: Balloon flowers emerge in late spring, and it's easy to dig into the clumps by mistake. Pinch back plants by half in late spring to reduce height.

These old-fashioned perennials are somewhat slow to become established, but mature plants demand little care. Don't fertilize plants, but do top-dress in spring with compost to keep the soil healthy. Mulch in fall, but don't cover the plant crowns. Plants need staking only if they are growing in rich soil or partial shade. Removing individual blossoms is a tedious job, but deadheading keeps the plants blooming. Cutting stems back stops future flowering, as the new buds form on the existing stem.

Established plants can be left in place for decades and resent being disturbed. If you must transplant, dig deeply and handle the clumps carefully. To propagate, take stem cuttings in summer, dig any rooted shoots that grow at the base of the main clump, or grow from seed—most cultivars come true. Sow seeds indoors in individual pots, six to eight weeks

before the frost-free date, or outdoors where they are to grow in warm regions; or sow in pots in fall and set them outdoors in a protected location to over-winter. Do not cover seeds, as light aids germination. Seedlings are fragile and should be handled carefully. Balloon flowers also self-sow if conditions are ideal, and seedlings can be transplanted.

Platycodons are highly insect and disease resistant.

WHAT TO GROW

Balloon flower (*P. grandiflorus*) is hardy in Zones 3 to 8. The species is about 2 feet tall; *P. grandiflorus* spp. *mariesii* (also sold as 'Mariesii') is semidwarf, to 1½ feet, with purple-blue flowers. 'Sentimental Blue' is another dwarf selection, to about 8 inches, with lilac-blue flowers; 'Shell Pink' bears pale, nearly white flowers on 2-foot plants; Fuji Series plants are a seed-grown strain with white, pink, and purple-blue flowers on 2- to 2½-foot plants; 'Fairy Snow' bears white flowers on 12-inch plants. There are double-flowered cultivars, too, including 'Hakone Blue', 'Double Blue', and 'Double White', all 2 feet.

IN THE GARDEN

Combine balloon flowers with daylilies, lavenders (*Lavandula* spp.), lamb's-ear (*Stachys byzantina*), catmints (*Nepeta* spp.), thread-leaved coreopsis (*Coreopsis verticillata*), and ornamental grasses. The blooms make fine cut flowers, too. Pick stems when at least two buds have opened. The stems exude white, milky latex, so sear the cut stem ends with a lighted match before conditioning them overnight in warm water.

Portulaca grandiflora

(*por-tyew-LAC-ah gran-dih-FLOOR-ah*)

Portulaca, rose moss, moss rose

Purslane family, Portulacaceae. Annual.

○ ▼

Portulaca is the Latin name for purslane (*P. oleracea*), a common garden weed with edible leaves that are rich in iron and sometimes used in salads or as a pot herb. Purslane also is a good source for omega-3 fatty acids, natural compounds thought to reduce heart attacks and strengthen the immune system. The

Moss rose, Portulaca grandiflora '*Sundial Mix*'

plants have been used in Chinese medicine since before A.D. 500 as an antibacterial and "cooling herb" to reduce fevers. Leaves of brightly colored common portulaca (*P. grandiflora*), the species grown in flower gardens, can be pressed for juice used to treat such ailments as insect and snake bites as well as burns and eczema.

Despite the delicate appearance of its satiny textured flowers, common portulaca is a tough, easy to grow, warm-weather annual. It is also one of the few succulents that are annual. The plant's common names are said to spring from the legend of an angel who became weary while walking and lay down under a rose to rest. When she awoke, she repaid the plant for its hospitality by creating a carpet of moss with roselike flowers around its base to keep its roots cool—thus the names moss rose and rose moss. In the scrublands of western Argentina—moss rose is a South American native—portulaca is one of the herbaceous plants that magically emerge when the rains begin. Wherever it grows, its flowers open in the morning but often close by midday, when temperatures rise. That trait has led to the common names eleven-o'clock and sun flower.

HOW TO GROW

Give portulaca full sun and poor to average, light soil that drains very well. This is a species that thrives in sandy, dry conditions and rots in rich, wet soil. Plants may not flower well in wet summers.

Pick up market packs of portulaca at garden centers or anywhere annuals are sold and set them out after the frost-free date. To start from seeds, sow indoors six to eight weeks before the last frost in individual containers, or sow outdoors after the last frost. The seed is fine, so barely press it into the soil. Transplant seedlings with care, as plants resent being disturbed. Water regularly until plants are established. After that, portulaca requires no regular care. Plants also self-sow, but hybrids don't come true; or propagate from stem cuttings, which root quickly.

WHAT TO GROW

Portulaca (*P. grandiflora*) is a 4- to 8-inch-tall annual. Plants have fleshy, cylindrical leaves and single or double, 1-inch-wide flowers from summer to frost. Blooms come in bright colors, including hot pink, red, purple, yellow, and white. The flowers normally open only in sunny weather. Sundial Series plants bear double flowers that tend to stay open longer than other selections. These are available as a mix or in separate colors. 'Sunnyside Mix' is an open-pollinated selection that yields a high percentage of double-flowered plants in a wide variety of colors. 'Calypso Mix', 'Magic Carpet', 'Sunglo', and 'Sunkiss' are other names to look for.

IN THE GARDEN

Plant portulacas in raised beds, rock gardens, as edgings, or along the top of walls where drainage is perfect. They are a good choice for tough, dry, hot sunny sites where few annuals will grow. They are also pretty in containers.

Potentilla

(*poe-ten-TILL-ah*)

Potentillas, cinquefoils

Rose family, Rosaceae. Hardy perennials.

Potentilla is a large genus—about 500 species in all—with shrubs and perennials the most commonly grown garden plants. The botanical name is from the Latin *potens,* for "powerful," and refers to the medicinal qualities of some species, especially *P. erecta*, formerly listed as *P. tormentilla* and commonly called tormentil and bloodroot. Tormentil and several other species contain tannins, and the roots have been used to control bleeding, reduce inflammation, and promote healing.

One early observer said of potentillas, "its character for ornament is not very high," but those who have grown these plants value them for their pretty, five-petaled flowers that are usually cup or saucer shaped and come in shades of yellow, orange, red, pink, and white. Blooms are borne over a long season from spring or early summer to fall and are carried both singly and in small clusters. Leaves are compound, meaning they have separate leaflets, and look rather like the leaves of strawberry plants.

Potentillas didn't get to Europe and England until early in the 19th century, late arrivals by most garden-flower standards, and have had an up-and-down career ever since. The common name cinquefoil refers to the five fingers of the leaves, the five petals of the flowers, and, according to some, the five senses.

HOW TO GROW

Potentillas are plants for full sun, although they'll grow in light shade, especially in the South, where afternoon shade protect plants from heat. Select a site with average, well-drained soil. Either sandy or loamy soils are fine; clay soils stay too wet for potentillas and should be heavily amended with organic matter. Good winter drainage is crucial.

Start with plants when adding potentillas to your garden, and plant them in spring or in fall. You'll find large container-grown specimens, but small plants in market packs are better option if you want to use potentillas as ground covers. The plants are smaller, but they grow quickly. Planting taller cultivars closely will provide support and eliminate the need to stake. Water regularly until plants are established; topdress them with compost in spring.

Dig the clumps in spring or fall to divide them if they outgrow their space or to propagate. Propagate from stem cuttings in early summer. Or sow seeds in fall or early spring in containers, and set in a warm location until germination occurs.

Potentillas seldom have pest or disease problems.

WHAT TO GROW

Himalayan cinquefoil (*P. atrosanguinea*) is a 1- to 1½-foot species with gray-green, silky-hairy leaves and branched clusters of 1¼-inch flowers in shades of yellow, orange, or red from early summer to fall. 'Vulcan' bears double red flowers, 'Yellow Queen', bright yellow ones, and 'Firedance', salmon-red blooms. 'Gibson's Scarlet' is a hybrid that produces red flowers on 15-inch plants. All are hardy in Zones 5 to 8.

Nepal cinquefoil (*P. nepalensis*), hardy in Zones 4 to 8, ranges from 1 to 3 feet tall and bears clusters of dark red, 1-inch-wide flowers mainly in early summer although plants bloom sporadically into fall. 'Miss Willmott' has bright reddish pink blooms on 1- to 1½-foot plants. 'Ron McBeath' produces carmine-red flowers on 1-foot plants.

P. neumanniana, formerly *P. tabernaemontana* and *P. verna*, is a creeping, 4-inch-tall species that forms dense, 1-foot-wide mats. Plants are topped by loose clusters of yellow, ½- to 1-inch-wide flowers from late spring into summer. Compact 'Nana' is 2 to 3 inches tall. Both are hardy in Zones 4 to 8.

Sulfur cinquefoil (*P. recta*), hardy in Zones 3 to 7, is a 1- to 2-foot-tall species with gray-green leaves and clusters of ½- to 1-inch-wide, pale yellow flowers from early to late summer. 'Warrenii', also listed as 'Macrantha', bears bright yellow flowers. Sulfur cinquefoil has become a problematic plant in some regions; check with local authorities before you add it to your garden.

Three-toothed cinquefoil (*P. tridentata*) is a vigorous, woody-based

Himalayan cinquefoil, Potentilla atrosanguinea

perennial hardy in Zones 2 to 7 and native to the Eastern United States as well as Greenland. Plants range from 6 to 12 inches in height, have evergreen leaves, and bear clusters of ¼-inch-wide white flowers in early summer. Compact 'Minima' is 4 to 6 inches tall.

IN THE GARDEN

Potentillas have attractive mounding habits and are effective when used as ground covers, in rock gardens, and as edging plants. They also can be used in mixed plantings and along the front of shrub borders. Combine them with lavenders, thymes, catmints (*Nepeta* spp.), and penstemons (*Penstemon* spp.).

Primula

(*PRIM-you-lah*)

Primroses, primulas

Primrose Family, Primulaceae.
Hardy perennials.

While the sight of primroses in the garden doesn't elicit the same response as, say, ripe tomatoes, these hardy, spring-blooming perennials are, in fact edible. Flowers of both cowslip (*P. veris*) and English primrose (*P. vulgaris*) can be added to salads. Both species also have a long history of medicinal use. The Roman Pliny recommended English primrose as a treatment for gout and rheumatism, and cowslip primroses, once commonly called *herba paralysis* and palsywort, were used as long ago as the Medieval Ages to treat spasms, cramps, and paralysis. The 17th-century English herbalist Nicholas Culpeper recommended taking the juice of primrose roots, which "being snuffed up the nose, occasions violent sneezing," and it supposedly was good for nervous disorders.

Even if you don't add them to salads or snuff them up your nose, primulas are pretty plants for the spring garden. And while the genus includes some finicky species best left to experts, the plants listed here are easy and satisfying to grow. The botanical name *Primula* is a reference to the early blooming nature of many of these plants—it's from the Latin, *primus*, or "first." Plants bear clusters of bell-, funnel-, or tube-shaped flowers that often

have flaring, flat faces. Blooms are borne on stalks either above low clumps of narrow or oval leaves or among the leaves.

Although culture varies from one species to another, you can't go too far wrong with the advice of the famous herbalist John Gerard, who wrote more than 400 years ago that primulas "joy in moist and dankish places, but not altogether covered with water." The common name cowslip is one born of the farm; it comes from the Old English *cu slippe*, or cow dung, because the flowers often grew in pastures. As for the primrose path, that comes from Shakespeare's *Hamlet*. "Do not," Ophelia says,

> . . . . *as some ungracious pastors do,*
> *Show me the steep and thorny way to heaven;*
> *Whiles, like a puff'd and reckless libertine,*
> *Himself the primrose path of dalliance treads,*
> *And recks not his own rede.*

Don't say Shakespeare didn't warn you.

Cowslip, Primula veris

HOW TO GROW

Primroses are perennials for cool temperatures, shade, and rich, evenly moist soil. They also need a site protected from wind. Before planting, work plenty of compost or well-rotted manure into the soil. If you're just getting started with primroses, purchase container-grown plants in spring. Water new plants deeply and mulch them to keep the soil moist and cool.

Once plants are established and growing, renew the layer of mulch annually, and feed in spring with well-rotted manure, compost, or an organic fertilizer. Water plants as necessary to keep the soil evenly moist, especially during spring and early summer when they are growing and blooming. Summertime heat and humidity will leave them bedraggled, and they can be cut back at that time.

Most primroses will grow for years without needing to be divided, but dig them in spring or early summer after the flowers fade if they become overcrowded. Division is also an easy way to propagate primroses. Fast-growing Polyanthus Group primroses are often best when divided every three to four years. To divide, lift the clumps and use your fingers to tease apart the individual plants. Always amend the soil with organic matter before replanting the divisions, and water regularly for several weeks so they become well established.

To grow primroses from seeds, which also is easy, sow them in pots in fall or early spring and set the pots in a cold frame or a protected location outdoors.

A variety of bugs can bother primroses, including aphids, flea beetles, and spider mites, but most problems are related to getting too little moisture.

WHAT TO GROW

Primula is a large genus, comprised of over 400 species, that botanists have divided into over three dozen sections. The best primroses to grow depends to some extent on where you live. Most prefer cool summers, so the Pacific Northwest is ideal primrose-growing territory. Unless otherwise noted, the primroses listed below want rich, evenly moist, well-drained soil, and partial or full shade, especially during the hottest part of the day. A few species can tolerate full sun in regions with cool summers.

Polyanthus Group primroses, also listed as *P. × polyanthus*, are the showy florist's pot plants available everywhere in spring. They produce clusters of 1- to 2-inch-wide flowers on 6-inch stems in a

Drumstick primrose, Primula denticulata

range of colors, including pale to deep yellow, red, orange, violet-blue, white, and pink, often with yellow eyes. Bicolors also are available. Generally hardy in Zones 4 to 8, they're crosses of several species, so hardiness varies. Pacific Giants Series come in a wide range of colors, both solids and bicolors. Plants produced for the florist trade are forced in greenhouses and can't be moved to the garden without being hardened off. Be warned that forced plants have been grown quickly and usually have depleted reserves by the time they're finished blooming, which means their chances of doing well in your garden are 50-50 at best.

English primrose (*P. vulgaris*, formerly *P. acaulis*) is hardy in Zones 4 to 8. Plants bear clusters of pale yellow, 1- to 1½-inch-wide flowers in early spring above rosettes of evergreen to semi-evergreen leaves. Many cultivars are available with both single and double flowers in white, orange, magenta, purple-pink, and yellow. Potsdam Strain produces flowers in a range of colors; 'Cottage White' bears white flowers; 'Quaker's Bonnet' has double lavender flowers; and 'Double Sulfur' features double yellow blooms.

Cowslip primrose (*P. veris*) bears clusters of small, nodding, fragrant, yellow, 1-inch-wide flowers.

English primrose, Primula vulgaris

require partial to full shade (but good light) and constantly moist to wet soil, but they will not grow in stagnant conditions. Set them so the crowns are above the water line but the roots can delve down for as much moisture as the plants desire. Plants self-sow and are hardy in Zones 3 to 8.

Another species worth trying is *P. auricula*, which grows to 8 inches and produces clusters of fragrant single or double flowers in a huge range of colors, often with contrasting centers. Auriculas are hardy in Zones 3 to 8, and there are dozens of named cultivars. Siebold primrose (*P. sieboldii*) is a good choice for gardeners short on shade, as it is more sun tolerant than most species. It is, according to one commercial grower, "a primrose than any idiot can grow." Plants reach 10 inches and bear flowers colored white, pink, lilac, and all shades between. They are hardy in Zones 3 to 8.

Hardy in Zones 4 to 8, plants bloom in early to midspring on 10-inch-tall stalks above rosettes of evergreen or semi-evergreen. Cowslips self-sow, and you'll be glad they do.

Drumstick primrose (*P. denticulata*) produces round clusters of small, bell- or trumpet-shaped, ¾-inch-wide flowers. Blooms come in lavender-purple, lilac, blue, carmine-red, and white with yellow eyes and appear in early spring on thick, 8- to 12-inch stalks. This species thrives in rich, constantly moist soil and also grows well in soil that is wet to boggy in spring and summer. Plants, which are hardy in Zones 2 or 3 to 8 and self-sow, require better drainage in winter, however, when wet conditions can rot the plants. 'Ronsdorf Mix' is a hybrid choice.

Another species for a constantly wet spot is Japanese primrose (*P. japonica*), which blooms in midspring to early summer. Classified as candelabra primroses, these bear ¾-inch-wide flowers in one to several tiers on erect stalks that can reach 1½ to 2 feet. Flowers come in red, white, and shades of pink. Named cultivars are available, including 'Miller's Crimson' and 'Postford White'. Japanese primroses

IN THE GARDEN

Use primroses to add a bright spot of spring color to shady beds and borders. They are lovely planted with other perennials that thrive in rich, moist soil, such as ferns, hostas, bleeding hearts (*Dicentra* spp.), lungworts (*Pulmonaria* spp.), epimediums, or barrenworts (*Epimedium* spp.), and named wildflowers. They also make fine companions for early spring bulbs. Use Japanese and drumstick primroses along streams, ponds, and in bog gardens.

Polyanthus primrose, Primula × polyanthus *Pacific Giant Series*

Pulmonaria

(*pull-mon-AIR-ee-ah*)

Lungworts, pulmonarias

Borage Family, Boraginaceae. Hardy perennials.

Bethlehem sage, Pulmonaria saccharata 'Mrs. Moon'

Medicine in the 16th and 17th centuries was governed by the Doctrine of Signatures, and *Pulmonaria* owes both its botanical and some of its common names to this tradition. According to the Doctrine, God gave plants to humankind to heal and treat human ills, and the use for each plant was indicated by its appearance. Thus lungworts, or pulmonarias, were used to treat diseases of the lungs because the silver-mottled foliage supposedly resembled diseased lungs. *Pulmonaria* is from the Latin *pulmo*, "lung." Practitioners in herbal medicine still use Jerusalem cowslip (*P. officinalis*) to treat bronchitis, coughs, and other complaints, but it is toxic in some applications and is legally restricted in many countries.

Gardeners grow lungworts for the season-long interest they add to garden. They are among the first perennials to emerge after winter, and their small clusters of dainty, bell-shaped flowers color garden beds and borders from late winter to late spring. Flowers come in shades of lavender or violet-blue as well as white, pink, and red. Flowers aside, these also are stunning foliage plants for shady sites. Most cultivated lungworts produce mounds of broadly oval, green leaves splashed with white or silver, and hybridizers have introduced cultivars with so much white on them that very little green is left. The largest leaves are produced in a low rosette at the base of the plant and smaller leaves are borne on the flower stems. The leaves are still quite small when the plants start flowering and may not extend fully until after the plants have stopped blooming. The foliage remains attractive until early winter, and some lungworts are evergreen in mild climates.

Common names abound with pulmonaria, many of which refer to their mottled leaves: spotted dog, Virgin Mary's milk, and Mary's milk-drops. Soldiers and sailors, lords and ladies, Mary and Joseph, and Joseph's coat of many colors are names that stem from the blooms of species, which begin pink and turn blue as they open.

HOW TO GROW

Lungworts are tough plants, asking only for shade—mandatory during the hottest part of the day—and good drainage. Add evenly moist, organically rich soil and success is pretty much guaranteed. Plant lungworts in spring or fall, and water until they are established. Water in dry weather to keep leaves healthy, and mulch plants to keep the soil moist and cool. Topdress plants in spring with compost. Deadheading won't extend flowering, but it will prevent plants from self-sowing. Remove tattered leaves to keep plants attractive. If plants are infected with powdery mildew—a problem in regions with humid summers—remove and destroy all diseased leaves. Lungworts hybridize freely, so seedlings will not be identical to the parents, but you may find attractive new plants among the volunteers.

Lungworts don't need to be divided regularly, but some gardeners dig the clumps every three or four years to keep them vigorous. Division in spring after flowering ends is the best way to propagate lungworts. Newly divided plants wilt dramatically, but don't give up: Water and shade them, and they recover. Pulmonarias are rarely grown from seed.

Plants are bothered by mildews in very humid conditions but are largely pest- and disease-free.

WHAT TO GROW

Bethlehem sage (*P. saccharata*), hardy in Zones 3 to 8, is the most commonly grown species. Plants have pink buds that open to purple-blue or red-violet flowers and low, 8- to 10-inch mounds of 10- to 11-inch-long, silver-spotted leaves. Foliage is evergreen in areas with mild winters. 'Mrs. Moon', with pink buds and bluish-lilac flowers, is the most commonly available cultivar. 'Pierre's Pure Pink' has shell pink flowers.

Most gardeners grow hybrid lungworts, and breeders are busily creating more to choose from. Hardiness can vary, so read labels when selecting. 'Polar Splash' bears pink buds, blue flowers, and white-splashed leaves; 'Victorian Brooch' has white spotted leaves with magenta-coral flowers. 'Raspberry Splash' has raspberry pink flowers and silver-spotted leaves. All are hardy in Zones 3 to 9. 'Roy Davidson', hardy in Zones 5 to 8, bears sky blue flowers and midgreen leaves evenly blotched with silver. 'Sissinghurst White', Zones 4 to 8, has white flowers. Terra Nova, an award-winning wholesale nursery in Oregon is responsible for many new hybrid pulmonarias hardy in Zones 4 to 9, including 'Dark Vader', 'Excalibur', 'High Contrast', and 'Milky Way', that have stunning foliage and pretty flowers and that are highly resistant to mildew.

Longleaf lungwort (*P. longifolia*), Zones 4 to 8, bears silver-spotted, 18-inch-long leaves that form broad clumps. Plants bear purple-blue flowers. 'Bertram Anderson' has narrower leaves than the species that are strongly marked with silver; the leaves of 'Diana Clare' are apple green marked with silver; flowers are violet-blue. Red lungwort (*P. rubra*), which has solid green leaves and is hardy in Zones 4 to 8, is one of the earliest pulmonarias to bloom; it produces reddish pink flowers from late winter to midspring. Look, too, for the Royal Horticultural Society medal winner 'Red Start'.

IN THE GARDEN

Add lungworts to shady beds and borders where they can be combined with epimediums, or barrenworts (*Epimedium* spp.), hostas, ferns, bleeding hearts (*Dicentra* spp.), hellebores (*Helleborus* spp.), and spring bulbs. They also make fine ground covers.

Rodgersia

(*rode-JER-see-ah*)

Rodgersias

Saxifrage family, Saxifragaceae. Hardy perennials.

Rodgersias, or Roger's flower, are vigorous, almost shrublike perennials that are native to mountainous

Bronze-leaved rodgersia, Rodgersia podophylla

areas in Burma, China, Korea, and Japan. The genus name honors Admiral John Rodgers, the American commander of the 1853 expedition to China during which the genus was discovered. Despite this distinction, Rogers is remembered by military historians as the man who led the 1871 invasion of Korea in retaliation for the slaughter of the crew of the General Sherman in 1866. After his initial success, the Korean army sent reinforcements armed with modern weapons, "and Admiral Rodgers wisely retreated."

Rodgersias are often overlooked, even by experienced gardeners, yet they offer handsome, bold foliage as well as fluffy clusters of midsummer flowers. They are closely related to astilbes (*Astilbe* spp.), and the blooms of several species look like astilbes on steroids. The individual flowers of rodgersias, which are petal-less, star-shaped, and only about ¼ inch wide, are borne in large, showy, branched panicles held well above the foliage. The huge leaves also add contrast in gardens: They're compound, with leaflets arranged either in a palmate (handlike) or pinnate (featherlike) fashion, and often are heavily veined or textured. Some species have foliage with a bronze or purple tint, and several exhibit excellent fall color. Few perennials offer bolder leaves. Established clumps form mounds ranging from 3 to 6 feet or more, and plants are 5 to 6 feet tall in bloom.

Such desirable qualities don't come without a price. Rodgersias only do their very best in areas with cool summers and wet conditions. As American botanist Allan Armitage nicely summed it up when he wrote that "placing these plants in dry soils is like potting up primroses in Miami."

HOW TO GROW

Give rodgersias a spot in light to full shade where they won't be hit by strong winds. They require rich soil that's evenly moist or even constantly wet. Plants can tolerate drier conditions provided they are planted in shade, and they will tolerate more sun if they have ample moisture and are growing in an area where summers are cool. For best results, plant them along a pond or stream or in a bog garden.

Start with plants to add rodgersias to your garden. Dig plenty of compost or other organic matter into the soil at planting time, and water plants deeply. Once established, rodgersias can thrive for years with minimal attention. Clumps spread from 3 to 6 feet with time. Remove the flower stems when blooming is finished so they don't detract from the handsome foliage. An annual spring mulching with compost helps keep the soil rich, and plants only need to be divided if they outgrow their space, begin to loose vigor, or die out in the center of the clumps. Cut off the foliage after the first killing frost. Dig clumps in spring as necessary to rejuvenate them or for propagation. To grow rodgersias from seeds, sow in pots in fall and set the pots outdoors in a protected location. Do not cover the seeds.

Plants have no serious disease or pest problems.

WHAT TO GROW

Fingerleaf rodgersia (*R. aesculifolia*), hardy in Zones 4 to 7, is a 4-foot-tall species with palmate, 2-foot-wide leaves that have a corrugated or crinkled texture. Plants bear 2-foot-long panicles of white flowers in mid- to late summer. Featherleaf rodgersia (*R. pinnata*), hardy in Zones 5 to 7, is a 2- to 3-foot-tall species producing mounds of heavily veined, rough-textured, 3-foot-long pinnate (featherlike) leaves. Plants bear 1- to 2-foot-long panicles of yellowish-white, pink, or red flowers in mid- to late summer. 'Superba' bears leaves that are bronze-purple when young and rose-pink flowers; 'Elegans' has creamy white flowers. Bronze-leaved rodgersia (*R. podophylla*,

formerly *R. japonica*), hardy in Zones 5 to 8, bears 1- to 1½-foot-long palmate leaves. Plants form 4-foot-tall mounds of foliage topped by 1-foot-long panicles of creamy flowers in mid- to late summer. Leaves turn bronze-red in fall. Good cultivars include 'Pagoda' and 'Rotlaub'.

IN THE GARDEN

Rodgersias are large plants best used in good-size drifts in wet spots, along streams, or in bog gardens. Combine them with hostas, ferns (especially *Osmunda* spp. or ostrich ferns, *Matteuccia struthiopteris*), and turtleheads (*Chelone* spp.).

Rudbeckia

(*rude-BECK-ee-ah*)

Orange coneflowers, rudbeckias, black-eyed Susans

Aster Family, Asteraceae.
Hardy perennials, biennials.

Although all *Rudbeckia* species are native to North America, their botanical name honors Swedish physicians and botanists, father and son, Olof Rudbeck the elder (1630–1702) and Olof Rudbeck the younger (1660–1740). Common names like orange coneflowers and black-eyed Susans have more obvious origins: The best known rudbeckias produce daisylike flowers with conelike, dark brown, raised centers.

Like other members of the aster family, the daisylike blooms are flower heads with petal-like ray florets that surround the spiny center of densely packed disk florets, which produce the seeds. Orange coneflowers are tough, easy to grow perennials that bloom in summer. Ragged coneflower (*R. laciniata*) was supposedly the first rudbeckia to get to Europe. It was sent by French settlers in Quebec to France from where it made its way to England and the garden of John Parkinson, author of the famous *Paradisi in Sole, Paradisus Terrestris* (1629), the first illustrated book in English devoted largely to ornamental plants. The first half of the title, as others have pointed out, was a self-serving pun on his on name, "Park-in-son."

Rudbeckias are astonishingly cooperative flowers. They have a long bloom time and don't mind

Orange coneflower, Rudbeckia fulgida *var.* sullivantii *'Goldsturm'*

Orange coneflowers require very little care once they're established. They don't need annual feeding and are rarely attacked by pests. Taller cultivars—including some cultivars of *R. hirta* and *R. laciniata*—may need staking. Or cut plants back in early spring to reduce their height. If plants flop, you can cut them to the ground after they finish flowering, but many gardeners leave them standing until spring because the seed heads add winter interest and are attractive to birds.

Rudbeckias don't need to be divided regularly. Dig clumps in spring or fall if they outgrow their space or die out in the centers of the clumps. Propagate by division in spring or fall: Discard older, woody growth, and replant the vigorous sections. Or propagate from stem cuttings or seeds.

To grow gloriosa daisies (*R. hirta*) from seeds, sow indoors six to eight weeks before the last spring frost date. Or sow outdoors in a prepared seedbed where the plants are to grow two weeks before the last spring frost date. Sow seeds for perennial species in pots in fall or late winter and set the pots in a cold frame or a protected spot outdoors. While seeds of the popular cultivar 'Goldsturm' are available, plants propagated vegetatively are more uniform.

Rudbeckias are sometimes subject to mildews (especially gloriosa daisies) but are largely without problems.

WHAT TO GROW

Of the perennial coneflowers, orange coneflower (*R. fulgida*), is the best known, especially because of its cultivar 'Goldsturm' (*R. fulgida* var. *sullivantii*

being neglected. And of all the rudbeckias, none is more obliging than 'Goldsturm', which is why you'll find it in gardens throughout North America. Although its roots are American, it was discovered in 1937 by Heinrich Hagemann among a group of *R. fulgida* var. *sullivantii* plants at a nursery in the Czech Republic. 'Goldsturm', which means "gold storm," was introduced in 1949, and it has received nothing but raves ever since. In 1999, the Perennial Plant Association named it Perennial of the Year, yet another good review for this superb cultivar.

HOW TO GROW

Select a site in full sun to light shade to grow rudbeckias. They thrive in average to rich soil and grow best in evenly moist conditions, although they are tolerant of some drought once established. Start with nursery plants or grow your own from seeds. Perennial species can be planted in either spring or fall. While perennial species spread in the garden, gloriosa daisies (*R. hirta*) are biennials or short-lived perennials; plant them in spring.

Gloriosa daisy, Rudbeckia hirta *'Gloriosa Mix'*

'Goldsturm'), which bears 3- to 4-inch flowers on 2-foot plants from midsummer until the first frost. The species, also known as black-eyed Susan, is 1½ to 5 feet tall and bears 2- to 2½-inch, orange-yellow flowers with chocolate-brown centers; it is especially tolerant of hot, dry summer weather. Both are hardy in Zones 3 to 9.

Ragged, or green-headed, coneflower (*R. laciniata*), which ranges from 3 to 6 feet tall, produces 3- to 6-inch-wide flowers with yellow petals and green centers from midsummer to fall. Double-flowered cultivars are especially popular, including 'Goldquelle', 2 to 4 feet. Old-timer 'Golden Glow', which requires staking and attracts aphids, is still widely sold, although there are better cultivars available. Giant coneflower (*R. maxima*) ranges from 5 to 8 feet tall and bears 3- to 5-inch-wide flowers. Blooms have orange yellow petals and cone-shaped centers that rise 1½ inches and more above the petals. Finally, the hybrid *R.* 'Herbstsonne' (commonly sold as 'Autumn Sun') is a wonderful 6- to 7-foot-tall species that bears an abundance of yellow flowers with green centers from midsummer to early fall. All of the perennial coneflowers listed here are hardy in Zones 3 to 9.

Gloriosa daisies, cultivars of *R. hirta*, are also popular garden plants. All are short-lived perennials or biennials, hardy in Zones 3 to 9, but are often grown as annuals. The species, which is about 2 feet tall, has orange-yellow petals and dark brown centers, but many cultivars are available that feature petals marked with combinations of gold, yellow, mahogany, and bronze, and flower from midsummer through fall. 'Cherokee Sunset', an All-America Selections winner, yields single and double flowers in shades

of yellow, red, orange, bronze, and mahogany. 'Indian Summer', another AAS winner, has single and semidouble golden yellow blooms on 3- to 3½-foot plants; 'Hot Chocolate' bears dark-centered blooms with yellow-tipped, mahogany-red petals on 18-inch plants. Dwarf forms also are available, including 10-inch 'Becky' and 'Maya' with dark-centered, golden yellow blooms.

IN THE GARDEN

Plant orange coneflowers in sunny beds and borders with perennials such as ornamental grasses, daylilies, purple coneflower (*Echinacea purpurea*), yarrows (*Achillea* spp.), and Russian sage (*Perovskia atriplicifolia*). They can be used in meadow plantings or sunny wildflower gardens with other natives, such as butterfly weed (*Asclepias tuberosa*) and goldenrods (*Solidago* spp.). *R. fulgida* can be used as a low-maintenance ground cover. All make superb cut flowers.

Salvia

(SAL-vee-ah)

Salvias, sages

Mint family, Lamiaceae.
Hardy perennials, tender perennials usually grown as annuals, annuals.

Long before salvias were grown as ornamentals, they were prized as medicinal plants, as the genus name indicates: *Salvia* is from the Latin *salvare*, "to save" or "to heal." There are about 900 species in the genus, many of which contain a rich array of volatile oils that make the foliage and flowers aromatic. Written records trace their use to at least 200 hundred years B.C. Sages were indispensable, as the 9th-century abbot Walahfrid Strabo made clear when he wrote, "Amongst my herbs, sage holds the place of honour, of good scent it is and full of virtue for many ills." Believed to improve memory, the word "sage" took on the more general meaning of being wise. Shakespeare, in *Richard III*, has the Earl of Gloucester address his audience as "sage grown men."

Not surprisingly, it was common sage (*S. officinalis*) that our practical forefathers and mothers brought to North America from England and elsewhere. They used it in the kitchen and to heal—including in

Scarlet sage, Salvia splendens *'Flare'*

teas for cooling lascivious desires, a roundabout way of indicating that it would cure venereal diseases. In 1631, the Puritan John Winthrop Jr., ordered ½ ounce of sage seeds to be sent to him from England, but there is no record of to what use he planned to put his plants.

Flower gardeners, of course, look to the bright blooms these plants bring to beds and borders. The genus features annuals and hardy and tender perennials, all of which make excellent additions to the garden. These mint-family plants feature two-lipped flowers, which are carried in erect clusters and arranged in tiered whorls, in shades of red, pink, white, yellow, violet, and true blue. Their square stems signal their mint-family allegiance.

HOW TO GROW

Give salvias a spot in full sun or very light shade. They grow best in average, well-drained, evenly moist soil. For the most part, these are tough,

drought-tolerant plants once established. Very rich soil and not enough sun cause lanky growth and reduce flowering.

Begin by purchasing plants or sowing from seeds. Popular scarlet sages (S. *splendens*) are available in market packs everywhere bedding plants are sold in spring; hardier species are available at garden centers. Wait until the ground warms before transplanting scarlet sages outdoors. Hardy types can go outside in early spring or, depending on their hardiness rating, can be planted in fall.

Salvias are easy plants in the garden. Feed perennial species in spring with a balanced organic fertilizer or topdress them with compost. Water only during extended drought. Deadhead plants to encourage new flowers to form and to keep plants neat looking. Cut back plants after the first frost. Perennial species rarely need to be divided, but divide clumps in spring (fall in warm regions) if they lose vigor or for propagation. Or propagate from stem cuttings taken in summer and rooted in a mix of half perlite and half vermiculite.

Salvia species and many salvia cultivars come true from seeds, especially those typically grown as annuals, such as cultivars of scarlet sage (S. *splendens*). Sow seeds indoors six to eight weeks before the last frost (12 weeks for S. *farinacea*) or sow outdoors in early spring in warm regions. Most gardeners treat tender salvias as annuals and purchase new plants each spring, although they're also easy to propagate and overwinter indoors from stem cuttings made in late summer or early fall. Overwintering entire plants indoors in a sunny, cool spot also is possible.

Salvias are subject to few pest or disease problems, although they are occasionally infested by aphids and Asiatic beetles.

WHAT TO GROW

Of the hardy perennial sages, hybrid sage (S. × *sylvestris*) is most commonly grown. Hardy in Zones 4 to 9, it bears an abundance of erect spikes of pinkish purple flowers on 2- to 3-foot plants from early to midsummer. 'East Friesland', a compact, 1½-foot selection, bears violet-purple flowers, while 'May Night' ('Mainacht') bears indigo flowers. 'Rose Queen' produces pink flowers on 2½-foot plants; 'Dwarf Blue Queen' bears blue flowers on 12-inch plants. Other perennial sages include meadow sage (S. *pratensis*), hardy in Zones 3 to 9, with violet spikes from early to midsummer on 1- to 3-foot plants. Blue, or azure, sage (S. *azurea*), hardy in Zones 5 to

9, bears blue or white flowers from late summer to fall on 3- to 4-foot plants.

Of the so-called annual sages, scarlet sage (*S. splendens*) is by far the best known. Actually a tender perennial grown as an annual, this is a 1- to 1½-foot species with dense spikes of flowers from summer to fall. Scarlet is often the color of choice, but this species also comes in shades of pink, salmon, pinkish purple, mauve-purple, lavender, burgundy, purple, and white. Both Salsa Series and Sizzler Series offer compact plants in a range of colors.

Mealycup sage (*S. farinacea*), another tender perennial grown as an annual, bears dense spikes of small violet or white flowers from summer to fall on 2-foot plants. 'Victoria' bears violet-blue flowers and 'Victoria White', white spikes.

Other tender perennial sages include pineapple sage (*S. elegans*) with scarlet flowers in fall on 4- to 6-foot plants and pineapple-scented leaves. Gregg, or autumn, sage (*S. greggii*), hardy from Zone 7 south, produces red, purple, violet, pink, or yellow flowers from late summer to frost on 1- to 2-foot plants and is another good choice. As is *S. guaranitica*, grown for its showy azure flowers with purple-blue calyxes

on shrubby 5-foot plants that are hardy from Zone 8 south. All can be cultivated as annuals or as tender perennials.

Texas sage (*S. coccinea*), an annual, bears graceful, loose spikes of red, pink, or white flowers from summer to fall on 2- to 2½-foot plants. 'Lady in Red', an All-America Selections winner is a good choice, as are 'Lady in Pink', 'Coral Nymph', and 'Snow Nymph'. All self-sow.

IN THE GARDEN
Salvias deserve a place in every sunny bed and border, where they will add summertime flowers and scented foliage. Grow them with coreopsis, dahlias, four-o'clock (*Mirabilis jalapa*), orange coneflowers (*Rudbeckia* spp.), daylilies, yarrows (*Achillea* spp.), and other annuals and perennials that thrive in well-drained conditions. Salvias also are excellent container plants, and the flowers of most species are attractive to hummingbirds, butterflies, and beneficial insects.

Scabiosa

(*scah-bee-OH-sah*)

Scabious, pincushion flowers

Teasel family, Dipsacaceae. Hardy perennials.

While many garden perennials are members of vast clans—the aster family, Asteraceae, and the mint family, Lamiaceae, for example—*Scabiosa* belongs to a less commonly grown family. One close relative is teasel (*Dipsacus* spp.), and several species are naturalized weeds in North America whose conelike flower heads are picked for use in dried arrangements and crafts. Only three other garden flowers belong to the teasel family—giant scabious (*Cephalaria gigantea*) and two species of knautia (*Knautia arvensis* and *K. macedonica*), all of which once belonged to the genus *Scabiosa*.

The common name mournful widow apparently stems from the Victorian language of flowers: Scabiosa blooms represented loss and were used in funeral wreaths. Scabiosas are decidedly pretty flowers but have a botanical name with an inelegant origin: *Scabiosa* is from the Latin *scabies*, "the itch," because some species were used to treat this once-common complaint.

Mealycup sage, Salvia farinacea 'Victoria'

Pincushion flower, Scabiosa columbaria

As the common name pincushion flower suggests, scabious bears rounded flowers that somewhat resemble pincushions. The blooms, which can be single or double, look something like daisies and are constructed in a similar fashion: They have small central florets that form the "pincushion" surrounded by larger petal-like florets. The leaves are either entire, lobed, or deeply cut in a featherlike fashion.

HOW TO GROW

Plant pincushion flowers in full sun and out of the wind, and give them moderately rich, well-drained soil with a pH that is neutral to slightly alkaline. Good drainage is essential, especially in winter. In the South, look for a site that receives afternoon shade.

Purchase container-grown plants or grow these perennials from seed. Once in the garden, they thrive with minimal care. Plants will flower for several weeks if deadheaded; water deeply during dry weather. Cut back stems to the basal foliage after the first frost. If plants outgrow their space or become crowded, dig the clumps in spring and divide them. Propagate by division, or take cuttings from shoots that arise at the base of the plant in spring and root them in a mix of half vermiculite and half perlite. Seed is another option: Sow indoors eight to ten weeks before the last frost or in containers in fall that are set outdoors in a protected location to overwinter.

OTHER CHOICES

Sweet scabious or annual pincushion flower (*S. atropurpurea*) is a 2- to 3-foot-tall warm-weather annual with fragrant, 2-inch-wide flower heads in shades of purple, lavender, white, pink, or purple-blue. Star flower (*S. stellata*), also a warm-weather annual, is grown for its round, 3-inch-wide, papery brown seed heads, which are handsome in dried arrangements. Plants reach 1½ feet and the bluish white or pink flowers are 1¼ inches wide. Both species need full sun and average, well-drained soil. Sow seeds indoors four to five weeks before the last spring frost date or sow outdoors after the last-frost date.

Another perennial teasel relative with flowers that resemble pincushion flowers is *Knautia macedonica* (formerly *Scabiosa rumelica*), which is a 2- to 2½-foot-tall perennial that bears maroon-red, buttonlike flowerheads from mid- to late summer. Hardy in Zones 4 through 8, plants thrive in sun and average well-drained soil. Cut them back in midsummer if they flop.

Watch for rot and mildews, leafhoppers, slugs, and snails.

WHAT TO GROW

Two perennial species are commonly called pincushion flower—*S. caucasica* and *S. columbaria*—both clump-forming perennials with featherlike leaves that reach 2 feet in height. *S. caucasica* bears rounded 3-inch-wide flower clusters in lavender, white, yellow, and rose-purple from summer to early fall, and it is hardy in Zones 4 to 9. Its cultivars 'Miss Willmott' and 'Alba' both bear white flowers. *S. columbaria*, hardy in Zones 3 to 8, bears lilac-blue, 1½-inch-wide flower heads from summer to fall. 'Butterfly Blue' and 'Pink Mist', also sold as 'Butterfly Pink', are outstanding, long-blooming cultivars sometimes listed under *S. caucasica*. 'Butterfly Blue' was selected as the plant of the year in 2000 by the Perennial Plant Association.

IN THE GARDEN

Plant pincushion flowers in sunny perennial beds, especially at the front of the garden. They can be combined with salvias, coreopsis, sedums, daylilies, and lavender (*Lavandula angustifolia*). Flowers are long-lasting in the vase, and regular cutting encourages plants to form more flowers. Butterflies and beneficial insects are attracted by the blossoms.

Sedum

(SEE-dum)

Sedums, stonecrops

Orphine family, Crassulaceae.
Hardy perennials.

○

Sedums would be near the top of any list of low-maintenance perennials. These tough, drought-tolerant, easy to satisfy succulents bring a no-nonsense constitution and colorful flowers to the garden. The genus is large—about 400 species. Sedums bear fleshy leaves that are often oval and somewhat flattened along with dense, showy clusters of tiny, star-shaped flowers. In addition to perennials suitable for beds and borders, the genus contains mat-forming, fast-spreading species, such as golden moss stonecrop (*S. acre*), hardy in Zones 3 to 8, that are widely used as ground covers. Leafy stonecrop (*S. dasyphyllum*) is a 4-inch-tall plant that is ideal for rock gardens or planting between the stones of stone walls. Its flowers are white with pink streaks; plants are hardy in Zones 7 to 9.

The botanical name is from the Latin, *sedo*, "to sit," and refers to the way some species grow on rock outcrops, cliffs, and walls. The common name stonecrop also alludes to their affinity for rocky locations and because many sedums have plump gray leaves that look like stones. Stonecrops don't have the look-at-me panache of bearded iris or lilies, but the plant has had its moment in the literary spotlight when it appeared in William Wordsworth's narrative poem "The Excursion" (1814). Describing an overgrown cottage, he wrote:

> . . . and that bright weed,
> The yellow stonecrop, suffered to take root,
> Along the window's edge, profusely grew,
> Blinding the lower panes.

Wordsworth likely was writing about the diminutive but vigorous-spreading *S. acre*, a.k.a. wallpaper, for obvious reasons.

HOW TO GROW

Give sedums full sun. Period. They thrive in poor, dry soil but prefer slightly rich soil. Wet soil, on the other hand, is their demise. If not set in a soggy site, in shade, or overfed, sedums typically merit their common name live-forever.

Add sedums by purchasing container-grown plants in spring or fall. If planting in summer, water

Autumn Joy sedum, Sedum 'Autumn Joy'

until plants become established. Once in the garden, they need almost no care: no feeding, staking, or regular watering. Keep mulch away from their stems, and don't divide plants unless they begin to die out in the centers of the clumps. Ground-cover types easily spread too far, but this isn't a problem as they are easy to pull.

Pinching back tall sedums like 'Autumn Joy' in spring will reduce height and prevent stems from flopping. If clumps too get too large, divide them in spring, discarding any woody portions, and replanting the vigorous sections. Division is not the best means of propagating, however, and plants are rarely grown from seeds. Stem cuttings made in spring are 99.9 percent successful. Take cuttings from nonflowering shoots and root them in a mix of half perlite and half vermiculite.

Occasionally subject to infestations of aphids, sedums generally have no serious pest or disease troubles.

WHAT TO GROW

Among the taller sedums for beds and borders, there's little doubt that 'Autumn Joy' is king. It's also listed as 'Herbstfreude', the name given to it by its German hybridizers. Whichever name you prefer, this hardworking perennial lends three seasons of interest to the garden. In summer, plants produce broccoli-like clusters of flower buds on 2-foot plants. The pale green buds open in early fall, forming rounded, 8-inch-wide heads of densely packed flowers that open to dark pink and gradually age to bronze. The red-brown heads stand through winter. There are other hybrid cultivars worth considering: 'Stardust' bears white flowers; 'Brilliant' bears very large pink flowers that age to rust red; 'Frosty Morn' has light pink blooms and variegated foliage; and 'Meteor' bears carmine red flowers and gray-green leaves. All are hardy in Zones 3 to 9.

S. telephium spp. *maximum* 'Atropurpureum' is also a 2-foot-tall sedum with purple-red leaves and airy, pale pink blooms. It is hardy in Zones 3 to 9.

Several slightly shorter sedums also are suitable for growing in the flower garden, including hybrid 'Ruby Glow', which bears loose, 2½-inch clusters of pinkish red flowers from midsummer to early fall on 10-inch plants. Hardy in Zones 5 to 9, the plants have oval, purplish green leaves borne on arching stems. Showy 'Vera Jameson', another hybrid, has rose-pink flowers and purplish to burgundy leaves. It is hardy in Zones 4 to 9. October daphne (*S.*

sieboldii) bears 2½-inch clusters of pink flowers in fall. Hardy in Zones 3 to 8, the plants have fleshy, blue-green leaves edged in pink.

IN THE GARDEN

Combine 'Autumn Joy' and similar hybrids with summer- to fall-blooming perennials such as coreopsis, daylilies, ornamental grasses, autumn monkshood (*Aconitum autumnale*), orange coneflowers (*Rudbeckia* spp.), and variegated yuccas (*Yucca* spp.). They also can be used as edging plants.

Stachys byzantina

(STAY-kuss bih-zan-TEE-nah)

Lamb's ears, stachys

Mint family, Lamiaceae. Hardy perennial.

The velvety leaves of lamb's ears make it a plant everyone has to touch. Botanists describe the silver-gray leaves as white-woolly. In addition to its most often used common name, others, inspired by the furry foliage, have sprung up including lamb's tongue, lamb's tails, lamb's lungs, and woolly betony. The leaves range from oblong-elliptical to lance shaped; plants form low mounds.

Flower spikes rise above the leaves from early summer to fall, and the botanical name refers to these: *Stachys* is from the Greek *stachys*, "spike." The small pinkish purple flowers are two-lipped and are arranged in what looks like whorls around the stem. Like other mint-family plants, lamb's ears have square stems.

Woundwort, another common name sometimes used to identify *S. byzantina*, really belongs to another member of the genus, *S. officinalis*. The name *officinalis* is a heads-up that this a utilitarian plant. It also is called betony and grown primarily for its edible or medical virtues. With betony, which is also called bishop's wort, the virtues are medical although the plant also bears showy flowers. Its reputation as a cure-all reaches back to ancient Egypt, Greece, and Rome. In his herbal (1649), physician-astrologer Nicholas Culpeper recommended betony in wine to "killeth the worms in the belly . . . [and] cureth stitches and pains in the back or sides." Today we would call Culpeper a quack, but Alice Coats pointed out in her book about the history of flowers (1956) "that he was perfectly sincere in his peculiar beliefs and, though poor himself, never grudged free medical assistance to those in need."

HOW TO GROW

Give lamb's ears full sun, or morning sun and afternoon shade in warm regions, and moderately fertile soil that is very well drained. Begin with nursery-grown plants in spring. Once established, lamb's ears require little care. Plants are drought tolerant, but if watering is necessary, avoid wetting the leaves. Some gardeners consider the flower stalks unattractive and remove them as they appear, growing the plant exclusively for its foliage. Prune plants in midsummer if the foliage looks diseased or the stems appear to be rotting. Do not cut back in fall; instead, rake or prune plants in the spring to remove any dead foliage.

Divide plants in spring (autumn in warm areas) if they outgrow their space or the clumps die out in the center. Discard the old, woody growth and replant the rest. Division is an easy way to propagate lamb's ears, or separate the rooted plantlets that arise around the main plant and transplant them.

Lamb's ears have no serious pest or disease problems except in hot, humid, rainy weather, when crown rot and mildews can affect the plants.

WHAT TO GROW

Lamb's ears (*S. byzantina*, formerly *S. lanata* and *S. olympica*) is a mounding perennial primarily grown for its 6- to 12-inch-tall rosettes of silver-gray leaves.

Lamb's ear, Stachys byzantina *'Countess Helene von Stein'*

Woolly, 1½-foot-tall spikes of flowers appear from early summer to fall. 'Countess Helene von Stein', also sold as 'Big Ears', has large, 10-inch-long, greenish white leaves with a feltlike texture. 'Primrose Heron' has yellow-gray leaves. 'Silver Carpet' has gray-white leaves and does not flower; it spreads quickly and makes a good ground cover. All are hardy in Zones 4 to 8.

IN THE GARDEN

Lamb's ears is one of the easiest of the silver-leaved perennials to grow. It is handsome in sunny beds and borders, where it can be used as an edging plant or combined with other perennials to add interest to the front of a garden. Combine lamb's ears with sedums, daylilies, coreopsis, lavenders (*Lavandula* spp.), thymes, and bearded irises.

Tagetes

(*TAH-jeh-teez*)

Marigolds

Aster family, Asteraceae. Annuals.

In England, the marigold is *Calendula*, but on this side of the Atlantic that common name belongs to *Tagetes*. All 50-odd species in the genus but one are American natives—from North, Central, and South America—and most have deeply cut, featherlike foliage. Like other aster-family plants, marigolds bear flower heads with disk florets and larger, petal-like ray florets. Flowers can be single, semidouble, or double, and they are borne either singly or in clusters. They come in hues of yellow, orange, mahogany, rust, maroon, and creamy white.

Wayne Winterrowd notes in *Annuals for Connoisseurs* (1992), that, "in most garden literature, the marigold has come to be *the* example of plants beyond the pale." A few dwarf marigolds equipped with colossal flowers may be beyond the pale, but there aren't many bad marigolds, although there are too many marigolds that look exactly like marigolds with different names. Moreover, some have misleading names. French marigolds (*T. patula*) are not French but Mexican, and the tall African marigold (*T. erecta*) also is a Mexican native, which may

French marigold, Tagetes patula *'Disco Granada'*

cultivars in its 130-year history, far more than anyone else; however, its two-decade quest for a white cultivar ended in 1957 when it awarded the $10,000 prize to Sully, Iowa, gardener Alice Vonk. The marigold also was a preoccupation of the late Everett Dirksen, an Illinois senator who never missed a chance to fill the pages of the *Congressional Record* with long, eloquent pleas to make it our national flower. Marigolds lost out to the rose, but they continue, as Dirksen phrased it, "tossing their heads in the sunshine and giving a glow to the entire landscape."

HOW TO GROW

Nothing could be easier or quicker to grow from seed or easier to keep going than marigolds. Plants tolerate poor soil, drought, and most other garden calamities as long as they get full sun and are dead-headed, which will keep them flowering from late spring until frost. No wet nursing required. Watering during dry spells will improve flowering. Excessive feeding will not improve flowering—although it will produce lots of succulent leaves. In the deep South, a spot that receives shade during the afternoon helps protect plants from excessive heat.

Add marigolds to your garden in spring by purchasing market packs anywhere bedding plants are sold. They're also very easy to grow from seeds. Sow seeds indoors six to eight weeks before the last spring

explain why many seed catalogs now list it as "American marigold."

The debate over the marigold's pungent scent has raged for centuries. John Parkinson wrote in the 17th century that the flower was "pleasant to the eye, and not to any other sense." A nose-twister it is, with the fragrance coming more from the leaf than the bloom, but a marigold wouldn't be a marigold without it. 'Odorless Mixed', we can be thankful, has disappeared from seed catalogs. Be prepared not to find your favorite in next year's seed catalog: Marigold breeders are as prolific as rabbits, and each season brings a new warren of cultivars.

Thankfully, the Burpee company has never lost its love of marigolds and has released more than 100

African marigold, Tagetes erecta *'Primrose Lady'*

frost date or outdoors about the time of the frost-free date. (Start African marigolds indoors, since they're slow to bloom from seeds.) All marigolds are warm-weather annuals, so don't move seedlings to the garden until the chance of frost has past.

Some marigolds, especially French types, stop blooming during very hot weather; water them and they will resume blooming when cooler fall weather arrives. Marigolds are problem free, so resistant to diseases and bugs that they are frequently planted among vegetable crops to prevent infections and infestations.

WHAT TO GROW

African marigolds (*T. erecta*) bear pinnate leaves on 1½- to 3-foot plants and produce showy, carnation-like double flowers that are 4 to 5 inches across. Flowers come in shades of yellow, gold, and orange. Good compact cultivars stay under about 20 inches and include the Lady Series; 'First Lady', an All-America Selections award winner; and 'Royal Hybrid Mix', a semidwarf. The Climax Series has extra-large flowers in shades of yellow and orange. 'Toreador', deep orange, is another AAS winner.

Newer white marigold cultivars from Burpee include 'Snowdrift' and two hybrids, 'Snowball' and 'French Vanilla'. All have 3-inch blooms and are as close to pure white as you can find. Burpee's white-flowered marigolds are African-type plants.

French marigold (*T. patula*) is a compact, well-branched, 6- to 12-inch-tall species. Most cultivars of French marigolds produce double flowers, but singles are charming, too. Good cultivars are 'Boy O' Boy Mix', with crested, semidouble blooms, and 'Queen Sophia', an AAS winner with dark rusty orange petals edged in gold. Singles include 'Mr. Majestick', with striped yellow-and-maroon flowers, and 'Jaguar', which has gold-yellow flowers with maroon throats; 'Scarlet Scarlet' has bronze-red petals edged in gold and gold centers.

Triploid marigolds are extra-vigorous selections developed by crossing African and French marigolds. They have dwarf, French-type habits (to about 1 foot) and single or double flowers that range from 2 to 3 inches across. They don't set seeds and thus continue blooming even in hot weather or other stressful conditions. Zenith Series and Nugget Series are good selections.

Finally, signet marigolds (*T. tenuifolia*) are bushy, mound-forming annuals that range from 9 to 12 inches tall but spread twice that far. They have very lacy, finely divided leaves topped by an abundance of dainty, single, ¾-inch-wide flowers. Gem Series cultivars, in gold, lemon-yellow, and orange, are widely available.

IN THE GARDEN

Add marigolds to sunny beds and borders, and combine them with both sun-loving annuals and perennials. Shorter French and signet marigolds make fine edging plants. Taller African, or American, marigolds are better planted at the back of the border; they are also excellent flowers to grow for arrangements in a cutting garden. Plant marigolds with lavenders (*Lavandula* spp.), salvias or sages (*Salvia* spp.), cosmos, daylilies, coreopsis, and nasturtium (*Tropaeolum majus*). Signet marigolds fit well in herb and rock gardens. Both butterflies and hummingbirds like to visit marigold flowers.

Signet marigold, Tagetes tenuifolia *'Orange Gem'*

Thalictrum

(tha-LICK-trum)

Thalictrums, meadow rues

Buttercup family, Ranunculaceae.
Hardy perennials.

It's only in the last decade that thalictrums, favorites of wildflower gardeners for many years, have found their deserved place in ornamental beds and borders. They are grown for both their airy, finely textured clusters of flowers and their lacy foliage, usually pinnate leaves with rounded leaflets and often gray-green in color. Their membership in the buttercup family makes them close relatives of clematis (*Clematis* spp.) and columbines (*Aquilegia* spp.), although thalictrums have never reached the popularity of those two species. Times, though, are a'changing in American gardens.

In England, thalictrums, or meadow rues, have a long history of cultivation, but there are scant records of their presence. It is known that *T. flavum* has been planted since earliest times, especially in country gardens located in sheep-raising areas, as the roots were used to dye wool yellow. The meadow rue that has garnered the most interest in the last few years, *R. aquilegifolium*, didn't reach England until the 18th century and was known as purple tufted columbine because of its pale purple blooms and *Aquilegia*-like leaves. Alpine meadow rue (*T. alpinum*) was used to produce red dyes, giving rise to the common name redshank. *T. majus* once was believed to be a cure for the plague, but its lack of efficacy is suggested by the fact that more than one quarter of the population of Europe perished during the epidemics in the 14th century.

HOW TO GROW

Give thalictrums a spot in partial shade that has rich, moist soil. Plants tolerate full sun as long as they are growing in constantly moist soil, but they are happiest with some shade. In the South, plant them where they will receive shade during the hottest part of the day.

Add thalictrums to your garden by purchasing container-grown plants in spring or early fall, or grow them from seeds. Mark plants' locations in the garden, as they emerge somewhat late in spring, and it's easy to damage their crowns by mistake. Topdress plants with compost in spring to keep the soil rich; mulch lightly to help keep the ground moist, and water plants during dry weather. If plants become ragged or lose vigor after flowering, prune them back to the emerging basal leaves. Cut down plants after the first frost.

Thalictrums will thrive for years without needing to be divided, but you can dig them in early spring if they outgrow their space or to propagate. Newly divided plants are slow to reestablish, so be patient. Or propagate from fresh seeds collected in fall and sown in containers. Set the containers outside in a protected location to overwinter. Plants also may self-seed.

Thalictrums are potentially subject to mildews and rust diseases but are mostly trouble-free plants.

OTHER CHOICES

Buttercups (*Ranunculus* spp.) are another buttercup-family plant that thrives in full sun or shade and rich, moist, well-drained soil. Plants bear five-petaled flowers that feature a cluster of showy stamens in the center, and while the species have single blooms, garden-grown forms have double flowers. Blooms are usually yellow, but buttercups also come in white, pink, orange, or red. Look for aconite buttercup (*R. aconitifolius*), also called bachelor's button, which reaches about 2 feet tall and spreads to 1½ feet. Hardy in Zones 5 to 9, plants bear white, ¾-inch-wide flowers in late spring and early summer. 'Flore-Pleno', with double flowers, is more often grown than the species. Both need partial to full shade and constantly moist soil. Double-flowered forms of tall buttercup (*R. acris*) also make pretty garden additions. The species is a European native that has naturalized in North America. Hardy in Zones 3 or 4 to 8, plants bear 1-inch-wide golden yellow flowers from early to midsummer and are 1 to 3 feet tall. Look for 'Flore Pleno', also sold as 'Plena' and 'Multiplex'.

Columbine meadow rue, Thalictrum aquilegifolium

WHAT TO GROW

Columbine meadow rue (*T. aquilegifolium*), hardy in Zones 4 to 8, produces large mounds of rounded, blue-green, columbine-like leaves and spreads by rhizomes. Plants are 3 feet tall and in early summer bear 6- to 8-inch-wide clusters of fluffy, ½-inch-long flowers with showy purple or white stamens. Yunan meadow rue (*T. delavayi*), hardy in Zones 4 to 9, is a 2- to 4-foot-tall species that bears fluffy branched panicles of flowers with purple sepals and creamy yellow stamens from summer to fall. 'Hewitt's Double' produces rounded, mauve-purple flowers with many petal-like sepals.

Yellow meadow rue (*T. flavum*), hardy in Zones 5 to 9, is a vigorous, 1- to 3-foot-tall species that spreads by rhizomes and bears panicles of lightly fragrant, ¼-inch-long, yellow flowers in summer. Lavender mist

(*T. rochebruneanum* 'Lavender Mist'), hardy in Zones 4 to 7, is a popular, 3- to 5-foot-tall species with loose panicles of ½-inch lilac-pink or white flowers in summer. Tiny alpine meadow rue (*T. alpinum*) has white flowers and grows 6 inches tall or less.

IN THE GARDEN

Plant thalictrums in lightly shaded beds along the edge of a woodland or in sunny gardens with rich, moist soil. Combine them with rose mallows (*Hibiscus* spp.), hostas, daylilies, ligularias (*Ligularia* spp.), and turtleheads (*Chelone* spp.).

Tradescantia

(*tray-des-CAN-tee-ah*)

Spiderworts

Spiderwort family, Commelinaceae.
Hardy perennials.

Native to North, South, and Central America, the members of this genus include tender trailers often grown as houseplants as well as hardy garden perennials. The botanical name, *Tradescantia*, honors two renowned 17th-century botanists, gardeners, and plant collectors: John Tradescant the elder, who gardened for a succession of titled individuals before landing a position as gardener for King Charles I of England, and his son, John Tradescant the younger, who continued plant collecting and followed his father as gardener to King Charles I. Their vast collections—which included such items as Guy Fawkes's lantern and a stuffed dodo as well as plants—became the basis for the Ashmolean Museum at Oxford University in England.

John Tradescant, the son, traveled to Virginia in 1637 to collect plants, one of the early English botanists to visit the American colonies, but spiderwort was already known in Europe and England before he crossed the Atlantic. The common name alludes to its use as a cure for spider bites. The name widow's tears refers to the flower: Enzymes in the plant result in flowers dissolving into wet blobs rather than shriveling. More recently, spiderworts have been identified as plants that are highly sensitive to pollution, including carbon monoxide, sulphur

Virginia spiderwort, Tradescantia virginiana *'Zwanenburg Blue'*

dioxide, and radioactivity, perhaps leading to a spiderwort in the buttonhole instead of a canary in a cage or a Geiger counter.

While tender spiderworts are sometimes used in containers, gardeners are more interested in the hardy species. These have strap- to lance-shaped leaves and bear clusters of saucer-shaped flowers in late spring and early summer. Each blossom has three petals and three sepals with a pair of boat-shaped bracts at the base. While the individual flowers only last half a day, they are numerous and produced over a long season, usually two months and longer.

HOW TO GROW

Give perennial spiderworts a sunny or partly sunny site—afternoon shade in southern gardens—with moderately rich, moist, well-drained soil. Since most plants grown in gardens are hybrids, add spiderwort

to your garden by purchasing nursery-grown plants in spring or fall.

Pinch plants back by one-third when they reach 1 foot to encourage compact growth, and keep them watered during dry weather. After the main flush of flowers has faded, cut plants to the ground to discourage self-sowing and encourage reblooming. In areas with cool summers, plants will regrow quickly; in regions with warm summers, they may not reemerge until fall. Plants not cut back should be pruned to the ground after the first frost.

Spiderworts can spread quickly—in some regions, gardeners consider them invasive. To keep plants in bounds and to maintain plant vigor, divide the dense clumps in spring (spring or fall in the South) every three to four years. Division is also the best way to propagate spiderworts; although they self-sow with enthusiasm, seedlings won't look like their parents. Plants grown from seed will bloom in their second year.

Rust sometimes affects spiderworts, but plants have no other pest or disease problems of consequence.

WHAT TO GROW

Most hybrids are classified in the *Tradescantia* Andersoniana Group. These are 1½- to 2-foot-tall plants that spread to 3 feet or more if not divided regularly. Plants bear clusters of saucer-shaped, 1-inch-wide flowers with three petals from early to midsummer in shades of violet, lavender-blue, pink, rose-red, and white. 'Iris Prichard' bears white flowers with pale lavender-blue shading; 'Red Cloud' has bright rose-red flowers; 'Purple Dome' bears violet-purple blooms; 'Snowcap' has large white blooms; 'Bilberry Ice' bears white flowers with a lavender blotch; and 'Blue and Gold' features chartreuse leaves and blue flowers that are sterile and thus set no seed. All are hardy in Zones 4 to 9, to Zone 3 with winter protection.

And look out for Virginia spiderwort (*T. virginiana*), a native North American wildflower and one of the parents of the hybrids grown in gardens. Hardy in Zones 4 to 9, plants form 1- to 2-foot-tall mounds of strap-shaped leaves that spread from 2 to 3 feet and bear clusters of 1-inch purple-blue flowers.

IN THE GARDEN

Plant tradescantias in shady beds and borders where they will get plenty of moisture. They can be combined with hostas, epimediums (*Epimedium* spp.), hardy geraniums or cranesbills (*Geranium* spp.), toad lilies (*Tricyrtis* spp.), foam flowers (*Tiarella* spp.), and annual impatiens.

Tropaeolum majus

(tro-pee-OH-lum MAY-jus)

Nasturtium

Nasturtium family, Tropaeolaceae. Annual.

|||||||||||||||||||||||||||||||||||||||||||||||||||||||||||||||||||||||||||||||||||

Although nasturtiums are the most cheerful and unassuming of summer-blooming garden annuals, these South American natives bear a name with warlike connotations. *Tropaeolum* is from the Greek *tropaion* or Latin *tropaeum*, both meaning "trophy." The name alludes to the rounded, shield-like leaves as well as the helmet-shaped flowers. Together they were thought to resemble the captured shields and helmets of enemy armies, which in ancient times were displayed by the victors on a pillar.

Nasturtiums are grown for their showy five-petaled, slightly scented flowers that have prominent spurs that stick out the back of the bloom. Flowers come in shades of red, orange, yellow, and cream. The plants bear round leaves that are peltate, meaning the stems are attached in the center of the leaves rather than at the edges. Nasturtiums can be bushy, trailing, or climbing.

In a confusing twist of nomenclature, the common name nasturtium also is the botanical name for another plant—watercress (*Nasturtium officinale*). Like watercress, common nasturtium (*T. majus*) bears edible leaves that have a peppery taste—and its flowers are edible as well. For many years it was relegated to the kitchen garden. The great 17th-century French botanist (and gourmet) J. Pitton de Torunefort wrote that the nasturtium's best use "is in Sallads, on account of its fine sharp taste, and beautiful look." It is that beautiful look that gardeners most value today.

HOW TO GROW

Give common nasturtiums full sun and plant them in thin, well-drained soil. If the soil is rich, plants will produce foliage at the expense of flowers. These annuals do best in areas with relatively cool summers and they tend to fail in the hot, humid Southeast or when summer temperatures rise.

Add nasturtiums to your garden by sowing seeds, or buy market packs from a well-stocked garden center in spring. Climbing types will need some training and support on their upward journey. Nasturtiums resent transplanting, so it's wisest to sow seeds outdoors one week after the last spring frost date where the plants are to grow. To start them indoors, sow in individual pots four to five weeks before the last-frost date and transplant carefully. Nasturtiums also can be propagated by cuttings taken in early summer; double-flowered forms cannot be grown from seed and must be propagated by cuttings. Rooted cuttings also can be used to overwinter plants indoors. Nasturtiums cut for vases often root in water.

Nasturtiums are subject to viruses and leaf miners.

WHAT TO GROW

Common nasturtium (*T. majus*), also called Indian cress, is a climbing, round-leaved, warm-weather annual with 2- to 2½-inch-wide flowers from summer to fall. Both bushy and climbing cultivars are available; many are hybrids, crosses with other species, and sometimes are listed as *T. nanum*.

Nasturtium, Tropaeolum majus *'Princess of India'*

Bushy types, which are about 1 foot tall, include 'Double Dwarf Jewel Mix', which yields double and semi-double flowers from seed in a mix of yellow, peachy pink, orange, and red. 'Peach Melba' features creamy yellow flowers marked with maroon, and 'Alaska Mix' bears green-and-white variegated leaves and flowers in orange-red, yellow, and orange.

Trailing types can climb or sprawl. Good choices include the Gleam Series, which contains a full range of colors; 'Jewel of Africa', which climbs to 8 feet and has variegated leaves; 'Tip Top Mahogany', with chartreuse leaves and mahogany flowers; and 'Moonlight', which scrambles to 7 feet and bears yellow flowers.

Darwin Hybrid tulip, Tulipa *'Golden Apeldoorn'*

IN THE GARDEN

Common nasturtiums are pretty annuals to use as edgings or at the front of a flower bed with other low-growing annuals and perennials. Allow plants to trail over walls or raised beds, and use them to add summertime color to rock gardens. They also are handsome in containers and window boxes. Train climbing types onto strings, trellises, shrubs, or other supports. Use nasturtiums to garnish salads or other dishes, or cut them for the vase.

Tulipa

(TOO-lip-ah)

Tulips

Lily Family, Liliaceae. Hardy bulbs.

Tulips are native plants of central Asia. The Persians cultivated them as early as 1050, but it was the Turks who likely carried the flower from Asia into Europe in the middle of the 16th century. The botanical name *Tulip* is the Latinized form of *tulipan*, or "turban," and alludes to the form of the flower. And what a flower it is!

Although they're beloved today, tulips have never regained the crazed popularity attained in Holland between 1634 and 1637, when a frenzy of buying and selling spun into bulbs and bulblets being traded like futures on a high-flying, unregulated commodities market. The tulips at the delirium's epicenter were "broken varieties," wildly colored and marked rogue blooms that unexpectedly appeared in gardens (we now know they were caused by a virus that weakens the bulb). The story of fortunes made and lost is detailed in Mike Dash's *Tulipomania* (1999), but a hint of the insanity of it all is that the highest price paid for a tulip was 20 times the *annual* income of a skilled carpenter. The Dutch government finally stepped in to curb the market, and the tulip industry in Holland is still strictly controlled. Bulbs are now produced in North American and England, but Holland is the major breeder and grower of tulips, producing more than 3.5 billion bulbs annually.

Gardeners have their own version of tulipomania each spring, when the showy flowers appear in beds and borders. There are plenty of tulips to choose from—more than 3,000 cultivars—and they exhibit some of the brightest hues of spring, including brilliant orange, red, and yellow, plus violet-purple, pale pink, and white. Tulips come in every color except true blue. Many feature bicolor blooms—red-and-white striped, for example. The most familiar tulips have cup-shaped blooms, but tulips with star-shaped and goblet-shaped flowers are available, as are bowl-shaped doubles, tulips with fringed petal edges, ruffled petals, and tulips that bear several blooms on a single stem.

Triumph tulip, Tulipa 'Blenda'

Triumph tulip, Tulipa 'Alba'

Most flowers have six petal-like tepals, three true petals and three sepals. The plants grow from teardrop-shaped bulbs that are covered with a brown skin, called a tunic. Popular hybrids have broadly oval leaves that are bluish or gray-green in color, but some tulips have strap-shaped, or long, very narrow leaves.

HOW TO GROW

Grow tulips in sun or partial shade—afternoon shade is recommended for southern gardens—and give them rich, well-drained soil. Well-drained soil is *the* essential consideration, as bulbs rot in wet conditions. Tall cultivars need a site that is protected from wind.

Tulip bulbs are available at garden centers in fall, but the best selection is available from mail-order suppliers. Bulbs should have no mold or black, rotted blotches, and their brown tunic cover should be intact. The flowers are already formed in the bulbs you buy, and proper storage is important. Storage at high temperatures—tulips resent temperatures above 70°F either above the ground or once planted in the soil—reduces or destroys the quality of the bulbs and the flowers they produce. Avoid buying tulips from displays where bulbs have been exposed to high temperatures, moisture, or other adverse conditions. Plant bulbs as soon as they are available and the ground is cool: fall in northern Zones, early winter in the South. If you can't plant immediately, store bulbs in a cool, dry, dark location.

Dig plenty of organic matter into the soil before planting, but don't add fertilizers, which can burn the bulbs. Set bulbs with their bases between 8 and 10 inches below the soil surface. Deep planting keeps bulbs cool in the summertime and discourages them from breaking up into lots of smaller, nonflowering bulbs after the first year. Bulbs that are being grown as annuals can be planted at a depth of 5 or 6 inches. If your goal is a drift of tulips that bloom at the same time, plant the bulbs at the same depth. Space bulbs 3 to 6 inches apart, depending on their size.

If you're not growing tulips as annuals, topdress with compost or composted manure. After the first frost, mulch the planting site with compost or another organic mulch. To keep chipmunks and other rodents from dining on tulip bulbs, lay hardware cloth on top of the planting area, under the mulch, then remove it in late winter. Or plant bulbs in mesh baskets that are sold at garden stores—or make your own from hardware cloth. Once plants have finished blooming, deadhead to prevent seed formation, but let the leaves ripen naturally if you want the bulbs to flower the following year. Topdress the planting site each fall with well-rotted manure or compost.

If you are treating tulips like annuals, you can cut back the foliage or dig the bulbs as soon as flowering ends. Tulip bulbs are relatively inexpensive, which makes them a good deal however you grow them. But be warned: Even with the best of care, most tulips don't have the long lives that daffodils do.

Plantings of tulips that behave as perennials are possible in Zones 3 to 7 or 8, but selecting the right species or cultivars is important. Among the best naturalizers—tulips planted for more than one year of flowers—are the Darwin hybrids as well as Kaufmanniana, Fosteriana, and Greigii tulips. Species that are especially dependable include *T. saxatilis, T. batalinii, T. humilis,* and *T. tarda.*

Most tulips are hardy in Zones 3 to 8, but perform best in Zones 4 to 6. In Zones 8 to 10, most tulip bulbs don't receive cold enough temperatures in winter to bloom, so buy precooled bulbs and treat them as annuals. *T. clusiana, T. saxatilis, T. sylvestris,* and *T. tarda* are species tulips that can be grown in southern zones and will flower without a cold treatment. Breeders have produced a bevy of new cultivars for warm-weather gardens. Lists of tulips for the South and for other special uses and locations—as well as information about other hardy and tender bulbous plants—are available at the Netherlands Flower Bulb Information Center web site (www.bulb.com).

Tulips are subject to botrytis and aphids but these problems arise only rarely.

WHAT TO GROW

There are about 100 species of tulips and thousands of named cultivars, which have been organized into 15 divisions based on flower shape and origin. Planting tulips from several divisions ensures a variety of shapes, sizes, and bloom times. Blooming season is from early to late spring, and careful selection will ensure tulips in bloom for as long as two months. Unless otherwise noted, the tulips below are hardy in Zones 3 to 8.

Single Early Tulips, Division 1. These bloom in early to midspring and bear cup-shaped, 3-inch flowers on 10- to 18-inch-tall plants. Many are fragrant, and Single Early tulips are good for forcing. Cultivars include fragrant 'Apricot Beauty', salmon with rose-pink flames; 'Christmas Dream', fuchsia pink; 'Flair', yellow and red; 'Generaal de Wet', an old cultivar with orange and yellow blooms; and 'Purple Prince', with purple and dusky lilac flowers.

Double Early Tulips, Division 2. Blooming in midspring and good for forcing, Double Early Tulips produce bowl-shaped, 3-inch-wide peonylike flowers on 12- to 16-inch-tall stems. They come in shades of red, yellow, pink, red-orange, and white, often marked with a contrasting color. Cultivars include 'Abba', orange-red; 'Monsella', yellow with red; 'Monte Carlo', a fragrant yellow; and 'Peach Blossom', an old cultivar with fragrant, rose pink flowers.

Triumph Tulips, Division 3. Mid- to late-spring bloomers, Triumph tulips have single, cup-shaped, 2½-inch-wide flowers and are among the best choices for forcing. Cultivars include 'Barcelona', fuchsia-purple; 'Calgary', snow white; 'Dreaming Maid', violet petals edged in white; 'Dynamite', red with white; 'Golden Melody', yellow; 'Negrita', red-purple; and 'New Design', pink with creamy yellow and leaves edged in pinkish white.

Darwin Hybrid Tulips, Division 4. These bloom in mid- to late spring and have single, rounded, 3-inch blooms. Darwin Hybrids are among the best tulips for perennializing. Cultivars include 'Apeldoorn', red; 'Banja Luka', yellow and red; 'Big Chief', salmon-rose; 'Daydream',

Single Late tulip, Tulipa 'Magier'

yellow; 'Ivory Floradale', ivory-white; 'Ollioules', rose-pink; 'Parade', red; and 'Pink Impression', pink.

Single Late Tulips, Division 5. Single Late tulips bear single, 3-inch flowers that are cup or goblet shaped in late spring on stems that can reach 30 inches. They come in a wide range of colors, and some cultivars bear more than one bloom per stem. Cultivars include 'Big Smile', yellow; 'Blushing Lady', orangey yellow; 'Dreamland', red with white; 'Georgette', yellow and bearing several blooms per stem; and 'Queen of the Night', an old cultivar with maroon blooms.

Lily-Flowered Tulips, Division 6. Grown for their single, goblet-shaped flowers, Lily-flowered tulips bloom in mid- to late spring. Good cultivars include 'Ballade', reddish purple; 'Ballerina', tangerine; 'Marilyn', creamy white with reddish purple; 'Red Shine', red; 'West Point', yellow; and 'White Triumphator', white.

Fringed Tulips, Division 7. Blooming in mid- to late spring Fringed tulips produce single, 3-inch-wide, cup-shaped flowers with fringed edges. Like most divisions, they come in a wide range of colors and the fringe is often a contrasting color. Good cultivars include 'American Eagle', red-purple with creamy fringe; 'Fringed Elegance', a fine perennializer with yellow blooms; and 'Swan Wings' pure white.

Parrot Tulips, Division 10. These bloom in late spring and produce cup-shaped, 4-inch blooms with tepals that are irregularly cut, fringed, curled, and twisted in a featherlike fashion. The flowers are heavy, and plants are best grown in a spot protected from wind. Cultivars include 'Black Parrot', an old cultivar with dark burgundy blooms; 'Blue Parrot', blue-violet; 'Carmine Parrot', red; and 'Estella Rijnveld', red marked with creamy yellow.

Double Late Tulips, Division 11. Also called peony-flowered tulips, these tulips bloom in late spring and have heavy, double, bowl-shaped blooms that can reach 5 inches across. Plant them in a spot protected from wind. Good cultivars include 'Angelique', pale

Fosteriana tulip, Tulipa *'Purissima'*

Persian pearl, Tulipa pulchella

Greigii Tulips, Division 14. These tulips bear single, 4-inch-wide flowers on 6- to 12-inch plants. The species usually has red flowers with a black blotch, but the cultivars come in a range of hues. Greigii tulips also have leaves that are handsomely mottled or striped with purple and are reliable perennials in the garden. Cultivars with purple-mottled leaves include: 'Cape Cod', yellow to apricot; 'Oratorio', watermelon pink; 'Pinocchio', creamy white with red; 'Red Riding Hood', red; and 'Sweet Lady', pink.

Species tulips. Species tulips fall into the Miscellaneous Tulips (Division 15), along with hybrids that don't fit in the other divisions. A few of the many appealing species tulips include *T. batalinii*, a 4- to 8-inch-tall species with narrow gray-green leaves and bowl-shaped, 3-inch-wide, pale yellow flowers. *T. saxatilis*, which spreads by runners, has 2½- to 3-inch, star-shaped flowers in mid- to late spring that are pink to purplish pink and are carried singly or in clusters. *T. saxatilis* needs poor soil, mild winters, and hot summers. Hardy in Zones 5 to 10, it doesn't require a cold period to bloom. *T. sylvestris*, hardy in Zones 4 to 10, also doesn't need a cold period to bloom. It has linear leaves and starry, 2½- to 3-inch, yellow flowers in midspring that are solitary or borne in pairs. *T. tarda* (formerly *T. dasystemon*) is a 4- to 6-inch-tall species with lance-shaped leaves and clusters of 4 to 6 star-shaped, 2½-inch-wide yellow flower with white tips.

IN THE GARDEN

Plant tulips in beds and borders, in containers, and in the cutting garden. They are handsome planted alone or combined with other spring-blooming bulbs and perennials, such as lungworts (*Pulmonaria* spp.), epimediums, or barrenworts (*Epimedium* spp.), bleeding heats (*Dicentra* spp.), and columbines (*Aquilegia* spp.). Overplant tulips with cold tolerant annuals such as pansies. To use tulips as cut flowers, cut the blooms just as the buds begin to open; recut the stem ends before placing them in the vase.

pink; 'Cream Upstar', yellow; 'Lilac Perfection', lilac-purple; and 'Maywonder', rose-pink.

Kaufmanniana Tulips, Division 12. Sometimes called waterlily tulips, these bloom in early to mid-spring. The species *T. kaufmanniana* bears creamy white flowers with a yellow base and tepals often streaked with rose-pink; both species and cultivars bear single, 2- to 5-inch-wide blooms that are cup or bowl shaped and resemble water lilies when fully open. All are dependable perennials that range from 6 to 12 inches tall. Cultivars include 'Heart's Delight', red, rose-pink, and yellow blooms plus handsomely mottled leaves; and 'Shakespeare', 'Showwinner', and 'Stresa' are all red with various color highlights.

Fosteriana Tulips, Division 13. Another group of good perennial tulips, Fosterianas, have solitary, single, 5-inch-wide blooms. *T. fosteriana* bears red, bowl-shaped flowers with a purple-black central blotch edged in yellow. The classic Emperor cultivars belong here, including 'Golden Emperor', 'Red Emperor', 'Orange Emperor', and 'White Emperor'.

Verbascum

(ver-BAS-kum)

Mulleins, verbascums

Figwort family, Scrophulariaceae.
Hardy perennials.

Mulleins are one of the new darlings of trendy garden designers, they are coming up fast. And it's a good thing, as mulleins are interesting, reliable plants. All are grown for their tall, erect flower stalks, which are densely packed with small, five-petaled flowers. *Verbascum* is the classical Latin name for these plants, which have been used medicinally for centuries.

When it comes to utility, few plants can outdo common, or wooly, mullein (V. *thapsus*), a biennial that has naturalized and become a roadside weed in

North America. Mulleins were reputed to cure warts, diarrhea, bronchitis, asthma, colds, consumption, and both "stiff sinews" and "fluxes of the body." And they were used as torches more than 2,000 years ago—people covered their stalks with suet or pitch and lit them—giving rise to the common names candlewick, torches, and hag's taper. Mulleins have also been used to cast spells and guard against witches, to make dyes, to stuff mattresses, and to protect cattle "from coughs of the lungs." Generations of children have fashioned doll blankets from mullein leaves while their parents were smoking them—the leaves, not the children. Mullein flowers were used to flavor drinks and—if tossed on a burning hearth—to protect houses against storms. If that weren't enough, mulleins were used to predict the weather: Mullein meteorologists claimed that a long winter and heavy snow were certain if the flowers clustered at the top of the stalks.

The mulleins grown in gardens today feature yellow or white flowers, and most species produce a rosette of hairy to woolly leaves. The effect is rather like a small-flowered hollyhock's (*Alcea rosea*), a far better known garden plant.

HOW TO GROW

Mulleins aren't particular, but they only do their best in full sun. Set them in poor to average, well-drained soil that is neutral or slightly alkaline. Good drainage is especially important in northern gardens. Plants are becoming more available in the nursery trade, but you won't find mulleins at every local garden center. Fortunately for gardeners, plants are easy to grow from seed. Mulleins have deep taproots, and are happiest if planted where they won't be disturbed. Cutting stalks back when flowering ends may help plants survive the upcoming winter, but it's probably wiser to leave them in place to allow seeds to self-sow. Mulleins are drought tolerant; overfeeding produces lanky plants.

To grow mulleins from seed, sow seeds in pots and set them outdoors in a protected location. Perennials can be propagated by division in spring or fall, and from root cuttings. Self-sown seedlings are easily transplanted, but their flower colors may vary.

Spider mites can be problematic, especially where summers are hot.

WHAT TO GROW

You're most likely to find hybrid mulleins at garden centers. Look for 4-foot 'Gainsborough', with pale

Nettle-leaved mullein, Verbascum chaixii

yellow flowers from early to late summer; 'Jackie', peach flowers in summer and 18 inches tall; and 'Summer Sorbet', light purple, and 20 inches tall. All are hardy in Zones 4 or 5 to 9.

Nettle-leaved mullein (*V. chaixii*), hardy in Zones 4 to 8, is a 3-foot-tall perennial that produces a low, 1½-foot wide rosette of gray-green leaves. Plants, which tend to be short-lived, bear branched panicles of densely packed, 1-inch-wide yellow flowers from mid- to late summer. *V. chaixii* f. *album* bears white flowers with mauve-purple eyes.

Olympic mullein (*V. olympicum*), hardy in Zones 6 to 8, is a 6-foot-tall perennial with a 2-foot-wide rosette of silver-white woolly leaves and stems. Plants produce branched, 3-foot-long bloom stalks with 1¼-inch-wide yellow blooms in summer. Although Olympic mullein is a perennial, the plants often die after they flower and must be replaced annually. Purple mullein (*V. phoeniceum*), 4 to 5 feet tall and hardy in Zones 4 to 8, blooms from late spring into summer; flowers are purple, pink, or white.

IN THE GARDEN
Plant drifts of mulleins in perennial beds and borders to add a vertical accent to plantings. Combine them with catmints (*Nepeta* spp.), sundrops (*Oenothera* spp.), sea hollies (*Eryngium* spp.), and orange coneflowers (*Rudbeckia* spp.). Mulleins attract hummingbirds and beneficial insects.

Verbena, Verbena × hybrida 'Homestead Purple'

Verbena

(ver-BEE-nah)

Verbenas, vervains

Vervian family, Verbenaceae.
Hardy perennials, tender perennials usually grown as annuals.

○ ▼

Summer-flowering verbenas have a history of medicinal use and names that reflect that tradition. *Verbena* is possibly the name used in classical Latin for *V. officinalis*. Another explanation is that verbena is a corruption of *herbena*, or *herba bona*, meaning "good plant." The common name vervain has Celtic origins and refers to the use of *V. officinalis* to remove bladder stones: It is from the Celtic *fer*, "to remove," and *faen*, "stone." Whatever the origins, verbena was used by both Greeks and Romans in religious rites and has been prescribed for bites of rabid animals, headaches, pleurisy, and rheumatism—and to quell desire. In Laurence Sterne's novel *Tristram Shandy* (1767), Uncle Toby is told to take vervain before sitting with the Widow Wadman.

Most verbenas are native to North, Central, and South America, although the all-important *V. officinalis*, which is not commonly grown as an ornamental, is from Europe. The genus contains about 250 species in all. Verbenas bear small, salverform flowers—blooms have a slender tube at the base and an abruptly flared and flattened face that has five petal-like lobes. Flowers appear on showy spikes or clusters over a long season and come in shades of purple, violet, pink, cream, scarlet, and magenta. Verbenas have square stems and usually bear opposite leaves that range from toothed to deeply lobed.

Verbenas were latecomers to English gardens. The tender species *V. peruviana* was an instant success, so much so that Mrs. J. C. Louden observed in *The Ladies' Companion to the Flower Garden* (1844) that "it is now rare to see a garden or a balcony without them." *V. peruviana* is one of the species used to produce hybrid garden verbenas (*Verbena × hybrida*), the most popular verbenas grown today.

HOW TO GROW

Plant verbenas in full sun—eight hours at least—and give them average soil that drains well. Blue vervain (*V. hastata*) also grows in moist, well-drained soil. Hardy verbenas are available as container-grown plants, but the garden verbenas, the tender hybrids that are grown like annuals in the north but are perennial in Zones 9 and warmer, are sold in market packs. Or begin plants from seed.

Water until plants are established or during extended dry weather. Deadhead or shear back verbenas after the main flush of flowers to encourage rebloom. *V. bonariensis* blooms until frost without deadheading. Plants growing in moderately fertile soil don't need fertilizer; overfeeding garden verbena produces leaves, not flowers.

Divide perennial species in spring if they outgrow their space, lose vigor, or to propagate. To grow garden verbena (*V. × hybrida*) from seed, sow indoors 14 weeks before the last spring frost date; transplant seedlings to the garden when nighttime temperatures remain above 50°F. To grow hardy verbenas, refrigerate seeds for two weeks before sowing indoors, about 14 weeks before the last frost. Verbenas are easy to grow from cuttings taken in late summer; cuttings also offer a way to overwinter species that are not hardy.

Verbenas are susceptible to spider mites and thrips.

WHAT TO GROW

Garden verbena (*Verbena × hybrida*) is a tender perennial that's grown as an annual in most gardens. It brings brilliant, 3-inch-wide clusters of small flowers to the garden from summer to frost. Blooms come in shades of violet-purple, pink, magenta, scarlet, and white and are carried above mounds of dark green leaves on 10- to 18-inch-tall plants. Many cultivars come true from seed, including 'Crystal Ball Mix', 'Novalis Mix', and 'Quartz Mix', all of which produce a full range of colors. 'Waterfalls Mix' includes flowers in shades of lavender, purple-blue, rose-purple, and white. 'Peaches and Cream' bears orange-pink flowers that age to apricot then yellow.

Perennial blue vervain (*V. hastata*) is the most widely grown cold-tolerant verbena. Hardy in Zones 3 to 7, it bears branched, 2- to 4-inch-wide clusters of flowers from early summer to early fall on 3- to 5-foot plants. Rose verbena (*V. canadensis*), hardy in Zones 4 to 10, is a perennial that is often grown as an annual. It produces a main flush of 2½-inch-wide, rose-pink flower clusters in early summer, then

blooms sporadically until fall if plants are deadheaded regularly. Rose verbena is a mounding species that spreads from 1½ to 3 feet; its spreading stems root where they touch the ground. Cut plants back hard if they spread too far or lose their leaves. 'Homestead Purple' is a mildew-resistant, purple-flowered cultivar.

V. bonariensis is grown for its airy clusters of rosy-purple flowers that grace the garden from midsummer to frost. It is hardy in Zones 7 to 9, but is grown as an annual in the North. Where hardy, this species attains shrublike proportions, and plants can range from 4 to 6 feet tall. Cut them back as necessary to encourage branching.

IN THE GARDEN

Use verbenas to add bright color to any sunny planting in dry, well-drained soil. Combine them with nasturtium (*Tropaeolum majus*), gazanias (*Gazania* spp.), and blanket flowers (*Gaillardia* spp.), lavenders (*Lavandula* spp.), yarrows (*Achillea* spp.), sedums, or stonecrops (*Sedum* spp.), purple coneflower (*Echinacea purpurea*), globe thistle (*Echinops ritro*), and yuccas (*Yucca* spp.). Garden verbenas make good edging and container plants. They also attract butterflies, beneficial insects, and hummingbirds to the garden.

Veronica

(*ver-ON-ih-kah*)

Speedwells, veronicas

Figwort family, Scrophulariaceae.
Hardy perennials.

Veronicas are vigorous, easy to grow perennials with flowers in shades of true blue, violet-blue, pink, and white. There are about 300 species of speedwells in all—annuals, perennials, and a few subshrubs primarily native to Europe. All have linear to lance-shaped or rounded leaves and produce bottlebrush-like spikes packed with tiny, ¼- to ½-inch-wide flowers. Garden-grown speedwells are mostly upright plants with erect flower spikes, but there also are low-growing, mat-forming species that can be used as ground covers or in rock gardens. As a group, they offer a variety of heights, textures, and colors to any garden.

As the name speedwell suggests, many of these plants are vigorous. While creeping speedwell (*Veronica filiformis*), a mat-forming, 2-inch-tall species with pale blue flowers, has become a serious weed in gardens and lawns, most species are well-behaved enough for any bed or border.

One explanation of the genus name is that it honors St. Veronica, today the patron of laundry workers and photographers. That unlikely duo is joined by the legend that Veronica wiped Jesus' face as he made his way to be crucified, an act that left his image on her handkerchief. The story of St. Veronica also may have something to do with other lore about the plants: If you stare at the flowers, you will go blind, and if you pull it, birds will pluck out your eyes. Whatever their origins, those superstitions are responsible for the common names blind flower and bird's-eye. Another other garden adage holds that if a plant is named after a saint, it must be good. And veronica is.

HOW TO GROW

Give speedwells full sun or partial shade and moist, average to rich soil that is well drained. They are shallow-rooted and not very drought tolerant, but are as unhappy in soil that is constantly moist as they are in arid soil.

You'll find speedwells offered for sale at good garden centers in spring or fall. Dig in plenty of compost or other organic matter at planting time to ensure rich soil that retains moisture, but also drains well. Speedwells do not need to be fertilized annually,

Spike speedwell, Veronica spicata *'Blue Peter'*

but they must be watered during dry weather. Taller cultivars will need staking, especially if grown in very rich soil. Tall speedwells can be cut back in spring to reduce their height.

Most speedwells need to be divided regularly—every three or four years—in spring or fall. Discard woody portions from the center of the clumps, and replant the vigorous sections. In addition to division, speedwells can be propagated from stem cuttings made in early summer. Or sow seeds indoors eight to ten weeks before the last spring frost date; do not cover seed. Self-sown plants of cultivars will not be identical to their parents.

Veronicas have no serious disease or pest problems.

WHAT TO GROW

One easy way to approach speedwells is to divide them into upright plants, which are used in beds and borders, and low-growing species, which can be used toward the front edge of plantings, as ground covers, or in rock gardens. (Even the taller speedwells spread to form broad mounds and can be used as ground covers.) Hungarian speedwell (*V. austriaca* subsp. *teucrium*) bears 4- to 6-inch-long spikes of deep blue flowers on 6- to 24-inch plants in late spring and early summer. Hardy in Zones 3 to 8, plants may rebloom if cut back after flowering. 'Crater Lake Blue', from 12- to 18-inches tall, is the best known selection. Gentian speedwell (*V. gentianoides*), Zones 4 to 8, produces loose, 10-inch-long spikes of pale blue to white flowers in late spring to early summer on 6- to 20-inch plants that form dense mats of foliage. Gentian speedwell requires evenly moist soil and should not be allowed to dry out.

Spike speedwell (*V. spicata*), Zones 3 to 7 or 8, produces 1-foot-long flower spikes from early to late summer on 2-foot plants. Flowers come in shades of blue, violet-blue, pink, and white, and are produced over a long season. 'Goodness Grows' bears dark blue flowers on 12- to 15-inch plants. 'Icicle' has white flowers on 2-foot plants, and 'Red Fox', or 'Rotfuchs', bears rose-pink flowers. 'Sunny Border Blue', a hybrid hardy in Zones 4 to 8, has violet-blue, 7-inch-long spikes of flowers from early summer to late fall on 18- to 20-inch plants.

Harebell speedwell (*V. prostrata*), hardy in Zones 5 to 8, is the most widely available of the low-growing species. It ranges from 3 to 6 inches tall and spreads to 1½ feet. Plants produce short spikes of blue flowers in late spring or early summer. Also blue-flowered, creeping speedwell (*V. repens*), Zones 5 to 8, is 1½ inches tall, but plants spread to 1½ feet. When in bloom in mid- to late spring, they reach 3 to 4 inches. This species requires rich soil and is less drought tolerant than *V. prostrata*. For a hot, dry spot, consider Turkish speedwell (*V. liwanensis*), hardy in Zones 4 to 9, which produces dense mats of thymelike leaves and blue flowers in spring. The plants reach only 2 inches but spread to 1½ feet.

IN THE GARDEN

Use taller speedwells in beds and borders with perennials that thrive in well-drained soil, such as daylilies, pinks (*Dianthus* spp.), hardy geraniums or cranesbills (*Geranium* spp.), coreopsis, balloon flower (*Platycodon grandiflorus*), and ornamental grasses. The taller species also make fine cut flowers. Low-growing speedwells make attractive edging plants and also can be used as ground covers or allowed to trail over rocks. Combine them with small spring bulbs, candytuft (*Iberis* spp.), and low-growing bellflowers (*Campanula* spp.).

Viola

(vy-OH-lah)

Violets, pansies, violas

Violet family, Violaceae.
Hardy perennials, biennials, annuals.

Pansies, Johnny jump-ups, and violets—they're all much-loved garden flowers. Pansies, especially, hold a special place in many gardeners' hearts, perhaps because of the cheerful flower faces that enchanted them as children. Shakespeare's famous phrase "And there is pansies—that's for thoughts," comes from the French word for "thought," *pensée*.

When it comes to common names, the violas have few equals: herb trinity, tickle-my-fancy, love-in-idleness, heartsease, kiss-her-in-the-pantry, three-faces-in-a-hood, flamy, bonewort, and that's just the tip of the cognomen iceberg. But whether violets, violas, or pansies, members of the genus *Viola* bear five-petaled flowers that have a spurred lower petal that forms the lip of the flower, as well as two petals that point up and two more that point sideways. The genus contains some 500 species in all—including annuals, biennials, perennials (both hardy and tender), plus a few subshrubs. Leaves range from rounded and toothed or lobed to heart-shaped but also can be cut in a featherlike fashion.

Violas were used medicinally in ancient times—and still are in some folk medicines—but that's not the reason to grow these delightful beauties. The reason, Mrs. C. W. Earle wrote in *More Pot-Pourri from a Surrey Garden* (1899), is clear when you visit the English cemetery in Rome in March, and "see a never-to-be-forgotten sight—the whole ground blue with the Violets, tall and strong above their leaves, the air one sweet perfume, and the sound (soft and yet distinct) of the murmur of spring bees." If you can't get to the English cemetery in Rome in March, the hundreds of flats filled with violets, violas, and pansies at the local garden center in March are a good substitute.

HOW TO GROW

Give pansies and Johnny jump-ups a spot in full sun, or partial shade where summers are hot, that has rich, moist, well-drained soil. Either start with the market-pack plants sold everywhere in spring, or start your own plants from seeds. Sow seeds indoors eight to ten weeks before the last spring frost date, set the sown pots in the refrigerator for ten days, and then move them to a warm location to germinate. Johnny jump-ups (*V. tricolor*) also can be sown outdoors in late summer to fall for bloom the following year. In warm climates, both Johnny jump-ups and pansies (*V. × wittrockiana*) can planted outdoors in fall for bloom in late winter and early spring (sow seeds in midsummer or start with plants). Johnny jump-ups can be grown on this schedule from about Zone 6 south and pansies, from Zone 7 south.

Deadhead pansies—or pick the flowers frequently—to keep them blooming. Pansies are usually removed when they stop flowering, but Johnny jump-ups can be cut back in midsummer as they get scraggly, which encourages new growth and reblooming when cool temperatures return in fall.

Violets need partial to full shade with rich, moist, well-drained soil, although they can grow in full sun with consistent soil moisture in cooler regions. Bird's foot violet (*V. pedata*) wants acid, very well-drained, light soil that is high in organic matter. Add these plants to your garden by starting with container-grown plants, or start from seeds. Like Johnny jump-ups and pansies, violets grow best when temperatures

Johnny jump-up, Viola tricolor

are cool. They spread by creeping rhizomes and also self-sow. Some can become invasive, but make a dense, weed-smothering ground cover if you have the proper site. Propagate by division in spring or fall, or sow seeds in fall or early spring in pots and set them in a protected location outdoors. The species hybridize readily, so self-sown seedlings may not resemble their parents.

WHAT TO GROW

Old-fashioned Johnny jump-up (*V. tricolor*) is also known as hearts-ease, love-in-idleness, and wild pansy. From early spring to fall, 3- to 5-inch-tall viola plants bear 1-inch-wide flowers marked with deep violet, purple, white, or yellow in a facelike pattern. Plants are hardy from Zones 3 to 8, and they are grown as a cool-weather annual, biennial, or short-lived perennial. 'Princess Mix' yields plants with yellow, lavender-purple, white, or violet flowers; 'Bowles Black' has near-black flowers with yellow eyes; 'Prince John' bears yellow blooms; and 'Prince Henry' has dark purple flowers

Pansies (*V. × wittrockiana*), grown as cool-weather annuals or biennials, are 6- to 9-inch-tall perennials with 2½- to 4-inch-wide flowers that come in a wide variety of patterns and colors including violet, maroon, bronze, yellow, orange, lavender, purple, lilac-blue, and white. Traditional pansies,

such as Swiss Giant Series, Faces Series, Bingo Series, and 'Festival' hybrids, produce flowers with a dark, velvety, facelike blotch at the center, but solid colors also are available. Clear Crystal Series and Crystal Bowl Series plants come in a range of solid colors, without faces. 'Chalon Supreme Mix' produces plants with ruffled flowers in a range of colors, and the typical dark blotch is striped with yellow. 'Antique Shades Hybrid' produces flowers in pale pink, creamy yellow, soft orange, and white.

It's not just wildflower gardeners who will want to try Canada violet (*V. canadensis*), hardy in Zones 3 to 8. This native species is 6 to 12 inches tall and forms a 1-foot-wide mound of heart-shaped leaves. In spring, plants bear white, ½- to ¾-inch flowers with yellow eyes in spring. Labrador violet (*V. labradorica*), hardy in Zones 2 to 8, is another native species. It is 1 to 4 inches tall and spreads via prostrate stems to form 1-foot-wide mounds of kidney- to heart-shaped, purplish leaves. In spring and summer, plants bear pale purple flowers. Bird's-foot, or crow-foot, violet (*V. pedata*), a native hardy in Zones 4 to 8, is a 2- to 6-inch-tall perennial that spreads by rhizomes to form 1-foot-wide mounds of deeply cut leaves with very narrow lobes. In late spring and early summer, it bears 1¼-wide, pale lavender blooms. Woolly blue violet (*V. sororia*), hardy in Zones 4 to 8, is a 3- to 6-inch-tall rhizomatous native that forms 8-inch-wide mounds of rounded, scalloped, densely hairy leaves. In spring and summer, plants bear ¾-inch-wide white flowers speckled and streaked with purple.

Horned violet (*V. cornuta*), hardy in Zones 6 to 9, is native to Spain. It is a 4- to 12-inch-tall species that spreads by rhizomes to form 12- to 14-inch-wide mounds of evergreen, oval, toothed leaves. Plants bear 1- to 1½-inch-wide lilac-blue flowers that look like small pansies. 'Chantreyland' bears apricot flowers; 'Jersey Gem', purple-blue blooms; 'Alba' and 'White Perfection', white flowers; and 'Blue Perfection', sky blue blooms.

Sweet, or English, violet (*V. odorata*), hardy only in Zones 7 or 8 to 9, is a rhizomatous, 2- to 8-inch-tall species that spreads to 1½ feet. Plants bear rounded to heart-shaped leaves and ¾-inch-wide lavender-blue or white flowers in spring. 'Czar' bears dark violet flowers.

IN THE GARDEN

Add violets to mixed plantings with other low-growing perennials such as lungworts (*Pulmonaria* spp.), but use them carefully as they can overwhelm their neighbors. They are pretty ground covers, excellent under deciduous trees, and can be used alone or with other plants such as ajugas (*Ajuga* spp.) and common periwinkle (*Vinca minor*). Use Johnny jump-ups anywhere you need an extra touch of color in spring—among other edging plants, with spring bulbs, in containers, and mixed beds and borders. Flowers are edible and can be added to salads or used to garnish plates. All violas—

Pansy, Viola × wittrockiana *Majestic Giant Series*

Pansy, Viola × wittrockiana *Melody Series*

Johnny jump-ups, pansies, and violets—can be grown in containers.

Zinnia

(ZIN-nee-ah)

Zinnias

Aster family, Asteraceae. Annuals.

This popular tribe of annual flowers was named in honor of Johann Gottfried Zinn, an 18th-century German professor of medicine and botany, although they were called Brazilian marigold at the time Linnaeus classified them because they were thought to have originated in Brazil. While about 20 species belong here, including annuals, perennials, and subshrubs, gardeners are primarily concerned with the annuals, especially the common zinnia (*Z. elegans*), which is grown throughout North America where its seeds are carefully saved in paper bags each fall to be replanted in spring.

Few annuals are as popular or as easy to grow as zinnias. Or colorful, for they bloom in a range of hot colors—orange, red, bronze, orange-red, and yellow-orange are common—and in cooler hues, including white, cream, rose, pink, and pale green. Flowers come in all colors, in fact, except blue. Most are native to Mexico, but there are zinnias from the American Southwest as well as farther south in

Dwarf zinnia, Zinnia elegans *'Peter Pan Orange'*

Central and South America. The showy, daisylike flowers can be single or double, and like other aster-family plants, they consist of petal-like ray florets that surround a center cluster of smaller disk florets. In zinnias, all of the ray florets are female flowers, while the disk florets are perfect, or bisexual. The ray florets do not drop; instead, they fade and remain attached to the seeds.

Today's cultivars are a far cry from the zinnias of 100 years ago, when the blooms were so ordinary that the plant was referred to as everybody's flower and poorhouse flower. The transformation has been enormous, from poorhouse flower to the first double zinnia in the 1880s through American botanist Luther Burbank's giant dahlialike zinnia in 1925 to the multi-prize-winning narrow-leaf Profusion Series zinnias produced in the last decade—a transformation so great that the zinnia has also been called garden Cinderella.

HOW TO GROW

Give zinnias full sun, average to rich, well-drained soil, and heat. And they need good air circulation to help prevent powdery mildew. Gardeners with humid summers should only plant the newer, disease-resistant cultivars.

While you can find zinnias everywhere bedding plants are sold in spring, they're among the easiest flowers to grow from seeds. Sow seeds outdoors after the last-frost date where the plants are to grow. Or sow indoors four to six weeks before the last frost. Transplant carefully—zinnias don't like being moved—and water seedlings regularly until they are established. After that, zinnias do not need watering except during extended droughts. Pinch plants to encourage branching, unless you are growing them exclusively for cut flowers and want long stems. Deadhead regularly to keep plants flowering until fall.

Zinnias are subject to powdery mildew and occasionally are visited by Japanese beetles, aphids, and mites.

WHAT TO GROW

Common zinnia (Z. *elegans*) is a bushy, warm-weather annual that ranges from 6 inches to 4 feet in height. Many cultivars are available, with single or double flowers, and blooms range from 1½ to 5 inches wide. Cactus-flowered cultivars, including the Zenith Series, range from 2½ to 3 feet and bear double and semidouble, 4-inch-wide flowers with narrow, curved petals. 'Burpeeana Giants Mix' and 'Cactus Flowered Mix' are two cactus-type cultivars. Dahlia-flowered cultivars have semidouble to double, 3- to 5-inch-wide blooms in both full-size

Zinnia, Zinnia elegans *Dreamland Series*

and dwarf plants. Mildew-resistant 'Purple Prince' and the pale green 'Envy' are two cultivars to look for. 'Blue Point Mix' bears 5- to 6-inch dahlialike blooms on 4-foot plants. Oklahoma Series and 'Cut & Come Again Mix' are globe-shaped cultivars, both 2 feet tall, that were developed for cutting gardens. Pulchino Series plants are 1 to 1½-feet tall with 2- to 3-inch-wide flowers; they are more disease-resistant than most cultivars. Profusion Series zinnias, which are All-America Selections winners, have 2-inch single blooms; the 18-inch plants spread to 2 feet and are vigorous and bushy, with very strong disease-resistance.

OTHER CHOICES

A zinnia relative and fellow aster-family member, creeping zinnia (*Sanvitalia procumbens*) is another annual native to Central America, from Mexico to Guatemala. The seven species in the genus grow naturally on rocky slopes and in dry river washes, and creeping zinnia is a perfect choice for a full-sun site with dry or sandy soil. Plants produce charming daisylike flowers, which resemble small zinnias or sunflowers, with golden yellow petals and dark centers, from early summer to fall. The flowers are about 3/4-inch wide and are produced in abundance atop 6- to 8-inch-tall plants that spread to 2½ feet. Either buy creeping zinnias in market packs from your local garden center, or start your own plants from seed. Plants resent transplanting, and are happiest if sown outdoors several weeks before the last spring frost date. Or start seeds indoors as you would zinnias. 'Mandarin Orange' bears flowers with orange petals, and 'Gold Braid' has yellow flowers with dark centers on 2- to 4-inch plants.

Creeping zinnia, Sanvitalia procumbens *'Gold Braid'*

Mexican zinnia, Zinnia haageana *'Chippendale'*

Narrow-leaved, or Mexican, zinnia (Z. *haageana,* also listed as Z. *angustifolia* and Z. *linearis*) is a bushy, 1- to 2-foot-tall warm-weather annual that exhibits outstanding resistance to diseases. It's also both heat and drought tolerant. Plants have linear- to lance-shaped leaves and bear an abundance of daisylike 1½-inch-wide flower heads in summer. Star Series plants bear 2-inch-wide flowers in gold, orange, and white. Profusion Series plants produce 2- to 2½-inch-wide flowers in cherry pink and orange.

Red spider zinnia (Z. *peruviana,* formerly Z. *pauciflora*) is one other species to look for, since it features linear- to lance-shaped leaves that resist mildew. This 2- to 3-foot-tall species bears 1- to 1½-inch-wide daisylike flowers with dark centers and red or yellow petals. 'Bonita Red' has brick- to soft orange-red blooms, while 'Bonita Yellow' bears yellow to gold blooms. The heirloom 'Old Mexico' bears bicolor pom-pom flowers and reds and golds, and it resists mildew.

IN THE GARDEN

Plant zinnias in mixed plantings with other summer-blooming annuals, or place small groups of zinnias among perennials. They are at home in cottage gardens and children's gardens, and they are often grown in cutting gardens. (Cut the stems before the flower is completely open.) Dwarf types make fine edging and container plants, and the flowers of all zinnias attract hummingbirds, butterflies, and beneficial insects.

PART III

Appendix

According to humorist Dave Barry, the first job in the garden is to prepare the soil. "The best tool for this is your neighbor's motorized garden tiller. If your neighbor does not own a garden tiller, suggest that he buy one." Ahh, were we all so bold.

Tillers and other high-quality equipment and accurate information are huge assets to gardeners. Digging with a shovel that is too heavy or watering with a hose that kinks is frustrating beyond words. As is planting a flower you think will be perennial, a dahlia perhaps, and later discovering it doesn't have a snowball's chance in you-know-where of surviving winter in your garden. And knowing where to find seeds and plants—most local stores and garden centers stock only a limited number of mainstream cultivars—is indispensable to creating a garden that will match your dreams. Information, as someone said, is power.

Just as no garden can contain every flower, no book can contain everything about every flower or everything about growing every flower. What follows are some of the best sources for additional information: weather and climate data for the United States and Canada, suggestions for further reading about gardening and flowers and how to grow them, and assortment of outstanding firms selling seeds, plants, and garden supplies and equipment, recommendations for getting in touch with other flower gardeners, and much more.

Think of these sources as stand-ins for fellow gardeners, people who invariably are willing to share their wisdom and their time. And even their tillers.

Appendix

Climate and Weather

Local newspapers and radio and television stations are the best sources for weather reports, but they rarely provide climate information. Weatherbase is an easy to use web site (www.weatherbase.com) that publishes weather records and averages for hundreds of North American cities: average temperatures, precipitation, and more.

For even more climate statistics, go to the National Weather Service (www.nws.noaa.gov), the National Climate Data Center (www.ncdc. noaa.gov/oa/ncdc.html), or, for Canadian data, the National Climate Data and Information Archive at Environment Canada (www.climate.weatheroffice. ec.gc.ca/Welcome_e.html).

A raft of other climate data for selected U.S. cities—average wind speeds, normal precipitation totals, mean number of clear and cloudy days, mean number of days over 90°F, and more—is available at ols.nndc.noaa.gov/plolstore/plsql/olstore.prodspecific? prodnum=C00095-PUB-A0001.

FROST DATES AND GROWING SEASON LENGTHS

This chart lists probable spring and fall freeze dates and growing-season lengths (frost-free periods). It is based on temperature data collected by official U.S. and Canadian sources and gives a 50 percent probability that freezing temperatures will occur *after* the date listed in spring or *before* the date in fall. The cities and towns with available data were selected to give as broad a weather picture in each state as possible. States and portions of states that do not experience frost are omitted.

Keep in mind that 50 percent probability means five years out of ten, freezing temperatures will occur after these dates in spring or before them in fall. Adding three weeks to the spring date improves your chances (to one year in ten) that tender transplants won't be damaged by frost. Data for many more cities are available at www.ncdc.noaa.gov/climatenormals/clim20supp1/states.

STATE/PROVINCE	CITY	FROST DATES Spring	Fall	NUMBER OF FROST-FREE DAYS
ALABAMA	Birmingham	April 10	Oct. 25	198
	Gadsden	April 14	Oct. 23	191
	Mobile	March 14	Nov. 14	244
	Valley Head	May 5	Oct. 10	157
ALASKA	Fairbanks	May 30	Aug. 27	88
	Juneau	June 3	Sept. 8	96
	Sitka	May 15	Oct. 14	151
ARIZONA	Flagstaff	June 21	Sept. 5	76
	Phoenix	March 1	Nov. 30	273
	Prescott	May 31	Oct. 1	122
	Tucson	March 23	Nov. 21	242
	Yuma	Feb. 2	Dec. 18	312
ARKANSAS	Fort Smith	April 13	Oct. 21	190
	Hot Springs	April 7	Oct. 31	207
	Jonesboro	April 10	Oct. 23	196
	Texarkana	March 27	Nov. 3	221
CALIFORNIA	Bakersfield	March 2	Nov. 23	265
	El Centro	March 10	Nov. 26	260
	Eureka	March 29	Nov. 28	244
	Fresno	March 29	Nov. 12	227
	Sacramento	March 25	Nov. 17	236
	San Francisco	Feb. 7	Dec. 10	307
	Santa Cruz	April 27	Nov. 9	196
	Yreka	June 3	Sept. 29	117
COLORADO	Boulder	May 18	Sept. 29	133
	Canon City	May 15	Sept. 30	138
	Durango	June 18	Sept. 9	82

(continues)

STATE/PROVINCE	CITY	FROST DATES Spring	Fall	NUMBER OF FROST-FREE DAYS
CONNECTICUT	Danbury	May 18	Sept. 24	129
	Hartford	May 13	Oct. 2	141
	Norwalk	May 9	Oct. 5	149
DELAWARE	Dover	April 23	Oct. 18	178
	Wilmington	April 25	Oct. 16	173
FLORIDA	Gainesville	March 16	Nov. 17	245
	Tallahassee	March 26	Nov. 4	222
	Tampa	Feb. 9	Dec. 8	301
GEORGIA	Albany	March 26	Nov. 1	220
	Athens	April 7	Oct. 29	204
	Augusta	April 11	Oct. 24	195
	Macon	April 1	Oct. 30	211
IDAHO	Boise	May 21	Sept. 27	129
	Coeur d'Alene	May 26	Sept. 20	116
	Pocatello	June 6	Sept. 8	93
ILLINOIS	Carbondale	April 29	Oct. 5	158
	Chicago	May 1	Oct. 14	165
	Peoria	May 6	Oct. 6	152
	Rockford	May 13	Sept. 30	140
	Springfield	April 30	Oct. 10	162
INDIANA	Evansville	April 23	Oct. 17	176
	Indianapolis	May 3	Oct. 9	158
	South Bend	May 12	Oct. 6	146
	Terre Haute	May 6	Oct. 6	152
IOWA	Ames	May 9	Sept. 29	142
	Decorah	May 18	Sept. 19	123
	Ottumwa	May 1	Oct. 10	161
KANSAS	Colby	May 14	Sept. 27	135
	Dodge City	April 27	Oct. 12	167
	Topeka	May 1	Oct. 6	157
KENTUCKY	Hopkinsville	April 22	Oct. 15	175
	Lexington	April 29	Oct. 14	167
	Middlesboro	May 7	Oct. 8	153
LOUISIANA	Alexandria	March 20	Nov. 5	229
	Lafayette	March 9	Nov. 12	248
	Monroe	March 28	Oct. 27	212
MAINE	Augusta	May 11	Sept. 28	139
	Bar Harbor	May 13	Oct. 2	141
	Portland	May 20	Sept. 19	122
	Waterville	May 25	Sept. 18	115

STATE/PROVINCE	CITY	FROST DATES Spring	Fall	NUMBER OF FROST-FREE DAYS
MARYLAND	Baltimore	April 9	Nov. 3	207
	Cumberland	May 6	Oct. 2	148
	Salisbury	April 25	Oct. 16	173
	Westminster	May 2	Oct. 17	167
MASSACHUSETTS	Framingham	May 8	Oct. 2	146
	Nantucket	May 9	Oct. 19	163
	New Bedford	April 18	Oct. 25	188
	Springfield	May 7	Oct. 5	150
MICHIGAN	Ann Arbor	May 10	Oct. 6	149
	Lansing	May 26	Sept. 21	117
	Midland	May 20	Sept. 24	126
	Sault Ste. Marie	June 8	Sept. 13	96
MINNESOTA	Albert Lea	May 11	Sept. 27	138
	Alexandria	May 17	Sept. 22	126
	Duluth	June 4	Sept. 11	98
	Little Falls	Mat 25	Sept. 16	114
MISSISSIPPI	Biloxi City	March 7	Nov. 20	257
	Meridian	April 4	Oct. 26	203
	Picayune	March 24	Oct. 31	221
	Tupelo	April 16	Oct. 19	185
MISSOURI	Hannibal	April 28	Oct. 13	168
	Joplin	April 21	Oct. 17	178
	Poplar Bluff	April 21	Oct. 13	174
MONTANA	Billings	May 26	Sept. 14	111
	Helena	June 4	Sept. 8	95
	Kalispell	June 12	Sept. 7	87
NEBRASKA	Beatrice	May 5	Oct. 5	153
	Chadron	May 24	Sept. 15	113
	Grand Island	May 8	Sept. 28	143
NEVADA	Carson City	June 18	Sept. 5	79
	Elko	June 24	Aug. 28	64
	Las Vegas	March 27	Nov. 14	232
NEW HAMPSHIRE	Lebanon	June 2	Sept. 13	103
	Nashua	May 30	Sept. 12	105
NEW JERSEY	Cape May	April 14	Oct. 31	199
	Plainfield	May 6	Oct. 7	153
	Trenton	April 17	Oct. 25	190
NEW MEXICO	Alamogordo	April 20	Oct. 22	184
	Los Alamos	May 23	Oct. 2	131
	Tucumcari	May 1	Oct. 15	166

(continues)

STATE/PROVINCE	CITY	FROST DATES		NUMBER OF FROST-FREE DAYS
		Spring	Fall	
NEW YORK	New York City	April 14	Oct. 30	199
	Poughkeepsie	May 18	Sept. 24	128
	Rochester	May 13	Oct. 2	140
	Watertown	May 21	Sept. 25	126
NORTH CAROLINA	Asheville	April 27	Oct. 14	170
	Greensboro	April 23	Oct. 17	176
	Morehead City	April 1	Nov. 6	218
NORTH DAKOTA	Bismarck	May 30	Sept. 11	103
	Minot	May 24	Sept. 13	112
OHIO	Akron	May 14	Oct. 8	146
	Cincinnati	April 27	Oct. 15	170
	Columbus	May 7	Oct. 4	150
	Sandusky	April 27	Oct. 17	172
OKLAHOMA	Ardmore	March 31	Nov. 6	219
	Bartlesville	April 21	Oct. 14	174
	Tulsa	April 11	Oct. 24	195
OREGON	Ashland	June 2	Sept. 29	119
	Eugene	May 19	Oct. 6	139
	La Grande	June 2	Sept. 13	102
	Portland	April 29	Oct. 20	174
PENNSYLVANIA	Allentown	May 4	Oct. 6	155
	Meadville	May 27	Sept. 23	119
	State College	May 8	Oct. 4	149
	West Chester	May 1	Oct. 6	157
RHODE ISLAND	Block Island	April 24	Oct. 27	185
	Kingston	May 22	Sept. 20	120
SOUTH CAROLINA	Anderson	April 11	Oct. 22	193
	Beaufort	March 24	Nov. 9	230
	Columbia	April 16	Oct. 24	190
SOUTH DAKOTA	Mobridge	May 16	Sept. 22	128
	Rapid City	May 18	Sept. 20	125
	Sioux Falls	May 20	Sept. 21	123
TENNESSEE	Clarksville	April 27	Oct. 14	169
	Knoxville	April 9	Oct. 27	200
	Memphis	April 3	Oct. 31	210
TEXAS	Amarillo	April 26	Oct. 20	176
	Austin	March 16	Nov. 16	244
	Brownsville	Feb. 6	Dec. 24	322
	Denton	April 1	Nov. 4	216
	Galveston	Feb 13	Dec. 16	304

STATE/PROVINCE	CITY	FROST DATES Spring	Fall	NUMBER OF FROST-FREE DAYS
UTAH	Cedar City	June 5	Sept. 21	108
	Logan	May 20	Sept. 27	129
	Moab	April 28	Oct. 9	164
VERMONT	Burlington	May 24	Sept. 21	119
	Montpelier	June 5	Sept. 11	98
VIRGINIA	Blacksburg	May 14	Sept. 28	136
	Norfolk	April 7	Nov. 4	210
	Winchester	May 3	Oct. 7	157
WASHINGTON	Aberdeen	May 8	Oct. 20	165
	Seattle-Tacoma	April 22	Oct. 29	189
	Spokane	May 23	Sept. 21	120
	Yakima	June 6	Sept. 16	101
WEST VIRGINIA	Beckley	May 29	Sept. 17	110
	Martinsburg	May 5	Oct. 2	148
	Parkersburg	May 4	Oct. 6	154
WISCONSIN	Ashland	June 14	Sept. 5	82
	Green Bay	May 24	Sept. 21	119
	La Crosse	May 11	Sept. 30	142
WYOMING	Laramie	June 22	Aug. 29	67
	Sheridan	June 8	Sept. 10	93
ALBERTA	Calgary	May 23	Sept. 15	114
	Edmonton	May 7	Sept. 15	138
	Peace River	May 26	Sept. 3	99
BRITISH COLUMBIA	Dawson Creek	June 5	Aug. 29	84
	Kamloops	June 1	Oct. 5	156
	Prince George	June 4	Sept. 3	91
	Vancouver	March 28	Nov. 5	221
	Victoria	April 19	Nov. 5	200
MANITOBA	Thompson	June 15	Aug. 16	61
	Winnipeg	May 25	Sept. 22	119
NEW BRUNSWICK	Edmundston	May 28	Sept. 18	112
	Fredericton	May 20	Sept. 22	124
	Saint John	May 18	Oct. 4	139
NEWFOUNDLAND	Corner Brook	May 22	Oct. 12	142
	Grand Falls	June 2	Sept. 26	115
	St. John's	June 2	Oct. 12	131
NORTHWEST TERRITORIES AND YUKON	Fort Simpson	June 3	Aug. 24	81
	Whitehorse	June 11	Aug. 25	74
NOVA SCOTIA	Halifax	May 6	Oct. 20	166
	Sydney	May 24	Oct. 13	141
	Turo	May 30	Sept. 21	113

(continues)

STATE/PROVINCE	CITY	FROST DATES Spring	Fall	NUMBER OF FROST-FREE DAYS
ONTARIO	Ottawa	May 6	Oct. 5	151
	Thunder Bay	June 1	Sept. 15	105
	Timmins	June 8	Sept. 6	89
	Toronto	May 9	Oct. 6	149
PRINCE EDWARD ISLAND	Charlottetown	May 17	Oct. 14	150
QUEBEC	Baie Como	May 28	Sept. 15	109
	Chicoutimi	May 17	Sept. 30	133
	Montreal	May 3	Oct. 7	156
SASKATCHEWAN	Moose Jaw	May 20	Sept. 18	120
	Prince Albert	June 2	Sept. 4	93
	Regina	May 21	Sept. 10	111

USDA PLANT HARDINESS MAP

Revised in 1990, the USDA hardiness zone map divides North America into 11 zones and "shows in detail the lowest temperatures that can be expected each year." Because of the large area involved, it wasn't possible to draw one map that is accurate; the portion representing the U.S., according to the USDA, "has the least distortion."

For a more accurate Canadian map, go to sis.agr.gc.ca/cansis/nsdb/climate/hardiness/intro.html, the Agriculture Canada web site that contains both the 1967 and the revised (2000) plant hardiness maps for that country. The revised USDA hardiness zone map for the United States, reprinted here, also can be accessed at www.usna.usda.gov/Hardzone.

AHS PLANT HEAT ZONE MAP

The American Horticultural Society published the first Plant Heat Zone map in 1997, an acknowledgment that plants are at the mercy of heat as well as cold. The map divides the United States into 12 zones based on the average number of days per year that are over 86°F, the temperature at which most plants begin to suffer physiological damage from heat. The map is based on statistics from the National Climatic Data Center that were collected between 1974 and 1995. The map can be downloaded at www.ahs.org/publications/heat_zone_map.htm.

Soil Testing

Local Cooperative Extension Services, which are listed in the telephone directory under the name of the county or state university, have information about taking soil samples and local testing laboratories. Most state universities do soil tests for home gardeners, usually at a price well below those charged by commercial firms. In Canada, check your telephone directory's yellow pages for local labs and garden centers, or contact one of these companies.

A & L Plains Agricultural Laboratory Inc.
P.O. Box 1590
Lubbock, TX 79408
806-763-4278
www.al-labs-plains.com

EarthCo, Inc.
P.O. Box 50084
St. Louis, MO 63105
314-994-2167
www.drgoodearth.com

Grotek Manufacturing, Inc.
#284-505-210th Street
Langley, BC
V1M 2Y2 Canada
604-882-7686
www.grotek.net

USDA Plant Hardiness Zone Map

AVERAGE ANNUAL MINIMUM TEMPERATURE

Temperature (°C)	Zone	Temperature (°F)
Below −45.6	1	Below −50
−42.8 to −45.5	2a	−50 to −45
−40.0 to −42.7	2b	−45 to −40
−37.3 to −39.9	3a	−40 to −35
−34.5 to −37.2	3b	−35 to −30
−31.7 to −34.4	4a	−30 to −25
−28.9 to −31.6	4b	−25 to −20
−26.2 to −28.8	5a	−20 to −15
−23.4 to −26.1	5b	−15 to −10
−20.6 to −23.3	6a	−10 to −5
−17.8 to −20.5	6b	−5 to 0
−15.0 to −17.7	7a	0 to 5
−12.3 to −14.9	7b	5 to 10
−9.5 to −12.2	8a	10 to 15
−6.7 to −9.4	8b	15 to 20
−3.9 to −6.6	9a	20 to 25
−1.2 to −3.8	9b	25 to 30
1.6 to −1.1	10a	30 to 35
4.4 to 1.7	10b	35 to 40
Above 4.5	11	Above 40

Scale in Kilometers
Scale in Miles
Scale 1:6,000,000 (approximately)

Garden Supplies and Equipment

Even the best-equipped local garden stores can't compete with the huge inventories of mail-order companies. These are some of the best firms that sell garden tools, equipment, and supplies.

Active Forever
10799 N. 90th Street
Scottsdale, AZ 85260
800-377-8033
www.activeforever.com
Ergonomic tools

A. M. Leonard, Inc.
241 Fox Drive
Piqua, Ohio 45356-0816
800-543-8955
www.amleo.com
No-nonsense selection of tools and equipment

Extremely Green Gardening Co.
49 Lincoln Boulevard, PMB 113
Abington, MA 02351
781-878-5397
www.extremelygreen.com
Biorational controls, fertilizers, soil amendments

Dirt Works
6 Dog Team Road
New Haven, VT 05472-4000
800-769-3856
www.dirtworks.net
Organic fertilizers, soil mixes, soil-mix ingredients, disease and pest controls

Fertile Garden
8349 Leslie Road
San Antonio, TX 78254
800-373-3880
www.fertilegarden.com
Organic garden supplies

Gardener's Supply Company
128 Intervale Road
Burlington, VT 05401
888-833-1412
www.gardeners.com
Tools and equipment, soil amendments, fertilizers, pest controls

GardensAlive!
5100 Schenley Place
Lawrenceburg, IN 47025
513-354-1482
www.gardensalive.com
Natural pest and disease controls, fertilizers, beneficials, garden supplies

Gardenscape Ltd.
2010A Queen Street East
Toronto, ON
M4L 1J3 Canada
888-472-3266
www.gardenscape.ca
www.gardenscapetools.com (U.S.)
Tools and equipment

Harrod Horticultural
Pinbush Road
Lowestoft
Suffolk NR33 7NL
England
01502 505300
www.harrodhorticultural.com
British tools and equipment, including traditional Sussex trugs

Home Harvest Garden Supply, Inc.
995 Potosi Road
Glen Rock, PA 17327
717-235-6653
www.homeharvest.com
Disease and pest controls, fertilizers, soil amendments, tools

Life with Ease
P.O. Box 302
Newbury, NH 03255
800-966-5119
www.lifewithease.com
Ergonomic tools

Magical Garden
159 Castlebar Court
Mableton, GA 30126
770-745-0933
www.magicalgarden.com
Garden ornaments and sculpture

Natural Gardening Company
P.O. Box 750776
Petaluma, CA 94975-0776
707-766-9303
www.naturalgardening.com
Natural controls and fertilizers, tools and equipment, seeds

Oregon Scientific, Inc.
19861 SW 95th Avenue
Tualatin, OR 97062
949-608-2848
www.oregonscientific.com
Weather instruments

Peaceful Valley Farm Supply
P.O. Box 2209
Grass Valley, CA 95945
888-784-1722
www.groworganic.com
Tools and equipment, organic controls and fertilizers, seeds

Wind and Weather
250 N. Main Street
Fort Bragg, CA 95437
800-922-9463
windandweather.com
Weather instruments

Yardiac
50A Littlejohn Glen Court
Greenville, SC 29615
866-927-3422
www.yardiac.com
Large selection of controls, fertilizers, tools, equipment, weather instruments

Beneficials for Sale

Gardeners wanting to reinforce their existing population of beneficial bugs can contact any of these suppliers—all of which also sell a wide range of organic products, including pest traps, soil amendments and fertilizers, and more.

Biocontrol Network
5116 Williamsburg Road
Brentwood, TN 37027
800-441-2847
www.biconet.com

Planet Natural
1612 Gold Avenue
Bozeman, MT 59715
800-289-6656
www.planetnatural.com

**Harmony Farm Supply
& Nursery**
3244 Highway 116 North
Sebastopol, CA 95472
707-823-9125
www.harmonyfarm.com

Richters
P.O. Box 26
Goodwood, Ontario
LOC LAO Canada
416-640-6677
www.richters.com

**Home Harvest Garden
Supply, Inc.**
3807 Bank Street
Baltimore, MD 21224
800-348-4769
www.homeharvest.com

Worm's Way, Inc.
7850 North State Road 37
Bloomington, IN 47404
800-274-9676
www.wormsway.com

Web Sites

It often seems that URLs change faster than the speed of light, but this group of free, useful web sites includes only addresses that have been around for several years. You can find tens of thousands of other flower and garden sites by using www.google.com or some other search engine. Don't forget that the sites of commercial seed companies and nurseries often are first-rate sources of information as well as seeds and plants.

Web Garden (www.webgarden.osu.edu) is the home of *PlantFacts*, which contains a search engine for more than 260,000 pages of plant information from land-grant universities in the United States and Canada; a searchable database of plant photographs; 200 short garden how-to videos; an illustrated glossary of horticultural terms; and a searchable data base of commonly asked gardening questions (FAQ). One of the most useful sites on the web.

Horticulture on the Internet (www.ces.ncsu.edu/depts/hort/consumer/hortinternet/index.html) is a collection of online gardening sites compiled by the Department of Horticultural Science, North Carolina State University. In addition to how-to information, it includes long lists of plant and seed companies, public and private gardens, plant associations and societies, and online garden classes.

Biocontrol Network (www.bioconet.com) offers timely information about IPM and other nonchemical methods for controlling garden pests and diseases.

Flowerweb (www.flowerbase.com) sponsors *Flowerbase*, a searchable, illustrated flower database sponsored by the Dutch Greenhouse Business Networks.

GardenWeb (www.gardenweb.com) is an "Internet garden community." The site includes plant and image databases; forums on scores of subjects; garden events calendars; plant and seed exchanges; a botanical glossary; a directory of horticultural organizations, gardens, and plant collections; and extensive lists of mail-order garden-related businesses.

USDA Home Gardening Page (www.usda.gov/news/garden.htm) is the gateway to government information for home gardeners. Site includes a link to the USDA Plant Hardiness Zone map and other useful sources of information.

Netherlands Flower Bulb Information Center (www.bulb.com) is a comprehensive source of information about growing all kinds of bulbous plants.

Explore Cornell: Home Gardening (www.explore.cornell.edu/scene.cfm?scene=home%20gardening) is a site that includes flowers, vegetables, garden design, and lawn care, including searchable databases of how-to information and a "flower finder" by color, size, hardiness, bloom time, and other characteristics.

Garden Organizations

Local garden clubs are a fine way to connect with other flower growers—check with Cooperative Extension, area nurseries, and local gardeners to locate one in your area. The granddaddy (or mommy) of such organizations is National Garden Clubs, which has more than 7,000 chapters (www.gardenclub.org).

Many flowers have their own organization—informal groups like the Crocus Club (email: crocusclub@webtv.net), which advertises "no meetings, no dues, just share seeds and plants with other gardeners," or more formal organizations, such as the American Peony Society (www.americanpeonysociety.org) and the American Iris Society (www.irises.org), which publishes bulletins and newsletters, maintains the official registry of named cultivars, and sponsors national conventions. A good list of plant societies is at the American Horticultural Society web site (www.ahs.org/horticulture_internet_community/plant_societies.htm).

There also are regional organizations, such as the Horticultural Society of Maryland (www.horticulturemd.org), as well as regional associations devoted to particular plants, such as the Quebec Hosta and Hemerocallis Society (www.hostaquebec.com). Not only are most of these organizations filled with helpful members, they sponsor meetings, newsletters, plant exchanges and sales, and more. Use a search engine to find an organization that fits your interests.

The electronic equivalents of local garden clubs are online garden forums. Some, such as the forum run by the University of British Columbia (www.ubcbotanicalgarden.org/forums), are sponsored by educational institutions, commercial firms, or organizations; others, such as Dave's Garden forum (www.davesgarden.com/forums), are maintained by dedicated individuals. You can find a long list of garden forums at the GardenWeb web site (www.gardenweb.com), which also runs one of the largest online garden forums.

In addition to the possibilities suggested above, you may want take advantage of one of these organizations.

American Community Gardening Association
c/o Council on the Environment of NYC
51 Chambers Street, Suite 228
New York, NY 10007
www.communitygarden.org
Nonprofit organization working to create community gardens

Flower and Herb Exchange
3094 North Winn Road
Decorah, IA 52101
563-382-5990
www.seedsavers.org
Nonprofit dedicated to saving and sharing heirloom flower varieties

Master Gardeners
Master Gardeners International
424 North River Drive
Woodstock, VA 22664
mgic@capaccess.org
Classes, online and face to face, for beginning and advanced gardeners

Garden Tourism

There's much to be learned by visiting gardens, everything from a neighbor's small patio garden to large botanic gardens, such as those in Montreal, Brooklyn, Chicago, and Denver. Most public gardens maintain a web site that includes information about their plant collections as well as details about visiting. A good list of public gardens and arboreta is maintained at the GardenWeb web site (www.gardenweb.com). The *National Geographic Guide to America's Public Gardens*, published in 1999, is out of print but may be available at your library. Nurseries, especially those with display gardens, also are a wonderful source of ideas that can be translated into your own garden.

Flower Shows

There is nothing in North America as over the top as England's Chelsea Flower Show, but there are superb shows worth attending. The oldest in the United States—and one of the largest and best—is the Philadelphia Flower Show, which is held in March. Canada's largest show, Canada Blooms in Toronto, also occurs in March, as does Boston's and Wichita's. Florence, South Carolina, sponsors a Southern Plant and Flower Festival in April, and the Cleveland Botanical Garden Annual Flower Show, billed as "the largest outdoor flower show in North America," takes place in late May. The American Horticultural Society web site maintains an extensive list of flower shows and other events (www.ahs.org/events/index.htm). Information about smaller, local flower and garden shows is usually published in newspapers.

Garden Books

There are book titles sprinkled throughout of *Burpee: The Complete Flower Gardener*, every one worth buying or borrowing from the local library. These are additional and commendable works, authoritative works that go beyond the information contained in this book.

Armitage, Allan M. *Armitage's Garden Perennials*, 2000.
Bennett, Jennifer, and Turid Forsyth. *The Harrowsmith Annual Garden*, 1990.
Bird, Lindy. *Dried Flowers: A Complete Guide*, 2003.
Breskend, Jean Spiro. *Backyard Design*, 1991.
Capon, Brian. *Botany for Gardeners*, 1990.
Di Sabato-Aust, Tracy. *The Well-Tended Perennial Garden*, 1998.
Forster, Roy, and Alex Downie. *The Woodland Garden*, 2000.
Harper, Pamela J. *Color Echoes: Harmonizing Color in the Garden*, 1994.
Hill, Lewis, and Nancy Hill. *Bulbs: Four Seasons of Blooms*, 1994.
Hobhouse, Penelope. *The Story of Gardening*, 2002.
Johnson, Hugh. *Principles of Gardening*, rev. ed., 1996.
Lima, Patrick. *The Harrowsmith Perennial Garden*, 1987.
Lloyd, Christopher. *Christopher Lloyd's Garden Flowers*, 2000.
Marinelli, Janet, ed. *The Brooklyn Botanic Garden Gardener's Desk Reference*, 1998.
Ottesen, Carole. *Ornamental Grasses: The Amber Wave*, 1989.
Powell, Eileen. *The Gardener's A-Z Guide to Growing Flowers from Seed to Bloom*, 2004.
Rice, Graham. *Discovering Annuals*, 1991.
Roth, Sally. *The Gardener's Weather Bible*, 2003.
Schenk, George. *The Complete Shade Gardener*, 2002.
Whistler, W. Arthur. *Tropical Ornamentals: A Guide*, 2000.
Weinstein, Gayle. *Xeriscape Handbook: A How-to Guide to Natural, Resource-Wise Gardening*, 1999.

Garden Magazines

The number of national garden magazines keeps declining, but good titles are still published. The magazines on this short list are those likely to be most interesting to flower growers. There also are regional magazines, such as *Pacific Horticulture* and *Texas Gardener*, as well as publications issued by plant societies and other horticultural organizations and by enthusiastic home gardeners. For a bit of fun, take a look at *GreenPrints*, which features the "human side of gardening" (P.O. Box 1355, Fairview, NC 28730; 800-569-0602; www.greenprints.com). For more garden periodicals, go to the list at the Gardening Launch Pad (www.gardeninglaunchpad.com).

The American Gardener
American Horticultural Society
7931 East Boulevard Drive
Alexandria VA 22308
www.ahs.org

Canadian Gardening
340 Ferrier Street, Suite 210
Markham, ON
L3R 2Z5 Canada
www.canadiangardening.com

Fine Gardening
The Taunton Press, Inc.
P.O. Box 5506
Newtown, CT 06470-5506
www.taunton.com/finegardening/index.asp

Horticulture
Horticulture
98 North Washington Street
Boston, MA 02114
www.hortmag.com

Mail-Order Seed and Plant Sources

There are hundreds of mail-order seed and plant companies, and nearly all are amazingly helpful and accommodating to home gardeners. Most publish both print (either free or for a small fee) and online catalogs. Included in this small sample are both generalists, such as W. Atlee Burpee & Co., and specialists like Schreiner's Gardens, which specializes in bearded irises. An online search will turn up dozens more firms; if you're looking for a specific genus, such as *Primula*, include that in your search request.

A&D Peony and Perennial Nursery
P.O. Box 2383
Snohomish, WA 98291
360-668-9690
www.adpeonies.com
Peonies, daylilies, hostas

Alpen Gardens
12010 NE Flett Road
Gaston, OR 97119
503-662-3951
www.alpengardens.com
Dahlia tubers

Ambergate Gardens
8730 County Road 43
Chaska, MN 55318-935
877-211-9769
www.ambergategardens.com
Perennial plants

André Viette
994 Long Meadow Road
Fishersville, VA 22939-3012
800-575-5538
www.viette.com
Perennial plants

Arrowhead Alpines
P.O. Box 857
Fowlerville, MI 48836
517-223-2581
www.arrowhead-alpines.com
Perennial plants, especially alpines

Ashwood Garden
18995 Hooper Ridge Road
Glouster, OH 45732
740-767-3946
www.ashwooddaylilies.com
Daylilies

Burpee
Warminster, PA 18974
800-888-1447
www.burpee.com
Seeds, perennial plants, hardy and tender bulbs

B & D Lilies
P.O. Box 2007
Port Townsend, WA 98368
360-385-1738
www.lilybulb.com
Lily bulbs

Bluestone Perennials
7211 Middle Ridge Road
Madison, OH 44057
800-852-5243
www.bluestoneperennials.com
Starter plants: perennials

Borbeleta Gardens
15980 Canby Avenue
Faribault, MN 55021-7652
507-334-2807
1rl.com/borbeleta.htm
Perennials, especially Siberian iris, lilies, daylilies, peonies

Botanus
2489 Wayburne Crescent
Langley, BC
V2Y 1B6 Canada
800-672-3414
www.botanus.com
Hardy and tender bulbs
(in Canada only)

Brent and Becky's Bulbs
7900 Daffodil Lane
Glouchester, VA 23061
877-661-2852
www.brentandbeckysbulbs.com
Hardy and tender bulbs

Busse Gardens
17160 245th Avenue
Big Lake, MN 55309
800-544-3192
www.bussegardens.com
Perennial plants

Canyon Creek Nursery
3527 Dry Creek Road
Oroville, CA 95965
530-533-2166
www.canyoncreeknursery.com
Perennial plants, especially violets,
salvias, dianthus

Carroll Gardens
444 East Main Street
Westminster, MD 21157-5540
800-638-6334
www.carrollgardens.com
Perennial plants, hardy and tender
bulbs

Cascade Bulb and Seed
P.O. Box 271
Scotts Mills, OR 97375
503-873-2218
www.open.org/halinar/cbs.htm
Lily bulbs and seeds, daylily plants
and seeds

Chiltern Seeds
Bortree Stile, Ulverston
Cumbria, LA12 7PB
England
www.edirectory.co.uk/chilternseeds
Perennial and annual seeds

Cooley's Gardens
P.O. Box 126
Silverton, Oregon 97381
800-225-5391
www.cooleysgardens.com
Bearded iris

Cricket Hill Garden
670 Walnut Hill Road
Thomaston, Connecticut, 06787
877-723-6642
www.treepeony.com
Garden and tree peony

The Crownsville Nursery
P.O. Box 309
Strasburg VA 22657
540-631-9411
www.crownsvillenursery.com
Perennial plants

Digging Dog Nursery
P.O. Box 471
Albion, CA 95410
707-937-1130
www.diggingdog.com
Perennial plants

Florabunda Seeds
Box 3
Indian River, ON
Canada K0L 2B0
705-295-6440
www.florabundaseeds.com
Heirloom seeds

Floyd Cove Nursery
1050 Enterprise-Osteen Road
Enterprise, FL 32725-9355
386-860-1230
www.floydcove.com
New daylily cultivars

Gardenimport Inc.
P.O. Box 760
Thornhill, ON
L4B 1C6 Canada
800-339-8314
www.gardenimport.com
Seeds, plants, bulbs

Garden Perennials
Route 1
Wayne, NE 68787
402-375-3615
gardenperennials.net
Perennial plants

Gilbert H. Wild and Son
P.O. Box 338
Sarcoxie, MO 64862-0338
888-449-4537
www.gilberthwild.com
Perennial plants, especially
daylilies, peonies, bearded iris

Harris Seeds
P.O. Box 22960
Rochester, NY 14692-2960
800-514-4441
www.harrisseeds.com
Seeds

**Hauser's Superior View
Nursery**
RR1, Box 199
Bayfield, WI 54814
715-779-5404
www.superiorviewfarm.com
Perennial plants

Heronswood Nursery
7530 NE 288th Street
Kingston, WA 98346
360-297-4172
www.heronswood.com
Unusual perennial plants, grasses

High Country Gardens
2902 Rufina Street
Santa Fe, NM 87507
800-925-9387
www.highcountrygardens.com
Perennial plants, especially
xeriscape plants

Hollingsworth Peonies
28747 290 Street
Maryville, MO 64468
660-562-3010
www.hollingsworthpeonies.com
Peonies

Hortico Nurseries, Inc.
723 Robson Road
Waterdown, ON
L0R 2H1 Canada
905-689-6984
www.hortico.com
Perennial plants

Johnny's Selected Seeds
955 Benton Avenue
Winslow, ME 04901
800-879-2258
www.johnnyseeds.com
Seeds and bulbs

John Scheepers, Inc.
P.O. Box 638
Bantam, CT 06750-0638
860-567-0838
www.johnscheepers.com
Hardy and tender bulbs

King's Mums
P.O. Box 368
Clements, CA 95227
209-759-3571
www.kingsmums.com
Chrysanthemums

Klehm's Song Sparrow Farm
13101 East Rye Road
Avalon, WI 53505
800-533-3715
www.songsparrow.com
Perennial plants, especially
peonies, daylilies, hosta

Lilypons Water Gardens
P.O. Box 10
Buckeystown, MD 21717-0010
800-999-5459
www.lilypons.com
Perennial plants for water gardens
and ponds

Mitsch Daffodils
P.O. Box 218
Hubbard, OR 97032
503-651-2742
www.web-ster.com/havens/mitsch
Narcissus bulbs

Nicholls Gardens
4724 Angus Drive
Gainesville, VA 20155
703-754-9623
www.nichollsgardens.com
Perennial plants, especially iris,
daylilies, hostas, peonies, cyclamen

Old House Gardens
36 Third Street
Ann Arbor, MI 48103
734-995-1486
www.oldhousegardens.com
Heirloom hardy and tender bulbs

Perennial Pleasures Nursery
P.O. Box 147
East Hardwick, VT 05836
802-472-5104
www.perennialpleasures.net/
contact.htm
Heirloom seeds and plants

Pinetree Garden Seeds
P.O. Box 300
New Gloucester, ME 04260
207-926-3400
www.superseeds.com
Seeds

Plant Delights Nursery, Inc.
9241 Sauls Road
Raleigh, NC 27603
919-772-4794
www.plantsdelight.com
New and unusual perennial plants

**Pleasant Valley Glads and
Dahlias**
P.O. Box 494
Agawam, MA 01001
860-798-8189
www.gladolia.com
Gladiolus corms, dahlia tubers

Savory's Gardens, Inc.
5300 Whiting Avenue
Edina, MN 55439
952-941-8755
www.savorysgardens.com
Hostas

Schreiner's Iris Gardens
3625 Quinaby Road, NE
Salem, OR 97303
800-525-2367
www.schreinersgardens.com
Bearded iris

Seeds of Change
P.O. Box 15700
Santa Fe, NM 87592-1500
888-762-7333
www.seedsofchange.com
Organic seeds

Seeds of Distinction
P.O. Box 86, Station A
Etobicoke, Toronto, ON
M9C 4V2 Canada
416-255-3060
www.seedsofdistinction.com
Unusual seeds

Siskiyou Rare Plant Nursery
2825 Cummings Road
Medford, OR 97501
541-772-6846
www.srpn.net
Unusual perennial plants, alpines,
grasses

**Southern Exposure Seed
Exchange**
P.O. Box 460
Mineral, VA 23117
540-894-9480
www.southernexposure.com
Heirloom flower seeds, organic

Specialty Perennials
481 Reflection Road
Apple Valley, MN 55124
952-432-8673
www.hardyplants.com
Perennial plants and seeds

Stokes Seeds, Inc.
P.O. Box 548
Buffalo, NY 14240-0548
in Canada:
P.O. Box 10
Thorold, ON
L2V 5E9 Canada
800-396-9238
www.stokeseeds.com
Seeds

Swallowtail Garden Seeds
122 Calistoga Road, #178
Santa Rosa, CA 95409
707-538-3585
www.swallowtailgardenseeds.com
Seeds

Swan Island Dahlias
P.O. Box 700
Danby, OR 97013
800-410-6540
www.dahlias.com
Dahlia tubers

T&T Seeds Ltd.
Box 1710
Winnipeg, MB
R3C 3P6 Canada
204-895-9964
www.ttseeds.com
Seeds, plants, bulbs (in Canada only)

**Thompson & Morgan
Seedsmen, Inc.**
P.O. Box 1308
Jackson, NJ 08627-0308
800-274-7333
www.thompson-morgan.com
Seeds

Underwood Shade Nursery
P.O. Box 1386
North Attleboro, MA 02763
508-222-2164
www.underwoodshadenursery.com
Perennials for shade

Vesey's Seeds Ltd.
P.O. Box 9000
Charlottetown, PE
C1A 8K6 Canada
902-368-7333
www.veseys.com
Seeds

Wayside Gardens
1 Garden Lane
Hodges, SC 29695-0001
800-213-0379
www.waysidegardens.com
Perennial plants, hardy and tender
bulbs

White Flower Farm
P.O. Box 50
Litchfield, CT 06759
800-503-9624
www.whiteflowerfarm.com
Perennial plants, hardy and tender
bulbs

William Dam Seeds Ltd.
Box 8400
Dundas, ON
L9H 6M1 Canada
905-628-6641
www.damseeds.com
Seeds (in Canada only)

Index

Page numbers in *italics* indicate illustrations.

A

Abelmoschus
  manihot, 342
  moschatus, 342
Acer palmatum, 87
Achillea, 32, 39, 66, 74, 173, *214*,
    214–215
  cultivars, 215
  filipendulina, 214–215
  millefolium, 214, 215
  ptarmica, 27
  tomentosa, 215
Aconite
  winter, 12, 170, 280, *280*
  See also Monkshood
Aconite buttercup, 438
Aconitum, 12, 141, 149, 173, 215–217
  carmichaelii, 216
  × *cammarum*, 216
  cultivars, 216
  ferox, 215
  lycoctonum spp. *vulparia*, 216
  napellus, 215–216, *216*
Adenophora
  confusa, 255
  lilifolia, 255
Aden, Paul, 343
African daisy, 39, *318*, 318, 326
Agastache foeniculum, 55
Ageratum
  hardy, 218, 306–307, *307*
  yellow, 326
Ageratum houstonianum, 10, 173, *217*,
    217–218
Ajuga
  genevensis, 272
  pyramidalis, 272
  reptans, 272
Alcea
  ficifolia, 220
  rosea, 21, 27, 119, 218–221, *219*, 384
Alchemilla mollis, 40, 68, 119, *221*,
    221–222
Alcott, Louisa May, 405
All-America Selections (AAS), 25
Allium, 222–224
  aflatunense, 222, 223
  caeruleum, *107*, 223
  cernuum, 224
  christophii, 21, 223
  giganteum, 223
  moly, 222, 223, 223–224
  schoenoprasum, 222–223, 224, *224*
  senescens, 224
  senescens var. *glaucum*, 224

thunbergii, 37, 224
tuberosum, 223, 224
virgunculae, 224
Allspice, Carolina, 50
Altitude, 31–33
Alumroot, 320, 339–341
  American, 339, 341
  small-flowered, *339*, 341
Alyssum, sweet, 10, 11, 39, 74, 137, 173,
    376–377, *377*
Amaranth, feathered, 260–261, *261*
Amaranthus caudatus, 74
Amaryllis belladonna, 149
American Community Gardening
    Association, 468
American Horticultural Society, Heat
    Zone Map of, 464
*American Horticultural Society A–Z
    Encyclopedia of Garden Plants*, 20
Ammobium alatum, 326
Amsonia
  ciliata, 225
  hubrechtii, 225
  tabernaemontana, 225, 225–226
  tabernaemontana var. *montana*, 226
  tabernaemontana var. *salcifolia*, 225–226
Analogous color schemes, 112, *114*
Anatomy, flower, 20–22
Anemone, 22, 141, 226–228
  grape-leaf, 59, 227–228, *228*
  Japanese, 27, 59, *227*, 227
  meadow, 32, 227
  poppy, 228
  snowdrop, 227
  wood, 227
Anemone, 22, 141, 226–228
  blanda, 226, 227
  canadensis, 32, 227
  coronaria, 228
  cultivars, 227, 228
  hupehensis, 37, 59, 227
  × *hybrida*, 27, 59, *227*, 227
  nemorosa, 227
  sylvestris, 227
  tomentosa, 59, 227–228, *228*
Angiosperm, 13, 14
Animal bedding mulch, 132
Animal manure, 73
Animal parts, dried, 74
Animals. *See* Wildlife
Anise hyssop, 55
Annuals
  buying, 128
  cool-weather, 16–17
  deadheading, 137
  in dry sites, 39

easy to grow, 10, 11, 44
  for edging, 96
  for high temperatures, 17, 38
  for season-long garden, 184
  for shade, 59
  tall, 102
  for thin soil, 74
  underplanting with, 108
  See also Plants; Plant selection; *specific
    names*
Anthemis
  sancti-johannis, 229
  tinctoria, 38, 170, 228–230, *229*
Antirrhinum, 152
  braun-blanquettii, 232
  majus, 24, 27, 230–232
Antitranspirants, 159
Aphids, 155, 162–163
Apical bud, 18–19
Aquilegia, 32, 40, 232–234
  caerulea, 233
  canadensis, 233
  chrysantha, 233, *233*
  hybrids, 234
  longissima, 233
  seeds, 119, 121
  vulgaris, 233, 234
Arabis caucasica, 74, 173
Arctotis
  fastuosa, 318
  × *hybrida*, 318
  venusta, 318
Arends, George, 240
Argemone grandiflora, 74
Arkell, Reginal, 52
Armeria maritima, 38, 39
Armitage, Allan, 214, 247, 290, 409, 427
Arnim, Countess von, 147, 195
Artemisia, 19
  vulgaris, 15
Arum lily, 84–85
Aruncus, 22, 44, 234–235
  aethusifolius, 235
  dioicus, 55, 59, 68, 170, 234–235, *235*
Asclepias
  incarnata, 55, 236
  tuberosa, 39, 141, 235–236, *236*
Asexual reproduction, 22–23
Aster, 37, 69, 237–240
  blue wood, 239
  calico, 240
  cornflower, *263*, 263
  Frikart's, 239
  heath, 240
  New England, 27, 34, 237–239, *238*
  New York, *237*, 237, 238, 239

Aster (continued)
  Tartarian, 238, 239
  white wood, 239–240
Aster, 37, 69, 237–240
  cordifolius, 239
  cultivars, 238–239
  divaricatus, 239–240
  ericoides, 240
  × frikartii, 239
  lateriflorus, 240
  novae-angliae, 27, 34, 237–239, 238
  novi-belgii, 237, 237, 238, 239
  tataricus, 238, 239
Astilbe, 12, 27, 40, 44, 55, 59, 68,
    240–242, 426
  Chinese, 14, 240, 242
  ostrich plume, 241, 242
  star, 242
Astilbe, 12, 27, 40, 44, 55, 59, 68,
    240–242, 426
  chinensis, 14, 240, 242
  cultivars, 242
  simplicifolia, 242
  thunbergii, 241, 242
Asymmetrical (informal) design, 90,
    92–93, 93
Attenborough, David, 21
Aulis, Jack, 83
Autumn garden, 37, 143, 145
Avens, 323, 323–324
  purple, 323
  water, 323
Azadirachtin, 159

B

Baby's breath, 58, 141, 327–329
  annual, 38, 328, 328, 329
  creeping, 328, 329
  perennial, 15, 21, 74, 328–329
Bachelor's button, 15, 27, 39, 74,
    261–263, 262, 326
Bacillus popilliae (Bp), 157
Bacillus thuringiensis (Bt), 157
Bacteria, 152
Bacterial wilt, 172
Balloon flower, 141, 418–419, 419
Balloon vine, 49, 352
Balsam, garden, 59, 350–351
Bamboo, 50
Bangs, John Kendrick, 63
Banister, Reverend, 299
Baptisia, 141, 242–244
  alba, 243
  australis, 243, 243–244
  bracteata, 243
  hybrids, 243
  lactea, 243
  sphaerocarpa, 243
  tinctoria, 242–243
Barberry, 50
  Japanese, 87
Bargon, Benjamin Smith, 339

Barrenwort, 302–303
Barry, Dave, 135, 458
Bartram, John, 252, 400
Bastard trenching, 83
Beard, Henry, 30, 201
Beard-tongue, 19, 407–409
  common, 409
  hairy, 66
  hybrid, 408, 409
Beautybush, 87
Beds and borders, 85–115
  autumn cleanup, 145
  clearing the soil for, 80, 80–82
  defined, 86
  edges, 96–97, 97, 136
  focus and balance in, 95–96
  formal, 88, 91–93
  informal, 90, 91, 92–93, 93
  mixed, 87
  placement of, 42–43, 48, 86, 88
  progression and sequence in, 95
  raised, 54, 69
  repetition in, 93–95, 94
  size and scale of, 90–91, 91
  spacing plants in, 131
  turning the soil for, 82–83, 83
  See also Garden design; Plant selection
Bee balm, 21, 27, 30, 55, 157, 387,
    387–388, 388
  wild, 388
Beetles, 151–152, 163
  flea, 164
  Japanese, 155, 163, 165, 165
  soldier, 158
Bégon, Michel, 244
Begonia, 22, 244–247
  hardy, 24, 246, 247
  rex, 246
  tuberous, 59, 244–245, 245–247
  wax, 59, 245, 246, 246, 247
Begonia, 22, 244–247
  grandis ssp. evansiana, 245, 246, 247
  rex, 246
  semperflorens, 59, 245, 246, 246, 247
  tuberhybridacultorum, 59, 244–245,
    245–247
Bellflower, 40, 252–255
  clustered, 253–254, 32
  creeping, 252–253
  Dalmatian, 253, 255, 255
  great, 253, 253, 254
  milky, 119, 253, 254
  peach-leaved, 253, 254, 254
  Serbian, 255
Bellis perennis, 40, 119
Belloc, Hilaire, 207
Bells of Ireland, 386
Bell vine, purple, 49, 352
Benches, 208
Beneficial insects, 153, 153, 156–158,
    160, 467
Berberis, 50
  thunbergii, 87

Bergen, August von, 247
Bergenia, 40, 59, 173, 247–248
  heart-leaved, 247, 248
Bergenia, 40, 59, 173, 247–248
  cordifolia, 247, 248
Beston, Henry, 135
Bethlehem sage, 425, 425–426
Bicarbonate sprays, 159–160
Biennials, 10–11
Bilateral symmetry, 92
Biocontrol Network, 467
Bird, Lindy, 186
Birds, insect-eating, 154
Bishop's cap, 302–303
Black cohosh, 269
Black-eyed Susan, 37, 38, 39, 68,
    100–101, 427–429
Black-eyed Susan vine, 49, 59, 352, 352
Blanket flower, 39, 66, 74, 119, 315, 315–316
Blazing star, 363–364
  dotted, 363, 364
  prairie, 364
Bleeding heart, 12, 44, 59, 121, 141, 149,
    173, 293–295
  common, 32, 293–294, 294
  dwarf, 130
  fringed, 295
  Western, 295
Blight diseases, 169
Blood meal, 74
Bloodroot, 59
Bloom time
  latitude and, 30
  plant selection and, 105–107
Bluebeard, 410
Bluebell, 141, 280–281
  English, 281
  Scotch, 252, 255
  Spanish, 12, 280–281, 281
Blue dawn flower, 353, 354
Blue flowers, 109
Blue mist shrub, 87
Blue star
  downy, 225
  willow, 225, 225–226
  willow, dwarf, 226
Bluet, mountain, 32, 262, 263
Boltonia asteroides, 37, 239
Bonemeal, 74
Books, gardening, 210, 469
Boots, gardening, 208, 210
Bordeau × mixture, 160
Borders. See Beds and borders
Borers, 163
Botany, basic, 17–20
Botrytis blight, 171
Bottle gourd, 49
Bouncing bet, 381
Boxwood, common, 50
Brachyscome iberidifolia, 248–249, 249
Bracteantha bracteata, 66, 249, 249–250, 326
Bracton, Henry de, 149
Britton, Nathaniel Lord, 342

Broom, Scotch, 15
Browallia speciosa, 59
Brunnera macrophylla, 40, 170
Buchanan, Rita, 191
Buckets, 200
Buddleja davidii, 87
Buds, 17–19
Bugbane
 American, 268–269, 37
 Kamchatka, 269
Bugleweed
 blue, 272
 common, 272
 pyramid, 272
Bugloss, Siberian, 40, 170
Bulbous plants
 for autumn garden, 37
 buying guidelines, 129
 division of, 142
 dying back, 138
 easy to grow, 44
 hardy/tender, 17
 little, 280–282
 overplanting, 107
 types of, 12–13
 wildlife-proof, 175
Burbank, Luther, 8, 324, 361, 455
Burpee Trial Gardens, 1
Butter-and-eggs, 74
Buttercup, 55, 438
 aconite, 438
 tall, 438
Butterfly bush, 87
Butterfly garden, 178
Butterfly weed, 39, 141, 235–236, 236
Buxus sempervirens, 50
Buying
 beneficial insects, 157, 467
 bulbs, 129
 equipment and tools, 196–197, 466
 plants and seeds, 120, 127–129, 470–474

C

Caladium, 19, 20, 104, 104
Calendula officinalis, 11, 39, 55, 250–251, 27, 251
Calicrachoa, 413
California poppy, 38, 58, 66, 74, 183, 304–306, 305
Calla lily, 6, 22
Callirhoe involucrata, 141
Calycanthus floridus, 50
Calyx, 21
Camassia
 cusickii, 369
 quamash, 369
Campanula, 40, 252–255
 americana, 252
 carpatica, 253, 254–255
 cochleariifolia, 253
 cultivars, 254–255
 glomerata, 253–254, 32
 lactiflora, 119, 253, 254

latifolia, 253, 253, 254
medium, 55, 252, 252, 253
persicifolia, 253, 254, 254
portenschlagiana, 253, 255, 255
poscharskyana, 253, 255
rapunculoides, 252–253
rotundifolia, 253, 255
Campion, 381–382
 Arkwright's, 382
 rose, 119, 381, 381, 382
Canary creeper, 49
Candytuft, 348–350
 evergreen, 32, 348, 349
 globe, 59, 349, 349
 rock, 349
 rocket, 349
Canna, 19, 256, 256–258, 257
Canna × generalis, 19, 256, 256–258, 257
Canterbury bells, 55, 252, 253, 353
Čapek, Karel, 54, 63, 71, 124
Capitulum, 21
Cardinal climber, 354
Cardinal flower, 374, 375, 376, 376
Cardiospermum halicacabum, 49, 352
Carduus nutans, 15
Carts, garden, 200–201
Caryopteris × clandonensis, 87, 410
Castor bean, 22, 149
Catalogs, seed and plant, 211
Catananche caerulea, 263
Catchfly
 German, 381, 382
 royal, 381
Caterpillars, 163
Catharanthus roseus, 15, 38, 59, 66, 258–259, 259
Cather, Willa, 57, 315
Catmint, 37, 45, 394–395
Celosia
 argentea, 10, 38, 39, 260, 260–261, 74, 74, 261
 cristata, 66
 spicata, 261
Centaurea
 globe, 15, 263
 Persian, 263
Centaurea, 261–263
 americana, 261, 262, 263
 cyanus, 15, 27, 39, 74, 261, 262, 262, 263
 dealbata, 263
 macrocephala, 15, 263
 montana, 32, 262, 263
Centranthus ruber, 119, 264, 264–265
Cephalaria gigantea, 431
Cerastium tomentosum, 66, 74, 170
Ceratostigma plumbaginoides, 272
Cercis canadensis, 87
Chagall, Marc, 6
Chamaemelum nobile, 230, 230
Chamomile, Roman, 230, 230
Charles I, King of England, 250
Chaucer, Geoffrey, 6
Checkered lily, 313, 313, 366

Chelone, 37, 55
 glabra, 311
 lyonii, 311
 obliqua, 311
Chemical controls, 148, 159–162
Chicabiddy, 49
Child's garden, 178–179, 179
Chinese lantern, 149
Chionodoxa luciliae, 12, 170, 280
Chives
 common, 222–223, 224, 224
 garlic, 223, 224
Chlorosis, interveinal, 72
Christmas rose, 334, 335
Chrysanthemum × morifolium, 265, 265–267, 267
Chrysogonum virginianum, 55, 272
Church, Thomas, 48
Cimicifuga, 55, 59, 268–269
 americana, 37, 268–269
 racemosa, 37, 173, 268, 269
 simplex, 269
Cineraria, 84–85
Cinquefoil, 85, 420–422
 Himalayan, 421, 421
 Nepal, 421
 sulfur, 15, 421
 three-toothed, 421–422
Citrus oils, 160
Clark, William, 34
Clarkia unguiculata, 74
Clay soil, 56, 64, 66, 68
Cleanup, garden, 144, 145, 150, 153
Clearing the soil, 80, 80–82
Cleome hassleriana, 10, 21, 38, 44, 66, 74, 121, 170, 173, 174, 269, 269–270
Climate and weather, 30–45
 average temperature, 39
 elevation and, 31–33
 growing season, 36, 459–464
 hardiness zone rating, 16, 34–36, 464, 465
 heat zone rating, 464
 high temperature, 36, 38, 39
 information sources on, 31, 458
 latitude and, 30, 31
 low temperature, 40
 microclimate, 41
 non-native species and, 14, 16, 34
 phenology data, 36
 precipitation, 39, 52
 recording, 207
Climbing plants, 102
Clogs, garden, 210
Clothing, gardening, 208
Coats, Alice, 372, 394, 434–435
Cobaea scandens, 49, 170, 352
Cockscomb, 10, 38, 39, 66, 74, 74, 260, 260–261
Cocoa hull mulch, 132
Coir (coco peat), 203
Colchicum
 autumnale, 37, 149, 282, 282
 speciosum, 282

Cold frame, *129*, 129, 205
Coleridge, Samuel Taylor, 389
Coleus, 19
Collinson, Peter, 211, 252
Color, 108–115
  blue, red, and yellow, 109
  combinations, 113
  light and, 58, 110–111
  neutral hues, 115
  repetitive, *94*, 94
  schemes, 111–115
  sequential, 95
  warm and cool, 109–110, *112*, 115
Color wheel, 108–109, *110*, *111*
Columbine, 32, 40, *232*, 232–234
  European, 234
  golden, *233*, 233
  hybrids, 234
  long-spurred, 233
  Rocky Mountain, 233
  seeds, 119, 121
  wild, 233
Common names, 8
Compass plant, 68
Complementary color schemes, 111–112
Composting, *75*, 79
  bins for, *77*, 77–78, *206*, 206
  cold composting, 77
  hot composting, 78–79
  mulch, *132*, 132
  nutrients in, 74, 78
  tips, 78–79
Compost tea, 127, 135
Coneflower
  giant, 429
  narrow-leaved, 300
  orange, 32, 119, 173, 427, *428*, 428–429
  pale, 300
  purple, 12, 39, 44, 68, 119, 173,
    298–300, *299*
  ragged, 12, 427, 429
  Tennessee, 300
Consolida ajacis, 289
Container garden, 192–193, *193*
Containers, for seed starting, 203, 205
Convallaria majalis, 13, 59, 74, 149, 170,
    270–272, *271*
  var. *rosea*, 271
Convolvulus tricolor, 354
Cool-weather annuals, 16–17
Cooperative Extension Service, 211, 464
Cooper, Susan Fenimore, 151
Copper-based fungicides, 160
Coral bells, 19, 40, 59, 339–341
Coreopsis, 119, 272–275
  lance-leaved, 66, 274
  large-flowered, *273*, 274, 274
  mouse-ear, *273*, 274
  pink, *273*, 273, 274
  plains, 10, 11, 38, 39, 74, 272, *273*,
    273–274
Coreopsis, 119, 272–275
  auriculata, *273*, 274
  cultivars, 274–275

  grandiflora, *273*, 274, 274
  lanceolata, 66, 274
  rosea, *273*, 273, 274
  tinctoria, 10, 11, 38, 39, 74, 272, *273*,
    273–274
  verticillata, 40, 173, 274–275, *275*
Corms, 12
Corncobs, ground, 132
Cornflower, 261–263
Cornflower aster, *263*, 263
Cornus alba, 87
Cornut, Jacques Philippe, 233
Corolla, 21
Coronilla varia, 15
Corydalis, 275–276
  blue, 276
  ferny, 276
  white, 276
  yellow, 276
Corydalis, 275–276
  cheilanthifolia, 276
  flexuosa, 276
  lutea, 58, 59, *275*, 275, 276
  ochroleuca, 276
  solida, 276
Cosmos, 173, 276–278
  annual, 10, 27, 38, 39, 66, *118*, 276,
    277, 277–278
  chocolate, 278
  sulphur, 10, 27, 66, 276, *278*, 278
Cosmos, 173, 276–278
  atrosanguineus, 278
  bipinnatus, 10, 27, 38, 39, 66, *118*, 276,
    277, 277–278
  sulphureus, 10, 27, 66, 276, *278*,
    278
Cotyledons, 19, 124
Cowslip
  Jerusalem, 425
  primrose, *422*, 422, 423–424
Crambe
  cordifolia, 328
  maritima, 328
Cranesbill, 12, 59, 319–322
  Armenian, 321
  bloody, 321–322, *322*
  Dalmatian, 322
  dusky, 322
  Endress, 322
  grayleaf, *320*, 322
  lilac, *321*, 321
  meadow, 321
  wild, 74, *320*, 322
  woody, 322
Crape myrtle, 60
Crockett, James, 327
Crocosmia, 369
Crocus, 12, 37, 279, 283–284
  autumn, 37, 149, *282*, 282
  Italian, 283
  saffron, 279, 283
  Scotch, 283, 284
  snow, 27, 283, 284
  spring, *279*, 279, 284

Crocus, 12, 37, 279, 283–284
  biflorus, 283, 284
  chrysanthus, 27, 283, 284
  cultivars, 283
  imperati, 283
  laevigatus, 284
  × *luteus*, 27, 283
  ochroleucus, 284
  sativus, 279, 283
  speciosus, 284
  tommasinianus, 283, 284
  vernus, 279, *279*, 284
Cross-pollination, 23, 24
Crown imperial, 12, 27, 311–312, *312*, 313
Crown vetch, 15
Cullins, Bill, 187
Culpeper, Nicholas, 250, 399, 422, 434–435
Cultivar names, 9
Cultural controls, 135–136, 149–150,
    153–154
Cultural disorders, 150–151
Cummings, E. E., 85
Cup-and-saucer vine, 49, 170, 352
Cupid's dart, 263
Cutting back, 138, 143, 145
Cutting garden, perennial, 189, *190*, 190
Cuttings, propagation by, 139, 140–141
Cutworms, 154, 164
Cyclamen, 40
Cypress vine, 353, 354
Cytisus scoparius, 15

D

Daffodil, 12, *13*, 149, 170, 390–394
  autumn, 37, *282*, 282
  cyclamineus, *392*, 393
  double, 393
  heirloom cultivars, 27
  hoop petticoat, 394
  jonquilla, 393–394
  large-cup, 390, *393*, 393–394
  paperwhite, 392
  pheasant's eye, *393*, 394
  poet's, 394
  small-cupped, 393
  tazetta, 394
  triandrus, 393
  trumpet, *391*, 392
Dahl, Andreas, 284
Dahlia, 16, 27, 284–287, *284–285*, 286
Daisy
  African, 39, *318*, 318, 326
  blue, 74
  common names for, 8
  English, 40, 119
  florets of, 21
  Gloriosa, 28–29, *428*, 428, 429
  Michaelmas, 238
  Nippon, 37, 362
  ox-eye, *15*, 15, 362
  painted, 32, *266*, 266
  Shasta, 107, 32, 119, 361–363, *362*
  Swan River, 170, 248–249, *249*

Dame's rocket, 15
Damping-off disease, 169
Dana, Mrs. William Starr, *22, 24,*
    235–236
Darwin, Charles, 64
Dash, Mike, 442
Daylily, *12, 44, 58, 66, 68,* 335–338
    citron, 338
    disease-resistance, *170,* 170
    heirloom, 27
    lemon lily, 338
    middendorff, 338
    reblooming, 105, 338
    tawny, *15, 26, 27,* 338
Deadheading, 130, *136,* 137
Deadnettle, spotted, *19,* 173, *272, 272*
Debudding, 137
Deer control, 173–175
Deerproof plants, 173, *174*
Delphinium, 40, 119, 149, 287–289
    × *belladonna,* 289
    cultivars, 289
    × *elatum, 32,* 287, *288,* 289
Democritus, 148
Design. *See* Garden design
Deutzia crenata, 87
Dianthus, 119, 290–293
    × *allwoodii, 290,* 292, *293*
    barbatus, 32, 290, 293
    chinensis, 290, 291, 293
    cultivars, 292–293
    deltoides, 74, 292
    gratianopolitanus, 290, 292
    plumarius, 292
Dibbles (dibbers), 200
Dicentra, 44, 59, 121, 141, 149, 173,
    293–295
    canadensis, 295
    cucullaria, 295
    eximia, 294, 295
    formosa, 130, 294, 295
    spectabilis, 12, 32, 293–294, *294,* 295
Dickinson, Emily, 14, 290
Dicotyledons (dicots), 14
Dictamnus albus, 12, 141, *170,* 295–296,
    296
    var. *purpurascens,* 296
Digging tools, 82, 197–199
Digitalis, 8, 149, 173, 296–298
    cultivars, 298
    ferruginea, 298
    grandiflora, 298
    × *mertonensis,* 298
    purpurea, 8, 21, 59, 91, 297, 297, 298,
        298
    seeds, 119, 121
Dimorphotheca
    pluvialis, 318
    sinuata, 39, 318, 318
Dioecious flowers, 22
Dioscoridis, 390
Dipsacus, 431
Dirksen, Everett, 436
Disease-resistant plants, *150,* 153, *170*

Diseases
    causes of, 152
    chemical fungicides, 159–160
    common, 169–173
    cultural controls, 135–136, 149–150,
        153–154
    organic fungicides, 155
Division, propagation by, 131, 138–139,
    141–142, *142*
Dogtooth violet, 280
    European, 280
Dogwood, red twig, 87
Doronicum, 170
Double-digging, 83
Drainage, 35, 52
Dried flowers, 186–187, *187,* 326
Drip irrigation systems, 52, 55, 56, 201
Driscoll, Louise, 287
Dropwort, 311
Drought-tolerant plants, 39, 53
Duke, James, 305
Dusty miller, *62, 104, 381,* 381, 382
Dutchman's breeches, 295
Dyer's garden, 191

E

Earle, Mrs. E. W., 210
Earthworms, 64
Easter lily, 34, 369
Eccremocarpus scaber, 49
Echinacea
    cultivars, 300
    pallida, 300
    paradoxa, 300
    purpurea, 12, 39, 44, 68, 119, 173,
        298–300, *299*
    tennesseensis, 300
Echinops, 170, 300–301
    bannaticus, 301, 301
    ritro, 39, 301
Eddison, Sydney, *44, 58, 108, 115, 136,* 192
Edging, 96–97, *97,* 136
Edible gardens, 182
Eiseley, Loren, 56
Elaeagnus umbellata, 50
Emerson, Ralph Waldo, 6, 177
English Daisy, 40, 119
Epimedium, 302–303
    alpine, 303
    bicolor, 303
    long-spurred, 303
    Warley, 303
    yellow, *302,* 302–303
Epimedium, 302–303
    alpinum, 303
    cultivars, 303
    grandiflorum, 303
    × *perralchicum, 302,* 302–303
    × *versicolor,* 303
    × *warleyense,* 303
Equipment and supplies, 195–211
    buying guidelines, 196–197
    cold frame, *129,* 129, 205

compost bins, *77,* 77–78, *206,* 206
    for digging, raking, and hoeing, 82,
        197–199
    ergonomic, 211
    for hauling, *200,* 200–201
    mail-order sources for, 466
    maintenance of, 145, 198
    miscellaneous, 206–207
    rototillers, 81, 83
    for seed starting, 123, 203–206, *204*
    sharpening, 199, 206
    short-handled, *199,* 199–200
    for watering, 201–203, *202*
Eranthis hyemalis, 12, 170, 280, 280
Eremurus, 369
    × *isabellinus,* 369
Ergonomic tools, 211
Eryngium, 141, 303–304
    agavifolium, 304
    alpinum, 304
    amethystinum, 39, 304
    aquaticum, 303
    eburneum, 304
    foetidum, 303
    giganteum, 303, 304
    maritimum, 303
    planum, 304
    yuccifolium, 303, 304
Erythronium
    americanum, 280, 366
    californicum, 280
    dens-canis, 280
    grandiflorum, 280, 280
Eschscholz, Johann Friedrich, 305
Eschscholzia californica, 38, 58, 66, 74,
    304–306, *305*
Eulalia grass, 95
Euonymus fortunei, 87
Eupatorium, 37, 55, 119, 306–308
    coelestinum, 218, 306–307, *307*
    fistulosum, 307
    maculatum, 307
    perfoliatum, 306
    purpureum, 306, 307
    rugosum, 307
Euphorbia, 173, 308–310
    amygdaloides var. *robbiae*
    cyathophora, 310
    dulcis, 309
    griffithii, 309
    marginata, 11, 19, 59, 66, 308, 309, 309
    myrsinites, 309
    polychroma, 308, 309
    pulcherrima, 22, 58, 308
Evelyn, John, 118, 385
Evening primrose
    common, 398
    Missouri, 399
    pink, 398, 399
    tufted, 399
    yellow, 21, 399
Everlasting
    pearly or winged, 326
    rose, 326

Everlasting garden, 186–187, *187*
Everlasting pea, 27
Exacum affine, 59
Exotic love, 354
Exotic plants, 14
Explore Cornell: Home Gardening
    (web site), 468

F

F₁ hybrid, 25
Fairchild, Thomas, 25
False indigo
    blue, *243*, 243–244
    yellow, 243
Farewell-to-spring, 74
Farrer, Reginald, 334
Fawn lily, 280
Feather grass, 95
Feather reed grass, 95
Feathertop, 95
Felicia amelloides, 74
Fences, 41, 175
Fernleaf, 274–275, *275*
Ferreniea, Vicki, 187
Fertility, soil, 64, 73
Fertilizing, 73, 75, 127, 134–135
Feverfew, 27, 121, 170, 266
Fibrous roots, 17
Filipendula, 310–311
    palmata, 311
    purpurea, 311
    rubra, 310
    ulmaria, *310*, 310, 311
    vulgaris, 310, 311
Firethorn, 50
Flax, 372 373
    annual, 373
    blue, 373
    Narbonne, 373
    perennial, *372*, 373
    yellow, 373
Flea beetles, 164
Flexitubs, 200
Floss flower, 217–218, *217*
Flower and Herb Exchange (FHE), 26,
    120, 210, 468
Flowers
    anatomy of, 20–22
    in art, literature and mythology, 6–7
    language of, 7
    as national symbol, 6
    See also Plants
Flower shows, 469
Flowerweb, 467
Fluorescent light, 125
Foam flower
    Allegheny, 59, *340*, 340
    Wherry's, 340
Foliage. *See* Leaves
Foliar feeding, 127, 135
Food traps, 155
Forget-me-not, 55, 59, 74, 119, 173,
    388–389, *389*

Forks, *197*, 197, 198
    hand, 199
Formal (symmetrical) design, 88, 91–93
Formosa lily, 370
Forsythia, 50
Fortune, Robert, 265, 294, 343
Foundation planting, 86
Fountain grass, 95
Four-o'clock, 38, 59, 74, 149, *386*, 386
Foxglove, 8, 149, 173, 296–298
    common, 8, 21, 59, *91*, 297, *297*, 298,
        298
    rusty, 298
    seeds, 119, 121
    strawberry, 298
    yellow, 298
Foxtail lily, 369
Friable soil, 68, 71
Fritillaria, 311–314
    imperialis, 12, 27, 311–312, *312*, 313
    meleagris, 12, *313*, 313, 366
    michailovskyi, 312, 313–314
    pallidiflora, 313
    persica, 312
    pontica, 313
Fritillary, 311–314
    checkered lily, *313*, 313
    crown imperial, 12, 27, 311–312, *312*, 313
Frost-free dates, 36, 459–464
Frost, Robert, 115
Fuch, Leonhart, 314
Fuchsia, *314*, 314–315
    × *hybrida*, *314*
Fungi, 152, 158
Fungicides
    chemical, 159–160, 162
    organic, 155
Fusarium wilt, 172

G

Gaillardia, 39, 66, 74, 119, 315–316
    aristata, 315, 316
    × *grandiflora*, *315*, 315, 316
    pulchella, 315, 316
Galanthus
    elwesii, 280
    nivalis, 12, *149*, 149, 170, 280
Galium odoratum, 21, 59, 72, 173,
    316–317
Garden design
    changes and adjustments to, 88
    diagram for, *42*, 42
    garden rooms, 90
    guidelines, 44
    hardscape and, 42
    information sources for, 43, 44, 88, 469
    inherited garden, 90
    location and, 60, 88
    microclimate and, 41, 43
    topography and, 48
    windbreaks in, 41, 49–51
    See also Beds and borders; Plant
        selection

Garden organizations, 43, 120, 210, 468
Garden rooms, 90
Garden tours, 468
GardenWeb, 467, 468
Garlic
    German, 224
    as insect repellant, 154–155
Gas plant, 12, 141, 170, 295–296, *296*
Gate, garden, 89
Gayfeather, 66, 68, 363–364
    Kansas, 364
    spike, 14, 55, *363*, 363, 364, *364*
    tall, 37, 39
Gazania, 39
    krebsiana, 319
    linearis, 319
    ringens, *317*, 319, *319*
Genders, Roy, 299
Gentian, closed bottle, 37
Gentiana andrewsii, 37
Genus name, 8
Geranium, 405–407
    apple, 407
    bigroot, 322
    Clark's, 321
    coconut-scented, 407
    hardy, 12, 59, 319–322
    ivy, *406*, 406
    nutmeg, 407
    peppermint, 407
    purple hardy, *320*
    regal, 407
    rose, 407
    scented, 407
    zonal, 34, 184, 405, *406*, 406
    See also Cranesbill; *Geranium*
Geranium, 12, 59, 319–322
    cinereum, *320*, 322
    clarkei, 321
    cultivars, 321–322
    dalmaticum, 322
    endressii, 321, 322
    himalayense, 321, *321*
    macrorrhizum, 322
    maculatum, 74, 320, 322
    × *magnificum*, *320*
    × *oxonianum*, 322
    phaeum, 322
    pratense, 321
    psilostemon, 321
    robertianum, 321
    sanguineum, 321–322, *322*
    sanguineum var. *striatum*, 322
    sylvaticum, 321, 322
    See also Pelargonium
Gerard, John, 214, 222, 261, 264, 270, 303,
    320, 323, 349, 354, 397, 399, 422
Geum, 40, 119, 323–324
    chiloense, 323, 323–324
    cultivars, 323–324
    rivale, 323
    triflorum, 323
Gilbert, Samuel, 385
Glacier lily, yellow, *280*, 280

Gladiolus, 324–326
  common, *325*, 325–326
  hardy, *324, 324, 325*
  heirloom cultivars, 27
Gladiolus, 324–326
  communis ssp. *byzantinus, 324, 324, 325*
  heirloom cultivars, 27
  × *hortulanus, 325*, 325–326
Globe amaranth, 326–327, *327*
Globe thistle, 39, 170, 300–301, *301*
Gloriosa daisy, *28–29, 428, 428, 429*
Gloriosa superba, 149
Glory lily, 149
Glory-of-the-snow, 12, 170, 280
Glory vine, Chilean, 49
Gloves, gardening, 208
Goat's beard, 22, 44, 55, 59, 68, 170,
    234–235, *235*
  dwarf, 235
Goethe, Johann Wolfgang von, 20, 109
Goldenrod, *37, 37*, 39, 68, 119, 239
  dwarf, 239
  European, 239
  rough-leaved, 239
  sweet, 239
  wreath, 239
Goldenstar, 55, 272
Gomphrena, 326–327
  globosa, 326–327, *327*
  haageana, 327
Grape hyacinth, 12, *281*, 281
Grass clipping mulch, 132
Grasses, ornamental, *95, 95, 144*
Grasshoppers, *162*, 164
Green-and-gold, 272
Greenhouse, 122
Grieve, Mrs. M., 270, 308, 398
Growing season, 36, 459–464
Guinea-hen flower, *313, 313*
Gumboots, 210
Gypsophila, 58, 141, 327–329
  cultivars, 329
  elegans, 38, 328, 328, 329
  paniculata, 15, 21, 74, 328–329
  repens, *328*, 329

H

Hagemann, Heinrich, 428
Hakone grass, variegated, 95
Hanging garden, 188–189
Hardening off, 129
Hardy bulbs, 17
Hardy perennials, 16
Harebell, Carpathian, 254–255
Harper, Pamela, 91
Harris, Moses, 108
Haughton, Claire Shaver, 14
Hay mulch, 132–133
Heating cables, 205
Heat zone rating, 36, 39, 464
Hedges, 41
Heims, Dan, 339
Heirloom plants, 27, 186

Helenium
  autumnale, 37, 55, 119, *329*, 329–331
  cultivars, 330–331
  hoopesii, 331
Helianthus, 37, 39, 331–333
  angustifolius, 333
  annuus, 11, 25, 38, 74, *57, 174, 331,*
    332–333, 333
  cultivars, 332–333
  decapetalus, 333
  divaricatus, 333
  maximilianii, 333
  × *multiflorus*, 333
  salicifolius, 333
  strumosus, 333
Helichrysum petiolatum, 53
Heliopsis helianthoides, 68, 119, 330
  spp. *scabra*, 330
Heliotrope, *413, 413*
Heliotropic plants, 57
Heliotropium arborescens, 413, 413
Hellebore, 40, 141, 149, 334–335
  stinking, 335
Helleborus, 40, 141, 149, 334–335
  foetidus, 335
  × *hybridus, 334*, 335
  niger, 334, 335
Hemerocallis, 12, 44, 58, 66, 68, 335–338
  citrina, 338
  cultivars, 106, 337–338
  disease-resistance, *170, 170*
  fulva, 15, 26, 27
  heirloom, 27
  lilioasphodelus, 338
  middendorfii, 338
  reblooming, 105, 338
Hemlock, dwarf, 87
Henry IV, King of England, 389
Herb garden, *185*, 185–186
Herbicides, organic, 81
Hesperis matronalis, 15
Heucher, Johann Heinrich von, 339
Heuchera, 19, 40, 59, *339*, 339–341
  americana, 339, 341
  × *brizoides*, 338–339, 341
  micrantha, 341
  sanguinea, 338–339, 341
Hibberd, Shirley, 418
Hibiscus
  coccineus, 55, 342
  moscheutos, 119, *341*, 341–342, 55
High-altitude gardens, 32
Hill, Thomas, 64, 123, 148
Hillside garden, 182, 184
Hobhouse, Penelope, 88, 108
Hoes, 198–199
Hogg, Thomas, 15
Holly, 50
  Japanese, 87
Hollyhock, 21, 27, 119, 218–221, *219*, 384
  fig-leaved, 220
Hollyhock mallow, 220, 384, *385*
Homer, 346, 391
Honesty, *378*, 378–379

Honeysuckle, fragrant, 50
Hood, Thomas, 143
Horticultural oils, 155, 160–161
Horticulture on the Internet, 467
Hoses, 201–202
Host, Nicholaus Thomas, 343
Hosta, 12, 19, 40, 44, 55, *343*, 343–346,
    344, 346
  cultivars, 346
  fluctuans, 346
  leaf features of, 103–104, 115
  montana, 346
  plantaginea, 346
  for shade garden, 59, 98–99
  sieboldiana, 346
  venusta, 346
Hudak, Joseph, 30
Hummingbird garden, 188–189
Humus, 71
Hyacinth bean, 49, *352, 352*
Hyacinth, Dutch, 12, 25, 149, 346–348,
    347
Hyacinthoides, 280–281
  hispanica, 12, 280–281, *281*
  non-scripta, 281
Hyacinthus orientalis, 12, 27, 149,
    346–348, *347*
Hybrids, breeding of, 25–26
Hydrangea
  bigleaf, 71–72
  peegee, 50
Hydrangea
  macrophylla, 71–72
  paniculata, 50
Hypericum
  androsaemum, 87
  frondosum, 87

I

Iberis, 348–350
  amara, 349
  cultivars, 349
  saxatilis, 349
  sempervirens, 32, 348, 349
  umbellata, 59, *349*, 349
Ilex, 50
  crenata, 87
Impatiens, 184, 350–351
  balsamina, 59, *350*, 351
  capensis, 350
  cultivars, 351
  New Guinea, 350, 351
  walleriana, 10, 14, 16, 55, 59, *350, 350, 351*
Indian tobacco, 375
Inflorescence, 20
Informal (asymmetrical) design, 90,
    92–93, *93*
Information sources
  books and magazines, 210, 469
  on climate and weather, 458
  on garden design, 43, 88, 469
  on public gardens, 468
  web sites, 467–468, 211

Ingham, Elaine, 127
Insecticidal soaps, 154, 160
Insects
    beneficial, *153*, 153, 156–158, *160*, 467
    chemical controls, 148, 159–162
    common pests, 151–152, 162–169
    cultural controls, 135–136, 149–150,
        153–154
    homemade remedies, 154–155, 162
    integrated controls, 150
    mail order controls for, 466
    physical controls, 154–156
    plants' defenses against, 148–149, 155
Integrated pest management (IPM), 150
*International Code of Botanical
    Nomenclature*, 9
Internodes, 19
Interplanting, 107–108
Invasive plants, 14, 15
Ipheion uniflorum, 12, 281
Ipomoea, 11, 49, 59, 74, 121, 149, 351,
        353–354
    acuminata, 18
    alba, 49, 354
    batatas, 353
    indica, 353, 354
    lobata, 49, *354*, 354
    × *multifida*, 354
    nil, 27, 58, 353
    purpurea, 353
    quamoclit, 353, 354
    tricolor, 353–354
Iris, 354–360
    bearded, 27, 66, 142, *355*, 355, 356, 358
    blue flag, 359
    blue flag, Southern, 55, 359
    bulbous, 359
    crested, 74, *359*, 360
    Danford, 359
    Dutch, 356, 359
    English, 359
    Japanese, 27, 356, 358, 359
    Louisiana Hybrid, 359
    reticulated, 359–360
    roof, 358–359
    Siberian, 32, 44, 55, 137, 170, *357*, 358,
        359
    Spanish, 359
    variegated sweet, 19
    yellow flag, *358*, 359
Iris, 354–360
    bearded, 27, 66, 142, *355*, 355, 356, 358
    bulbous, 359
    cristata, 74, *359*, 360
    cultivars, 356, 358
    danfordiae, 359
    ensata, 27, 356, 358, 359
    × *germanica*, 356
    × *germanica* var. *florentina*, *355*
    Louisiana Hybrid, 359
    pallida, 19
    pseudacorus, *358*, 359
    reticulata, 359–360

sibirica, 32, 44, *55*, 137, 170, *357*, 358,
        359
    subgenus, 356, 359
    tectorum, 358–359
    versicolor, 359
    virginica, 55, 359
Iron phosphate, in pesticides, 161
Ironweed, 37, 307
Irrigation, drip, 52, 55, 56, 201
Island beds, 86
Itea virginica, 50

J

Japanese beetles, 155, 163, *165*, 165
Jefferson, Thomas, 14, 135, 233, 252,
        260, 290, 350, 353, 400
Jekyll, Gertrude, 33, 94, 108, 232, 256, 353
Jerusalem cross, 381, 382
Joe-Pye weed, 37, 55, 119, 306–308
    hollow, 307
    spotted, 307
Johnny jump-up, 8–9, 452, *453*, 453
Johnson, Hugh, 148
Johnson, Louisa, 208
Jonquilla, 393–394

K

Kerria japonica, 87
Klinkenborg, Verlyn, 164
Knapweed, American, 261, 262, 263
Knautia
    arvensis, 431
    macedonica, 431, 432
Knife, 206
Kniphof, Johann Hieronymus, 360
Kniphofia uvaria, 21, 66, 119, *360*,
        360–361
Kourik, Robert, 201
Kudzu, 15
Kunst, Scott, 26

L

Labels, plant, 206–207
Lablab purpureus, 49, *352*, 352
Lacewings, 151–152
    green, 158
Ladybell
    common, 255
    lilyleaf, 255
Ladybugs, *153*, 157, 158
Lady's mantle, 40, 59, 68, 119, *221*, 221–222
Lagenaria siceraria, 49
Lamb's ear, 19, 53, 97, 119, 434–435, *435*
Lamium maculatum, 19, 173, *272*, 272
Landscape design. *See* Garden design
Landscape fabric, 133
"Language of flowers," 7
Larkspur, 289, *289*
Lateral buds, 19
Lathyrus
    latifolius, 27
    odoratus, 27, 49, 55, 141, *352*, 352

Latitude, 30, 31
Lavandula angustifolia, 53, 173, *410*, 410
Lavatera trimestris, 220, *220*, 384
Lavender, *53*, 173, *410*, 410
Lavender mist, 439
Lawrence, Elizabeth, 8, 117, 211
Layering, propagation by, 141
Leaf cuttings, 140
Leafhoppers, 165
Leaf miners, 151–152, 165–166
Leaf mold, 79, 133
Leaf spot diseases, 169–170
Leaves
    anatomy of, 18–19
    colors, 115
    foliar feeding, 127, 135
    as mulch, 133, 145
    nitrogen depletion, 76
    photosynthesis, 19
    potassium deficiency, 150–151
    texture of, 103–105
    variegated foliage, 19, 20, 108
Lee, Laurie, 405
Leek lily, 222, *223*, 223–224
Leighton, Ann, 237
Lemmon, Robert, 342
Le Nôtre, André, 92
Lenten rose, 59, *334*, 334–335
Leopard's banes, 170
Leucanthemum
    cultivars, 362
    lacustre, 361
    maximum, 361
    × *superbum*, 32, 107, 119, 361–363, *362*
    vulgare, 15, *15*, 362
Leucojum
    aestivum, 281
    vernum, 281
Lewis, Meriwether, 34
Liatris, 66, 68, 363–364
    punctata, 363, 364
    pycnostachya, 364
    scariosa, 37, 39
    spicata, 14, 55, *363*, 363, 364
Licorice plant, 53
Light, color and, 110
Light exposure, 57–60
Ligularia, 55, 59, 364–365
    big-leaved, 365
Ligularia, 55, 59, 364–365
    dentata, *365*, 365
    przewalskii, 365
    stenocephala, *365*, 365
Ligustrum, 50
Lilac
    common, 50
    Korean, dwarf, 87
Lilium, 366–370
    Asiatic Hybrids, *366*, 368
    Aurelian Hybrids, 369–370
    canadense, 55, 370
    candidum, 366, *367*, 368
    concolor, 366
    cultivars, 27, 368–370

formosanum, 370
heirloom, 27
interplanting, 107–108
L.A. Hybrids, 369
longiflorum, 34, 369
martagon, 368, 368
martagon var. *album*, 368
Martagon Hybrids, 368–369
Oriental Hybrids, 368, 369
regale, 366
speciosum, 370
superbum, 370
Trumpet Hybrids, 369–370
Lily, 366–370
  arum, 84–85
  belladonna, 149
  calla, 6, 22
  Canada, 55, 370
  checkered, 12, *313*, 313, 366
  division of, 142
  Easter, 34, 369
  fawn, 280
  Formosa, 370
  foxtail, 369
  glory, 149
  heirloom, 27
  Japanese, 370
  leek, *222*, 223, 223–224
  Madonna, 366, 367, 368
  magic, 366
  naked lady, 369
  plantain, *343*, 343–346, *344*, *346*
  regal, 370
  toad, 37, 345
  torch, 21, 66, 119, *360*, 360–361
  trout, 280, 366
  trumpet, *367*, 369–370
  turf, 19, 59, 97, *373*, 373–374
  Turk's cap, *368*, 368
  Turk's cap, American, 370
  yellow glacier, *280*, 280
  See also Daylily
Lily-of-the-valley, 13, 59, 74, 149, 170,
  173, 270–272, *271*
Lilyturf, 19, 59, 97, *373*, 373–374
Limonium, 370–372
  latifolium, 66, 141, 326, 328, 370–371
  perezii, *371*, 372
  sinuatum, 38, 39, 66, 370–371, *371*
Linaria
  maroccana, 27
  vulgaris, 15, 74
Linnaeus, Carolus, 8, 250, 272, 284, 342
Linum, 372–373
  flavum, 372
  grandiflorum, 373
  lewisii, 372
  narbonense, 372
  perenne, *372*, 373
  usitatissimum, 372
Liriope, 19, 59, 97, *373*, 373–374
  muscari, 373, 374
  spicata, 374
Lloyd, Christopher, 225, 364, 370

Lobelia, 55, 119, 374–376
  edging, 59, *91*, 374, *375*, 375, 376
  great blue, 376
  perennial, 375, 376
Lobelia, 55, 119, 374–376
  cardinalis, 374, 375, *376*, 376
  cultivars, 376
  erinus, 59, *91*, 374, *375*, 375, 376
  siphilitica, 375, 376
  × *speciosa*, 376
Lobularia maritima, 10, 11, 39, 74, 137,
  173, 376–377, *377*
Loewer, Peter, 192
Lonas annua, 326
Longfellow, Henry Wadsworth, 290
Longgood, William, 134
Lonicera fragrantissima, 50
Loosestrife, 382–383
  dense-flowered, 383
  fringed, 383
  gooseneck, *382*, 383
  purple, 14, 15
  whorled, *383*, 383
Louden, Mrs. J. C., 449
Loudon, Jane, 82
Love-in-a-mist, 170, *397*, 397–398
Love-lies-bleeding, 74
Lowell, Amy, 4
Lunaria
  annua, *378*, 378–379
  rediviva, 378
Lungwort, 19, 40, 44, 59, 425–426
  longleaf, 426
Lupine, 27, 32, 40, 119, 141, 149, *379*,
  379–380, *380*
  Carolina, 379
  wild, 66, 380
Lupinus, 27, 40, 119, *379*, 379–380, *380*
  perennis, 66, 380
  polyphyllus, 32
  Russell Hybrids, *380*, 380
  texensis, 380
Lychnis, 381–382
  × *arkwrightii*, 382
  chalcedonica, 381, 382
  coronaria, 119, *381*, 381, 382
  × *haageana*, 382
  viscaria, *381*, 382
Lycoris squamigera, 366, 369
Lysimachia, 382–383
  ciliata, 383
  clethroides, *382*, 383
  congestiflora, 383
  punctata, *383*, 383
Lythrum salicaria, 14, 15

M

Madonna lily, 366, 367, 368
Magazines, gardening, 210, 469
Magic lily, 366
Mail-order sources
  beneficial insects, 157, 467
  plants and seeds, 120, 128–129,
  470–474

supplies and equipment,
  466
Malcolmia maritima, 386
Mallow, 384–385
  annual, *220*, 220
  hollyhock, 220, 384, 385
  musk, 220
  tree, 14, 220, 384, 385
Malva, 384–385
  alcea, 384, 385
  alcea var. *fastigiata*, 220, 385
  moschata, 220
  sylvestris, 14, 220, 384, 385
Manures, animal, 73
Maple, thread-leaved Japanese, 87
Marguerite, golden, 38, 170, 228–230,
  229
Marigold, 10, 11, 27, 39, 44, 173,
  435–437
  African, 17, 435–436, *436*, 437
  French, 435, 437
  pot, 11, 27, 39, 55, 250–251, *251*
  signet, *437*, 437
  triploid, 437
Mass plantings, 93
Master Gardeners, 43, 468
Mat-forming plants, 102
Matthiola
  incana, 385, 385–387
  longipetala, 11
  longipetala spp. *bicornis*, 386
Mattiolo, Piesandrea, 385
Maurandella antirrhiniflora, 49
Maurandya scandens, 49
McCrae, John, 403
McKenny, Margaret, 237
McKie, Roy, 30, 201
McMahon, Bernard, 290, 350
Meadow rue, 55, 438–439
  alpine, 438, 439
  columbine, 438, *439*, 439
  yellow, 438, 439
  Yunan, 439
Meadowsweet, *310*
  Japanese, 311
  Siberian, 311
Medium. *See* Soil media
Mendel, Gregor, 25
Mertensia, 141
Mexican poppy, 74
Mexican sunflower, 27, 170, *332*, 332
Microclimate, 41
Microorganisms, 152
  beneficial, 156, 157
Mignonette, 59, 386
Mildews, 170–171
Milkweed, swamp, 55, 236
Millay, Edna St. Vincent, 396
Milton, John, 346
Mimulus × *hybridus*, 33, 34, 55, 59, 231
Mirabilis jalapa, 38, 59, 74, 149, 386, *386*
Miscanthus sinensis, 95, *95*
Mitchell, Henry, 115, 148
Mites, 158, 166

Mithridates Eupator, 306
Mock-orange, 50
Mold diseases, 171
Molucella laevis, 386
Monarch of the veldt, 318
Monarda, 21, 30, 55, *157*, 387–388
   cultivars, 388
   didyma, 27, 387, *387*, 388, 388
   fistulosa, 68, 387, 388
Monardes, Nicholas, 387
Money plant, *378*, 378–379
Moneywort, *378*, 378–379
Monkey flower, 33, 34, 55, 59, 231
Monkshood, 12, 141, 149, 173, 215–217
   azure, 216
   common, 215–216, *216*
Monochromatic color schemes, 112, 114
Monocotyledons (monocots), 14
Monoecious flowers, 22
Moonflower, 49, 354
Moon garden, 192
Morning glory, *18*, 27, 49, 59, 74, 149,
      351, 353–354
   dwarf, 354
   Japanese, 58, 353
   seed, 11, 121
Moss rose, 10, 38, 39, 66, 74, 419–420, *420*
Mounded plants, 101, *102*
Mugwort, 15
Mulch
   in autumn, 145
   cubic yards, calculating, 131
   dyed, 133
   pros and cons of, 76, 131–132
   types of, 132–133
   water retention and, 41, 56, 153
Mullein, 448–449
   common, 15, 448
   nettle-leaved, 448, 449
   Olympic, 449
   purple, 449
Mum, garden, *265*, 265–267, *267*
Mumford, Lewis, 6
Muscari, 12
   armeniacum, *281*, 281
   botryoides, 281
   latifolium, 281
Musk mallow, annual, 342
Myosotis sylvatica, 55, 59, 74, 119, 173,
      388–389, *389*
Mythology, flowers in, 7

N

Naked lady, 369
Names
   common, 8
   cultivar, 9
   scientific, 8–9
Nandina domestica, 50
Narcissus, 12, *13*, 149, 170, 390–394
   bulbocodium, 394
   bulbocodium spp. *conspicuus*, 394
   cultivars, 392–394

   cyclamineus, 392, 393
   papyraceus, 392
   poeticus, 391, 394
   poeticus var. *recurvus*, *393*, 394
Nasturtium, 10, 11, 27, 39, 49, 66, 74, 173
   common, *441*, 441–442
Nasturtium officinale, 441
National flowers, 6
National Weather Service, 458
Native species, 14
Neem (azadirachtin), 159
Nematodes, *157*, 166–167
Nemesia strumosa, *231*, 231
Nepeta, 394–395
   cataria, 394, 395
   × *faassenii*, 45, 394, 395, *395*
   sibirica, 395
   subsessilis, 37
Netherlands Flower Bulb Information
      Center, 468
Newsprint, soil clearing with, 81
Newton, Isaac, 108
Nichols, Beverly, 139, 207
Nicot, Jean, 395
Nicotiana, 74, 121, 173, 395–397
   alata, 27, 59, *396*, 396
   glauca, 149
   × *sanderae*, 396
   sylvestris, 396
Nigella damascena, 170, *397*, 397–398
Nipponanthemum nipponicum, 37, 362
Nippon daisy, 37, 362
Nitrogen
   in compost, 78
   depletion, 76
   in fertilizer, 73
   sources of, 73
Nodes, stem, 18
Non-native species, 14, 16, 94
Nutrient deficiency, 134–135, 150–151
Nutrients, 72–75

O

Oat grass, blue, 95
Obedient plant, 19, 37, 417–418
Oehme, Wolfgang, 256
Oenothera, 398–399
   biennis, 398
   caespitosa, 399
   fruticosa, 398, 399
   fruticosa spp. *glauca*, 399
   macrocarpa, 21, *139*, 399
   speciosa, 398, 399
Oil and soap spray, 162
O'Keefe, Georgia, 6
Old-fashioned garden, 186
Olive, autumn, 50
Onion, ornamental, 222–225
   blue globe, *107*, 223
   giant, 223
   Japanese, 37
   nodding, 224
   October, 224

   Persian, *222*, 223
   star of Persia, 21, 223
Open-pollinated cultivars (OPs), 25
Organic pest management (OPM), 150
Oriental poppy, 27, 40, *40–41*, 173, 403,
      403–404
Ornaments, garden, 207–208
Ornithogalum, 12, 149
   nutans, 282
   umbellatum, *281*, 281–282
Osteospermum
   ecklonis, 318
   jucundum, 318
Overplanting, 107
Ovid, 373
Ox-eye, 68, 119, 330
Ox-eye daisy, *15*, 15, 362
Oyster shell mulch, 133

P

Paeonia, 12, 21, 32, 141, 399–402
   cultivars, 27, 400, 401, 402
   interplanting, 107
   lactiflora, 48, 107, 402
   mascula, 399
   officinalis, 399, 402
   tenuifolia, 402
Page, Ruth, 151
Painted daisy, 32, 266, *266*
Pampas grass, 95
Pansy, 59, *452*, 453, *454*
Papaver, 141, 402–405
   alpinum, 32, 403, 404, 404–405
   croceum, 32, 404
   cultivars, 404
   orientale, 27, 40, *40–41*, 107, 173, 403,
      403–404
   rhoeas, 74, 403, 404, *404*
   seeds, 119, 121
   somniferum, 8, *9*, 9, 402–403
Paperwhite, 392
Parkinson, John, 219, 231, 264, 310, 427,
      437
Parsons, Frances Theodora, 268
Pasque flower, 32, 40, 170
Paths and walkways
   border gardens, 184–185
   edging for, 46–47
   in formal design, 92–93
   in informal design, 92–93
Patio garden, *91*
Payne, J. Howard, 47
Pea
   everlasting, 37
   sweet, 27, 49, 55, 141, *352*, 352
Peat containers, 205
Peat pellets, 204
Pelargonium, 405–407
   cultivars, 406–407
   × *domesticum*, 407
   × *fragrans*, 407
   graveolens, 407
   grossularioides, 407

× *hortorum*, 34, 184, *405, 406, 406*
odoratissimum, 407
peltatum, 406, *407*
tomentosum, 407
Penstemon, 407–409
beardlip, 409
foxglove, 19, *408*, 409
mountain, 409
Small's, 409
Penstemon, 407–409
barbatus, 409
cultivars, 409
digitalis, 19, *408*, 409
hirsutus, 66, 409
hybrid, *408*, 409
smallii, 409
strictus, 409
Peony, *11, 12*, 32, 44, 141, 399–402
fernleaf, 402
garden, *401*
heirloom cultivars, 27
interplanting, 107
Japanese, *48*
Memorial Day, 402
tree, *400*, 402
Pepper spray, for pest control, 154
Perennials, 11–12
for autumn garden, 37
buying, 128
for clay soil, 68
for cool weather, 40
cutting garden, 189–190, *190*
deadheading, 137
dividing, 131, 138–139, 141–142
for dry conditions, 39, *53*
easy to grow, 44
for edging, 96–97, *97*
hardy, 16
for high-altitudes, 32
long-lasting, 12
medium height, 103
salt-tolerant, 42
for sandy soil, 66
from seed, 119
for shade, 59, *100–101*
tall, 102
tender, 16
for thin soil, 74
for wet conditions, 55
See also Plants; Plant selection; *specific
names*
Perényi, Eleanor, 156
Periwinkle, 15, 149
Madagascar, 15, 38, 59, 66, 258–259, *259*
Perlite, in soil media, 203
Perovskia atriplicifolia, 37, 65, 66, 68, 170,
173, 409–411, *411*
Pesticides, 148, 160, 161–162
Pests. *See* Insects
Petals, 21, 22
Peterson, Roger Tory, 237, 374
Petiole, 20
Petunia, 411–413

cultivars, 412–413
× *hybrida*, 10, 38, *38*, 39, 66, 74, *412*,
412–413
integrifolia, 413
pH, soil, 71–72
Phaseolus coccineus, 49, 352
Phenological signs, 36
Pheromone traps, 155
Philadelphus coronarius, 50
Phlox, 39, 414–417
annual, 10, 38, 414, 415, *416*
cleft, 416
creeping, 59, 74, *414*, 415–416
garden, 27, 32, 68, 414, *415*, *415*,
416–417
Siberian, 414
thick-leaved, 417
wild blue, 59, 119, 414, *416*, *416*
wild sweet William, 416, 417
Phlox, 39, 414–417
bifida, 414, 415, 416
carolina, 415, 416, 417
cultivars, 415–417
divaricata, 59, 119, 414, *416*, *416*
douglasii, 414, 415
drummondii, 10, 38, 414, 415, *416*
maculata, 415, 416, 417
paniculata, 27, 32, 68, 414, *415*, *415*,
416–417
sibirica, 414
stolonifera, 59, 414, 416
subulata, *414*, 414–416, 74
Phosphorus, sources of, 73
Photinia glabra, 50
Photoperiodism, 58
Photosynthesis, 19, 72, 138
Phyllostachys, 50
Physiological disorders, 150–151
Physostegia, 417–418
Physostegia virginiana, 19, 37, *417*, 417–418
Picea
abies, 87
glauca, 87
pungens, 87
Pinching back, 130, 137–138
Pincushion flower, *91*, 431–433, *432*
annual, 432
Pine
Japanese red, 87
white, dwarf, 87
Pine needle mulch, 133
Pink, 119
Allwood, *290*, *292*, 293
Cheddar, *290*, 292
China, 290, *291*, 293
cottage, 293
maiden, 74, 292
sea, 38, 39, 170
Pinus
densiflora, 87
strobus, 87
Pistil, 22
Plantain lily, *343, 343–346, 344, 346*

Plant collars, 154
Plant collectors, 14
Planting hole, 130
Planting and transplanting
in autumn, 143
frost-free dates, 36, 459–461
guidelines for, 130
hardening off, 129
spacing in, 131
timing of, 153
Plant problems
cultural/physiological, 150–151
wildlife, 148, 151, 173–175
See also Diseases; Insects
Plants
anatomy of, 17–20
beneficial insect attracting, 156
biennials, 10–11
buying tips, 127–129
deerproof, 173, *174*
disease and pest resistant, 150, 153, 170
hardiness zone ratings, 16, 34–36, *464, 465*
heat zone ratings, 36, 39, *464*
heirloom, 27, 186
insect repellant, 148–149, 155
invasive, 14, 15
from mail-order nurseries, 128, 470–474
names, 8–9
native, 14
non-native species, 14, 16, 34
nutrient deficiency in, 134–135, 150–151
nutrients for, 72–75
pollination of, 22–24
reproduction of, 22–25, *See also*
Propagation
terminology, 16–17
for themed gardens. *See* Themed gardens
tropical, 13–14
See also Annuals; Bulbous plants;
Flowers; Perennials; *specific names*
Plant selection, 97–115
bloom time and, 105–107
cultural requirements in, 99
easy to grow plants, 10, 11, 44
for edges, 96–97, *97*
for garden rooms, 90
for interplanting, 107–108
for mixed beds and borders, 87
for overplanting, 107
for pest and disease control, 149–150
proportion and, 90–91, 101
size and shape in, 99–103
texture and, 103–105
for underplanting, *107*, 107
See also Climate and weather; Color
Plant supports, 120–131, 136–137, 207
Plant traps, 155–156
Plastic, soil clearing with, 81
Platycodon grandiflorus, 141, 418–419, *419*
Pliny, 290, 342
Pliny the Elder, 148
Plumbago, 272
Plumier, Charles, 244, 314

Poinsettia, 22, 58, 308
  annual, 309–310
Pollination, 23–24
Polychromatic color scheme, *112*, 114–115
Polygonatum
  biflorum, 59, 345
  odoratum, 19, 345
  odoratum var. *thunbergii*, *345*, 345
Pope, Alexander, 41
Poppy, 141, 402–405
  alpine, 32, 403, *404*, 404–405
  California, 38, 58, 66, 74, *183*,
    304–306, *305*
  celandine, 59
  corn, 74, 403, *404*, 404
  Iceland, 32, 404
  Mexican, 74
  opium, 8, 9, 402–403
  oriental, 27, 40, *40–41*, 107, 173, *403*,
    403–404
  seeds, 119, 121
Poppy mallow, 141
Porosity, soil, 52
Portulaca, 419–420
Portulaca grandiflora, 10, 38, 39, 66, 74,
  419–420, *420*
Potassium
  deficiency, 150–151
  sources of, 73
Potentilla, 420–422
  atrosanguinea, *421*, 421
  cultivars, 421–422
  erecta, 420–421
  fruticosa, 87
  nepalensis, 421
  neumanniana, 421
  recta, 15
  tridentata, 421–422
Pot maker, 205
Pot marigold, 11, 27, 39, 55, 250–251,
  251
Potting soil. *See* Soil media
Prairie smoke, 323
Praying mantises, 158
Precipitation, 39, 52, 55
Primrose, 40, 59, *146–147*, 422–424
  auricula, 424
  cowslip, *422*, 422, 423–424
  drumstick, *423*, 424
  English, 34, *422*, 423, *424*
  Japanese, 55, 424
  polyanthus, *119*, 423, *424*
  seed, 119, *120*, 121
  Siebold, 424
  See also Evening primrose
Primula, 40, 59, *146–147*, 422–424
  auricula, 424
  cultivars, 423–424
  denticulata, *423*, 424
  japonica, 55, 424
  × *polyanthus*, *119*, 423, *424*
  seed, 119, *120*, 121

sieboldii, 424
  veris, *422*, 422, 423–424
  vulgaris, 34, *422*, 423, *424*
Private Life of Plants, The, 21
Privet, 50
Propagation, 22, 139–143
  artificial selection and, 24–26
  by cuttings, 139, 140–141
  by division, 131, 138–139, 141–142, *142*
  by layering, 141
  from seed. *See* Seed, starting from
  seed saving, 143
Prostrate plants, 102
Proust, Marcel, 92
Provinces (Canada), frost dates/growing
    seasons in, 463–464
Pruners, 206
Psylliostachys suworowii, 326
Public gardens, visiting, 468
Pueraria lobata, 15
Pulmonaria, 19, 40, 44, 59, 425–426
  cultivars, 425–426
  longifolia, 426
  officinalis, 425
  saccharata, 425, 425–426
Pulsatilla
  patens, 32
  vulgaris, 40, 170
Puschkinia scilloides, 282
Pycnanthemum tenuifolium, 65
Pyracantha, 50
Pyrethrins (pesticide), 161

Q

Quaking grass, 95
Queen-of-the-prairie, *310*, 310–311
  Japanese, 311
  Siberian, 311

R

Rain daisy, 318
Rainfall, 39, 52, 55
Rain gauge, 55
Rain water, 56
Raised beds, 54, 69
Rakes, 197, 198
Ranunculus, 55, 438
  aconitifolius, 438
  acris, 438
Rattail, 326
Rattlesnake master, 303, 304
Ravenna grass, 95
Redbud, eastern, 87
Red flowers, 109
Red-hot poker, *360*, 360–361
Reed grass, giant, 95
Regale lily, 366
Reinelt, Frank, 287
Reproduction
  asexual (vegetative), 22–23
  sexual, 23–25
  See also Propagation

Reseda odorata, 59, 386
Rhizomes, 12–13
Rhodanthe
  chlorocephala, 326
  manglesii, 326
Rhodochiton atrosanguineum, 49, 352
Ricinus communis, 22, 149
Robinson, William, 93
Rodgers, John, 426
Rodgersia, 59, 426–427
  bronze-leaved, 426, 427
  featherleaf, 427
  fingerleaf, 427
Rodgersia, 59, 426–427
  aesculifolia, 427
  pinnata, 427
  podophylla, 426, 427
Roethke, Theodore, 11, 405
Root cuttings, 139, 140
Rooting hormone powder, 141
Root rot, 35
Roots, anatomy of, 17
Rosa. *See* Rose
Rose
  floribunda, 87, 87
  Polyantha, 87
  Rugosa, 50
Rose mallow, 55
  common, 119, *341*, 341–342
  scarlet, 55, 342
Rosemary, Victoria, 53
Rose moss, 419–420, *420*
Rossetti, Gabriel, 308
Rot diseases, 171–172
Rotenone pesticide, 161–162
Rototillers, 81, 83
Row covers, 154, *168*
Rudbeck, Olof the elder and younger, 427
Rudbeckia, 11, 119, 119, 121–129
  cultivars, 428–429
  fulgida, 32, 37, 68, 428, 428
  fulgida var. *sullivantii*, 428–429
  hirta, 24, 28–29, 38, 39, 68, *100–101*,
    428, 428, 429
  laciniata, 12, 427, 428, 429
  maxima, 429
Russian sage, 37, 65, 66, 68, 170, 173,
  409–411, *411*
Rust diseases, 172

S

Sackville-West, Vita, 93, 147, 154, 203
Sage, 429–431
  azure, 430–431
  common, 429–430
  Gregg, 431
  hybrid, 14, 430
  meadow, 430
  mealycup, 430, *431*, 431
  pineapple, 431
  scarlet, 38, 39, 66, *100–101*, *116*, 430,
    430, 431
  Texas, 431

Saline soil, 68
Salt-tolerant perennials, 42
Salvia, 429–431
 azurea, 430–431
 cultivars, 430–431
 elegans, 431
 farinacea, 430, *431*, 431
 greggii, 431
 guaranitica, 431
 officinalis, 429–430
 pratensis, 430
 splendens, 38, 39, 66, *100–101*, *116*,
  430, 430, 431
 × *sylvestris*, 14, 430
Sand, in soil media, 203
Sandy soil, 64, 66
Sanvitalia procumbens, 39, 66, *456*, 456
Saponaria officinalis, 170, 381
Sarton, May, 5
Scabiosa, 91, 431–433
 atropurpurea, 432
 caucasica, 433
 columbaria, *432*, 433
 stellata, 326, 432
Scabious, giant, 431
Scales, 167
Scarlet runner bean, 49, 352
Scientific names, 8–9
Scilla, 149
 bifolia, 282
 siberica, 12, 282
Sea holly, 141, 303–304
 alpine, 304
 amethyst, 39, 304
 flat, 304
 Miss Wilmott's ghost, *303*, 304
 rattlesnake master, 303, 304
Sea kale, 328
Sea lavender, 66, 141, *326*, 328, 370–371
Sea pink, 38, 39
Sedum, 12, 37, 39, 58, 66, 433–434
 acre, 433
 cultivars, 27, 32, 68, *433*, 434
 dasyphyllum, 433
 kamtschaticum, 65
 sieboldii, 434
 telephium spp. *maximum*, 434
 variegated foliage, 19
Seed
 All-America Selections, 25
 color and size of, *118*, 119–120
 exchanges, 120
 germination rate for, 120–121
 mail-order sources, 120, 470–474
 saving, 143
 scarifying, 121
 self-seeding plants, 10–11
 stratification, *120*, 121
Seed, starting from
 guidelines for, 123
 indoors, 122–124, 203–206, *204*
 outdoors, 11, 122
 outdoors (in pots), 120, 121

 soil media, 123, 125–126, 127,
  203–205, *204*
 timing of, 121–122
Seedlings, *124*, 124–127, *125*
Seed Savers Exchange, 26
Self-pollinating plants, 23
Self-seeding plants, 10–11
Sepals, 21, 22
Sexual reproduction, 23–25
Shade gardens
 color in, 110–111
 plants for, 58–60, 98–99
 under-a-tree, 181–182
 woodland, 186–187
Shade traps, 155
Shakespeare, William, 80–81, 117, 290,
  422, 429
Shasta daisy, 107, 119, 361–363, *362*
Shearing, 138
Shelley, Percy Bysshe, 347
Shoes, gardening, 208
Shovels, 197–198
Shrubs
 in mixed bed and border, 87
 underplanting, 107
 as windbreak, 50
Silene regia, 381
Silphium laciniatum, 68
Skipwith, Jean, Lady, 348
Slugs, 167
Snails, 167
Snakeroot, 55, 59, 173, 268–269
 autumn, 269
 black, 37, 269
 button, 303
Snakes, 147–148, *158*
Snakeshead, 311
Snapdragon, 24, 27, 152, 230–232
 twining, 49
Sneezeweed
 common, 37, 55, 119, *329*, 329–331
 orange, 331
Sneezewort, 27
Snow cover, 36
Snowdrop, 12, *149*, 149, 170
 common, 280
 giant, 280
Snowflake, 281
 spring, 281
 summer, 281
Snow-in-summer, 66, 74, 170
Snow-on-the-mountain, 11, 19, 59, 66,
  308, *309*, 309
Soapwort, 170, 381
Sod, removal of, *80*, 80–82
Soil, 64–83
 clay, 56, 64, 66, 68
 clearing for beds, 80, 80–82
 fertility of, 64, 73
 health, 135–136, 150, 153
 organic amendments to, 56, 68, 73,
  75–76, 135, *See also* Composting
 organisms, 69–70

 pH, 71–72
 porosity, 35, 52
 in raised beds, 54
 rototilling and, 81
 sandy, 64, 66
 solarizing, 81–82, 156
 structure of, 67–68
 testing, 72, 464
 texture of, 64, 66–67, *67*
 turning, 82–83, *83*
Soil blockers, 204
Soil media
 for seedlings, 125–126
 seed-starting, 123, 203–205, *204*
Solarizing soil, 81–82, 156
Soldier beetles, 158
Solenostemon scutellarioides, 19
Solidago, 37, 39, 68, 119, *239*
 caesia, 239
 odora, 239
 rugosa, 239
 sphacelata, 239
 virgaurea, 239
Solomon's seal, 59, 345
 fragrant, *345*, 345
 variegated, 19
Sowing. *See* Seed, starting from
Spades, 82, 197, 198
Spanish flag, 49, *354*, 354
Species names, 8–9
Speedwell, 40, 68, 449–452
 creeping, 452
 harebell, 74, 451–452
 spike, 14, *32*, *451*, 451
Sphagnum peat moss
 mulch, 133
 in soil media, 203
Spider flower, 10, *21*, 38, 44, 66,
  74, 121, 170, 173, *174*, *269*,
  269–270
Spider mites, 166
Spiderwort, 55, 439–440
 Virginia, *440*, 440
Spirea, 50
 Japanese, 87
Spittle bugs, 167
Split-complementary color scheme,
  111–112
Sprinklers, 54, 203, 208
Spruce, dwarf
 Alberta, 87
 Blue, 87
 common, 87
Spurge, 173
 cushion, *308*, 309
 Griffith's, 309
 wood, 309
Squill, 149
 Siberian, 282
 striped, 282, 282
 twin-leaf, 282
Squirrel corn, 295
Stachys, 434–435

Stachys
 byzantina, 19, *53*, 97, 119, 434–435, *435*
 officinalis, 434
Staking, 130–131, 136–137, 207
Stamen, 22
Star flower, 326, 432
Starflower, spring, 12, 281
Star glory, 354
Star-of-Bethlehem, 12, 149, *281*, 281–282
Star-of-the-veldt, *318*, 318
Star of Persia, 21, 223
States (U.S.), frost dates/growing seasons
 in, 459–463
Statice, 38, 39, 66, 370–372, *371*
 Russian, 326
 seafoam, *371*, 372
Stem cuttings, 140–141
Stems, 17–19
Sternbergia lutea, 37, *282*, 282
Sterne, Laurence, 449
Sticky traps, 155
St. John's wort, golden, 87
Stock
 common, *385*, 385–387
 night-scented, 11, 386
 Virginia, 386
Stokes' aster, *263*, 263
Stokesia laevis, *263*, 263
Stonecrop, 12, 37, 39, 58, 66, 68,
 433–434
 golden moss, 433
 Kamtschat, 65
 leafy, 433
Strabo, Walahfrid, 429
Strawflower, 66, *249*, 249–250, 326
Straw mulch, 133
Stylophorum diphyllum, 59
Succession of blooms, 105–107
Sulfur fungicide, 162
Sundrops
 common, *398*, 399
 Ozark, *139*, 399
Sun exposure, 39, 48, 57–60
Sunflower, 37, 39, *57*, 331–333
 annual, 11, 25, 38, 74, *331*, 332–333, *333*
 many-flowered hybrid, 333
 Maximillian, 333
 Mexican, *332*, 332
 pale-leaved wood, 333
 swamp, 333
 thin-leaved, 333
 willow-leafed, 333
 woodland, 333
Sunflower heliopsis, 330
Sunscreen, 208
Sunset hibiscus, 342
Swan River daisy, 170, 248–249, *249*
Sweet alyssum, 10, 11, 39, 74, 137, 173,
 376–377, *377*
Sweet pea, 27, 49, 55, 141, *352*, 352
Sweet potato, 353
Sweet shrub, 50
Sweet spire, Virginia, 50

Sweet William, 32, 290, 293
 wild, 416, 417
Sweet woodruff, 21, 59, 72, 173, 316–317
Symmetrical (formal) design, 88, 91–93
Syringa
 meyeri, 87
 vulgaris, 50

T

Tabernaemontanus, J. T., 225
Tagetes, 10, 11, 39, 173, 435–437
 cultivars, 437
 erecta, 17, 435–436, *436*, 437
 patula, 27, 435, 437
 tenuifolia, *437*, 437
Tall plants, 102
Tanacetum
 coccineum, 32, 266, *266*
 parthenium, 27, 121, 170, 266
Taproots, 17
Taxonomy, 9
Taxus, 50
Teasel, 431
Temperature
 average, 39
 high, 36, 38, 39
 low, 40
Tender bulbs, 17
Tender perennials, 16
Tepals, 22
Texas bluebonnet, 380
Texture, foliage, 103–105
Thalictrum, 55, 438–439
 alpinum, 438, 439
 aquilegifolium, 438, *439*, 439
 delavayi, 439
 flavum, 438, 439
 majus, 438
 rochebruneanum, 439
Thaxter, Celia, 24, 119
Themed gardens, 1, 177–193
 butterfly, 178
 child's, 178–179, *179*
 container, 192–193, *193*
 dyer's, 191
 edible, 182
 everlasting, 186–187, *187*
 fragrant, 180
 hanging, 188–189
 herb, *185*, 185–186
 hillside, 182, 184
 hummingbird, 188–189
 moon, 192
 old-fashioned, 186
 path, 184–185
 perennial cutting, 189–190, *190*
 season-long, 184
 under-a-tree, 180–182, *180–181*
 woodland, 187–188
Theodore of Gaza, 319
Theophrastus, 319, 390
Thermopsis villosa, 379

Thinning out, 138
Thistle
 globe, 39, 170, 300–301, *301*
 nodding, 15
Thomas, R. S., 88
Thoreau, Henry David, 119, 208, 243
Thrift, common, 38, 39, 170
Thrips, 167–168
Thunbergia
 alata, 49, 59, *352*, 352
 grandiflora, 49
Tiarella
 cordifolia, 59, *340*, 340
 wherryi, 340
Tickseed. *See Coreopsis*
Tithonia rotundifolia, 27, 170, 332
Toadflax
 common, 15
 fairies', 27
Toad lily, 37, 345
Tobacco, flowering, 27, 59, 74, 121, 173,
 395–397, *396*
 tree, 149
Tools. *See* Equipment and supplies
Topsoil, 64
Torch lily, 21, 66, 119, *360*, 360–361
Tornefort, J. Pitton de, 441
Tradescant, John the elder, and the
 younger, 235, *237*, 439
Tradescantia, 55, 439–440
 virginiana, *440*, 440
Transplanting. *See* Planting and
 transplanting
Trapping, wildlife, 175
Traps, pest control, 155–156
Treasure flower, 317, *319*, 319
Triadic color scheme, 112
Tricyrtis, 37, 345
Tropaeolum
 majus, 10, 11, 27, 39, 49, 66, 74, 173,
 441, 441–442
 peregrinum, 49
Tropical plants, 13–14
Trout lily, 280, 366
Trowels, *199*, 199
Trumpet lily, *367*, 369–370
Trumpet vine, blue, 49
Tsuga canadensis, 87
Tuberous plants, 13
Tulip, 12, 442–447
 Darwin Hybrid, *442*, 445–446, *444*
 Double Late, 446–447
 Fosteriana, *444*, *446*, 447
 Fringed, 446
 Greigii, *444*, 447
 heirloom, 27
 Kaufmanniana, *444*, 447
 Lily-Flowered, 446
 Parrot, 446
 Single Early, *444*, 445
 Single Late, *445*, 446
 Species, 447
 Triumph, *4–5*, *443*, 445

Tulipa, 12, 442–447
  batalinii, 444, 447
  clusiana, 444
  cultivars, 27, 445–447
  fosteriana, 447
  heirloom, 27
  humilis, 444
  kaufmanniana, 447
  pulchella, 447
  saxatilis, 444, 447
  sylvestris, 444, 447
  tarda, 444, 447
Tulipomania, 7, 442
Turf, removal of, 80, 80–82
Turf lily, 19, 373, 373–374
Turk's cap lily, 368, 368
  American, 370
Turning the soil, 82–83, 83
Turtlehead, 37, 55, 311
Tutsan, 87

U

Umbel flowers, 21
Under-a-tree garden, 180–182, *180–181*
Underplanting, *107*, 107, 180–182
USDA Hardiness Zone Map, 16, 34, 464, *465*
USDA Home Gardening Page, 468
USDA Soil Texture Triangle, 66, 67

V

Valerian
  common, 264
  red, 119, *264*, 264–265
Valeriana officinalis, 264
Van Sweden, James, 256
Variegated foliage, 19, *20*
Verbascum, 448–449
  chaixii, *448*, 449
  olympicum, 449
  phoeniceum, 449
  thapsus, 15, 448
Verbena, 38, 39, 66, 173, 449–450
  garden, 450
  rose, 450
Verbena, 38, 39, 66, 173, 449–450
  bonariensis, 450
  canadensis, 450
  hastata, 55, 450
  × *hybrida*, 449, *449*, 450
  officinalis, 448
  peruviana, 449
  stricta, 66
Vermiculite, in soil media, 203
Vernonia, 307
  noveboracensis, 37, 307
Veronica, 40, 68, 450–452
  filiformis, 451
  prostrata, 74, 451–452
  repens, 452
  spicata, 14, *32*, 451, 451
Vertical plants, 101
Verticillium wilt, 172

Vervain, 449–450
  blue, 55, 450
  hoary, 66
Viburnum, 50
Vinca, 15, 149
Vines, 49, 352
Viola, 40, 59, 452–454
  biflora, 8
  canadensis, 453
  cornuta, 454
  labradorica, 55, 453
  odorata, 454
  pedata, 452, 453
  sororia, 453–454
  tricolor, 8–9, 452, *453*, 453
  × *wittrockiana*, 59, 452, 453, *454*
Violet, 59, 452–453
  bird's foot, 452, 453
  bush, 59
  Canada, 453
  dogtooth, 280
  horned, 454
  Labrador, 55, 453
  Persian, 59
  Sweet, 454
  twin-flowered, 8
  woolly blue, 453–454
Viruses, 152, 172
Vonk, Alice, 436

W

Walkways. *See* Paths and walkways
Walls, 41
Ward, Nathaniel, 294
Warm-weather annuals, 17
Warner, Charles Dudley, 156, 211
Washington, George, 260
Wasps, parasitic, 158
Watercress, 441
Water gardens, *176*
Watering
  with compost tea, 127
  drip irrigation, 52, 55, 56, 201
  equipment, 201–203, *202*
  guidelines, 54–56, 135, 153
  by hand, 54, *209*
  for seed germination, 124
  seedlings, 125, *126*, 126
  before transplanting, 130
Watering cans, 201, *202*
Watering wands, 202
Weather. *See* Climate and weather
Weather instruments, 207
Weather prophet, 318
Web Garden, 467
Web sites, 467–468, 211
Weeders, hand, 199
Weeding, 80–81, 135, 153
Weeds, herbicides for, 81
Wellingtons, 208, 210
Westringia rosariniformis, 53
Wet conditions, plants for, 55
Whealy, Kent, 26
Wheelbarrows, *200*, 200

White, Katharine S., 211, 230
Whiteflies, 168
White flowers, *113*, 115, 192
Whittle, Tyler, 198
Wilder, Louise Beebe, 411
Wild indigo
  plains, 243
  prairie, 243
  white, 243
Wildlife
  beneficials, *152*, 154, 157, 158
  control of, 148, 151, 173–175
Wilson, E. H., 14, 366
Wilts, 172–173
Wind, 35–36
Windbreaks, 41, 49–51, *51*
Windflower, 22, 226–228
  Grecian, 12, 226, 227
Wintercreeper, 87
Winter garden, *144*
Winterrowd, Wayne, 435
Winthrop, John Jr., 218, 430
Wireworms, 168–169
Wolfsbane, 215–217
Wolseley, Frances Garnet, 208
Wood bark mulch, 133
Wood chip mulch, 133
Woodland garden, 187–188
Woodruff, sweet, 21, 59, 72, 173, 316–317
Wood shaving mulch, 133
Woolflower, Chinese, 261
Wordsworth, William, 391, 433
Wright, Richardson, 10, 408

X

Xeriscaping, 52

Y

Yarrow, 32, 39, 40, 66, 74, 173, *214*, 214–215
  common, 214, 215
  fernleaf, 214–215
  woolly, 215
Yellow flowers, 109
Yew, 50

Z

Zantedeschia, 22, 84–85
Zinn, Johann Gottfried, 454
Zinnia, *10*, 10, 38, 39, 66, 173, 455–456
  common, 11, 32, 62, *455*, 455–456
  creeping, 38, 39, 66, *456*, 456
  Mexican, *456*, 456
  prairie, 39
  red spider, 456
Zinnia, *10*, 10, 38, 39, 66, 173, 454–456
  cultivars, 455–456
  elegans, 11, 32, 62, *455*, 455–456
  grandiflora, 39
  haageana, *456*, 456
  peruviana, 456